Do not misunderstand me, but understand me fully [and] my affection for the land. I never said the land was mine to do with as I chose. The one who has the right to dispose of it is the one who has created it. I claim a right to live on my land, and accord you the privilege to live on yours.

Chief Joseph

Eastward I go only by force; but westward I go free. . . . I should not lay so much stress on this fact if I did not believe that something like this is the prevailing tendency of my countrymen. I must walk toward Oregon. . . . And that way the nation is moving. . . .

Henry David Thoreau

NARRATIVE BY

GEOFFREY C. WARD

BASED ON A
DOCUMENTARY FILM
SCRIPT BY

GEOFFREY C. WARD
AND DAYTON DUNCAN

WITH A PREFACE BY

STEPHEN IVES
AND KEN BURNS

AND CONTRIBUTIONS BY

DAYTON DUNCAN

JOHN MACK
FARAGHER

DAVID G. GUTIÉRREZ

JULIE ROY JEFFREY

PATRICIA NELSON
LIMERICK

N. SCOTT MOMADAY

T. H. WATKINS

RICHARD WHITE

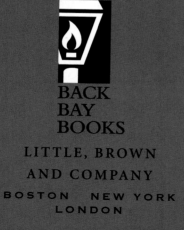

BACK
BAY
BOOKS

LITTLE, BROWN
AND COMPANY

BOSTON   NEW YORK
LONDON

THE WEST

AN ILLUSTRATED HISTORY

Back Bay Books / Little, Brown and Company
Hachette Book Group
237 Park Avenue, New York, NY 10017
Visit our Web site at
www.HachetteBookGroup.com

Originally published in hardcover by Little, Brown and Company, September 1996
Published by Back Bay Books in a text-only paper-back edition, September 1999
First illustrated Back Bay paperback edition, October 2003

Back Bay Books is an imprint of Little, Brown and Company. The Back Bay Books name and logo are trademarks of Hachette Book Group, Inc.

The author is grateful for permission to include the following previously copyrighted material:

Excerpts from *We Pointed Them North* by E. C. Abbott and Helena Huntington Smith. Copyright 1939. By permission of the University of Oklahoma Press.

Excerpts from *Cabeza de Vaca's Adventures in the Unknown Interior of America* trans. and edited by Cyclone Covey. Copyright © 1961 by Macmillan Publishing Company. By permission of Simon & Schuster.

Excerpts from *The World Rushed In: An Eyewitness Account of a Nation Heading West* by J. S. Holliday. Copyright © 1981. By permission of Simon & Schuster.

Letters of Julia Luisa Lovejoy. By permission of the Kansas State Historical Society.

Letters of the Oblinger Family. By permission of the Nebraska State Historical Society.

Excerpts from *With the Nez Perces: Alice Fletcher in the Field, 1889–1892* by Jane E. Gay, Joan Mark, and Fread Hoxie, eds. By permission of the University of Nebraska Press.

Excerpts from *The Way to Independence: Memories of a Hidatsa Indian Family* by Carolyn Gilman and Mary Jane Schneider. Copyright © 1987. By permission of the Minnesota Historical Society Press.

Excerpts from *We Were 49ers!: Chilean Accounts of the California Gold Rush* trans. and edited by Edwin A. Beilharz and Carlos V. Lopez. Copyright © 1976 by Ward Ritchie Press. By permission of Mrs. Edwin Beilharz.

Library of Congress Cataloging-in-Publication Data

Ward, Geoffrey C.
    The West : an illustrated history / narrative by Geoffrey C. Ward; based on a documentary film script by Geoffrey C. Ward and Dayton Duncan ; with contributions by Dayton Duncan . . . [et al.].
        p.   cm.
    ISBN 978-0-316-92236-4 (hardcover) / 978-0-316-92485-6 (text-only paperback) / 978-0-316-73589-6 (illustrated paperback)
    1. West (U.S.) — History. I. Duncan, Dayton. II. Title.
F591.W27   1996
978 — dc20   96–4323

The Back Bay Books name and logo are trademarks of Little, Brown and Company.

10 9 8 7 6 5 4 3 2

IM-TH

Designed by Wendy Byrne
Picture research and art assistance by Victoria Gohl

Printed in Thailand

Overleaf: Two citizens of Helena, Montana, chatting at the corner of Cutler and Water streets, 1870

COLONEL W. F. CODY.

"Buffalo Bill."

CONTENTS

Preceding pages:

Chief Joseph, Nez Percé

Westerners (clockwise from top left):
Texas Ranger;
Hispanic woman, California, 1856;
San Francisco peace officer and his daughter;
Sarah Smith Griffin, Mormon pioneer

Sam Houston, 1851

The family of Don Vicente Lugo, California, 1870

Chinese immigrant, 1851

Texas cowboys in Denver, 1901

William F. "Buffalo Bill" Cody

Pretty Nose, Cheyenne, 1878

Mormon children, about 1900

Lumberjacks, Pacific Northwest, 1907

Following page:

July Fourth, Fort Belknap, Montana, 1906

THE DREAMING PLACE

In a conversation with us several years ago, the Kiowa poet N. Scott Momaday remarked that the American West is "a dream. It is what people who have come here from the beginning of time have dreamed. . . . It is a landscape that has to be seen to be believed, and may have to be believed in order to be seen."

For five years we have traveled that landscape, photographed its vistas, talked to its people, sought out its history, all as part of our production of *The West,* an eight-part documentary series for public television. Now — 100,000 air-miles, 72 filmed interviews, 74 visits to archives and collections, and more than 250 hours of film later — we have begun to understand at least something of what Momaday meant. In the West, everything seems somehow larger than life, and we now can see why so many different peoples have come to consider their own innermost lives inextricably linked with it. Over the centuries, the West has been the repository of the dreams of an astonishing variety of people — and it has been on the long, dusty roads of the West that those dreams have crisscrossed and collided, transforming all who traveled along them, rewarding some while disappointing others.

The story of the West was once told as an unbroken series of triumphs — the victory of "civilization" over "barbarism," a relentlessly inspirational epic in which greed and cruelty were often glossed over as enterprise and courage. Later, that epic would be turned upside down by some, so that the story of the West became another — equally misleading — morality tale, one in which the crimes of conquest and dispossession were allowed to overshadow everything else that ever happened beyond the Mississippi. The truth about the West is far more complicated, and much more compelling.

America without the West is unthinkable now. Yet there was nothing inevitable about our taking of it. Others had prior claim to its vastness, after all, and we could quite easily have remained forever huddled east of the Mississippi. In resolving to move west and become a continental nation we would exact a fearful price from those already living on the land. But we also became a different people, and it is no accident that that turbulent history — and the myths that have grown up around it — has made the West the most potent symbol of the nation as a whole, overseas as well as in our own hearts.

Of course, no film series, no book — no library of books, for that matter — can ever encompass the whole story of the West. There are as many valid approaches to telling it as there are able historians willing to try. We believe that history really is biography, and in this volume — and in the script for the twelve-hour film series upon which it is based — we have chosen to focus on the experiences of individual men and women, many of whom tell their own stories in their own words, through diaries and letters and autobiographical accounts.

Our cast is deliberately diverse — there are explorers and soldiers and Indian warriors, settlers and railroad builders and gaudy showmen, but there are also a Chinese ditch digger and a rich Mexican American landowner, a forty-niner from Chile and a Texas cowboy born in Britain, a woman missionary to the Indians who loathed the West and a Wellesley graduate who loved it in spite of everything it did to her and her family. Some of our subjects are celebrated figures. Others will be new to most readers. None plays the stereotyped part one or another of the West's contradictory myths dictates. All were selected because they seemed to us both to illuminate the times through which they lived and to tell us something important about the West, as well.

Our subjects were chosen, too, to demonstrate that in the often stirring story of the West, a human price was paid for every gain. The stories we've tried to tell in these pages and on the television screen at least suggest, we hope, the outlines of a more inclusive story of the West than is conventionally told; a story that is more frank about our failures and more clear-eyed about the cost of even our greatest successes than the old one, but also a story in which each of us can find a place and all can take pardonable pride.

The story of the American West, we believe, is at once the story of a unique part of the country and a metaphor for the country as a whole. With all its heroism and inequity, exploitation and adventure, sober realities and bright myths, it is the story of all of us, no matter where on the continent we happen to live, no matter how recently our ancestors arrived on its shores.

Stephen Ives and Ken Burns

By the time this Blackfoot village was photographed around the turn of the twentieth century, the Indian world had already changed forever.

CHAPTER ONE

THE NORTHERN MYSTERY

The native peoples of the West were far more varied than were the Europeans who, out of ignorance, would one day call them all "Indians." Each group had its own distinctive story of how it came to exist, and its own special name, which most often translated simply as "the people." And each had proved its ability to adapt to change — shifts in climate, new terrain, pressure from neighboring peoples. But nothing could have prepared any of them for what was about to happen to their world.

Most of the men, women, and children of the Cocos Indian village on Galveston Island were away from their homes, setting traps for fish and gathering roots, one early November day in 1528, and so they did not see the pale, half-naked man with hair on his face slip in among their huts. Moving warily, he stole an earthen cooking pot from one dwelling, grabbed fish from the rack on which they had been drying in the sun, tucked a squirming puppy under his arm. Then he fled toward the beach.

Three warriors did spot him and followed at a distance. When they reached the beach they were astonished to see nearly forty strangers much like the one they'd followed, huddled around a driftwood fire. Some were eagerly tearing at the half-dried fish, others were preparing to roast the stolen dog. Still others were simply sprawled on the beach, apparently too weak to move.

The Cocos were accustomed to trading with other native peoples living far inland, but none of them had ever seen men like these before: most of them were pale and hairy, a few were dark skinned, all spoke a barbarous, incomprehensible tongue. The Indians hurried off for reinforcements. Soon, some one hundred warriors — tall men who pierced their ears and lower lips with reeds and were armed with bows and arrows — had gathered to see the curious newcomers.

One of the strangers tottered toward them, holding out a handful of beads and tiny bells. The warriors accepted them, delighting in the tinkling sound they had never heard before, and they offered arrows in return as a sign of friendship. By hand signals they made it clear that they would bring food and water in the morning.

The grateful, desperate strangers were Spanish soldiers and Moorish slaves, all that survived of a land expedition of some three hundred men that had sailed north from Cuba a year earlier with orders to conquer all of "Florida" — the whole fifteen-hundred-mile Gulf coast from the Florida peninsula to the Panuco River in what is now Mexico. The expedition's commander, a one-eyed conquistador named Panfilo de Narvaez, had proved a disaster in the field. In his overeagerness to find treasure, he had led his army too far inland from their landing place near Tampa Bay for it to be resupplied by sea, then lost touch entirely with the vessels that might have rescued him. His high-handed dealings with the Apalachee Indians of the Tallahassee region had finally led their skilled archers to open fire. Without hope of rescue and in terror of Apalachee arrows, suffering from malaria and reduced to eating his horses and stealing parched corn from Indian towns simply to survive, Narvaez had finally abandoned any thought of further exploration and ordered his men to fashion barges

The New World as seen by a Spanish cartographer in 1526, two years before Cabeza de Vaca and his companions were washed up on the Texas coast to begin their extraordinary journey across the Southwest

from hollowed-out trees in which to flee. With sails sewn together from the men's shirts, they had set out from Apalachicola Bay and tried to sail their way west to Mexico. They had been on the water for more than a month, subsisting on half a fistful of corn a day as fierce winds shredded their sails. Only hours before the wind blew them onto the beach at Galveston Island, the survivors had watched it overturn a second vessel, drowning more than forty of their friends.

When the Cocos returned to the beach the next day they brought with them so much food that the man now in command of the strangers, a veteran of half a dozen wars in Europe named Alvar Nuñez Cabeza de Vaca, thought he and his men might still be able to continue their journey. They clawed their log boat out of the sand and pushed it back out into the water, then climbed in and began again to row. But the wind came up once more, a big wave tore the oars from their weakened hands, and a

second turned the barge over. Three men were pulled under and drowned. The rest scrambled to shore and collapsed again on the sand.

Watching from shore, the Cocos were so moved by the strangers' plight, Cabeza de Vaca remembered, that "they sat down and lamented for half an hour so loudly they could have been heard a long way off." Then they motioned for the newcomers to follow them to their camp. The Spanish feared the Indians planned to kill them; instead, they offered only sympathy and hospitality: "Supporting us under our arms, they hurried us from one to another of four big fires they had built along the path [to their village]. At each fire, when we regained a little warmth and strength, they took us on so swiftly our feet hardly touched ground."

These men — their bodies now "so emaciated," Cabeza de Vaca remembered, "we could easily count every bone and looked the very picture of death" — were the first Europeans ever to set foot in the vast region that would one day be called the West.

It was not an auspicious beginning, and all but four of them would soon die. But the adventures that befell those four over the next seven years, and the accounts they gave when they finally reached safety in Mexico, would help to fuel more than two centuries of Spanish adventuring in the region. Their experiences hinted, too, at what the history of the whole West might have been had European assumptions about the people already living there not been so circumscribed, had humility and respect not so often been outweighed by greed and arrogance.

Fourteen ninety-two had marked two great milestones for Ferdinand of Aragon and Isabella of Castile, the rulers of Spain: nearly eight centuries of warfare between Christians and Moorish Muslims on the Iberian Peninsula had ended in victory for the Cross that year, and Christopher Columbus had stumbled upon a whole New World. Surely, the Spanish argued, two such momentous events in a single year were proof that God favored their cause. The following year, Pope Alexander VI, himself a Spaniard, lent that belief his official approval; citing the "authority of the mighty God," he solemnly awarded to his homeland the right to claim the entire New World so that all of its inhabitants could be brought to Christ — by kindness and exhortation if possible, by force of arms if necessary. The same religious zeal that had finally

Encounters: Three engravings of life among the Timucuan people of Florida — based on the firsthand observations of Jacques Le Moyne de Morgues, who visited them with a French expedition in 1564 — suggest something of the complexity of the Indian world Cabeza de Vaca and his contemporaries knew. At left, the Timucuan "king" shows his visitors a pillar, set up by an earlier French party, to which his people continue to make obeisance as a sign of friendship with the exotic strangers. In the center, he leads his men into battle. At right, he comforts the widows of those slain by his enemies.

driven the Moors from Spain would now be loosed upon a whole host of new nonbelievers.

Conquest promised material rewards as well as spiritual ones. To persuade them to finance their holy war against the Moors, the kings of Castile had offered soldiers licenses, entitling them to a handsome share in the spoils. Now, the Spanish king made the same offer to entice adventurers to try their luck across the Atlantic. As Christianity's fortunes improved, so would the fortunes of its soldiers.

The conquistadors seized the island of Española first, then Puerto Rico, Jamaica, Cuba. Hernán Cortés conquered the Aztecs, taking Mexico and with it almost unimaginable riches. Francisco Pizarro crushed the Incas of Peru and commandeered their still richer treasure. By the time Cabeza de Vaca had set out for Florida in 1527, Spain laid claim to the Caribbean and Central America and most of South America, and was eager to probe still farther northward. "We came here to serve God and his Majesty," one conquistador said, "to give light to those who were in the darkness and to get rich, as all men desire to do."

Cabeza de Vaca and his companions shared that desire, and had expected to come as conquerors. Instead, they soon entered the Indian world as supplicants and slaves. The Cocos fed and housed them willingly at first, and Cabeza de Vaca was struck by their tender feelings and generosity: "These people love their offspring more than any in the world and treat them very kindly. If a son dies, the whole village joins the parents and kindred in weeping. The parents set off the wails each day before dawn, again at noon, and at sunset for one year. . . . The people are generous to each other with what little they have."

But when cholera, carried by the Europeans, swept through the Indians' camp, killing all but fifteen of the strangers and almost half the Cocos' own number, the status of the newcomers changed. The surviving Spaniards and Moors scattered, Cabeza de Vaca recalled, and "my life [became] unbearable. In addition to much other work, I had to grub roots in the water or from underground in the canebrakes. My fingers got so raw that if a straw touched them they would bleed. The broken canes often slashed my flesh. I had to work amidst them without benefit of clothes."

In February of 1530, Cabeza de Vaca escaped from his first masters and became a trader instead of a slave, carrying shells and mesquite beans from the coast to the tribes of the interior, and bringing back in exchange flint for arrowheads and red ochre and deer-hair tassels for decoration. "The various Indians would beg me to go from one quarter to another for things they needed," he recalled. "Their incessant hostilities made it impossible for them to travel cross-country. . . . This served my main purpose, which all the while was to determine an eventual road out."

He kept servicing his customers and learning all that he could about the countryside until the summer of 1532, when he came upon three other survivors of his expedition: two soldiers, Alonso del Castillo and Andres Dorantes, and a Moorish slave named Estevanico, who belonged to Dorantes. They were living among a hard-living Tonkawa people called the Mariames, of whom Cabeza de Vaca wrote:

They cast away their daughters at birth; the dogs eat them. They [say they] do this because all the nations of the region are their enemies, with whom they war ceaselessly; and that if they were to marry off their daughters, the daughters would multiply their enemies. . . . We asked why they did not themselves marry these girls. They said that marrying relatives would be a disgusting thing; it was far better to kill them than give them to either kin or foe.

On September 22, 1534, the four men determined to make a break for the Spanish settlements in Mexico, hundreds of miles away. They had been gone for seven years now and would wander for nearly two more, through present-day Texas, northward along the Rio Grande, then south again into what would become northern Mexico, moving from one tribe to the next.

"They all differ," Cabeza de Vaca wrote of the peoples he and his companions met, "in their habitations, villages and tongues." Some menaced the strangers. Others greeted them as honored guests. Still others asked for their help: "Surely extraordinary men like us, [they said,] embodied . . . powers over nature. . . . Some Indians came [begging us] to cure them of terrible headaches. . . . Our method . . . was to bless the sick, breathe upon them, recite a *Pater Noster* and *Ave Maria* and pray earnestly to God our Lord for their recovery. When we concluded with the sign of the cross, He willed that our patients should directly spread the news that they have been restored to health."

In the end, both Cabeza de Vaca and his companions and their Indian patients came to believe in the travelers' healing powers. They were hailed as the Children of the Sun, showered with food and gifts:

At sunset we reached a village of a hundred huts. All the people who lived in them were awaiting us at the village outskirts with terrific yelling and violent slapping of their hands against their thighs. They had with them their precious perforated gourd rattles (pebbles inside) which they produce only at such important occasions. . . . This people hysterically crowded upon us, everyone competing to touch us first; we were nearly killed in the crush. Without letting our feet touch ground, they carried us to the huts they had made for us.

In the Valley of the Sonora they were received by the people of the Ures pueblo, who gave them turquoises and arrowheads fashioned from other green stones that resembled emeralds and which they said came from somewhere far to the north.

By the spring of 1536, some six hundred Pima Indian admirers were escorting them from one settlement to the next. Then they entered the valley of the Rio Sinaloa. Here no crowds turned out to greet them. Indian villages stood empty. "With heavy hearts we looked out over the lavishly watered, fertile and beautiful land," Cabeza de Vaca noted, "now abandoned and burned, and the people thin and weak, scattering and hiding in fright. . . . All along the way we could see the tracks of the Christians and traces of their camps." The "Christians" were Spanish slavers who had already managed to seize "half the men and all the women and boys" to work their gold and copper mines.

Cabeza de Vaca sought out the Spanish commander, a conquistador named Diego de Alcaraz. He was "dumbfounded by the sight of me," Cabeza de Vaca recalled,

The hardships I endured in this journeying business were long to tell — peril and privation, storms and frost, which often overtook me when alone in the wilderness. By the unfailing Grace of God our Lord I came forth from all.

Alvar Nuñez Cabeza de Vaca

THE ANASAZI

Several great peoples — remembered collectively as the Anasazi, the Navajo word for "the Old Ones" — once ruled the high country where the present states of New Mexico, Colorado, Utah, and Arizona come together. For centuries, their civilization thrived, trading turquoise with other cultures to the north and south, east and west. They felled trees to make way for fields of corn and beans and squash, dammed streams to water their crops, laid out hundreds of miles of broad, straight roads across the desert, and built towns where thousands lived in houses several stories high.

But by A.D. 1300 — most likely because years of drought had simply made life untenable — they abandoned it all and moved south to establish new towns along the Rio Grande. (The present-day Pueblos, Zuni, and Hopi are believed to be their descendants.) Meanwhile, newcomers — ancestors of the Navajo and Ute and Apache — eventually took over much of the region the Anasazi had occupied. The Old Ones were not the first people to be displaced by others in the West, nor would they be the last.

Anasazi ruins in Canyon de Chelly, New Mexico, photographed by Timothy O'Sullivan in 1873

"strangely undressed and in company with friends." But the commander was frankly delighted by the sight of Cabeza de Vaca's Indian companions, six hundred men, women, and children, ripe for the taking. There were precious few potential slaves in the picked-over region, he explained, and "he was completely undone, having been unable to catch any Indians in a long time; he did not know which way to turn; his men were getting too hungry and exhausted." Seizing Cabeza de Vaca's Indian escort would make the whole expedition worthwhile.

But Cabeza de Vaca refused to cooperate. If Indians were to be converted to Christianity, his travels had now taught him, "they must be won by kindness, the only certain way." He urged his followers to return to their homes as quickly as possible. The Indians hesitated at first, fearful of leaving their healer among such barbaric strangers. They could not believe that these brutal slavers and the men who had healed them could be the same sort of people:

> Conferring among themselves, they replied that the Christians lied: We had come from the sunrise, they from the sunset; we healed the sick, they killed the [healthy]; we came naked and barefoot, they, clothed, horsed, and lanced; we coveted nothing but gave whatever we were given, while they robbed whomsoever they found and bestowed nothing on anyone.

Cabeza de Vaca persisted in urging them to go home, and the Pimas finally agreed. The slavers waited till he and his companions were on their way to the nearest Spanish settlement under escort, then seized the Indians anyway.

By appealing to the Spanish authorities when he got to Mexico City, Cabeza de Vaca managed to win freedom for all of his former followers, but the viceroy was far less interested in his views on how Indians should be treated than he was in the possibility of new treasure. The returned wanderer was careful not to exaggerate. Most of the lands through which he had passed, he said, were "remote and malign, devoid of resources." But he also reported that the Indians had told him of "populous towns and very large houses . . . and many turquoise stones" farther to the north than he had gone.

There had long been rumors in Europe of Seven Cities of Gold, said to have been established by seven fugitive bishops from Portugal and now believed to lie somewhere north of Mexico. Cabeza de Vaca's account was all the would-be treasure-hunters needed. The Seven Cities did exist; here was proof of it. In 1539, the slave Estevanico was asked to guide a priest, Fray Marcos de Niza, and a large scouting party in hopes of finding them somewhere in the region the Spanish called the Northern Mystery.

THE SEVEN CITIES OF GOLD

In the spring of that year, the one hundred Zuni families who made Hawikuh pueblo in what is now Arizona their home were preparing to begin their planting ritual, as they had done for centuries. Their sacred spirits — *katsinas* — were to be evoked to ensure fertility and bring the rain that made life in that arid land possible.

But just as the ceremonies got under way, a lookout spotted a jostling crowd of some three hundred Indians approaching. They were escorting a man unlike anyone they had ever seen before — tall and dark skinned, dressed in pelts and wearing bits of turquoise, walking two greyhounds on a leash. His escorts said he was a great healer, but the people of Hawikuh tried to bar his entry by pouring a line of sacred cornmeal across his path.

The stranger stepped right over it. Declaring himself a Child of the Sun, he demanded turquoise and women, and warned that more of the Sun's children were on their way. As a token of his unearthly power he had sent ahead of him a decorated gourd rattle.

The chief of the pueblo was not impressed. He recognized the rattle as having been fashioned by a people far to the south, with whom his people had no friendly rela-

Dancers assembled to invoke rain as part of the annual summer solstice ceremony at Zuni pueblo, 1899

THE PEOPLE

It stretches from the Pacific Ocean to the Mississippi River, from the Rio Grande to what is now the border of Canada — 2,168,930 square miles of the most extraordinary landscape on earth.

To the Spanish priests and soldiers who rode into it from Mexico, it was the North. To the Russians and British who first sailed along its coast in search of furs to sell to China, it was the East. And to the French and British trappers who wandered into it from Canada, it was the South.

To the Native Americans it was simply home. Yet because its most recent conquerors came from the east, it has come to be called the West.

Its terrain has always beckoned — and repelled. It is a land of grasslands and deserts and mountain barriers: the Rockies and Wasatch, the Bitterroots and Bighorns, the Sierra Nevada and Sangre de Cristo, the Confusions, the Crazies, and the Black Hills.

It is a land of rivers: the Colorado and Columbia and Missouri; the Carson, the Humboldt, and the Dismal; the Big Sandy and the Little Sandy; Sand Creek and the Greasy Grass; the River That Scolds All Others and the River of No Return.

And it is also a land of too little water.

The West exists on a scale virtually unknown elsewhere. It is a land of unimaginable distances and infinite horizons.

But it was never empty. No one knows how many hundreds of thousands of native people occupied it before the coming of the first Europeans, perhaps as many as 3 million. But they had lived there for a thousand generations since their arrival by land from the Asian mainland across the Bering Strait.

Counterclockwise from left: Many Horns, Teton Lakota, 1872; Navajo boy, 1905; Mattie Tom, Apache, 1899

The photographs on these and the following pages, made in the late nineteenth and early twentieth centuries, can only hint at the richness and variety of the Indian world before the coming of the conquistadors.

Devils Tower in Wyoming, sacred
to several Indian peoples

Right: Modisi, Hopi, 1879;
Chief Washakie, Shoshone

There were those among them who lived in isolated shelters fashioned from brush, and others who occupied large houses made from the tallest trees on earth. Some knew only skin teepees that could be put up and pulled down in minutes; others dwelt in elaborate cliff-top cities that had stood for centuries.

Some prayed to the spirits of the animals they hunted and did not dare alter the earth they believed to be their mother. Others transformed the landscape, burning valleys and hillsides to increase the grasslands — and the deer that fed upon them. Still others built dams and diverted streams to irrigate their crops.

In some tribes, war was considered the highest calling, and wealth was measured in slaves. In others, women owned all the property, and when a couple married, the man joined his wife's family.

Pawnee earth lodge village in present-day Nebraska

Havasupai dwelling made of brush, Southwest

Cheyenne painted for a sun dance

Spokane village, Washington

Two Whistles, Crow

Hopi dancer

Zuni snake priest

Webs of ancient trading trails stretched in every direction and covered every corner of the West. Precious seashells from the Pacific Northwest were harvested by people who rode the seas in immense canoes and traded the shells for elk hides with a people who flattened their babies' heads as a sign of beauty and prestige. From tribe to tribe, the shells were passed inland — exchanged for salmon with a merchant people who held a yearly trading fair on the Columbia River.

Kwakiutl wearing mask, Northwest coast

Skidegate village of the Haida tribe, Queen Charlotte Island, British Columbia, 1878

Haida shamans

Umatilla woman, Columbia Basin

Nez Percé woman

Gros Ventre woman drying meat,
Fort Belknap reservation, 1906

Omaha village

Lakota women decorated with
porcupine quills and dentalium shells

The shells were also traded for powerful bows fashioned from the horns of mountain sheep by a tribe who called themselves the Namipu but who would one day be called the Nez Percé, who each year climbed through the Bitterroots to hunt; for buffalo meat provided by people who followed the great herds across the Plains on foot and depended on dogs to haul their few belongings; for corn, grown along the Missouri River by the Mandan people, who lived in large towns of rounded earth lodges; and for wild rice and deerskins, brought from the woodlands east of the Mississippi by the Lakota, a people who would one day migrate west themselves and be renamed the Sioux by their enemies.

And so, people who worshiped different gods, inhabited entirely different worlds, and were sometimes unaware of one another's existence were linked together nonetheless: buffalo robes warmed people who had never seen a buffalo; cornmeal was eaten by people who had never planted corn; and ocean shells decorated the clothing of people who lived a thousand miles from the sea.

Kutenai duck hunter, Montana

Lakota woman and dog travois of the kind used before the coming of the horse, Rosebud reservation

Sia buffalo mask, Southwest

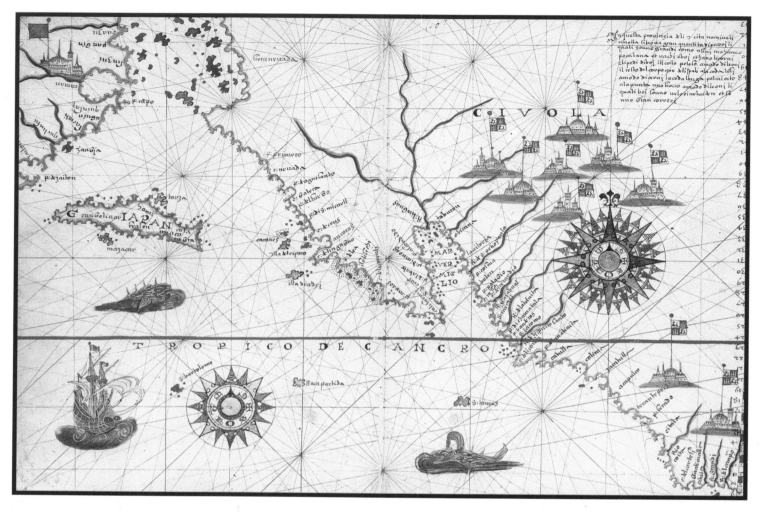

The Seven Cities of Gold were still optimistically included in this detail of a Spanish map showing the Southwest in 1578, nearly four decades after Coronado had failed to find them.

tions. Now believing the stranger either a spy, a madman, or a witch, the chief ordered him killed. Afterward, some of the people of the pueblo wondered if they had done the right thing, whether the dead man's warning of more mysterious strangers on the way would come true. They would have to wait just a little over a year for their answer. They could not have known it then, but nothing in their lives — or the lives of the other peoples who occupied the lands newcomers would one day call the West — would ever be the same again.

The dark-skinned stranger the Zuni of Hawikuh had killed was the Moorish slave Estevanico, and when Fray Marcos got word of his guide's fate, he determined to return to Mexico as fast as he could. But before he fled, he slipped up close enough to have at least a glimpse of Hawikuh, or so he would later claim:

> It had a very fine appearance. . . . The houses, as the Indians have told me, are all of stone, built in stories and with flat roofs. Judging by what I could see from the height where I placed myself to observe it, the settlement is larger than the city of Mexico. . . . It appears to me that this land is the best and largest of all those that have been discovered.

Hawikuh, he assured the authorities in Mexico City, was indeed one of the Seven Cities of Gold and satisfyingly filled with treasure: "I was told that there is much gold there and the natives make it into little vessels and jewels for their ears, and into little blades with which they wipe away their sweat."

The friar's gaudy stories grew with the telling — he confided to a fellow priest that he had also seen a temple filled with idols, its walls covered "inside and outside with precious stones" — and in February of 1540, the Spanish viceroy sent Fray Marcos north again, escorted this time by 292 Spanish soldiers, 3 priests, more than a thousand Indians, and big hungry herds of sheep and cattle and horses. In command was the thirty-year-old governor of a Mexican province who had married a woman of great wealth and was now eager to amass a fortune of his own — Francisco Vásquez de Coronado.

It took Coronado's expedition four months, following Indian trails across deserts and through the mountains, but he finally reached Hawikuh in July.

The Zuni saw them coming, the sun slanting off their helmets. The black stranger had been right: they *were* the Children of the Sun. And this time they came riding on monstrous animals no Native American in the region had ever seen before — horses. The warriors went down to face them, nonetheless. Through an interpreter, Coronado explained that he had come on a sacred mission. He warned that the Indians must submit to the Spanish crown and adopt Christianity. If they did not, "with the help of God we shall forcefully . . . make war against you . . . take you and your wives and children and . . . make slaves of them . . . and shall do to you all the harm and damage that we can."

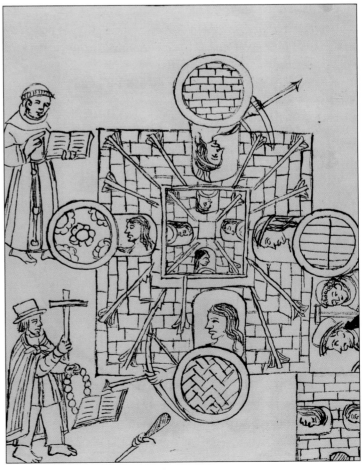

A mestizo artist from Mexico — half-Spanish and half-Tlaxcalan — made this drawing of the Zuni defending their pueblo against Coronado to impress Phillip II of Spain with the part Mexican Indians had played in Spanish efforts to dominate the Southwest.

The Zuni refused to allow the strangers to enter their pueblo, perhaps having heard from their trading partners to the south rumors about the depredations of Spanish slavers. Instead, they began to throw stones and shoot arrows. "They . . . grew so bold," Coronado remembered, "that they came up almost to the heels of our horses to shoot their arrows. On this account, I saw that it was no longer time to hesitate, and as the priests approved the action, I charged them." The Spanish shouted "Santiago!" — St. James — as they went into battle, their war cry invoking the patron saint who they believed had brought them victory over the Moors.

The Indians fled from Spanish lances and from Spanish guns, whose thunderous sound they had never heard before. Several were killed. The rest retreated within the town walls and hurled rocks down on their attackers. Coronado himself was twice knocked to the ground: "If I had not been protected by the very good headpiece," he recalled, "the outcome would have been very bad for me." But the Spanish soon overran the Indians, seized their stores of food, and set up a cross — to which the Zuni began to make frantic offerings.

Christianity had come to the American West.

Coronado renamed Hawikuh "Granada," but quickly realized it was no City of Gold. Instead, one of his disillusioned soldiers remembered, it was "a little crowded village, looking as if

it had been crumpled all up together. There are ranch houses in New Spain which make a better appearance at a distance."

There was no treasure. Nor did Coronado's men find any in neighboring pueblos. Furious, Coronado sent Fray Marcos back to Mexico for fear one of his frustrated soldiers might kill him if he stayed. "He has not told the truth in a single thing that he said," he wrote to the viceroy, "but everything is the opposite of what he related. . . ."

From Hawikuh, Coronado sent expeditions into the surrounding countryside. One explored the Colorado Plateau and crossed the Painted Desert into the land of the Hopi. Another, with Hopi guides to show them the way, marched for twenty days to the edge of a great gorge — the Grand Canyon of the Colorado. Nothing in the European experience had prepared them for its sheer size. The Spanish determined to cross it, and when the Indians tried to tell them how wide the river and its canyon really were, one member of the party remembered, they refused to believe their guides:

Strangers: Navajo artists painted these Spanish soldiers and their mounts in Canyon del Muerto in what is now Arizona sometime in the late eighteenth or early nineteenth century.

> . . . Captain Melgosa, with Juan Galeras and another companion, . . . undertook to clamber down at a place that appeared to them the least difficult. They kept descending in sight of the men left above until they were lost to view. . . . At four o'clock in the afternoon they returned, without having been able to reach the bottom because of the great obstacles they encountered, for what from above had appeared to be easy, proved to be, on the contrary, rough and difficult. They said they had only been a third of the way down, but from the place they reached, the river looked very large indeed; indeed, judging from what they saw, it must be as wide as the Indians had said. The men who remained above estimated that some rocks jutting out from the canyon must be about as high as a man; but those who went down swore that when they reached them they were found to be taller than the highest tower of Seville.

As winter approached, Coronado sent his army northward toward the Tiwa country on the Rio Grande, halting only long enough to search each pueblo he came upon. His men commandeered the pueblo of Alcanfor, demanded food and clothing, allowed their herds to destroy Indian crops, and molested Indian women. When the nearby pueblo of Arenal rose against them, one of Coronado's lieutenants set it afire, then burned one hundred warriors at the stake and killed many more as they fled in terror. Twelve villages were destroyed before the Spanish had finished, and many of their occupants driven into the Sangre de Cristo Mountains.

In the spring, Coronado moved still farther north, determined to salvage his reputation, his dream of treasure rekindled by a Pawnee captive of the Pueblos whom the Spanish called "the Turk" because, one Spaniard explained, "he looked like one." The Turk told wondrous tales of his homeland far to the north, a place he called Quivira. "The lord of that land took his siesta under a large tree from which hung numerous golden . . . bells," he promised, and "the common table service of all was generally of wrought silver, and . . . the pitchers, dishes, and bowls, were made of gold."

In the spring of 1541, Coronado set out for Quivira. He crossed the panhandle of what would one day become Texas, mostly unimpressed by the nomadic bands of hunters his men encountered; they "have no permanent residence anywhere," wrote the expedition's chronicler, Pedro de Castañeda, and used "troops of dogs" to drag their meager belongings. But the Spanish were astounded by the great herds of buffalo — "cows," Castañeda called them — which parted just long enough to let his columns pass.

Coronado led his men on, through an ocean of grass so vast and featureless they had to navigate with a "sea-compass," onto the great plains of what is now Kansas. Like all the newcomers who arrived in the West after them, these Spanish conquistadors and their Mexican Indian allies were stunned by the grand scale of the landscape through which they passed:

> Who could believe [Castañeda remembered] that 1,000 horses and 500 of our cows and more than 5,000 rams and ewes and more than 1,500 friendly Indians and servants, in traveling over those plains, would leave no more trace when they had passed than if nothing had been there — nothing — so that it was necessary to make piles of bones and cow dung, so that the rear guard could follow the army.

Here, too, the promised treasure failed to materialize. Quivira turned out to be a Wichita village on the bank of the Arkansas River, just another cluster of huts surrounded by corn and bean fields. Under questioning, the Turk admitted it had all been a lie. There had never been any gold or silver. To rid themselves of the Spanish, the Tiwa had evidently urged him to lead the foreigners as far as possible onto the plains — "to take us to a place," one of the soldiers remembered, "where we and our horses would starve to death."

Coronado's men strangled the Turk, then began the long march back to Mexico and safety. There Coronado faced charges of having mismanaged his expedition. "Holy Catholic Caesarian Majesty," he wrote to his sovereign. "I have done all that I possibly could to serve Your Majesty and to discover a country where God Our Lord might be served and the Royal Patrimony increased, as . . . Your Majesty's humble servant and vassal, who would kiss the royal feet and hands." A court of inquiry exonerated Coronado of all charges, but he died in obscurity a dozen years later and his failure to find treasure discouraged further explorations of the Northern Mystery for nearly half a century. Conquest without profit was too costly even for the viceroys of Mexico.

The country itself is the best I have ever seen for producing all the products of Spain . . . the land itself being very fat and black and . . . very well watered by the rivulets and springs and rivers. . . . [But] what I am sure of is that there is not any gold nor any other metal in all that country, . . . nothing but little villages, and in many of these they do not plant anything and do not have any houses except of skins and sticks, and they wander around with the cows; so that the account [the Indians] gave me was false. . . .

Francisco Vásquez de Coronado

The army passed the great rock of
Acoma. As it was at peace, the
people entertained us well, giving
us provisions and birds. . . . Many
soldiers climbed up to the top to see
the pueblo. They found it very difficult
to climb the steps in the rock, not
being used to them. The natives, on the
other hand, go up and down so freely
that they carry loads of provisions,
and the women carry water, and
they do not seem to touch the walls
with their hands. Our men had
to hand their weapons to one another
when they tried to make the climb.

Pedro de Castañeda

The ruins of Acoma, photographed in 1904

THE PUEBLO REVOLT

By 1629 — 101 years after Cabeza de Vaca and his companions were washed up on the Gulf coast, 87 years after Coronado returned to Mexico City in disgrace, and 9 years after English Puritans began settling Plymouth and the Massachusetts Bay Colony on the Atlantic coast — the Spanish-speaking presence in the Southwest still numbered well under a thousand persons, most of whom were Indian or part-Indian servants.

The notion of large-scale settlement had been abandoned, but a handful of soldier-settlers had established *haciendas* along the Rio Grande and exacted labor from nearby Pueblos, just as Spanish landowners worked their serfs at home.

New Mexico was now officially a royal colony, ruled from a village on a tributary of the Rio Grande called Santa Fe — the city of "Holy Faith" — and maintained at royal expense to provide protection for a handful of priests who claimed already to have brought some 20,000 Indians to Christ. More than fifty pueblos had churches of their own now, all built by Indian hands.

Then, a new expedition reached Santa Fe from Mexico, a band of thirty Franciscan friars escorted by a handful of soldiers and filled with fresh zeal to see to it that their faith was spread to the farthest reaches of the province. They had come, they told all those they encountered, to liberate them from "the miserable slavery of the demon and from the obscure darkness of their idolatry. . . ."

By now, the people of the pueblos had learned through bitter experience that it was better to tolerate the presence of the Spanish than to defy them openly, simpler to demonstrate exclusive fealty to the friar's god in public, and then, in the privacy of their kivas — the circular, partially underground chambers reached by ladders that symbolized life emerging from Mother Earth — treat "Dios, the Mexican god" as just one of many deities.

There were tense moments between the priests and the people of the pueblos, but there was also continuous conflict between the friars and the secular officials meant to protect them. Settlers charged that the priests took up too much of the Indians' time that might better be spent working their fields. The priests responded that the settlers — and the royal governors who usually sided with them — were interrupting God's work of converting unbelievers. Meanwhile, white man's diseases to which the Indians had no immunities tore through the pueblos — smallpox, measles, tuberculosis, diphtheria. Twenty thousand died in 1638 alone — one-third of the pueblo population. Ten thousand more Indians died in 1640, and those who survived could not help but notice that the prayers of the priests seemed to have no effect on these new enemies that none of them could see.

Then, beginning in 1660, a drought further seared the already parched landscape. It refused to rain, summer after summer. And with the drought came raids by the Pueblos' traditional enemies, nomadic hunting bands who spoke the Athabascan language and whose ancestors had wandered south from Canada. These raiders called themselves *Diné* — "the People" — but the Pueblos called some of them *apachu,* "the enemy," and others *apachu nabahu,* or "enemies of the cultivated fields." Soon, they would be known as the Apache and the Navajo. Driven off the plains and into Pueblo territory by drought, some survived by raiding, sometimes burning crops

Hopi watch a party of strangers approach the stone steps that lead to their mesa-top home at Walpi, Arizona, 1873.

and killing the livestock they could not carry off with them. Again, the friars' prayers seemed powerless against these raiders.

All these misfortunes coming at once suggested to some among the Pueblos that by accepting Christianity even in part they had displeased their own divinities, and one Tiwa spiritual leader of the San Juan pueblo began preaching in secret that the Spanish would have to be driven out before life could be made good again. His name was Popé, which means "ripe planting," and his normal ritual duties included blessing crops but not fighting battles. That such a man should have come to advocate violent resistance was evidence of how deeply unhappy his people were. Soon, urged on by Popé and others, young men everywhere were dancing in honor of the *katsinas* that had always brought them prosperity, thumping their feet hard on the earth to awaken the gods who dwelled beneath it.

Meanwhile, the Spanish came to believe they had displeased *their* God. Convinced that their colony's troubles grew out of the lack of Christian unity between priests and governors, the Franciscans redoubled their efforts to blot out the Pueblo religion. Ritual dances were forbidden, religious objects burned.

Twice, the Spanish had Popé flogged publicly, but they could not silence him. The Spanish governor finally ordered him and forty-six others sold into slavery for cast-

Martyrs: In 1758, Comanche and their Tonkawa and Hasinai allies — armed with French weapons and angry that Spain had forged an alliance with their Apache enemies — attacked the Spanish mission at San Saba in present-day Texas. Eight persons were killed, including two Franciscans, Fray Terreros (left) and Fray Santiestéban, whose deaths are exhaustively commemorated in this anonymous painting made in Mexico City five years later.

ing spells. But when a large delegation of armed Tiwa descended upon Santa Fe and demanded the Indians' release, the governor felt he had no choice but to give in. With fewer than a thousand colonists in all New Mexico, he could not risk a full-scale uprising.

That was just what Popé had in mind, and from his post inside the kiva at Taos he began secretly spreading his message from pueblo to pueblo: the people must forget their differences, band together, and finally rid themselves of Spain.

On August 10, pueblos all across northern New Mexico rose up and overthrew their priests: at Taos, Santa Clara, Picuris, Santa Cruz, they killed the friars and razed or profaned their churches. Twenty-one of the thirty-three Franciscans in New Mexico were killed. So were 375 settlers and their servants. Terrified colonists and their allies fled to Santa Fe and huddled together inside the adobe-walled Palace of the Governors, where 2,500 warriors surrounded them, cut off their water, burned the rest of the capital, and sang the Catholic liturgy in Latin to mock their captives. After eleven days of siege, the surviving Spaniards fought their way out and set out for the mission of El Paso, far to the south.

The Pueblos let them go. It was enough that New Mexico was theirs again. Popé had inspired the most successful Indian revolt in North American history — but his victory would not last long.

The record of what happened next is only fragmentary. If Spanish sources are to be believed, Popé, like other revolutionaries in other lands, became a despot who ordered all Spanish buildings razed — except for the governors' palace, which he claimed for himself. Determined that everyone should return as swiftly as possible to "the state of their antiquity," he insisted that his followers forget everything they had learned from the Spanish, renounce their baptisms and dissolve their Christian marriages, abandon the metal hoes that made bigger crops possible, even tear up their fruit trees. Some Indians resisted. Others noted that although they had returned to the old ways, the sky still withheld its rain.

In any case, by the time General Diego de Vargas led a detachment of just sixty soldiers and a hundred Indian auxiliaries back to Santa Fe in the summer of 1692, Popé was dead. The Pueblos had fallen out among themselves and were again unable to fend off the Apache and the Navajo. After a bloody battle to wrest the capital from the Tanos — which ended with the execution of seventy warriors and the distribution of their wives and children among the new colonists as slaves — and a second revolt in 1696 in which all but five of the pueblos joined, most of the Indians acquiesced in the restoration of Spanish power.

The Franciscans eventually managed to build a string of new missions in what is now southern Arizona, and the threat of giving up any of the territory Spain claimed to a European rival could still stir Madrid and Mexico City into action: when French traders dared move into what is now Texas from the east, Spain sent expeditions to establish outposts, including the presidio San Antonio de Bexar and its accompanying mission, San Antonio de Valero — whose chapel would one day be remembered as the Alamo.

But Spain had abandoned hope of full-scale colonization: it was too expensive and promised too few rewards. The colonists and the Pueblos needed one another to fend

The Christian Indians of this kingdom are convoked, allied and confederated for the purpose of rebelling, abandoning obedience to the crown and apostasizing from the Holy Faith. They plan to kill the priests, and all the Spaniards — even women and children — thus to destroy the total population of this kingdom. . . .

Headmen of three pueblos loyal to Spain, to the Spanish governor of New Mexico, August 9, 1680

off the Apache and the Navajo, and a brisk trade began in selling one another Indian slaves captured from their mutual enemies. The Pueblos were tacitly permitted to practice their own faith alongside Catholicism: church and kiva, *katsinas* and Christ all came to coexist in relative harmony. Colonists and colonized intermarried. The boundaries between the Indian and Spanish worlds had begun to blur.

SWEET MEDICINE

According to Cheyenne tradition, there was once a prophet named Sweet Medicine who warned that strangers called "Earth Men" would one day appear among them, light skinned, speaking an unknown tongue. And with them would come a strange animal that would change the Cheyenne way of life, forever:

> It has a shaggy neck and a tail almost touching the ground. Its hoofs are round. This animal will carry you on his back and help you in many ways. Those far hills that seem only a blue vision in the distance take many days to reach now; but with this animal you can get there in a short time, so fear him not. Remember what I have said.

The Pueblo Revolt had been confined to one remote corner of the West, but its aftershock would help make that prophecy come true — for the Cheyenne and for most of the other native peoples of the West. It brought them the horse.

A painted buffalo hide memorializes the victory of a party of mounted Pawnee over some horseless Kansa Indians.

Opposite, top: A Gros Ventre family demonstrates for the photographer Edward Curtis how households moved from place to place after the coming of the horse, 1904.

Opposite, bottom: Plenty-Coups, Crow, 1880

Some Spanish horses had already been stolen or illegally traded to other tribes before the revolt began, but when the Spanish were driven out of their lands, the Pueblos, who had little need for the big herds that devoured the grass their sheep required, started trading them off to the Apache and the Navajo, who, in turn, soon began trading them to tribes farther north. And so it went, hunters swapping with farmers, farmers with hunters. By the 1690s, the horse had already reached the Plains tribes of Texas. By 1700, it had reached the Kiowa and Comanche in what is now Colorado.

The Cheyenne had been farmers, dwelling in permanent villages on the banks of rivers in what is now Minnesota, growing corn and beans and squash, until the Lakota began driving them westward. By 1700, they were living in what is now South Dakota, still tending crops and hunting buffalo on foot. Then the horse came. "The first Cheyenne who ever saw horses saw them come to water at a lake . . ." a man named John Stands-in-Timber would remember being told:

> He went down closer to look, and then he thought of the prophecy of Sweet Medicine, that there would be animals with round hoofs and shaggy manes and tails, and men could ride on their backs into the Blue Vision. He went back to the village and told the old Indians and they remembered.
>
> So they fixed a snare, and when a horse stepped into it they ran to him and tied him down. . . . After they got the first horses they learned there were more of them in the South and they went there after them. That was when they began the religion they called the Horse Worship.

Suddenly, a mounted hunter could in one day kill enough buffalo to feed and clothe his family for months. Soon, the Cheyenne were following the buffalo on horseback and raiding other tribes to add to their pony herds. The Great Plains, which had been sparsely occupied mostly by agriculturists, suddenly became a crowded meeting ground for some thirty tribes from every direction. Some, like the Pawnee, would use the horse to move from one campsite to another, hunting buffalo from horseback just twice a year, and otherwise continue to rely on their crops for survival. But others — including the Cheyenne and Crow — abandoned their fields and permanent villages altogether to become nomadic hunters. A Crow chief named Plenty-Coups summed up what his mount meant to him.

My horse fights with me and fasts with me, because if he is to carry me in battle he must know my heart, and I must know his or we shall never become brothers. I have been told that the white man, who is almost a god, and yet a great fool, does not believe that the horse has a spirit. This cannot be true. I have many times seen my horse's soul in his eyes.

Soon, the horse was so central to the lives of some western peoples that they literally could no longer imagine a time when they had managed to survive without it.

There were other signs of white men besides horses. French trappers probed northern lakes and rivers in search of furs, built missions and trading posts down the Mississippi and its tributaries, and armed the tribes with whom they traded. Their rivals, the English, armed and supplied their Indian allies, as well. Guns gave some tribes a sudden, deadly advantage over others, just as European trade goods — blankets, knives, kettles, axes — made some tribes wealthier than others overnight.

But if some Indian peoples were strengthened by the coming of the horse and the gun and trade goods, all were threatened by still another legacy of the Europeans: disease for which they had no immunities. Smallpox swept across the Plains well in advance of the whites who had brought it with them, and reached the Northwest in 1782. There, it may have killed half the Blackfeet — as well as half their sometime enemies, the Nez Percé, occupants of the grassy plateau between the Cascades and the Rockies in what is now Idaho, who had yet even to see one of the white men who had now twice transformed their world; they would not see one for almost another quarter of a century. Some scholars suggest that most of the people who inhabited the West — and the rest of the New World — succumbed to epidemic disease before serious white settlement began.

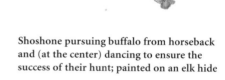

Shoshone pursuing buffalo from horseback and (at the center) dancing to ensure the success of their hunt; painted on an elk hide

Opposite: A Ute warrior and his son, photographed in 1871, some 200 years after the horse and firearms had begun the transformation of their world

Sweet Medicine of the Cheyenne had foreseen the coming of the horse. But he also predicted the corrosive impact upon his people of those who had brought the horse with them into the West:

> Some day you will meet a people who are white. They will try always to give you things, but do not take them. At last I think you will take these things that they offer you, and this will bring sickness to you. . . .
>
> Your ways will change. You will leave your religion for something new. You will lose respect for your leaders and start quarreling with one another. . . . You will take the Earth Men's ways and forget good things by which you have lived and in the end become worse than crazy.

THE TERRESTRIAL PARADISE

European legends held that California was an island, a strange and exotic place, the home of beautiful Amazons, each of whom had only a single breast so that she could draw her bow more effectively. In fact, it was the most densely populated region in North America, home to more than 300,000 people, belonging to countless bands, speaking more than eighty mutually unintelligible languages.

In 1769, rumors reached Mexico City that fur traders from Russia were building outposts along California's coast, and the visitor-general of New Spain, alarmed that the Russians and the British might challenge Spain's claim to the region, sent

A man could not even court a girl unless he had proved his courage. That was one reason so many were anxious to win good war records. . . . The women even had a song they would sing about a man whose courage had failed him. The song was: "If you are afraid when you charge, turn back. The Desert Women will eat you." . . . It was hard to go into a fight, and they were often afraid, but it was worse to turn back and face the women.

John Stands-in-Timber, Cheyenne

On May 15, 1769, Father Junipero Serra (below) encountered California Indians (left) for the first time: "I gave praise to the Lord," he remembered, "kissing the ground, and thanking His Majesty for the fact that, after so many years of looking forward to it, He now permitted me to be among the pagans in their own country. . . . I found myself in front of twelve of them, all men and grown up, except two who were boys. . . . I saw something I could not believe. . . . It was this: They were entirely naked as Adam in the garden, before sin. . . . We spoke a long time with them, and not for one moment, while they saw us clothed, could you notice the least sign of shame in them."

an expedition northward to establish missions and garrisons with which to guard them. With them, on what would later be called the "sacred expedition," came Father Junipero Serra.

Serra was a former teacher of philosophy, nearsighted, badly handicapped by an ulcerated leg, and further weakened by his pious habit of scourging his own flesh in atonement for the sins of others. He was so frail at the outset of the journey that he had to be lifted onto his mule, and sometimes had to be carried on a stretcher. But nothing could quell his missionary fervor, and whenever he spotted Indians along the way he rang a little bell to attract them to his side so that he could preach the gospel to them.

Father Serra and his successors would establish twenty missions in all, scattered along five hundred miles of the California coast — including San Diego, San Gabriel, San Luis Obispo, San Antonio de Padua, San Jose, and San Francisco de Asis. Near the mission San Gabriel, where earthquake tremors were so strong they shook the Spanish off their feet, a small town sprang up in 1781, settled by forty-six persons whom the mission fathers considered lazy and corrupt, interested mainly in drinking, gambling, and pursuing women. It was called El Pueblo de Nuestra Senora La Reina de Los Angeles.

The California missions were run very differently from those in New Mexico. There, the priests had attached themselves and their churches to already-established pueblos and often relied on them as allies against raids by other tribes. But in California, the coastal peoples — the Ipais and Tipais, Salinans, Chumash, Constanoans, Gabrielinos, and the rest — lived for the most part in scattered

Retrato del Rev. Padre Fray Junipero Serra Apostol de la Alta California, tomado del original que se conserva en su Convento de la Santa Cruz de Querétaro.

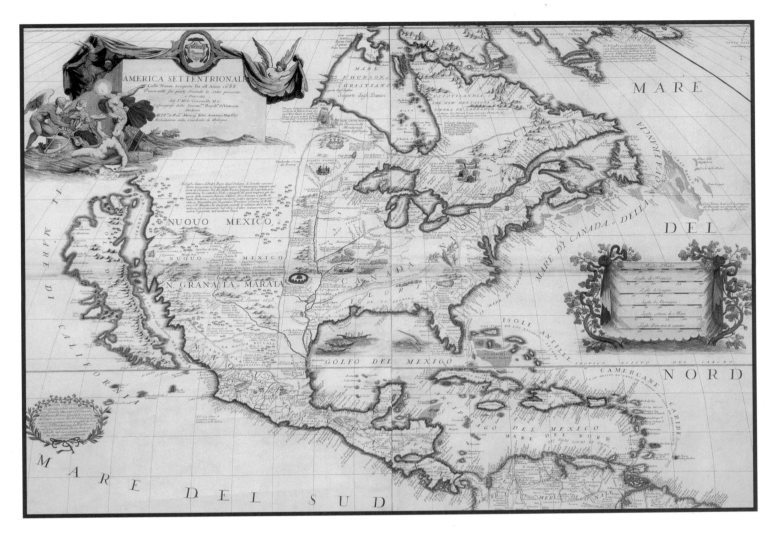

Until Spain sent missionaries north from Mexico, cartographers remained stubbornly convinced that California was an island, as shown in this 1688 rendering.

bands or small villages. To curtail what they called the Indians' "free and undisciplined state," and thereby bring them to Christ, the friars used soldiers to round them up and force them into the missions. There, the Indians — "neopyhtes," the friars called them — had little choice but to do as they were told. They were given new Spanish names, crowded together in sexually segregated barracks, and made to labor without pay or hope of freedom. Those who tried to flee were hunted down and flogged. Such apparent cruelty, the friars held, was really a great kindness because it would lead their converts to Paradise instead of the eternal damnation they were certain awaited all unbelievers.

Those who managed to escape and flee into the hills often joined forces with the Yokuts and other hunting tribes who lived there in raiding the missions, stealing horses, destroying crops, sometimes killing priests.

The fathers managed to baptize some 54,000 California Indians during the mission era, but few survived more than a few years of mission life. The Indian population between San Diego and San Francisco declined from perhaps 72,000 to as few as 18,000, victims of poor food, poor treatment, and European diseases fostered by overcrowding. "They live well free," a puzzled friar said, "but as soon as we reduce them to a Christian and community life . . . they fatten, sicken and die."

Christ bearing the cross (top) and being nailed to it, painted by Indian neophytes at Mission San Fernando

THE MISSION

By 1804, white visitors were nothing new to the Mandan, who occupied two great walled towns at the confluence of the Missouri and Knife rivers in what is now North Dakota. When combined with the five nearby villages belonging to their allies, the Hidatsa, theirs was the largest community west of the Mississippi, home to 4,500 people, more than then lived in St. Louis or Washington, D.C. The Mandan had long been the middlemen for trade on the upper Missouri, growing corn for barter and providing neutral ground on which the Cheyenne could trade horses for furs with the Assiniboin and Crow, and the Lakota could swap buffalo meat for French firearms. And ever since the Frenchman Pierre Gaultier de Varennes, Sieur de La Vérendrye, had visited the Mandan in 1738 — under the mistaken impression that they were a mysterious tribe of blue-eyed Welshmen somehow transplanted to the

New World — they had been doing a profitable business with individual traders from England and France.

In fact, a Scottish trapper and several French-Canadians were living in their villages when, on October 15, they looked down from their log ramparts on something they had never seen before — a keelboat so big it took twenty-two men to row it. A red, white, and blue cloth fluttered above a swivel gun that jutted from the bow. No such expedition had ever appeared on the Missouri before, and men, women, and children all hurried down to see it.

The leader of the newcomers — a tall man whose men called him Captain Lewis — distributed gifts and explained that the Mandan's old "Fathers," the Spanish and the French, had recently "gone beyond the great lake toward the rising Sun" and would never return. A new great chief would soon be sending some of his children to live among them:

> The great chief of the Seventeen great nations of America, impelled by his parental regard for his newly adopted children on the troubled waters, has sent us out to clear the road. . . . [He] has commanded us his war chiefs to under-

Mandan women in skin boats skim across the frozen surface of the Missouri in search of firewood during the winter of 1834–35, thirty years after Lewis and Clark wintered with their people. This aquatint was made after a watercolor by the Swiss artist Karl Bodmer.

take this long journey. You are to live in peace with all the white men, for they are his children. . . . Injure not the person of any trader who may come among you. . . . Do these things which your great father advises and be happy. Avoid the councils of bad birds; turn on your heel from them as you would from the precipice of a high rock . . . lest by one false step you should bring down upon your nation the displeasure of your great father . . . who could consume you as the fire consumes the grass of the plains.

The Mandan were less impressed by what the two American captains had to say than they were by their boat. After all, over the years they had heard from the representatives of many far-off "fathers," and it had not affected business much. They simply added the Americans to their list of potential customers. But they also made them welcome, allowing them to build themselves a palisaded fort on the outskirts of their village in which to spend the winter.

Meriwether Lewis and his second-in-command, William Clark, represented a new country, but they were on what was now a very old mission: trying to find a waterway to the Pacific.

Meriwether Lewis (above) and William Clark, both painted from life by Charles Willson Peale

Of all the myths about North America that fueled Europe's avarice, the one that lasted longest was that there was a Northwest Passage that cut right through the continent, linking the Pacific with the Atlantic. Everyone agreed that the nation that first found it and then controlled its traffic would so dominate trade between the Old World and the New that it would dominate the continent, as well.

John Cabot had been looking for it in 1497 when he touched at Newfoundland and laid claim to all of North America for England, and Sir Francis Drake had been on the same search when he skirted the coast of California in 1578. When the first conquistador marched north to claim New Mexico officially for Spain, he carried with him sails and rigging, just in case the waterway ran through the southwestern desert. Samuel de Champlain fitted out an expedition to find it for France in the vicinity of the Great Lakes in 1634, and La Vérendrye had been trying to locate it when he visited the Mandan.

On July 12, 1776 — just eight days after the thirteen American colonies declared their independence from Great Britain — two British vessels had set out from England with orders to search for the elusive passage along the Northwest coast. In command was England's greatest explorer, Captain James Cook. He proved no more successful than his predecessors — and soon sailed on to the Sandwich Islands, where he was killed — but he anchored long enough off Vancouver Island to stake a British claim to the whole Northwest, and word spread fast of the plentiful furs that his men had obtained there from the Indians.

Soon, Yankee seafarers — "Bostons," the coastal tribes called them — outnumbered British traders along the Northwest coast. To reassert their supremacy in the trade, the British reasoned, they needed to find a passage — a series of rivers, if not an actual sea — that would link the coast with their Canadian trading posts. Their American rivals, said the Scottish fur trader Alexander Mackenzie, "would instantly disappear from before [such] a well-regulated trade." Mackenzie himself determined to find the passage that would make that British triumph possible. In 1789, he

became the first man to cross the Rockies — only to reach the Arctic Ocean, not the Pacific. He named the river he had followed the River of Disappointment.

The following year, an American seaman named Robert Gray came upon the Columbia River; his discovery would be the basis for the United States' claim to the region. Two nations now asserted their ownership of the Northwest.

For Britain, there was no time to lose. Mackenzie tried again to find a passage in 1793, and made it to the Pacific this time, but he had to do so mostly on foot; the rivers he found and followed were too swift and turbulent to carry canoes. Despite his failures, Mackenzie continued to argue that the search be pressed: British power in North America depended upon it.

No one had followed Mackenzie's journeys more avidly than the new President of the United States, Thomas Jefferson. He was interested in everything — from dinosaurs to chamber music, fine wines to politics — but the West especially had fascinated him since his boyhood and, although he had himself never ventured more than fifty miles west of his home in the Virginia mountains, he had amassed the largest collection on earth of books about the region, and had three times tried to organize American expeditions to cross the continent before he took office as President.

Now he faced a delicate political situation, fraught with danger but also filled with possibility. The United States ended at the Mississippi. Britain occupied Canada and now claimed the Oregon Country, spreading west from the Rockies to the Pacific, and north from Spanish California to Russian Alaska. Spain also claimed the rest of the vast, mostly unmapped territory that stretched from the mouth of the Mississippi to the Pacific and from Minnesota to the Rio Grande.

In 1802, Madrid threatened to close the all-important port of New Orleans to American trade. That was ominous enough. But then Jefferson learned that Spain had secretly ceded to France all of "Louisiana," the vast tract that ran north and west from New Orleans all the way to the Rockies. Spain was a comparatively weak power. But France was vigorous and expansive, and its emperor, Napoleon Bonaparte, dreamed of carving out a vast New World empire, centered in New Orleans and stretching far into the Caribbean. Britain was certain to try to stop him, and when war between the Old World's mightiest powers came — as it had twice before in recent memory — the President feared the United States would have to wed itself to the British fleet.

To forestall that threat, Jefferson sent diplomats to Paris in the hope of purchasing New Orleans outright. Meanwhile, he persuaded Congress to authorize $2,500 to mount an expedition that would venture into foreign territory to search out a route between the Mississippi and the Pacific before the British could do so.

To lead it, he turned to his own personal secretary and young Virginia neighbor, Meriwether Lewis. The serious-minded son of a planter who had died during the Revolution, responsible since boyhood for the welfare of his mother, brothers, and sisters, he was a skilled hunter and amateur scientist who had joined the regular army on the frontier and made a name for himself as a promising officer before Jefferson brought him to the White House.

As his second-in-command, Lewis picked his old army commander and fellow Virginian Lieutenant William Clark. The younger brother of the Revolutionary War

The object of your mission is to explore the Missouri River, & such principal streams of it, as, by its course & Communications with the waters of the Pacific Ocean may offer the most direct & practicable water communication across this continent for the purpose of commerce. . . .

Thomas Jefferson

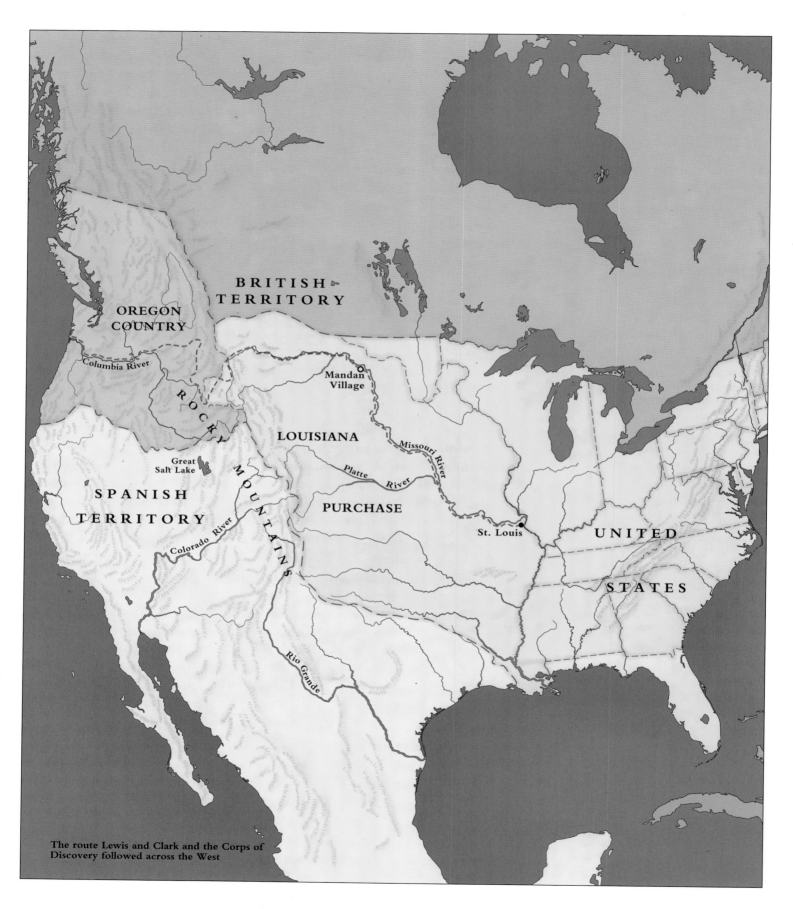

OREGON
COUNTRY

BRITISH
TERRITORY

Columbia River

ROCKY

Mandan
Village

LOUISIANA

Missouri River

Great
Salt Lake

Platte River

SPANISH

MOUNTAINS

PURCHASE

TERRITORY

Colorado River

St. Louis

UNITED

Rio Grande

STATES

The route Lewis and Clark and the Corps of
Discovery followed across the West

May 14, 1804. I set out at 4 o'clock p.m., in the presence of many of the neighboring inhabitants, and proceeded on under a gentle breeze up the Missouri. . . .

William Clark

"A Memorandum of Articles in Readiness for the Voyage," in William Clark's hand. Among the hundreds of items that had to be carefully packed and stowed for the journey were 50 kegs of salt pork, 30 half-barrels of flour, 21 bales of gifts for Indians, 7 barrels of fat, 14 bags of parchment, 2 boxes of candles, and a bag of wicks.

general George Rogers Clark, red-haired and gregarious, he had learned his woodcraft campaigning against Indians in the Ohio country, and was delighted by the prospect of the great adventure Lewis proposed. "My friend," he wrote Clark, "I do assure you that no man lives with whom I would prefer to take such a trip."

At Jefferson's urging, Lewis studied up on botany, zoology, emergency medicine, and navigating by the stars. He was authorized to take with him no more than a dozen soldiers. The rest of the party, he told Clark, was to be made up of "good hunters, stout, healthy, unmarried men, accustomed to the woods and capable of bearing bodily fatigue in a pretty considerable degree." In the end, there would be some forty-five men in all: twenty-nine members of what was called "the permanent expedition," who had signed on for the whole journey; nine French voyageurs, accustomed to river travel but hired to go only as far as the Mandan villages; six soldiers to provide protection against unfriendly Indians; and York, a slave who belonged to William Clark.

Lewis was in Washington in early July of 1803 when he learned that events elsewhere had suddenly changed everything. Napoleon's dream of a New World empire had collapsed with the defeat of a French army in Haiti. Now he wanted to ensure that Louisiana never fell to Britain; he was willing to sell New Orleans to the United States — provided it bought all of the Louisiana Territory as well. Jefferson could not believe his luck. For $15 million he bought some 800,000 square miles between the Mississippi and the Rockies. Jefferson's political opponents charged he would bankrupt the country. Why, they asked, spend money — of which the government had too little — for land — of which they had too much. "I would rather the Mississippi were a running stream of burning lava," said former congressman Harrison Gray Otis of Massachusetts, "over which no human being could pass, than that the treaty should be ratified." But it was ratified in the end, and Jefferson had more than doubled the size of his country.

And so, when Lewis and Clark's little fleet swung out into the main current of the Missouri on a May afternoon in 1804, its members were traveling not as glorified spies scouting lands claimed by a foreign power but as the Corps of Discovery, American citizens eager to see what their money had bought.

It had taken them more than five months rowing upstream through waters already familiar to British, French, and Spanish trappers to reach the Mandan, months during which they'd endured bouts of dysentery, swarms of mosquitoes, torrential rains. One man had been bitten by a rattlesnake; another, named Charles Floyd, died of a burst appendix and was buried on a bluff in what is now Iowa, the first American soldier to die west of the Mississippi. There had been problems with discipline, too: one man got fifty lashes for breaking into the whiskey supply, another received seventy-five for nodding off on sentry duty.

But their encounters with Indians had been almost uniformly peaceful. Like the Mandan, the Oto, Missouri, Yankton Dakota, and Arikara had all enjoyed the gifts the strangers brought, delighted in

New Year's Day, 1805. About 9 o'clock, fifteen of the party went up to the 1st village of Mandans to dance, as it had been their request. Carried with us a fiddle and a tambourine and a sound[ing] horn . . . then went into a lodge and danced a while, which pleased them very much. They then brought victuals from different lodges . . . also a quantity of corn and some buffalo robes which they made us a present of. So we danced in different lodges until late in the afternoon. Then a part of the men returned to the fort. The remainder stayed all night in the village.

John Ordway

watching them fire an air rifle that seemed never to need reloading, and listened politely — if without much conviction — as the newcomers declared themselves to be the representatives of their new, far-off "Father." Only the Brulé Lakota gave the expedition any trouble. They lived near the mouth of the Bad River in what is now South Dakota, were allied with the British Northwest Company, and made it their business to stop any trapper from St. Louis who dared try to get past their villages and force him to turn over his trade goods.

Lewis and Clark were expected to persuade them to forsake the British and forge a new alliance with the Americans that would allow American trappers to pass peacefully through their territory. But when several of their chiefs, invited aboard the keelboat and given whiskey, began to demand the vessel's stores and threatened to attack when they were not handed over, Clark drew his sword. On shore, nearly a hundred warriors notched their arrows. The fate of the expedition seemed to hang in the balance.

Captain Clark [a member of the expedition recalled] spoke to all the party to stand to . . . arms. The large swivel [gun was] loaded well with buck shot. Cap-

Several members of the Lewis and Clark expedition wrote accounts of their journey. These woodcut illustrations, depicting a distinctly formal parley with Indians (top) and one man's ignominious retreat from a wounded grizzly, originally appeared in *Journey of Voyages and Travels of Corps of Discovery* by William Gass, published in 1810.

Interior of a Mandan lodge by Karl Bodmer. The weapons, shield, and medicine symbols at the right were especially prized by the man seated at the fire, who shared his home with his dogs and horses as well as his family.

tain Clark used moderation with them. Told them that we must and would go on, that we were not squaws but warriors. The chief said he had warriors, too, and if we were to go they would follow us and kill and take the whole of us by degrees.

Then, Captain Clark told them that we were sent by their great Father, the president of the United States, and that if they misused us . . . he or Captain Lewis could, by writing to him, have them all destroyed as it were in a moment.

The Brulé hesitated, backed down, then welcomed the explorers to their camp. Clark was carried, seated on a buffalo robe, from the riverbank to the Brulé's council fire as a sign of respect. The expedition stayed with the Brulé for three days, but the Indians made no promises of future peace, and the Americans were in no position to force them to abandon the British. Months later, Clark was still calling the Lakota "the vilest miscreants of the savage race"; until American power could be brought to bear on them, he wrote, they "must ever remain the pirates of the Missouri."

From his new log stockade near the Mandan village, Meriwether Lewis wrote his mother a letter that would not make its way eastward until spring.

Fort Mandan, 1609 miles above the entrance of the Missouri,
Dear Mother,

. . . The near approach of winter, the low state of the water, and the known scarcity of timber which exists on the Missouri for many hundreds of miles above the Mandans, . . . determined my friend and companion Captain Clark and myself to fortify ourselves and remain for the winter in the neighborhood of the Mandans . . . who are the most friendly and well disposed savages that we have yet met with. . . .

I request that you give yourself no uneasiness with respect to my fate, for I assure you that I feel myself . . . perfectly safe; and the only difference between three or four thousand miles and 130 is that I can not have the pleasure of seeing you as often as I did while at Washington. . . . [R]est assured . . . of [my] most devoted and filial affection. . . .

Now, ice blocked the river. The temperature dropped to forty-eight below. A bottle of whiskey left out in the snow froze solid in fifteen minutes. Members of the party used the winter weeks to garner as much information as they could from the Indians about what lay ahead. They would have to find their way around a great waterfall, one chief told them, and then would have to get through a great mountain range. But, he continued, the Missouri was navigable almost all the way to its source, and he had heard that within half a day's march of that source there was another great river, running south to north. Lewis and Clark were convinced that river must be the Columbia, the waterway that would lead them directly to the Pacific.

O! THE JOY

On April 7, Lewis and Clark started west again. They thought they were nearing their goal. Actually, they had barely gone halfway, and the worst was yet to come. There were just thirty-three members of the party now, including three new travelers: a French trapper, Toussaint Charbonneau, who was to act as translator; one of his Indian wives, a sixteen-year-old Shoshone named Sacagawea, who had been captured by the Hidatsa as a small girl and then sold to the Frenchman; and their infant son, Jean-Baptiste.

Things went well enough at first. The riverbanks swarmed with game. Beaver swam heedlessly near the boats. On May 26, Lewis clambered up a hill and saw the Rockies spread out before him: "These points of the Rocky Mountains were covered with snow and the sun shone on it in such a manner as to give me the most plain and satisfactory view. While I viewed these mountains I felt a secret pleasure in finding myself so near the head of the heretofore conceived boundless Missouri. . . ."

The Mandan had told Lewis and Clark of the mountain barrier they faced, but they had said nothing about what suddenly confronted them just one week later. The Missouri split in two. No one in the party could be sure which branch was the great river, which a mere tributary. A wrong choice "would not only lose us the whole of this season," Lewis wrote, "but would probably so dishearten the party that it might defeat the expedition altogether." One branch ran north, the other south. Because the northernmost was muddy, just as the Missouri had been all the way from St. Louis, most of the men believed they should follow it. But Lewis followed it for some forty

This little fleet although not so respectable as those of Columbus or Captain Cook, were still viewed by us with as much pleasure as those deservedly famed adventurers ever beheld theirs; . . . we were now about to penetrate a country at least two thousand miles in width on which the foot of civilized man had never trodden; the good or evil it had in store for us was for experiment yet to determine; . . . [yet] entertaining as I do, the most confident hope of succeeding in a voyage which had formed a darling project of mine for the last ten years, I could but esteem this moment of departure as among the most happy of my life.

Meriwether Lewis, April 7, 1805

The great canoe that so impressed the Mandan and Hidatsa, sketched by William Clark

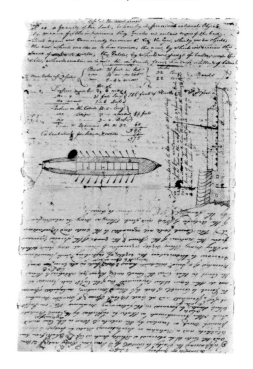

The Missouri winds westward toward the distant Bear Paw Mountains in what is now central Montana in this painting by Karl Bodmer. Only a few miles farther on, the waterway divides, and Lewis and Clark had to decide which branch to follow.

miles, far enough to convince himself that it led not westward toward the Pacific, but northward, toward the endless Canadian plains. He then led another party down the south fork, hoping to come upon the great Falls of the Missouri the Mandan had told him about. It took him three days to find it. Three hundred yards wide and eighty feet high, Lewis wrote, it was "the grandest sight I ever beheld," but the expedition now had to find a way around it, hauling their supplies and dugouts. Thickets of cactus pierced the men's moccasins. Grizzlies twice attacked members of the party. Their supply of whiskey ran out. The distance around the falls was just 18¼ miles, but it took them more than three weeks.

On August 12, Lewis led a small advance party along a well-worn Indian trail that wound west into the Rockies. Coming upon an ice-cold spring, he called it "the most distant fountain of the mighty Missouri . . . one of those great objects on which my mind has been unalterably fixed for many years." Then he climbed toward the sharp ridge behind it. From that vantage point, he believed, he might well see the watershed of the Columbia and beyond it, perhaps, a great plain leading down to the sea. Here, if anywhere, should lie the Northwest Passage that had been the goal of explorers for more than three hundred years, the great prize that Thomas Jefferson had sent Lewis and Clark to claim for the United States.

Instead, there were just more mountains. Lewis was the first American to cross the Continental Divide — the spine of the Rocky Mountains — beyond which the rivers flow west. But his party was more than three hundred miles farther from the Pacific than they had thought they were, there were several more ranges of mountains still to cross, and summer was fast disappearing. The Louisiana Territory ended at the western edge of the Missouri watershed; from here on, Lewis and Clark would be making their way through lands to which Britain had as legitimate a claim as their own country did.

Lewis hurried down the western slope, his mind concentrated not on geography or politics now but on his desperate need to find the Shoshone and buy horses from

. . . all the canoes put into the water and loaded, fixed our canoes as well as possible and set out.

William Clark
October 7, 1805

The Clearwater River, which sped Lewis and Clark on their way west again after they were rescued and resupplied by the Nez Percé, photographed almost a century later

them, so that he and his exhausted men might complete their journey before snow trapped them in the mountains:

> If we do not find them or some other nation who have horses I fear the successful issue of our voyage will be very doubtful. We are now several hundred miles within the bosom of this wild and mountainous country . . . without any information with respect to the country, not knowing how far these mountains continue, or where to direct our course to pass them to advantage or intercept a navigable branch of the Columbia.

The next morning, with nothing left but a little flour and some parched meal to forestall starvation, he chanced upon three Shoshone women. He handed them gifts, smeared their cheeks with vermilion as a sign of peace, and gratefully let himself be led to their menfolk, sixty warriors "mounted on excellent horses, who came in nearly full speed." A herd of some four hundred horses grazed near their village, but the Shoshone had never seen a white man and were suspicious of the strangers. What then occurred is one of the most extraordinary coincidences in American history. Sacagawea, the French trapper's wife who had joined the expedition at the Mandan villages, suddenly recognized first a girlhood friend among the Shoshone and then their chief. He was her brother, whom she had not seen since she had been captured by the Hidatsa. They embraced, and he quickly agreed to provide her odd-looking companions with horses and guides.

Lewis and Clark had now been traveling for sixteen months. The dream of a Northwest Passage had died, they were still not certain they would ever reach the Pacific, and frost already covered the ground each morning.

Now it fell to Clark to hurry ahead of the main party, hoping to find a navigable river to speed them through the Bitterroots. He soon sent word back that there was none. The Salmon was a roaring torrent that would dash their boats to pieces. They would have to go on horseback. Lewis asked the Shoshone how Indians on the far side of the Bitterroots managed to come east to hunt buffalo. There was a steep trail, they said, but it was rocky, heavily timbered, and with little game to shoot.

Despite the risks, Lewis determined to take it. "Knowing that Indians had passed and did pass at this season," he wrote, ". . . my route was instantly settled in my own mind. . . . I felt perfectly satisfied that if the Indians could pass those mountains with their women and children, that we could pass them."

Clark and an advance party of six men started up the old trail through swirling snow, desperate with hunger. They shot and ate a coyote, a raven, scrambled after crayfish in an ice-covered stream, killed and ate some of their horses, devoured even their candles, and finally stumbled down out of the mountains eleven days later, more dead than alive.

There, the Nez Percé found them. Like the Shoshone, they had never seen a white man but did not hesitate to help. They gave the starving strangers dried salmon and the roots of the camas plant to eat, assured them it was possible to reach the sea by water from their territory, and permitted them to fell five trees from which to make canoes for the journey. They even agreed to look after their horses until the following spring. Lewis and Clark never forgot the generosity of the Nez Percé: "I think we can

The eulachon, or candlefish, traded to the expedition by the Klatsop Indians. New to science, it was also "superior to any fish I ever tasted," said William Clark, who carefully drew it in his notebook.

justly affirm, to the honor of this people," Lewis wrote, "that they are the most hospitable, honest and sincere [people] that we have met with on our voyage."

The expedition moved fast now, down the Clearwater, then the Snake, through currents, one member of the expedition remembered, "swifter than any horse could run," and finally onto the broad Columbia itself. Winter rain fell steadily. There was little to eat except dogs, purchased from the Indians who came out to watch them pass.

By late October, there were signs that they were nearing the coast. Some Indians were dressed in blue jackets and round hats obtained through trading with British and American sailors. Brass teakettles hung over cook fires. "The persons who usually visit the entrance of this river for the purpose of traffic or hunting I believe are either English or American," Lewis wrote. "The Indians inform us they speak the same language with ourselves and give us proofs of their veracity by repeating many words of English, as 'musket,' 'powder,' 'shot,' 'knife,' 'file,' 'damned rascal,' 'son of a bitch,' et cetera."

On October 31, the river started to widen still further, and Clark thought he detected signs of tidal movement. The party kept going.

> November 7, Thursday 1805. A cloudy foggy morning. Some rain. We set out early . . . the fog so thick we could not see across the river. . . . We landed at a village. . . . It contains 7 indifferent houses. . . . Here we purchased a dog, some fish . . . and I purchased 2 beaver skins for the purpose of making me a robe, as the robe I have is rotten and good for nothing. . . . [W]e with difficulty found a place clear of the tide and sufficiently large to lie on . . . round stones on which we lay our mats. Rain continued . . . all day.

> Then the fog lifted a little.

> Ocean in view! O! the joy. . . . We are in view of the Ocean, this great Pacific Ocean which we [have] been so long anxious to see, and the roaring or noise made by the waves breaking on the rocky shores . . . may be heard distinctly.

Since 1528, Europeans from different nations had been entering the West from different directions, pursuing different myths. Without help from the native peoples who had lived on these lands for thousands of years, none would have survived for long. Yet each intruder had laid claim to the region as if he were the first to discover it, as if the people already living on it whose worlds had been changed forever did not exist. A conquistador named Juan de Oñate had etched his name for Spain on El Morro Rock in New Mexico. On behalf of France, the two sons of La Vérendrye had buried a lead tablet with his name on it somewhere on the northern Plains. Alexander Mackenzie had painted his name on a rock to claim the Northwest coast for England.

Now it was the Americans' turn. At a point overlooking the surf, Clark carved a message in the bark of a tree: "William Clark, December 3rd, 1805. By Land. From the U States. . . ."

Our party from necessity having been obliged to subsist some length of time on dogs have now become extremely fond of their flesh. . . . For my own part I have become so perfectly reconciled to the dog that I think it an agreeable food and would prefer it vastly to lean venison or elk.

Meriwether Lewis

As for my own part I have not become reconciled to the taste of this animal as yet.

William Clark

OTHER WESTS

RICHARD WHITE

The West could have been different. Events are patterned; history is not random; but the world is also surprising. Historians devote their careers to explaining how the world came to be the way it is; at best, they give only idle moments to thinking how easily it might have been otherwise.

I am an historian of the American West. I have tried in my work to explain how the federal government came to play such a large role in the West. I have examined conflict between Indian peoples and whites. I have looked at environmental change and destruction. I write about these things because they link the past and the present. They explain the present. But this focus on the present is, at least in part, a problem.

In one way or another the events in the West that academic historians research, that popular historians endlessly retell, and that readers find "relevant" are those past events that seem connected to the present, which seem to produce it. It is certainly a legitimate function of history to produce, as the cliché goes, a usable past. But there is a danger in our obsession with mapping out the routes to the present, because in doing so, we slice off all that is not "relevant" and thus distort the past. We eliminate its strangeness. We eliminate, most of all, its possibilities. History should do more than just validate the inevitability of the present.

What I am attempting in this essay is quite simple. I am looking for crossroads, points where history might have gone in another direction, but did not. I am looking for contingency in the routes between the western past and present, but the contingency I am after is not chance. It is instead the multiple possibilities that reside in most situations and the occasional fragility of the causes that produce one outcome rather than another.

The contingency of the present has become a staple of science fiction plots: time travelers make a small change in a past event and thus create a very different present. The plots, as in *Back to the Future*, with time machines and variants on mad scientists, are far-fetched. The premise is not. Small changes in one period can yield significant differences in another. Contingency is not the whole story, but it is part of the story.

Because the nineteenth-century West did not hold within it a single genetic code that caused the modern West to flower like a rose, western historians should at least show a decent curiosity about how it might have been, about other potentials resting within the western past. My technique here will be to look at both what we take for granted or regard as intrinsic to the West (such as its boundaries) and events we regard as inevitable (for example, chronic conflicts between whites and Indians and the near extermination of the bison) and try to demonstrate how other possibilities once existed.

If we need any evidence of the contingency of particular movements along the route from western past to western present, we need only to look at the boundaries of the West. The American West is a bounded place. Western historians constantly quarrel about the eastern boundary — "where the West begins" — but they rarely quibble about the other boundaries. The West is south of Canada and north of Mexico, but where south of Canada or north of Mexico begins is not necessarily a simple question. It took much of the first half of the nineteenth century to draw the lines we have today.

In the imperial competition of the nineteenth century, the North American continent sat like a carcass waiting to be divided. Different calculations, slightly different turns of events, a little more intransigence or weakness on one side or another could easily have yielded a very different division of the spoils and thus a different West. Although some Americans regarded themselves as darlings of providence entitled to the entire continent (which was what the claim of Manifest Destiny originally involved), most Americans were more finicky in their territorial appetites. Americans quarreled among themselves, with Mexico and with Britain, and, of course, with the Indian peoples who actually occupied the land. The actual boundaries had about the same logic, and the same predictability, as the division of spoils between predators and scavengers competing over a kill.

The United States at one time demanded much more land than it now claims in western North America and at other times was willing to settle for much less than it now possesses. That the boundaries came out where they did has often surprised both nineteenth-century observers and modern historians.

In 1872 J. W. Boddam-Whetham, a British traveler, took the newly opened Northern Pacific Railroad from Kalama on the Columbia River to Sinio, which was as far as the railroad had gotten on its way to Tacoma in Washington Territory. Boddam-Whetham was not bothered by the western boors who squabbled on the train. He expected westerners to be boorish; they were local color. What bothered him was that these particular boors of the American West were in a region that by all rights should be British.

"It is not easy," Boddam-Whetham wrote, "to conceive what reasons for claiming the country north of the Columbia could be urged by the United States Government." The dispute over the Oregon Country had not been British diplomacy's finest moment. Boddam-Whetham repeated a story then current in British Columbia, that Britain had lost the region because the brother-in-law of a British minister had written home that the salmon in the Columbia would not rise to a fly and thus the country was not worth bothering about.

The route from the past to the present is a precarious one, but not so precarious that the fishing failures of ministerial brothers-in-law are likely explanations for the ultimate nationality of large chunks of real estate. Still Boddam-Whetham's bewilderment was understandable. David Pletcher, a modern historian who has studied the annexation of Oregon with great care, concluded that "the United States had obtained a wedge of territory to which she had little real claim from exploration or effective settlement."

As it happens, I am sitting as I write this on the wedge of territory that put Boddam-Whetham in such a funk: the large scoop of land north and west of the Columbia River that today comprises all of western Washington and a good chunk of eastern Washington. Seattle could have been in Canada. David Pletcher suggested that the boundary very nearly came out quite differently a number of times. If negotiations had continued in 1811, for example, the Americans might have accepted a compromise along the watershed between the Columbia River and Puget Sound. Between 1825 and 1827 the two sides seemed on the verge of a similar compromise, with the British throwing in some American ports on the west side of the Olympic Peninsula. Daniel Webster, then secretary of state, thought in 1842 that the lands north of the Columbia were negotiable, and Pletcher proposed that Webster might very well have given Britain much of western Washington if he could have secured the special mission to Britain he wanted. Our southern boundary with Mexico showed the same tendency to waver over hundreds, indeed thousands, of miles.

The person most responsible for fixing the northern and southern boundaries of the West was James K. Polk. Polk, it may seem, was the man with his hand on the horizontal hold of history. Supposedly armed with an expansionist mandate, he took the wavering lines on the historical screen and resolved them into a clear picture. But precisely because James K. Polk did have such an influence on western boundaries, he takes us deeper into the vagaries of contingency.

Polk was an unlikely president with a dubious mandate and a shifting policy. Twice defeated as candidate for the governor of Tennessee, Polk was the darkest of dark horses seeking the Democratic presidential nomination in 1844. The seeming certainty of Martin Van Buren's nomination scared off stronger rivals and a seemingly meaningless shift in the date of the Democratic convention kept Polk alive. The spectacularly bad judgment of his rival, Silas Wright, resulted in Polk's nomination on the ninth ballot. Polk's electoral

French explorers landing in the New World

victory was equally narrow. The opposition Whigs were certain they could beat him. His triumph over the Whig nominee, Henry Clay, required "a political miracle." Polk did not get a majority of the popular vote, but he did get his miracle. The antislavery Liberty party took critical votes away from the Whigs in New York and threw that key state to the Democrats and Polk. The unlikely happened. Polk was president. The election, however, hardly represented a clear endorsement of his expansionist foreign policy.

The Polk of political legend was a man who, if he knew nothing else, certainly knew his own mind. James K. Polk was an ardent expansionist, but he seems to have had no clear plan for securing Oregon, Texas, and California. He improvised, he shifted. He was not necessarily bent on war. He would have, at various times, settled for something other than the boundaries he eventually got. He was dealing with fluid political situations both at home and in Mexico and Europe. Timing made a great deal of difference. What was possible one month might be impossible the next.

Securing the land north of the Columbia was a great triumph, but Polk had promised much more. The whole Oregon Country was in dispute in the early nineteenth century, and the Oregon Country was a big place. It ranged from Alaska to California and from the crest of the Rockies to the Pacific. By the early nineteenth century, the contestants had been reduced to two: Great Britain and the United States. In one of the more unique imperial arrangements, the two powers agreed to share the region — joint occupation — until a permanent boundary could be drawn. Either side could terminate the agreement on twelve months' notice.

Despite the fact that few Americans or British citizens actually lived in the Oregon Country, the European rules for dividing up other people's countries seemed to make the ultimate division of the area clear. South of the Columbia the United States had a strong claim, but north of the Columbia the advantage went to the British. The British had been there before the Americans, the British had mapped and charted the area, and the British had settled it. The United States had only the claims it inherited by treaty from Spain, the sporadic presence of oceangoing fur traders in the region, and the burning desire for a safe deep-water port to serve as a gateway to Asia. The Oregon coast, despite its wonderful and forbidding beauty, did not offer any safe ports.

The British wanted the boundary drawn on the basis of exploration and possession; Polk simply claimed the whole thing: the entire Oregon Country. He demanded a border at 54°40', the present southern boundary of Alaska. The slogan "Fifty-four Forty or Fight," for all its alliteration, did not give the United States British Columbia. The Americans had no desire to fight over British Columbia. And in the end, the British had no stomach for a fight over a patch of forest, water, and mountain south of the forty-ninth parallel. The boundary came out on the forty-ninth parallel. The area north of the Columbia, which Americans had neither first explored nor settled nor conquered, became part of the American West.

The southern boundary of the West was just as contingent, just as surprising. There were in 1845 and 1846 numerous alternate boundaries afloat. If Polk had offered an envoy other than John Slidell to settle the Texas boundary, if Mexico and the United States could have resolved a diplomatic quarrel over the envoy's title, if Mexico had not been plagued by a revolution, then the American offer to negotiate the Texas boundary and acquire California for $40 million might have at least provided a start for negotiations. President Jose Joaquin Herrera of Mexico, while eager to preserve Mexican honor, did not want to push his own impoverished and divided country into war.

When John Slidell left for Mexico, his instructions asked him to obtain the Rio Grande boundary including much of New Mexico, and a California boundary that took in San Francisco. But Polk provided him with several alternate boundaries. Southern California, parts of Nevada, New Mexico, and Utah, and virtually all of Arizona remained negotiable. After the Mexican War started, Polk continued to offer different boundaries.

Ultimately the Mexican boundary was the work of as unlikely a set of events as Polk's election. The American envoy Nicholas Trist, already recalled and disavowed by Polk, negotiated a boundary that the President rejected. But Polk felt compelled by political pressure and American war weariness to submit the Treaty of Guadalupe Hidalgo to Congress. Congress approved the treaty. At the end of the war, Polk himself wanted Baja California. He was inclining toward a southern boundary well to the south of the modern boundary. He was not the most extreme. There were those who wanted all of Mexico. There were also those who would have settled for San Francisco Bay and the surrounding area.

In the end, the American engine of Manifest Destiny ran out of steam well short of taking in all its advocates desired. A last flurry of expansion produced the Gadsden Purchase in 1853, but President James Buchanan's attempt to buy Baja failed. That the West is where it is turns out to be the sum of American power, interest, and contingency.

As contingent as the boundaries might be, they influenced all that followed. The vast new territory forced the United States to face the issue of slavery in the territories. The Mexican War thus begat the Civil War. And the Civil War deflected what had seemed the most dependable of the traits of American westering. Before the Civil War, American settlement produced two Wests: a southern backcountry and a northern backcountry. After the Civil War, all this changed. There was a single West when Americans crossed the Missouri. The triumphant North and the new and stronger federal government, not the defeated South, shaped the West. And migration now came from all directions.

This migration seemed to have the inevitability of a natural force. We speak of it as flowing as if it were a river, or a flood, or a volcanic eruption. And we, prisoners of our metaphors, expect that nothing could have stood in front of it. It was destined to overwhelm all who opposed it.

When we pick our symbols of this encounter, we encapsulate our assumptions. We think of mounted warriors of the Great Plains confronting covered wagons. We think of the Battle of the Little Bighorn. We think of Wounded Knee. We think of constant and inevitable conflict.

There were, however, other encounters in the West that indicate other possibilities. Dr. Charles Pickering is not a prominent name in the annals of American exploration. Although born in Pennsylvania, he was the child of an old and illustrious Massachusetts family. He graduated from Harvard Medical School, but his real love was botany, and he had a reputation as a zoologist. He was in nineteenth-century terms a naturalist, yet he gained appointment as an ethnologist to the Great United States Exploring Expedition of 1838–42 (or the Wilkes expedition, as it was commonly called). He was to study human beings and not plants or animals. His appointment yielded a book: *The Races of Men*. Only one hundred copies were originally published.

In hindsight, joining the Wilkes expedition was one of those choices that Pickering might have better passed by. Lieutenant Charles Wilkes was not the only problem, but he was most definitely a problem. Wilkes, described rather forgivingly by one historian as a "paranoid martinet," had formidable skills as a navigator and chart maker, but he also imagined himself a competent scientist, and he hated the "scientifics" who recognized neither his talents nor his qualifications. That the commander of a scientific expedition hated scientifics might have served as storm warning, but it was hard really to distinguish among Wilkes's hatreds and dislikes, there were so many of them. He brutalized his crew, browbeat his officers, slaughtered South Sea Islanders, and alienated most everyone he met. One of his midshipmen called him more of a monster than a man. All of this lay in the expedition's long bloody wake when the ships reached the Northwest coast in 1841.

Charles Wilkes was the kind of man who seems a walking trump card when it comes to arguments about the inevitability of racial conflict in the West. He was impatient with what he regarded as inferior races and inferior classes. Wilkes operated in a customary world of Indian deficiency. He assumed a chasm between peoples. This unbridgeable chasm is a lingering cliché. We hold it still. Although we are likely to make the Indians virtuous where Wilkes saw them as vicious and deficient, we presume a "clash of cultures."

Wilkes, however, forms only the conventional background to an astonishing foreground that Pickering revealed in his book. Wilkes's certainty and utter faith in his own prejudices makes Pickering stand out all the more clearly. Unlike Wilkes, Pickering could be surprised.

When Wilkes, anchored in Puget Sound, ordered Lieutenant Robert E. Johnson to lead a foray across the Cascade Mountains and "explore the interior," he expected not only an exploration of "wilderness" but an exploration of "savagery." That is why he ordered Pickering, the ethnologist, to accompany Johnson. The whole party consisted of seven men. They accomplished nothing of any moment. But on this obscure side-trip of this obscure expedition, there occurred a small and revealing jewel of a moment. The moment stuck with Pickering. He included it in his *Races of Man.*

Conquistadors and Indians

The moment came at the end of Johnson's journey as the returning party descended the western slope of the Cascades. In 1841 physical culture was beginning to make organized exercise a part of American education. Doctors argued that fresh air and exercise were essential to warding off tuberculosis, the most feared killer of the nineteenth century. Whatever the reason, during this journey Pickering and others engaged in "gymnastic exercises."

"Gymnastic exercises" was an elastic term in the early 1840s. It applied to the "more active species of exercise." It included Catherine Beecher's emphasis on exercises that demanded parallel bars, climbing ropes, and other equipment that were not part of the expedition's outfit. More likely, these gymnastic exercises were calisthenics that operated on a military model and demanded "military postures." But then again, they also might have been simply sports or games of one kind or another. There is no way to be sure, but let's imagine that the gymnastic exercises were calisthenics.

At their last encampment, twenty miles from Puget Sound, the Johnson party met some Nisqually Indians who were camped nearby for purposes of their own. And at this encampment it occurred to someone "to [initiate] the Indians in gymnastic exercises." There on a prairie in the shadow of Mount Rainier were American sailors, marines, and scientists in military posture with Nisqually men and women lined up alongside them. And they all began to do synchronized gymnastic exercises. The Indians, Pickering said, "entered into the sport very willingly and with some spirit."

We can take that moment of Indians and whites, synchronized and spirited, and use it as a prism for the rest of that journey. From Pickering's account we can imagine a set of circumstances and possibilities in which Indians and whites exercising and playing on the prairies seems ordinary instead of an odd and surprising moment of harmony where we expect to find conflict. Pickering and Johnson traveled in and recorded a mixed world in which the later categories and boundaries of white/Indian, conqueror and conquered had not yet hardened. Pickering saw a world, a set of possibilities, that Wilkes seemed congenitally unable to see.

Johnson's party explored lands already long, if sparsely, settled by Indians and more recently settled by a smaller number of other peoples: some Britons and Scots, Canadians, Hawaiians, Indians from the east, and a few Americans. This settlement had already produced a group of children of mixed descent. But these divisions into whites, Indians, and mixed-race individuals were all Pickering's distinctions. He was told that "no idea of difference of race such as is recognized by Europeans, ever enters into the heads of the natives."

"The natives" were hardly a simple lot. Johnson, Pickering, and their companions met Indian women gathering camas and Indian men fishing for salmon. In other lodges they saw buffalo robes, evidence of hunts made eastward across the Rockies. At Spalding's mission Pickering saw Indian farms and farmers, and Spalding "gave them the character generally of being 'an exceedingly industrious people.'" A few days later he saw four generations of another Indian family gathered under a canopy "hardly sufficient to shelter a sheep." He saw lodges made of mats, and teepees like those of the Plains, and Indians living in log cabins. All of these diverse people were Indians and around them were Hudson's Bay Company forts and American Board missions. In short, there was, on the eve of American settlement, a complicated world in place.

This particular western world contained numerous possibilities. Pickering had witnessed Indian peoples independently working out accommodations to change. Some Indians used European introductions such as the horse to gain access to resources of the Plains. And, once on the Plains, they adopted aspects of the Plains cultures and brought them back to the Columbia Plateau. Other Indians adopted European technology and agriculture and set them to work raising crops and cattle. Still other Indians lived much as their ancestors had lived before there were either Europeans or horses. And as for Europeans and Americans, their lives were intimately involved with Indians. Their prosperity and well-being depended on Indians. Everywhere there was exchange and interchange. This was a mixed world. These were people fully aware of difference but disinclined to structure these differences around race.

I introduce Pickering and his gymnastic Indians and his seemingly inconsequential journey to underline a second simple point about the western past, the American past. It was not only contingent, it also contained possibilities that we forget because these possibilities are not always realized in the present. The western past is fuller than our popular histories often make it. Pickering's response does not, of course, erase Wilkes's more typical and scornful reaction. Moments of gleeful surprise do not erase Little Bighorn, or Wounded Knee, or innumerable other conflicts and atrocities that scar the western past. But that is not the point. The point is that this West was a world that contained gymnastics *and* slaughter.

The contingency of the borders of the West, the possibilities of accommodation between Indians and whites before the tidal waves of settlement broke over the West, are, it might be objected, well and good, but do they really alter our views of American expansion? Even if expanding Americans didn't achieve all their own ambitions, even if whites temporarily accommodated rather than conquered, the American desire to dominate remained uncomplicated and supreme. But was it?

American domination involved not only other peoples but nature itself, and the great symbol of that domination was the near-extinction of the bison, or buffalo. These herds once existed in their millions, then, in a seeming blink of an eye, they were gone. We, with a different environmental consciousness, sometimes lament the slaughter of the bison as tragic but inevitable. It is a tawdry stance; it is, in effect, to enjoy the luxury of simultaneously condemning and excusing the slaughter. Nineteenth-century Americans thought they could preserve the buffalo.

The history of the destruction of the bison has recently become far more complicated than simple slaughter by white hunters. The decline of the bison began long before the white hide-hunters arrived. Drought, exotic diseases transmitted by horses and cattle, competition with horses for critical winter habitat in the river valleys, increasing Indian population of the Great Plains all depleted the herds before the hide-hunters administered the coup de grâce following the Civil War.

With the buffalo in decline, the nation neither greeted the final slaughter with equanimity nor saw it as the inevitable price of progress. In the West the Santa Fe *New Mexican* editorialized during 1873 against "the buffalo slaughter going on the past few years on the plains and which increases every year" as "wantonly wicked" and a development that "should be stopped by the most stringent enact-

Indian neophyte painting of the archangel Raphael, Mission Santa Ines, California

ments." Even some of the hunters felt guilt in what they did, although they sought to justify their actions to themselves and others. Revulsion at a slaughter seen as unnecessary, excessive, immoral, and expensive even appeared in Congress. Congressman Greenbury Fort of Illinois submitted bills "to prevent the useless slaughter of buffaloes within the Territories of the United States." The arguments for preserving buffalo were simple and straightforward. The "useless and wanton destruction" was a "cruel waste." Many military officers stationed in the West contended that the slaughter of the buffalo caused expensive wars with the Indians and forced the government to supply them with beef to replace the vanished bison. The buffalo should be a larder for Indians, settlers, and travelers.

There were arguments in favor of extermination. Some congressmen and military men contended it desirable. Representative John Hancock of Texas offered that "the sooner we get rid of the buffalo entirely the better it will be for the Indian and the white man too" because removing the buffalo would remove an obstacle to "humanizing and civilizing [the Indian] and making him [self-sustaining]." The Orwellian logic of making Indians self-sustaining by eliminating the source of their sustenance did not go unchallenged. Fort did not think that "in order to civilize the Indian" it was necessary to "reduce him to starvation." And if this were true, why stop with the buffalo, why not kill all that lived and breathed in the West? "Why not also kill all the deer, the elk, and beautiful antelope? Why not poison the rivers and kill all the fish? Why not destroy all the game?"

Under the terms of Fort's bills, Indians would retain a free hunt. Settlers and travelers would be able to take bulls but in no "greater number . . . than needed for food by such person, or than can be used, cured or preserved for the food of other persons, or for the market." There would be a one-hundred-dollar fine for each offense. Slaughter for the hides alone would be prohibited. A second bill providing for a tax on hides would finance wardens to police the hunt. Since the heavy hides had to go out on the railroads, policing would be relatively easy.

In 1874 as the slaughter of the southern herd reached a climax, Congressman Fort's bill actually passed both houses of Congress. It needed only President Grant's signature to become law. The signature never came. President Grant voiced no opposition to the bill; he did not veto it. He simply did not sign it, whether from his own objections or inefficiency or other causes. This pocket veto killed the bill. It was resurrected in 1876, but this was the year that Custer died, and arguments that involved preserving buffalo for Indians did not go far. And so the slaughter went on unimpeded. A substantial roadblock had been only a signature away. Certainly the buffalo would have declined, law or no law, but with protection they would probably never have reached the desperate straits they eventually did.

These examples of the contingency of the western past and present, of the lost possibilities the past contained, are important. Historical accounts often re-create the semblance of contests, but because we know the ending, the alternate possibilities of the past never seem quite real. History ordains and explains the winner; the other possibilities become only token possibilities. The further the past recedes from us, the more we regard these lost peoples, these lost dreams, these lost ideas, these lost possibilities as mere curiosities. Often these possibilities disappear entirely. History becomes a thoroughfare leading to the present. It is lined by graveyards of failed possibilities.

Writing history in terms of the present has its virtues, but it can be an odd procedure. Presentism can yield what might be called the horseshoe crab theory of history, where signs of the present in the past come to define the past. The horseshoe crab is an arthropod related to the spider. It is very old, first appearing in the Upper Silurian period of the Paleozoic Era, about 425 million years ago. Trilobites and much of the other life that once shared the seas with horseshoe crabs appear now only as fossils. The horseshoe crab is still around. As evolutionary winner, it has survived while the vast majority of what once surrounded it has vanished. But to think that we can understand that Silurian past as if its true significance resides in producing the horseshoe crab for posterity is slightly mad. In the past the horseshoe crab mattered no more than the rest of the teeming life of ancient seas. Its survival into the present doesn't alter its role in the past. The past existed on its own terms.

By revealing to us the contingency of the present, how different alternatives existed in the past, history indicates that small changes in one time can yield large differences in another. It restores agency without eliminating the large forces that shape all our lives. In this wider past among the unmarked graves of the West we might make history more than a way either of celebrating ourselves or of resigning ourselves to the present.

Pioneers like these, photographed in 1866 near Coleville, in what is now Utah, owed much to the men and women who blazed the trail two decades earlier.

CHAPTER TWO

THE MOST
AVID NATION

1806–1848

The vast territory Thomas Jefferson had bought from France gave the United States title to half the West, at least on paper. Yet besides Lewis and Clark, only a handful of U.S. citizens had ever been beyond the Missouri, had ever seen the West's forbidding landscape or been intoxicated by its mysteries. Most of the first Americans who did move west — to trap beaver in mountain streams, to trade in New Mexico, to settle in Texas and California and the Oregon Country — seemed less concerned with conquest than with simply making their way in other people's worlds. And after 1821, when Mexico won its independence from Spain, there were two rival republics as well as a host of Indian nations with claims to parts of the region. But before long, the Americans would determine to make the West — all of it — theirs, and theirs alone.

On August 12, 1806, the Lewis and Clark flotilla was nearing the Mandan villages again, moving down the Missouri this time, on its way home from the Pacific, when the men were startled to see two Americans in a canoe, paddling hard the other way. They were Forest Handcock and Joseph Dickson, would-be trappers from Illinois bound for the Yellowstone River and eager to begin building a fortune in furs even before the rest of the country had heard of all that the Corps of Discovery had found.

Americans had come last to the Rocky Mountain fur trade — Indian trappers had been supplying skins to British, French, and Spanish traders on the Missouri and the Columbia for decades — and they meant to make up for lost time. The demand by the gentry of England and Europe and the eastern cities for the beaver pelts from which their fashionable felt hats were made seemed limitless.

No one knows what happened to Handcock and Dickson, but soon scores of other American trappers were on their way up the Missouri. In 1807, Manuel Lisa, a Spanish merchant in St. Louis who had helped supply Lewis and Clark, established the first American trading post, Fort Raymond, at the confluence of the Yellowstone and Little Bighorn rivers in present-day Montana: it was his notion that Americans could do much of the trapping themselves rather than rely on the Plains tribes to do their work for them. Two years later, William Clark himself joined Lisa and others in forming the Missouri Fur Company. And in 1811, the German-born entrepreneur John Jacob Astor established an outpost at the mouth of the Columbia; it failed during the War of 1812, but its brief presence further strengthened America's claim to the Oregon Country.

General William Henry Ashley, the lieutenant governor of Missouri, had made one fortune manufacturing gunpowder during the War of 1812, and was confident he could make another in the fur business. In 1822, he placed an advertisement in a St. Louis newspaper:

To Enterprising young men: The subscriber wishes to engage one hundred men, to ascend the river Missouri to its source, there to be employed for one, two or three years. For particulars, inquire of Major Andrew Henry, near the Lead Mines in the County of Washington, . . . or to the subscriber at St. Louis.

Among those who had most eagerly answered Ashley's call was a pious, well-read twenty-three-year-old named Jedediah Strong Smith. A Methodist storekeeper's son from southern New York State, Smith had devoured the official two-volume history of the Lewis and Clark expedition while still a boy; it was his dream to see the country his boyhood heroes had traveled and then, perhaps, to make new discoveries of his own:

> I informed [Ashley] that I was entirely unemployed. He said that he wished then that I would assist him in engaging men for his Rocky Mountain expedition which I accordingly did, getting instructions as to where I would most probably find men willing to engage . . . grog shops and other sinks of degradation. . . . A description of our crew I cannot give, but a Falstaff's Battalion was genteel in comparison.

Ashley's first venture into the mountains ended in disaster. In the spring of 1823, with some seventy men, he started up the Missouri. One of his keelboats had already struck a snag and sunk, carrying with it thousands of dollars' worth of supplies. Now, the Arikara, angered that a small band of American trappers had sided with their enemies, the Lakota, in a recent skirmish, opened fire on the party, killing twelve and wounding twelve more. "Before meeting with this defeat," one survivor of the battle recalled, "I think few men had stronger ideas of their bravery and disregard of fear than I had, but standing on a bare and open sand bar to be shot at from behind a picketed Indian village was more than I had contracted for and somewhat cooled my courage."

The Missouri was now closed. If Ashley's new company were to keep from going under, his men would have to find some other way to enter the Rockies on foot or horseback. He named Jed Smith to command one of two expeditions with orders to look for a likely overland route. It, too, very nearly ended not long after it began. An enraged grizzly broke several of Smith's ribs and seized his whole head in its mouth, tearing off most of his ear, before roaring off again into the wilderness. Another young trapper offered to do what he could for his commander:

> I asked the captain what was best. He said, "One or two go for water and if you have a needle and thread get it out and sew up my wounds around my head" which was bleeding freely. . . . One of his ears was torn from his head out to the outer rim. After stitching all the other wounds in the best way I was capable and according to the captain's directions,

Habitual watchfulness destroys every frivolity of mind and action. They seldom smile: the expression of their countenances is watchful, solemn and determined. They ride and walk like men whose breasts have been so long exposed to the bullet and the arrow, that fear finds within them no resting place.

Thomas J. Farnham

Jim Beckwourth, one of the most flamboyant of the mountain men, in a previously unpublished daguerreotype

the ear being the last, I told him I could nothing for his ear. "Oh, you must try to stitch it up some way or other," said he. Then I put in my needle and stitched it through and through and over and over laying the lacerated parts together as nice as I could with my hands. . . . This gave us a lesson on the character of the grizzly bear which we did not forget.

Despite his wounds, Jed Smith was back on the trail within ten days and, with the help of Crow and Cheyenne from whom he purchased pelts, eventually came upon South Pass, a treeless valley twenty to thirty miles across that would allow wagons to make it through the mountains. Smith had shown that the Rockies were not quite the daunting barrier that even his heroes, Lewis and Clark, had believed them to be. And better than that from his employer's point of view, he also found the Green River country, just west of the pass, swarming with beaver.

Soon, thanks to Smith and his companions, Ashley and his investors were becoming wealthy men and rival entrepreneurs were eagerly fitting out their own trapping expeditions. Black trappers as well as white trooped into the central Rockies and beyond. There were Iroquois and Delaware Indians, too; Hawaiians; men from Scotland, England, and Mexico. French-Canadians outnumbered Americans four to one. But they were all called mountain men and, wrote one who knew them well, "had little fear of God and none at all of the devil."

Some became legends. Jim Bridger was called "Old Gabe" by his white friends and "Blanket Chief" by the Indians because of the red-and-blue robe he liked to wear on ceremonial occasions. He gave up a safe life as a St. Louis blacksmith to join Ashley's first expedition into the mountains and never looked back. He was the first white man ever to see the Great Salt Lake — which he was sure, after tasting it, must be an inlet of the Pacific Ocean. He was rarely so confused; after twenty-one years in the fur trade he may have known more of the West firsthand than any other man.

Jim Beckwourth was the slave — and the illegitimate son — of a Virginia planter who took him west to St. Louis and set him free. He began his career in the fur trade working as General Ashley's servant, but soon became a mountain man in his own right and was adopted by the Crow after convincing a chief that he was really his long-lost son who had been captured by the Cheyenne and sold to whites — or so Beckwourth later liked to claim.

Joseph LaFayette Meek was born in Washington County, Virginia, one of fifteen children of a prosperous planter. But when his mother died and his father brought home an overly stern and domineering stepmother, he ran off to the West, where three of his older brothers were already working the beaver streams. He would spend just over a decade in the mountains, traveling relentlessly — from the Snake River to what is now southern Utah, and once into a landscape, the Yellowstone plateau, filled with such wonders that no one would credit his descriptions of them:

The artists' West: Charles Deas, who painted the gravity-defying *Death Struggle* (above) about 1845, assumed that trappers and Indians were invariably at one another's throats. Alfred Jacob Miller, the French-trained artist from New Orleans who painted *The Trapper's Bride* (opposite), was a good deal more realistic. He ventured into the Rockies in 1837 in search of his subjects and here portrays a mountain man being accepted into the clan of his new wife. Without Indian help, Americans had little chance of surviving for long in the mountains.

The whole country . . . was smoking with the vapor from boiling springs, and burning with gasses, issuing from small craters, each of which was emitting a sharp whistling sound . . . like that place the old Methodist preacher used to threaten me with. . . . [But] the warmth of the place [was] most delightful, after the freezing cold of the mountains; [so] if it was hell, it was a more agreeable climate than I had been in for some time.

The life Meek and his fellow mountain men led was extraordinarily dangerous. They fell victim to grizzlies, froze to death after wading waist-deep in icy streams to retrieve their traps, were killed by the Blackfeet and other tribes allied with their British rivals. "I have held my hands in an ant-hill until they were covered with ants, then greedily licked them off," Meek recalled. "I have taken the soles of my moccasins, crisped them in the fire, and eaten them. In our extremity, the large black crickets which are found in the country were considered fair game. We used to take a kettle of hot water, catch the crickets and throw them in, and when they stopped kicking, eat them."

"When the pie was opened then the birds began to sing." When Captain Sublette's goods were opened and distributed . . . then began the usual gay carousal; and the "fast young men" of the mountains outvied each other in all manner of mad pranks. . . . The horse-racing, fine riding, wrestling and all the manlier sports, soon degenerated into the baser exhibitions of a "crazy drunk" exhibition.

Joe Meek

Joe Meek

For all their tenacity, the mountain men would never have survived without help. Almost half of them married Indian women, who provided sex and companionship, helped prepare skins, and, perhaps most important, provided them with family ties to the people through whose lands they moved. Joe Meek's first wife was a Shoshone named Umentucken, or Mountain Lamb. She was "the most beautiful Indian woman I ever saw," he recalled, "and when she was mounted on her dapple gray horse, which cost me three hundred dollars, she made a fine show." After she was killed in a fight with the Bannocks, he wed a Nez Percé, who soon abandoned him because he drank too much. His third wife was also a Nez Percé, whom he called Virginia, in honor of his native state. She stayed with him for the rest of his life and bore him eight children.

The summer rendezvous, held in the mountains every year from 1825 to 1840, was the reward for all that he and his fellow trappers had been through, Meek remembered:

> The lonely mountain valley was populated with the different camps. The Rocky Mountain and American Companies with their separate camps; . . . the Nez Perces and Flatheads . . . friends of the whites, had their lodges all along the streams; so that altogether there could not have been less than one thousand souls, and two or three thousand horses and mules. . . .
>
> It was always chosen in some valley where there was grass for the animals and game for the camp. . . . The waving grass of the plain, variegated with wild flowers; the clear summer heavens flecked with white clouds that threw soft shadows; . . . gay laughter and the murmuring of Indian voices, all made up a most spirited and enchanting picture. . . .

Following the trail across South Pass, supply trains from St. Louis arrived at the rendezvous loaded with goods to exchange for beaver pelts. A pound of tobacco, which cost a few cents in Missouri, was worth more at the rendezvous than a pound of beaver fur, which sold for nearly four dollars. Scarlet cloth of the kind favored by Indian women cost six dollars per yard. Whiskey, bought for fifteen cents a gallon in St. Louis, was heavily watered down, then resold for up to four dollars a pint. "The men drank together," one of their employers remembered, "they sang, they laughed, they whooped; they tried to out-brag and out-lie each other. Now and then, familiarity was pushed too far, and would effervesce into a brawl, and a 'rough and tumble' fight; but it all ended in cordial reconciliation and maudlin endearment. . . ."

By the time the annual revels had ended, most of the mountain men were broke again. In later years, they would be romanticized as free spirits, roaming at will and answerable to no man. In fact, most mountain men were "mere slaves," as one of them admitted, hired "to catch beavers for others." But in their frenzied search for furs they did range over much of the West. "Not a hole or corner but has been ransacked by these hardy men," wrote George F. Ruxton a few years later. "From the Mississippi to the mouth of the Colorado of the West, from the forest regions of the North to the Gila in Mexico, the beaver-hunter has set his traps in every creek and stream. All this vast country, but for the daring and enterprise of these men, would be even now a *terra incognita* to geographers." And in pushing and probing beyond the borders of the United States, into California and New Mexico, they also saw firsthand how rich and how thinly defended those regions were.

By 1840, the mountain men had mostly moved on. Many streams had simply been trapped out. Besides, the stylish gentlemen of London and New York and Paris had finally wearied of beaver hats. They preferred silk now, and so the mountain men had to find other uses for their skills. Jim Bridger began guiding wagon trains through the vast territory he had helped to chart. Jim Beckwourth drifted into the California mountains and became a horse thief.

The 1837 rendezvous on the Green River, painted by Alfred Jacob Miller. "The whole city was a military camp," a nervous eastern visitor remembered, "every little camp had its own guards to protect its occupants from being stolen by its neighbor. The arrow or the ball decided the only disputes that might occur. The only law for horse-stealing was death to the thief. . . ."

Joe Meek had had enough of the mountains, too. In 1840, he took his children and his Nez Percé wife, and went all the way west, settling near a British trading post in the disputed Oregon Country, which a handful of American settlers were already talking about making part of the United States. "I was born in Washington County, Virginia, . . ." Meek said. "I want to live long enough to see Oregon securely American, and then I want this section, where I expect to die, to be named Washington County, so I can say that I was born in Washington County, United States, and died in Washington County, United States."

TEJAS

Anglo-Americans had kept an eye on the province the Spanish called *Tejas* for a long time. It seemed to have everything — dense forests in the east; rich soil on the central plains, ideal for corn and cotton; vast herds of wild horses and cattle; navigable rivers; natural ports on the Gulf of Mexico. By 1800, the Spanish-speaking populace numbered well under 3,000, most of them living in or around just three towns — San Antonio, Goliad, and Nacogdoches.

American settlers were not welcome, but Spain's grip was weakening everywhere. In 1800, Madrid had turned over the vast Louisiana Territory to France — only to have Napoleon sell it off to the Americans three years later. In Florida, so many Americans had settled illegally that Spain felt it necessary to sell it, too, to the United States. In return, Washington vowed it had no designs on Texas.

Spain did not believe it, and restless frontiersmen in Louisiana, Mississippi, and Tennessee, many of them desperate to get out of debt and eager for new lands on which to make a new start, refused to accept it; the Louisiana Purchase, they claimed, had encompassed all the territory watered by the Mississippi system — including the Red River and each of its tributaries. At a protest meeting in Natchez, Mississippi, three hundred men volunteered to seize Texas for the United States. Their leader was a surgeon with grandiose dreams, Dr. James Long. In July of 1819, he led his army into the border town of Nacogdoches, seized it from its astonished citizens without firing a shot, proclaimed it the capital of the "Republic of Texas" and himself its first president, then hurried off to see if he could persuade the notorious French pirate Jean Lafitte to join forces with him. Lafitte saw no profit in doing so, and while Long was away, Spanish troops took back their town.

Meanwhile, Moses Austin, a bankrupt Missouri mine owner eager to start over, determined to use persuasion instead of force. He traveled to Mexico City, seeking official permission to bring three hundred American families to Texas. All would be Roman Catholics, he promised, and all would pledge their loyalty to Spain. The Spanish authorities agreed, granting him a vast parcel of land on the Brazos River, but Austin died of pneumonia before he could gather his followers for the journey, and so it was his son, Stephen F. Austin, just twenty-seven, who brought the first handful of American families with him to East Texas in 1821.

Then, shortly after he began laying out his colony, San Felipé de Austin, Mexico won its independence from Spain. Tejas was now a province within the Republic of Mexico and the Austin land grant from Spain was no longer valid. Austin hurried to Mexico City to persuade the new government that it should allow him and his colonists to remain in Texas. "I arrived in Mexico City in April," he remembered,

The department of Texas is contiguous to the most avid nation in the world. The North Americans have conquered whatever territory adjoins them. In less than half a century, they have become masters of extensive colonies which formerly belonged to Spain and France, and of even more spacious territories from which have disappeared the former owners, the Indian tribes.

General Manuel de Mier y Teran

Stephen F. Austin

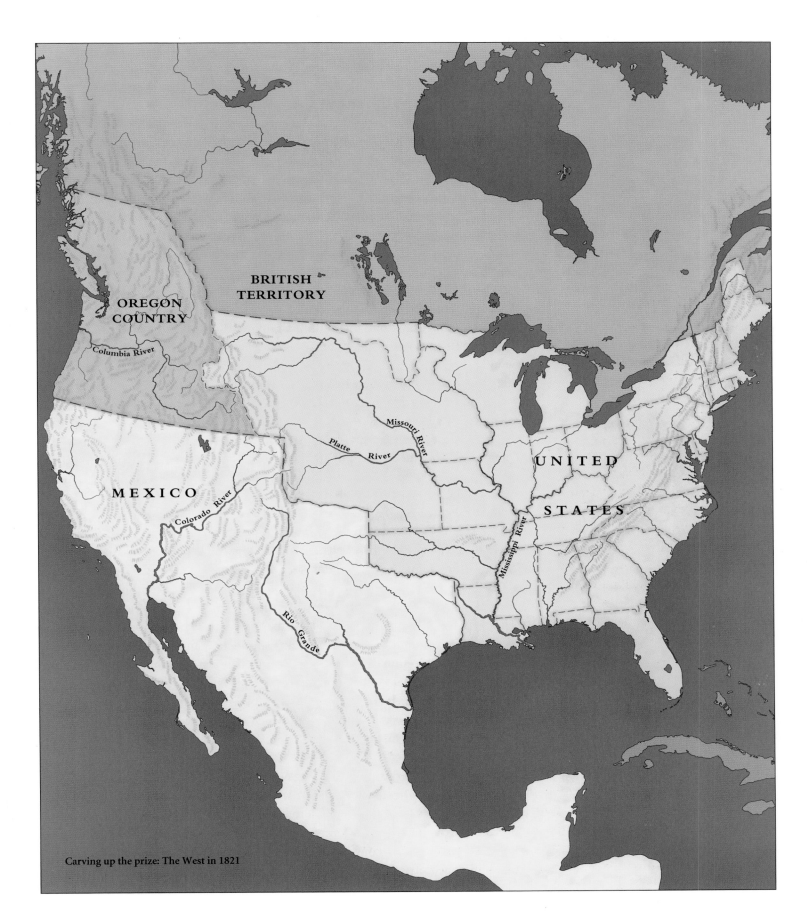

OREGON
COUNTRY

BRITISH
TERRITORY

Columbia River

MEXICO

Colorado River

Platte River

Missouri River

UNITED

STATES

Mississippi River

Rio Grande

Carving up the prize: The West in 1821

The names of the early settlers shown in the daugerreotypes on this and the opposite page have long been lost, but they run true to Texas type: all are young, lean, and conspicuously armed.

"without acquaintances, without friends, ignorant of the language, of the laws, the forms, the dispositions and feelings of the government. . . . I found the city in an unsettled state, the whole people and country still agitated by the revolutionary convulsion, public opinion vacillating, party spirit raging."

It took Austin almost a year, but in the end the new government of Mexico proved eager to see its northern frontier settled. Permanent, legal colonies of Anglo-Americans, it reasoned, would help provide protection against Indians and American adventurers alike. To attract still more legitimate settlers, Mexico would exempt Anglo-Americans from taxes for four years, award huge tracts of land to anyone who pledged to settle one hundred new families, pretend not to notice when Protestants as well as Catholics came, even permit settlers to keep their slaves as lifetime "indentured servants" — though the Mexican constitution expressly forbade involuntary servitude.

The lives of Austin's settlers, who called themselves "Texians," were hard at first, and they fought skirmish after skirmish with the Karankawa Indians, who resisted the settlers' intrusion onto their hunting grounds. But the land was fertile, the grasslands seemed "inexhaustible," Austin wrote, "and green, winter and summer," and wildflowers carpeted the clearings. "It does not appear possible," one of the first settlers wrote home, "that there can be a land more lovely."

Soon, there were other American *empresarios* with sprawling colonies of their own. American squatters came, too, carving out homesteads in the Red River country without anyone's permission. Austin dismissed them as "leatherstockings" and "longrifles," unlettered and impatient men likely to make trouble. ". . . [N]o frontiersman who has no other occupation than that of hunter will be received [by me]," he said, "no drunkard, no gambler, no profane swearer, no idler."

They kept turning up, anyway: dirt-poor debtors with dreams of becoming wealthy planters, land speculators, lawyers — and fugitives from the law. "The Sabine River is a greater savior than Jesus Christ," one man wrote. "He only saves men when they die from going to Hell, but this river saves men from prison."

By the end of the decade, there would be some 7,000 American-born Texians and their slaves in Texas — more than twice the Spanish-speaking *Tejano* population. They kept mostly to themselves, and saw themselves as a wholly superior people, sent to conquer a wilderness that the Mexicans and their Spanish forebears had failed to tame over three centuries. Even Stephen Austin privately thought most Mexicans "want nothing but tails to be more brutes than the apes."

Many *Tejanos,* in turn, found the newcomers overbearing, impatient, ignorant even of the language of the country in which they had come to live, and likely to secede from it at the first opportunity.

Stephen Austin never married — "Texas is my mistress," he said — but he saw himself as the father of his colony and took with deadly seriousness his pledge to remain a loyal citizen of Mexico. He barred Protestant clergymen from San Felipé de Austin because he feared they might foment trouble, and when Tejas lost its separate status under the new Mexican constitution of 1824, and was combined with the more populous province of Coahuila to form the new state of Coahuila y Texas, he urged patience rather than angry words and threats of defiance. And when an erratic American *empresario* named Haden Edwards took Nacogdoches in 1826, and proclaimed it the capital of an independent "Republic of Fredonia," Austin sent one hundred American-born militiamen to help quell the rebellion. "I consider that I owe *fidelity and gratitude to Mexico*," he wrote. "That has been my motto, and I have impressed it upon my colonists."

Other settlers began to develop other ideas. Jim Bowie was a tall, alcoholic Louisianan who, before coming to San Antonio in 1828, had made a fortune selling slaves and land to which he had no title, and had killed several men in duels with a broad-bladed knife said to be of his own design. He converted to Catholicism in Texas, married the wealthy nineteen-year-old daughter of the Mexican lieutenant governor, and hoped to make himself rich once more speculating in land and mining for silver.

William Barrett Travis was quick-tempered, too. A young lawyer who had deserted a wife and child in South Carolina after killing the man he accused of being his wife's lover, he was fond of gambling and women, fiercely ambitious, and so fascinated by himself that he wrote an autobiography at the age of twenty-three.

On December 2, 1832, a tall thirty-nine-year-old Tennessean stepped aboard the Red River ferry, crossing from Indian Territory into Texas. He was Sam Houston, a former member of Congress and governor of Tennessee who had been spoken of as a possible successor to his friend and political mentor, President Andrew Jackson, until scandal and alcoholism ended his political career. He hoped Texas would provide him with new and glorious opportunities. "An eagle swooped down near my head," he remembered later, "and then, soaring aloft with wildest screams, was lost in the rays of the setting sun. I knew that a great destiny waited for me in the West."

THE ROAD TO SANTA FE

Like the *Tejanos,* the Spanish-speaking people of New Mexico had long felt isolated and neglected by Spain. They were farmers and ranchers, mostly, living in and around small towns scattered along the Rio Grande and its northern tributaries, the Chama and the Pecos. The authorities had been unable to shield them effectively from Comanche and Navajo raiders. All commerce with the United States was barred, and legitimate trade limited to a trickle of pack trains that moved back and forth from Chihuahua, far to the south. When Mexican independence came, only a few had much faith that their lot would greatly improve; the 5,000 citizens of Santa Fe would not get around to celebrating their freedom for a full five months.

On September 1, 1821, a St. Louis trader named William Becknell set out for Santa Fe with some thirty mounted companions, carrying axes, knives, and bolts of bright cotton to swap for horses and mules. They followed the Arkansas River into the Raton Mountains — where they were suddenly surrounded by a squadron of uniformed dragoons. Becknell knew he was deep into Spanish territory and feared the fate that had befallen earlier American smugglers — arrest, confiscation of his goods, imprisonment. Instead, the soldiers smiled and made clear the Americans were to follow them into Santa Fe. There, the governor greeted Becknell warmly and told him everything had changed. The Spanish had been overthrown. He was now in Mexican territory, and Missouri traders henceforth would be welcome at Santa Fe.

The town itself, with its single-story adobe houses, struck one trader as looking "more like a prairie dog village than a capital," but its citizens eagerly bought up all of

Santa Fe: Missouri traders arriving in the capital of New Mexico (above), and the town itself as it looked in 1848 after the Americans had taken over and the Stars and Stripes was raised above the old Palace of the Governors.

The caravan at last hove into sight, and, wagon after wagon, was seen pouring down the last declivity at about a mile's distance from the city. . . . The arrival produced a great bustle and excitement among the natives. "Los Americanos!" — "Los Carros!" — "Le entrada de la caravana!" were to be heard in every direction; and crowds of women and boys flocked around to see the new-comers. . . . The wagoners were by no means free from excitement. . . . [T]hey were prepared with clean faces, sleek combed hair, and their choicest Sunday suit, to meet the "fair eyes" of glistening black that were sure to stare at them as they passed.

Josiah Gregg

Becknell's trade goods, and when he and his companions rode home, their saddle-bags were heavy with Mexican silver pesos.

Becknell set out for New Mexico again the next spring, this time bringing three oxcarts laden with goods. Because the wagons couldn't be hauled through the mountains, he blazed a new trail across the Cimarron desert — and almost didn't make it. Comanche harassed his men. They ran out of water, became so desperate that they lopped off their mules' ears to quench their thirst with blood, and were saved only when they shot a buffalo, its stomach still filled with water from the Cimarron.

Still, Becknell already had several Missouri rivals for the Santa Fe trade. In 1824, they joined forces to form one well-defended caravan. The Indians held off, and the traders, who had invested $30,000, brought back $190,000 in gold, silver, and furs.

Thereafter, season after season, the traders made the thousand-mile trek to Santa Fe, sometimes one hundred wagons at a time, bringing with them handkerchiefs and shawls, pots and pans and wallpaper, even window glass. There were rock slides on the mountain route, sudden rainstorms on the Cimarron Cutoff that turned the dusty flatland into a morass of mud and caused flash floods that swept wagons away.

The risks were great. But the rewards were greater, and Mexican traders were soon on the move as well, driving herds of horses, sheep, and mules northward for sale in Missouri. Soon, while the region's cultural and political ties to Mexico remained strong, its economy was increasingly dominated by the Americans, who carried home so many silver pesos that New Mexico virtually ran out of coins by the mid-1820s.

COME AND TAKE IT

Americans continued to pour into Texas, so many now that when the letters "G.T.T." appeared on the walls of empty cabins throughout the southern United States, everyone knew it meant "Gone to Texas."

Some wealthy *Tejanos* still saw American settlement as the best way to develop the state. "I cannot help seeing advantages," wrote one citizen of San Antonio, "which, to my way of thinking, would result if we admitted honest hard-working people, regardless of what country they come from . . . even hell itself."

But Mexico City soon began to take a very different view and sent the former minister of war, General Manuel de Mier y Teran, north to survey the situation. Riding across the state in a splendidly carved coach inlaid with silver, he was appalled by what he found:

> The whole population here is a mixture of strange and incoherent parts without parallel in our federation: numerous tribes of Indians, now at peace, but armed at any moment ready for war . . . colonists of another people, more progressive and better informed than the Mexican inhabitants, but also more shrewd and unruly; among these foreigners are fugitives from justice, honest laborers, vagabonds and criminals, but honorable and dishonorable alike travel with their political constitution in their pockets, demanding the privileges, authority and officers which such a constitution guarantees.

The more the American population of Texas is increased, the more readily will the Mexican Government give it up. A gentle breeze shakes off a ripe peach. Can it be supposed that the violent political convulsions of Mexico will not shake off Texas so soon as it is ripe enough to fall? All that is now wanting is a great immigration of good and efficient families. . . . [Then] . . . the peach will be ripe.

Stephen F. Austin

Land grants (opposite, top) formally given to Stephen Austin and his fellow *empresarios* by Mexico in the years before the Texas Revolution

General Antonio Lopez de Santa Anna (opposite, bottom) served as president of Mexico eleven times over the course of his long and turbulent career, despite his inglorious loss of Texas.

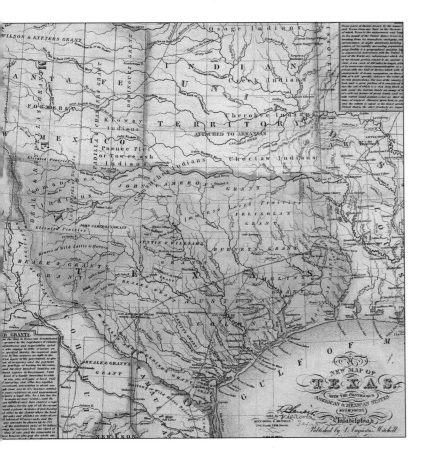

Such people were sure to foment a revolution. "Either the government occupies Texas *now*," the general wrote, "or it is lost forever." Lucas Alaman, the Mexican secretary of state, agreed: "Where others send invading armies," he wrote, ". . . [the Americans] send their colonists." And when President Andrew Jackson sent an emissary to Mexico City, prepared to buy Texas for $5 million, the Mexican government indignantly rejected the offer.

The next year, Anglo-American settlement was barred altogether. Instead of Americans, Mexican citizens and Europeans would now be encouraged to colonize Texas. Convict-soldiers were to be sent north, too, first to enforce the law and then to become settlers themselves. A handful of Irish colonists managed to establish two settlements, Refugio and San Patricio Hibernia — St. Patrick of Ireland. An English settlement was started, too, only to be wiped out by the Comanche.

But the flow of illegal American squatters just increased. Between 1830 and 1834, the population of Texas more than doubled, to better than 20,000. By 1835, 1,000 Americans a month were pushing into Texas at one river crossing alone. The next year, there were 35,000 Anglo-Americans and their slaves in Texas — ten times the number of *Tejanos*. Trying to stop American immigration, Stephen Austin wrote, was "like trying to stop the Mississippi with a dam of straw." Tensions rose. Rumors spread that Mexico intended to insist the Texians' slaves be freed. Mexican troops offered little protection against Indians but insisted on collecting duties, which the colonists resisted paying, and some among the settlers began to compare the Mexican troops newly stationed among them with British redcoats.

The Texians began to divide into two camps: a "war party," headed by impetuous young men like William Travis, who openly urged revolution and independence, and a "peace party," which looked to Stephen Austin for leadership and still hoped for some sort of compromise with Mexico.

Then everything seemed to change. General Antonio Lopez de Santa Anna, the self-styled "Napoleon of the West" who had once destroyed a Spanish army sent to overthrow the Mexican revolution, was elected president of Mexico, promising to restore the old states' rights constitution. Moderate Texans were jubilant, sure their grievances would at last be heard. They drew up a resolution asking that the law against American settlement be repealed, that Texas be allowed to separate itself from Coahuila with a state constitution modeled closely on that of the United States. Austin was appointed to take the petition to Mexico City. Once again, events moved more slowly than he liked, and he wrote an uncharacteristically blunt letter to the mostly *Tejano* city council of San Antonio. "If our application is refused . . ." he said, "I shall be in favor of organizing without it. I see no other way of saving the country from total anarchy and ruin. I am totally done with conciliatory measures and, for the future, shall be uncompromising as to Texas."

Sam Houston, painted by George Catlin in 1840

Santa Anna finally agreed to end the ban on American settlement, at least, but news of Austin's indiscreet letter made its way back to Mexico City. He was arrested and clapped in jail for eighteen months. Meanwhile, Santa Anna betrayed his own revolution and, like his hero, Napoleon Bonaparte, declared himself dictator. Then he sent an army northward under the command of his brother-in-law, General Martin Perfecto de Cos, with orders to crush all resistance to his rule wherever he found it.

Texas-style minutemen began to drill. "Nothing is heard but 'God damn Santa Anna,'" one anxious Mexican official reported. Another warned that Texians would arm "even the children" rather than allow a Mexican army to cross the Rio Grande. Even Stephen Austin's patience had run out. Returning to Texas in the summer of 1835, he declared, "Santa Anna is . . . a base, unprincipled bloody monster. . . . War is our only recourse. No halfway measures, but war in full."

On October 2, as General Cos and his army moved into San Antonio, a detachment of one hundred Mexican cavalrymen was sent to Gonzales to reclaim an aged brass cannon the settlers had borrowed to defend themselves against Indians. The men of Gonzales hung out a banner reading "Come and Take It," and when the Mexicans tried to do just that, they touched it off, sending a load of nails, wire, and horseshoes slashing through the Mexican ranks. The survivors fled.

The Texas Revolution had begun.

At first, it seemed that more easy Texan victories lay in store. They seized the Mexican garrison at Goliad. Stephen Austin himself accompanied a force of 300 to 500 that he called "the Army of the People," bent on besieging General Cos and his army of 800 at San Antonio. Among them were some 160 *Tejanos*, just as eager as the American colonists to restore the Mexican constitution. The Texian army ringed San Antonio and settled in for a siege.

Meanwhile, Austin called for a "general consultation" at San Felipé to map a united defense. The war party called openly for independence, but the moderates were still in the majority: the "consultation" asked only for a return to the Constitution of 1824. Austin was sent east to the United States to rally volunteers and arrange credit with which to finance a war.

Sam Houston was named commander of the Texas forces. He had a distinctly mixed reputation. Some remembered only the bright promise of his youth. Raised by his widowed mother in the Tennessee canebrake and informally adopted by the Cherokee, he survived three serious wounds to distinguish himself in battle against the Creek, then became a general of militia, congressman, and governor, thanks in part to the patronage of his old commander, Andrew Jackson.

But others could not forget the complications of his private life. He had been abandoned by his young wife and had resigned his governorship immediately afterward without explanation: "This is a painful but a private affair," was all he would say.

"I do not recognize the right of the public to interfere." He later beat a congressman senseless with his cane for daring to question his honesty, and drank so heavily that his Cherokee friends nicknamed him "Big Drunk."

No one questioned his courage. But they did worry about his steadiness and some challenged his authority. He had opposed the march on San Antonio as premature, but the forces now shivering in the cold outside the town did not report to him.

On December 5, spurred on by a hot-tempered old settler named Ben Milam, the Texians roared into Goliad. Milam was killed early on, and it took five days of vicious house-to-house fighting, but General Cos and his men were finally driven into an old mission called the Alamo on the far side of the San Antonio River, where they finally surrendered. The Texians gallantly allowed Cos and his defeated soldiers to leave town unmolested after they vowed never to return to Texas — and even gave them powder and shot to ward off any Indians they might meet on their way back to Mexico. The war was over — or so many Texians thought. Most of the volunteers went home.

Sam Houston knew better. The fighting had just begun. Humiliated by his brother-in-law's defeat, General Santa Anna now determined to crush the Texians in person, at the head of an army of 4,000 men. Another 1,500 waited to join forces with him on the Rio Grande.

Santa Anna's army rode north beneath a black flag that meant no quarter. "The foreigners who wage war against the Mexican Nation have violated all laws and do not deserve any consideration . . ." the general warned. "They have audaciously declared a war of extermination to the Mexicans and should be treated in the same manner."

As Santa Anna's mighty army moved closer, Houston called for more men, from Texas and from the United States. "Let each man," he said, "come with a good rifle and one hundred rounds of ammunition — and come soon." "Texas meetings" were held all over the country. Funds were raised in New York, Mobile, Columbus, Boston. "Texas, Texas," wrote the editor of the Philadelphia *Courier,* "crowded meetings and gun-powder speeches calling down vengeance upon the oppressors of the Texonians is the order of the day." Impetuous young men signed up by the battalion: Captain Duval's Kentucky Mustangs, Captain Shackleford's Red Rovers of Alabama, the New Orleans Greys. "If we succeed," wrote one volunteer, "a fertile region and a grateful people will be for us a home and secure us our reward. If we fail, death in defense of so just and so good a cause need not excite a shudder or a tear."

From Tennessee came Colonel Davy Crockett — hunter, frontiersman, teller of tall tales, and Whig congressman. He had lost his most recent election after announcing that if his constituents didn't reelect him, they could go to hell and he would go to Texas. Now he was on his way.

Davy Crockett, frontiersman and Tennessee politician, painted by John Gadsby Chapman. According to several eyewitnesses, Crockett and five other defenders of the Alamo survived the fighting and surrendered to the enemy, only to be hacked to death at Santa Anna's orders.

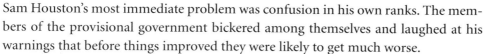

San Antonio de Bejar and the outlying Alamo (top, left), diagrammed by Santa Anna's chief military engineer during the siege, and two of the Alamo's defenders: Jim Bowie (top, right), whose refusal to follow orders and blow up the old mission eventually led to his death and those of almost two hundred of his companions; and Juan Seguín (above), the *Tejano* who slipped through the Mexican lines in search of reinforcements and later distinguished himself at the battle of San Jacinto

Sam Houston's most immediate problem was confusion in his own ranks. The members of the provisional government bickered among themselves and laughed at his warnings that before things improved they were likely to get much worse.

The strategy he favored was simple. He would harass Santa Anna's army from a distance — just as the American revolutionaries had once harassed the British redcoats — stretch the enemy's supply lines, and then hope to defeat him in one climactic battle. "It is better," he said, "to do well . . . *late* . . . than never."

But others refused to see it that way. James Fannin, a former slave runner from Georgia who had once attended West Point and therefore had a dangerously exalted view of his own martial skills, insisted upon starting south with half the army to seize the border town of Matamoros. Houston was violently opposed but powerless to stop him. Halfway to his goal, Fannin himself hesitated and settled in with his army at Goliad.

The Texians were now dangerously divided, and Santa Anna's army was nearing San Antonio, bent on revenge.

Houston knew the Alamo was too isolated, too big, too badly designed and poorly armed to be successfully defended. He sent Jim Bowie to blow it up. But Bowie did not do so. Instead, he and some 123 men prepared to hold the old mission until reinforcements could reach them. There were New Yorkers and Pennsylvanians as well as Kentuckians and Tennesseeans among them, immigrants from England and Ireland and Germany, as well as Davy Crockett and at least six *Tejanos* willing to risk everything for the Texian cause.

William Travis, now a colonel in the Texian army, assumed command, bringing with him some thirty cavalrymen, and on February 24, 1836, when Santa Anna

The battered farmhouse at Washington-on-the-Brazos in which the Texas Declaration of Independence was adopted, photographed many years later

reached San Antonio and demanded that the Alamo's occupants surrender or be annihilated, he answered with a cannon shot.

A steady Mexican shelling began.

Travis scribbled out requests for reinforcements and smuggled them through the gate. One was carried from the Alamo to Gonzales by Juan Seguín, the son of the former mayor of San Antonio, who had organized a force of *Tejano* ranchers to fight for independence. Twenty-nine men responded to Travis's appeals and managed to slip into the Alamo under cover of darkness. Travis now had some 182 men. There would be no more.

The Mexican artillery continued to batter the walls and hurl shells into the courtyard.

On March 2, 1836, fifty-nine Texians gathered in a crude frame building in the tiny settlement of Washington-on-the-Brazos. Cloth was stretched across the windows to keep out the howling wind. It was "a disgusting place," one visitor wrote. "It is laid out in the woods, about a dozen wretched cabins or shanties constitute the city; not one decent house in it, and only one well-defined street, which consists of an opening cut out of the woods, the stumps still standing. A rare place to hold a national convention in."

There, over the course of the next two weeks, the delegates declared Texas an independent republic, hammered out a constitution closely modeled after that of the United States, elected a frail, tubercular planter named David Burnet as interim president, and named Sam Houston commander in chief of the army.

EVEN THE WOLVES WILL SHRINK

The Four Bears, a Mandan chief, shown here in two portraits by Karl Bodmer, was a formidable warrior. He had killed five chiefs of other nations in hand-to-hand combat. Unarmed, he had wrested a knife from a Cheyenne warrior and used it to kill its owner. He also had taken many prisoners, survived an enemy arrow and six gunshot wounds. But he had never shown anything but friendship to the Americans. "Ever since I can remember," he once said, "I have loved the whites. I have lived with them ever since I was a boy and to the best of my knowledge I have never wronged a white man. . . ."

No Indian people had been more cordial to whites than the Mandan. They welcomed traders and trappers of all nations, sheltered Lewis and Clark during the bitter winter of 1805, served as trusted middlemen for the Missouri fur trade.

In the autumn of 1837, they paid a fearful price for their hospitality. When the American Fur Company brought its steamboat filled with supplies to their villages for its annual visit, the smallpox virus was inadvertently harbored among the crew. It raged through the Mandan villages, felling men, women, and children.

"About fifteen days afterward," a trader at Fort Union recalled, "there was such a stench in the fort that it could be smelt at the distance of 300 yards. It was awful — the scene in the fort, where some went crazy, and others were eaten up by maggots before they died; yet, singular to say, not a single bad expression was ever uttered by a sick Indian. Many died, and those who recovered were so much disfigured that one could scarcely recognize them."

When the epidemic had finally run its course, the once-mighty Mandan nation was reduced to barely thirty individuals, huddled together with remnants of the Arikara and Hidatsa, wholly dependent on the U.S. government for their survival.

The Four Bears was among the last to contract the disease. As he was dying, he lamented that he had ever befriended the men who had brought such devastation to his people:

> The Four Bears never saw a white man hungry, but what he gave them to eat, drink and a buffalo skin to sleep on in time of need . . . and how they have repaid it! With ingratitude! I have never called a white man a dog, but today I do pronounce them to be a set of black-hearted dogs. They have deceived me. Them that I always considered as brothers have turned out to be my worst enemies. . . . I do not fear death, my friends, you know it. But to die with my face rotten, that even the wolves will shrink from horror at seeing me, and say to themselves, "That is the Four Bears, the friend of the whites."
>
> Listen well to what I have to say, as it will be the last time you will hear me. Think of your wives, children, brothers, sisters, friends, and in fact all that you hold dear. All are dead or dying, with their faces all rotten, caused by those dogs the whites. Think of all that my friends, and rise together and not leave one of them alive.

Still, the chances for Texian independence now seemed slim. All that stood between the Mexican army and the settlements in East Texas were James Fannin's 420 men, shut up in Goliad, and William Travis's 182 volunteers surrounded inside the Alamo.

There, at five in the morning, March 6, 1836, a Mexican bugler blew the *Deguello*, the signal for death in the bullring, and 2,600 men charged the old mission. The Texians shot them down as they came on, clubbed them as they clambered over the walls, fought them hand-to-hand and room-to-room. At least six hundred Mexican soldiers would fall that morning — many of them shot in the back by their poorly led comrades, coming along behind — though afterward, Santa Anna would officially admit to just seventy deaths among his men. But in the end, the odds proved overwhelming. The Alamo was taken, and Bowie, Crockett, Travis, and all their companions lay dead.

The news galvanized the southern frontier. Many of the dead had been U.S. volunteers and there were calls for revenge up and down the border. New volunteers poured across the Red River and the Sabine.

But Santa Anna was already on the march again, heading straight for the American colonies in East Texas.

The Texas cause now rested squarely on the shoulders of Sam Houston, who refused to say what he would do. "Had I consulted the wishes of all," he said, "I should have been like the ass between two stacks of hay. I consulted no one — I held no councils of war. If I err, the blame is mine." He began an erratic, zigzagging retreat across Texas, keeping his tiny force just out of range of the advancing Mexicans, in the hope that the winter rains would slow them down enough to let fresh volunteers reach his army before battle was joined.

As Houston fell back, word came of still another disaster. Fannin's force of four hundred men at Goliad had been surrounded and disarmed. They were mostly American volunteers, not Texians, and Santa Anna considered them no better than pirates. At his orders, more than three hundred of them were shot and their corpses set ablaze.

Thousands of frightened settlers and their families began fleeing for the border. "We passed a house with all the doors open," one woman remembered. "The table had been set, all of the victuals on the table, and even the chairs set up in their places. On the table was a plate of biscuits, a plate of potatoes, fried chicken. . . ." Old-timers would remember the exodus as "the Runaway Scrape."

The civilian government panicked, too, retreating to the tiny East Texas town of Harrisburg, then demanding that Houston stand and fight. "Sir: The enemy are laughing you to scorn," President Burnet told Houston. "You must fight them. You must retreat no further. The country expects you to fight. The salvation of the country depends on your doing so." Settlers jeered Houston from the roadside. Rumors spread that alcohol had undercut his courage. Some of his men wept with frustration as they marched. Others deserted in order to escort their families out of harm's way.

Still he kept his own counsel, gnawing on the raw ears of corn with which he filled his saddlebags, poring over Caesar's *Commentaries*. Some soldiers feared he meant simply to flee across the U.S. border and abandon Texas to Santa Anna. Officers threatened to seize command — and Houston threatened to shoot anyone who dared try it.

Then Santa Anna veered off to seize Harrisburg, where he believed the provisional government was hiding. The town was empty when he got there. Santa Anna burned it down, but Houston and his army had now slipped up behind him. The hunter was about to become the hunted.

Late in the afternoon of April 21, 1836, Santa Anna and some 1,250 men were resting in a shady grove of trees near the river crossing at San Jacinto, confident that they had cut off Houston's escape route. It was the moment Houston had been waiting for.

Misinformation: This poster, issued in New Orleans before the Alamo's fall and intended to spur recruitment in Louisiana, alleges that the mission's defenders have fought off Santa Anna's army, killing or wounding five hundred Mexicans, without suffering a single casualty themselves, and that a Texian army is already marching to relieve the siege. None of it was true.

The Texian battle flag, carried into the thick of the fighting by Houston's men and sewn by Kentucky women who sympathized with their cause

Ever since Texas has unfurled the banner of Freedom, and commenced a Warfare of liberty or death, our hearts have been enlisted in her behalf. . . . If we succeed, the country is ours, it is immense in extent and fertile in its soil, and will amply reward all our toil. If we fail, death in the cause of liberty and humanity is not a cause for shuddering.

Daniel Cloud

San Jacinto: Sam Houston (waving his hat at center left, as an aide holds the wounded Saracen) leads his men into battle against the stunned Mexican army, while General Santa Anna (conveniently wearing a white sombrero so the onlooker can't miss him) gallops furiously away at center right. Despite the hand-to-hand heroics rendered here, the real thing was a one-sided slaughter. "I sat there on my horse and shot them until my ammunition gave out," a Texas private recalled. "Then I turned the butt of my musket and started knocking them in the head."

When Alfonso Steele (above), a Kentucky-born volunteer, was photographed at ninety-four, he claimed to be the last living veteran of San Jacinto. His memories included Santa Anna's surrender to Sam Houston, painted by William Huddle in 1866. Houston had been shot in the leg and was unable to stand when the Mexican commander was brought before him by his captors. "I was lying on my left side in a kind of haze," Houston recalled, "when I felt some person clasp my right hand. I looked up as Santa Anna stood before me. He announced his name and rank."

He ordered the bridge behind the Mexicans destroyed. ". . . [I]t cut off all means of escape for either army," he remembered. "There was now no alternative but victory or death." The enemy was cut off by water on three sides and Houston's eight hundred men held the fourth.

Mounted on a white stallion called Saracen, he rallied his troops. "Victory is certain!" he told them. "Trust in God and fear not! The victims of the Alamo and the names of those who were murdered at Goliad cry out for vengeance. Remember the Alamo! Remember Goliad!" Then he led the charge, swinging his saber. When Saracen fell, hit by five musket balls, Houston climbed onto another horse. It, too, was killed, and this time his own right leg was splintered by a ball. But the Mexican army was already in full flight, and the vengeful Texians were right behind them.

The fighting lasted just eighteen minutes, but the slaughter went on for another hour or so. "If Jesus Christ were to come down from Heaven and order me to quit shooting Santanistas," one soldier told an officer, "I wouldn't do it, sir!" A Texian sergeant remembered the special quality of the savagery:

A young Mexican boy (a drummer I suppose) [was] lying on his face. One of the Volunteers . . . pricked the boy with his bayonet. The boy grasped the man around the legs and cried out in Spanish "Hail Mary, Most Pure! For God's sake, save my life!' I begged the man to spare him, both of his legs being broken already. The man looked at me and put his hand on his pistol, so I passed on. Just as I did so, he blew out the boy's brains.

When it was all over, six hundred Mexican soldiers were dead, nearly seven hundred more had surrendered. The surprise had been so complete, the blow so sudden, that only six Texans died in the battle of San Jacinto. Santa Anna himself was Sam Houston's prisoner and was forced to sign a document ceding Texan independence, which the Mexican legislature indignantly withdrew.

Nonetheless, North America was now divided into five parts — Alaska, claimed by Russia; British Canada; the United States; Mexico; and the brand-new Republic of Texas. "The loss of Texas will inevitably result in the loss of New Mexico and the Californias," warned José Maria Tornel y Mendivil, the Mexican secretary of war. "Little by little our territory will be absorbed until only an insignificant part is left to us. . . . Our national existence, recognized after so many difficulties, [will] end like those weak meteors from time to time, shine fitfully in the firmament and disappear."

IN THE MIDST OF SAVAGE DARKNESS

From the moment Lewis and Clark had first appeared among them, the Nez Percé had been friendly toward the Americans. They trapped with them, attended their rendezvous, even fought alongside them against their rivals, the Blackfeet and Gros Ventre. And they had come to admire their weapons and tools and their ability to communicate with one another over hundreds of miles by making marks on paper.

Clearly, the whites had special medicine, and the Nez Percé began to mimic some of their practices in hopes of sharing in it. Two Nez Percé boys, returning home from a Hudson's Bay school in Canada, explained that the white man's secrets were to be found in a black book called the Bible. Soon, trappers were startled to find that their Nez Percé allies stopped to pray twice a day, said a sort of grace before meals, and would no longer work on Sundays. "They even had a rude calendar of the fasts and festivals of the Romish church," Captain Benjamin L. E. Bonneville remembered, "and some traces of its ceremonials. These have become blended with their own wild rites, and present a strange medley; civilized and barbarous. On the Sabbath men, women and children array themselves in their best style and assemble round a pole erected at the head of the camp. Here they go through a wild fantastic ceremonial, strongly resembling the religious dance of the shaking Quakers."

In 1831, four Indians — three Nez Percé and a member of the Flathead tribe — made their way east to St. Louis, hoping to learn more of the white man's ways and

George Catlin painted the St. Louis waterfront (left), as well as portraits of two of the four Indians — Rabbit's Skin Leggings (top) and No Horn on His Head, both Nez Percé — who came there in 1832 to seek the white man's Black Book.

perhaps to see if they could find someone willing to come west to explain to their people the secrets contained in the Black Book. They sought out their old friend William Clark, now the Commissioner for Indians, and spoke with several Catholic priests. Two of the Nez Percé died of disease while still in St. Louis, a third died aboard a steamboat trying to get home. The fourth survived long enough to find a Nez Percé band hunting in Montana and tell them that white men might soon be coming with the Black Book, before he, too, died, at the hands of the Blackfeet.

The Reverend Henry Spalding (top, right) grips both Bible and hoe, twin symbols of his mission to the Indians.

The six-foot-high "learning ladder" (above) was drawn by Spalding's wife, Eliza, and meant to impress upon the Nez Percé the superiority of Presbyterianism over the faith preached by the Spaldings' Roman Catholic rivals. The straight and narrow path on the right represents the one true route to salvation, while a greedy and obese pope blocks the broader thoroughfare. Catholic missionaries countered with ladders of their own, in which Protestants were shown tumbling into hell.

In St. Louis, a Methodist member of the Wyandot tribe named William Walker heard of the Indians' visit and wrote a highly colored account of it to a friend back East. The friend embellished it still further and published it in the missionary press: the Nez Percé were pleading for salvation, he said. The whole of Oregon lay open to Protestant Christianity if only missionaries could be found to go west and spread the Gospel. "Hear! Hear!" wrote the editor of *The Christian Advocate and Journal.* "Who will respond to the call from beyond the Rocky Mountains? . . . [W]e are for having a mission established there at once. . . . All we want is men. Who will go? Who?"

The Methodists were the first to answer, sending Jason Lee to the Oregon Country in 1834. He set up a mission among the Chinook, but soon proved a disappointment to his church, more interested in colonizing the Willamette Valley with fellow Methodists from New England than saving Indian souls, and was eventually dismissed.

In late 1836, a party of five Presbyterian missionaries from the American Board of Foreign Missions made the 2,000-mile trek from Missouri to Fort Vancouver along the route that would soon be called the Oregon Trail. It was an arduous journey made still more arduous because, while the missionaries agreed on the importance of carrying the Gospel westward, they agreed on very little else. One missionary, William Gray, proved quarrelsome and petulant; trained in carpentry and mechanics and ill-prepared for life among the Indians, he would soon abandon the ministry for farming. Another, the Reverend Henry Spalding, was a rigid and embittered man from upstate New York. Born out of wedlock to a woman who neglected him and a father who would have nothing to do with him, he was newly married to Eliza Gray, but still nursed a grievance against the woman who had turned down his first proposal of marriage, Narcissa Prentiss. That same Narcissa Prentiss and her new husband, Dr. Marcus Whitman, made up the rest of the party, and the two couples were forced to share the same tent all across the continent.

As soon as the party reached Oregon it split up. The Spaldings settled among the Nez Percé. The Whitmans chose to begin their work 120 miles away, at Walla Walla, among the Nez Percé's neighbors, the Cayuse.

Narcissa Whitman was pious and eager and possessed of a fine voice for singing hymns, but, like the rest of her missionary companions, utterly ignorant of the West and of the people she and her husband hoped to convert to Christianity. "Some [of the Indians] feel almost to blame us for telling about eternal realities," she noted. "One said it was good when they knew nothing but to hunt, eat, drink and sleep; now it was bad. [. . . Still,] we long to have them know of a Saviour's pardoning love."

The Cayuse, like the Nez Percé, to whom they were closely related, had hoped to be taught the practical secrets of white civilization — modern weaponry, better tools. Instead, the Whitmans told them they must abandon hunting and fishing and take up the plow, denounced their medicine men as charlatans, and warned that they were doomed if they failed to repent of their sins.

The Indians came to resent the missionaries' refusal to pay for the land they occupied or to offer gifts, as was the Cayuse custom when visitors came to call. They were insulted when, not long after giving birth to a daughter, Alice, Narcissa barred them from her parlor because, she said, "they would make it so dirty and full of fleas that we could not live in it," and were further baffled when the Whitmans began quarreling with Catholic missionaries over who had a monopoly on religious truth. During their first years in Oregon, the Whitmans managed to convert a Scottish visitor, a French-Canadian Catholic, and several Hawaiian laborers who worked for the mission. But they failed to make a single convert among the Cayuse.

> Never [wrote Narcissa] was I more keenly sensible to the self denials of a missionary life. Even now while I am writing, the drum and the savage yell are sounding in my ears, every sound of which is as far as the east is from the west from vibrating in unison with my feelings. . . . Dear friends will you not sometime think of me almost alone in the midst of savage darkness.

Meanwhile, Henry Spalding did a little better with the Nez Percé. On November 17, 1839 — three years after the Spaldings' arrival in Oregon — he officiated at the baptism of his first two converts. Both were chiefs. He named one Joseph and the other Timothy. The following year, Joseph had a son, whom he named *Hin-mah-too-yah-lat-kekht* — Thunder Rolling from the Mountains. Spalding baptized the infant as Ephraim, but he would one day be known throughout the West as Chief Joseph.

TRAIL OF TEARS

Since Thomas Jefferson's time, Washington had hoped that the Indian peoples of the East might learn the ways of the whites and thus gradually be absorbed among them. But if they could not be absorbed, then they might gradually be moved west of the Mississippi, to a "permanent Indian frontier" carved from the prairies. There, the theory was, they could flourish free from further white encroachment.

Whites disagreed over the degree of kindness or coercion that should be applied to bringing about the Indians' removal, but virtually all agreed that their own wish to expand westward into lands to which they believed the Indian peoples had only the vaguest sort of title should always come first. That, after all, had been how the East was settled; why should the West be any different? "What is the right of a huntsman to the forest of a thousand miles over which he has accidentally ranged in quest of prey?" asked John Quincy Adams. ". . . Shall the field and valley, which a beneficent

[The Indians] listened to our professions of friendship. We called them brothers and they believed us. They yielded millions of acres to our demands and yet we crave more. We have crowded the tribes upon a few miserable acres of our southern frontier: it is all that is left to them of their once boundless forests; and still, like the horse-leech, our insatiated cupidity cries, give! give! give!

Senator Theodore Frelinghuysen of New Jersey

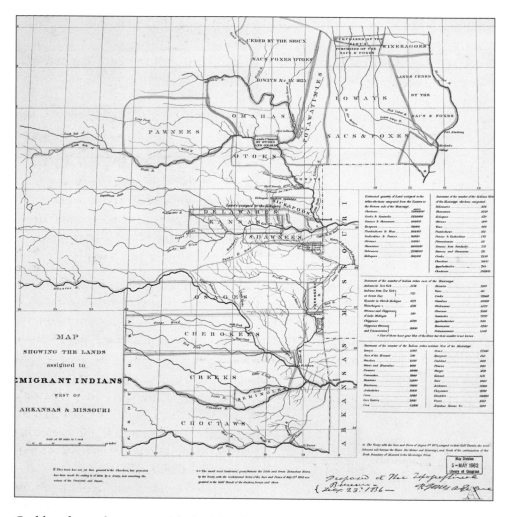

Map Division
5 – MAY 1962
Library of Congress

We ask [the President] to protect us, agreeable to treaties. Inclination to remove from this land has no abiding place in our hearts, and when we move we shall move by the course of nature to sleep under this ground which the Great Spirit gave to our ancestors and which now covers them in their undisturbed repose.

Legislative Council of the Cherokee

Indian Territory in 1836, parceled out among euphemistically titled "Emigrant Indians" — actually peoples from eastern and midwestern tribes compelled to leave their homes and move west

God has formed to teem with the life of innumerable multitudes, be condemned to everlasting barrenness?"

On May 28, 1830, President Andrew Jackson had signed the Indian Removal Act, which empowered him to make treaties with all tribes east of the Mississippi to cede their lands in exchange for lands in the West. One by one, Indian bands found themselves forced to move from their old homes — Ottawa, Shawnee, and Potawatomi, Sac and Fox, Miami and Kickapoo.

Indian peoples already living in the West were not consulted about this involuntary invasion. When the newcomers edged too far west in search of buffalo, Kiowa and Comanche attacked them, and federal troops had to be called in to impose a tenuous peace. The Cheyenne and Arapaho also sought to drive the Potawatomi from their hunting grounds but got more than they bargained for; the easterners, trained by the British during the War of 1812, formed ranks, fired organized volleys, and took a terrible toll on their attackers before driving them from the field.

The southern states were home to the peoples whom whites called the "Five Civilized Tribes." The Choctaw were the first to be moved west, followed by the Chickasaw. Some of the Creek had to be driven from their land. So did the Seminoles.

The Cherokee, living on 40,000 acres in the heart of Georgia, sought to resist Removal by legal means. No other Indian people had ever so successfully adopted the white man's ways. Some lived on large plantations worked by black slaves. They had constructed smithies and sawmills and factories for weaving cloth, built public schools and miles of good roads. Many had intermarried with whites. They had their own constitution and government and courts, too, their own written language, their own newspaper.

"Even in our distant state," wrote Ralph Waldo Emerson from Concord, Massachusetts,

> some good rumor of [the Cherokee's] worth and civility has arrived. We have learned with joy of their improvements in the social arts. We have read their newspapers. We have seen some of them in our schools and colleges. . . . [W]e have witnessed with sympathy the painful labors of these red men to redeem their own race from the doom of eternal inferiority and to borrow and domesticate in the tribe the arts and customs of the Caucasian race.

None of this mattered to white Georgians. They wanted Cherokee land and methodically went about taking it. Cherokee land titles were declared illegal. Cherokee were forbidden to testify against whites, even to dig for gold on their own lands. Those who resisted were beaten, jailed, killed.

The Cherokee took their case to the U.S. Supreme Court — and won at least a limited victory. The Indians were "domestic dependent nations," wrote Chief Justice John Marshall, subject to the United States, which was responsible for protecting their rights, but not subject to the individual states themselves. Georgia could not simply seize their lands.

But Andrew Jackson refused to intervene. To him, even the Cherokee were an obstacle to American expansion: no matter how hard they had tried to make their civilization match that of the whites who surrounded them, they would have to move. Indians, Jackson believed, had "neither the intelligence, the industry, the moral habits, nor the desire for improvement which are essential to any favorable change in their condition . . . they must necessarily yield to the force of circumstances and ere long disappear."

Some Cherokee, including prosperous mixed-blood planters certain that only disaster awaited them if they resisted, and traditional hunters who hoped to re-create their old lives in new surroundings, had already moved west on their own. The rest of the Cherokee people now began to divide into two camps. A treaty party, led by several members of one influential family — Major Ridge, a wealthy planter and tribal orator, his son, John Ridge, and nephews Elias Boudinot and Stand Watie — had reluctantly come to the conclusion that further resistance would only prolong the tribe's agony: it was time to admit defeat, give up their lands, and move west.

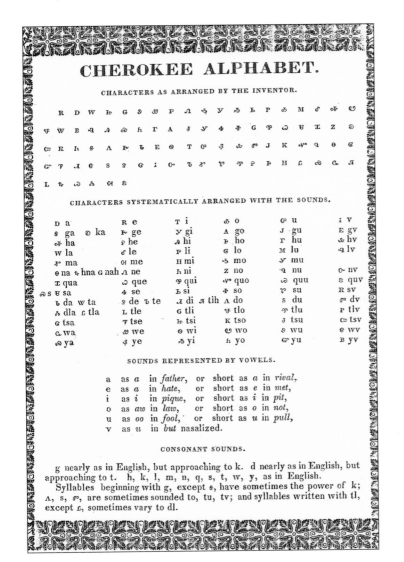

The Cherokee alphabet, introduced in 1821 by Sequoyah, the son of a Cherokee mother and a white trader, had a separate character for each of the eighty-six syllables of the tribal tongue.

Cherokee rivals: John Ross (far left), who adamantly opposed Removal, and Stand Watie, who reluctantly came to favor it

The Georgians have shown a grasping spirit lately; . . . I know the Indians have an older title than theirs. . . . Yet they are strong and we are weak. We are few, they are many. We cannot remain here in safety and comfort. I know we love the graves of our fathers. . . . We can never forget these homes, I know, but an unbending, iron necessity tells us we must leave them. . . . There is but one path of safety, one road to future existence as a Nation. That path is open before you. Make a treaty of cession. Give up these lands and go over beyond the great Father of Waters.

Major Ridge

But John Ross, the principal chief of the Cherokee, was opposed to any treaty. He was the son of a Scottish immigrant and only one-eighth Indian, and had once served under Andrew Jackson against the Creek. But his followers were mostly full-bloods, generally less well off than the leading members of the treaty party, and adamantly against leaving the land where their ancestors were buried.

On December 29, 1835 — with Ross away in Washington still trying to plead his people's case — the leaders of the treaty party gathered in the parlor of Elias Boudinot's home and signed a treaty ceding all their lands in exchange for $5 million. Fully 80 percent of the tribe — almost 16,000 Cherokee — issued a protest afterward disavowing the treaty: John Ridge and his allies had spoken only for themselves, they said.

Andrew Jackson ignored them. The eastern Cherokee nation, he said, no longer existed. They were given two years to move. Two thousand went voluntarily, including the members of the treaty party. The rest held out to the end. In the spring of 1838, soldiers began to round them up.

. . . [A]fter all the warning and with soldiers in their midst [an officer remembered], the inevitable day found the Indians at work in their houses and in their fields. . . . Two or three dropped their hoes and ran as fast as they could when they saw the soldiers coming. . . . The men . . . picked them up in the road, in the field anywhere they found them . . . the cows and calves lowing to one another; the poor dogs howling for their owners; the open doors of the cabins as we left them — to have seen it all would have melted to tenderness a heart of stone.

A few Cherokee escaped to the hills and stayed behind. But some 15,000 were kept penned up inside log stockades all summer, subject to measles, whooping cough, and cholera. Then the day came to start west. ". . . [I]n the chill of the drizzling rain on an October morning," one private wrote, "I saw them loaded like cattle or sheep into six hundred and forty-five wagons and started toward the west. . . . Chief Ross led in prayer and when the bugle sounded and the wagons started rolling many of the children . . . waved their little hands good-bye to their mountain homes."

It was 1,200 miles to what is now Oklahoma. Cold autumn rain fell all along the way. Many fell ill and some 4,000 died. The survivors rebuilt their lives, and it is one of the more remarkable ironies of western history that among the first communities to carry the trappings of eastern civilization into the region — churches, schools, slavery, the printing press — were people thought hopelessly "primitive" by their white neighbors.

The Cherokee never forgot the Trail of Tears. Nor did those who had never agreed to give up their old lives forget or forgive those they held responsible for their misery. On the morning of June 22, 1839, Cherokee assassins dragged John Ridge from his bed and stabbed him to death. Others stabbed Elias Boudinot and shot Major Ridge.

Still, it was not over. Stand Watie of the treaty party survived. The conflict over Removal would continue to divide the Cherokee for generations. And even before they began their westward march, a small-town blacksmith from Illinois named John Deere had fashioned for a neighbor a new kind of plow, made of steel and capable of turning the rich matted soil of the prairie that had resisted the old wrought-iron plows settlers brought with them from the East. It would take him ten more years to begin mass-producing his invention, but it would transform farming in the West — and one day encourage whites to think of taking over lands the Indians had been assured would be theirs forever. Meanwhile, the permanence of the "permanent Indian frontier" was already being violated as white settlers began to cross it on their way to Oregon and California.

THIS WONDERFUL COUNTRY

John Bidwell was just a twenty-one-year-old schoolteacher in 1840, but he had already moved from New York to Pennsylvania to Ohio to Weston, Missouri — where a claim-jumper stole his land. Unwilling to return to Ohio in disgrace and with nothing much to lose, he heard a French-Canadian trader tell of the wonders he had seen in California and was spellbound:

> At that time when a man moved out West, as soon as he was fairly settled he wanted to move again, and naturally every question imaginable was asked in regard to this wonderful country. Generally, the first question . . . was whether there was any fever and ague. I remember his answer distinctly. He said that there was but one man in California that had ever had a chill there, and it was a matter of so much wonderment to the people of Monterey that they went eighteen miles into the country to see him shake.

A few weeks later, a widely published letter from an American resident of California, Dr. John Marsh, made it seem still more alluring. "The Agricultural capabilities [of California] as yet are but very imperfectly developed," he reported.

> The whole of it is remarkably adapted to the culture of the vine. *Wine & brandy* are made in considerable quantities. Olives, figs & almonds grow well. Apples, pears & peaches are abundant & in the southern part, *oranges. Cotton* . . . suc-

The only thing we lack here [in California] is a good Government. . . . If we had fifty families here from Missouri, we could do exactly as we pleased without any fear of being troubled. . . . The difficulty of coming here is imaginary.

Dr. John Marsh, 1840

John Bidwell, who went west armed with "nothing more formidable than a pocket knife" and eventually became one of California's richest men

ceeds well. . . . I think [California] cannot long remain in the hands of its present owners. . . . [A]lthough nominally belonging to Mexico [it] is about as independent of it as Texas and must ere long share the same fate.

California was still only sparsely colonized and poorly defended. Boston-based merchants were making a killing peddling crockery and clothing, coffee and sugar, silks and satins and pins to the *Californios* in exchange for shiploads of tallow and hides. And small numbers of foreigners — Americans, Britons, Europeans, many of whom had married into influential *Californio* families — already dominated commerce from offices in Monterey and Los Angeles.

It all sounded wonderful to John Bidwell. He helped form a "Western Emigration Society." Some five hundred Missourians signed up to go to California the following

Emigrants Crossing the Plains by Alfred Bierstadt, one of the most celebrated of many paintings extolling the pioneer. "The march of emigration is to the West," wrote Alfred Robinson in 1846, "and naught will arrest its advance but the mighty ocean."

spring. But during the winter there were disturbing reports that an American had been imprisoned in California for daring to suggest that the United States might one day seize it, and in the end, of the original five hundred, only Bidwell turned up in the spring, armed and ready to start for the Pacific.

He was undeterred, though it took several weeks to recruit sixty-eight other would-be pioneers, as eager as he to go to California but just as unsure how to get there. "We were ready to start," he recalled, "but no one knew where to go, not even the captain. Our ignorance of the route was complete. We knew that California lay west, and that was the extent of our knowledge."

Then they chanced upon a former mountain man, Thomas Fitzpatrick, whom the Cheyenne called "Broken Hand" because he'd lost three fingers when his rifle blew up, already employed to guide a party that included the Jesuit priest Father Pierre-Jean De Smet to Oregon. He agreed to lead them as far as the point where the trails diverged.

The journey had its share of excitements: a cyclone that dipped down dangerously close to the wagons; buffalo herds so immense the party feared it might be trampled; the death of one man who accidentally shot himself; and an encounter with Cheyenne who turned out to be perfectly friendly but whose sudden appearance so unnerved one of the party's hunters that he stripped off his clothes in terror — and was forever after called "Cheyenne" Dawson.

At Soda Springs, the northernmost bend of the Bear River, the party divided in two: when Fitzpatrick and Father De Smet and their contingent turned north toward Oregon, fully half of Bidwell's original party decided to go with them, frightened of venturing into unknown territory without a guide.

Bidwell and his thirty-one remaining companions determined to struggle south alone. They almost didn't make it. They had to slaughter their oxen for food and abandon their wagons, then ate crows, a wildcat, a coyote, even a pulpy paste, prepared by helpful local Indians, that turned out to be mashed insects. They soldiered on, nonetheless, over the Sierras and down into the San Joaquin Valley, stumbling at last onto the farm of Dr. John Marsh, the same man whose rosy letters had helped lure them to California.

Marsh's enthusiasm for California had been real enough, but he himself turned out to be something of a fraud. A Harvard graduate who practiced medicine without ever having attended medical school, he now asked to be paid for the few rations he allowed the half-starved pioneers to have, then demanded an exorbitant fee for Mexican passports it had cost him nothing to obtain. Bidwell declared him the most "selfish" man he'd ever met.

John Bidwell stayed on, nonetheless, and soon got a job in the Sacramento Valley, a hundred miles to the north, working as chief clerk for John Augustus Sutter, the most important foreigner in California. Sutter had been an utter failure before he got to California, a bankrupt German-Swiss storekeeper on the run from his creditors and from the wife and five children he had left behind in Switzerland. But he was hard to discourage — and persuasive. In 1839, he had arrived at Monterey from Hawaii with a considerable entourage — two Germans and ten Hawaiians, including his mistress — but without any apparent prospects. Nonetheless, he put on a worn French military uniform he had bought for a single beaver skin, asked to see the Mexican governor, and somehow talked him into granting him nearly 50,000 acres at the junc-

John Augustus Sutter and the fortress
from which he ruled his California empire

tion of the Sacramento and American rivers in the uncolonized Sacramento Valley, where he hoped to establish a colony called Nueva Helvetia — "New Switzerland."

Bidwell's first task for Sutter was to complete the transfer of the contents of Fort Ross, one of two former Russian coastal outposts that Sutter had bought using an unsecured loan that he never managed to repay. The fort was stripped of everything except its apple trees: furniture, tools, lumber, herds of sheep and cattle, military uniforms, and, most important, several French cannons the Russians had captured from Napoleon, which Sutter used to make his new fort impregnable against Indians and suspicious Mexican authorities alike.

Sutter ran his sprawling domain like a European barony — drilling an army of Indians, dispensing a crude kind of justice, encouraging his workers to plant fields and orchards and harvest timber, and taking very young girls to bed. But he also provided supplies and shelter to the Americans who had begun to follow John Bidwell's footsteps into California. One hundred and twenty-five Americans made it through the next year. In 1845, nearly 3,000 followed. "We find ourselves threatened by hordes of Yankee emigrants, who have already begun to flock into our country, and whose progress we cannot arrest," warned California's governor, Pio Pico. "Already have the wagons of that perfidious people scaled the almost inaccessible summits of the Sierra Nevada, crossed the entire continent and penetrated the fruitful valley of the Sacramento. What that astonishing people will next undertake, I cannot say."

Mariano Guadalupe Vallejo belonged to one of the oldest Spanish families in the Americas. One ancestor had sailed with Columbus, another with Cortés, and his father had been one of the first soldiers to settle in California. The rarified life of the *Californios* that was their legacy to him seemed to him idyllic. "There was never a more peaceful or happy people on the face of the earth than the Spanish, Mexican and Indian population of Alta California," he would write one day. "We were the pioneers of the Pacific coast, building pueblos and missions while General Washington was carrying on the war of the Revolution. . . ."

Born at Monterey on July 4, 1807, Vallejo spent most of his early years as a soldier, concerned with defending that life against anyone who threatened it, and the Mexican government had rewarded him for his services with grants of land that made him one of California's wealthiest men by the age of thirty — 450,000 acres, most of the Sonoma Valley, belonged to him and to the members of his family, which would eventually include sixteen children. It was a magical region when he arrived there in 1833, he remembered. "The face of the earth in all those splendid valleys and mountain sides was a mass of clover and . . . wild oats . . . standing more than waist high. All the bays and creeks were literally alive with fish. . . . I came instructed by my Government to do what I could for the inhabitants of the country and to ward off incursions from Russia on the one hand, and from the people over the Rocky Mountains on the other."

The Russian threat had dissipated after 1842, when John Sutter bought the Russian outposts at Fort Ross and on Bodega Bay. The Americans were another matter. Mexico City seemed as distant and removed to the *Californios* as it had to the people of Texas and New Mexico, and as the Americans continued to

Above: Mariano Guadalupe Vallejo with two daughters (upper left and lower right) and three granddaughters. Below: Lachryma Montis — "Tear of the Mountain" — the New England–style farmhouse and outbuildings Vallejo built for himself near Sonoma after the coming of the Americans.

file through the mountains, Vallejo begged in vain for the men and arms he knew would be necessary to forestall an American invasion:

> The total population of California does not exceed 6,000 souls and of these two thirds must be counted as women and children, leaving scarcely 2,000 men. We cannot count on the 15,000 Indians . . . because they inspire more fear than confidence. This is the lamentable situation in a Country worthy of a better fate. . . . Excuse this burst of feeling in a soldier who laments not having arms, when he sees the treasure being stolen.

NOT CONTENT TO REMAIN IN ONE PLACE

In 1841, instead of going to California, half of John Bidwell's overland party had split off for the Oregon Country. There, in the broad valley of the Willamette River, south of the Columbia, they found a rich soil, a mild climate, and only about two hundred other newcomers — a few American missionaries, some employees of the British Hudson's Bay Company, and a handful of former mountain men, including Joe Meek, living with his Indian wife.

Britain and the United States both still claimed the Oregon Country, but Americans soon began to stream in as though the whole region was already theirs. In 1843, in the first major American migration into the West, nearly a thousand pioneers arrived from Missouri. The next year, almost twice as many came. For many of them, pioneering was nothing new: they had moved steadily westward with the nation's frontier from the Allegheny Mountains to the Missouri River. Now, 2,000 miles from the States, they were repeating a familiar pattern. They built homes out of logs, started schools and churches, bartered crops and labor in exchange for supplies because of the lack of hard currency, and founded towns with names that reminded them of their eastern origins: Salem, Albany, and Portland — which got its name when those in favor of Boston lost a coin toss to those with roots in Maine.

And they joined together to form the rudiments of a government. In 1843, a meeting held to organize a community hunt to rid the countryside of wolves, bears, and mountain lions evolved into a proposal to write a provisional constitution. It provided for jury trials, freedom of religion, 640 acres of land for anyone who filed a claim and built a cabin, and barred slavery — though it also forbade free black people from settling in the region. All taxes were prohibited; the new government was to be supported by voluntary donations — payments in wheat were entirely acceptable.

More and more Americans were heading for Oregon now. "Hundreds are already prepared to start in the spring," the Boston *Daily Evening Transcript* reported in 1844, "while hundreds [more] are anxiously awaiting the action of Congress in reference to that country as the signal for their departure. . . . The Oregon fever has broken out, and is now raging like any other contagion."

Henry Sager had moved his growing family four times in as many years, always a little farther west in search of land that was more fertile and less expensive. By 1844, the Sagers and their six children were in St. Joseph, Missouri, ready to move again. "Father," his daughter Catherine would remember, "was one of those restless men who are not content to remain in one place long at a time. . . . [He] had been talking of going to Texas. But mother, hearing much said about the healthfulness of Oregon, preferred to go there, being willing to endure the hardships and privations of the journey for the sake of finding a country where she could enjoy this great blessing."

Sager was determined to take his family to Oregon, and joined a group of equally eager pioneers who called themselves the "Independent Colony." There were 323 persons and 72 wagons in the party. Catherine Sager recalled their leave-taking:

> Some wept for departing friends, and others at the thoughts of leaving all they held dear for a long and uncertain journey, and the children wept for fear of the mighty waters that came rushing down and seemed as though it would swallow [us] up; so that, taken altogether, it was a sad company that crossed over the Missouri River that bright spring morning. . . .

In eastern Kansas, rain turned the prairies to mud, and flood-swollen rivers proved dangerous and slow to cross. Henry Sager had trouble controlling his oxen.

The emigrants were nervous about Indians — needlessly, it turned out — and guards fired into the night at the slightest sound, once narrowly missing two young women out for a midnight stroll. Five weeks out, Naomi Sager gave birth to her seventh child — and in her weakened condition caught a cold she seemed unable to shake.

Farther on, the skies cleared. On July 4, the caravan rested near the Platte River, in what is now Nebraska. A young couple used the occasion to get married. The party came across its first herd of buffalo, and in a frenzy of excitement halted two days to shoot far more than they could use. The wanton destruction disgusted several members of the party, and tensions that had been building since Missouri broke out into bitter arguments. Two days later, the captain resigned his post. From then on, the Independent Colony would proceed without a leader.

After fording the South Platte, Sager again lost control of his ox team. This time the wagon overturned, injuring his wife. Then, just past Scotts Bluff, young Catherine, age nine, tried to hop off the wagon: "The hem of my dress caught on an axe-handle, precipitating me under the wheels, both of which passed over me, badly crushing the left leg before Father could stop the oxen. . . . A glance at my limb dangling in the air as he ran revealed to him the extent of the injury I had received, and in a broken voice he exclaimed, 'My dear child, your leg is broken all to pieces!' " A doctor from another wagon train was found, Catherine's leg was put in a splint, and for the remainder of the trip she either rode in the jolting wagon or walked with crutches.

Oregon was still weeks away. A sickness called "camp fever" struck the caravan. Two women died. Then a little girl. Henry Sager and three of his children came down with the disease. "One day four buffalos ran between our wagon and the one behind us," Catherine recalled.

> Father, although feeble, seized his gun and gave chase. This imprudent act again prostrated him, and it soon became apparent to all that he must die. . . . The evening before he died we crossed the Green River and camped on the bank. . . . Looking upon me as I lay helplessly by his side, he said, "Poor child! What will become of you?" Father expired the next morning, and was buried on the bank of the Green River, his coffin consisting of two troughs hastily dug out of the trunk of a tree. . . .

Survivors: Three of the Sagers' daughters (top) lived to attend the fiftieth anniversary of the Whitman Massacre in 1897. The eldest, Catherine Sager Pringle, is in the center, flanked by Elizabeth Sager Helm (left) and Matilda Sager Delaney. Above: The youngest of the children, Henrietta Naomi Sager Sterling, born on the Oregon Trail, became an actress and grew apart from her family. She toured the California goldfields and is said to have died there later, shot to death by a tragically inaccurate assailant who had been aiming at her husband.

There is enchantment in the word [Oregon]. It signifies a land of pure delight in the woody solitudes of the West. . . . That is a country of the largest liberty, the only known land of equality on the face of the earth . . . there is a place to build anew the Temple of Democracy.

Cleveland *Plain Dealer*, 1843

Wagons along the route to Oregon

It is palpable homicide to tempt or send women and children over this thousand miles of precipice and volcanic sterility to Oregon. . . . This migration wears an aspect of insanity. . . .

Horace Greeley

Now fatherless, the Sagers pushed on. Naomi hired a young man to drive their wagon, but after a few days, he disappeared to join his girlfriend in the wagon train ahead of them. He took Henry's rifle with him.

Then, somewhere on the dusty trail along the Snake River in what is now Idaho, Catherine remembered, her mother became delirious with fever: "The day she died we traveled over a very rough road, and she moaned pitifully all day. When we camped for the night . . . [her] pulse was nearly gone. . . . She lived but a few moments more, and her last words were, 'Oh, Henry, if you only knew how we have suffered!'"

Men from the other wagons buried Naomi Sager, wrapped in a bedsheet, in a shallow grave by the side of the trail, with willow brush and a wooden headboard to mark the spot. "The teams were then hitched to the wagon and the train drove on," Catherine recalled, "leaving her to her long sleep. Thus in twenty-six days both our parents were laid in the grave, and we were [seven] orphans, the oldest fourteen years old and the youngest five months old."

Under the care of the other families in the wagon train, the seven Sager children pressed on. It was now September, and the first snows were falling in the mountains. They were in Cayuse country, nearing the Whitman mission. One member of the caravan rode ahead to inform the Whitmans that a needy wagon train was approaching — and to talk with them about the Sager children. The Whitmans' own two-year-old daughter, Alice, had drowned, and after a long siege of grieving, Narcissa had already taken in four other children, including the half-Indian daughters of the mountain men Joe Meek and Jim Bridger. But she had to think hard about taking in seven more children. "Husband thought we could get along with all but the baby," she noted. "He did not see how we could take that; but I felt that if I must take any, I wanted her as a charm to bind the rest to me." In the end, the Whitmans took all seven. "The Lord has taken our own dear child away," Narcissa Whitman wrote, "so that we may care for the poor outcasts of the country."

A few days later, after seven months and 2,000 miles, the wagon in which Henry and Naomi Sager's children were riding stopped in front of their new home in Oregon. Narcissa Whitman came out to meet them. "She was a large, well-formed woman," Catherine Sager remembered, "fair complexioned, with beautiful auburn hair, nose rather large, and large grey eyes. She had on a dark calico dress and gingham sunbonnet; and we thought as we shyly looked at her that she was the prettiest woman we had ever seen."

TO SAVE OUR PEOPLE

The Whitmans had largely abandoned their work among the Cayuse, whom Narcissa now believed irredeemably "insolent, proud, domineering, arrogant." Instead, they kept busy ministering to the needs of the settlers who now rolled steadily past their doorstep. "It does not concern me so much what is to become of any particular set of Indians," Marcus Whitman told his superiors back in Boston. "I have no doubt our greatest work is to be to aid the white settlement of this country and help to found its religious institutions."

The Whitman mission compound, all of it built on land the Cayuse still considered their own, eventually grew to include a handsome house as well as corncribs, henhouses, a smokehouse, an apple orchard, a blacksmith shop, sawmill, gristmill,

Early pioneers like the Sagers started the steady westward rush of restless families like this one, captured momentarily at rest by an unknown photographer.

thirty acres of fenced fields of wheat and corn, and sizable herds of cattle and sheep and hogs.

The American Board was not impressed. "We are glad to hear of your prosperity in secular matters," its secretary wrote Whitman in the spring of 1846,

> and that you may be able, by means of your grain and your stock, to defray a large part of your expenses. All this is well. Still we are not quite sure that you ought to devote so much time and thought to feeding the emigrants, and thus make your station a great restaurant for the weary pilgrims on their way to the promised land. Such a work is very humane & good work; but the work of guiding men to Christ is a better one and coincides better with the vocation of a missionary laborer.

The Cayuse were unhappy with the Whitmans, too. They had always resented their presence. Now they complained of the newcomers who camped near the Whitmans' house. Marcus Whitman dismissed their muttering. They had failed to heed the Gospel and were reaping the fruits of their stubborn disbelief: "When a people refuse or neglect to fill the designs of Providence," he said, "they ought not to complain of the results."

Then, in 1847, measles, carried west with the emigrant trains, swept through the Cayuse villages. The Indians noticed that while white children usually survived its ravages, their own children — and many adults, as well — did not. Despite Marcus Whitman's tireless attendance, more than half the tribe died, and rumors began to spread among the survivors that instead of trying to cure the disease, Whitman was secretly spreading it.

On the afternoon of November 29, 1847, three Cayuse appeared at the door and asked to see the doctor. One of them, a man called Tiloukaikt, who had once considered converting to Christianity, had now lost three children to the white man's illness. When he and his companions got inside they shot and hacked Marcus Whitman to death.

"Mother was standing looking out at the window," Narcissa's adopted daughter Catherine Sager remembered, "when a ball came through the broken pane, entering

Nancy Osborn, who survived the Whitman Massacre by concealing herself beneath the floorboards of one of the mission buildings, later drew this sketch of the compound as it looked when the Cayuse attacked. The Whitmans lived in the structure she labeled number one; emigrants were housed in number three, and their wagons were repaired in number two.

The poor Indians are amazed at the overwhelming numbers of Americans coming into the country. They seem not to know what to make of it.

Narcissa Whitman

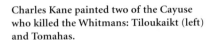

Charles Kane painted two of the Cayuse who killed the Whitmans: Tiloukaikt (left) and Tomahas.

her right shoulder. She clapped her hand to the wound . . . and fell backwards. She now forgot everything but the poor, helpless children depending on her, and . . . poured out her soul in prayer for them: 'Lord, save these little ones!' was her repeated cry."

Warriors carried the wounded woman out of the house on a settee, killed her, then lashed her dead face with a quirt. Besides the Whitmans, eleven other whites were killed before it was over, including the two Sager boys. Hannah Sager, age six and ill with measles at the time of the massacre, died soon afterward from lack of medical attention. So did the daughters of Joe Meek and Jim Bridger. The four surviving Sager girls were orphans once more. They and the rest of the survivors were carried off as captives.

The Cayuse ransomed them after a time. Then those who had taken part in the massacre fled to the mountains. A pioneer militia pursued them, and eventually five warriors — including two of the men who had killed Marcus Whitman — turned themselves in so that the rest of their people would not be hunted down. Before Tiloukaikt was hanged, someone asked him why he had surrendered: "Did not your missionaries teach us that Christ died to save his people?" he answered. "So we die to save *our* people."

Joe Meek, still grieving for his daughter, was dispatched across the Rockies in the dead of winter to bring Washington news of the Whitman Massacre — along with a renewed demand that Congress make Oregon a United States territory and provide its American residents with protection.

THE BASTARD

On a warm June day in 1841, two very different men chanced to fall into conversation on the deck of the steamboat *Rowena* as she nosed her way up the Missouri from St. Louis. One was a short, unprepossessing former mountain man named Christopher Carson, known to his friends as Kit. He was born on a Kentucky farm — he was a distant relation of Daniel Boone — and had been supporting himself on the frontier since, at the age of fourteen, he had run away from the Missouri saddle maker to whom his family had apprenticed him. He had been a drover on the Santa Fe trail, a short-order cook, a hunter, and a trapper, familiar with beaver streams all over the West. Now he was on his way back to the West after leaving his half-Indian daughter at a convent school.

The other man was a handsome, dark-haired young army officer named John Charles Frémont. He was about to begin a government expedition, he told Carson, to survey South Pass and measure the highest peaks of the Rockies. He had his whole party assembled — hunters, voyageurs, even a cook — but he lacked a guide.

"I told [him]," Carson remembered, "that I had been some time in the mountains and thought I could guide him to any point he would wish to go."

Frémont offered him one hundred dollars a month. Carson accepted. That decision would forever change the lives of both men — and the future of the West, as well.

John Charles Frémont was born out of wedlock in a Georgia boardinghouse in 1813. His mother had been married for a dozen miserable years to an elderly veteran of the Revolution when she ran off with a French dancing master who called himself Charles Frémon. He soon died, leaving her to raise their three children on her own, in the face of polite society's steady scorn.

Frémont's illegitimacy left him with a lifelong distrust of almost everyone and an inbred hatred of older men with power over him. As a young man, he fell in and out of love with alarming regularity, studied natural history, joined the Army Corps of Topographical Engineers, and dreamed of making a name for himself in the West. Then he met the Bentons. Senator Thomas Hart Benton of Missouri was as imposing as he was important. Six foot four, with a voice that could reach the back of the biggest crowd and had earned him the nickname "The Old Thunderer," he had devoted his career to peopling the West. In 1839, he happened to stop by the young engineer's worktable and began to talk of the need for new surveys of western lands. "The thought of penetrating into the recesses of this wilderness region filled me with enthusiasm," Frémont recalled. "I saw visions."

Benton invited Frémont home for dinner, where he met Benton's beautiful, strong-willed daughter, Jessie, and fell instantly in love. In the spring of 1841 she agreed to marry him. He was twenty-eight; she was only seventeen. Senator Benton was appalled: he did not wish to give up his daughter, especially to a much older, half-French, bastard soldier with no family, no fortune, no apparent prospects. He barred Frémont from his home. So powerful was Senator Benton in Washington that the couple could find no Protestant clergyman brave enough to perform the ceremony. On October 19, 1841, they were secretly married by a Catholic priest.

It was weeks before Jessie dared tell her father she was married. When she did, he ordered her and her new husband out of his house. But Jessie Benton was her father's daughter. If he did not give the couple his blessing, she said, her father would never see her again. Benton had met his match — and, as chairman of the Senate Committee on Military Affairs, he soon became his son-in-law's patron. On New Year's Day, 1842, Frémont was given command of an expedition to the Rockies.

Before he set out from St. Louis, he forbade any member of his party to keep a diary; he planned a book of his own and wanted no rivals. But the expedition's cartographer, a German named Charles Preuss, secretly kept a journal in the form of

Frémont is the damndest scoundrel who ever lived, but in the infinite mercy of Providence, also the damndest fool.

Abraham Lincoln

Partners in pioneering: Senator Thomas Hart Benton of Missouri, noisy champion of western exploration and expansion (left), and his protégé and son-in-law, John Charles Frémont, who was able to realize many of his patron's dreams

letters to his wife. In it, he expressed strong opinions about both the country he was crossing and the man in charge of the expedition: "Eternal prairie and grass with occasional groups of trees," he wrote on June 12. "Frémont prefers this to every other landscape. To me it is as if someone would prefer a book with blank pages to a good story. . . ."

With Kit Carson in the lead, the expedition moved along the Platte to Fort Laramie, where Jim Bridger warned Frémont that Lakota war parties had been seen farther west. Frémont was unmoved. He "informed them," Carson recalled, "that he was directed by his government to perform a certain duty, that it mattered not what obstacles were in his advance, that he was bound to continue his march in obedience to his instruction, and that he would accomplish that for which he [was] sent or die in the attempt. . . ."

Such bravado did not reassure Charles Preuss:

July 9. [Bridger] advises very earnestly not to continue from Laramie with such a small crew. . . . Daily, several people, white and Indian, have been killed there. . . . It would be ridiculous to risk the lives of 25 people just to determine a few longitudes and latitudes and to find out the elevation of a mountain range. . . .

[July 20] Tomorrow we'll start, straight toward the Indians. Nothing can be done about it, my dear *Trautchen*. To be sure, I could stay here . . . — but what a disgrace, what a disgrace! . . . Of course if I had known it, I should not have come along. I see no honor in being murdered by this rabble. But all that is too late now.

It proved a false alarm: the Sioux had split up, some going to fight the Crow, others to hunt buffalo.

Finally, Frémont's party reached the Continental Divide at South Pass, the easiest way through the Rockies and the goal of the expedition. Frémont's orders were to measure its height, map it for travelers, and return home. It failed to live up to his expectations:

> The ascent had been so gradual, that . . . we were obliged to watch very closely to find the place at which we had reached the culminating point. . . . From the impression on my mind at this time . . . I should compare the elevation which we surmounted immediately at the Pass, to the ascent of the Capitol Hill from the avenue at Washington. . . .

Disappointed by the gentle rise of South Pass, Frémont looked for something that would add luster to his reputation as an explorer. In the nearby Wind River Range, he climbed a peak that he claimed was "the loftiest" of the Rocky Mountains. Fifty-five other peaks would later prove to be higher, but Frémont was enraptured.

> Here, on the summit, where the stillness was absolute, unbroken by any sound, . . . we thought ourselves beyond the region of animated life; but while we were sitting on the rock, a solitary [bumble] bee came winging his flight from the eastern valley, and lit on the knee of one of the men. It was a strange place, the icy rock and the highest peak of the Rocky Mountains, for a lover of warm sunshine and flowers; and we pleased ourselves with the idea that he was the first of his species to cross the mountain barrier, a solitary pioneer to fore-tell the advance of civilization. . . .

The expedition set out for home the way it had come. Frémont had brought along a novelty, an inflatable rubber boat with which he was determined to run the rapids of the Platte. ". . . Singing, or rather shouting, we dashed along," he remembered, "and were . . . in the midst of a chorus when the boat struck a concealed rock imme-diately at the foot of a fall, which whirled her over in an instant."

Charles Preuss was horrified:

> What a depressing sight! The boat was upside down; some men held on to it, while others hung, like me, on projecting rocks. . . . Everything swam swiftly to the next rapids. . . . Where were the sextant, the pair of compasses, the large tele-scope . . . the journal with astronomical and barometric observations? Every-thing gone to the devil. . . . It was certainly stupid of the young chief to be so foolhardy where the terrain was absolutely unknown.

Miraculously, the book of observations turned up downriver, soaked but intact.

In 1843, Congress printed 10,000 copies of Frémont's official report, its prose much improved by his wife's literary skill and illustrated with Charles Preuss's metic-ulously accurate maps. It was a best-seller, the beginning of Frémont's reputation as "the Pathfinder." "Frémont has particularly touched my imagination," wrote Henry Wadsworth Longfellow. "What a wild life, and what a fresh kind of existence! But, ah, the discomforts!"

Frémont was unaware of his new fame. He and Kit Carson and thirty-seven hand-picked men were already back in the mountains. This time, they would be gone for fourteen months and cover 3,500 miles. It was the most important expedition since

And from this place ye shall go forth into the regions westward; and inasmuch as ye shall find them that will receive you, ye shall build up my Church in every region, until the time shall come when it shall be revealed unto you from on high, where the city of the New Jerusalem shall be prepared, that ye may be gathered in. . . .

Joseph Smith

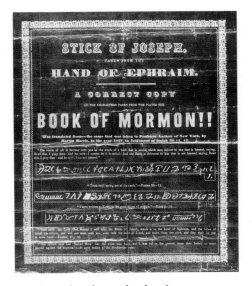

Joseph Smith and an early advertisement for the Book of Mormon, which he said he had translated from tablets buried in upstate New York

Lewis and Clark's nearly forty years before — an almost complete circuit of the West, from Missouri to the Great Salt Lake, into Oregon, across the Sierras in the dead of winter and into California (where they found temporary shelter at Sutter's Fort), then south round the southern flank of the Sierras, along the Old Spanish Trail, across the Colorado Plateau, through the Rockies, and home again.

Indians and mountain men had already seen most of what Frémont saw, but through his maps and writings, he was now making the American people see it, too.

LIKE A STONE FROM A SLING

In 1820, a great revival had swept through the small towns of western New York. At Palmyra, a fourteen-year-old boy, eager for salvation but troubled by the claims and counterclaims of the revivalists, knelt in a grove behind his father's house to pray for guidance. A pillar of light appeared before him. Within it were two figures, he said. They told him to join no sect — "all their creeds were an abomination" — but instead to prepare himself for a great work.

The boy's name was Joseph Smith, and he grew to manhood on his father's farm, doing odd jobs, sometimes digging for treasure, and experiencing what he said were divine visitations. In one of them, an angel appeared to him:

> He called me by name and said unto me . . . that his name was Moroni, that God had work for me to do; and that my name should be had for good and evil among all nations, kindreds and tongues. He said there was a book deposited, written upon gold plates, giving an account of the former inhabitants of this continent and the source from which they sprang. . . .

No existing denomination represented God's will, he was told; Christ's church had been withdrawn from earth. God had selected Joseph Smith to restore it. Engraved plates of gold, buried on a hillside near Manchester, New York, held the sacred history. In 1827, Smith said, he dug them up, then spent three years translating the ancient writing upon them. The Indians, according to the tablets, were the lost tribes of Israel. Jesus had preached in America after the Resurrection and would return to it after a new true church was constituted. Smith himself was to be its prophet.

Smith published the Book of Mormon in 1830 and established the Church of Jesus Christ of Latter-day Saints for those who believed its promises. It grew fast, from just six members to several hundred before the year was out. Unbelievers — scorned as "gentiles" by the faithful — resented the new church, denounced its prophet as a fraud, and called the book he claimed to have discovered blasphemous.

Smith decreed that the New Jerusalem was to be found somewhere in the West and began moving his flock, first to Ohio, and after mobs attacked them there, to Missouri — where things only grew worse.

Missouri clergymen denounced their faith. Missouri settlers feared their growing numbers. Rumors spread that they were stealing, stirring up the Indians, planning to free the slaves, printing counterfeit money. "The Mormons," one Presbyterian minister told his flock, "are the common enemies of mankind and ought to be destroyed." Smith himself was beaten, tarred, jailed. There were shootings and fires and calls for vengeance by both sides. Finally, the governor of Missouri himself ordered the Mormons to leave his state or be "exterminated."

Smith next led his followers back across the Mississippi, to the tiny town of Commerce, Illinois. He renamed it Nauvoo and within five years had transformed it into the second largest city in the state. By 1844, Joseph Smith had 35,000 disciples and more were on their way, converts gathered by Mormon missionaries dispatched to continental Europe and Great Britain. An armed legion of 4,000 men marched to his orders, and he pronounced himself ready to run for president.

But again, neighboring communities had other ideas. And there was dissension within Nauvoo itself now, charges that Smith had become too dictatorial and that he secretly practiced "plural marriage" — polygamy. When dissidents attacked him in print, he ordered their press destroyed. Finally, in the spring of 1845, Smith was arrested for inciting a riot and locked up with his brother, Hyrum, at Carthage, Illinois, to await trial. On June 27, a mob of militiamen, their faces blackened in disguise, broke into the jail and shot them both to death. The Mormon Church had lost its prophet.

Some disciples, including Smith's own first wife and son, now split away over the issue of polygamy and formed the Reorganized Mormon Church. But most placed their hopes in a big, Vermont-born farmer and sometime carpenter named Brigham Young. A veteran of the Missouri fighting and one of the twelve apostles appointed to take charge of what was left of the church, he had married eight of the dead prophet's widows. It would soon be time, he said, for the Mormons to move west again, and some who heard him swore that when Brigham Young spoke, he now spoke in the voice of Joseph Smith:

> And from this place ye shall go forth into the regions westward; and inasmuch as ye shall find them that will receive you, ye shall build up my Church in every region, until the time shall come when it shall be revealed unto you from on high, where the city of the New Jerusalem shall be prepared, that ye may be gathered in. . . .

Young bided his time before leading the Mormons on their next journey toward Zion, working to complete the great temple Joseph Smith had started at Nauvoo and puzzling over just where they should go. California and Oregon, Vancouver Island and Texas were all considered, then rejected: Young was determined to lead his people where no troublesome gentiles had preceded them — and where none were likely to follow them, either. Then he read Frémont's description of the Valley of the Great Salt Lake, sheltered from the east by the Wasatch Range, and said to be suitable for "civilized settlement."

He would take his Saints there. The journey began in the spring of 1846. Young proved as practical as he was pious. "Prayer is good," he said, "but when baked potatoes and pudding and milk are needed, prayer will not supply their place," and he and his advisers mapped out in advance every detail of the new Mormon exodus. The Saints would go west in separate caravans, following one another at regular intervals. Each wagon train was divided into "hundreds" or "fifties," each commanded by a captain, and each in turn subdivided into "tens," supervised by a lieutenant. ". . . At 5:00 in the morning," Young's instructions began, "the bugle is to be sounded as a signal for every man to arise and attend prayers before he leaves his wagon. Then cooking, eating, feeding teams, etc. till seven o'clock, at which time the camp is to move at the

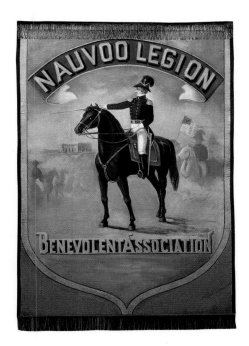

Nauvoo: The existence of the well-armed, well-drilled Nauvoo Legion, whose banner appears above, alarmed the Mormons' neighbors in Missouri and Illinois. In 1846, not long after the daguerreotype opposite was made, they would burn the Mormons' hilltop temple to the ground.

sound of a bugle. Each teamster to keep beside his wagon with his loaded gun in his hands or in his wagon, where he can get it at any moment. . . ." The first wagons were to halt from time to time to plow fields and sow seeds so that those who followed could reap a harvest and, in turn, replant the fields for those who came after. "If you do these things," Young promised his people, "faith will abide in your hearts; and the angels of God will go with you, even as they went with the children of Israel, when Moses led them from the land of Egypt."

Soon, a steady procession stretching nearly three hundred miles was strung out across the flat landscape. Before the snow began to fall, some 16,000 Mormons had made it all the way to Winter Quarters in Indian country — a log town of almost a thousand cabins, which Young's men had readied for them — or had taken shelter in one of the way stations built at regular intervals all across what would become Iowa. But even Brigham Young could not control the prairie weather, and before spring came, some seven hundred Mormons had died in the bitter cold.

In April of 1847, Young himself led forth a "Pioneer Band" — 143 men, 3 women, and 2 children — who were to seek the Valley of the Great Salt Lake and select the site on which all would settle. To avoid contact with their old enemies the Missourians, now plodding along the Oregon Trail on the south bank of the Platte, they blazed their own route along its north bank. It would become known as the Mormon Trail.

Nothing deterred Young. As his company entered South Pass, they conferred with Jim Bridger, who warned that the Valley of the Great Salt Lake was too cold at night to grow the corn Young expected to plant. Young paid no heed. A few miles farther on, Young's party came upon Sam Brannan, a Mormon elder who had escorted a party of Saints to California by sea the year before. Brannan, too, urged Young to abandon any notion of settling in Utah: the San Joaquin Valley was the place to start over; he would lead them there. Young turned him away: "God has made the choice — not Brigham Young," he said.

My people must be tried in all things, that they may be prepared to receive the glory that I have for them, even the glory of Zion, and he that will not bear chastisement is not worthy of my kingdom.

Brigham Young

Exodus: Carl Christensen, a Danish convert to Mormonism, painted the tidy version of *Winter Quarters* (opposite) in 1857, ten years after the Mormons built it as the jumping-off place for their journey to the Valley of the Great Salt Lake. Techniques of travel worked out on that first trek made the journey at least marginally more comfortable for those who came later, like this Mormon family, photographed on the trail in the 1860s.

Mormon pioneers on the Plains, 1866

On July 12, the prophet took to his wagon, shivering with Colorado tick fever, but he sent an advance party on ahead to find a way through the Wasatch. They probed canyon after canyon before settling on a trail that brought them finally to the Valley of the Great Salt Lake. Their first glimpse of it was not encouraging: only a "broad and barren plain hemmed in by mountains," one man remembered, "blistering in the burning rays of the midsummer sun . . . a seemingly interminable waste of sagebrush . . . the paradise of the lizard, the cricket and the rattlesnake." One of the women in the party was still more blunt: "We have traveled fifteen hundred miles to get here," she wrote, "and I would willingly travel a thousand miles farther to get where it looked as though a white man could live."

But Mormon faith held. The advance party went to work, and by the time Young arrived in the valley on July 24, potatoes had already been planted and a dam was being built across a stream to irrigate them. "We have been thrown like a stone from a sling," Young said, "and we have lodged in the godly place where the Lord wants his people to gather. . . . If the Lord should say by His revelation this is the spot, the Saints would be satisfied if it was a barren rock."

On the evening of July 27, Young set forth his vision of the Mormon future:

We do not intend to have any trade or commerce with the gentile world. . . .
The Kingdom of God cannot rise independent of the gentile nations until we
produce, manufacture and make every article of use, convenience, or necessity

among our own people. . . . I am determined to cut every thread of this kind and live free and independent, untrammeled by any of their detestable customs and practices.

The next morning, he began to pace off the streets and squares of the great city he would soon begin to build on the shore of the Great Salt Lake.

OUR TRUE TITLE

Sam Houston had assumed that the Texas Republic would have a very short life, that Texas would become a state within a few months of his victory at San Jacinto. "The people of Texas had," he said, "with a unanimity unparalleled, declared that they will be reunited to the great Republican family of the North. . . . We are cheered by the hope that they will receive us . . . and hail us welcome into the great family of freemen." But seven years went by as the struggle in Congress over the extension of slavery thwarted his plans. Northern congressmen opposed the annexation of a new slave state, while many whites, both northern and southern, were no less hostile to incorporating within the United States a large new population of Indians and Hispanics.

To change their minds, Houston the soldier became Houston the subtle statesman: he feigned indifference about statehood, toyed with obtaining a guarantee of Texan independence from Britain, even flirted with promising Mexico City that Texas might be willing to submit again to its rule. And he encouraged more and more emigrants, from the States and from overseas as well: 2,000 French settlers built homes between the Nueces and the Rio Grande, and more than 5,000 Germans settled in and around the settlements of Fredericksburg and New Braunfels.

Meanwhile, the national attitude had begun to shift toward expansion. Southerners feared that if Houston succeeded in obtaining a British guarantee of Texan independence, London would eventually insist on abolishing slavery. Some northern congressmen came to fear that, too, but for a different reason: they did not want emancipated Texas slaves migrating northward. And many, in and out of Congress, were increasingly drawn to the notion that the United States not only had a duty to extend the blessings of its form of government to encompass new lands and peoples, but that God Himself favored that effort. John O'Sullivan, the editor of the New York *Morning News,* would provide these expansionists with a rallying cry:

> Away, away with all these cobweb tissues of rights of discovery, exploration, settlement, contiguity, etc. . . . The American claim is by the right of our manifest destiny to overspread and to possess the whole of the continent which Providence has given us for the development of the great experiment of liberty and federative self-government entrusted to us. It is a right such as that of the tree to the space of air and earth suitable for the full expansion of its principle and destiny of growth. . . . It is in our future far more than in our past or in the past history of Spanish exploration . . . that our True Title is found.

In 1844, James Knox Polk was elected President. He was a humorless, hardworking Democrat from Tennessee, an admirer of Andrew Jackson, and utterly committed to expanding the United States as far as he could. His victory was narrow: he won only a plurality of the popular vote; had the ballots of his two opponents been combined,

Young America demands the immediate annexation of Texas at any and every hazard. It will plant its right foot upon the northern verge of Oregon, and its left upon the Atlantic rag, and waving the stars and the stripes in the face of the once proud mistress of the Ocean, bid her, if she dare, "Cry havoc, and let slip the dogs of war."

United States Journal, 1845

the history of the West might have been very different. But he insisted on seeing his election as a mandate for expansion.

In this new climate, Sam Houston's maneuvering finally paid off: on December 29, 1845, Texas was admitted to the Union as the twenty-eighth state. The editor of the Dublin *Freeman* saw the real significance of what had happened:

> The Government of the United States have passed their arm down to the waist of the continent, and, now that they have got it there, they certainly will not hesitate to pass it round. [W]hen settlers from the United States swarm upon the borders of California (as of necessity they soon will), can it be doubted but the people of California . . . will find abundant inducements to fall into the body of that vast confederacy whose happy constitution confers all the protection and all the pride of imperial greatness, without derogating a particle from local independence? . . . We regard the annexation of Texas as a step that at once opens to the Americans the horizon of California.

President Polk would soon prove the *Freeman* right. Through a combination of public bluster and private willingness to compromise, he persuaded Britain to abandon its claim to the region that would one day become Oregon, Washington, and Idaho. And he determined to take New Mexico and California as well — by purchase if possible, by force if necessary. The Mexican government wasn't interested in selling, and refused even to receive the American envoy sent to Mexico City to make an offer. "Be assured," the envoy told Polk, ". . . nothing is to be done with these people until they shall have been chastised."

American presidents: Sam Houston (above), president of the Republic of Texas, and James Knox Polk, chief executive of the United States

THE HORIZON OF CALIFORNIA

Thomas O. Larkin, the American consul at Monterey, was much admired by the *Californios,* and he was armed in the spring of 1846 with secret orders from Washington to see if he couldn't encourage his friends among them to help throw off Mexican rule and join the United States.

It might have worked. Mariano Guadalupe Vallejo, for one, had now come to favor it. "To rely any longer upon Mexico to govern and defend us would be idle and absurd . . ." he said. "Why should we shrink from incorporating ourselves with the happiest and freest nation in the world, destined soon to be the most wealthy and powerful? . . . When we join our fortunes to hers, we shall not become subjects, but fellow-citizens. . . ."

But Larkin had not foreseen the sudden, intrusive presence of the Pathfinder. In the spring of 1845, John Charles Frémont undertook a third expedition into Mexican territory. He believed California was soon likely to fall into American hands, and he, his wife, and his father-in-law were all determined that he play a central role in its conquest. But after a tense confrontation with Mexican forces near Monterey, Frémont quietly withdrew, leading his party northward into southern Oregon.

Then, on May 8, 1846, near Klamath Lake, a rider from the east suddenly appeared at Frémont's camp — a Marine officer disguised in civilian clothes. Negotiations for the purchase of California and New Mexico had failed. Mexico would not sell. Nor would it agree to the Rio Grande as its border with Texas, and President Polk had dispatched an army to occupy the disputed region. Mexico could be expected to resist.

"I saw the way opening clear before me," Frémont recalled. "War with Mexico was inevitable; and a grand opportunity presented itself to realize . . . the far-sighted views of Senator Benton, and make the Pacific Ocean the western boundary of the United States. I resolved to . . . return forthwith to the Sacramento Valley in order to bring to bear all the influences I could command." Frémont immediately turned his party around and started back to California, ready for a fight.

That same day, far to the southeast, a Mexican army splashed across the Rio Grande and attacked an American patrol. President Polk announced that "American blood had been shed on American soil" and three days later asked Congress for a declaration of war: Mexicans, he said, had invaded American territory. Mexico understandably saw it the other way around. "The time to fight has come," declared President Mariano Padres. "Soldiers! A rapacious and grasping race have thrown themselves upon our territory and dare to flatter themselves that we will not defend."

Polk's strategy was straightforward: while armies occupied Mexico's northern provinces, and assaulted her from both coasts to force her to relinquish her territories north of the Rio Grande, a 2,700-man "Army of the West," commanded by Colonel Stephen Watts Kearny, would seize the Southwest, then join forces with the navy and take California.

New Hampshire volunteers for the war with Mexico parade through Exeter, 1846. New Englanders like these would come late to the fighting; most of the first men to sign up were from southern and western states.

Mexican forces melted away in front of Kearny's advancing army. He left one regiment to hold New Mexico, sent a second force south to take El Paso, then personally led three hundred men toward California. On the trail, he met Kit Carson, heading east with news from Frémont: California had already fallen to the Americans.

It had all happened very fast. Early in the morning of June 14, 1846, there had been a loud knock on the door of the home of General Mariano Guadalupe Vallejo at Sonoma. One of his daughters answered the door. "[There stood] a large group of rough-looking men," she remembered, "wearing on their heads caps made with the skins of coyotes or wolves, some wearing slouch hats full of holes, some wearing straw hats as black as charcoal. . . . [S]everal had no shirts, shoes were only to be seen on the feet of 15 or 20 of the whole lot."

The strangers were Americans — trappers, settlers, squatters who proudly called themselves "floaters" — and they demanded that Vallejo, as nominal commander of northern California, surrender to them. They flew a crude flag emblazoned with a grizzly bear sketched in blackberry juice and said they were declaring California a republic — the "Bear Flag Republic."

Hospitable as always, Vallejo ushered in the leaders and offered them so much brandy and wine they soon could no longer walk. He also signed the surrender happily enough; tired of appealing to Mexico City for arms and aid that never came, he had already enthusiastically endorsed peaceful annexation by his friends, the Americans. But the strangers had something else in mind. They told him he was under arrest. "And they tied me to a chair!" he remembered many years later. "Me! Vallejo!"

Then Frémont arrived at Sonoma, declared himself in charge of the revolt, and clapped Vallejo in jail for eight weeks. Even John Sutter was confined to his quarters.

There was no serious fighting at first — the outnumbered, outgunned regular Mexican forces elected to return to Mexico — and on June 24, Frémont marched into San Francisco, where he grandly spiked ten obsolete cannons and renamed the harbor "the Golden Gate." On July 7, American naval forces occupied Monterey, raised the American flag, and declared that "henceforward, California will be a portion of the United States." The Bear Flag Republic had lasted less than a month. Commodore Robert Stockton formally mustered Frémont's band into a "California Battalion of Mounted Riflemen" and placed the Pathfinder in charge.

Meanwhile, the stubborn imperiousness of the American officer in command at Los Angeles had driven its people to rise up and retake their town. And when Kearny and his men finally arrived in California, they were met near the pueblo of Pasqual by a volunteer force of skilled *Californio* lancers riding fast horses. Twenty-two of the invaders were killed, and seventeen were wounded, including their commander. This battle marked the high point of *Californio* resistance. Their leaders began to fall out among themselves, Kearny and Stockton finally managed to join forces, and on January 13, 1847, the last *Californio* forces surrendered to Frémont at Cahuenga Pass, on the outskirts of Los Angeles.

Commodore Stockton, a pompous soldier whose men privately called him "Gassy Bob," appointed Frémont the first American governor of California. But Kearny saw himself as Stockton's superior, and thought Frémont a showy amateur who owed his celebrity to political connections. He ordered him to disband his battalion and give

The Mexican-American War was the first to be photographed. An anonymous daguerreotypist captured Major Lucien B. Webster's battery (above) in the mountains north of Buena Vista, where they had helped smash larger but less well armed Mexican forces. The anonymous portrait opposite is believed to be the only one to show a Texas Ranger in battle dress. No photographs survive of the skirmishing that captured California for the United States, but the flag inset above was carried by the founders of the short-lived Bear Flag Republic, who started it all.

up the governorship. Frémont was an army officer, not a navy man, and should have obeyed. But he liked being governor, hated taking orders from any man, refused to resign. When Kearny sent an intermediary to demand that he surrender his papers, Frémont challenged the man to a duel, with shotguns.

The duel never took place, but Kearny won the political struggle. President Polk had empowered him, not Stockton, to set up a civilian government. Frémont resigned the governorship but refused to apologize for his insubordination. "The younger officers," Lieutenant William Tecumseh Sherman remembered, "had been discussing what the General would do with Frémont, who was supposed to be in a state of mutiny. Some thought he would be tried and shot, some that he would be carried back in irons; and all agreed that if anyone else than Frémont had put on such airs and acted as he had done, Kearny would have shown him no mercy."

Kearny didn't show much: he ordered Frémont's arrest for mutiny. When Kearny left California for the East with part of his victorious army in the summer of 1847, Frémont, facing court-martial, was ordered to ride at the rear of the column, eating his enemy's dust as they made their way back along the trail. Angry and bitter, he found some solace in the praise showered upon him by many of the emigrants who recognized him along the trail. "They were using my maps on the road," he wrote to a friend, "traveling by them, and you may judge how gratified I was to find that they found them perfectly correct. . . ." At Truckee Lake, high in the Sierras, Frémont saw horrific evidence of what could happen to travelers moving through the West without a good map — the bones of California-bound pioneers remembered as the Donner Party, men and women who had taken an untried cutoff and perished in the snow, lay scattered over the countryside, gnawed white by wolves and coyotes.

Meanwhile, the war in Mexico stretched on for another year — a bloody, desperate struggle that cost thousands of Mexican lives and ended only after American troops stormed into Mexico City. On February 2, 1848, Mexico signed the Treaty of Guadalupe Hidalgo, formally ending the war. It had lost nearly half its territory to the invaders from the north.

On July 4, 1848, in Washington, D.C., thousands turned out to see President Polk lay the cornerstone of a new monument — a giant stone shaft modeled after the obelisks of ancient Egypt to honor the nation's first president, George Washington. Washington's America had ended at the Mississippi. But now, as Polk spoke to the crowd, he was the president of a nation three times as large, a continental United States that stretched from sea to sea. In only a generation — by bluff and intimidation, by sacrifice, and by outright conquest — Americans had seized almost all of the West.

Standing near the President at the ceremony was Joe Meek, whose fondest wish had now come true. Born in Washington County, Virginia, the old mountain man was now sheriff of the brand-new Washington County — in Oregon Territory. A month later, even more good news arrived from the newest section of the country. In California — on a stream named the American River — gold had been discovered. Nothing in the West would ever be the same again.

THE MISSION AT WAIILATPU: A MEETING PLACE FOR WESTERN WOMEN

JULIE ROY JEFFREY

Once, a long time ago, there were two old Cayuse women. While the men went hunting for game, these old women were searching for camas roots. Some they would dry for the winter, but they were using others to make delicious hot mush.

Now at that time, the Snake were on the warpath, and one of the Snake warriors met up with these women. And what do you think the women did? Why, they poured the hot mush all over the enemy's face. The warrior fell back, and these two old women, they just took a knife and scalped him and then escaped to the Walla Walla Valley.

When they got home and told what they had done, all the Cayuse shouted with joy for the feat of these old women, these brave old Cayuse women. Then, they named the creek for them, and that's why it's named Squaw Creek.

In the Cayuse longhouses, each one home to an extended family during the winter months when the tribe camped near the Walla Walla River, you could hear this kind of story and many others during the long dark evenings. Elders, with the wisdom of many years, were the favored storytellers. And while everyone crowded around the fire to listen to them, children and young people were encouraged to pay especially close attention. For it was through stories that Cayuse children were instructed about what was important in life. The story of the two old women, for example, contained many lessons: it taught the importance of heroism, bravery, and quick thinking, defined the character of the Snake, and reflected the power of tribal ties and the people's love for the Walla Walla Valley, their home. Then, too, children could learn to appreciate the critical role women played in sustaining tribal life and to admire female strength and courage.

On cold winter evenings in the mid-1840s, not far from the Indian encampment, quite different scenes of domestic life were taking place in the comfortable mission house. If it were a Thursday night, you could see Narcissa Whitman, the wife of the Presbyterian medical missionary, Marcus Whitman, and an assistant missionary to the Indians herself, leading a religious meeting for her large family of adopted children. She was hoping to alert them to the dangers of their sinful natures and to the promise of God's loving forgiveness. Without a spiritual awakening, they could never experience the conversion she believed necessary for salvation. On other nights, she might lead them in singing, and, when there were guests, show them off a bit, by having them line up according to height as they performed. They were her "family stairway," she said. If she was proud of them for their singing and their neat attire, and if she monitored

their spiritual progress very closely, you could hardly blame her. Most of the children had been wild and untutored when she had taken them in, not at all like her own dead child, Alice, who had loved singing hymns and talking of Jesus. The last ones she had adopted, a whole family of children named the Sagers, orphaned during the long overland journey to the West, had been a real challenge — seven of them at once, ignorant and unruly after months of travel. But then, perhaps their dead mother, Naomi Sager, had not taken her obligations as a mother quite so seriously as Narcissa did her own.

These two domestic scenes, so different in character yet unfolding so close to one another in the Walla Walla Valley in eastern Oregon Territory, hint at the diversity of family life and female experience in the nineteenth-century West. While the Whitman mission at Waiilatpu lasted just eleven years, it was a place where Native American, white, and métis women of mixed racial parentage mingled. Even though common experiences like childbirth tied the different women together, were we to visit the mission, we might well have been struck more by the differences than the similarities between them.

Narcissa Whitman's middle-class values, her notions of appropriate roles for women and men, her evangelical background, her education and training in New York State provided the vantage point from which she viewed and judged the Indian women among whom she lived and worked. On the one hand, she pitied Indian women, whom she thought were "slaves to their husbands." Unused to labor outside of the house and garden, Narcissa, like many white women, was horrified at the heavy work that Indian women performed and the many tasks for which they were responsible. On the other hand, she condemned them for being neglectful mothers, bemoaning the fact that she could not see "one savory example" of proper childrearing among the Cayuse. The ease of divorce, the sexual freedom tolerated before marriage, the practice of polygamy all violated her beliefs about morality, female chastity, and marital fidelity.

Frustrated by the Cayuse women's unwillingness to emulate her own domestic habits and routines, believing that she was offering them the comforts of both civilization and salvation, she could only interpret their resistance as either the work of Satan or rival Roman Catholic missionaries. Her exasperation impressed one white observer, who remarked that Narcissa entertained for the "Indians in her charge the feelings of a mother towards ungrateful children." While there were harmonious moments — Narcissa recorded buying berries from Indian women and reading the Bible to them, and she possessed a decorated Indian fan — an underlying current of mutual misunderstanding and frustration simmered below the surface.

A good correspondent, Narcissa has provided us with ample evidence of her own activities and her perceptions of others. But what of the Indian women who left no written record? Although their perspective needs some imaginative effort to recover, there are enough clues to allow us to reconstruct their lives and to speculate about their views. While native women's routines were very different from those of white women like Narcissa, as the story of the two old women suggests, Cayuse women were neither slaves nor drudges. Their activities were crucial to their people's welfare. They were not tribal leaders, but they were eligible to hold important positions within the tribe. Some even became "medicine squaws" and performed the sacred healing rituals that drew out evil spirits from the sick.

The Cayuse were one of several seminomadic Indian tribes living in the plateau area of the Columbia River. Because they were not agriculturalists, hunting and gathering activities determined the tribe's annual movements. During the spring and summer, the tribe was constantly on the move, but in the fall the Cayuse split into small groups of kin and family and erected communal longhouses, where they would spend the winter months. One of these groups had its winter quarters close to the Whitman mission house.

While gender determined the division of labor, men and women had complementary but equally important roles in ensuring that the tribe had enough food for the winter. Men fished for salmon and hunted game. Women dried the fish for future use, butchered game and dried it, cured skins, and, most importantly, gathered and preserved roots, wild plants, and fruits. About half the food the tribe ate came from the plants women obtained. Perhaps in partial recognition of the significance of this female work, Indians attributed to it a sacred dimension. As a Cayuse called Young Chief pointed out, the Great Spirit himself "had named the roots that he should feed the Indians on."

This division of labor stretched back to the days of myth and legend. With the introduction of horses, the character of tribal life had changed, but the basic structure of male and female roles was only modified. Cayuse men became successful horse breeders and traders, able now to join in the great buffalo hunts on the plains and to roam farther in pursuit of their enemies. Cayuse women continued to perform their essential functions in tribal life, but their tasks, too, were made less onerous by the presence of horses. They learned to dry buffalo meat and cure the skins that they decorated with beadwork and shells for their own clothes. As explorers and fur traders made their way into the West in the early decades of

Nez Percé women and schoolteachers, Idaho, 1890

the nineteenth century, other changes occurred. New tools and implements became available. But the essential contours of female life remained the same.

By the standards of white middle-class society, Indian culture represented the antithesis of civilization. The Whitmans viewed the Walla Walla Valley as a wilderness and referred to the Cayuse as heathens and occasionally as savages. The missionaries implored the Cayuse to turn away from traditional religious beliefs and attacked their medicine men as Satan's minions. They urged the tribe to abandon their seminomadic life and to settle permanently as farmers around the mission. While the Whitmans argued that settled agricultural life would ensure that the tribe never went hungry during the winter, staying at the mission would obviously eliminate women's work as food providers and the prestige and power that went along with it. The Cayuse soon recognized that the Whitmans' goal was one of transformation. As Narcissa pointed out, "We have come to elevate them and not to suffer ourselves to sink down to their standard."

While none of the Cayuse abandoned their yearly cycle of travel, some took the Whitmans' advice and planted a field or two. But the undertaking was problematic. Some men resisted the whole idea of farming, reminding the Cayuse that the earth was their mother. As a member of a closely related tribe asked, "Shall I take a knife and tear my mother's bosom?" Others regarded working in the fields as unmanly and left the labor to their wives and children or slaves. For the women who tended the crops, the agricultural experiment meant new burdens added to their usual round of work. And unlike their gathering activities, labor in the fields, rejected by men as demeaning and dishonorable, did not bring prestige to the women who did it.

Given the weight of Cayuse cultural values and the importance of traditional female activities, we can understand why many Cayuse women did not respond positively to Narcissa's instruction. Certainly it was hard to view her as a friend. Narcissa's refusal to exchange gifts as was customary in Indian society, and her insistence that the Cayuse must work or pay for goods, symbolized for them her lack of interest in friendship.

Consider some of the implications of her work for the lives of Cayuse women. Like most missionaries, Narcissa was determined to replace polygamy with the nuclear family. As she noted, one of the Cayuse men "thinks he is a Christian, but we fear to the contrary. His mind is somewhat waked up about his living with two women. I would not ease him any, but urged him to do his duty." But what was to happen to the wives who would be so dutifully discarded? What would loss of the labor of several wives mean for a family's diet and health? What would compensate a woman who lost the prestige that accompanied marriage to a chief, one of the men most likely to have more than one wife?

Eager to encourage Indian women to adopt her own construction of womanhood, Narcissa never really considered why Cayuse women might not benefit from the changes she suggested. When they failed to exhibit sufficient interest in acquiring white domestic skills, Narcissa was disgusted. "The Indians do not love to work well enough for us to place any dependence upon them," she remarked. In particular, "the Kayuse ladies are too proud to be seen usefully employed." They even looked askance at having their children perform suitable chores. "The moment they hear of the children doing the least thing," Narcissa reported, "they are panic-stricken and make trouble."

Cayuse women must have wondered where it would all end. Did Narcissa want them to abandon their longhouses, which she obviously found dirty and poorly arranged, for a house like her own? Longhouses provided space for husbands, wives, children, grandparents, cousins, aunts, and uncles to live together as an extended family. They were open and accessible to friends and kin. Narcissa's house had closed doors, windows covered with blinds, and fences to keep people away. Cayuse women knew that they were not welcome there. Why should they want to replicate Narcissa's arrangements and the work that went along with them? Would they even be urged to leave off their familiar clothes in order to wear the kinds of dresses the missionary favored, the ones that needed continual washing? Would she expect them to keep their children close by, as she did her own, forcing them to work and punishing them as no Indian mother would do? (Shaming a child, rather than punishment, was the Indian way of discipline.)

There were a few women who listened and became "good" Indians. But most native women apparently found Narcissa's advice and the manner in which she gave it unappealing. "Firmness in her was natural," observed one white, "and to some, especially the Indians, it was repulsive." In the aftermath of Narcissa's violent death at the hands of the Cayuse, the Indian women played out their hostility to the white missionary who had lived in their midst. One witness recollected the terrible scene, "white women running and screaming, and the Indian women singing and dancing."

The gloomy spiritual lessons both the Whitmans taught also colored the Cayuse perspective of the missionaries. Although many members of the tribe willingly adopted some of the Christian practices introduced at the mission, their religious performances were always judged wanting. The Whitmans continually reminded the Cayuse that they had not experienced the requisite change of heart. They were doomed to hell. Not surprisingly, Indians denounced this "bad talk." "Instead of yielding to the truth," Narcissa wrote, "they oppose it vigorously."

More pliable and positive than the Cayuse women who so frustrated Narcissa was her friend Catherine Pambrun. In the early years of mission life when the sight of white women was a rarity at the mission, Narcissa had depended upon Catherine, the wife of Pierre Pambrun, the factor at the Hudson's Bay Fort Walla Walla, about twenty-five miles distant. At her daughter's birth in 1837, Narcissa had only her husband and Catherine to help her.

Catherine Pambrun was a métis woman, the result of two generations of intermarriage between white fur traders and Indian women. Marriages of this sort were common in the fur trade in the 1820s and 1830s. There were few white women as potential marriage partners in the West, and native and mixed-blood women had family ties and skills that were useful to white traders, who depended on Indians to procure furs and horses, to serve as guides, interpreters, and go-betweens. Marriage with an Indian woman cemented business ties and provided a trader with an ideal racial and cultural intermediary. Mixed marriages were also valued in Indian society, not only for the contacts that a woman possessed in the white world but also for the goods and skills that she could pass along to her Indian relatives.

Catherine Pambrun's material life and habits symbolized her position somewhere between two racial and cultural worlds. The house in which she lived with her husband was "half-native, half-French." When Narcissa met her, Catherine was still washing her clothes in a stream and using cradleboards for her newborn children. Stories suggest she even smoked tobacco. In her household, as was also true at other fur-trading outposts, the men did most of the cooking and housework. Such an arrangement violated Narcissa's understanding of the proper roles for men and women, and she wrote that fur-trade wives were "not first rate housekeepers." While Catherine was fluent in her mother's language and French, she could speak little English.

Narcissa, who was well treated by the head factor of the Hudson's Bay Company and his mixed-blood wife when she arrived in the West, liked Catherine Pambrun and began to teach her English. She taught her other things as well: how to wash her clothes in a bucket instead of in a stream and the importance of not confining a baby in a cradleboard. She felt a great sense of achievement when Catherine abandoned the practice and gave "the blessed privilege of liberty" to her newborn.

Despite the friendship between the women, and the sense that cultural and racial boundaries in the West were permeable, the racial easiness of the métis fur-trade world was fast disappearing as more white women came west and judged métis women by their own standards. Pierre Pambrun sensed, if his wife did not, that times were changing. If women like Catherine were to survive in the white world, they would have to adopt white standards, and even then, they would probably face discrimination. It was Pierre who set the English lessons in motion and tried to persuade Catherine to give up smoking in exchange for diamond earrings. Certainly, Narcissa's own toleration of racial mixing had limits. Although Catherine remained her friend, by 1846 Narcissa was condemning men who were "disposed to degrade themselves" by taking "a native" woman as a spouse.

The uneasiness of Pierre Pambrun, who sensed his world was being undermined by white migration, was matched by that of Indian tribes whose territories lay in the path of the overland wagon trains. The Cayuse, like other tribes, grew restive in the 1840s as the number of white emigrants crossing their lands increased. Some of the whites stopped at the mission station, where the Whitmans gave them supplies for which the Indians had to pay. They even occupied the room that had been set aside as the Indian room. During the winter, emigrants lived at the mission, where the Whitmans organized a school for their children.

Lakota and a missionary

Blaine, who had come from Seneca Falls, New York, to Portland, Oregon, proclaimed, "This is an awfully wicked country and if it doesn't meet with the fate of Sodom and Gomorrah or Pompeii, it won't be because the people don't deserve it."

The importance Narcissa attached to the domestic sphere and the re-creation of a genteel lifestyle would also be shared by other middle-class emigrants. Narcissa's first home had been a simple adobe building with a log lean-to. Even in these modest surroundings, Narcissa managed to provide some domestic comforts. She put glass in her windows, made feather beds for the bedsteads, for which there were also sheets — a rarity in the West at that time — and had separate pots for brewing coffee and tea. Her washtub, which she believed one of only two west of the Rockies, symbolized her intention to uphold familiar housekeeping standards. She objected to the Cayuse partly because "they are so filthy they make a great deal of cleaning wherever they go." The work they created "wears out a woman very fast." Her attitude toward cleanliness could hardly have escaped Cayuse notice, for she refused to let her daughter Alice crawl on the floor and carried the child around in her arms for the first year of her life.

The Cayuse must have sensed how much the attitudes of the missionary couple had shifted. Originally, they had come as missionaries to the Indians. Now they welcomed the emigrants and acted as the white people's trusted friends and defenders. Perhaps some of them even suspected that the Whitmans had consigned them to oblivion. As Marcus wrote candidly in an 1844 letter, "I am fully convinced that when a people refuse or neglect to fill the designs of Providence, they ought not to complain at the results; and so it is equally useless for Christians to be anxious on their account. The Indians have in no case obeyed the command to multiply and replenish the earth, and they cannot stand in the way of others doing so." While Narcissa continued to refer to the "poor Indians" dutifully in her letters, she busied herself with her large family of children and all but removed herself from contact with them.

For Narcissa, the emigration pointed to a hopeful future. She had never felt comfortable in her missionary work, and when her daughter had accidentally drowned, she had gone into a deep depression. A long visit in the more settled Willamette Valley had only made her more aware of the real character of the mission station. Upon her return to Waiilatpu, she had written to a friend despairingly. "What sounds fall upon my ears and what savage sights do I behold every day around me. . . . [E]ven now . . . the drum and the savage yell are sounding in my ears." Now, it seemed possible that civilization as she understood it could be established in the West.

While Narcissa's original missionary vocation marked her as exceptional, her understanding of the female sphere and its obligations was shared by other white women moving west. Although there were few female missionaries, many women, especially those from a middle-class eastern background, agreed with Narcissa that a woman had a duty to reform the world. They would judge western society and find it wanting. In 1856, nine years after Narcissa's death, Kate

As the mission became a successful farming operation, a new house was constructed. One of the Sager orphans was amazed at her first sight of it. "We expected to see log houses, occupied by Indians and such people as we had seen about the forts. Instead we saw a large white house surrounded with palisades." Inside Narcissa had both a parlor and a dining room. Floors were tastefully painted yellow and trim was slate gray. Furniture included settees, clothes presses, and rocking chairs. There was even a cabinet for Narcissa's curiosities, English china for the dining table, and, of course, books. Most of the appurtenances for genteel living were now present.

Despite the fact travelers and other missionaries were occasional visitors, this home was, as the Indians recognized, a private space set aside for family life. Like other middle-class women, Narcissa saw her house as a haven from the bustle and confusion of public life that, in the mission setting, the Indians represented. Soon after the Whitmans' arrival, Narcissa had decided that "as soon as we are able [we will] . . . prepare a separate room" for the Cayuse. "They will not be allowed to come in any part of the house at all," she declared. Her insistence on family privacy, so different from the relaxed attitudes of her Indian neighbors, led inevitably to conflict. The Cayuse insisted on access to the house, which the Whitmans refused. In 1841, the Indians hacked in the mission house's door and broke windows but failed to sway the Whitmans. "We told them," reported Narcissa, "that . . . we should order our doors."

Her house was the setting for all the domestic activities that normally were part of a white middle-class woman's domain: cooking on the cookstove (a "luxury in those days"), sewing, spinning, knitting, washing clothes, cleaning, and caring for the garden. Although she had hired help when she could, Narcissa insisted that her adopted children take on domestic chores. She considered it part of her responsibility to teach her girls the housewifely skills that would be expected of them when they married.

The house was also the place where Narcissa exercised her authority as mother and moral guide. By the time she came west in the mid-1830s, there were specific cultural expectations for middle-class motherhood. Unlike her Cayuse neighbors, who spread childrearing responsibilities among members of the extended family, Narcissa believed that training the children was a mother's duty. How well she did the job would determine the future health and welfare of the nation and of the West.

Approaching her task with all the seriousness it required, Narcissa sought help from periodicals like *Mother's Magazine* and shared her challenges and triumphs in letters with family and close friends. The children she adopted had all suffered from neglect or inadequate maternal supervision. Several came to her filthy and in poor health. The youngest Sager child, only a few months old, arrived malnourished and weak. Her brothers and sisters had had little discipline and often appeared willful.

Narcissa established a strict regime that included stringent standards for personal cleanliness (a cold bath daily) and for behavior. Some of the children needed "long and tedious" efforts to be trained properly although others were "easily governed." She expected obedience. "There was no danger of any of us being spoiled," wrote Matilda Sager. "She would point to one of us, then point to the dishes or the broom, and we would instantly get busy." "Any deviation from the laid down rule," remembered Matilda's sister, Catherine, "met with instant and severe punishment." When they looked back on their childhood, the Sager children used the word "puritan" to describe Narcissa's approach, very different, in their opinion, "from the way of the plains" and presumably of their own parents.

Most emigrants who came to the Whitman mission saw only the couple's graciousness and hospitality. The Whitmans were "fine, friendly people," Joseph Williams wrote, "with all kinds of garden vegetables, which they gave us very freely." Emigrants appreciated not only the supplies (sometimes given outright, sometimes sold) but also the medical care and advice the Whitmans provided. For some, like Sarah Cummins, whose party Marcus Whitman helped out of a threatening encounter with Indians, the doctor, at least, took on heroic proportions. Sarah recollected him rising before the Indians to "almost super-human height."

But both Narcissa and her husband harbored private doubts about the character of most emigrants and the society they were likely to establish in Oregon. As Marcus wrote to the missionary board, the Whitmans wanted good men (and women), especially from New England, to "hold a good influence over the Indians & sustain religious institutions as a nucleus for society." Only if the right sort of people came to Oregon, Narcissa asserted in 1844, could the country "be saved from becoming a sink of wickedness and prostitution."

While Narcissa certainly did not judge emigrants as harshly as she judged Indians, many violated the norms and values that were a product of her class, religious commitment, and regional background. Narcissa regarded the woman who had cared for the newborn Sager infant after her mother's death on the Oregon Trail as an "old filthy woman" with "a wicked, disobedient family around her to see to." We can imagine what she might have said about Naomi Sager herself. Naomi, perhaps partly as a result of the family's frequent moves, from Ohio to Indiana to eastern and then western Missouri, had never instructed her children in Christianity, nor had she disciplined them effectively. The three oldest could scarcely read when they joined the Whitman family.

Although Naomi never made it to Oregon, she was probably more typical of white women emigrating to the West than Narcissa was. As the Oregon census of 1850 revealed, while many New Englanders could be found in the territory's towns, the majority of settlers did not come from the Northeast but from the Midwest and the Mississippi Valley. Their roots lay in the South, among self-sufficient white yeoman farmers, not plantation owners.

Narcissa saw that the multitudes who were "hastening to this far-distant land to seek their fortune of worldly goods" were coming "regardless of their treasure in heaven." The Gay family, from Kentucky and Virginia via Springfield, Missouri, were just such a family. They had no vision of establishing a godly society in the West. Like most emigrants they were headed to Oregon for material reasons. Martha Gay remembered her father's western fever and his goals. "He had talked about Oregon and the Columbia River for many years and wanted to go there. He wanted to take his nine sons where they could get land." Land to establish a family, perhaps even to replicate the powerful connections between land and family that characterized the plantation South, this was the cherished dream.

Typically, emigrants like the Gays set off to the West with kinfolk and neighbors. When they left Missouri, there were sixteen in their party, "Father, mother, twelve children, one daughter-in-law and one young man who came all the long way with us." Once in Oregon, they searched out family members who had gone ahead or friends from home. The Gays went first to "the home of an old friend who had come out . . . some years before" and had a "joyous meeting" before moving on "to another old neighbor's place who had sent for us to come and stay in their home. . . . Father and his old neighbor were so moved by this meeting that they lost their power of speech."

The women of such migrant families were tough, adaptable, hardworking, and essential partners in the family dream. The trip west could hardly be undertaken without their cooperation. Martha's mother, despite her husband's enthusiasm, was reluctant "to undertake the long and dangerous journey with a large family of small children." Only when she agreed could Martin Gay "set about making arrangements for the journey." Ann Gay gave birth on the trail, but she also did her share of cooking, minding the children, packing and unpacking the wagons, and perhaps even driving on occasion. Her daughter remembered that her father spent much of his time hunting.

An Assiniboin family — Sampson, Frances Louis, and Leah Beaver, 1907

While these women did not differ from Narcissa in their fundamental understanding of what was proper for women to do, they did not share her reformist and evangelical zeal. Emigrants rarely commented on the spiritual aspect of the missionary operation, suggesting that they had little interest in it. Nor did women share all of Narcissa's demanding middle-class standards. Her comment that those who stopped for any length of time at the mission had "a disposition not to work, at any rate, not more than they can help" may have had more to do with a disagreement with the Whitmans' exacting requirements than with any disinclination to do for themselves. Many were neither literate nor genteel. They were often unkempt, too, at least in Narcissa's eyes. Even the young woman who worked as a cook for the Whitmans was deficient, "not as neat and tidy in her person and work as I could wish and as would be well for her."

The regional and cultural differences that Narcissa noticed pointed to the creation of a more complicated white society in Oregon than reminiscences of pioneer days might suggest. In the 1850s, Kate Blaine was remarking upon social and cultural distinctions in language similar to Narcissa's. A visit with "a poor family from Missouri" prompted Kate to write to friends at home, "I often think when we are with people of this class . . . [that] I wish you could hear them talk. I know you would laugh to hear their negro and western phrases." But Kate herself did not always feel like laughing. At the home of a family from Iowa, the woman of the house asked Kate whether she slept in sheets. "Many of the people from the west sleep between these Indian blankets without any sheets, but I would about as soon have caterpillars on me as to have those blankets touch me."

The circle of female life on the early Oregon rural frontier encompassed family, friends, and neighbors and was intensely local in character. Social and religious activities centered in homes and nearby schoolhouses. While female associational life was weak, interest in religion was not. Although Narcissa had decried the religious credentials of most of Oregon's future settlers, many women were not so much irreligious as weakly connected to any particular denomination. Indeed, women often supported family religious observances and encouraged the visits of itinerant preachers. Remembering how his mother and a neighbor from Missouri arranged a preaching service, one Oregonian described how "our cabin, being large, was for years the preaching place for the neighborhood."

Both women and their menfolk also attended camp meetings. At one, female behavior shocked George Atkinson, a minister from New England, who was engaged in just the sort of missionary work among settlers in the Willamette Valley that Narcissa and Marcus Whitman thought was so necessary. Comfortable with genteel worship, Atkinson was taken aback by the style of camp meetings and women's participation in them. He recorded that "two [women] screamed very loud and grasped hands, uttering many things incoherently." The hymns were almost unrecognizable. "Old tunes are changed. Very few are sung as nearly correct as in country churches at home. Some are barbarously altered. Other tunes are framed apparently for the occasion. I suppose many sung daily here never were expressed as notes."

Atkinson's shock reminds us that the West was home to diverse peoples. Although the mission at Waiilatpu does not figure in most narratives of western history, it allows us to glimpse women from different groups and to see the similarities and contrasts between them. It also shows us the ways in which culture, social and regional loyalties, and, of course, race shaped the perspectives and interactions of the women whose paths crossed at the Whitman mission station. And while following the women in their daily and seasonal routines reveals the misunderstandings and tensions they experienced as they dealt with one another, perhaps there are also lessons we can learn from them about the ways in which groups can and do coexist despite the strains between them.

An entrepreneur named R. Lowe opened this impromptu store in the California diggings. The surest way to riches in gold rush California was not to pan or dig for gold but to cater to the needs of those who did.

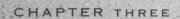

CHAPTER THREE

SEEING THE ELEPHANT

1848–1855

By 1848, the United States claimed almost all of the West. The Louisiana Purchase, the annexation of Texas and Oregon, and the war with Mexico had stretched the nation's boundaries all the way to the Pacific. But the West was still American in name only. Few people east of the Mississippi were anxious to venture into its forbidding interior. It still seemed too distant, too dangerous. Then gold was discovered at Sutter's Mill and everything changed — for California, for the West, and for the country. "It revolutionized America," wrote one man who had seen it all. "It was the beginning of our national madness, our insanity of greed."

According to the legend written on the back of this hand-tinted daguerreotype, "This nugget of pure gold was mined in the early 1850's by the man holding it: James Warner Woolsey. His mine was near Nevada City, California. [The nugget] was worth $1900.00. It weighed over eight pounds."

John Sutter was never satisfied. He had created an empire for himself in California — 50,000 acres of land, fields, and orchards, a fort and an Indian army to defend his holdings, and a sloop for sailing the Sacramento River. Now he wanted a sawmill with which to produce lumber for still more projects, and sent his foreman, James Marshall, forty-five miles north to build it at a bend of the South Fork of the American River.

On the morning of January 24, 1848, Marshall and his crew were deepening the millrace to speed up the wheel that was to drive the new saw when his eye noticed something out of the ordinary. "My eye was caught by something shining in the bottom of the ditch . . ." he recalled. "I reached my hand down and picked it up; it made my heart thump, for I was certain it was gold. The piece was about half the size and shape of a pea. Then I saw another. . . ." He rode off to Sutter's Fort to show his employer what he had found.

Together, they quietly consulted an encyclopedia, performed tests it suggested, and proved to their private satisfaction that the nugget was almost pure gold. Meanwhile, Marshall's men found more and more of it. Sutter tried to keep it all a secret — he wanted his mill finished and he didn't want anyone else digging for gold until he got clear title to the land on which it had been found — but rumors about the discovery began to spread in spite of him. His workers laid down their tools to look for gold. Gold-seekers began filtering in from others parts of California, as well — too many for Sutter to drive away.

One of them was Sam Brannan, the acquisitive Mormon whom Brigham Young had sent to California by sea with 238 fellow believers. Brannan already owned a flour mill and California's first newspaper, the *Star*. He found gold all right, but he also saw a surer path to further riches: he opened a store right next to Sutter's sawmill, fully stocked with picks and pans and shovels to cater to the needs of the treasure-seekers he was sure would follow him into the goldfields once word got out.

Then he made sure word did get out. He returned to San Francisco and on May 12 walked through the streets waving a quinine bottle filled with gold dust and shouting, "Gold! Gold! Gold from the American River!"

The gold rush was on. By the middle of June, three-quarters of the men living in San Francisco had left for the American River to look for gold. "The great rush from San Francisco arrived at the fort . . ." Sutter remembered. "My cook left me, like everybody else. The merchants, doctors, lawyers, sea captains, . . . all left their wives and families in San Francisco and those which had none locked their doors, abandoned their houses [or] offered them for sale, cheap. . . . The recently opened school had to be closed: teacher and pupils had gone off to the mines."

Gold seemed to be everywhere, lodged among rocks, glittering in sandbars, swirling in pools and eddies. Some made fortunes using nothing but spoons or jackknives to scoop it up. Others brought in crude machinery and hired Indians to do the work: seven men employing fifty Indians dug out 273 pounds of gold in just two months. "My little girls can make from 5 to 25 dollars per day washing gold in pans," a miner wrote home to Missouri. "My average income this winter will be about 150 dollars a day." And there seemed to be new discoveries every day — at Bidwell's Bar on the Feather River, on the Trinity River, on tributaries of the Sacramento, and along the streams that flowed through the foothills of the Sierra Nevada.

Lieutenant William Tecumseh Sherman, just twenty-eight, accompanied Colonel R. B. Mason, the military governor of California, on an official tour of the new goldfields. Four thousand men were already at work, they reported, and they were pulling out $30,000 to $50,000 worth of gold every day.

Soldiers began to desert for the goldfields. So did sailors from ships that docked at San Francisco. Two-thirds of the American men living in Oregon raced south in search of gold. Hawaiians and Chinese came to work the streams. So did gold-seekers from Peru, Mexico, Chile.

Sherman and Mason were stunned by what they saw. "I have no hesitation now," Mason wrote, "in saying there is more gold in the country drained by the Sacramento and San Joaquin rivers than will pay the cost of the war with Mexico a hundred times over." In August, the report Mason and Sherman had written was sent to Washington by ship, along with a tea caddy packed with gold dust.

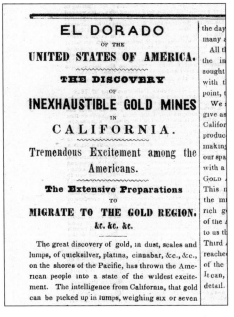

James Marshall (left) and the sawmill on the American River where he spotted the first particle of California gold. "It made my heart thump," he remembered, and he began to dream of getting rich quick. But newspaper headlines like those above quickly spread the word of what he'd found, an international stampede began, and in the end Marshall never earned a cent from his discovery.

It was put on display at the War Department. "The accounts of the abundance of gold in that territory [California]," President Polk told Congress, "are of such extraordinary character as would scarcely command belief were they not corroborated by authentic reports of officers in the public service."

Thousands of young men — and a handful of young women — now wanted to get to California right away. The only question was how best to get there. It was impossible to travel overland until spring thawed the prairies and mountain passes, so the most impatient argonauts started off by sea. There were two water routes. The longest — 18,000 nautical miles — went all the way around South America and took so much time that when one captain made the voyage in seventy-six days he asked that his record be engraved on his tombstone. The other route took less time but involved sailing aboard one vessel to Panama, risking death from tropical diseases while crossing the isthmus by mule-back and canoe, then boarding another ship for San Francisco.

Some 25,000 gold-seekers took one sea route or the other in 1849, and most were subjected to the same storms, seasickness, stale water, and worse food. "The passengers [on the steamer] were fed like hogs . . ." a gold-seeker named Isaac Lord remembered. "Some of the hard bread was of good quality, some moldy, and much of it was infested with black bugs burrowing into it like woodchucks in a sand bank."

The vessels were often unsafe, as well as uncomfortable and unhealthy: one woman and her husband were forced to climb aboard four different ships before they

A frenzy seized my soul. . . . Piles of gold rose up before me . . . castles of marble, thousands of slaves . . . myriads of fair virgins contending with each other for my love — were among the fancies of my fevered imagination. The Rothschilds, Girards, and Astors appeared to be but poor people; in short, I had a very violent attack of the gold fever.

Hubert Howe Bancroft

Getting there: In the 1849 lithograph opposite, top, a cartoonist working for the printmaker Nathaniel Currier proposes a "Grand Patent India-Rubber Air Line" to hurl eager gold-seekers all the way across the continent by air. The reality was only slightly less daunting — an arduous overland trek or the long, uncomfortable, sometimes dangerous journey by sea advertised cheerfully opposite, bottom, and rendered more realistically above.

finally reached San Francisco; the first three had to be scuttled after, one by one, their cargoes of coal burst into flame.

Vicente Pérez Rosales and his three younger brothers, members of a landed Chilean family that had fallen on hard times, set out from Valparaiso by sea that winter. "All told," Rosales noted, "we are 149 — 90 men, plus 4 cows, 8 pigs, 12 sheep, a few dozen chickens, 3 dogs, 7 sailors, the captain and the mate. We are a mixed lot in this little tower of babel: Frenchmen, Englishmen, Germans, Italians, Chileans; nabobs and beggars. . . . Seasickness is widespread. . . . The sides of the ships are covered with dripping vomit, and the cabin and the ladders, as well. Everywhere you see green faces and hear the sounds of men retching." Rosales had tried everything he could think of to restore his family's fortunes — ranching, distilling whiskey, making barrels, glass, pottery, even smuggling. Nothing had worked. Now he had staked everything on California gold.

DETERMINED TO HAVE MY SHARE

In April of 1849, some 30,000 Americans started for the goldfields by land. Among them was William Swain, a twenty-seven-year-old farmer's son from Youngstown, New York, and a graduate of Lewiston Academy. His wife, Sabrina, was against it. She did not know if she and her infant daughter, Eliza, could bear to be apart from him so long. His widowed mother refused to intercede — it was his decision, she said, his alone — and his older brother, George, was for his going. If pickings were as easy as the newspapers said they were, George would go west, too, the following spring.

Swain carried with him a guidebook to the Overland Trail, a Bible, and a diary.

April 11, 1849. All my things being ready last night, I rose early and commenced packing my trunk, preparatory to leaving home on my long journey, leaving for the first time my home and my dear friends with the prospect of absence from them for many months and perhaps for years. . . .

I had fortified my mind by previous reflection to suppress my emotions, as is my custom in all cases where emotion is expected. But this morning I learned by experience that I am not master of my feelings in all cases. I parted from my family completely unable to restrain my emotions and left them all bathed in tears, even my brother, whose energy of mind I never saw fail before.

The next day, as Swain and his friends boarded a lake steamer from Buffalo for Detroit, his wife began her first letter to him:

Dear, dear William,

I want very much to describe my feelings as near as I can, but in doing so I hope not to crucify yours. I feel as though I was alone in the world. The night you left home I did not, nor could not, close my eyes to sleep. Sis [their daughter] slept very well, awoke in the morning, and looked over at me seeming to welcome a spree with her father, but to her disappointment the looked for one was absent. She appears very lonesome, and seems to miss you very much. . . .

I received your daguerrian. . . . I think I never saw anything but life look more natural. I showed it to little Cub, and to my astonishment and pleasure she appeared to recognize it. She put her finger on it, looked up at me and laughed, put her face down on yours, and kissed it several times in succession. Every time it comes in her sight she will cry after it.

William, if I had known that I could not be more reconciled to your absence than I am, I never could have consented to your going. However, I will try to reconcile myself as well as I can, believing God will order all things for the best. . . .

From Detroit, Swain took the train, then a canal boat, and finally river steamers down the Illinois and on to Independence, Missouri, where he and his friends planned to outfit themselves for the journey.

May 6, 1849. We came up from St. Louis with a company of Californians from Marshall, Michigan. They are got up on the joint stock principle and are going with ox teams. On learning that we are going on oxen, they proposed that we should join them by paying $100 each into the fund, furnishing a wagon and thus becoming members of their company, having one equal share in the company, which we have done.

This company was got up last January. We now consist of sixty-three members, Americans, mostly eastern and some western men, but mostly smart and intelligent. There are among them two ministers and two doctors, one of whom is said to be well educated and very successful in his practice. There are also blacksmiths, carpenters, tailors, shoemakers and many other mechanics. They are men of good habits and are governed by the regulations of civilized life. They are not to travel on the Sabbath and are to have preaching on that day.

The members of Swain's company printed "Wolverine Rangers" on their wagons with axle grease. Other emigrants, one remembered, printed slogans — "Wild Yankee," "Rough and Ready," "Live Hoosier," "Never Say Die," and "Have You Seen the

William and Sabrina Swain (left) in daguerreo-type portraits they carefully had made in the spring of 1849 just before he left for California in case they never saw one another again. On April 12, Swain and his companions boarded the side-wheeler *Arrow* (above) at Buffalo, New York. "At half past two o'clock we took passage for Detroit," he wrote. "The lake is very smooth, — the boat shoots along like an arrow, and as she leaves far in the distance objects familiar to me and bears me on to those that are strange, I feel that she bears me to my destiny."

Elephant?" Those who set out for the California goldfields had a phrase for what they were about to experience: they called it "seeing the elephant." It may have come from an old joke. When an eastern farmer heard a circus was coming, he loaded his farm wagon with produce and hurried to town. On the way, he met the circus parade, led by an elephant. His horses bolted at the strange sight, tipping over the wagon and spilling vegetables all over the road. "I don't give a hang," the farmer said, "for I have seen the elephant."

The long road ahead of them had been charted by the mountain men, by Kit Carson and John Frémont, and by the pioneers who carved out the Oregon and California trails. The first leg — thirty days and 320 miles across the rolling prairie to Fort Kearny — passed through Oto, Potawatomi, and Shawnee lands whose fertile soil did not escape the notice of the onetime farmers on their way to the goldfields. "This land . . . will soon be on the market," one noted. "It is inevitable. . . . Some of these Indians do a little farming, but they will never develop the resources of a great state that might lie directly west of Missouri."

"It is said by alarmists that different tribes intend opposing the emigrants," another traveler wrote. "They might as well oppose the whirlwind." In fact, few Indians were seen. They kept away from the wagon trains, fearing that the cholera raging through them might spread to their camps as well. No one knew it then, but cholera, with its soaring fevers, chronic diarrhea, and ghastly death from dehydration, is spread by contaminated water and by flies attracted to raw sewage and the fouled bedding of the dead and dying. It was rampant all across the United States that year, but so virulent among the men and women who now proudly called themselves forty-niners that more than fifteen hundred of those who set out that spring are thought to have died of it.

It tore through Swain's company, too:

> Sabbath. May 27, 1849. In violation of our principle, we travel today on account of the sickness on the route. The health of our company is improving, and it is thought advisable to keep the company in active operation to keep their minds from getting engaged on cholera. I hope we may not have to break the Sabbath again.

> May 31. I was attacked at noon by dysentery very badly. I . . . got Reverend Hobart to make me a composition tea. . . .

> June 1. Still taking medicine, opium and astringent powders. . . . Today I have thought much of home and of my little girl, who is today one year old.

> June 4. This morning I am very unwell. I am very weak. . . . The mess fixed a good bed for me in the wagon, where I rode all day. . . .

> June 7. I am . . . on the gain, but very weak. . . . My appetite is good but I cannot eat hearty for fear of the consequences.

Swain and his companions reached Fort Kearny on June 13. Some gold-seekers had already had enough and turned around. "They had seen the *tail* of the Elephant," one more determined traveler wrote, "and can't bear to look any farther. Poor, forsaken beings they are." Most pressed on.

On June 20, Swain's company saw its first buffalo:

The whole emigration is wild and frantic with a desire to be pressing forward. . . . Whenever a wagon unluckily gets stuck in the mud in crossing some little rut, the other trains behind make a universal rush to try to pass that wagon and to get ahead of each other. Amid the yelling, popping of whips and cursing, perhaps a wagon wheel is broken, two or three men knocked down in a fight, and twenty guns drawn out of the wagons. All of this occasioned by a delay of perhaps two minutes and a half.

James Evans, 1849

Most gold-seekers who set out overland to California rode in wagons drawn by oxen, like those advertised on the opposite page, but the two men from Michigan above, Charles W. Cox and Walter Brewster, chose to chance it in the handsome conveyance drawn by two teams of horses with which they posed for a daguerreotypist at Battle Creek in March 1849. Both men — and all the horses — would make it through.

About eight o'clock the cry "buffalo" ran along the line. . . . [A] drove of nine . . . [were sighted] coursing along the flat. . . . Every man who could gave them his fire as they passed. . . . Some thirty shots aimed at the head of the first one finally brought him to the ground and [another] was soon dispatched.

All returned to the train loaded with buffalo meat, which we cut into pieces and hung along the sides of our wagons, on the reach, and along the tops of the covers. In such a fix we look like living.

We stopped to noon early and all hands struck a fire and had a fine buffalo steak dinner, which certainly is the sweetest and tenderest meat I have ever eaten.

Before the day was over Swain's companions had slaughtered more than fifty animals, though only three were needed for food. "Such wanton destruction of buffalo, the main dependence of the Indians for food, is certainly reprehensible," one of Swain's company recalled. "But, the desire by the emigrant of engaging once at least in a buffalo chase can scarcely be repressed."

That same afternoon, Swain noted, black clouds swept out of the west:

> The men all clad themselves in India-rubber or oil-cloth . . . all things looked likely for a cooling thunder-storm. But as the clouds advanced, . . . the whole air resounded with a noise resembling a shower of stones falling on a floor of boards. . . . In a moment after the first hail fell, the air was literally *filled* with balls of ice from the size of a *walnut* to that of a *goose egg*, . . . rebounding from whatever they struck. . . . When the storm had subsided sufficiently to permit investigation, it was found that the damage done . . . consisted of . . . one wagon upset, two [wagon] tongues broken, and one wheel smashed, with sundry bruises and gashed heads, black eyes, pounded and swollen backs, shoulders and arms. . . . "No great evil without some good" was our motto, so we filled our pails and kettles with hail and had icewater the rest of the day, a luxury we little expected on this route.

On Independence Day, Swain wrote home again.

> Dear Sabrina,
> I have just left the celebration dinner table, where the company are now drinking toasts to everything and everybody and cheering at no small rate. I enjoy myself better in conversing with you through the medium of the pen. . . . I often think of home and all the dear objects of affection there. . . . I am hearty and well, far more so than when I left home. . . . I am also more fleshy. . . .
>
> Your affectionate husband till death

Fort Laramie was the last stop before the Rockies, and the forty-niners paused there to lighten their loads before they began to climb. Some switched from wagons to mule-back, anxious that there might no longer be grass enough for oxen ahead. Others jettisoned everything they no longer thought they'd need. The trail was lined with boxes, barrels, anvils, cast-iron stoves, sidesaddles, India-rubber boats, rancid slabs of bacon.

Communications: When William Swain wrote to Sabrina from Fort Laramie on July Fourth, he worried that she might never get the letter: "You may or may not have received some of the many letters I have sent you by traders and others, on many of which I have paid a postage of 25 cents." Sabrina had no address for William in California and so had to send her replies to him (above, right) care of "Sutter's Fort on the American River" and hope that they would somehow be passed on to him. Somehow they were.

DESERET

At Salt Lake City, John D. Lee smelled opportunity in the air. He had joined the Church of Jesus Christ of Latter-day Saints during the troubles in Missouri, had followed them to Nauvoo, where he had displayed such devotion that Brigham Young himself had adopted him as his spiritual son, and was still settling his family in the new Zion. The Mormons were planning a celebration for July 24, 1849, marking two years since they had first entered the Salt Lake Valley. But instead of attending it, Lee hitched one of his wagons and set out on the trail — traveling against the tide of forty-niners heading toward California. He was amazed at what he saw.

> . . . [T]he road was so lined with wagons . . . that one would be scarcely ever out of sight of some train. Dust very disagreeable but not to compare with the stench from dead carcasses which lie along the road, having died from fatigue and hunger. Destruction of property along the road was beyond description, consisting of wagons, harness, tools of every description, provisions, clothings, stoves, cooking vessels, powder, lead, & almost everything, etc. that could be mentioned.
>
> Very frequently some 20 or 30 persons would surround [my] wagon and plead for a moment's instructions, some of them with consternation depicted on their countenances, their teams worn out, women & children on foot & some packing their provision[s], trying to reach some point of refuge. The general cry was, "Are you from the Mormon city or valley? Yes. What is the distance? Is there any feed by the way? What will be the chance to get some fresh animals, provisions, vegetables, butter, cheese, &c. & could we winter in the valley? Do pray tell us all you can that will benefit us, for we are in great distress. . . . We will pay you all you ask."
>
> Apples, peaches, coffee, sugar, tea, rice, flour, bacon, &c., was often brought & presented. The writer here observes truly what one of the ancients said that the love of money was the root of all evil. It was the love of it that has caused thousands to leave their pleasant homes & comfortable firesides & thus plunge themselves into unnecessary suffering & distress.

Farther on, Lee met the foreman in charge of a Mormon ferry on the North Platte, hurrying back to Brigham Young with $10,000 his crew had earned from forty-niners desperate to get across the swollen river. Near Devil's Gate, Lee turned around for home himself, picking up discarded items as he traveled.

> [I] found an excellent Premium stove No. 3 worth about $50 dollars. . . . Commenced loading up with powder, lead, cooking utensils, tobacco, nails, sacks, tools, bacon, coffee, sugar, clothing, small irons, some trunks, bootlegs, axes, harness, etc. . . . Surely the Lord is mindful of His people, and they that trust in Him will not be forsaken, neither will their seed be found begging bread.

By the time he returned to Salt Lake City, Lee had been gone a month and had missed the anniversary celebration. But the booty in his wagon was worth more than he could have earned in two years of work.

———————

John D. Lee,
photographed toward the end of his life

Brigham Young had led the Mormons west to get away from the Americans who had persecuted them in Missouri and Illinois, and they had hung on in the Valley of the Great Salt Lake during the terrible winter of 1848–49, shivering in tents and wagons and dugouts, surviving on roots and thistles and soup made from boiling old ox hides. "Glue soup," one family called it.

But if the Mormons were to survive and prosper in their new home, Brigham Young decreed, they could only do so as a disciplined and cooperative society. The church became the government and, as its president and prophet, Young himself became the supreme authority in all matters, temporal and spiritual. "An old woman," wrote one visitor, exaggerating only slightly, "will go to the president to know whether she had better change her cloak for a tippet, or the new calf for a pig."

Young seemed everywhere at once, laying out and overseeing the building of his city, parceling out lands according to each settler's needs — five acres for unmarried men, ten for heads of families — dispatching missionaries to England, France, Denmark, and Sweden in search of new converts, establishing a Perpetual Emigrating Fund to lend them money with which they might pay their passage to Utah, and founding new towns all across the landscape.

But the rush of events now threatened to destroy everything Brigham Young had built. The nominally Mexican lands on which he had initially settled now belonged to the United States. Thousands of Americans were passing through Mormon country on their way to California. Young forbade his people to join them. "We are gathered here not to scatter around and go off to the mines or any other place," he said, "but to build up the Kingdom of God. . . . [Salt Lake] is a good place to make Saints and it is a good place for Saints to live. It is the place the Lord has appointed and we shall stay here until He tells us to go somewhere else. . . . If you Elders of Israel want to go to the gold mines, go and be damned."

Surrounded once again by the enemy he had gone so far to flee, Young petitioned Congress to establish a sprawling new provisional state encompassing all of Utah and Nevada, and stretching from San Diego to South Pass, the Gila River to Oregon. He called it "Deseret," the Book of Mormon's word for the honeybee, a symbol of industry and cooperation. Within its boundaries, he hoped, the Mormons could continue to build their Zion unmolested by outsiders. "If the people of the United States will let us alone for ten years," he said, "we'll ask no odds of them."

STAY AT HOME

Beyond the Platte, William Swain and the other forty-niners endured fifty miles of treeless sagebrush dotted with pools of alkaline water fatal to oxen. Dead animals lay everywhere, filling the air with a hideous stench. Then they started through the mountains.

Swain and his companions were late and they knew it. Snow would soon begin to fall, closing the mountain passes. The men began to follow shortcuts that seemed likely to speed them through to the goldfields: Sublette's Cutoff, Hudspeth's Cutoff. Lassen's Cutoff looked likely, too. The original trail plunged south before it went west, and it passed through the Humboldt Sink, a fearsome desert where travelers were known to have died. But Lassen's Cutoff promised a more direct route, and after the middle of August, most forty-niners chose to take it.

We do not intend to have any trade or commerce with the Gentile world, for so long as we buy of them we are in a degree dependent upon them. . . . I intend to cut every thread of this kind and live free and independent, untrammeled by any of their detestable customs and practices.

Brigham Young

More than a decade after the rush to California set the pattern for the whole West, these wagons carried gold-seekers to new finds in Montana and Idaho.

In looking behind over the road just traveled, . . . or forward over that to be taken, for an indefinite number of miles there seemed to be an unending stream of emigrant trains, whilst in the still farther distance along these lines could be seen great clouds of dust, indicating that yet others of these immense caravans were on the move. It was a sight which, once seen, can never be forgotten; it seemed as if the whole family of man had set its face westward.

William G. Johnston, 1849

Senator Benton and other big men may talk and humbug the country . . . about a railroad to the Pacific, but if you and I live a thousand years we will never see the resemblance even of any such thing. . . . Men who could build a railroad to the moon perhaps could build one over these mountains, but I doubt it . . . and it is said the worst is yet to come. But never mind, Gold lies ahead.

William Wilson

Before and after: Charles E. Mitchell (above) as he left Middletown, Connecticut, for the gold-fields in 1849, and (right) as he looked — richer in experience than in cash — when he got back eight years later

Opposite: The High Sierra

On September 21, the Wolverine Rangers joined the stream of gold-seekers starting down Lassen's Cutoff. It would prove a bad mistake.

The disappointments came fast. Swain's company avoided the Humboldt Sink but they were forced to cross the Black Rock Desert, where both sides of the trail were lined with abandoned wagons and dead oxen. Then the trail itself, which had begun by going west, started leading them farther and farther north, instead. Days stretched into weeks. Ice began to form on the streams. Winter was very close now. Swain and the Rangers voted to throw away "the blacksmith tools and many other articles which we can do without."

On October 11, they started the steep climb to the pass they were sure would finally lead them to the summit of the Sierra Nevada. "Up we ascended," Swain wrote, "slowly but surely, by the toilsome climbing of the teams and by the lifting of the members of the mess at the wheels. Dreadful was the lashing our poor teams received. . . ." When they finally staggered to the summit and looked down, expecting to see spread out before them the comforting green of the Sacramento Valley, they saw only more miles of mountains. A little band of horsemen was waiting for them, sent from Sacramento to provide food and urge the travelers to keep moving as fast as they could. "We should hurry on for our lives," one of the Wolverine Rangers wrote. "[I]t is useless for us to try to get our teams through."

The Rangers agreed to split up into small groups. It would be every man for himself. Some now carried only backpacks. Others still tried to drive their oxen. The roads were made up of almost equal parts mud and boulders. Wagons broke down. Then, on the night of November 1, it began to snow. Oxen and mules collapsed. Then a steady, icy rain soaked the emigrants and flooded the trail. Swain now had no time for writing, but later he would recall his journey's end.

November 6. Morning came and all but nine men, who were selected to stay with the teams, bade farewell to everything but a small pack of clothes and three or four days' rations, which each packed on his back. . . . I carried a change of underclothes, both of flannel and of cotton, two pairs of socks, one coat, one pants, one neck handkerchief, my journal, pocket Bible, pocketbook and a few day's provisions.

We commenced, our way in ten inches of snow. . . . The storm increased as the day advanced. Had manhood in its strength been doomed to surmount these dangers alone human suffering would have been less. But there were the infirm and aged, for even here were gray heads. Many of the emigrants were palsied by that terrible disease scurvy. Here too were females and children of every age. Here might be seen a mother wading through the snow and in her arms an infant child. . . . There might be seen a mother, sister or a wife, winding along the mountain path. . . .

At dawn we arrived at Antelope Creek, eight miles from [Lassen's Ranch, which had become an unofficial receiving station for gold-seekers] and found it not fordable. The sky cleared. We kindled a rousing fire, dried and rested ourselves till noon when [two other men and] myself — with our clothes lashed to our shoulders — forded the stream with setting poles. None of the others would attempt it. It was the hardest job I ever had. When I stepped onto the opposite shore I thought my flesh would drop from by bones as high as the water came to my waist.

We arrived at Lassen's at sundown, tired and worn with toil and exposure.

"There was some talk between us of your coming to this country," Swain wrote to his brother.

For God's sake think not of it. Stay at home. Tell all whom you know that are thinking of coming that they have to sacrifice everything and face danger in all forms, for George, thousands have laid and will lay their bones along the routes to and in this country. Tell all that "death is in the pot" if they attempt to cross the plains and hellish mountains. Say to Playter never to think of the journey; and as for you, STAY AT HOME, for if my health is spared, I can get enough for both of us.

THE DIGGINGS

By then, Swain was already at Long's Bar, the nearest diggings on the Feather River, eager to begin gathering gold at last. "It seemed that every rock had a yellow tinge," a fellow miner recalled, "and even our camp kettle, that I thought the most filthy . . . I had ever seen, now appeared to be gilded. . . . During the night, yellow was the prevailing color in my dreams."

An unidentified miner with the tools of his trade and (opposite) just some of the gold-seekers gathered at one camp, each hoping to strike it rich. "Bought a pick for $6.50, — wood for a handle for .50. Made the handle myself," wrote one man. "Got a second hand wash bowl or pan for $1.00, — the selling price of new tin bowls being from $4 to $7.50. Had not money enough left to buy a shovel. I borrowed one . . . [s]elected a spot on the creek bank . . . filled the bowl once to pan out just for an experiment. I did not expect I had reached any gold, yet I was surprised to find when I 'panned out' at twilight, nearly a dollar's worth of gold in the pan. . . ."

In the diggings: A woman — a great rarity in the goldfields — brings lunch to miners in Auburn Ravine, 1852; an unidentified miner (left) shows off his prize — a nugget big enough to balance on the handle of his shovel — while another (below) has done well enough to buy himself a shirt emblazoned with picks and shovels.

Men at work: "You can scarcely form any conception of what a dirty business this gold digging is and of the mode of life which a miner is compelled to lead," one man wrote home. "We all live more like brutes than humans."

In their frenzy to get at the gold, these men slept packed together in the brush shelter behind them.

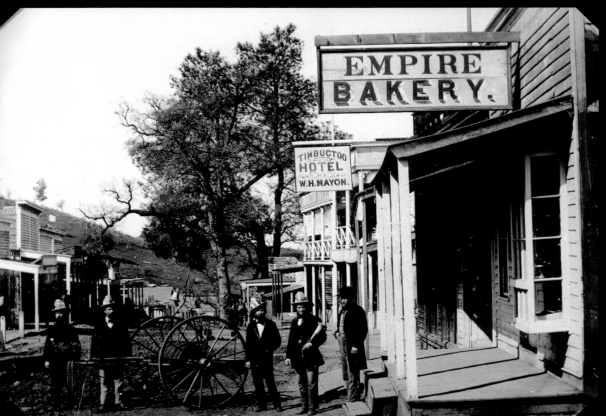

Gold camps were born overnight and sometimes died just as fast: Yuba, the site of A. J. Preston's Livery Stable (above) survived the gold rush to become today's Yuba City, but Timbuctoo, shown here about 1857, burned to the ground the following year.

Orlando Balou of Illinois came west in 1852 and
stayed five years in the goldfields.

The name of the miner above and those of the bearded men
below, who look enough alike to have been brothers, have been
lost, but their determination is unmistakable. "Our object here is
to get rich and stay that way," said one of their fellow forty-niners.

*Not one man in a hundred . . . ever puts a razor to his phiz. The
truth is, something looks wrong to see a white shirt or a shaven
face. . . . With the help of shears to keep the road open to our
mouths and a little trimming to keep our faces a little shipshape,
we are at the top of fashion. Barbers are about as useful here as
would be a penny whistle under the falls of Niagara.*

Henry Page, 1849

An unidentified but obviously contented argonaut, hung with a gold chain perhaps fashioned from ore he'd mined himself.

Mail from home: "Dear Husband. This is only the 25th of August," Sabrina Swain wrote William in 1849. "What a long summer. O!! how I want to see you. Sometimes I almost imagine myself with you, but alas it is only the dream of fancy. . . . O! William, if I could see you this morning, I would hug and kiss you till you would blush."

The Louisiana Hotel in Jackson, California, ca. 1851. The minimally clad woman lounging near the staircase at the right at least suggests that more than board and room may have been available inside.

Charles McNight hurried west in 1849, only to die in the diggings three years later. He was only thirty-five, and his wife begged his mother for this daguerreotype — "it is the only good one that has ever been taken" — so that she could at least remember how he had looked.

Your advice, Father, is in good time, for here a boy is truly in the very gates of destruction, as all kinds of vices hold unlimited sway in the cities and mines. But I hope and trust I shall be able to leave this country as pure and innocent as I came in — and that ain't anything to brag on, is it?

Lucius Fairchild, 1850

*Oh, Matilda, oft is the night when
laying alone on the hard ground with a
blanket under me and one over me that
my thoughts go back to Ohio and I
think of you and wish myself with you.
But I am willing to stand it all to make
enough to get us a home and so I can
be independent of some of the darned
sonabitches that felt themselves above
me because I was poor. Cuss them, I say.
I understand they prophesy that I will
never come back. Darn their stinking
hides. If God spares my life, I will
show them to be false prophets, for as
sure as I live we will shake hands
and give a warm embrace by spring
anyhow, and before if you say so.*

Captain David Dewolf
July 30, 1850

A lone miner fills the time with music, 1851.

But there were already 40,000 miners at work in the goldfields, and the surface gold that had made so many men rich the year before was harder and harder for newcomers like Swain to find.

January 6, 1850. South Fork of Feather River. After prospecting two days, we located a spot favorable for damming and draining the river. We made our claim and then built a house as soon as possible to shelter our heads from the soaking rains. So here we are, snug as schoolmarms, working at our race and dam. Whenever the rain will permit, a fall of the river will enable us to get into the bed of the river and know what is there. If there is no gold, we shall be off to another place, for there is an abundance of gold here, and if we are blessed with health, we are determined to have a share of it.

Some 80,000 men swarmed into California in 1849. More than half of them in their twenties — "a grey beard was almost as rare as a petticoat," one man remembered — and most hurried to one or another of the small, single-street settlements that grew up almost overnight wherever gold was found — Jimtown and Jesus Maria, Coyote Diggings and Grizzly Flats and Mad Mule Gulch, Angels Camp and Murderer's Bar, Whiskey Diggings and Delirium Tremens, Slumgullion, Shirt Tail Canyon, Bedbug, and You Bet.

Gold-seekers were delighted by the weather and dazzled by the landscape — "It's a glorious country," one miner remembered hearing over and over again. But everything cost too much: a dollar a pound for potatoes, eggs at fifty cents apiece; twenty dollars for a bottle of rum; two dollars to the expressman for every letter brought from San Francisco.

Digging for gold was hard, monotonous — and mostly unrewarding. It combined, one miner said, "the various arts of canal-digging, ditching, laying stone walls, ploughing and hoeing potatoes. . . ."

Roughly two-thirds of the forty-niners came from the United States and two-thirds of *them* were from New England. They included whites, free blacks, African-American slaves, and Indians. The rest, one wrote, "came from every hole and corner in the world." So many Mexican miners and their families were trooping into the southernmost goldfields, an American officer noted, that it seemed as if "the whole state of Sonora is on the move, passing us in gangs daily." Some 30,000 Frenchmen made it to California. There were Germans, Irishmen, Russians, Italians, West Indians, ex-convicts from Aus-

This stretch of a California stream was worked by a mixed crew that included two men who may have been either black or Indian and — possibly — a woman (center), whose name, "Mary Mc . . . ," is scratched into the back of the plate. The card that gleams in the right foreground advertises the daguerreotypist, "Sterrett & Company."

Opposite: Three panels from a wry broadsheet titled "The Miner's Ten Commandments," popular among the forty-niners. Top to bottom: The elephant, which every miner who made it through to California could claim he'd seen; just one of the dangers the men faced in getting there; miners entertain themselves as best they can while dreaming of womenfolk back home.

tralia. California now had more immigrants than any other part of the United States. Nine out of ten of them were men.

One of the first foreign gold-seekers to head for Sutter's Mill had been a young man from Canton named Chun Ming. He struck it rich and wrote home to say so. Soon young Chinese were setting sail for the land they called "Gold Mountain": 323 in 1849, 450 in 1850. In 1852, 20,000 came, 2,000 of them in a single day, striding ashore "bearing long bamboo poles across their shoulders," a newspaperman noted, and "wearing new cotton blouses and baggy breeches . . . slippers or shoes with heavy wooden soles [and] broad-brimmed hats of split bamboo."

The Chinese were mostly farmers from Guangdong Province and deeply in debt to Chinese credit merchants from whom they had borrowed their passage. They were tough, disciplined, and far more accustomed to backbreaking toil than most of their American counterparts. Working from dawn to dusk in bands of fifty or more, they often managed to sift gold from sites American miners had abandoned as played out.

Others never made it to the diggings, preferring to make money in San Francisco and Sacramento, instead. "The best eating houses in San Francisco are those kept by Celestials and conducted Chinese fashion," one miner recalled. "The dishes are mostly curries, hashes and fricassees served up in small dishes and as they are exceedingly palatable I was not curious enough to enquire as to the ingredients."

A man named Wah Lee opened the first large hand-laundry at the corner of Washington and Grant in 1851. There were few laundresses in the gold camps and the wealthiest San Franciscans were said to be sending their best shirts all the way to Hong Kong and Honolulu to have them washed and ironed for rates that ran as high as twelve dollars a dozen. Wah Lee charged just five — and made himself a rich man.

Chinese and American
miners at work

THE CIVILIZING AND DOMINANT RACE

Gold rush Californians were a "percussion people," one of them wrote, "living in a percussive country." They were impatient, energetic, eager to grow. With their rich gold deposits and an "instant" population of 90,000 American citizens, they demanded immediate statehood. A convention at Monterey drew up a proposed state constitution that prohibited slavery, not because most forty-niners were sympathetic to African-Americans, but because they did not want to compete with slaves in the diggings. Blacks in California would be forbidden to vote, serve on juries, and attend school with white children, just as they were in many northern states back East. Also included in the constitution was the nation's first provision for married women to own property — both because that was the Mexican tradition and because, it was argued, it might attract prosperous prospective wives to California.

But Congress itself was split over the question of slavery, and California's statehood threatened that balance. Congress had once hoped that the issue of slavery's extension had been settled forever by the Missouri Compromise of 1820, which barred slavery in most of the West. But the defeat of Mexico — and the sudden acquisition of so many hundreds of thousands of square miles — had changed everything.

Again, Congress sought to settle the issue through a complex bargain that came to be called the Compromise of 1850. It would not restrict slavery in the new territories of New Mexico and Utah, whose citizens would be allowed to decide the question for themselves in the future, and a new, stringent fugitive slave law allowed southerners to retrieve runaway slaves even from free states. In return, California was admitted to the Union without the usual territorial waiting period.

The American newcomers were not satisfied with statehood alone. "Indians, Spaniards of many provinces, Hawaiians, Japanese, Chinese, Malays, Tartars, and Russians," said the *Annals of California,* "must all give place to the resistless flood of Anglo-Saxons [and] American progress. These peoples need not, and most of them probably cannot, be swept from the face of the earth; but undoubtedly their national characteristics and opposing qualities and customs must be materially modified, and closely assimilated to those of the civilizing and dominant race."

One by one, the Americans saw to it that their rivals were driven out or stripped of their power. "The ill will of the Yankee rabble . . . against sons of other nations was rising," the Chilean Vicente Pérez Rosales remembered. "This mutual bad feeling explains the bloody hostilities and atrocities we witnessed every day in this land of gold and hope." It began in 1850, when American miners pressured the California legislature into enacting a monthly tax of twenty dollars on all miners who were not United States citizens, far more than most could possibly pay. The bill was aimed at Mexicans, and most of them left the goldfields. But many Chileans and Peruvians were driven out, too, and when a group of French miners dared display their flag, they in turn were forced to abandon their claims. "The Yankee regarded every man but an . . . American as an interloper," Rosales wrote, "who had no right to come to California and pick up the gold of 'free and enlightened citizens.'" Despite discriminatory taxes and intimidation, Rosales and his brothers hung on in the goldfields.

Even the Chinese, whom the Americans had once welcomed, came under attack. "The manners and habits of the Chinese are very repugnant to Americans in California," said a San Francisco newspaper. "Of different language, blood, religion, and character, and inferior in most mental and bodily qualities, the Chinaman is looked upon by some as only a little superior to the Negro, and by others as somewhat inferior. . . ." The Chinese kept to themselves, cooked their own kind of food, practiced their own religion, rarely learned English. When they paid the tax and continued to stay on in the goldfields, whites resorted to intimidation to drive them out. They hacked off the Chinese miners' queues, burned down their shacks, beat and flogged and murdered them.

Mexicans, too, felt the Americans' wrath. At Downieville, a Mexican woman — remembered only as Josepha — awoke to find a drunken American in her bedroom. She reached for a

Chinese working abandoned tailings

One of the volunteer fire companies that tried — without much success — to keep San Francisco safe: large sections of it burned down several times. "You have heard of our fires," a local lawyer wrote. "They throw light on our character. We burn down a city in a night and build it in a day. Contracts for new buildings are signed by the light of the fire that is consuming the old."

A resident surveys the San Francisco waterfront in the early 1850s. In the fall of 1849 San Francisco had had just over 2,000 citizens. Barely one year later, it was home to nearly 35,000 — including about 2,000 women — and had become the West's first full-fledged city. It would soon have a dozen daily newspapers, 15 fire companies, 16 hotels, 20 bathhouses, 3 hospitals, 18 churches, and an orphanage. There were also 537 drinking establishments, including 48 brothels and 46 gambling dens. Everything was brought in by sea at first — whiskey, shovels, lumber carried all the way from the forests of Maine, prefabricated houses ready to be banged together, even a cargo of cats, ferried in to take on the rats that ruled the waterfront.

knife and stabbed him to death. A mob immediately seized her and, when she failed to express regret for what she had done, watched as she was hanged. "Had this woman been an American instead of a Mexican," one newspaper wrote, "instead of being hung for the deed, she would have been lauded for it. It was not her guilt which condemned this unfortunate woman, but her Mexican blood."

A few displaced Mexican miners took to the hills, returning just long enough to raid the goldfields and ride away again. Somehow, these raiders became fused in the American mind into one daring — and perhaps mythical — bandit named Joaquin Murietta. The governor offered a thousand-dollar reward for Murietta's head, and the legislature outfitted an armed posse of twenty men to hunt him down. They hunted somebody down, cut off his head, pickled it in whiskey, and took it on a tour of the gold camps.

The Treaty of Guadalupe Hidalgo had pledged the United States to honor the land grants awarded by Spain and Mexico, but the titles of the *Californios* were often challenged in court and sometimes simply ignored by avaricious newcomers. They lie "prostrate before the conqueror," one wrote,

> and ask for the protection of the few possessions which remain to them in the bad luck to which they [have] fallen. . . . They are unfamiliar with the prevalent language now spoken in their country. . . . I have seen old men of sixty and seventy years of age weeping because they have been cast out of their ancestral home. They have been humiliated and insulted. They have been refused the privilege of cutting their own firewood. . . .

No *Californio* had been more accommodating to the Americans than Mariano Guadalupe Vallejo. The descendant of Spanish soldiers who had conquered Mexico and colonized California, he had built himself a vast empire on Indian labor, and had welcomed the first American settlers in his homeland, provided hospitality to the first gold-seekers, even served in the first state senate. But his new allies soon abandoned him, nonetheless: lawsuits and an invasion of squatters eventually reduced his sprawling estate from a quarter of a million acres to fewer than three hundred.

> Australia sent us a swarm of bandits [he wrote] who . . . dedicated themselves exclusively to robbery and assault. . . . France, desiring to be rid of several thousand lying men and corrupt women [sent them] to San Francisco. . . . China poured upon our shores clouds and more clouds of Asiatics . . . [who are] very harmful to the moral and material development of the country. . . . But all these evils became negligible with the swollen torrents of shysters who came from Missouri and other states of the Union. . . . These legal thieves, clothed in the robes of the law, took from us our lands and our houses, and without the least scruple enthroned themselves in our homes like so many powerful kings. For them existed no law but their own will and caprice that recognized its right by that of force.

Like other *Californios,* Vallejo was now viewed as an alien in his own land. He remained a realist: "He who calls the bull," he said, "must endure the horn wound."

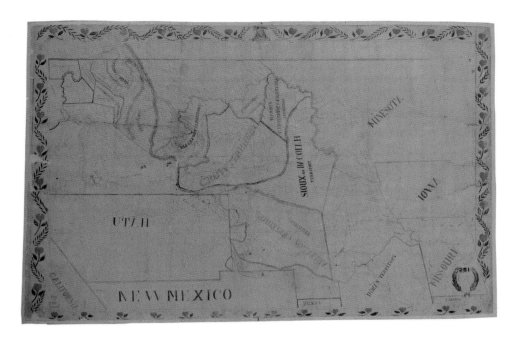

Since the white man has made a road across our land and killed off our game, we are hungry, and there is nothing for us to eat. Our women and children cry for food, and we have no food to give them.

Chief Washakie, Shoshone

Father Pierre-Jean De Smet, a Belgian-born Catholic missionary who accompanied Assiniboin, Arikara, Crow, and Hidatsa delegations to the great convocation of Indians held at Fort Laramie in 1851, drew this map to help work out a tidy division of the Plains among the tribes. What he remembered most about the talks, however, was not the negotiations but the ceremonial feasting, which, he said, brought about "the greatest massacre of the canine race" in history.

THIS GROUND DOES NOT BELONG TO YOU NOW

The permanence of the "Permanent Indian Frontier" had not lasted long, as the lines of wagons headed for California and Oregon cut broad rutted trails through tribal lands. Some Indian peoples made a good thing of the invasion, at least at first. They acted as guides, sold the gold-seekers horses, mules, and firewood. The Sac and Fox collected fifty cents for every wagon that passed through their land, and the Pawnee did the same for every wagon that traveled over their bridge across the Shell River.

But the gold rush proved a disaster for many peoples of the Plains. The Pawnee's crops were devoured by the emigrants' livestock, and when they went off to hunt buffalo they found that the herds along the main trail had been scared off. Some Pawnee starved to death on the way back to their villages. The Lakota, who had only recently driven the Pawnee from the fork of the Platte, were growing increasingly angry to see the whites cutting down the groves of trees beneath which they liked to shelter in summer; their oxen and horses and mules devouring the grass; their hunters shooting buffalo, taking only the best meat and leaving the rest to rot in the sun.

White diseases took a fierce toll, too. A party of Cheyenne came upon an encampment of forty-niners, several of whom were clearly dying from cholera. They rode away as fast as they could, but several had contracted the disease and died before they reached their villages. They called the sickness the Big Cramps. Several bands gathered for the sun dance on Smoky Hill River in Kansas in the summer of 1849 — Cheyenne, Arapaho, Comanche, Kiowa, Osage, prairie Apache. On the last day of the ceremonies, a Kiowa sun dancer suddenly collapsed and died. Then an Osage fell to the ground. The Cheyenne fled for the Cimarron River but it was too late. Scores died. A celebrated warrior named Little Old Man tried to make war upon the sickness. He put on his scalp shirt and sacred war bonnet, decorated his horse, and rode through the camp shouting, "If I could see this thing, if I knew where it was, I would go there and kill it!" Then the sickness found him; the first cramps hit him as he got down from his horse, and he was dead before nightfall.

Fearing that growing Indian resentment of the emigrants might burst out into open warfare against them, and that intensified conflicts between the tribes over ever-scarcer resources might engulf the wagon trains, the Department of Indian Affairs had begun to talk of dividing up Indian lands into small, well-defined tribal "colonies" or "territories" — the term "reservations" would come later — where they would be safe from whites and where they could be slowly but steadily persuaded to abandon their ways of life in favor of farming and Christianity. "There should be assigned to each tribe, for a permanent home," said the commissioner of Indian affairs in 1850,

> a country adapted to agriculture, of limited extent and well-defined boundaries; within which all, with occasional exceptions, should be compelled constantly to remain. . . . In the meantime, the government should cause them to be supplied with stock, agricultural implements, and useful material for clothing, encourage and assist them in the erection of comfortable dwellings, and secure to them the means and facilities of education, intellectual, moral and religious.

The first step on the Plains was to persuade Indian peoples — accustomed to a life of nomadism, whose culture was built on the display of courage in combat — that they should forthwith end their wanderings and give up warfare.

The U.S. Indian agent for the Upper Platte and Arkansas Agency was the former mountain man Tom "Broken Hand" Fitzpatrick. He knew and liked Indians and privately thought the effort to pen them up doomed; they did not fully understand what was really being proposed, he complained; and there was no way to get them to comply without the presence of an armed force far larger than any Congress was likely to send west. But he nonetheless summoned as many bands as would come to Fort Laramie on the North Platte in September of 1851.

They camped together in a grassy valley near the fort under the wary eyes of just 270 nervous soldiers — more than 10,000 Lakota, Cheyenne, Arapaho, Crow, Gros Ventre, Blackfeet, Shoshone, and a handful of Assiniboin, Mandan, and Hidatsa, all dressed in their ceremonial finery. (It was one of the largest gatherings in Indian history and would have been still larger had the Pawnee not refused to attend because they were afraid the Lakota would kill them all. The Comanche and Kiowa also stayed away; they had too many horses, one chief said, to risk "among such notorious horse thieves as the Sioux and Crows.")

The government gave those who attended a mountain of gifts and the promise of a total of $50,000 worth of supplies every year for fifty years, plus the promise of swift punishment for any white who trespassed on Indian land. In return, the Indians were to promise not to harass the wagons and grant the government the right to build forts (something it had already begun to do in any case). And each people must agree to stay within the territory assigned to it and stop warring against its neighbors. With the help of a crude map sketched by Jim Bridger, Fitzpatrick explained how the Plains were to be divided up.

A great issue of government presents was made to the Cheyennes. . . . We were given beef, but we did not care for this kind of meat. Great piles of bacon were stacked up on the prairie and distributed to us, but we used it only to make fires or to grease robes for tanning. . . . We liked the sugar presented to us. They gave us plenty of it, some of it light brown and some dark brown.

Iron Teeth

The Lakota seem to have understood more fully than most what was being asked of them, and they would have none of it. They, like the Americans, were a restless, aggressive people who had spilled onto other peoples' lands, taken them over, and then saw no reason to give them up. "You have split my land and I don't like it," a Lakota leader named Black Hawk told the government negotiators when he first saw Bridger's map. "These lands once belonged to the Kiowas and the Crows, but we whipped these nations out of them, and in this we did what the white men do when they want the lands of the Indians." Faced with Lakota intransigence, the Americans backed down. The Lakota were allowed to hunt south of the Platte and were given rights to sole occupancy of the rolling country between the Bighorn Mountains and the Black Hills, until recently the home of the Crow, which the Lakota had come to see as their most sacred ground.

To conclude the treaty, each tribe was asked to name a head chief who could sign for his people. None of them acknowledged a single leader, so the Americans picked chiefs for them. A Brulé warrior named Conquering Bear was chosen to represent the Lakota.

For two years the treaty with his people held. Then, in August of 1854, the Brulé came to Fort Laramie to collect their supplies and a calf strayed from a Mormon wagon train and wandered into their camp. A warrior shot it with an arrow. Its owner complained to the commander. Conquering Bear apologized and promised to pay the owner more than the animal was worth. The army brushed him aside and a young lieutenant named John L. Grattan, with twenty-nine soldiers and two howitzers, marched off to the Lakota camp to arrest the man who had shot the calf.

The warrior resisted. Forty-five anxious minutes went by. Finally, Grattan panicked and ordered his men to open fire. Conquering Bear was the first to fall. The outraged Lakota turned on the soldiers. Only one managed to crawl back to Fort Laramie before he died. Jefferson Davis, the secretary of war, declared the tragedy "the result of a deliberately formed plan" and ordered the army to exact revenge. Troops under General William S. Harney attacked the band that Conquering Bear had led at Blue Water Creek, killing eighty-six and carrying off seventy women and children. Half a century of peace between the Lakota and the Americans had come to an end; nothing between them would ever be the same again.

THE WOLF AND THE LAMB

"The Natives of these mountains," wrote William Swain from California,

> are wild, live in small huts made of brush and go naked as when they are born. They are small in stature, and . . . when they visit the camps of the miners, they evince the most timid and friendly nature. The miners . . . are sometimes guilty of the most brutal acts [against them], such as killing squaws and papooses. Such incidents have fallen under my notice that would make humanity weep and men disown their race.

Exploitation was nothing new for the Indian peoples of California. The Spanish had forced the coastal tribes to labor at their missions, and the *Californios* had used them as servants on their ranchos. But the Indians of the interior had never seen any-

By the time these photographs were made near San Bernardino in southern California by the photographer for a government survey in 1863, the once-plentiful Indians of the region had been reduced to a handful of scattered bands dependent on whites for their survival.

thing like this sudden onslaught of whites. They "formerly subsisted on game, fish, acorns, etc.," an Indian agent wrote,

but it is now impossible for them to make a living by hunting or fishing, for nearly all the game has been driven from the mining region or has been killed by the thousands of our people who now occupy the once quiet home of these children of the forest. . . . The rivers of tributaries of the Sacramento formerly were clear as crystal and abounded with the finest salmon. . . . But the miners have turned the streams from their beds and conveyed the water to the dry diggings and after being used it is so thick with mud that it will scarcely run.

Desperate for food, Indians began raiding the diggings, stealing horses and cattle, and angering the miners, who retaliated in a variety of ways. Slavery had officially been outlawed by California's constitution, but California law now made it legal to declare any jobless Indian a vagrant, then auction off his or her services for up to four months. And it permitted whites to force Indian children to work for them, provided the permission of a parent or a "friend" was obtained first. Enterprising whites hunted down adult Indians in the mountains, kidnapped their children, and sold them as "apprentices." "Indians seven or eight years old are worth $100," one Californian noted. "It is a damn poor Indian that's not worth $50."

"If ever an Indian was fully and honestly paid for his labor," another settler remembered, "it was not my luck to hear of it." Indians could not complain in court because by another California statute "no Indian or black or mulatto person" was "permitted to give evidence in favor of or against a white person." When the federal government negotiated treaties that would have provided sanctuary for eighteen tribes, California's congressional delegation blocked their ratification in the Senate. There was no longer room in California for the first Californians.

Thousands of Indians died from diseases the white man had inadvertently introduced among them, but thousands more were killed deliberately. A group of men from Cottonwood who called themselves the Squaw Hunters spent their weekends assaulting Indian women — and killing any men who objected. The towns of Marysville and Honey Lake paid bounties for Indian scalps. Shasta City offered five dollars for every Indian head brought to city hall.

"The Indians . . . had been living at a place called Roff's Ranch," a reporter wrote after covering an incident in the Pitt River valley in January of 1860. "There the 'bold' volunteers crept on them before day, . . . [and] killed about nine men, the balance escaping. The women and children remained, trusting [that an American] would not murder women and children. In this they were mistaken. . . . [T]hey searched around among the haystacks with the hatchet and split the children's heads open. In this way there were over forty women and children butchered. . . ."

Before the forty-niners came there were some 150,000 Indians in California. By 1870, there would be fewer than 30,000. It was the worst slaughter of Indian people in United States history.

On the night of 19th February 1857 two men (one named Lewis, commonly called "Squire" and the other Lawson, generally known as "Texas") came to an Indian ranch about a mile above this camp. . . . They commenced abusing the Indian squaws, and one squaw, while endeavoring to protect her daughter, was stabbed by Lewis very severely in the back and shoulder, who also stabbed the father of the girl twice in the arm. They then seized two other squaws whom they forced to remain with them all night. . . . [Later,] Lewis seized a club and without provocation, attacked and brutally beat an Indian boy named Tom, so that it is doubtful he will recover. I immediately stationed a guard to protect the Indians from future outrage. The man Lawson was subsequently shot by Captain Young, and Lewis has been bound over for trial. . . . He is, I believe, the first white man who has ever been arrested for anything of this kind in this neighborhood, though his offense, compared with others that have taken place on this river is a mere trivial matter. . . .

C. H. Rundell, Lieutenant 4th Infantry
Klamath, California

BE FAITHFUL AND TRUE

The Mormons had asked for immediate statehood for the vast territory they called Deseret because they thought it the best way to ensure that they would be left alone. They were confident, in fact, that if they waited long enough the American government itself would be destroyed, since it had failed to prevent the martyrdom of Joseph Smith. "God Almighty will give the United States a pill that will puke them to death," said Brigham Young. "I am prophet enough to prophesy the downfall of the government that has driven us out.... Woe to the United States! ... I see them greedy after death and destruction."

But Congress was not inclined to grant statehood to an empire so distant and so huge, ruled by a leader whose religion — and loyalty — many of its members questioned. Instead, it reduced the size of Deseret by more than three-quarters, changed its name to Utah — after the Ute Indians — and assigned it the lesser status of territory. Brigham Young was bitterly disappointed, though President Millard Fillmore named him territorial governor and superintendent of Indian affairs.

His policy toward the Goshute, Ute, Paiute, Shoshone, and other native peoples of his region was mixed. When they resisted giving up lands for Mormon settlements he ordered in the Nauvoo Legion to crush them, and he later tried to persuade Congress to remove all Indians from the territory. But Joseph Smith had taught that the Indians were "Lamanites," a lost tribe of Israelites ripe for conversion, and so Young also sent missionaries among them and urged his people to be forbearing when Indians raided their livestock: "The loss of a few cattle does not justify a retaliation sufficient

Gathering in the Saints: Mormons break ground for their new temple at Salt Lake City, April 6, 1853.

Opposite, top: Brigham Young with Margaret Pierce, one of five women he married in 1846 and the eleventh to bear him a child

Opposite, bottom: an 1897 parade through the streets of Salt Lake City by survivors of the handcart brigades who walked all the way to Utah to people the Mormon kingdom

for White men to kill the offenders." Such orders were eminently practical: "It's cheaper to feed 'em than fight 'em," Young said. And he hoped that if the Americans — the "Mericats," the Paiute called them — ever assaulted his desert stronghold, he could count on them to help him resist.

With a population of 10,000, Salt Lake City was now the second-largest city west of Missouri — eclipsed only by gold-rush San Francisco — and the nearby canyons of the Wasatch Range were stripped of trees because of the growing city's insatiable demand for lumber, fence posts, and firewood. At the city's center, ground was broken in 1853 for a new Mormon temple. Young wanted it built for the ages — far grander than the temple sacked by the gentile mobs in Nauvoo — with footings sixteen feet wide and eight feet deep, and walls eight feet thick.

The Mormons were proud of their growing prosperity. But in the West, as in the East, many gentiles resented it. The emigrants who passed through Utah complained of the high prices the Saints charged them for supplies. Non-Mormons who sought to settle complained of being frozen out by their Mormon neighbors. And there was growing opposition back East to the Mormons' doctrine of plural marriage. Joseph Smith had secretly preached polygamy since 1831, and revelations about his practice of it had helped bring about his murder at Nauvoo, but at Salt Lake City in 1852, Brigham Young publicly announced it as an integral part of Mormon doctrine. Young himself had 27 wives — he was eventually "sealed" to some 50 more women, to whom he expected to be joined in Heaven — and he had 56 children. His chief lieutenant, Heber Kimball — known as America's "most-married" man — had 43 wives, including five sets of sisters, 20 daughters, and 45 sons (16 of whom were named Heber, for their father). They lived in a dozen different households — "twelve teapots," he called them, "each holding different quantities of good tea, yet differing in form."

Despite the example set by some Mormon leaders, four out of five married Mormon men remained monogamous, and even most polygamists had no more than two wives. Still, the practice turned many Americans against them. Polygamy and slavery, reformers charged, were equally wicked; both needed to be expunged from American soil.

By 1855, so many Mormons had been helped to travel from the States and Europe to Utah that the Perpetual Emigrating Fund had run dangerously low. Brigham Young was undaunted: "Let them come on foot with handcarts or wheelbarrows," he said, "let them gird up their loins and walk through and nothing shall hinder them."

The Mormons took him literally at his word. In the spring of 1856, thirteen hundred Britons — Welsh coal miners, Scottish crofters, paupers from big English cities — volunteered to sail to America, take the train to Iowa City, and then simply start walking westward to Salt Lake City, nearly fourteen hundred miles away. "The fire of emigration blazes throughout the Pastorate," one British observer noted, "to such an extent that the folks are willing to part with all their effects, and toddle off with a few things in a pocket handkerchief."

They were an unlikely band of pioneers; most were either very young or past middle age, city dwellers, ill-prepared for carving a new life in the outdoors: bookbinders, bakers, butchers, dollmakers, even an expert in the rigging of sailboats.

The first three companies made it through to Salt Lake City, but two other companies — four hundred men, women, and children, from England, Scotland, Germany, and Scandinavia — started late and half of them didn't make it at all. Brigham Young wept when he saw the condition of the survivors, but he blamed others for what had befallen them — and then called for more handcart companies — seven in all, by 1860. Nothing was to slow the peopling of his Zion, for he knew he would need all the followers he could get for the struggle that seemed about to begin.

Pressure was building back East to remove him from the governorship. In 1855, three new federal judges were appointed for the Utah Territory. Two were apostate Mormons, eager to wreak vengeance on those who had remained true to their former faith. The third, W. W. Drummond, was a political appointee so enamored of his mistress that he liked to have her sit next to him as he presided from the bench. Young ordered his followers simply to ignore Drummond's presence and continue to bring their cases before the county probate courts — controlled by the church — just as they always had. "We have got a territorial government," he said, "and I am and will be Governor, and no power can hinder it, until the Lord Almighty says, 'Brigham, you need not be Governor any longer,' and then I am willing to yield to another Governor."

THE DAYS OF '49

Everything had gone wrong for William Swain in California. He'd spent the whole cold, rainy winter of 1849–50 in a claustrophobic cabin on the Feather River. In the spring, he and his partners moved to Foster's Bar on the Yuba River, only to be kept from panning by a heavy spring snowmelt that turned the clear stream into a roaring brown river. "Five months' rain," he wrote, "four months' high water, and three months . . . almost too hot to work."

The miners shown at work here may have come to California hoping to strike it rich on their own, but they ended up working for a weekly paycheck, pushing wheelbarrows of sand up to water-powered trommels (screen drums) that sifted out the gold and dropped it into flumes waiting below.

In the end, it was men like these unidentified San Francisco investors who reaped most of the profits from California's streams and gulches; only they had the kind of money needed to pay for the large-scale machinery needed to extract ore once the surface gold was gone.

Day after day without success taxed him. But so did his fear of returning home a failure, and when his brother, George, wrote to ask how he was doing, it was hard for him to admit the truth for fear that those back home would think ill of him: "My specific answer to your kind question is that my expectations are not realized. We have been unlucky — or rather, by being inexperienced, we selected a poor spot for a location and staked all on it, and it has proved worth nothing. . . . I mostly regret the necessity of staying here longer."

His brother proved understanding:

Dear William,

. . . Keep your courage up. If you fail there, you are not to blame. You have tried your best to do well, and if you can't do it there, you are better off than many who have gone there with their all and left nothing behind to fall back on. You have something, and friends who will meet you just as cordially unsuccessful as successful. . . . To tell the plain truth, I wish most sincerely you were out of that (if you are alive) and at home, no matter if you haven't got a single mill.

By November of 1850, Swain had been away from home for more than eighteen months. Then, reassured by his brother's letter, he headed for San Francisco. He had just five hundred dollars to show for all his hard work, and by the time he'd paid for his passage home by sea, he had no more cash in his pockets than he'd had when he left Youngstown. "I have got enough of California," he wrote his wife just before boarding his ship, "and am coming home as fast as I can."

By 1852, the surface gold in California was all but gone. Most of what gold remained could no longer be retrieved by a single miner with pick or shovel or pan, no matter how hard he worked. It lay at the bottom of rivers, in veins of quartz that could only be reached by deep shafts, or hidden in hillsides from which it had to be blasted by powerful streams of water.

Big machinery required big money. California's goldfields were soon controlled by investors with headquarters in San Francisco, and worked by miners who labored for a weekly paycheck. Meanwhile, discouraged forty-niners began to head home, some pausing to pan for gold in areas they had bypassed in their hurry to California. They made their biggest strike in the Colorado Rockies, and nearly 100,000 hopeful prospectors, many in wagons painted with the slogan "Pike's Peak or Bust," swarmed in. They founded Denver and soon organized the territory of Colorado, with 35,000 citizens. By treaty, it was Cheyenne land, but with only 4,000 people, the Cheyenne could do little to stop the invasion. There were strikes in other parts of the West, as well: in Montana, Oregon, New Mexico, Arizona, Nevada. And following a pattern set in California that would be repeated again and again all over the West, wherever gold was discovered, Indian peoples suddenly found themselves outnumbered in their own land.

John Bidwell, who had helped lead the American emigrants to California back in 1841, struck it rich in the goldfields and got out fast, then used his fortune to buy himself a 20,000-acre plantation he called Rancho Chico on which he raised every-

And now, my dear, allow me to ask, are your most sanguine expectations realized or at least being so? Or do you find things very much exaggerated? Would you advise anyone to go to California? There are many anxious to hear from you and learn the prospects. . . .

Sabrina Swain

thing from cattle and sheep and hogs to figs and grapes — which he insisted be made
into raisins since he did not approve of wine.

The Chilean gold-seeker Vicente Pérez Rosales and his three brothers stubbornly
stayed on in California, despite the hostility of the Americans, until one of San Francisco's frequent fires finally burned them out. "Two and a half months later," Rosales
wrote, "we were [back] in peaceful Chile, tenderly embracing our mother, poor as
ever, but satisfied that we had not abandoned the fort before the last shot was fired."

The gold rush proved a disaster for John Sutter. Squatters arrived on his land and
refused to move. He lost town sites he'd owned in Sacramento. Creditors dogged him.
"Stealing began," he wrote. "Land, cattle, horses, everything began to disappear. There
is a saying that men will steal everything but a milestone and a millstone. They stole
my millstones." He turned over what was left of his fortune to his son, John Jr., who
promptly lost most of it. He began to drink heavily. Sutter's Fort had once been the
gateway to California; now no one bothered to stop there. A meatpacking company
made a fortune rustling his cattle and he seemed powerless to stop them. Finally,
someone burned his house down. He haunted Congress for years before he died,
seeking compensation he said he was owed for having come to the aid of so many
American emigrants and for having once owned the land on which gold was found.

William Swain had found no gold in California and had gone home and resumed
farming, as if he'd never even been away. He and his wife, Sabrina, had three more
children, and in partnership with his brother, George, Swain eventually became the
biggest peach grower in Niagara County, New York. But in the evenings on his farm,
when the work was done, he never tired of telling his wife and children about the great
adventures he had had crossing the country when it, and he, had both been young.

MYTH AND MYOPIA:
HISPANIC PEOPLES AND WESTERN HISTORY

DAVID G. GUTIÉRREZ

When my paternal great-grandparents Antonio Gutiérrez and Lola Gallardo Camucci met and began courting in Los Angeles in the early years of this century, they probably had little sense of themselves as actors in a sweeping historical drama. Indeed, in many ways, they were just doing what came naturally. Like so many immigrants from Mexico, Antonio had come to the United States from his home in Yucatán to work on one of the West's rapidly expanding railroads, and he naturally gravitated to the old Mexican American neighborhood surrounding Los Angeles's central plaza that had been established when the region was still part of the Spanish empire. Drawn by the familiar sounds of Mexican music and Spanish conversation, the welcome aromas of savory Mexican food, and by a network of Mexican American–run mom-and-pop restaurants, stores, and saloons, Antonio entered a world that at least in some ways must have felt similar to the world he had left behind. However many butterflies he may have felt when he met Lola, he must have felt fairly at home in her world in Los Angeles's ethnic Mexican enclave.

It was just as natural for Lola to be attracted to Antonio. After all, unions between Spanish-speaking people from "Old Mexico" and Hispanic inhabitants of Texas, New Mexico, and California had been almost an everyday occurrence ever since Spanish colonists had begun settling the northern frontier in 1598. Although Antonio was more darkly complected than Lola, probably spoke a slightly different variant of Spanish, and most likely grew up following different customs than those familiar to Mexican Californians, it was not at all uncommon or unusual that the two should fall in love and decide to marry. Thus, when my great-grandparents married in 1905 and had their first son, my grandfather, on Valentine's Day, 1906, they were simply repeating a pattern that had helped to sustain a significant and unbroken Hispanic presence in the region over more than three centuries.

While these events must have seemed perfectly natural and normal to Lola and Antonio and to people like them who lived in Los Angeles's expanding Mexican barrios, my great-grandparents began their life together in a social world that was far removed from the experience of most of their Anglo-American neighbors. Indeed, even though Lola's family had lived in southern California for generations, and Antonio was part of an immigrant influx that would soon increase the Mexican population of the Southwest by more than a million people, ethnic Mexicans seemed invisible to most Americans.

On one level, this inability to "see" Mexicans like my great-grandparents can be explained as the more or less logical result of the severe social polarization between ethnic Mexicans and Americans that occurred in the West after the United States annexed Mexico's northern territories in 1848. Over the years, this tendency toward mutual avoidance contributed to the gradual emergence of neighborhoods so segregated along ethnic lines that Mexican Americans and Anglo-Americans rarely came into direct contact with one another. By the turn of the century, the social distance between the two groups had grown so great that many Anglo-Americans had come to believe that Mexicans had simply disappeared. There was, however, much more to this story. Although residential segregation provides at least a partial explanation for the gradual disappearance of Mexicans from the social landscape of the West, the erasure of ethnic Mexicans from American consciousness was part of a longer, more complicated process.

Before the early nineteenth century, Americans had little reason to think about the Spanish-speaking inhabitants of the trans-Mississippi West. Although some harbored vaguely negative opinions about Hispanics — a legacy of British prejudice against Spain, laced with their own distaste for the practice of miscegenation between Spaniards and Indians in Latin America — such attitudes were of little practical consequence. But once American trappers, traders, and travelers began to eye Mexican territory for themselves in the 1820s and 1830s, their casually negative attitudes about Mexicans began to harden into more serious stereotypes that, in turn, helped provide a rationale for territorial expansion.

Among the most influential shapers of public opinion on life on the northern Mexican frontier was Richard Henry Dana, whose *Two Years Before the Mast* (published in 1840) introduced a generation of Americans to life in Mexican California. Although Dana expressed qualified admiration for some aspects of *Californio* society, he ultimately dismissed the Mexican Californians as "thriftless, proud, and very much given to gaming" and therefore utterly unworthy of holding such valuable territory. "In the hands of an *enterprising* people," he mused, "what a country this might be." Other Americans were more brutal in their assessments. After a visit to Taos, New Mexico, in 1846, New Englander Rufus Sage was moved to write that "there are no people on the continent of America, with one or two exceptions, more miserable in condition or despicable in morals than the mongrel race inhabiting New Mexico. . . . Half naked and scantily fed . . . [and] possessed of little moral restraint and interested in nothing but the demands of present want, they abandon themselves to vice, and prey on one another and those around them." After a visit to Mexican California, another traveler from New England, Thomas Jefferson Farnham, voiced similar opinions. "Thus much for the Spanish population of the Californias," he noted,

> in every way a poor apology of European extraction; as a general thing, incapable of reading or writing, and knowing nothing of science or literature, nothing of government but its brutal force, nothing of virtue but the sanction of the Church, nothing of religion but ceremonies of the national ritual. Destitute of industry themselves, they compell the poor Indian to labor for them, affording him a bare savage existence for his toil, upon their plantations and the fields of the Missions. In a word, Californians are an imbecile, pusillanimous, race of men, and unfit to control the destinies of that beautiful country.

Ironically, the pervasiveness of negative attitudes among the few Americans who actually had had direct contact with Mexicans presented expansionists with some nettlesome problems when the debate over possible westward expansion into Mexican lands began to heat up during the 1840s. Given the increasing tension over the potential expansion of slavery into newly acquired territories and Americans' general sensitivity about racial issues, the possible incorporation into U.S. society of large numbers of such seemingly racially and culturally inferior people raised troubling questions. Indeed, once war erupted between the United States and Mexico, public discussion about "what to do" with the region's mixed-blood Spanish-speaking population became a key political issue.

Journalists, politicians, and members of the general public all advanced different theories about what was to become of people who might come with any annexed territory. Some of the more idealistic advocates of continental expansion argued that, with proper training in the principles of republicanism, most Mexicans eventually could be integrated into American society. Others were not so optimistic. Convinced, as another observer suggested, that Mexicans were "scarcely a visible grade, in the scale of intelligence, above the barbarous tribes by whom they are surrounded," many Americans believed that, like Indians, Mexicans either should be removed to reservations or exterminated altogether. Most expansionists, however, simply tried to sidestep the tricky question by predicting vaguely that the indigenous populations of the West would somehow "recede" or "fade away" before the advance of American civilization. New York senator Daniel Dickinson, for example, simply dismissed Mexicans as one part of "the fated aboriginal races, who can neither uphold government [n]or be restrained by it; who flourish only amid the haunts of savage

José Antonio and Grisselda Talamantes Sepulveda, Los Angeles, late nineteenth century

indolence, and perish under, if they do not recede before, the influences of civilization. . . . Like their doomed brethren, who were once spread over the several States of the Union, they are destined by laws above human agency to give way to a stronger race from this continent or another."

Such attitudes played a powerful role in ordering interethnic relations in the West after the Mexican War. Although the United States officially guaranteed by treaty that Mexican nationals who came with the transfer of territory would be granted "all the rights of American citizens" (including suffrage, religious freedom, and protection of their private property), when issues of control over economic resources and political power arose — as they soon did in California, New Mexico, and Texas — it became clear that most American settlers had no intention of observing, much less protecting, Mexicans' personal or property rights. While it is true that pockets of Spanish-speaking people in South Texas, northern New Mexico, and southern California were able to hold their own and maintain some social and political influence for a short period after the war, widespread racial antagonism, the imposition of new legal and taxation systems, the crushing pressure of squatters, and subsequent loss of much of their land combined to push ethnic Mexicans to the margins of society. As a result, by the late 1870s and early 1880s the vast majority of this first generation of Mexican Americans had been divested of their property, politically disfranchised, and socially ostracized and segregated as a racialized minority. As Texan Juan Seguín noted after experiencing the brunt of these processes himself, Mexicans in the West had been reduced to "foreigners in their native land."

Although the specific circumstances of the erosion of Mexican Americans' political and economic position varied from place to place, a pattern soon became distressingly clear. Local elites gradually lost their lands to taxes, lawyers' fees, and squatters, and as their land base dwindled, so did their ability to intercede on behalf of working-class Mexican Americans who had once looked to them for leadership. Events in Nueces County, Texas, provide a good illustration of these processes at work. While in 1835 Mexican landowners held title to fifteen large land grants covering tens of thousands of square acres, by 1859 only one of the original grants remained in Mexican hands.

The more successful Anglo-Americans were in marginalizing Mexican Americans, the more Americans' notions of their own racial and cultural superiority seemed self-evident. In a classic case of circular logic, the conquest and military occupation of the West and the subsequent social, political, and economic subordination of the region's indigenous populations seemed to "prove" to Americans that they were naturally superior to the people they displaced. And, as dispossessed Mexican Americans became more concentrated in segregated urban enclaves or isolated rural settlements, they seemed to disappear from the social landscape of the West. Thus, within twenty-five years of the annexation of the Southwest it seemed that Indians and Mexicans had in fact "melted away" before the advance of a superior civilization, just as the proponents of Manifest Destiny had predicted they would.

Had this been the extent of the social subordination of ethnic Mexicans in the West, the damage done them would have been bad enough. But just as their superior military might and control of economic resources had enabled Americans to consolidate their control over the West, such disparities in power also bestowed upon them the ability to rewrite its history from their own point of view. Freed from the necessity of viewing Mexicans as any kind of military or political threat, westerners began to spin romanticized versions of the not-too-distant history of the region.

The most important catalyst was the publication in 1884 of Helen Hunt Jackson's famous novel *Ramona*. Set in southern California, it told the story of two star-crossed lovers — an Indian named Alessandro and a beautiful Mexican-Indian maiden, Ramona — during the tumultuous transfer of California from Mexico to the United States. Jackson, a prominent champion of Native American rights, spent several months in 1882 and 1883 touring southern California's impoverished Mexican barrios and isolated Indian settlements, then resolved to expose the horrible conditions she had seen in a novel that she hoped would stimulate the sort of concern for Indians and Mexican Americans that Harriet Beecher Stowe's *Uncle Tom's Cabin* had elicited for African-American slaves.

Jackson's historical romance was an overnight success, the most popular American novel of its time, but much to Jackson's chagrin, the public reacted to *Ramona* very differently than she had anticipated. Missing entirely Jackson's implicit calls for reform, readers were transfixed instead by the novel's depictions of a magical, bygone age in which gentle, contented Indians worked a bountiful land under the benevolent supervision of saintly Spanish missionaries and a wise and generous landed gentry.

Many came to accept Ramona's story as the "true history" of "Spanish California" and, by extension, of the Spanish Southwest. Within months of the novel's publication, tourists began turning up in California eager to see "Ramona's country" for themselves. Some westerners at first attacked Jackson for her critical portrayal of the American takeover of the region, but it didn't take long for local entrepreneurs to recognize the commercial possibilities growing out of the craze she had inspired. Within two years of publication an entire cottage industry had sprung up around *Ramona*: railroads and local chambers of commerce promoted elaborate tours, promoters ground out tens of thousands of postcards allegedly depicting "Ramona's birthplace," "Ramona's school," and "the bed in which Ramona slept."

Eventually, promoters all over the Southwest were busily publicizing the region's Hispanic past. There were parades, rodeos, and cultural exhibitions; elaborate historical extravaganzas like the Los Angeles Fiesta, San Gabriel's "Mission Play," "Old Spanish Days" in Santa Barbara, and similar festivals in Santa Fe, Taos, and other towns in the newly named "Land of Enchantment."

The creation of what the writer Carey McWilliams called the "Spanish fantasy heritage" ultimately had a powerful effect on the public's imagination. Virtually overnight, aspects of the Hispanic past that had been portrayed just ten or twenty years earlier as distasteful remnants of a primitive and backward culture were transformed into icons of romantic and nostalgic fascination. The Spanish and Mexican Franciscan missionaries, who had long been painted by American travelers as tyrannical, even sadistic exploiters of Indians, were now re-created in the Anglo imagination as benevolent, patient friars who not only converted the primitive Indians, but as the Los Angeles booster Charles F. Lummis wrote in 1903, "taught them to read and write, to sing, to play musical instruments, to spin, weave, and make clothing, . . . to dwell in houses instead of brush hovels, . . . and otherwise trained them in all the handicrafts necessary for a self-supporting community."

Ruins, too, took on new meanings. "Looked at with the cold eye of one indifferent to material," Gertrude Atherton had written after visiting what was left of California's Mission San Antonio de Padua at mid-century, "it is doubtful if there is any structure on earth colder, barer, uglier, dirtier, less picturesque, less romantic than a California mission; so cheap are they; so tawdry, so indescribably common, so suggestive of mules harbored within, and chattering unshorn priests, and dirty Mexicans, with their unspeakable young." By the early 1890s, the missions had been transmuted into potent positive symbols of both the state of California and the greater "Spanish Southwest" itself, "embodiments," as one contemporary writer put it, "not only of the purposes of their founders, but of the faith which built the great cathedrals of Europe."

And it didn't end there. Organizations like the Association for the Preservation of the Missions sprang up everywhere because, as Charles Lummis wrote, "[the missions] are as a group by far the most imposing, the most important, and the most romantic landmarks in the United States, architecturally and historically." A regional architectural renaissance known as the Mission Revival brought to life in adobe, stucco, and concrete the fantastic images Jackson, Lummis, and subsequent promoters had imagined. Ranging from monumental projects such as the synthetic Romanesque–Spanish Mission design of Stanford University to more utilitarian structures, the Mission Revival style was well on its way to becoming a southwestern cliché by the 1910s; by the 1930s, nearly a million "Spanish-style" homes had been built in California alone. "Who would live in a structure of wood and brick if they could get a palace of mud?" wrote one eastern journalist of buildings modeled more or less after those the pioneers had deprecated as hovels unworthy of civilized people. "The adobes to me [make] the most picturesque and comfortable [homes] . . . and harmonize . . . with the whole nature of the landscape."

While many present-day Americans think of the Mission Revival and the plethora of community celebrations built around romanticized Spanish themes as innocuous examples of "local color" (or more cynically, as harmless cases of good old-fashioned American hucksterism), few stop to consider the effects the Spanish fantasy heritage may have had on the living representatives of that authentic tradition. Over the years, however, Americans of Hispanic Mexican descent have understandably developed a different point of view about such ostensible "celebrations" of their cultural heritage. Although a few members of the surviving Mexican American elite participated in the first of these observances — believing that such distorted recognition was better than no recognition at all — others realized early that the most insidious aspect of the Spanish fantasy heritage was that rather than rehabilitate the image of Mexican Americans who still lived around them, the fantasy helped to obscure them even more. Just as vague notions that Indians and Mexicans were providentially destined to disappear had helped free an earlier generation of Americans from suffering guilt for having expanded into their homelands, the creation of a mythical history between the 1880s and 1920s helped their inheritors to perform the even more remarkable feat of rendering invisible the ethnic Mexicans who actually still lived in the West.

In fact, the Spanish fantasy seems to have worked like a sort of neutron bomb, allowing westerners to celebrate quaint monuments to a past safely cleansed both of the people who had built them and of their living, breathing descendants. As a San Diego *Union* editorial celebrating the opening of the 1915 Panama California Exposition unself-consciously put it,

> [I]n California the weaker was absorbed by the stronger; but with the passing of the weaker they left a legacy of their art and culture, which the survivor has gladly possessed to beautify and decorate his own. They left us their tradition, their romance, and their musical nomenclature. . . . We have received this tradition gladly; we have made this romance the background of our own history.

The facts, of course, were very different. Mexican culture not only survived but grew and flourished during the decades when its practitioners were supposed to have disappeared. Rates of growth varied from place to place, but the Hispanic population expanded throughout the West. In New Mexico, for example, the American takeover actually seems to have stimulated an expansion of Hispano settlement: as local Indians such as the Ute, Navajo, Comanche, and Apache were forced from some of their homelands, Hispanos filled the vacuum. By the early 1870s, Hispano small farmers and ranchers had established a far-flung network of settlements such as San Luis, Madrid, San Miguel, and Trinidad in what is now southern Colorado, as well as similar settlements in the panhandles of Texas and Oklahoma. By 1900, their numbers had nearly tripled to more than 140,000.

In Texas, similar patterns emerged. Although stigmatized and subjected to racial violence to a degree matched nowhere else in the West, the ethnic Mexican population managed to survive and grow, particularly in South Texas, where Mexicans remained a numerical majority until the turn of the century.

In California too, despite the influx of nearly a quarter of a million American, European, Asian, and Latin American gold-seekers that first transformed the resident Mexican population of the new state into a tiny minority and then drove them from the goldfields, they refused to disappear. In fact, natural increase — combined with the little-known but significant migration of at least 15,000 to 20,000 forty-niners from the northern Mexican state of Sonora — actually helped the population of ethnic Mexicans in California to grow from an estimated 10,000 in 1848 to approximately 40,000 by the turn of the century.

Although invisible to most Anglos, the growth of the West's Hispanic population shaped the social, cultural, and political evolution of the region in important ways. Mexicans had to walk a very fine line in their efforts to survive and assert themselves in the midst of the American society that was growing around them, but just as they had learned to survive under the harsh conditions of Mexico's northern frontier over the previous two centuries, they now quietly worked to adapt to life under the Americans. Ironically, in some ways, social isolation and residential segregation worked as a kind of perverse guarantee that Mexicans would continue to follow traditional Mexican cultural practices as central components of their everyday lives. Since most Mexicans had little contact with Anglo-Americans and received little formal schooling, the overwhelming majority naturally continued to speak Spanish as their primary (or only) language throughout the nineteenth century. For similar reasons, local architectural styles utilizing adobe and roughly hewn lumber, popular forms of entertainment, traditional Mexican cuisine, and music, dance, and other forms of expressive culture remained the norm in ethnic Mexican enclaves across the region.

And of course, the majority of Spanish-speaking people in the West continued to practice regional variants of folk Catholicism and a traditional system of godparentage known as *compadrazgo*. Under the system, biological parents choose close friends to "sponsor" their children as *compadres* (godparents) during key Catholic rites of passage such as baptism, confirmation, and marriage. In theory, the godparents are then obligated to see to it that children are cared for in case anything happens to the children's parents. In practice, the system helps people of meager means to pool their resources to provide the food, drink, entertainment, and gifts necessary for the proper celebration of culturally meaningful events. By linking kin and close family friends in intricate networks of mutual obligation and support, Mexican Catholics not only provided an added level of emotional and financial security for their children, but also helped foster community cohesion during a particularly stressful period.

The growth of the Spanish-speaking population in enforced isolation from the mainstream of western American life had other important consequences. Anglo control of politics, ownership of much of the best land, and a virtual monopoly on skilled jobs placed clearly defined upper limits on what Mexicans reasonably could expect to achieve in the nineteenth-century West, but they doggedly filled whatever economic niche they could carve out. In areas where lines of social and economic discrimination were particularly harsh, such as in South Texas, ethnic Mexicans were often forced by circumstance to provide for their own

Feast day at Mission San Juan Capistrano, early twentieth century

needs. Thus, over time, they developed an informal economy, selling goods and services otherwise difficult to acquire: they offered agricultural products grown on their own small plots and prepared foods such as tamales, tacos, and *pan dulces* (sweet baked goods); ran *carnicerías* (butcher shops), *tienditas* (small grocery or dry goods stores), or cantinas in Mexican neighborhoods. Although few made much, ethnic Mexican entrepreneurs nevertheless built a resilient alternative economic and social infrastructure composed of local networks of religious confraternities, mom-and-pop stores, restaurants, saloons, barbershops, boardinghouses, bordellos, Spanish-language newspapers, even informal rotating credit and mutual life insurance companies. In the process, they created a parallel Hispanic society in the West that was largely unnoticed by Anglo-Americans.

Of course, social isolation exacted its costs from the first generation of Mexican Americans and their children. Systematically barred from most of the best-paid and highest-skilled occupations, ethnic Mexicans were slowly but surely forced to take the most arduous and lowest-paid jobs. And having been socially erased from the landscape, Spanish-speaking westerners faced extremely painful challenges when it came to making decisions about their future — and their children's future — in the United States. Although life in urban barrios and rural ranch communities provided them with a relatively safe social space in which to foster cultural cohesion and solidarity, exclusion from the American mainstream also meant that ethnic Mexicans had very few ways to articulate political or legal grievances. Thus, they learned early on that before they could even take the first tentative steps toward regaining a political voice as citizens (or at least as potential citizens) they first had to get other Americans to recognize that they actually existed.

Mexicans tried several different ways to do this. Some took up arms to defend what they perceived to be their basic political and property rights. For example, although Anglo Californians (and some Mexicans) considered the violent depredations of the cattle rustler and stagecoach robber Tiburcio Vásquez in the 1850s and 1860s to be the acts of a simple brigand, Vásquez himself argued that he was engaged in revolutionary resistance to American oppression. Awaiting his execution after being convicted of robbery and murder by a San Jose court in 1874, he insisted that his violent behavior "grew out of the circumstances by which I was surrounded." As Americans had become more numerous in California after the Mexican War, he argued, and began "to shove the native born men aside, a spirit of revenge took possession of me. [After that,] I had numerous fights in defense of my countrymen. The officers were continually in pursuit of me [but] I believed we were unjustly and wrongfully deprived of the social rights that belonged to us."

Others favored more symbolic resistance. One of the most satisfying symbolic forms was the Mexican *corrido,* or folk ballad. Corridos tell all sorts of stories, but after the Mexican-American War, their subject matter shifted dramatically from love and romance to conflict with *norteamericanos.* Sometimes protesting injustice and sometimes reveling in feats of bravery, Mexican balladeers also took great pleasure in poking fun at arrogant *gringos.* For example, in a corrido that first became popular in the late 1860s known as "El Corrido de Kiansis" — The Kansas Corrido — the *corridista* boasts:

Five hundred steers there were,
All big and quick;
Thirty American cowboys
Could not keep them bunched up.

The five Mexicans arrive,
All of them wearing good chaps;
And in less than a quarter hour,
They had the steers penned up.

Other corridos told of outnumbered but courageous Mexicans fighting against all odds to protect their families and preserve their honor. One of the most famous of all corridos, "The Ballad of Gregorio Cortez," commemorates the desperate flight in 1901 of a *Tejano* whose brother had been shot down in cold blood by a local sheriff. Cortez killed the sheriff in self-defense and then eluded a large posse of Texas Rangers over nearly five hundred miles before turning himself in near Laredo.

> They set the bloodhounds on him
> So they could follow his trail,
> But trying to overtake Cortez
> Was like following a star.
>
> He struck out for Gonzales
> Without showing any fear,
> "Follow me, cowardly rangers,
> I am Gregorio Cortez."

Beyond such symbolic statements of protest and pride, however, most ethnic Mexicans in the West generally tried to accommodate themselves to the new order, if for no other reason than that they recognized the superior military and police power of the American interlopers. Concerned primarily with the welfare and future of their American-born children, they tended either to avoid political activity altogether or pursued moderate community-based political goals. Over the long run, their modest political efforts, built upon the internal resources of their communities, proved more effective in gaining recognition and relief than the more dramatic efforts of their compatriots. In southern Arizona's rich copper mining region, for example, mutual aid associations provided ethnic Mexican workers with the institutional framework from which to organize and launch strikes for better wages and working conditions. Similarly, farm and railway workers in California and Texas used mutual aid associations both as strike headquarters and as prototypes for more modern community-based advocacy organizations. These initial labor protests produced few immediate victories, and could not completely alleviate ethnic Mexicans' deep sense of alienation and political and cultural ambiguity in a society that largely continued to ignore them, but they did provide a foundation for the gradual emergence, early in the twentieth century, of a powerful new sense of collective identity. Building from there, community activists initiated a sweeping Mexican American civil rights movement that would gain momentum until its peak in the 1960s and early 1970s.

For all the concrete gains that ethnic Mexican civil rights leaders ultimately achieved in the century after annexation, their most important contribution may have been their insistence on challenging the mythology Americans had constructed about what had happened to Mexicans in the West. By demanding not only that they be "seen" but that they at long last be extended their full rights as U.S. citizens, ethnic Mexican activists took the first steps toward reclaiming their suppressed history. The ultimate legacy of their efforts may lie in their success in gaining belated recognition from other Americans that the "real" West is much more complicated, culturally diverse, and interesting than the distorted picture painted by promoters of the Spanish fantasy heritage could ever be.

Still, one does not have to look long to recognize that Americans' historical myopia about Hispanics continues to color their perceptions, and it is difficult not to view the recent debate over Mexican immigration as another case in which Americans' inability to "see" a process that has unfolded over the past century has blinded them to the fact that the resident ethnic Mexican population has grown from the approximately one-half million people who lived in the United States when my grandfather was born to a population estimated in 1990 to be more than 14 million. The current spate of blaming Mexican immigrants for all the Southwest's ills — and the severe restrictions on immigration that may soon follow — may slow the growth of the United States' ethnic Mexican population, but it will also allow westerners — and Americans in general — the dangerous luxury of avoiding the reality that they already live in an extremely diverse, multiethnic, and multicultural society, and will eventually have to deal with the political and social consequences of that fact.

As any visitor knows who has sipped a margarita or otherwise lingered in the restored missions or "Old Town" sections of present-day Santa Fe, San Antonio, Los Angeles, San Diego, or Santa Barbara, despite the current hysteria over the increasing "Mexicanization" of the American West, the romantic image of the West's Hispanic past remains alive and well as a highly visible component of the region's historical mythology and tourist industry. And while the hundreds of thousands of tourists who travel through the Old Spanish Southwest each year to experience a taste of "Hispanic culture" may have a more sophisticated understanding of that complex culture than did their counterparts in the late nineteenth century, one need only think about the huge gulf between such popular attractions and the increasingly violent rhetoric concerning immigration, the poverty and violence of segregated inner-city barrios, and the general persistence of anti-Mexican sentiment in American life to recognize the extent to which American images of Hispanics remain polarized.

Border warfare: In the late spring of 1859, Dr. John Doy (seated) was kidnapped while trying to lead thirteen runaway slaves to freedom in Kansas and locked up in the St. Joseph, Missouri, jail. He is seen here, safely back in Kansas, with the band of armed antislavery men who slipped across the Missouri border and rescued him.

A Hell of a Storm

1855–1865

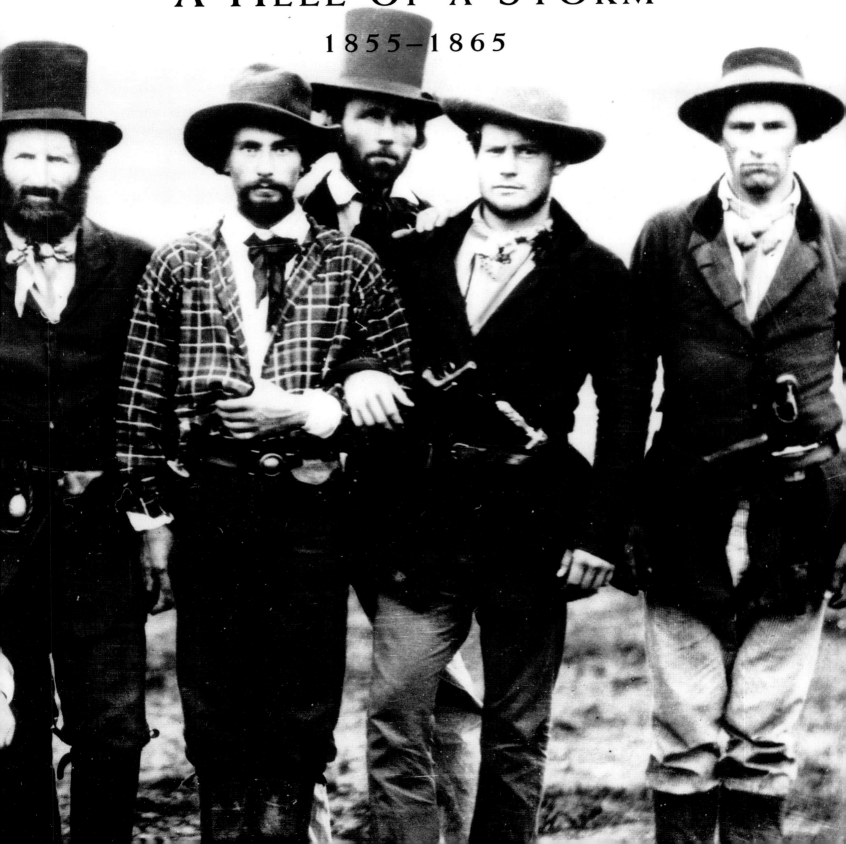

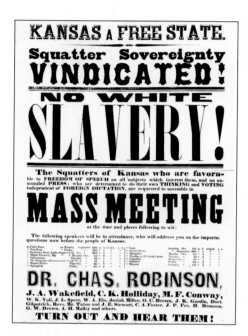

The Free-Soil party plastered this poster in and around Lawrence in the weeks leading up to the vote that was to decide the territory's fate in the autumn of 1855.

It seemed at first that the new lands the United States had won from Mexico would be peopled in the orderly fashion that the law appeared to dictate: first, treaties with the Indians were to legitimize settlement; then official surveys would map resources to be exploited; finally, under federal protection, settlers could spread peacefully across the region. And in the years that followed the gold rush, Americans did move west in ever-larger numbers, and many believed the opportunities opening up there would help heal the growing tensions between North and South. But in the end, the new settlers brought with them the nation's oldest, most divisive issue — slavery. The federal government, engaged in a struggle simply to hold the country together, was hard put to impose its will in the West. And the largely unprotected region became the breeding ground for bloodshed that would eventually engulf the whole nation. The spark that ignited the Civil War in the East was struck in the West, and the war years there witnessed a kind of savagery largely unknown in the East, as neighbor slaughtered neighbor and Indian peoples found themselves swept up in the conflict — forced to take sides, driven from their lands, trapped in a violent world where it seemed that no man's word could be trusted.

In the spring of 1855, the Reverend Charles H. Lovejoy and his wife, Julia Louisa, began to build themselves a home on the Big Blue River in the brand-new settlement of Manhattan in Kansas Territory. They had come all the way from Croydon, New Hampshire, under the auspices of the New England Emigrant Aid Company, and were a different kind of American pioneer — not interested in gold, land, or glory. They were abolitionists, and not even the death of their four-year-old daughter during the long overland passage had undercut their antislavery ardor. "A great work is to be done," Mrs. Lovejoy wrote to the editor of her former local newspaper in New England, "and Kansas is the great battlefield where a mighty conflict is to be waged with the monster slavery, and he will be routed and slain. Amen and Amen."

The Lovejoys — and hundreds of other men and women also willing to give up their old lives in order to keep the soil of Kansas free from slavery — were reacting to the relentless ambition of one man, Senator Stephen A. Douglas of Illinois, who said *he* did not care whether slavery was voted up or voted down. The chairman of the Committee on Territories, Douglas was a little man — his admirers called him "the Little Giant" — with big plans, for himself, for Chicago, and for the West. He had already used his influence to help make Chicago the hub of a railroad web, but still he was not satisfied. Ever since the gold rush, Californians had been clamoring for a railroad to link San Francisco with eastern cities. Douglas was determined that that line, too, should run through Chicago.

But the old question of slavery had stood in his way. The Missouri Compromise of 1820 had barred slavery from lands north of Missouri's southern border, lands through which Douglas's railroad would have to pass. The South would have voted down any plan that promised to bring new settlers onto free soil and thereby strengthen the hand of the North. And so Douglas had overturned the old compromise. To secure southern support, his bill proposed to carve from part of the old Permament Indian Territory two altogether new territories, Kansas and Nebraska. The people of those territories, not Congress, were to be allowed to decide for themselves about slavery. Douglas told a friend his bill would cause "a hell of a storm," but he was also sure it would enrich his region and himself — he had invested heavily in the line he hoped to build — and, by linking the Atlantic and Pacific and making possible the settlement of the lands in between, he believed it would also help unite the country. Instead, by leaving it to a few thousand settlers to decide the momentous question of slavery in the western territories, it would tear the country apart.

Each side readied for the showdown. "Come on then, Gentlemen of the Slave States," said Senator William A. Seward of New York, "since there is no escaping your challenge, I accept it in behalf of the cause of freedom. We will engage in competition for the virgin soil of Kansas, and God give the victory to the side which is stronger in numbers as it is in right."

"We are playing for a mighty stake," answered Senator David Atchison of Missouri. "The game must be played boldly. . . . If we win, we can carry slavery to the Pacific ocean. . . ."

When the day to vote came, Atchison and nearly 5,000 armed pro-slavery men from Missouri — "border ruffians," their enemies called them — flooded across the

The 700 block of Massachusetts Street in downtown Lawrence, a Free-Soil stronghold peopled largely by transplanted New Englanders who named its thirty-two streets for the thirty-two states previously admitted to the Union

Kansas border, seized polling places, cast four times as many ballots as there were voters in the territory, and installed a legislature that made it a crime even to criticize slavery. Free-Soilers countered with their own election. They drew up a constitution that outlawed slavery, and applied for admission to the Union as a free state. Kansas now had two governments. Its people were about to go to war with one another.

In the fall of 1855, a pro-slavery settler shot and killed his neighbor, an antislavery man. They had quarreled over the ownership of a stand of timber, not over slavery, but it was all that was needed to spark off the fighting. After someone wounded the pro-slavery sheriff of Douglas County the following spring, eight hundred armed Missourians stormed into the Free-Soil stronghold of Lawrence, Kansas, got drunk, destroyed two newspaper offices, and burned down the hotel and the home of the Free-Soil governor. When Massachusetts senator Charles Sumner denounced what he called this "Crime against Kansas," committed by "murderous robbers from Missouri," a South Carolina congressman strode onto the Senate floor and beat him senseless with a cane.

Three days later, on the night of May 24, on Pottawatomie Creek, a strange, driven man named John Brown called five settlers said to favor slavery out of their cabins and, with the help of his sons, hacked them to death with broadswords. It was a war to the death between good and evil, Brown said. "We must fight fire with fire." (In fact, at least two of his hapless victims may have been Free-Soilers themselves.)

During the next three months, some two hundred more men would die in "Bleeding Kansas." "We are in the midst of war — war of the most bloody kind — a war of extermination," wrote Julia Lovejoy. "Freedom and slavery are interlocked in deadly embrace, and death is certain for one or the other party. The hour has come, and freedom's martyrs will be strewn along the rivers of Kansas . . . or slavery will be driven across the Missouri River. . . . A crisis is just before us and only God knoweth where it will end."

Julia Louisa Lovejoy, photographed many years after the troubles in Kansas had ended

UP, AWAKE, YE DEFENDERS OF ZION

On July 24, 1857, 2,500 Mormons gathered near Salt Lake City for a great anniversary celebration: it had been ten years since Brigham Young had brought the first Saints to their desert sanctuary. Then, four horsemen arrived with startling news. The United States Army — 2,500 men — was marching on Utah.

Young's announcement that polygamy was part of church doctrine had turned still more Americans against him, so many, both North and South, that when John C. Frémont ran as the first Republican presidential nominee in 1856 he had sought to broaden his support by promising an end to both polygamy and slavery. The Democrat who had beaten him, James Buchanan, now sought to deflect the public's attention from the divisive issue of slavery by mounting an all-out assault on the practice of polygamy, which most Americans deplored. John Tyler, son of the former president, spelled out the strategy for Buchanan:

The Popular Idea is rapidly maturing that Mormonism . . . should be put down and utterly extirpated. I believe that we can supercede the Negro-Mania with the almost universal excitement of an Anti-Mormon Crusade. Should you . . . seize this question with a strong, fearless and resolute hand, the Country I am sure will rally to you with an earnest enthusiasm and the pipings of Abolitionism will hardly be heard amidst the thunders of the storm we shall raise.

The Mormons, their memories of the violence that they had experienced in Missouri and Illinois still raw, prepared for the worst. "Woe, woe to those men who [come] here to unlawfully meddle with me and this people," said Brigham Young. "I swore in Nauvoo when my enemies were looking me in the face, that I would send them to hell . . . if they meddled with me; and I ask no more odds of all hell today." Young declared martial law, formed a new guerrilla organization called the Mormon Raiders, and strengthened his alliance with the Paiute against the federal invaders.

While federal troops made their slow way west, a wagon train from Arkansas and Missouri on its way to California happened to enter the southern part of Mormon territory. Among them were a band of horsemen who called themselves the "Missouri wildcats." "They [were] the worst set that ever crossed the plains," one Mormon recalled. "They swore and boasted openly that they helped shoot the guts out of Joe Smith . . . and that Buchanan's whole army was coming right behind them, and would kill every God Damn Mormon in Utah. . . . They had two bulls which they called one 'Heber' and the other 'Brigham' and whipped 'em through every town, yelling and singing, blackguarding and blaspheming oaths that would have made your hair stand on end."

When the wagon train reached a grassy area called Mountain Meadows on September 7, 1857, some two hundred Paiute attacked it, convinced the Missourians had poisoned some of their watering holes. The emigrants drove them back. The Indians settled in for a siege, then asked the Mormons to join them in destroying the common enemy. Local officials sent a message to Salt Lake City, asking Brigham Young what they should do. Young sent a courier pounding back with orders to let the wagons go. But the message arrived two days late.

God almighty helping me, I will fight until there is not a drop of blood in my veins. Good God! I have wives enough to whip out the United States.

Heber Kimball

The central tithing office and church store in Salt Lake City, 1850s. Mormon doctrine required that every Saint voluntarily donate one-tenth of his or her earnings to the church — though most only partially complied.

The blood of American citizens cries for vengeance from the barren sands of the Great Basin. The insulted dignity of the nation demands retribution from their infamous murderers. Virtue, Christianity and decency require that the vile brood of incestuous miscreants who have perpetrated this atrocity shall be broken up and dispersed. And the tide of popular opinion, now rolling up from every end of the land, calls loudly upon the Government to let no longer delay ensue before beginning the good work.

San Francisco *Evening Bulletin*

The site of the town of Ogden, thirty-five miles northwest of Salt Lake City, was purchased by the Mormons from a mountain man named Miles Goodyear in 1847. It soon became the second-largest Mormon settlement in the region.

Meanwhile, a Missourian had managed to slip away in search of help — only to be shot dead by young Mormons. If word of that got out, the Mormons knew, the advancing federal army would surely seek revenge. To make sure news did not reach the outside world, local leaders resolved to wipe out the wagon train, then blame everything on the Paiute. John D. Lee was ordered to lure the emigrants into the open.

Lee had been a loyal Mormon since the troubles in Missouri twenty years earlier, and Brigham Young had adopted him as a son, both in this world and the next. He was, as he himself said, "as clay in the hands of the potter" when it came to carrying out the wishes of the church leaders. But this was something else again. The orders were to "*decoy* the emigrants from their position," Lee remembered, "and kill all of them that could talk. This order was in writing. . . . I read it, and then dropped it on the ground, saying, 'I cannot do this. . . .' I then left the Council and went away to myself and bowed myself in prayer before God and asked him to overrule the decision of that Council. . . . If I had then had a thousand worlds to command, I would have given them freely to save that company from death."

Lee agonized so long and so tearfully that the impatient Paiute gave him the nickname *Nah-gaats* — "Cry Baby" — but in the end he agreed to do as he was told. On the morning of September 11, he rode out to the besieged wagon train under a flag of truce. The Indians would not attack, he promised the emigrants; all they needed to do was put down their arms and follow him away from the wagons. They did so.

Then, someone gave the signal and the Mormons opened fire on the men, then stepped out of the way so that the Paiute could kill the women and all the children over the age of five. In less than half an hour, 120 people were butchered. Lee himself shot and killed all the sick and wounded. Seventeen children survived; thought too young ever to tell the horrible story, they were adopted by local Mormon families.

"Thanks be to the Lord God of Israel, who has this day delivered our enemies into our hands," said Lee, who then rode to Salt Lake City to report to Brigham Young.

Precisely how much Young was then told of the Mormons' part in the massacre is unclear. But publicly, Young blamed everything on the Indians. With the American army coming closer every day, he showed little interest in punishing anyone: "The more you stir a manure pile," he is said to have told a friend, "the worse it stinks."

The Mormons went on to raid military supply trains, raze Fort Bridger and Fort Supply, and burn forage in front of the advancing federal troops. The army was forced to halt for the winter at the site of Fort Bridger. In the end, there was no Mormon war. The President thought it best to back off, and struck a deal with the Mormon patriarch in the spring: Young resigned as governor and agreed to let troops be stationed at Fort Floyd, forty miles from Salt Lake City, but Young and his followers were pardoned for inciting rebellion and he remained president of the Church of Jesus Christ of Latter-day Saints and unchallenged patriarch of his people. James Buchanan's attempt to divert the nation's attention away from slavery had failed.

Four years later, Young would stop at Mountain Meadows on an inspection tour. Federal troops had erected a makeshift monument to those who had been murdered. On it were the words "Vengeance is mine saith the Lord, and I will repay." Young gazed at it for a time, muttered, "Vengeance is *mine* — and I have taken a little." Then he ordered the monument torn down. On his way home to Salt Lake City, he and fifty members of his party stopped to dine at the home of John D. Lee.

ACTUAL WAR ON THE BORDER

The treaty that ended the Mexican War had promised all the benefits of United States citizenship to Mexican Americans, and it had also pledged to recognize the Spanish and Mexican grants that gave them title to their lands. In practice both were routinely ignored, even in regions, like the lower Rio Grande valley of Texas, where Mexican Americans still greatly outnumbered Anglos.

Juan Nepomuceno Cortina, a cattle rancher and the great-great-grandson of one of the first Spanish settlers of the valley, had fought to keep the Americans out during the Mexican-American War, and afterward battled with them over the ownership of stray livestock. And he had watched as American squatters and American courts reduced his family's lands to a fraction of what they once had been.

On July 13, 1859, Cortina rode into Brownsville, Texas, to buy supplies and came upon the city marshal pistol-whipping a Mexican laborer who had once worked for the Cortina family. When the sheriff refused to stop, Cortina shot him in the shoulder, swept his prisoner onto the back of his horse, and rode off with him. A little over two months later, with some seventy-five armed followers, he rode into town again, freed twelve Mexican prisoners from jail, seized arms and ammunition, and shot dead three Americans whom he said had killed Mexicans while the law looked the other way.

Then he returned to his ranch and issued a proclamation.

Mexicans! . . . There are . . . [Anglo-American] criminals covered with frightful crimes, but . . . to these monsters indulgence is shown, because they are not of our race, which is unworthy, as they say, to belong to the human species. . . . When the State of Texas [became] . . . part of the Union, flocks of vampires, in the guise of men, came and scattered themselves in the settlements. Most of you

Juan Cortina

Jack Ford (above), who led the Texas Rangers in pursuit of Juan Cortina, was known as "RIP" because during the Mexican-American War it had been his duty to inform the families of men who had died that they would now "rest in peace." He got little help in his mission from the Mexican Americans struggling to survive in small settlements along the Rio Grande (top, left and right) who believed his elusive quarry a hero.

have been robbed of your property, incarcerated, chased, murdered and hunted like wild beasts, because your labor was fruitful and your industry excited . . . [their] vile avarice. . . . Mexicans! Is there no remedy for you?

When a force of Anglo settlers and Mexican national guardsmen attacked Cortina's ranch, he and his men sent them limping away, leaving behind two artillery pieces. "Our personal enemies," Cortina vowed, "shall not possess our land until they have fattened it with their gore."

Anglo bands lynched one of his lieutenants in retaliation and began burning Mexican Americans' homes. But they could not catch Cortina himself: when the state militia, known as the Texas Rangers, came after him, he ambushed them, then drove the survivors from the field.

For several months, Cortina managed to hold on to the lower Rio Grande valley with the help of food and supplies secretly provided by sympathetic Mexicans on both sides of the border. "Rio Grande City is almost depopulated . . ." wrote an army officer. "There have been fifteen Americans and eighty friendly Mexicans killed. . . . The whole country from Brownsville to Rio Grande City . . . has been laid waste. . . ." "ASTOUNDING NEWS FROM THE RIO GRANDE!" said the San Antonio *Herald.* "THE MEXICAN POPULACE ARMING TO EXTERMINATE THE AMERICANS AND RECONQUER OUR COUNTRY TO THE COLORADO RIVER! ACTUAL WAR ON THE BORDER!"

"Cortina was now a great man," one of his pursuers recalled. "He had defeated the 'Gringo,' and his position was impregnable; he had the Mexican flag flying in his camp and numbers were flocking to his standard. . . . [H]e was received as the champion of his race — as the man who would right the wrongs the Mexicans had received; that he would drive back the hated Americans to the Nueces. . . ."

CAPTIVE

By 1860, Texans had driven most of the native peoples from their state into Indian Territory. But some Comanche bands refused to leave their homeland and continued to raid settlements, seizing horses and cattle and sometimes killing those who dared resist, just as they had for centuries. One of the most feared Comanche leaders was named Peta Nocona, and a ragtag sixty-man force made up of regular army soldiers, Texas Rangers, and civilian volunteers under Captain Jack Cureton (below) was sent to hunt him down. On December 18, 1860, on the shore of the Pease River they caught up with members of his band — mostly women and children — drying meat for the winter. Nocona and his warriors were away hunting.

The overall commander of the sixty-man force, Captain Lawrence Sullivan Ross, promised a shiny new Colt revolver to the first man to kill an Indian. Then his men attacked. At least sixteen women were cut down. One woman, weeping and holding a baby girl (right), was spared because she had blue eyes. When she was questioned through an interpreter it slowly became clear that she was a white woman — Cynthia Ann Parker — who had been kidnapped nearly a quarter of a century earlier at the age of nine. Her family had never given up looking for her, and there had been several attempts at ransom and rescue. But she had always refused to leave the Comanche: she was happy to be the wife of Peta Nocona, she said,

proud to be the mother of his daughter and two sons. Now, she wanted only to go back to the Pease River and see if she could find the rest of her family.

Instead, her uncle, Isaac Parker, insisted that she return with him to his home at Birdville, where he and his wife did all they could to make her forget the life she had led as a Comanche. She was instructed in the Bible, made to wear clothing suitable to a white woman, finally locked up at night to keep her from fleeing back to the Plains. The Texas legislature voted her a plot of land and a pension of one hundred dollars a year as compensation for the supposed "suffering and woe" she had endured. But she was unable to forget the only life she'd known and yearned to see her husband and sons again. She was no happier living with her brother, Silas, whose wife disliked having a half-Indian child in the house and called Topsannah, her daughter, "Little Barbarian." "She had a wild expression and would look down when

people talked to her . . ." a neighbor recalled. "She thought her two boys were lost on the prairie . . . this dissatisfied her very much."

In 1863, Topsannah died suddenly of pneumonia. Her mother was devastated. Alone now and grieving amid uncomprehending relatives and curious neighbors, never knowing what had happened to the rest of her Comanche family, she lived on until 1870, when influenza ended her misery.

Peta Nocona never remarried and died shortly after his wife did without ever knowing what had happened to her. One of her sons died, too. But her second son, Quanah Parker (below), grew up to become a Comanche chief. He would fight to drive the buffalo hunters from the southern Plains, but he also longed for his mother, just as she longed for him, and forbade his raiders to harm white women for fear they might inadvertently harm her. When he finally surrendered in 1875 and learned that she was dead, he advertised for a photograph of her, then located her remains, and in 1910 had them reinterred in the cemetery on the Comanche reservation in Oklahoma. His mother, he said, through tears, had loved her life among the Comanche, had never wanted to return to the white world. But, he added, he knew that "people all same anyway"; he was himself living proof of it. Quanah Parker died just one month later, and was buried alongside the mother he had sought for so long.

Finally, a large, combined force of federal troops and Texas Rangers chased Cortina and his men to Rio Grande City and closed in for the kill. "Cortina was the last to leave the field," John S. Ford, commander of the Texas Rangers, remembered. "He faced his pursuers, emptied his revolver and tried to halt his panic-stricken men. . . . One shot struck the cantle of his saddle, one cut a lock of hair from his head, a third cut his bridle rein, a fourth passed through his horse's ear, and a fifth struck his belt. [But] he galloped off unhurt."

Cortina got away into Mexico, from where he continued to launch raids and steal Texas cattle for another fifteen years. Americans denounced Cortina as a murderous traitor, but to Mexican Americans along the border he would be remembered as the Robin Hood of the Rio Grande.

HAM AND EGGS AND SCENERY

"Our New England friends," Julia Lovejoy wrote to her hometown newspaper from Kansas, "may wonder that the warlike spirit has taken such hold upon those who, until they came to Kansas, were as complete non-resistants as the most orthodox Quaker; but sir, such individuals only need a little Kansas experience to understand the matter." On October 16, 1859, John Brown brought that experience east to Harpers Ferry, Virginia, where he tried to start a slave rebellion. Ten people were killed. Brown was captured, tried, and sentenced to hang.

The whole country was now experiencing the fear that had gripped Kansas for so long. On April 12, 1861, rebel guns fired on Fort Sumter. Carried by pony express, the news took thirteen days to travel from Missouri to San Francisco — even longer to reach other corners of the West. It was not until mid-July that Granville Stuart, a miner at Deer Lodge Valley in Montana Territory, heard that his country had gone to war with itself: "July 15, 1861. [We] went to Dempsey's ranch after two . . . cows [and] borrowed a small fragment of a newspaper that Tolman and Jackson brought from Fort Owen on the Bitterroot. . . . Bad news from the states. The North and South are fighting."

Samuel Clemens, not long after becoming Mark Twain

Just as the Civil War was getting under way that spring, a twenty-four-year-old some-time riverboat pilot named Sam Clemens and his elder brother, Orion, set out for the West from St. Joseph, Missouri. Two weeks in the Confederate militia had convinced Sam that he was not cut out for warfare. Orion had just been named secretary of the newly created Nevada Territory and asked his younger brother to come along as his assistant — provided he pay for both tickets. Two seats aboard the Central Overland and Pike's Peak Express Company stagecoach cost three hundred dollars, and they could carry just fifty pounds of baggage between them.

They left St. Joseph on July 26, 1861, and spun through Kansas and Nebraska beside the winding Platte, making eight to ten miles an hour through an unbroken sea of grass. "Ham and eggs and scenery," Sam remembered, "a 'down grade,' a flying coach, a fragrant pipe and a contented heart. . . . It is what all the ages have struggled for." A pony express rider galloped past. Coyotes howled. They saw buffalo, encountered their first Indians, talked with a real-life outlaw momentarily pursuing an honest living as a division superintendent for the stagecoach company. And they experienced for the first time the hugeness of the land that had staggered new arrivals from the time of Coronado:

> Imagine a vast waveless ocean stricken dead and turned to ashes. Imagine this solemn waste tufted with ash-dusted sage brushes; imagine the lifeless silence and solitude that belong to such a place; imagine a coach creeping like a bug through the midst of this shoreless level, and sending up tumbled volumes of dust as if it were a bug that went by steam.

Sam Clemens loved it all. "There was a freshness and breeziness" about heading west, he noted, "and an exhilarating sense of emancipation from all sorts of cares and responsibilities that almost made us feel that the years we had spent in the close, hot city, toiling and slaving, had been wasted and thrown away."

It took the Clemens brothers twenty days to reach Carson City, the small town that was the capital of the new territory. It was something of a letdown, Sam told his mother:

> [Nevada Territory] is fabulously rich in gold, silver, lead, coal, iron, quicksilver, . . . thieves, murderers, desperadoes, ladies, children, lawyers, Christians, Indians, Chinamen, Spaniards, gamblers, sharpers, coyotes, poets, preachers and jackass rabbits.
>
> I overheard a gentleman call it "the damnedest country under the sun" — and that comprehensive conception I fully subscribe to. It never rains here, the dew never falls. No flowers grow here, and no green thing gladdens the eye. . . .
>
> Our city lies in the midst of a desert of the purest, most unadulterated and uncompromising sand — in which infernal soil nothing but that fag-end of vegetable creation, "sage-brush," is mean enough to grow. . . . The houses are mostly frame, and unplastered; but "papered" inside with flour-sacks sewed together [and] engravings cut from "Harper's Weekly." . . . On account of the dryness of the atmosphere, the shingles on the houses warp until they look very much like they would be glad to turn over and lie awhile on the other side.

Working for his brother was not enough for Sam Clemens. With three friends, he claimed a large tract of forest on the shore of Lake Tahoe and dreamed of becoming a lumber king until he got careless with a cook fire and saw his forest burn.

Then he spent a fruitless month prospecting for gold or silver in the Humboldt region, buying and trading shares in mines with gaudy names and disappointing yields — the Columbiana, Branch Mint, Universe, Treasure Trove, Golconda, Monarch of the Mountains. Somehow, he remembered, it didn't matter. "We were stark mad with excitement — drunk with happiness — smothered under mountains of prospective wealth — arrogantly compassionate toward the plodding of millions who knew not our marvelous canyon — but our credit was not good at the grocer's."

The same story was being told all over the West. "The miners . . . were like quicksilver," the historian Herbert Bancroft, who had once been one of them, recalled. "A mass of them dropped into any locality, broke up into individual globules and ran off after any atom of gold in their vicinity. They stayed nowhere longer than the gold attracted them." California, Idaho, Colorado, Nevada, Utah, Arizona, New Mexico —

Sage brush is very fair fuel, but as a vegetable it is a distinguished failure. Nothing can abide the taste of it but the jackass and his illegitimate child the mule. But their testament to its nutritiousness is worth nothing, for they will eat pine knots, or anthracite coal, or brass filings, or lead pipe, or old bottles, or anything that comes handy, and then go off looking as grateful as if they had oysters for dinner.

Mark Twain

Hope dies hard: This lone prospector was still panning Clear Creek in Colorado more than twenty years after gold was first found there in 1859.

miners continued to scour the western landscape for gold and silver as though there were no Civil War back East, as if no treaties with the tribes had ever been signed to keep them out of Indian lands.

In April of 1862, six miners who had wandered into southwestern Montana in search of gold were captured by the Crow and then let off with a stern warning. Even that did not discourage them. They paused to prospect in a shallow creek that ran through a ravine they called Alder Gulch and found five dollars' worth of gold glinting in the bottom of a single pan. One of the partners, a man named Barney Hughes, was sworn to secrecy and sent to Bannack, the nearest town, to pick up supplies. He kept quiet, but somehow, other miners detected the excitement underlying his silence, and when he started back to the site, some two hundred men were strung out along the trail behind him. Hughes called a halt and said he would not take another step until his pursuers agreed that he and his partners were each to have exclusive rights to two hundred feet of land along the creek bed. By the end of June, full-fledged towns lined both sides of the trickling creek, and miners were moving out into the surrounding countryside in search of more likely sites.

Sam Clemens spent six months with three partners in a ten-by-twelve-foot cabin, panning, digging, drinking, going more and more heavily into debt. Then, he would claim later, he became a multimillionaire — for just ten days. One of his partners discovered a "blind lead" — a subterranean vein of silver on public land — and claimed it for himself and his friends. They stayed up all night talking about what they would do with the money:

> What kind of house are *you* going to build?
>   Brick.
>   Bosh!
>   Why? What is your idea?
>   Brown stone front — French plate glass — billiard room off the dining room — statuary and paintings — shrubbery and two-acre grass plat — greenhouse — iron dog on the front stoop — gray horses — landau and a coachman with a bug on his hat!
>   The news was all over town. . . . I walked the streets serene and happy. Higbie said the foreman had been offered two hundred thousand dollars for his third of the mine. I said I would like to see myself selling for any such price. My ideas were lofty. My figure was a million.

The law required that work begin within ten days of filing a claim. Otherwise, anyone else could claim it as his own. Clemens was called away to tend a sick friend. Each of his partners somehow thought the other had started work. No one so much as scratched the surface of the earth, and when Clemens returned he found fourteen armed men had taken over the claim — or so he later liked to say.

"I had been a private secretary," he wrote, "a silver miner and a silver mine operative, and amounted to less than nothing in each, and now what to do next?"

Virginia City would provide the answer. It stood astride the Comstock Lode, the richest body of ore yet discovered in America, and it had grown from a tiny town to a city in less than two years. Fifteen thousand people now lived there. They had put

in gaslights, built stock exchanges, three theaters, four churches — and forty-two saloons. And there was a newspaper, the *Territorial Enterprise.* Sam talked himself into a job as a reporter, then wrote his mother:

> . . . I have just heard five pistol shots down the street — as such things are in my line, I will go and see about it. . . . PS — 5 AM — The pistol did its work well — one man, a Jackson County, Missourian, shot two of my friends (police officers) through the heart — both died within three minutes. Murderer's name is John Campbell.

Soon, Sam was covering everything from candy pulls to shootings, Indian attacks to theatrical performances. He was also writing light pieces — "I have had a 'call' to literature of a low order — i.e. *humorous,*" he told his mother. "It is nothing to be proud of but it is my strongest suit." He had begun to sign his articles "Mark Twain."

Texas had seceded from the Union before the inauguration of Abraham Lincoln, and federal forts and supplies there had been meekly turned over to the Confederates. Now, some within the Confederacy dreamed of stretching their new republic far beyond Texas, north to the Colorado goldfields, and all the way west to California.

In early July of 1861, Confederate colonel John R. Baylor, who had learned his warfare fighting Comanche on the Texas plains, made the first move, sending a Texan force north to seize Fort Bliss without firing a shot and to declare New Mexico's southern half the Confederate Territory of Arizona. The Confederate conquest of the Southwest was off to an early and promising start. Next, the Confederates had to rid the rest of New Mexico Territory of federal troops and seize control of the Rio Grande. Brigadier General Henry H. Sibley eagerly accepted the assignment. A Louisianan who fought almost as hard as he drank — one soldier called him a "walking keg of whiskey" — he drew up a straightforward plan: starting out from El Paso, he would follow the winding river northward all the way to Santa Fe, take the Colorado goldfields, then head west for California. He moved out at the head of four regiments — 3,700 Texans who had coveted the mostly Mexican American settlements of New Mexico for years — on January 4, 1862. Their motto was "on to San Francisco."

Within the adobe walls of Fort Craig, Lieutenant Colonel Edward R. S. Canby and some 4,000 poorly trained Union volunteers waited nervously for Sibley and his army to arrive. Canby and Sibley had been classmates at West Point; Canby had been Sibley's best man, had married Sibley's wife's first cousin, had fought alongside him against the Navajo. Now, it was up to Canby to stop his old friend. He sent messages to the governors of the California, Utah, and Colorado territories, pleading for reinforcements, then settled in to wait.

The first Confederate regiment appeared across the river on February 19, and the federal commander, fearful that Sibley meant simply to bypass his fort and plunge on toward Santa Fe, reluctantly left the protection of its walls to attack him near a mesa called Valverde.

The Confederate commander could not believe his luck. At the end of two bloody days of what one soldier remembered as fighting "terrific beyond description" that left the surface of the Rio Grande littered with the bobbing corpses of men and horses, the Texans drove Canby and what was left of his force back inside their fort.

Sibley continued his march. Supplies were growing scarce now, and federal troops destroyed the depots from which the rebels had hoped to replenish them. The pro-Confederate volunteers Sibley had assumed would rally to him failed to materialize — the mostly Spanish-speaking people of the region had little affection for Texans.

Still, the Confederate conquest of the Southwest seemed to be moving forward. Sibley took Albuquerque and plundered Santa Fe. All that now stood between him and the Colorado goldfields was Fort Union. He sent an advance force to the mouth of Apache Canyon to hold it until his whole army was in place and they could pour through together to crush federal resistance forever. But he had not reckoned on the last-minute arrival of the 1st Colorado Volunteers, mostly miners from the goldfields, hastily trained and hard drinking but itching for a fight. They had marched

Private Simeon Jasper Crews of the 7th Texas Mounted Volunteers, who took part in the Confederate invasion of New Mexico. "The country is worthless," wrote one of his fellow soldiers. "Think this country never was intended for white folks. The first man that ever came . . . ought to have been killed by the Indians."

Mining the Comstock Lode (opposite): In two of the first flashlit photographs ever made, Timothy O'Sullivan caught six miners on their way down a mine shaft belonging to the Savage Silver Mining Works at Virginia City in 1868, as well as one of their comrades at work deep beneath the earth. "It was as if a wondrous battle raged," wrote one visitor to Virginia City, "in which the combatants were man and earth. Myriads of swarthy, dust-covered men are piercing into the grim old mountains, ripping them open, thrusting murderous holes through their naked bodies. . . ."

Sergeant Alexander Coker (above), 2nd Texas Mounted Rifles. "We heeded not their great renown," one Confederate volunteer remembered of the rebel triumph at Valverde. "We charged them with a yell,/We turned their tactics upside down,/And gave the regulars hell."

Costume change: General Henry H. Sibley (center), wearing the Confederate uniform he put on after leaving the Union army, and the Reverend John M. Chivington, dressed as he customarily was before transforming himself into a Union soldier

forty miles a day to get there, through ice and snow and freezing winds. Now, four hundred of them started through the narrow canyon toward the waiting Texans.

In the lead was Colonel John M. Chivington, a big, bearish Methodist parson, the presiding elder of the Rocky Mountain District of his church and as famous for his flamboyance as for his fiery sermons. He sometimes preached with a revolver resting on the pulpit and had refused to serve as regimental chaplain, demanding a "fighting commission" instead, because he thought it would serve better to boost the career in politics he now wished to pursue.

Now, he would get his chance to show what he could do. The Confederates opened fire as soon as they saw Chivington's men, and the Union volunteers fell back for a moment. But then they regrouped and Chivington sent some of his men scurrying up the canyon sides so that they could fire down on the enemy. "They were up on the walls on both sides of us," one Texan remembered, "shooting us down like sheep." Then, Chivington, waving two revolvers, ordered in his cavalry. He "chawed his lips with only less energy than he gave his orders," one of his men recalled. "He seemed burdened with a new responsibility, the extent of which he had never before realized, and to have no thought of danger. Of commanding presence, dressed in full regimentals, he was a conspicuous mark for the Texan sharp sharpshooters. . . . As if possessed of a charmed life, he galloped unhurt through the storm of bullets. . . ."

A Confederate who saw the Coloradans charge was impressed, too:

On they came to what I supposed certain destruction, but nothing like lead or iron seemed to stop them, for we were pouring it into them from every side like hail in a storm. In a moment these devils had run the gauntlet for a half mile and were fighting hand to hand with our men in the road.

The Texans withdrew. Sibley's success no longer seemed quite so assured.

The two main armies met the following day at Glorieta Pass, "a terrible place for an engagement," a federal officer remembered, "a deep gorge with a narrow wagon-track running along the bottom, the ground rising precipitously on each side, with huge boulders and clumps of stunted cedars interspersed." They slammed at each other amid the rocks for five hours, neither side willing to give an inch to the other, until the Texans suddenly called a truce.

Behind their lines, Chivington and his Coloradans had dealt the Texans a fatal blow. With a Mexican guide to show them the way, they had marched sixteen miles through the mountains to a cliff that overlooked the Texans' supply wagons. There, they lowered themselves by ropes, drove off the guards, set eighty-five wagons filled with provisions on fire, bayoneted five hundred horses and mules. Sibley's Confederate army, so close to victory only a few days before, now suddenly faced starvation and thirst as well as a hostile enemy.

The Confederate invasion had been halted. The battle of Glorieta Pass came to be called "the Gettysburg of the West" and Colonel Chivington — "the Fighting Parson" — and his Coloradans emerged as its heroes.

Sibley now just wanted to get his battered army back to Texas. On April 12, he ordered his men to begin the long retreat. Canby and his army followed at a discreet distance, content for the most part to let the weather and terrain do their deadly work.

Columns got lost. Boots wore out. Men had to stagger through burning sand in bare feet. There was little to eat, still less to drink. There were sandstorms, mountain blizzards. Some Texans mutinied. Others abandoned their weapons, collapsed from exhaustion, dehydration, sunstroke. Thirty-seven hundred Texans had marched north with Sibley. Fifteen hundred of them never returned.

The dream of a Confederate Southwest was dead.

Private Bates of the Texas Mounted Volunteers. He and his comrades vowed to "fight as long as [General] Sibley said fight," one of them declared after their defeat at Glorieta Pass, "but the moment he said surrender, they were going . . . into the mountains and make their way to Texas."

THE WATER RISING ALL AROUND

By 1861, the so-called Five Civilized Tribes that had been forced to crowd together onto Indian Territory had rebuilt much of the world they had left behind: schools, churches, newspapers, plantations worked by slaves. But they were still divided between those who had agreed to come west and those who had opposed it, and now they faced another bitter choice — whether to side with the North or the South.

No people were more deeply split than the Cherokee. John Ross, their principal chief, had fought the Removal treaty, and when in 1861 a Confederate agent called upon him to support the Confederacy, he refused. He wished to remain neutral in this white man's war; he owned slaves himself and had little love for the federal government that had driven his people west, but it still owed them a million dollars and he did not want to forfeit it. "I am — the Cherokees are — your friends," he told two Confederate agents sent to win him to their cause, "but we do not wish to be brought into the feuds between yourselves and your northern brethren. Our wish is for peace. Peace at home and peace among you."

Meanwhile, his ancient enemy Stand Watie, the only prominent signer of the treaty that had ceded the Cherokee lands in Georgia to have escaped assassination by those who had opposed it, pledged his loyalty to the South, and began raising a regi-

White man's war: A Union recruiter swears in recruits somewhere in Indian Territory, while an unidentified Native American (above) displays his loyalty to the Confederacy.

ment of mixed-bloods. Other tribes were signing on with the Confederacy, too — the Chickasaw, Choctaw, Seminoles. The Creek split into two factions, one pro-Union, the other pro-Confederacy. Then came word of Southern triumphs at Bull Run, and again at Wilson's Creek in southwest Missouri, where Stand Watie's Cherokee followers helped turn the tide against the Union. With neighboring Missouri in rebel hands, neutrality no longer seemed practical.

Ross reluctantly forged an alliance with the South in return for a Confederate pledge to honor the Union debt to the tribe and provide white troops, should northern soldiers invade Indian Territory. He prayed he'd chosen the winning side. "We are in the situation of a man standing upon a low naked spot of ground," he wrote, "with the water rising all around him. . . . The tide carries by him, in its mad course, a drifting log. . . . By refusing it he is a doomed man. By seizing hold of it he has a chance for his life."

Indians from all over the country fought in the Civil War. These Union veterans, all members of the Menominee tribe, belonged to the Joseph Lederberger Post No. 267 of the G.A.R.

There soon broke out a bloody civil war within Indian Territory itself that cost the region proportionately more men than any state, North or South. Settlements were burned, crops ravaged. White intruders carried off thousands of head of livestock. John Ross was captured early and spent most of the war as a prisoner in Washington. His nemesis, Stand Watie, took time out from fighting an invading Union force to destroy Tahlequah, the Cherokee capital, and burn Ross's house to the ground.

In the end, the Cherokee and their neighbors would gain nothing by their involvement in the Civil War. After the fighting finally ended, Congress would punish rebel and loyal Indians alike by forcing them to give up still more of their land.

LAWRENCE

No Civil War fighting was more savage than that between pro-slavery and anti-slavery settlers along the Kansas-Missouri border — and none had a more lasting impact on its region.

The most notorious leader of the Union guerrillas — called Jayhawkers by their enemies — was James H. Lane, a cadaverous former senator from Kansas who thought Missourians "wolves, snakes, devils" whom he wanted to see "cast into a burning hell." He did his best to cast them there, haunting the trail of rebel armies, first to ravage the homes of anyone who had dared help them, then sacking and burning whole towns.

Confederate guerrillas — called Bushwhackers because they hid in the bush — responded in kind. Their most celebrated leader was William Clarke Quantrill, a former schoolteacher from Ohio with little interest in slavery but limitless enthusiasm

Appearances: William Quantrill (left), in a previously unpublished daguerreotype made when he was fifteen, seems incapable of hurting anyone, while Bloody Bill Anderson (right) seems eager for the carnage to begin.

for looting and killing. He came to Kansas before the war, seemed to favor the abolition of slavery, even helped plan a raid into Missouri to free some slaves, then — for reasons never satisfactorily explained — he betrayed his co-conspirators, led them into a fatal ambush, and went over to the enemy. For helping Confederate regulars take Springfield in 1861, he was made a captain, then raised a loosely knit army of wild young men — some as young as seventeen — and went to war on his own, swearing he would burn Jim Lane at the stake. Union farmers, he warned that autumn, should not bother to plant crops the following spring; they would not live to harvest them.

Quantrill's raiders so angered the local Union commander, Thomas Ewing, that he proposed to exile their families to the South in the hope that the guerrillas would follow them there. "About two thirds of the families on the occupied farms," Ewing reported, "are of kin to the guerrillas and are actively and heartily engaged in feeding, clothing and sustaining them. . . . The families of several hundred of the worst of these men should be sent, with their clothes and bedding, to some rebel district south. . . . The men will follow. . . ."

Ewing arrested several of the wives and sisters of Quantrill's men. Somehow, the old brick building in which some of them were locked up in Kansas City collapsed. Five women died; several others were badly injured. One had been the cousin of Cole Younger, a young Bushwhacker already eager for revenge against the Jayhawkers, who had burned his family home. Another was the sister of an accused horse thief named Bill Anderson, who had already proved himself an adept killer and would soon earn

Unidentified but heavily armed settlers, thought to have been photographed near Lawrence in 1855. No one knows whether these men favored slavery or free soil, but their like could be seen all across the region. "The prairies are ablaze," one Kansas newspaper said. "There is nothing talked about here except war."

himself the nickname "Bloody Bill." His sister's death in federal custody seems to have driven him to madness: he began wearing a garland of Yankee scalps into battle, laughed as he and his followers gunned down unarmed prisoners, then ordered his men to scalp and mutilate their corpses. "I will kill you," he wrote to the readers of one antislavery newspaper. "I will hunt you down like wolves and murder you."

William Quantrill, too, was eager for revenge. "Blood and revenge are hammering in my heart," he said. And Lawrence, Kansas, seemed the ideal target: it had always been a free-soil stronghold and was the headquarters of the hated Jayhawkers. Runaway slaves had found sanctuary there, too, and it was the home of Jim Lane. "Let's go to Lawrence," Quantrill said. "We can get more money and more revenge there than anywhere else in the state of Kansas."

On the morning of August 21, 1863, Quantrill and some 450 men drew up just outside Lawrence. Riding with them were Bloody Bill Anderson, Cole Younger, and a distant cousin of his, Frank James. Along the way, Quantrill had kidnapped ten farmers, forced them to show him the way to town, then murdered them all. And he had just begun to kill.

Quantrill's massacre at Lawrence is almost enough to curdle the blood with horror. In the history of the war thus far, full as it has been of dreadful scenes, there has been no such diabolical work as this indiscriminate slaughter of peaceful villagers. . . .

New York *Daily Times*

The expedition to Lawrence was a gallant and perfectly fair blow at the enemy . . . as the population of Kansas is malignant and scoundrely beyond description.

Richmond *Examiner*

The Bushwhackers surrounded a downtown hotel. A guest hung a white sheet from the window and asked Quantrill what he wanted. "Plunder!" he answered. The guests were ordered out and robbed. The hotel was set afire. Waving two of the six pistols he carried, Quantrill rose in his stirrups and shouted, "Kill! Kill! Lawrence must be cleansed, and the only way to cleanse it is to kill!" Then, while he ordered the terrified staff of another hotel to cook him a big breakfast, his men carried out his orders. Unarmed men were shot down as they ran. Some were dragged from their houses and murdered in front of their families; others were smothered or burned alive inside their homes. Two wounded men who had managed to crawl out of the flames were thrown back in.

"One lady threw her arms around her husband," Julia Lovejoy was told,

Free-soil citizens of Lawrence: John F. Griswald (top, left) was killed in Quantrill's raid. As an agent of the Emigrant Aid Company, Charles Robinson (top, right) helped pick the site for the town and was later arrested and put on trial for treason by pro-slavery forces at their capital of Lecompton. James and Annie Gleason helped publish the *Kansas Herald of Freedom*, whose weekly antislavery message helped bring the wrath of the Confederate guerrillas down upon their village.

and begged of them to spare his life. They rested the pistol on her arm as it was around his body, and shot him dead, and the fire from the pistol burnt the sleeve of her dress. Mrs. Reed put out the fire six times to save her house, and they would fire it anew, but she by almost superhuman exertions saved it. Mrs. Fisher, wife of the Rev. H. D. Fisher, of the Kansas Conference, . . . a spunky little Dutch-Irish woman from Pennsylvania, by her own exertion saved the L part of her house, whilst the front, a splendid new brick establishment, was burnt, worth $2,000 probably. All the business houses, banks, stores, &c., in the city were robbed and burned save one, and most of the business men killed. It is estimated that half a million in money has been carried off.

Quantrill's men, many of them drunk from commandeered whiskey, rode up and down the streets with American flags dragging in the dust behind their horses. Jim Lane, the principal target of the raid, had managed to escape through a cornfield in his nightshirt, but 183 men and boys were killed — fewer than 20 of whom had been soldiers — and 185 homes were burned before Quantrill and his men rode out of town, leaving behind 80 widows, 250 fatherless children.

To avenge the Lawrence Massacre and to crush Confederate resistance in Missouri once and for all, General Ewing now issued Order Number 11, which forced from their homes every man, woman, and child living in three Missouri border counties, and half of a fourth. Federal troops drove thousands of people onto the open prairie, while Jayhawkers followed in their wake, burning and looting the empty houses they left behind, raiding the refugee columns, stealing even wedding rings. For years, the region would be known as the "Burnt District." "The very air seems charged with blood and death," a newspaperman wrote. "Pandemonium itself seems to have broken loose, and robbery, murder, . . . and death runs riot over the country."

Seeking vengeance: In October 1864 — just a little over a year after Quantrill's raid — volunteers from Lawrence march north on Massachusetts Street to join federal forces near Kansas City. A few weeks later they would help destroy a rebel army at the battle of Westport.

Now, it was the Confederates' turn to seek revenge. General Sterling Price returned to Missouri with 12,000 regulars. With him rode Quantrill and many of his raiders, whom Price had complimented for their "gallant struggle" at Lawrence. Union forces stopped them at the battles of Pilot's Knob and Westport. Quantrill fled to Texas and was later fatally wounded during a raid into Kentucky; his raiders broke up into small, savage outlaw bands. Bloody Bill Anderson was hunted down by federal troops and shot in the back of the head after charging through their lines. Organized Confederate resistance eventually ended, but the bitterness the bloodshed had produced would persist for generations.

THE WORK OF GOD

In the spring of 1863, a delegation of sixteen Plains Indian leaders was invited to Washington. They were photographed with Mrs. Abraham Lincoln, and the President himself received them in the White House. He hoped to persuade them not to be tempted to side with the Confederacy or take advantage of the Civil War to drive out white settlers.

A Cheyenne named Lean Bear addressed Lincoln. "He wished to live in peace for the balance of his life," a reporter for the Washington *Evening Star* remembered his saying, "on the buffalo, as his fathers had done, . . . and again urged the President to counsel his white children, who were annually encroaching more and more upon

Kiowa and Cheyenne leaders gather in the conservatory of the Executive Mansion in Washington, March 27, 1863, to be photographed with Mary Todd Lincoln (standing, far right). The four Cheyenne leaders seated in the front row all had less than eighteen months to live. Yellow Wolf (right) died of tuberculosis, but the rest were killed by whites: Lean Bear (second from right) would be shot down by regulars as he protested his peaceful intentions; War Bonnet (far left) and Standing in the Water were killed by Colorado volunteers at Sand Creek.

their tribes, to abstain from acts of violence and wrong towards them. He deplored, he said, the war between the whites, now being waged, and expressed the determination of the tribes not to take part or sides in it, and said that its end would be hailed with joy by them."

The President replied that

the palefaced people are numerous and prosperous because they cultivate the earth, produce bread, and depend upon the products of the earth rather than wild game for subsistence. This is the chief reason of the difference [between the numbers of the two races]; but there is another. Although we are now engaged in a great war between one another, we are not, as a race, so much disposed to fight and kill one another as our red brethren.

You have asked for my advice. I really am not capable of advising you whether, in the providence of the Great Spirit, who is the great Father of us all, it is for you to maintain the habits and customs of your race, or adopt a new mode of life. I can only say that I can see no way in which your race is to become as numerous and prosperous as the white race except by living as they do, by the cultivation of the earth.

Lincoln presented Lean Bear with a medal, which he wore proudly from that day forward as a token of his friendship with the White Father at Washington.

Lean Bear was a peace chief, one of forty-four who worked for the benefit of all the Cheyenne bands, settling internal quarrels, working for the general welfare, urging the younger warriors to avoid war with the whites. So was his friend Black Kettle. He had once led raids against the Kiowa and Ute, had been entrusted with the tribes' sacred arrows in battle against the Delaware when they strayed too far west from their new home in Indian Territory, and had fought white soldiers on the Solomon River in 1858. But he had watched white settlers and gold-seekers crowd onto the lands between the North Platte and the Arkansas that had been promised to the Cheyenne by the Fort Laramie Treaty, and realized that there were too many whites to fight, that some way must be found to live with them. "The whole force of his nature was concentrated in the one idea of how best to act for the good of his race," a regular army officer remembered; "he knew the power of the white man, and was aware that thence might spring most of the evils that could befall his people, and consequently the whole of his powers were directed toward conciliating the whites, and his utmost endeavors used to preserve peace and friendship between his race and their oppressors."

And so, when a new treaty was hastily drawn up at Fort Wise in 1861, ceding all the Cheyenne and Arapaho lands except for a small reservation along Sand Creek southeast of Denver, Black Kettle was one of just six Cheyenne chiefs to sign. "The whites presumed to treat these six chiefs as the head chiefs of the tribe," the trader George Bent recalled, "and as this was against custom the Cheyennes refused to abide by the treaty. They called the signers of this treaty the 'Six Chiefs,' as a sort of nickname. The whites also wished to consider Black Kettle as head chief, and this too, was against custom. . . . The whites had the wrong idea about Indian chiefs." In any case, the treaty proved a bad bargain: the reservation was small, sandy, barren, empty of game, unsuited to agriculture. Whites were not kept out, as the commissioners had

THE FEARING TIME

In the Southwest, Indians saw the withdrawal of regular troops as a signal to drive out all outsiders. Mescalero Apache and Navajo bands stole livestock, attacked settlements, raided mining camps, even ambushed a column of California volunteers that had been sent against Henry Sibley's Confederates. Ute, Zuni, and Mexican Americans joined white settlers in demanding that the government do something.

The commander of the Department of New Mexico, Brigadier General James Carleton, launched a campaign to restore federal control of the region. He had little patience with Indians. A decorated hero of the Mexican War, grim and demanding, he had fought them for nearly two decades before the war and saw nothing to be gained from negotiations. They must surrender and agree to stay on a reservation of his choosing — an arid stretch of land along the Pecos River called Bosque Redondo — or they would be killed, he said.

Kit Carson, now a colonel of the New Mexico Cavalry, was named to carry out his orders. He began with a grueling but successful campaign against the Mescalero, then turned his attention to the Navajo, some 12,000 of them, scattered across thousands of square miles of rugged country. Riding back and forth across Navajo country for six exhausting months, Carson had poor luck hunting down the elusive Navajo themselves, but he burned their homes, blankets, and grain, rounded up their sheep, hacked down their peach orchards. The Navajo began to starve.

Winter came. The cold began to kill the old people and the children. Carson was ordered to pursue the Navajo into their sacred stronghold, Canyon de Chelly.

There, the Indians stood helplessly on the cliffs, hurling curses and stones, as Carson's men methodically destroyed everything they owned on the canyon floor.

Unable to find food, shivering with cold but afraid to build fires for fear the smoke would give them away, the Navajo began to surrender to Carson, in small groups at first, then by the hundreds, convinced that at least he would not murder them if they put themselves in his hands.

Four thousand Navajo held out for two more years in the remote western reaches of their lands

Kit Carson (above) and some of the Navajo he brought to Bosque Redondo

before surrendering. But most of the tribe — more than 8,000 men, women, and children — gave themselves up and were made to march three hundred miles across New Mexico to Bosque Redondo. Carleton was not prepared for such numbers of desperate people. There was not enough food, no clothes or other supplies. Hundreds died along the way. Ute and New Mexicans shadowing the slow-moving columns seized stragglers and sold them as slaves.

Despite the hardships of getting there, Carleton was confident that Bosque Redondo would soon become "the happiest and most delightfully located pueblo of Indians in New Mexico — perhaps in the United States."

Instead, it was a disaster. There was no game, not enough fertile land for farming, too little grass even for goats. The meager crops that did grow fell victim to cutworms and sudden downpours. Thin government clothing kept no one warm in winter. Bickering between the army and the Indian bureau meant supplies often arrived late, or not at all. There was constant fighting, too, between the Navajo and the outnumbered Mescalero — who finally fled the reservation and returned to the hills from which Kit Carson had driven them.

Carleton insisted that the Navajo live in adobe houses, but they refused, preferring even holes in the ground because their religion forbade them to continue to live in a structure in which someone had died — and they were dying fast.

The Navajo would remain at Bosque Redondo for four ghastly years — they called them *Nahonzod,* "the Fearing Time." In 1868, a new policy would permit them to return to their homeland. By then, more than one-quarter of them had died.

An American flag — blurred by the slow shutter of the camera — marks the wagon in which Arapaho and Cheyenne chiefs, including Black Kettle, ride into Camp Weld, near Denver, to talk peace in September of 1864.

promised they would be. Annuities and goods often failed to arrive. Some Cheyenne were reduced to begging for food from white settlers. Soon, even Black Kettle had moved his lodges back to the old hunting grounds. Despite the best efforts of the peace chiefs, young men from the warrior societies began raiding settlers.

Governor John Evans of Colorado Territory was an ambitious man: he wanted to be Colorado's first senator and saw a winning issue in ridding his region of its Indians. He warned that any Indian found outside the reservation would henceforth be considered hostile, and called upon the federal government for troops to back up his threat. When they did not come — Washington now had no soldiers to spare — Evans called for volunteers. Hundreds signed up.

Parson John Chivington — now Colonel Chivington after his triumph at Glorieta Pass — continued to preach to big appreciative congregations. But he, too, had his sights set on bigger things. One victory had made him a Colorado hero; two might

make him a congressman once Colorado entered the Union. But first he needed a war, and, as military commander in the territory, he was perfectly situated to start one. He ordered his men to burn every Indian village and kill every Indian they came upon.

In May, Black Kettle, Lean Bear, and their bands were hunting buffalo in Kansas. A column of troops appeared near their camp. Lean Bear and another peace chief named Star rode out to meet them. Lean Bear wore the peace medal Lincoln had given him as a sign of his friendship and he held up papers attesting to his loyalty, signed by the President. When the two chiefs were within twenty feet of the soldiers the commanding officer ordered his men to fire. Lean Bear and Star tumbled from their horses; a second volley killed them where they lay.

The younger men wanted to attack the soldiers, but Black Kettle managed to stop them. Even now, there must be no war with the white men, he said; there was no way to win. They held off. But soon, other warriors were seeking revenge. They plundered wagon trains, burned ranches, raped and kidnapped women, and killed some two hundred settlers.

Peace talks: At Fort Weld, Major Edward W. Wynkoop kneels at the feet of Black Kettle (partially obscured by Wynkoop's big hat). At the time, war seemed to have been averted.

One family was butchered just outside Denver, one city resident recalled:

> . . . About 100 yards from the ranch they discovered the body of the murdered woman and her two dead children, one of which was a little girl of four years and the other an infant. The woman had been stabbed in several places and scalped, and the body bore evidence of having been violated. The two children had their throats cut, their heads being nearly severed from their bodies. [The bodies were brought to Denver and] placed in a box, side by side, the two children between their parents, and shown to the people from a shed where the City Hall now stands. Everybody saw them and anger and revenge mounted all day long as the people filed past or remained to talk over Indian outrages and means of protection and reprisal.

The old trader William Bent, married to a Cheyenne woman and the father of three half-Cheyenne sons, feared what was coming and tried to stop it. He warned Chivington that what had already happened was bad enough, but that if the Indians were further provoked they would unite among themselves — Cheyenne and Kiowa, Arapaho and Lakota — and then no power on earth could protect the whites from their anger. "In reply," Bent remembered,

> [Chivington] said he was not authorized to make peace, and that he was then on the warpath. . . . I then stated to him that there was great risk to run in keeping up the war; that there were a great many government trains traveling to New Mexico and other points; also a great many citizens, and that I did not think there was sufficient force to protect the travelers, and the citizens and the settlers of the country would have to suffer. He said the citizens would have to protect themselves.

Colonel John M. Chivington

In September of 1864, Black Kettle and six other Cheyenne chiefs came to Fort Weld, near Denver, wanting to talk peace, and bringing with them four white captives they had ransomed from other bands as evidence of their good faith. "We have come with our eyes shut . . ." Black Kettle told the fort's commander, "like coming through the fire. All we ask is that we may have peace with the whites; we want to hold you by the hand. You are our father; we have been traveling through a cloud; the sky has been dark ever since the war began. . . . I want you to give all the chiefs of the soldiers here to understand that we are for peace, and that we have made peace, that we may not be mistaken for enemies."

This did not fit well with the war plans Evans and Chivington had already made. " . . . [W]hat shall I do with the Third Colorado Regiment if I make peace?" the governor asked privately. "They have been raised to kill Indians and they must kill Indians."

Some of Black Kettle's own young men had been among the raiders, the chief admitted, but he remained determined not to have a war. He brought his band back to the reservation in November, and reported to Major Edward Wynkoop at Fort Lyon.

Wynkoop, also eager to avoid conflict, promised him protection as well as food and supplies, for which he had no authorization. The Indians would have to be

Blackfoot winter camp, Montana Territory,
ca. 1890. It was during the winter that the Plains
peoples were most vulnerable to attack.

made "to suffer more" before they could have peace, his superiors said. Wynkoop was replaced.

The new commander, Major Scott Anthony, cooperated with Evans and Chivington. He told Black Kettle to move his band twenty-five miles away, to a bend in Sand Creek. They would be safe there, he said. Then he waited for reinforcements from Denver.

Chivington and some seven hundred volunteers arrived at Fort Lyon on November 26, 1864, eager for a fight before their hundred-day term of enlistment ran out. Some officers protested that to attack the peaceable encampment would betray the army's pledge of safety. "Damn any man that sympathizes with Indians," Chivington said. "I have come to kill Indians and believe it right and honorable to use any means under God's heaven. . . ."

At dawn on November 29, 1864, Chivington and seven hundred men, many of them full of the whiskey they had swallowed to keep them warm during the icy all-night ride, reached the edge of Black Kettle's sleeping camp. "Kill and scalp all," Chivington told his men, "big and little; nits make lice." His men needed little encouragement.

One of William Bent's sons, Robert, was riding with them, commandeered against his will to show the way to the Cheyenne camp. Three of Bent's other children — Charles, Julia, and George — were staying in it. George Bent watched the soldiers come:

> From down the creek a large body of troops was advancing at a rapid trot . . . more soldiers could be seen making for the Indian pony herds to the south of the camp; in the camps themselves all was confusion and noise — men, women, and children rushing out of the lodges partly dressed; women and children screaming at the sight of the troops; men running back into the lodges for their arms. . . . Black Kettle had a large American flag tied to the end of a long lodgepole and was standing in front of his lodge, holding the pole, with the flag fluttering in the gray light of the winter dawn. . . .
>
> All the time Black Kettle kept calling out not to be frightened; that the camp was under protection and there was no danger.

Robert Bent was watching, too:

> I saw the American flag waving and heard Black Kettle tell the Indians to stand around the flag, and there they were huddled — men, women, and children. This was when we were within fifty yards of the Indians. I also saw a white flag raised. These flags were in so conspicuous a position that they must have been seen. . . . I think there were six hundred Indians in all. I think there were thirty-five braves and some old men, about sixty in all. . . . [T]he rest of the men were away from camp hunting. . . .

The volunteers began firing into the lodges. Warriors did all they could to defend their families. "I never saw more bravery displayed by any set of people on the face of the earth than by these Indians," a regular soldier recalled. "They would charge on the whole company singly, determined to kill someone before being killed themselves. . . . We, of course, took no prisoners."

"After the firing," Robert Bent remembered,

the warriors put the squaws and children together, and surrounded them to protect them. I saw five squaws under a bank for shelter. When the troops came up to them they ran out and showed their persons to let the soldiers know they were squaws and begged for mercy, but the soldiers shot them all. I saw one squaw lying on the bank whose leg had been broken by a shell; a soldier came up to her with a drawn saber; she raised her arm to protect herself, when he struck, breaking her arm; she rolled over and raised her other arm, when he struck, breaking it, and then he left her without killing her. There seemed to be indiscriminate slaughter of men, women and children. There were some thirty or forty squaws collected in a hole for protection; they sent out a little girl about six years old with a white flag on a stick; she had not proceeded a few steps when she was shot and killed. All the squaws in that hole were afterwards killed. . . .

"In going over the battleground the next day," a regular army lieutenant testified later,

I did not see a body of a man, woman, or child but was scalped, and in many instances their bodies were mutilated in the most horrible manner. . . . I heard one man say that he had cut out a woman's private parts and had them for exhibition on a stick; I heard another man say that he had cut the fingers off an Indian to get the rings on his hand; according to the best of my knowledge and belief these atrocities that were committed were with the knowledge of J. M. Chivington, and I do not know of his taking any measures to prevent them; I heard of one instance of a child a few months old being thrown in the feedbox of a wagon, and after being carried some distance left on the ground to perish; I also heard of numerous instances in which men had cut out the private parts of females and stretched them over the saddle-bows and wore them over their hats while riding in ranks.

Chivington and his men returned to Denver in triumph, claiming to have killed five hundred warriors — instead of ninety-eight women and children and a handful of mostly old men. The *Rocky Mountain News* pronounced it a "brilliant feat of arms." "All did nobly," Chivington said, and one evening during intermission at the Denver opera house, one hundred Cheyenne scalps were put on display while the orchestra played patriotic airs and the audience stood to applaud the men who had taken them.

Regular army officers were appalled by Sand Creek. General Ulysses S. Grant himself privately declared it nothing more nor less than murder. There were separate investigations by Congress and the army. "As to Colonel Chivington," said the official report of the Senate Committee on the Conduct of the War, "your committee can hardly find fitting terms to describe his conduct. Wearing the uniform of the United States, which should be the emblem of justice and humanity . . . he deliberately planned and executed a foul and dastardly massacre which would have disgraced the veriest savage among those who were the victims of his cruelty." But by the time the tribunals reached their verdicts, Chivington was a civilian again and beyond the reach of military justice. In the end, no one was ever punished for the slaughter of Black Kettle's

Lawrence reborn: the south-southwestern side of town, photographed by Alexander Gardner in 1867 from a gentle rise the townspeople had grandly named Mount Oread

Cheyenne. Nor did Chivington ever admit he had done anything wrong. Speaking before a reunion of Pike's Peak pioneers nearly twenty years later, he would declare, "I stand by Sand Creek."

Word of what had happened there spread fast. Cheyenne runners carried war pipes to all the Lakota, Arapaho, and Cheyenne bands. Soon, the whole region was at war: stagecoaches were burned, telegraph wires pulled down. Denver was cut off from the outside world. Cheyenne sacked the little town of Julesburg, Colorado, twice. Soldiers who tried to stop them were killed or driven off. "Since this . . . horrible murder by Chivington," said Major Wynkoop, "the country presents a scene of desolation; all communication is cut off with the States, except by sending bodies of troops, and already over one hundred whites have fallen as victims to this fearful vengeance of these betrayed Indians. All this country is ruined; there can be no such thing as peace in the future."

Still, Black Kettle wanted no part of further fighting. "Although wrongs have been done me," he said, "I live in hopes. I have not got two hearts. . . . I once thought that I was the only man that persevered to be the friend of the white man, but since they have come and cleaned out our lodges, horses, and everything else, it is hard for me to believe white men any more." He took the survivors of Sand Creek south, instead of north, as far from the fighting as he could get.

On April 9, 1865, Robert E. Lee at last surrendered his army at Appomattox Court House in Virginia. The transcontinental telegraph now brought the news west to San Francisco instantaneously, and fireworks were launched from Fisherman's Wharf in celebration. In Los Angeles, there was a parade, and Denver celebrated with a two-hundred-gun salute. All over the West, lives interrupted by war resumed again.

Julia Louisa Lovejoy, now living with her family in the town of Baldwin City in what she proudly called "the *State* of Kansas," expressed her pleasure and pride in another letter to her old New England paper:

Towns are starting up as by magic all along the valley. . . . Things now look quite city-like, and the sound of the hammer is heard on every hand. . . . I wish to say to our friends in New Hampshire, one and all, we have never regretted coming to Kansas. . . . We have never wavered — never flinched — not even when three times in twenty four hours we were compelled to flee from our house. . . . I tell you all, though we have felt the horrors of war, if we were not in Kansas already, we would come as soon as steam could bring us.

Believing in the American West

Patricia Nelson Limerick

GROWING UP POST-MORMON

My father and I are not Mormons. This fact is true of many other people in the American West, but it is particularly true of us. My father was raised Mormon in Brigham City, Utah. Although it is common for fallen-away members of the Church of Jesus Christ of Latter-day Saints to become fervent believers in other churches, my father took a different path. When he cut his ties to the Mormon Church and moved to California, he turned away from all organized religion.

My sisters and I thus grew up with a particular opportunity to drive our father batty. Here was our distinctive and very gratifying channel of rebellion: we could insist on our First Amendment right to freedom of religion, get dressed up for church, and demand that Father drive us there. The peak of this soul-satisfying mutiny came in asking him for money to put in the collection plate. And, since Mother was (and is) a non–church-attending Congregationalist and thus nearly as vulnerable as Father to the abrasive powers of our piety, there was also considerable pleasure to be gained from coming home from church, sitting down to Sunday dinner, and delivering an earnest prayer on behalf of our parents' redemption.

Such rebellion, however, came at a cost. For me, the cost was repeated exposure to the misery of the unbaptized heathen. Churched or not, our parents had installed into our thinking a great devotion to justice and fairness. And so the dilemma of the poor souls in Africa and Asia, living and dying and heading off to hell without the opportunity to hear the Christian gospel, weighed heavily on me. If God really had decided to let salvation hinge on the basis of the arbitrary facts of place of birth (a fact that He, in His omnipotence, had determined), then God seemed to be following rather questionable values Himself, showing a pretty tenuous understanding of the concept of fairness.

The pleasures of bugging my father were, therefore, already wearing thin on a memorable day in 1962 at the First Baptist Church in Banning, the day on which my rebellion ended. The membership of the First Baptist Church was entirely white. On this Sunday, a black woman, new in town, came to church. I happened to be behind her in the line, waiting to shake hands with the minister. We had spent some time, in Sunday school, singing about Jesus' transcendence of racial prejudice:

> Red and yellow, black and white,
> They're all sacred in His sight.
> Jesus loves the little children of the world.

This little song was not easy to reconcile with the dilemma of the unbaptized heathen, and our minister had, himself, not gotten very far in reconciling Jesus' sentiments with his own. When the black woman shook hands with him, the minister told her that *her* church was on the other side of town.

Since that Sunday, I have learned more about the ways in which race relations in the American West came to bear an unhappy resemblance to race relations in the rest of the country. In religious terms, it was not simply a matter of segregation in western churches, it was often a matter of the active use of the church as a social institution to maintain racial separation and inequality. The minister of the First Baptist Church not only gave me a memorable introduction to this topic, he also persuaded me that my rebellion against my father had gone far enough. Since then I have taken the path leading away from organized religion and toward what I will call disorganized religion. My father and I remain post-Mormon and unchurched, but nonetheless driven by convictions about right and wrong.

For decades, I thought that Father and I had placed ourselves on the margins of conventional religious behavior. But, like so many other westerners who treasured a picture of themselves as odd birds, we have turned out to be birds positioned right at the center of the flock. "[P]oor church attendance is characteristic of westerners generally," the historian Michael Quinn has written. This is the West's principal claim to distinctiveness in religious terms: it is the region with the lowest rates of church participation, in both the nineteenth and the twentieth centuries. In the nation as a whole, "the West as a region has the lowest attendance (36 percent) in church or synagogue." The West thus holds the status of the nation's "Unchurched Belt." In this region, participants in disorganized religion have held and hold a considerable numerical advantage over participants in organized religion.

My father and I turn out to be not rebels and eccentrics, but representative westerners. Still, without official papers of membership, we and our many disaffiliated comrades are not likely to register in the records of western religious history. Contemplating the prospect of one's invisibility, one finds good reason to question how much the fact of church membership reveals about a matter as subjective and private as religious belief. Churches are, of course, the places where *records* of official religious performance accumulate. Historians of religion, oriented to written documents, have had good reason to place churches and their members at the center of their inquiry, in the manner of labor historians who, for a time, hinged their history of the working class on the much more narrow topic of membership in unions.

"In comparison with Whites in the United States today," the anthropologist Harold Driver once wrote, "the Indians [of the past] were at least ten times as religious." Of all the improbable proclamations of academics made over the last forty years, this one is my personal favorite, an example of confident, social-scientific thinking at its goofiest. And yet, whatever Harold Driver meant by this memorable assertion, one suspects that he did *not* mean that Indians were ten times as religious because they were ten times more likely to join formally chartered and organized churches. On the contrary, Driver thought (and he shared this conviction with many others) that Indian people were more religious because they unmistakably and consistently demonstrated their faith, observing little separation between the secular and the spiritual. They did not need to join churches and attend formal services, because they lived virtually every moment in a religious way. By contrast, in Driver's equally widely shared but considerably more questionable assumption, modern white American people have been a very secular group, driven primarily by economic motives. For a group of people holding their souls on such a tight leash, religious conviction could only appear in official membership in an institutional church, with even that level of religious commitment often confined to attendance at Sunday services, cresting at Easter and Christmas.

Consider, by contrast, the state of affairs in mid-nineteenth-century rural Oregon. True to the western pattern, church membership there was very limited. But a low percentage of church attendance, historian Dean May has argued, "does not imply . . . an absence of religious sentiment and feelings." The settlers' religious activity was, emphatically, local, often practiced within households, "involving them rarely, if at all, in any broader community." They had Bibles in their homes, and recorded significant family events in those Bibles. "Blessings on food, prayers, prayer meetings, hymn singing, and exhortation were held in home and schoolhouse for gatherings of families and close neighbors." Preachers sent by home missionary societies found Oregon's "seeming incoherence of religious organization" both puzzling and frustrating. In a curious convergence of opinion, historians would come to share the judgment of the preachers: "religion in any setting other than an established congregation was to them hardly religion at all."

Few of the people of the Oregon settlements were joining churches, but they gave many other signs of religiousness. The pattern of Oregon may well be the pattern of the western United

Kansas baptism

States. "[E]xcept in Mormon territory, the majority of far westerners have cared little about traditional religious institutions and practices," the historian Eldon G. Ernst put it. "They form the most secular society in the United States if gauged by church membership statistics, yet when questioned they claim to be religiously concerned and find religion to be important in their personal lives."

We return to the common difficulty faced by anyone exploring this topic: in its subjectivity and privacy, religious belief is very hard to track. A few groups — Indians, missionaries, and Mormons — have made the task easier: for all their differences, these groups were believers who consistently and visibly demonstrated their faith in frequent public rituals, steering by religious principles in everyday activities. Whether the ritual was a dance, a hymn, or a ward-house meeting, whether the consecrated activity was hunting, teaching, or irrigated farming, Indians, missionaries, and Mormons placed their faith front and center, where no one could miss it. Thus, western historians fell into a perfectly logical habit of confining the explicit discussion of religion to topics where it simply could not be avoided. For all the other westerners — for the sizable numbers who were *not* Indians, *not* missionaries, and *not* Mormons — the most resolutely secular history is all they seemed to deserve, and generally all they got.

The fact that American westward expansion was so strongly governed by economic motives reinforced the apparent wisdom of this strategy of reserving religious history for the few, and leaving secular history for the majority. The daily experience of overland travel during the gold rush had many of the qualities of a sacred pilgrimage, testing determination and persistence in a thousand ways. But a journey undertaken as a tribute to Mammon surrendered its credentials as pilgrimage. Fervent participation in mineral rushes and land rushes, in timber booms and cattle speculation deepened the impression that the determination of white Americans to develop the West's natural resources left very little room for the development of their souls. Often invoked in support of these expanding commercial enterprises, God's name looked as if it had become little more than another product endorsement.

Consider, as a striking example of this linkage of religion with commerce, the memorable song "The Cowboy's Prayer":

Lord, please help me, lend me Thine ear,
The prayer of a troubled cowman to hear.
No doubt my prayer to you may seem strange,
But I want you to bless my cattle range. . . .

As you O Lord my fine herds behold,
They represent a sack of pure gold.
I think that at least five cents on the pound
Would be a good price for beef the year round.

When God was asked to intervene on behalf of rising cattle prices, the theological seemed to have made a full surrender to the secular. But then again, when whites asked God to bless their economic undertakings, was this *entirely* different from an Indian hunter's hope that the right gestures of respect would recruit the spirits as the sponsors of a successful hunt? Didn't both practices serve as examples of a people's refusal to draw a hard line between the spiritual and the worldly? If God wanted the best for His Chosen People, wouldn't He *want* them to prosper in the cattle market?

In 1973, my husband and I were driving west, crossing the country on yet another secular pilgrimage. Through the journey, we had invested a great deal in the services of auto mechanics, purchasing, among other things, an entire replacement engine for our VW Bug. We were not entirely sure that we had enough money left to get to California. On a Sunday morning, we turned on the radio and found an evangelist in the middle of a prayer that spoke directly to our dilemma: "Lord," the evangelist asked, "heal our families; heal our hearts; and heal our finances." When my father wired us money in Laramie, we felt that prayer had been heard.

WESTWARD THE COURSE OF CHAOS TAKES ITS WAY

The year after I parted with the First Baptist Church, a remarkable event occurred in the demography of Banning, California. A bunch of kids appeared out of nowhere. Banning was a town of eight or nine thousand people, and I thought I knew most of them; I certainly knew the ones around my own age. But when we left the sixth grade at Central Elementary School and moved on to the seventh grade at Susan B. Coombs Junior High School, some fifteen or twenty strangers joined us. Had a large caravan of families all moved to town over the summer? On the contrary, and very mysteriously, the strangers claimed that they had lived in Banning most, in some cases all, of their lives. But where had they been? How had they stayed hidden all those years?

The strangers were, it turned out, Catholics. They had been hidden in parochial school, but parochial school — whatever that was — ended in sixth grade, and so now they were out of hiding. The term "Mormon" I understood, but "Catholic"? Or, even more puzzling, "Jew"? In the First Baptist Sunday School, our education on that particular topic had been *very* brief. One of the children had said to the Sunday school teacher, "We keep seeing the word 'Jew' in the Bible, but we don't know what it means." The teacher looked unhappy, and then seized on her way out. "You all know Jeff," she said, pointing to one member of the class. "Jeff used to be a Jew, but now he's a Baptist."

The extent of my Sunday school teacher's — and my — ignorance in these matters was at a cosmic scale, and quite surprising, given the West's great history of religious diversity. This diversity represented the realization of the worst fears of many Protestants in the nineteenth-century West. Protestant clergymen in the West confronted a region in which every moment in daily life told them that they were working against a great disadvantage. White American Protestants in the nineteenth-century West knew that they were outnumbered. They knew that they had before them a long struggle to find a permanent place in a society in which neither Episcopalians nor Baptists, Presbyterians nor Congregationalists could dominate. In many western areas, Catholics and Mormons had gotten the jump in timing, as well as in membership, on Protestants of any denomination. Jews were early arrivals in many western settlements. At the same time, American Indian religions and the Buddhism, Taoism, and Confucianism of Asian immigrants stretched the categories of faith along an extraordinarily wide continuum. In the nineteenth-century West, as historian Ferenc Szasz has written, the mainline Protestant groups "confronted the greatest challenge of their day: dealing with religious diversity." Several decades before their counterparts in the eastern United States would come to face a comparable challenge, western Protestant ministers "dealt with pluralism on a daily basis." In religious terms, the West was the American future.

For many of those getting an advance look at this future, religious pluralism proved to be fruitful soil for discomfort and doubt. Where we might see an extraordinary and fascinating mosaic of religious practice, the Protestant ministers were more inclined to see chaos, and dangerous chaos at that. Take the concerns and worries recorded by the Reverend Josiah Strong. After two years' service as a Congregationalist minister in Cheyenne, Wyoming, the reverend came down with a pronounced case of western Protestant anxiety. The West, he wrote in his book *Our Country* (1886), was "peculiarly exposed" to the principal "dangers" of the times: "Mammonism, materialism, luxuriousness, and the centralization of wealth." The region was particularly burdened, as well, with the threats posed by socialism, the saloon, Mormonism, Catholicism, and foreign immigration. Not only were the dangers greatest in the West, the Protestant churches were at their weakest, ill-equipped to respond to any of these challenges.

If this was a region in which all its enemies ganged up on Protestant Christianity, might the good news be that the region's sparse population rendered its religious condition irrelevant to the nation's well-being? On the contrary: in Rev. Josiah Strong's judgment, the West determined the national future. With its vast resources, ready to support an equally sizable population, the West "is to dominate the East"; in the near future, "the West will direct the policy of the Government, and by virtue of her preponderating population and influence will determine our national character and, therefore, destiny."

If Protestant Christianity could not save the West, then nothing could save the nation. And the stakes went considerably beyond the national. In the reverend's vision, the settling of the American West would be only one test of the Anglo-Saxon's "instinct or genius for colonizing," a genius that would finally work its way around the entire planet in *the final competition of races, for which the Anglo-Saxon is being schooled* [his emphasis]." Through the religious challenge posed by the American West, "God was training the Anglo-Saxon race for an hour sure to come in the world's future."

Full of distrust for European immigrants, for Mormons, and for New Mexican Hispanics, Rev. Josiah Strong nonetheless reserved his greatest distrust for the actions and beliefs of his fellow Anglo-Saxons, those "church-members who seem to have left their religion behind when they crossed the Missouri." Of course, the reverend would worry about all those "others," but it is, at first, a surprise to see how doubtful he was about the religious reliability of his fellow whites. Given the continued status of the West as the nation's unchurched region, he was right to be worried. My father and I, and our many disaffiliated fellow westerners, are the reverend's worst nightmare come true.

In the intervening century, few writers have been able to produce texts that can match *Our Country* in its remarkable mixture of confidence and doubt. In the space of a few pages, Rev. Josiah Strong could shift from a cosmic confidence in Anglo-Saxon destiny to rule the world and to install God's kingdom in the process to a dark vision of a West soon to collapse before the pressures of evil and disorder. How could he be at once so confident and so anxious? The paradox here was a great one. On the ground level the American West had the greatest religious diversity of any part of the nation, and the heightened anxiety of the nineteenth-century Protestant clergy testified to the challenge posed by that diversity. And yet, in the broader sweep of history, expansion into the American West seemed to have shown white American religious belief at its most homogeneous, combining a Christian sense of mission with patriotism to form a virtual state religion. Faith in the United States' Manifest Destiny had long ago melted the division between the sacred and the secular. And yet, by a considerable irony, when Protestant fervor merged into national policy, it ended up producing the region in which Protestant denominations had their weakest hold.

Whites had an indisputable claim on the West, Senator Thomas Hart Benton had said, because they used the land "according to the intentions of the CREATOR." As historian Albert Weinberg observed, "[T]heological literature was scarcely more abundant in reference to Providence than was the literature of expansionism." To one typical expansionist during the Mexican-American War, war was "the religious execution of our country's glorious mission, under the direction of Divine Providence, to civilize and christianize, and raise up from anarchy and degradation a most ignorant, indolent, wicked and unhappy people." And yet one outcome of this enterprise was not the redemption of the Mexican people, but the slide into religious "anarchy and degradation" of many of the Americans who were supposed to be the agents of the West's redemption. As William Jennings Bryan put it after the start of the Philippine insurrection, "'Destiny' is not as manifest as it was" a while ago.

THE *KIVA* IN MY SOUL

In New Mexico, it was never possible to draw a firm border between the secular and the sacred. For centuries, Indian religious belief erased any line between faith and worldly activity. In the Spanish colonization of the sixteenth and seventeenth centuries, missionaries played a role in conquest as important as, if not more important than, the role of soldiers. For the Spanish, religious motives came interwoven with economic and political motives; even when governors fought with friars for the control of colonies, those struggles dramatized the central role that religion played in the whole undertaking. In the nineteenth century, when white Americans entered the scene, Protestant disapproval of Catholicism added to the contest over land and labor and to the frictions of nationality and race. In the history unrolling in New Mexico, religious belief had been everywhere, shaping and being shaped by even the most secular elements of human thought and behavior.

In the summer of 1992, Santa Fe — the town called "Holy Faith" — permitted me a memorable visit to the blurred border between the secular and the sacred. I was meeting with a group of international scholars studying American regionalism. From Senegal to Thailand, from Belgium to the Philippines, all of my companions had grown up watching western movies, and watching them with feelings that bordered on reverence. No conventionally religious mission society, one could learn from the testimony of these visitors, has ever come close to matching the achievements of the Hollywood western in global proselytizing and conversion.

On our last day of class, the participants were having a competition to see who had been the most influenced or tainted by the Wild West myth. We had heard a number of eloquent statements from men whose childhoods had included frequent visits to "Old West" tourist towns in Germany and Austria, where they had cheerfully fired away at the Indian targets in shooting galleries. Then a woman from Poland suddenly and urgently announced her candidacy as the most mythically influenced. "The first thing I can remember," she told us, "is my father reading to me from Karl May's western novels. As soon as I could read, I read them for myself. I loved old Shatterhand, and even after I saw a movie with a fat Frenchman playing his part, my love for him did not change. You may tell me they are factually wrong, but Karl May's novels are . . ." Here she paused and searched for the right word, seizing on a term she had learned the day before during a tour of a pueblo. "Karl May's novels," she ended, with the right word firmly grasped, "are the *kiva* in my soul."

Here was yet another piece of testimony from Santa Fe, reminding me of the hopelessness of trying to separate faith from worldly fact in western America. Once again, Santa Fe offered a reminder that of all the places on the planet where the sacred and the secular meet, the American West is one of the hot spots. One could argue (as indeed one had, and at length) that the vision of the West as a romantic place, where strong and good men went down to Main Street or out to the wilderness to take their courageous stands, held little connection to historical fact. And yet, if Karl May's western fantasies had provided a spiritual and emotional sanctuary for a young woman growing up in Poland in tough times, then we were clearly talking about a realm of belief out of reach of historical fact checking.

Trained in movie theaters in Senegal or Thailand, New York City or Denver, the human spirit has developed the conditioned response of soaring when it confronts certain images: horses galloping across open spaces; wagon trains moving through a landscape of mesas and mountains; cruel enemies and agents of disorder defeated by handsome white men with nerves of steel and tremendous — and justified — self-esteem. And when the human spirit undertakes to soar, it is not necessarily the obligation of the historian to act as air traffic controller and force the spirit down for a landing. Improbable as it may seem to the prosaic historian, an imagined and factually unsubstantiated version of western American history has become, for many believers, a sacred story. For those believers, a challenge to that story can count as sacrilege.

In American life today, lots of groups have made a heavy emotional investment in the proposition that history is a sacred, not a secular, tale. The best and clearest example of this comes from the Mormons. In the last few years, historians who are Mormon believers but who try to write searchingly and critically about Mormon history have had a rough time. Some of them have been excommunicated for their failure to write what the church's General Authorities call faith-affirming history. But the pattern seen among the Mormons appears everywhere. Consider, for instance, how similar the Mormon call for faith-affirming history is to the Afro-centric call for a history of African-American people that consistently praises their accomplishments and affirms their self-esteem. Or consider the desire, on the part of some American Indian people, for a writing of Indian history that enshrines Indian people as ecological and environmental saints and traces an unbroken line of nobility and solidarity among tribal people. When white politicians condemn "revisionist" or "multicultural" history and call for a narrative of the past that affirms the achievements and virtues of white Americans, those politicians show a striking kinship to the Afro-centric intellectuals and to the General Authorities of the Mormon Church. *Every-*

Episcopal worshipers, Wichita, Kansas

one wants faith-affirming history; the disagreement is just a question of which faith any particular individual wants to see affirmed. Each group wants history to provide guidance, legitimacy, justification, and direction for its particular chosen people.

These contests over history, often focused on the West, resemble and echo more familiar contests over religious faith. Different versions of history have become creation stories or origin stories for the people who treasure them, and, with so much feeling at stake, the clash between these sacred tales grows increasingly bitter. And yet, while these separate and contesting claims on history proliferate, more and more evidence emerges from the historical record to counter these assertions of exclusivity. Explorations of western American history reveal many examples of unexpected kinship, mixed heritage, cultural trading, syncretism, and borrowing. It is not simply a matter of the blending of the West's people through intermarriage, though this is certainly an enormous part of the region's story. It is also a matter of reciprocal influence and mutual assimilation. The various peoples of the American West have been bumping into each other for an awfully long time, and it cannot be a surprise to discover that their habits and beliefs have rubbed off on each other.

Indian religious movements — from the ghost dance to the Native American Church with its use of peyote — show many Christian elements. Perhaps the best example of this complexity in religious identity is the Lakota religious leader Black Elk. Thanks to the writer John G. Neihardt's telling of his life story in *Black Elk Speaks,* Black Elk came to stand for the most traditional practice of Indian religion, a practice brought to a tragic end by conquest. But his daughter, Lucy Black Elk Looks Twice, hoped to correct and deepen the standing image of her father, and, working with the anthropologist Michael Steltencamp, Lucy told the post-conquest story of Nicholas Black Elk, who became a leading Catholic convert and cathechist on his reservation. This was not a matter of Black Elk "selling out" or betraying his traditional beliefs; this was a matter of sincere religious conviction responding to new beliefs in new times.

In the nineteenth-century West, white Americans had denounced the religions of the "others," labeling other systems of belief as paganism, heathenism, superstition, barbarism, or savagery, and struggling to convert American Indians and Asian immigrants to Protestant Christianity. In the late-twentieth-century West, the tide seems to be reversing, as a number of white Americans have developed an enthusiasm for tribal religions, as well as for the varieties of Asian Buddhism. Particularly well represented in the West, "New Age" religion has appropriated pieces and parts of American Indian religions, with both Indian and white claimants to enlightenment, in the familiar area of overlap between commerce and religion, cashing in on the opportunities so presented. Rev. Josiah Strong and his colleagues were presumably tossing in their graves, but all over the West, the lines dividing the vision quest from communion, the *kiva* from the church, were shifting and wavering.

DREAM OTHER DREAMS, AND BETTER

To many white Americans in our times, belief in the mythic Old West has come to resemble belief in more conventional religious doctrines. For these believers, the Old Frontier is the nation's creation story, the place where the virtues and values of the nation were formed. And yet, for all the faith now invested in it, the mythic version of the Old West had little room for ministers and pastors, congregations and parishes. In a story full of cowboys, sheriffs, saloon girls, outlaws, gunfighters, prospectors, and stagecoach drivers, the church was, at best, the place where the frightened townspeople gathered to sing hymns and await rescue by the all-too-worldly hero. The church, after all, was aligned with the forces of respectability, the forces that would eventually tame the Wild West and end all the fun and adventure of the glory days. If one went in search of the classic heroes in the mythic turf of the Old West, one would not bother to look among the clergy.

In the quest for western heroes, there is good reason now to look in unexpected, less explored places. The old heroes are a pretty battered and discredited lot, with their character flaws on permanent display. The examples they provide often affirm the wrong faith entirely — the faith in guns and violence — or serve solely as individual examples of courage and determination, attached to no particular principle. Driven by the values of conquest and domination, or purely by the goal of personal fortune-seeking, the old heroes are looking pretty tired — depleted, exhausted, and ready for retirement. In truth, they deserve a rest.

And yet, when the critics of academic historians say that we have discredited the old heroes and failed to replace them with any new ones, they are right. But this is not because we lack the resources. We have all the material we need to put

Chinese American congregation, California

forward a better team, people whose examples affirm a faith of considerably greater promise. It is time for a different kind of western hero: the sustainable hero who can replace the old, exhausted, and depleted western heroes. As Wallace Stegner said of the old western myths, "dream other dreams, and better."

Sustainability in a hero means, very concretely, providing inspiration that sustains the spirit and the soul. While inconsistency can disqualify a conventional hero, a degree of inconsistency is one of the essential qualifications of a sustainable hero. Models of sustainable heroism are drawn from the record of people doing the right thing *some of the time* — people practicing heroism at a level that we can actually aspire to match. The fact that these people fell, periodically, off the high ground of heroism but then determinedly climbed back, even if only in order to fall again, is exactly what makes their heroism sustainable. Because it is uneven and broken, this kind of heroism is resilient, credible, possible, reachable. Sustainable heroism comes only in moments and glimpses, but they are moments and glimpses in which the universe lights up.

Assigned in 1867 to preside over the vast district of Montana, Idaho, and Utah, Bishop Daniel Tuttle "traveled more than forty thousand miles" by stagecoach. "Most times I enjoyed that mode of traveling," he remembered, "many times I grimly endured it, a few times I was rendered miserable by it." Think about what it meant to ride with strangers for hours and hours, jammed into an inflexible, jostling container, and the fact that Bishop Tuttle kept his temper and most of the time enjoyed the ride is its own measure of sustainable heroism.

While misery most often derived from the rough road conditions or the inadequacy of stagecoach shock-protection, fellow passengers could sometimes match the bumps in the road in their power to annoy. In one case, a fellow passenger "by manner and act was insulting to a colored woman in the coach." Bishop Tuttle firmly "reproved him." When words proved insufficient and the passenger "repeated the offense," Tuttle reported, "I shook him soundly." If this demonstration of muscular Christianity failed to produce a conversion, it still made for a happier ride. "At the next station," the offender "got out and slunk entirely away from our sight."

Bishop Tuttle was a complicated man, full of self-righteous disapproval in his appraisal of Mormon belief and earnestly committed to the growth of his denomination. But when Bishop Tuttle took his stand on behalf of the right of African-American women to travel with dignity, he offered a memorable demonstration of sustainable heroism, an episode in faith-affirming history for those trying to hold on to a belief in an American commitment to justice and fairness.

And then there is the remarkable example of heroism set by Rev. Howard Thurman. An African-American who was the chaplain at Howard University, he headed west to team up with a white man as co-pastor of a new and courageous church. As a young child, he had attended his father's funeral and listened to a preacher condemn his father as an example of an unredeemed, unchurched sinner. Ever since then, Thurman had been on a campaign against exclusivity in Christian practice, fighting the exclusivity of the smugly saved as persistently as he fought the exclusivity of race. When he learned of an effort to form a church in San Francisco uniting people of all races and backgrounds, he felt called. The year was 1943, more than ten years before the Montgomery, Alabama, bus boycott.

The location and the timing were both crucial. "Segregation of the races," Thurman wrote, "was a part of the mores, and of the social behavior of the country." "San Francisco with its varied nationalities, its rich intercultural heritages, and its face resolutely fixed toward the Orient" was the ideal place to undertake a trial run toward a better future in American race relations. War work had brought a much increased black population to San Francisco and heightened the prospects of community friction. Responding to these challenges, an interracial group had decided to form the Church for the Fellowship of All Peoples, and Thurman joined them, following his quest to find out "whether or not it is true that experiences of spiritual unity and fellowship are more compelling than the fears and dogmas and prejudices that separate men." There was considerable risk, financial and otherwise, in the "mission" that brought him and his family "three thousand miles across the continent." And there were constant tests of the spirit, as the Fellowship Church and its founder faced the prospects of sponsoring interracial marriages and other challenges to the social order. Simply visiting a member of the congregation in the hospital could prove to be a test of Thurman's spirit; hospital staffs repeatedly stumbled over and resisted the notion that a white believer could be in the care of a black pastor.

Fellowship Church under Rev. Howard Thurman's leadership proved to be a great success, navigating its way through the difficult divisions between denominations as well as those between races. In God's presence, Thurman always insisted, "the worshiper is neither male nor female, black nor white, Protestant nor Catholic nor Buddhist nor Hindu, but a human spirit laid bare." "Religious experience," he believed — and he had lived this gospel — "must unite rather than divide men."

The examples set by heroes like Bishop Tuttle and Reverend Thurman encourage me to believe in the real American West, a place — in the past and in the present — of dazzling human and natural possibility. Believing in the other West, the mythic and imagined West, has never been much of an option for me. Instead, the very notion of investing any faith in a simple, romantic, glorified West always brought to mind the verse that I learned from my father when I was very young:

With this bright, believing band,
I have no claim to be.
What seems so true to them,
Seems fantasy to me.

This verse has kept me on course in the company of those who have fallen head over heels in love with a western illusion; and yet, in the presence of more traditional religious believers, it gives me much less comfort. The company of people secure in their faith, whether that faith is a tribal religion, Catholicism, Judaism, Mormonism, or a Protestant denomination, can make me melt with envy. But then the verse — "With this bright, believing band, I have no claim to be" — comes to mind and interrupts the melting. I remain a member of a battered, disorganized, but still pretty bright, believing band of my own, churched and unchurched, composed of all races and backgrounds — people who hold on to a faith that fairness and justice might someday prevail in this region and in this nation. That faith, the faith of my father and my mother, of Bishop Tuttle and Reverend Thurman, is the *kiva* in my soul.

The Union Pacific works its way past Citadel Rock on the Green River in Wyoming Territory, 1868. Work trains like the one shown here ran over a temporary wooden bridge until the permanent one under construction below could be completed.

CHAPTER FIVE

THE GRANDEST ENTERPRISE
UNDER GOD

1865–1874

With North and South reunited, Americans were free to move west as they never had been before. Settlers from around the world would soon be stepping off at Red Cloud and Lone Tree and Broken Bow and starting to sow foreign strains of wheat in rich, matted prairie soil that had never known anything but grass. Hundreds of thousands of lean, long-horned cattle would be driven north from Texas and shipped to eastern markets — and the dusty, saddle-sore men who herded them would be transformed into the idols of every eastern schoolchild. Isolated outposts would change overnight into raucous boomtowns, and buffalo hunters would swarm onto the Great Plains and drive the animal that sustained its native peoples to the brink of extinction. The railroads would make it all possible. But first, someone had to build them.

The dreamer: Theodore Judah, photographed when he still believed the transcontinental railroad would one day make him rich. "I have always had to pit my brains . . . against other men's money . . . ," he boasted to his wife. But in the end, other men's money would win.

Railroads had already transformed life in the East, but at the end of the Civil War the rails still stopped at the Missouri. Without them, the development of the West could proceed only slowly. To make the region's mines and forests, farms and ranches pay, westerners needed a transportation system that could dependably haul great loads over long distances.

Americans had been calling for a line all the way across the continent for half a century. In 1817 — eleven years before the first mile of American track was laid — a New Yorker named Robert Mills was already urging that a railroad be built between the headwaters of the Mississippi and Oregon Territory. Thomas Hart Benton, Stephen A. Douglas, and other western politicians had built whole careers on the bright promise of linking the coasts by rail. It would help people the West, they argued, and it would provide a direct route to the Orient, ending Europe's domination of trade with the Far East. "America will be between Asia and Europe," wrote John C. Frémont, "the golden vein which runs through the history of the world will follow the track to San Francisco, and the Asiatic trade will finally fall into its last and permanent road."

But no lines could be built without congressional permission to cross federal land, and no man — or combination of men — was rich enough to undertake such a vast enterprise without massive federal loans and grants of land. Before the war, Secretary of War Jefferson Davis had dispatched teams of topographical engineers to survey five possible routes, but bitter sectional quarrels over which one should be followed had kept Congress from choosing one, let alone voting for either land or loans with which actual construction could begin. Now, the South could no longer block legislation, and in 1862 lobbyists descended on Washington with valises full of schemes.

None had more of them than a California railroad man named Theodore Judah. For more than a decade, he had talked about building a transcontinental railroad with such obsessive fervor that behind his back people called him "Crazy Judah." Born in New England and mad about trains since boyhood, he had laid tracks through the Niagara River gorge in New York State and persuaded himself that laying them through the western mountains would be only a little more difficult. He built California's first line, the Sacramento Valley Railroad, hoping that it might become the first leg of a transcontinental railway, and when that dream died for lack of funds, refused to be discouraged. He made twenty-four lonely mule-back forays into the Sierras in search of a likely route through the mountains before settling on the Donner and Emigrant passes that had first brought Americans into California. Then he set up a paper line called the Central Pacific with himself as chief engineer, and began stumping the state in search of investors.

He found no takers in San Francisco, the financial capital of the West. No such thing as a transcontinental railroad had ever been attempted anywhere — some 1,780 miles of track would have to be laid from Sacramento to Omaha. Fifteen tunnels would have to be cut through mountains higher than any railroad builder had ever faced, while, beyond the Sierras, a roadbed would have to be made across deserts where there was no water for the crews and treeless prairies where Indians were sure to resist their passage.

Then, one June evening in 1861, Judah finally found four Sacramento merchants willing to put up enough money to get started at least. They were Leland Stanford, a grocer with political ambitions (he would be elected California's first Republican governor that November), Charles Crocker, a dry goods merchant and sometime Republican legislator, and Mark Hopkins and Collis P. Huntington, who together owned the hardware store above which the businessmen met.

With their backing — and armed with $100,000 in company stock earmarked for distribution among pliant legislators — Judah hurried to Washington to do all he could to influence the nonpartisan Pacific Railroad Act about to emerge from Congress at last. Few lobbyists in American history can have been more effective: he managed to make himself clerk to both the House and Senate committees that were to

The Sacramento hardware store at 54 K Street above which, just a few weeks after the Civil War began, Theodore Judah talked four storekeepers into investing in his Central Pacific Railroad

*The great Pacific Railway is com-
menced. . . . Immigration will soon
pour into these valleys. Ten millions
of emigrants will settle in this golden
land in twenty years. . . . This is the
grandest enterprise under God!*

George Francis Train

Labor and management: Union Pacific surveyors (opposite) claw their way up a Wyoming
rock face in search of the best line along which
the track gangs would lay the rails, while the
directors of their railroad (above) confer in the
quiet comfort of their private car. Seated, from
left to right: Silas Seymour, Sidney Dillon,
Thomas C. Durant (who oversaw the financing
of the road's construction), and John Duff.

draft the final bill, and not surprisingly, his Central Pacific was awarded the contract
to build through the Sierras when it was enacted on June 20, 1862. Meanwhile, an
eastern-based line, the Union Pacific, was to start from the one hundredth meridian
in Missouri, cross the Great Plains, and cut through the Rockies.

The point at which the two lines were to meet was not designated; from the first,
the two companies would be in a race to see who could lay the most track — and
therefore make the most money. Each railroad was to receive 6,400 acres of federal
land laid out in checkerboard parcels on either side of the tracks for every mile completed, plus vast loans from the treasury as they went along — $16,000 per mile of
level track, $32,000 across the plateaus, $48,000 per mile in the mountains.

Both lines resorted to some singularly creative financing in order to get going. The
officers of the Union Pacific set up a holding company, the *Crédit Mobilier* of America, through which they siphoned into their own pockets the funds for building their
line, and then bought congressmen wholesale to ensure that no one objected. The
Crédit Mobilier, wrote the reformer Charles Francis Adams, Jr., "is another name for
the Pacific Railroad Ring. The members of it are in Congress; they are trustees of the
bondholders; they are contractors; in Washington they vote the subsidies, in New

York they receive them, upon the plains they expend them. . . . Ever-shifting characters, they are ubiquitous; they receive money into one hand and pay it into the other. . . ."

Meanwhile, the Big Four made sure that not a penny of potential profits would escape them by awarding the Central Pacific construction contract to one of their number, Charles Crocker, despite the fact that he had no experience whatsoever building railroads and had never managed anything larger than a small Indiana iron foundry. (In the end, the partners would pay themselves some $90 million for work estimated actually to have cost about a third of that.) Using all of their political influence, they then persuaded a malleable state geologist named Josiah Whitney officially to declare the gently sloping Sacramento Valley a mountainous region so that the Central Pacific could collect the highest possible rate for laying track across it; Whitney dutifully ruled that the Sierras began abruptly to rise just seven miles from Sacramento, when the real distance was at least twenty-two miles.

Theodore Judah, who had proved himself a master manipulator in Washington, now objected to the way the Big Four were doing business, and in October of 1863 set out for New York by sea, determined to find enough Wall Street investors to buy them out. But he contracted yellow fever in Panama and was dying when his ship finally docked at New York on November 2, the same day construction began at Sacramento on the railroad that he had championed for so long.

That same year, the Union Pacific staged an elaborate ground-breaking ceremony at Omaha, meant to impress potential investors. Cannons were fired. Nebraska's governor spoke. A telegram from Abraham Lincoln was read. A shovelful of earth was turned. But the East was still preoccupied with the war. The Union Pacific managed to lay just forty miles of track before Appomattox.

But once the shooting stopped, the race began in earnest. Each line faced unique problems. The endless miles of prairie across which the Union Pacific had to lay its tracks provided neither timber for ties nor iron nor provisions, and at first, everything had to be shipped up the Missouri by boat, then hauled overland to the crews. And there was an understandable reluctance to venture too far too fast into the valley of the Platte, which vengeful Cheyenne and Arapaho and Lakota had virtually swept clean of white settlement after the massacre at Sand Creek. A newspaperman who traveled along just thirty miles of the proposed roadbed through Nebraska claimed to have counted "ninety-three graves; no less than twenty-seven of which contain the bodies of settlers killed within the past six weeks. Dead bodies have been seen floating down the Platte."

Indians were soon attacking railroad men, as well — picking off surveyors, graders, whole section gangs. Many years later, a Cheyenne warrior named Porcupine recalled an encounter near the town of Plum Creek in Nebraska Territory:

> We were feeling angry. . . . We looked at [the train] from a high ridge. Far off it was very small, but it kept coming and growing larger all the time, puffing out smoke and steam; and as it came on, we said to each other that it looked like a white man's pipe when he was smoking. . . . After we had seen this train and watched it come near us and grow large and pass by and then disappear . . . we went down . . . to see what sort of trail it made. . . .
>
> . . . [W]e said among ourselves: "Now the white people have taken all we had and have made us poor and we ought to do something. In these big wagons that go on this metal road, there must be things that are valuable — perhaps clothing. If we could throw these wagons off the iron they run on and break them open, we should find out what was in them and could take whatever might be useful to us."
>
> Red Wolf and I tried to do this. We got a big stick, and just before sundown one day tied it to the rails and sat down to watch and see what would happen. Close by the track we built a big fire. Quite a long time after it got dark we heard a rumbling sound.

A handcar was approaching in the dark. Six men were aboard, returning from a day spent repairing telegraph wires. They began pumping furiously when they saw the fire and the shadowy figures of the Cheyenne waiting alongside the track. They never saw the log.

"When the car struck the stick it jumped high in the air," Porcupine remembered. "The men got up from where they had fallen and ran away." The Cheyenne killed five of them instantly. The sixth man, a Briton named William Thompson, got a bullet through his arm before a warrior rode him down, stabbed him in the neck, then began methodically to saw off his scalp while Thompson, fully conscious, did his best to seem dead.

The Cheyenne, delighted with their success, then spied the distant light of an approaching freight. They pried up the rails and waited. The train, too, jumped the track. Two crewmen were killed. As the warriors began to loot and burn the boxcars, Thompson managed to stagger to his feet and set out along the tracks for the nearest

General Grenville Dodge (above), chief engineer and surveyor of the Union Pacific, and some of the Shoshone and Pawnee (opposite) he hired to help guard his crews against their common enemies, the Cheyenne and the Arapaho, 1868

railhead, pausing just long enough to pick up his own scalp, evidently mislaid in the excitement of derailing the train by the warrior who'd taken it.

Thompson eventually made it to safety and was carried to Omaha by rail, along with the charred bodies of the derailed train's engineer and fireman. His scalp rode beside him in a bucket of water; a reporter who saw it said it somewhat resembled "a drowned rat, as it floated, curled up. . . ."

HELL ON WHEELS

General Grenville M. Dodge was in overall command of getting the Union Pacific rolling. He was an ideal choice for the job, tough, resourceful, implacable. He had built railroads before the Civil War, rebuilt railroad bridges and southern lines to aid the northern army during it, and then had come west to fight Plains Indians. He armed his crews, hired Pawnee and Shoshone to help drive off their enemies, the Lakota and Cheyenne, and called for military protection; eventually, 5,000 troops would guard the line as it inched its way west.

He picked two tough red-bearded ex-soldiers, General Jack Casement and his brother, Dan, to be the construction bosses. Their crews were mostly Irish — immigrants from eastern slums, many of whom had fought for the Union in the Civil War and were eager for a second new start in the West — but they also included ex–Confederate soldiers, Mexicans and Germans, Englishmen and former slaves. There were some 10,000 men in all, an army of workmen moving across the plains with soldierly precision. First came the surveying parties — each with a chief engineer and his assistant, as well as rodmen, flagmen, chainmen, axmen, teamsters, hunters, and a military escort. Then came the location men, whose task it was to stake out the grades and curves, followed by the big grading crews, who worked well ahead of the tracklayers, getting everything ready.

Finally, the tracklaying could begin. A twenty-two-car work train housed and fed the men, who rose at dawn. A supply train nosed up behind it, carrying all the supplies needed that day — rails, ties, spikes, rods, fishplates — all of which had to be loaded onto flatcars and run up to the railhead where the "iron men" were already waiting.

Each rail weighed seven hundred pounds. Five men were needed to lift it off the flatcar and into place. Then, even before the men with the hammers drove the spikes all the way home, the flatcar rolled forward over the new rails so that the next ones could be unloaded and dropped into place. "It is a grand anvil chorus that these sturdy sledges are playing across the Plains," wrote an awed newspaperman. "It is in triple time, three strokes to a spike, four hundred rails to a mile, eighteen hundred miles to [California] — twenty-one million times are they to come down with their sharp punctuation before the great work of modern America is complete."

"The time is coming, and fast, too," one Union Pacific engineer noted in his diary, "when, in the sense it is now understood, THERE WILL BE NO WEST."

As the crews moved across the prairie, a movable city followed right along behind — hundreds of prostitutes, pimps, gamblers, saloon keepers, gunmen — "a carnivorous horde," one man recalled, "hungrier than the native grasshoppers" and eager to devour the men's weekly pay. The succession of base camps the Union Pacific built

Jack Casement, the ex-soldier who drove the Union Pacific crews, and one of his construction trains. Prefabricated parts of the portable town he carried with him are piled on top of the cars, ready to be set up farther down the track. The crews shown inset below are digging a tunnel near Echo Canyon (left) and constructing the footings for a permanent bridge across the Green River.

A light car, drawn by a single horse, gallops up to the front with its load of rails. Two men seize the end of a rail and start forward, the rest of the gang taking hold by twos until it is clear of the car. They come forward at a run. At the word of command, the rail is dropped into its place, right side up, with care, while the same process goes on on the other side of the car. Less than thirty seconds to a rail for each gang, and so four rails go down to the minute. . . .

William A. Bell

The steady progress Grenville Dodge (far left) hoped to make suffered every kind of interruption, including time-consuming visits by dignitaries. Here, at Fort Sanders in Dakota Territory, Generals Philip Sheridan (third from left), Ulysses Grant (at center, wearing straw hat), and William Tecumseh Sherman (framed by the doorway) and their entourages have all come to see how the great work is going. Grant, about to become the Republican nominee for president, also helped resolve a dispute between Dodge and Thomas Durant (sixth from right), who wanted to lengthen the line unnecessarily to augment company profits. Grant sided with Dodge.

roughly seventy miles apart each had a different name — Elk Horn, Fremont, Columbus, Grand Island, Kearney, Plum Creek, North Platte, O'Fallon's, Oglala, Julesburg, Sidney, Cheyenne, Sherman, Laramie, Rawlins, Bitter Creek, Green River — but the men called them all "Hell on Wheels."

Hundreds of workers contracted venereal disease. There were drunken brawls, shootings, knifings. The journalist Henry Morton Stanley took an after-dinner stroll through Julesburg in August of 1867:

> . . . At night new aspects are presented in this city of premature growth. Watch-fires gleam over the sea-like expanse of ground outside the city, while inside soldiers, herdsmen, teamsters, women, railroad men, are dancing, singing, or gambling. I verily believe that there are men here who would murder a fellow-creature for five dollars. Nay, there are men who have already done it, and who stalk abroad in daylight unwhipped of justice. Not a day passes but a dead body is found somewhere in the vicinity with pockets rifled of their contents. . . .

When things got too bad, Dodge dispatched Jack Casement and a band of two hundred armed men to clean things up. This, Dodge remembered, "was fun for Casement," and after a shoot-out in Julesburg he proudly showed his employer through the town's burgeoning cemetery: "General," he said, "they all died in their boots and Julesburg has been quiet ever since." Julesburg did quiet down. But the next base camp was already being banged together up ahead, and when the crews finally reached it, they would find Hell on Wheels waiting for them all over again.

I WANT THE GREAT FATHER TO MAKE NO ROADS

Red Cloud of the Oglala Lakota was no stranger to war. He had counted eighty coups in battle against the Crow, Pawnee, and Ute, and had earned himself a reputation for both daring and ferocity: his followers liked to recall the time he chased a Ute on a wounded horse into a river; when his quarry fell off his mount, Red Cloud rode into the fast-moving current, hauled him out by the hair, hacked off his scalp, then scornfully let the terrified warrior drop back into the water.

Now, he watched with growing anger as whites surveyed a wagon road through the Lakota country. It was meant to link the Oregon Trail with the new Montana mining towns of Bozeman and Virginia City, but it also threatened one of his people's favorite hunting grounds, the rolling foothills of the Bighorn Mountains along the Powder River. For him, the matter was simple:

> Whose voice was first sounded on this land? The voice of the red people who had but bows and arrows. . . . What has been done in my country I did not want, did not ask for it; white people going through my country. . . . When the white man comes in my country he leaves a trail of blood behind him. . . . I have two mountains in that country — the Black Hills and the Big Horn Mountain. I want the Great Father to make no roads through them.

When two whites seeking to map a route ventured too far into the hills, Red Cloud's warriors surrounded them, demanded their clothes and tools, then sent them running, naked, back toward the fort from which they'd come.

The Dale Creek Bridge on the western slope of the Black Hills epitomized the Union Pacific's somewhat casual attitude toward construction. A company engineer blithely suggested that "when the bridges shall decay," iron or rock should be substituted. "It strikes me," wrote a federal investigator, "that waiting for the bridge to decay would be rather hazardous. Its decay might . . . be discovered by its giving way under a train. . . . [It] is so fixed now that the unsuspecting passengers will not see their danger, nor know that the yawning chasm, granite-bottomed, into which they are plunging is one hundred and twenty feet deep!"

*In the ripeness of time the hope
of humanity is realized. . . . [This]
continental railway . . . will bind the
two seaboards to this one continental
union like ears to the human head;
[to plant] the foundation of the
Union so broad and deep . . . that
no possible force or stratagem can
shake its permanence.*

William Gilpin

Handsomely decorated and highly polished
by its proud crew, Engine No. 23
waits at a short-lived Union Pacific depot
called Wyoming Station, 1868.

In June of 1866, Red Cloud and several other Lakota leaders were called to Fort Laramie to discuss a new treaty aimed at persuading the Sioux to permit the road to be built. If they would permit safe passage along it, the commissioners promised, the Indians would be given presents and permitted to hunt in peace, as they always had. The talks went cordially enough until a battalion of seven hundred infantrymen arrived unexpectedly under Colonel Henry R. Carrington; he already had orders to protect whites traveling along a road that had not yet officially been begun. Red Cloud felt betrayed: the government clearly planned to have its road, whether or not the Lakota agreed. He angrily denounced the commissioners for "treating the assembled chiefs as children," an eyewitness recalled. The whites were "pretending to negotiate for a country which they had already taken by Conquest. . . .

[H]e told them that the white men had crowded the Indians back year by year and forced them to live in a small country north of the Platte and now their last hunting ground, the home of their people was to be taken from them. This meant that they and their women and children were to starve, and for his part he preferred to die fighting rather than by starvation. . . . [If] the combined tribes would defend their homes they would be able to drive the soldiers out of their country.

Some Lakota leaders who thought resistance futile or who lived south of the Platte and therefore had little interest in the Powder River country signed the treaty anyway, in exchange for annuities of $70,000 every year for twenty years. Some Cheyenne signed, too.

But many Lakota, led by Red Cloud and Man-Afraid-of-His-Horses, refused to sign and rode off to the Powder River, determined to make life impossible for travelers and the soldiers sent to protect them. Cheyenne who had dared favor peace were made to suffer, too: when a band of Lakota chiefs came upon a group of warriors who had agreed to abandon the road to the soldiers, they beat them with the flat of their bows as a sign of their contempt.

Colonel Carrington succeeded in completing three forts along the proposed route before winter set in — Fort C. F. Smith on the Bighorn River in southern Montana, and Forts Reno and Phil Kearny in Wyoming. But Lakota and Cheyenne warriors raided his small, scattered force again and again, picking off stragglers, seizing supply wagons, driving off stock, attacking the men when they ventured out to cut hay or firewood.

Even inside Carrington's headquarters at Fort Phil Kearny some feared for their lives, an officer's wife named Mrs. Frances Grummond remembered:

More than once the Sioux crawled up to the stockade covered with wolf skins and imitating the wolf cry, and on one occasion actually shot a sentry from his platform with an arrow that noiselessly pierced his heart.

The organs of sight and hearing grew to be extremely acute in that dry and rarefied atmosphere, involving an almost overpowering sense of stillness, especially at night. . . . The sight of the daily wood-party leaving for their accustomed duty, the interval of anxious waiting, and the reassuring bugle notes signaling their safe return. . . . No less [gratefully received] was the sentry's call at night, "All's well."

Hear me, Lakotas . . . before the ashes of the council fire are cold, the Great Father is building his forts among us. You have heard the sound of the white soldiers' ax upon the Little Piney. His presence here is an insult and a threat. It is an insult to the spirits of our ancestors. Are we to give up their sacred grounds to be plowed for corn? Lakotas, I am for war.

Red Cloud

Red Cloud

But thirty-three-year-old Lt. Col. William J. Fetterman, a Civil War veteran, claimed to be unafraid. "Give me 80 good men," he said, "and I can ride through the whole Sioux nation." Four days before Christmas, a daring young Oglala named Crazy Horse led an attack on wagons bringing firewood back to the fort. Fetterman saw his chance: he asked Colonel Carrington for permission to ride to the rescue. His commander agreed, but carefully warned him not to allow himself to be drawn out of sight of the fort: "Support the wood train. Relieve it and report to me. Do not engage or pursue Indians at its expense. Under no circumstances pursue over Lodge Trail Ridge."

But not long after Fetterman led his men through the gate, Crazy Horse and a handful of companions appeared in the distance and began taunting the soldiers, waving blankets, shouting curses, even getting off their ponies and ostentatiously adjusting the bridles despite the army bullets that pattered all around them. Then they remounted and raced over the ridge. Fetterman galloped after them. On the far side, nearly 2,000 warriors were waiting for him — Lakota, Cheyenne, and a handful of Santee exiles from Minnesota.

Mrs. Grummond and the other women in the fort could not see the brief, furious battle that followed, but they could hear it: "A few shots were heard, followed up by increasing rapidity . . . a desperate fight was going on in the valley below the ridge . . . in the very place where the command was forbidden to go. Then followed a few quick volleys, then scattering shots, and then, dead silence. Less than half an hour had passed, and the silence was dreadful."

A nervous search party edged over the ridge late that afternoon and found Fetterman and his whole command dead, their bodies mutilated. Fetterman and his second-in-command lay close together. Each had been shot through the temple at close range. They had evidently killed one another rather than fall into Indian hands.

Private John Guthrie was among those who gathered up the dead:

[We found] all the Fetterman boys huddled together on the small hill. . . . We packed them . . . on top of [the ammunition boxes in the wagons]. Terrible cuts left by Indians. Could not tell Cavalry from the Infantry. All dead bodies stripped naked, crushed skulls, with war clubs, ears, nose and legs had been cut off, scalps torn away and the bodies pierced with bullets and arrows, wrists, feet and ankles leaving each attached by a tendon. . . . Sergeant Baker of Company C 2nd Cavalry, a gunny sack over his head, not scalped, little finger cut off for a gold ring; Lee Bontee, the guide, body full of arrows which had to be broken off to load him. . . . We walked on their internals and did not know it in the high grass. Picked them up, that is their internals, did not know the soldier they belonged to, so you see the cavalry man got an infantry man's guts and an infantry man got a cavalry man's guts. . . .

Back at the fort, Mrs. Grummond remembered,

[t]he ladies clustered in Mrs. Wand's cabin as night drew on, all speechless from absolute stagnation and terror. Then the crunching of wagon wheels startled us to our feet. The gates opened. Wagons were slowly driven within, bearing their dead but precious harvest from the field of blood and carrying . . . lifeless

One half of the headquarters building, which was my temporary home, was unfinished, and this part was utilized by carpenters for making pine cases for the dead. I knew that my husband's coffin was being made, and the sound of hammers and the grating of saws was torture. . . . My husband had a picture of myself in a choice setting that he always wore, and I have often wondered what Indian . . . has it now in his possession to wear as a trophy. . . .

Mrs. Frances Grummond

bodies to the hospital, with the heart-rending news, almost tenderly whispered by the soldiers themselves, that "*no more were to come in. . . .*"

On the central Plains, the celebrated soldiers who only recently had defeated the Confederacy weren't doing much better. Winfield Scott Hancock — "Hancock the superb," who had broken Pickett's charge at Gettysburg — was in overall command with orders to drive the Cheyenne from Kansas and Nebraska. He was a tenacious soldier, but he knew nothing about Indian warfare. In four months of frustrating patrolling, his men managed to kill precisely two Indians. Meanwhile, the Cheyenne they were trying to find killed better than two hundred white settlers.

Conspicuous among Hancock's commanders was another hero of the Civil War, George Armstrong Custer. An Ohio blacksmith's son, impulsive and high-spirited, charming but self-absorbed, he had just scraped through West Point, accumulating 726 demerits and graduating last in his class. "It was all right with him," a classmate remembered, "whether he knew his lessons or not; he did not allow it to trouble him." And he was an unlikely-looking soldier: his hair swept to his shoulders in golden ringlets, he carried a toothbrush in his jacket pocket so that, no matter what was going on around him, he could polish his gleaming teeth after every meal, and he had worn into battle a gaudy uniform of his own design — Confederate hat, red kerchief, velveteen jacket, and trousers decorated with gold lace.

George and Libbie Custer and their cook, Eliza, for whom the colonel would bring home a Cheyenne blanket as a souvenir of the battle of the Washita in 1868

But he was born for war. His judgment would often be called into question, but no one ever questioned his headlong courage. Again and again, he led the charge — at Bull Run, Gettysburg, Yellow Tavern, Winchester, Fisher's Hill, Five Forks — as though no bullet or saber could touch him. Eleven horses were shot from under Custer, and at twenty-three, he became the youngest general in the Union army, and perhaps its best-known divisional commander. Abraham Lincoln himself called Custer the man who "goes into a charge with a whoop and a shout," and his men — many of whom admired him so much that they, too, wore red kerchiefs into battle — also suffered some of the Union army's highest losses. And when, at the Grand Review, the great Washington parade that celebrated the war's end, three hundred admiring girls all dressed in blue showered him with blossoms and his horse bolted, he became the only man in the Union army to ride past the reviewing stand twice. "In the sunshine," a newspaperman wrote, "his locks, unskeined, stream[ed] a foot behind him. . . . It was like the charge of a Sioux chieftain."

His wife, Elizabeth — "Libbie" — was his match in charm and spirit and ambition. Lovely, well-educated, adoring but strong-minded, she was the daughter of an Ohio judge who took a dim view of soldiers in general and Custer in particular, and she had refused to marry him until he swore that he would never drink — a promise he kept — and that he would never curse or gamble, either — pledges he largely ignored. She had stayed as close to his side as she could throughout the war, living in tents, farmhouses, boardinghouses just to be near him, and when he decided to stay in the army and go west to take command of the Seventh Cavalry afterward, she came, too, bringing with her to Fort Riley, Kansas, Custer's worshipful brother, Tom, a black cook, a serving boy, a pack of staghounds, and three blooded horses.

At first, Custer professed to love the West, and he designed for himself a new distinctively western costume, meant to catch the eye of visiting newspapermen. Indians especially admired it and, marveling at his curls, began to call him "Yellow Hair." And when he had important visitors he loved to put his men through their paces on the parade ground. One dazzled onlooker, Libbie Custer recalled, "kept turning to take in the rare sight, declaring that nothing in our prosaic nineteenth century was so like the days of chivalry, when some feudal lord went out to war or to the chase, followed by his retainers."

But the glory Custer assumed would once again be his as soon as he faced Indians in battle proved maddeningly elusive. Out hunting one day with his hounds, far from his column and in the heart of Indian country, he galloped after a buffalo, aimed his revolver — and somehow shot his own horse through the head. On foot, bruised and totally lost, he had to be rescued by his own men. Catching Indians was no easier. A Lakota warrior named Pawnee Killer and his band attacked Custer's column, stole several horses, and got away clean. After weeks of fruitless campaigning, forage and supplies failed to materialize. There were endless delays: "The inaction to which I am subjected now . . ." Custer wrote Libbie, "is almost unendurable." The pitiless prairie sun took a heavy toll on Custer's men and horses, and they began to desert in ones, twos, and threes. Then, thirteen troopers left camp together. Custer ordered them hunted down and shot. One was killed outright, two more were brought back wounded. For two days, Custer refused them medical attention. One subsequently died. Custer, Captain Albert Barnitz told his wife, was "the most complete example of a petty tyrant that I have ever seen. You would be filled with utter amazement, if I were to give you a few instances of his cruelty to the men and discourtesy to the officers."

Custer had been on the march for nearly two months with precious little to show for it when, inexplicably, he left most of his command behind and with a personal escort set off at a furious pace for Fort Riley, 275 miles away. When a favorite horse fell behind, he sent six men on worn-out mounts back to find it. Indians attacked them. One trooper was killed, another wounded and left for dead. Custer refused to go back for their bodies — and later blamed them for bringing about their own deaths. He would offer a number of contradictory excuses for this strange forced march, but the real reason seems to have been nothing more than a desperate desire to see his wife.

Custer was arrested, found guilty of "conduct prejudicial to good order and military discipline," and suspended from the service for a year. Libbie dismissed the verdict as "nothing but a plan of persecution" of her husband, the act of envious officers seeking to cover up the shortcomings of the Hancock campaign. The couple moved back East, to Michigan, where Custer did his best to forget his current disgrace by recalling earlier triumphs on other battlefields. "I am like Mr. Micawber," he wrote to a friend, "waiting for something to 'turn up,' meanwhile I am preparing . . . a memoir of my experiences from West Point to Appomattox. Arrangements for this are concluded with Messrs Harper & Brothers."

Sand Creek. The loss of Fetterman's whole command. Hancock's failed campaign. Clearly, something had gone terribly wrong with United States policy toward the Indians. General William Tecumseh Sherman, now in overall command of the army between Canada and Texas, the Mississippi and the Rockies, was neither a patient nor a sentimental man. Wars were to be won, enemies conquered, he believed, before there could ever be peace. He had helped destroy the Confederacy by acting upon those beliefs, and the blackened chimneys of hundreds of homes between Atlanta and the sea attested to his effectiveness against civilians of his own race. The peoples of the Plains could expect no gentler treatment. "I do not understand," he wrote to his friend General Ulysses S. Grant, "how the massacre of Colonel Fetterman's party could have been so complete. We must act with vindictive earnestness against the Sioux, even to their extermination, men, women and children. Nothing less will ever reach the root of the case."

Sherman took up his new duties with a deceptively simple plan: the Lakota were to be confined north of the Platte; the Arapaho, Cheyenne, and Comanche pushed south of the Arkansas. "This," he explained, "would leave for our people exclusively the use of the wide belt, east and west, between the Platte and the Arkansas, in which lie the two great railroads, and over which pass the bulk of travel to the mountain territories."

But Indian policy remained in the hands of the Interior Department, and for the moment, the advocates of less harsh treatment of the Indians seemed to have the upper hand. Memories of the Civil War were still fresh. Many voters found the soaring cost of hunting Indians without catching them absurd. Accordingly, in the late summer of 1867, a peace delegation headed west, empowered by Congress to remove the causes of war with the tribes, and pursue "the hitherto untried policy of conquering with kindness."

At Medicine Lodge Creek in Kansas, a new agreement was outlined to leaders of the southern Plains peoples — Cheyenne, Arapaho, Kiowa, Comanche. The Great Plains were no longer to be considered one great reservation through which they could roam and hunt as they always had. In exchange for agreeing to move out of the way of white settlement and onto reservations in what is now western Oklahoma, the tribes were to receive food and supplies for thirty years, as well as schools to teach them the white man's language and resident farmers to show them how to work the land.

One by one, the chiefs agreed to sign the treaty — Satank and Kicking Bird, Woman's Heart and Standing Bear of the Kiowa; Ten Bears, Silver Brooch, Horse Back, and Iron Mountain of the Comanche; Little Raven of the Arapaho; and the Cheyenne leaders, Bull Bear, Tall Bull, White Horse, Black Kettle. All were eager for a halt to years of sporadic violence and pleased by the gifts the commissioners distributed among them. But few fully understood what was being asked of them, and

fewer still could imagine abandoning their old ways. "I remember in particular one Indian who looked disdainfully on the white man's gifts," one officer recalled:

> There was apparently nothing among the paraphernalia of the white man that Kick-a-Bird wanted. Nothing until his eye chanced upon a high silk hat that seemingly delighted him. Setting his symbol of a conquering civilization firmly on his oiled hair he strutted for hours up and down for the amusement of his grinning companions. But presently he grew tired of his selection, and the last we saw of the glossy, high silk hat, Kick-a-Bird and his companions were contemptuously using it for a football.

Farther north, at Fort Laramie on the Platte, the commissioners also signed a treaty with a number of Brulé, Oglala, and Miniconjou Lakota bands. They agreed to remain within a vast Sioux reservation that encompassed all of present-day South Dakota and much of North Dakota and Nebraska, west of the Missouri. In turn, the government recognized their right to hunt buffalo on lands north of the Platte and on the Republican River "so long as buffalo may range there in numbers sufficient to justify the chase."

Red Cloud refused even to meet with the commissioners, but he sent word that all three forts in the Powder River country would have to be abandoned before he touched the pen. "If the Great Father kept white men out of my country," he said, "then peace would last forever. The Great Spirit has raised me in this land and has raised you in another land. What I have said I mean. I mean to keep this land." The commission yielded. The soldiers marched away. Gleeful Lakota burned all three

Parley at Fort Laramie: Peace commissioners (left), including Generals William S. Harney (white beard) and William Tecumseh Sherman (seated next to Harney), came west in 1868 to seek an end to hostilities with the Cheyenne and the Lakota. Among the Indian leaders attending (opposite, from left) were Spotted Tail, Brulé Lakota; Roman Nose, Cheyenne; and Man-Afraid-of-His-Horses, Oglala Lakota, who is also shown above, smoking a ceremonial pipe.

forts — only cemeteries remained to mark where they once had stood — and the Bozeman Trail was closed. Still, Red Cloud disdainfully stayed away from Fort Laramie all summer and into the autumn, preferring to hunt buffalo as he always had rather than meet with the soldiers. It was not until November 6, 1868, that he and some 125 other chiefs and headmen finally rode in to sign the treaty. Even then, he was ambivalent as to whether he would really agree to live on the reservation, submit to being fed and housed by white men, or be taught how to farm.

By 1872, when this portrait was made in Washington, D.C., by Alexander Gardner, Red Cloud had become a national celebrity and whites vied with one another to be photographed with him. His companion here is an Englishman named William Henry Blackmore.

In the spring of 1870, to convince Red Cloud of the futility of further resistance, he and a delegation of twenty-one Lakota were escorted to Washington, to meet with the new Great Father, President Grant. Everything was arranged to awe the Indians with American might, but none of it seemed to impress them much. A huge cannon that lobbed a shell four miles down the Potomac made a satisfying noise, but the Lakota pointed out that they could simply ride around it while it was being laboriously reloaded; they were quickly bored by the debate on the Senate floor and brightened only when they saw the busts of two Indian chiefs in the Capitol; and an elaborate meal served at the Executive Mansion only demonstrated, one of the chiefs said, that whites had not been sending them the best of their food and drink.

And when Jacob Cox, the secretary of the interior, told his visitors that because of what they had been shown, "Red Cloud and his people . . . will now know that what the President does is not because he is afraid but because he wants to do that which is right and good," the Lakota leader remained unmoved: "The white people have surrounded me," he said through an interpreter, "and left me nothing but an island. When we first had this land we were strong. Now we are melting like snow on the hillside while you are growing like spring grass. . . ." Still, he claimed he had never understood what he had signed at Fort Laramie; the paper was "all lies"; the interpreters had misrepresented everything to him. His people would never go to the agency on the Missouri to collect their gifts; it was an unhealthy place. He would trade only at Fort Laramie.

One goal of the treaty had been to move the Lakota away from the Platte, but the government, anxious to hold on to the fragile peace, again relented: Red Cloud's people would not have to go to the agency to collect their gifts. Instead, a new agency would be built especially for Red Cloud and the Oglala in northwestern Nebraska.

Given the chance to visit New York in order to buy presents before returning home, Red Cloud at first scornfully turned it down: "The whites are the same everywhere," he said. "I see them every day." But in the end he did go, even agreed to parade with his friends on horseback through Central Park past cheering, dazzled crowds, and on the afternoon of June 14, 1869, stood on the stage of Cooper Union, where Abraham Lincoln had delivered the address that first brought him to national attention, and spoke for his people:

> We came to Washington to see our Great Father that peace might be continued. The Great Father that made us both wishes peace to be kept; we want to keep peace. Will you help us? In 1868, men came out and brought papers. We could not read them, and they did not tell us truly what was in them. We thought the treaty was to remove the forts. . . . [We] did not want to go to the Missouri, but wanted traders where we were. . . .
>
> Look at me. I am poor and naked but I am the Chief of the Nation. . . . The riches that we have in this world, Secretary Cox said truly, we cannot take with us to the next world. I wish to know why the Commissioners are sent out to us who do nothing but rob us and get the riches of this world away from us? I was brought up among the traders . . . and I had a good time with them. But by and by, the Great Father sent out a different kind of men; men who cheated and drank whiskey; men who were so bad the Great Father could not keep them at home. . . . I have sent a great many words to the Great Father but they never reached him. They were drowned on the way, and I was afraid the words I spoke lately . . . would not reach you [either], so I came to speak to you myself and now I am going away to my home.

The abuses about which Red Cloud spoke at Cooper Union were all too familiar to members of the Grant administration, and at the time he spoke it had already begun to try to do something about them. Even the Indians' most unyielding enemies knew that the reservation system was profoundly corrupt. Unscrupulous agents, appointed purely because of their political connections, wielded near-absolute power over their charges' lives. Some sold off Indian timber and mineral rights for their own profit; others skimmed off funds meant for buying supplies and food for their charges — or stole them wholesale. "The Indian agent they have sent us is so mean," said one Plains chief, "that he carries around in his pocket a . . . rag into which he blows his nose, for fear he will blow away something of value."

Grant would seek to end the worst abuses of the old patronage system by turning over at least some of the agencies to the churches — Quakers, Presbyterians, Methodists, Catholics, Lutherans, Congregationalists, Episcopalians, Baptists. Some of the agents sent west under this so-called "peace policy" would prove genuinely dedicated to Indian welfare (though they were also almost always woefully ignorant of Indian ways). But the sects quarreled with one another, some of the agents they chose were no more honest than their predecessors, and three heads of the Indian bureau were forced from office under the shadow of scandal. Conditions for agency Indians showed little improvement.

Red Cloud had dictated terms to the United States and understandably saw himself as the victor in the war over the Bozeman Trail. But by the time he agreed to end his war the advancing Union Pacific had already made the hated road superfluous. Trains now carried more and more settlers west; they could also haul the soldiers and supplies General Sherman already planned to use against the scattered peoples of the Plains. The Peace Policy, Sherman believed, was doomed to failure, and the Peace Commission responsible for the treaties with Red Cloud and others, he said privately, had been merely "killing time" before the inevitable, final conquest of the Lakota and Cheyenne and their allies could begin. "We will be kind to you if you keep the peace," he warned at one treaty council. "But if you won't listen to reason, we are ordered to make war upon you in a different manner from what we have done before."

Sherman was not alone in his skepticism about the new agreements. Captain Barnitz, who had acted as secretary during the talks at Medicine Lodge Creek, also thought them largely a waste of time:

> [T]he Cheyennes were with great difficulty persuaded to sign the treaty. They were superstitious in regard to touching the pen, or perhaps they supposed that by doing so they would be "signing away their rights" — which is doubtless the true state of affairs, as *they have no idea* they are giving up, or that they have ever given up, the country which they claim as their own, the country north of the Arkansas. The treaty all amounts to nothing, and we will certainly have another war sooner or later with the Cheyennes, at least, and probably with the other Indians, in consequence of misunderstanding of the terms of present and previous treaties.

Barnitz was right. The treaty with the southern tribes proved just another piece of paper. Congress, caught up in politics, failed to ratify the document so that no funds were available to sustain the people in their new homes. Some bands left the reservations in search of food. Others never bothered to go there at all. And in the late summer of 1868, when the Indian agent at Fort Larned refused to hand over arms and ammunition used for hunting, to which the Cheyenne believed themselves entitled by the treaty, warriors began raiding settlers along the Saline and Solomon rivers again, burning cabins and running off stock. Fifteen men were killed. Five women were carried off and raped. More raids and more killing followed. Kansas settlements lived in fear.

Above all things, the plainsman had to have a sense — an instinct for direction. . . . Few men have this instinct. Yet in the few it is to be trusted as absolutely as the homing instinct of a wild goose. . . . I never had a compass in my life. I was never lost.

Charles Goodnight

LAID AWAY IN A FOREIGN COUNTRY

Charles Goodnight was twenty-eight when the Civil War ended, and used to tough times. A dirt farmer's son, he had ridden bareback all the way from Illinois to Texas at the age of nine, and had been working full-time to support his widowed mother since he was eleven. At nineteen, he and his stepbrother went into the beef business. Cattle had come north with Coronado in 1540, and the Spanish and Mexican ranchos had established the cattle business and most of its distinctive customs — from the roundup to branding irons, the boots on a vaquero's feet to the wide-brimmed sombrero on his head — long before the United States expanded beyond the Mississippi.

But by the 1850s, Americans were taking over, and the largest herds were in South Texas, in the region around San Antonio, Corpus Christi, and Laredo. Eastern markets were thought too far away to be reached by land, so most ranchers drove cattle south, to ports on the Gulf of Mexico, where hides and tallow were shipped to eastern manufacturers. During the gold rush, more than half a million Texas cattle were herded west, to the mining camps of California. (A roughly equal number of sheep were driven to the goldfields from New Mexico by Mexican American herdsmen.)

Still too poor to buy their own herd, Goodnight and his stepbrother agreed to watch over someone else's — receiving every fourth calf as pay — and had managed to collect 180 head before Texas left the Union and Texas cattlemen found themselves cut off from their markets by the Union blockade of southern ports. Goodnight served as a scout for the Texas Rangers during the war, fighting Comanche and learning lessons about surviving in inhospitable country that would serve him well for the rest of his life. Most important was reading the signs of nearby water: the presence of mesquite bushes, he discovered, meant there was likely to be water within three miles; a swallow flying low, with an empty beak, was headed toward water; one with mud in its beak was coming straight from it.

When he returned to his small ranch at war's end, he found the cattle business in ruins. Texas herds had multiplied wildly — from 3.5 million head to perhaps 6 million. Rustlers were everywhere. "It looked like everything worth living for was gone," he remembered. "The entire country was depressed — there was no hope. . . . In a year or two's time, stealing or so-called mavericking became public. You could count the honest ones on your fingers and still have one hand left."

Goodnight prized honesty and hard work. "Only the weak steal," he once said, and the only way to make an honest profit in cattle was to try to take them north to better markets. He needed a partner and enlisted the help of Oliver Loving, twenty-five years older than he, who had taken Texas herds all the way to Chicago before the war, something no other cattleman had ever done. What Goodnight now proposed was a new, seven-hundred-mile route to new destinations — the Indian reservation at Bosque Redondo, the mining camps of Colorado, and finally the Union Pacific crews working their way across Wyoming. Loving agreed to try it: Goodnight's plan, which required that herds be driven across Comanche hunting grounds, was full of risk, but also possibility.

In 1866, with 2,000 cattle and eighteen cowboys, the two men set out along what would soon be called the Goodnight-Loving Trail. To avoid the Comanche of the panhandle, they first went southwest, across an arid eighty-mile plain toward the Pecos River — "the most desolate country," Goodnight remembered, "that I ever

Charles Goodnight when he was still a young, threadbare cattleman. Before his long career ended, he would be the master of some 20 million acres of Texas rangeland.

*The danger of swimming rivers is that the cattle will
get to milling, and the first you know they will start to
jump up and ride one another, trying to climb out,
and down they will go and you will lose a lot of them.
You have to keep them pointed for the opposite bank,
which means that in the water each man has to hold
his place alongside the herd, just like on the trail.*

Teddy Blue Abbott

Cattle drive, ca. 1900

Right: An army officer distributes rations to Navajo captives at Bosque Redondo.

explored." It took three days and three nights in choking dust without stopping to cross. Newborn calves slowed down the herd, so Goodnight had them killed each morning. (On subsequent drives he would bring along an extra wagon just to carry the calves — each one wrapped in a burlap bag, so that it kept its own scent and its mother could find it when the calves were turned loose to feed at night.) Three hundred cattle died in the heat; a hundred more drowned when the thirst-crazed herd finally smelled the Pecos River and stampeded over its banks into quicksand and swirling waters.

Goodnight and Loving pointed the survivors north, into New Mexico Territory, and at last reached Bosque Redondo, where some 8,000 Navajo were on the verge of starvation and government agents gladly paid top dollar for Texas beef to feed them. The partners now had a $12,000 profit and half the herd still in their possession. They drove them even farther north, into Colorado, fattening their animals on range grasses as they traveled, then sold them in Denver. There, Loving learned that good grazing extended all the way to Montana, where other Indian agencies and military outposts were paying high prices. Excited about their prospects and $24,000 richer, the partners returned to Texas, bought more cattle, and hurried back up the trail they'd blazed.

"Loving was a man of religious instincts and one of the coolest and bravest men I have ever known," Goodnight recalled, "but devoid of caution." This time he insisted on pushing ahead to get in the partners' bid for new government beef contracts at Bosque Redondo before rival ranchers got there. Comanche caught him on the open plain, shot him in the wrist and side, and chased him to the riverbank, where he held them off for several days, then managed to crawl to safety in the night. He was picked up by a passing wagon and taken to the military hospital at Bosque Redondo.

Loving refused an amputation until he could talk to his partner. By the time Goodnight finally reached his bedside, gangrene had set in. The operation was too late to save him. The night Loving died, "his mind turned back to Texas," Goodnight recalled, "and at last he said: 'I regret to have to be laid away in a foreign country.' I assured him that he need have no fears; that I would see that his remains were laid in the cemetery at home. He felt this would be impossible, but I told him it would be done."

Goodnight had his men fashion a tin casket out of flattened cans. They put Loving's wooden coffin inside, covered it with charcoal, sealed the top, and placed it in a wagon. Flanked by a cowboy escort, Goodnight started back south for Texas. Word of the profits Goodnight and Loving had cleared had spread throughout cattle country, and other outfits were already streaming north, headed now for the nearest railheads from which cattle could be shipped east. But in February of 1868, Charles Goodnight, the man who had helped start it all, was headed in the other direction. Keeping his promise to his dead partner, he was taking Oliver Loving home.

THE WHOLE ARTILLERY OF HEAVEN

While the Union Pacific worked its way west across the Great Plains, the Central Pacific, after a fast start, had gotten stuck in the Sierra Nevada. The mountains still looked impenetrable, and Charles Crocker, whose job it was to break through them, could not seem to hold on to his workers: three out of five stuck with him just long enough to get a free ride to the railhead, then set out on their own for the Nevada goldfields. His plans called for a workforce of 10,000. He had fewer than 600 upon whom he could depend.

Desperate, he suggested to his superintendent of construction, James Strobridge, that he try the Chinese, many of whom who were eking out a living working California gold tailings abandoned by others. Strobridge was an ex–forty-niner, loud and profane, accustomed to carrying a pick handle as what he called his "persuader," and unaccustomed to having his judgment questioned. "I will not boss Chinese," he said; they were too small, too frail; they had no training as railroad builders.

Crocker insisted the Chinese be given a chance; their ancestors had, after all, built the Great Wall. Strobridge was to try fifty of them for a month to see how they stood up. They did fine.

Before long, 11,000 of them were at work on the Central Pacific, and Crocker was advertising for still more in China. "They do not drink or fight or strike," wrote the journalist Charles Nordhoff, ". . . and it is always said of them that they are very cleanly in their habits. It is the custom among them, after they have had their suppers every evening, to bathe with the help of small tubs. I doubt if the white laborers do as much."

The Chinese had other advantages over their white counterparts. They arrived at the work site already divided into smoothly efficient work gangs, usually from the same province and speaking the same dialect. They fell ill less often, too, because they drank only tea made from boiled water, and consumed a varied diet instead of the daily ration of beef and potatoes washed down with river water that sustained their white counterparts.

Before the Central Pacific could get through the Sierras the crews had to carve and gouge and blast fifteen tunnels out of solid granite. It sometimes took them twenty-four hours and five hundred kegs of explosives to move ahead eight inches; in an average week they used more explosives than were heard at Antietam. Then they came up against a face they called Cape Horn: solid rock, nearly straight up and down, more than 3,000 feet above the tumbling American River. There were no

Chinese workers and their white foreman. "Systematic workers these Chinese," said the *Alta California*, "competent and wonderfully effective, tireless and unremitting in their industry."

The greater proportion of the laborers employed by us are Chinese who constitute a large element in the population of California. Without them it would be impossible to complete the western portion of this great national enterprise within the time required by the Acts of Congress.

Leland Stanford

End of the line: Union Pacific crews at work and encamped along the newly laid track

The mouth of Tunnel No. 10 in the High Sierra

footholds, but the Chinese still somehow managed to blast and carve out a ledge along the cliff wide enough for a train to pass. To do it, Chinese workers were swung down over the rock face in wicker baskets to gouge holes, pack them with explosives, set the fuses, then hope the explosives did not go off before their comrades above could haul them up and out of harm's way.

A reporter remembered watching the pyrotechnics above Donner Lake:

Through the gathering shades of night, immense volumes of fire and dense clouds of smoke from the mountainside, as if a mighty volcano was rending it to atoms. Huge masses of rocks and debris were rent and heaved up in the commotion; then . . . came the thunders of explosion like a lightning stroke, reverberating along the hills and canyons, as if the whole artillery of Heaven was in play. Huge masses of rock rolled far down the steep declivity, and pieces weighing two hundred pounds were thrown a distance of a mile. Sometimes the peo-

There was a dance at Donner Lake at a hotel and a sleigh-load of us went up from Truckee and on our return, about 9 a.m. next morning, we saw something under a tree by the side of the road, its shape resembling that of a man. We stopped and found a frozen Chinese. As a consequence, we threw him in the sleigh, with the rest of us and took him into town and laid him out by the side of a shed and covered him with a rice mat, the most appropriate thing for the laying out of a Celestial.

A. P. Partridge

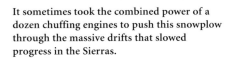

It sometimes took the combined power of a dozen chuffing engines to push this snowplow through the massive drifts that slowed progress in the Sierras.

ple at the hotel, a mile from the scene of destruction, were obliged to retire to avoid the . . . falling fragments.

The crews kept at it right through two of the worst winters in memory. "Snow storms, forty-four in number," remembered a railroad official in 1866, "varied in length from a short . . . squall to a two-week gale. . . . [T]he heaviest storm of the winter, began February 18th, at 2 p.m., and snowed steadily until 10 p.m. of the 22nd, during which time six feet fell. . . ." The Chinese tunneled beneath sixty-foot drifts, working by lamplight, breathing through air shafts. ". . . [S]now slides carried away our camps and we lost a good many men in those slides," another official recalled. "[M]any of them we did not find until the next season when the snow melted." No one kept a precise count, but more than twelve hundred Chinese are believed to have died building the Central Pacific.

In the spring of 1867, some 3,000 Chinese workers struck, demanding an eight-hour day and the same terms as the whites who took fewer risks than they did. (Whites were fed by the railroad, for example; Chinese workers had to feed themselves.) Charles Crocker would not hear of it. He let it be known that he was looking into the possibility of bringing in freed slaves from the South to replace any Chinese who would not go back to work, charged that the whole strike had been inspired by agents of the rival Union Pacific, and cut off the strikers' food supply. But in the end, it was Crocker, not his Chinese workers, who retreated at least a little: his men still had to work a twelve-hour day and got no free food, but he raised their pay two dollars to thirty-five dollars a month.

By the side of the grade are the camp fires of the blue-clad laborers waiting for the signal to start work. These are the Chinese, and the job of this particular contingent is to clear a level roadbed for the track. They are the vanguard of the construction forces. Miles back is the camp of the rear guard — the Chinese who follow the track gang, ballasting and finishing the roadbed.

Alta California
November 9, 1868

Some of the first Chinese to work for the Central Pacific, laboring to complete the Secret Town Trestle on the western slope of the Sierras in the summer of 1866

Finally, in September of 1868, after three long years of backbreaking, dangerous labor, the Central Pacific crews did what few had believed even they could accomplish — they broke out of the High Sierra and onto the Nevada desert. The *Territorial Enterprise* paid heartfelt if patronizing tribute to the men who had made it possible: "John [Chinaman], with his patient toil, directed by American energy and backed by American capital, has broken down the great barrier at last and opened over it the greatest highway yet created for the march of commerce and civilization around the globe."

The hardest part was now behind them. The Central Pacific was back in the race.

NOTHING BUT THEIR EYES TO WEEP WITH

General Philip Henry Sheridan — "Fighting Phil" — had now assumed command of the Department of the Missouri, which included Kansas, Oklahoma, New Mexico, and Colorado. The diminutive son of an Irish tenant farmer and trained at West Point — from which he had been suspended for a year for trying to stab another cadet with his bayonet — he was hard, hot-tempered, and still less sentimental about the soldier's task than was his friend Sherman. "The proper strategy," he once said, "consists in the first place in inflicting as telling blows as possible upon the enemy's army, and then causing the inhabitants so much suffering that they must long for peace, and force their government to demand it. The people must be left nothing but their eyes to weep with over the war."

During the Civil War, he had applied his grim theory to the Shenandoah Valley, stripping its people of so much, he boasted, that a crow wishing to fly over the valley had to carry its own rations. Now Sherman asked him to apply similar tactics in the West, wherever Indians continued to resist. They would begin with the Cheyenne, and would attack them in the winter, when they were most vulnerable. "In taking the offensive," Sheridan assured Sherman, "I have to select that season when I can catch the fiends; and if a village is attacked and women and children killed, the responsibility is not with the soldiers, but with the people whose crimes necessitated the attack."

Sherman heartily approved:

Go ahead in your own way and I will back you with my whole authority. . . . I will say nothing and do nothing to restrain our troops from doing what they deem proper on the spot, and will allow no mere vague general charges of cruelty and inhumanity to tie their hands, but will use all the powers confided to me to the end that these Indians, the enemies of our race and of our civilization, shall not again be able to begin and carry out their barbarous warfare on any kind of pretext they may choose to allege.

To lead his winter campaign, Sheridan sent for Custer. It was all the younger man had hoped for — a chance to redeem himself, erase the bitter memory of the Hancock campaign, and win a great victory. Three separate columns were to force the Cheyenne back onto their reservation, but Sheridan meant for Custer to do the real fighting, attacking the Cheyenne villages when they least expected it. "I rely in everything upon you," he told Custer, "and shall send you on this expedition without giving you any orders, leaving you to act entirely on your own judgment."

I have always done my best to keep my young men quiet, but some will not listen, and since the fighting began I have not been able to keep them all at home. But we want peace, and I would be glad to move all my people down this way; I could then keep them all quietly near camp.

Black Kettle

Custer drove his men relentlessly through the snow. An old Osage scout asked him what he would do if they were to find "more Indians than we can handle."

"All I am afraid of is we won't find half enough," Custer answered. "There are not Indians enough in the country to whip the Seventh Cavalry."

Then, his scouts reported they had found a Cheyenne village of some fifty lodges. Custer ordered his men to prepare for a dawn attack. Though he didn't know it at the time, Custer had come upon Black Kettle's band, encamped along the Washita River, well within the Cheyenne reservation. A white flag flew above the peace chief's teepee. But some of his young men had slipped away to steal livestock and raid settlers. It was their pony tracks that had led Custer's scouts to the edge of the camp, and four white hostages, women and children, were being held by the Indians.

At dawn on November 27, 1868, just two days short of the fourth anniversary of the Sand Creek massacre, Custer's buglers sounded a somewhat muffled charge — their lips froze to the mouthpieces of their instruments in the fierce cold — and six hundred mounted men started toward the village, firing as they came.

Black Kettle mounted his pony, pulled his wife up behind him, and tried to ride away. A volley of fire hurled him, his wife, and the pony into the river. The soldiers rode over their bodies and on into the camp. The killing went on for half an hour.

Custer (seated at center, in profile) and his officers enjoy the autumn sun at the beginning of the 1868 campaign that ended at the Washita.

The survivors hid in the tall grass. "The soldiers would pass back and forth near the spot where I lay," one Cheyenne girl remembered. "As I turned sideways and looked, one soldier saw us, and rode toward where we lay. He stopped his horse and stared at us. He did not say a word, and we wondered what would happen. But he left and no one showed up after that. I suppose he pitied us, and left us alone."

The surprise had been complete, but Custer had failed to realize that Black Kettle was not alone on the Washita. Some 6,000 Cheyenne and Arapaho, Kiowa and Comanche were camped just downriver, and warriors soon began to swarm out to attack him. Under cover of darkness that evening, Custer managed to escape with some prisoners — including a Cheyenne woman whom he would soon take as his mistress — but not before a foolhardy young major charged headlong into the Indians and was cut down with eighteen volunteers. Custer never even tried to rescue them.

He sent a boastful report to his superiors, nonetheless:

> The Indians left on the ground 103 warriors, including Black Kettle, whose scalp was taken by an Osage guide. 875 horses and mules were captured, 241 saddles . . . 573 buffalo robes, 390 buffalo skins, 160 untanned robes. . . . [All] the winter supply of dried buffalo meat, all the meal, flour and other provisions; in fact, all they possessed was captured, as the warriors escaped with little or no clothing. Everything of value [to them] was destroyed.

Cheyenne survivors said only eleven warriors were killed. The rest of the dead were women and children and old men. Two of the white hostages were dead, too, stabbed to death by Cheyenne women as soon as the shooting began.

"If we can get in one or two more [such] blows," said Sheridan, "there will be no more Indian troubles in my department." The blows were eventually struck, and by the autumn of 1869 Indians had been driven off the plains between the Platte and the Arkansas. But many of Custer's own officers and men never forgave him for abandoning their comrades on the Washita battlefield. "The honor of his country weighed lightly in the scale against the 'glorious' name of 'Geo. A. Custer,'" wrote a private who

Lieutenant-General Sherman,
St. Louis, Mo.
War Department,
Washington City,
December 2, 1868
I congratulate you, Sheridan, and Custer on the splendid success with which your campaign is begun. Ask Sheridan to send forward the names of officers and men deserving of special mention.

J. M. Schofield
Secretary of War

Cheyenne survivors of the Washita, mostly women and children, under guard at Camp Supply in Indian Territory, 1868

served under him, "the hardships and danger to his men, as well as the probable loss of life were worthy of but little consideration when dim visions of an 'eagle' or even a 'star' floated before [his] excited mind. . . ."

The following spring, the last Cheyenne holdouts from the unremitting winter campaign began to come in. One band was led by a chief named Rock Forehead. He held two white women as captives, so Custer decided to talk him into giving up, rather than risk having them killed in another attack.

Custer entered the village with only an interpreter, and was taken to the chief's teepee. He told the Cheyenne that if they released their captives and returned to the reservation, no one would be harmed and peace could be restored.

Eventually, Rock Forehead would agree to give up. But on that day he was not convinced that Custer was trustworthy. He tapped out the pipe's ashes on the general's boots, to bring Custer bad luck and to drive home a warning. "They told him," a Cheyenne woman named Kate Big Head recalled, ". . . that if ever afterward he should break that peace promise and should fight the Cheyennes, the Everywhere Spirit would cause him to be killed."

DONE!

By the spring of 1869, the Central Pacific and the Union Pacific were converging at last in Utah. Speed and distance were still everything: "I would build the road in the cheapest possible manner," Collis P. Huntington told Charles Crocker, "then go back and improve it . . . , because the Union Pacific have built the cheapest kind of road." (Huntington was right about the Union Pacific, which was forced to come up with an extra $7 million for repairs even before the line was completed; by 1887, Grenville Dodge admitted, the original tracks of the line he'd built were "two dirt tracks ballasted with streaks of rust.")

Rival armies of railroad men vied to cover the most ground — and earn the most money for their employers — before the two lines finally met. Still, no fixed rendezvous point had been established, so grading crews, working far ahead of the men who laid the track, passed each other in opposite directions and pushed on for miles, sometimes working so close to one another, the Deseret *Evening News* reported, that blasts set off by one work gang often spattered its rival with dirt:

> [W]hen Sharp & Young's men first began to work for the Central Pacific, [they] would give [the Union Pacific crews] no warning when they lit the fuse. Jim Livingston, Sharp's able foreman, said nothing, but went to work and loaded a point of rock with nitroglycerine, and without saying anything to the Central Pacific "let 'er rip." The explosion was terrific. The report was heard in the Dry Tortugas, and the foreman of the Central Pacific came down to confer . . . about the necessity of each party notifying the other when ready for a blast. The matter was speedily arranged to the satisfaction of both parties.

Finally, government engineers intervened and picked Promontory Summit, fifty-six miles west of Ogden, as the place where the two lines would finally meet.

By May 8, 1869, the rails were at last ready to be joined. Leland Stanford of the Central Pacific had already arrived for the ceremony in his private railroad car. But

May God continue the unity of our country as this railroad unites the two great oceans of the world.

Engraved on a ceremonial spike

Vice President Thomas C. Durant of the Union Pacific was nowhere to be seen. His train had been halted in Wyoming by a crew of angry tie cutters who had not been paid for five months. They chained the wheels of his car to the tracks and would not let him pass until the cash was in their hands.

The Union Pacific sent a special train with the payroll, Durant was released, and on May 10 everything was finally ready at Promontory Summit. The last two lengths of rail were brought up — one by the Union Pacific's Irishmen, the other by the Central Pacific's Chinese. A telegrapher stood by to signal the driving of the final spike to both coasts and all points in between:

TO EVERYBODY, KEEP QUIET. WHEN THE LAST SPIKE IS DRIVEN AT PROMONTORY POINT, WE WILL SAY "DONE!" DON'T BREAK THE CIRCUIT, BUT WATCH FOR THE SIGNALS OF THE BLOWS OF THE HAMMER.

Four spikes — two gold, one silver, and the fourth a blend of gold, silver, and iron — were to be gently tapped into position to mark the occasion, and then a fifth and final spike — an ordinary one but wired to the telegrapher's key — was to be hammered into the ground.

ALMOST READY. HATS OFF PRAYER IS BEING OFFERED.

A clergyman intoned what seemed to be an interminable prayer:

. . . O Father, God of our fathers, we desire to acknowledge Thy handiwork in this great work, and ask Thy blessing upon us here assembled, upon the rulers of our government, and upon Thy people everywhere; that peace may flow

Climax at Promontory Summit, May 10, 1869. Above, left: With the final spike driven at last, Leland Stanford (center) brandishes the silver-headed maul with which he managed to hit it the second time he tried.

Above, right: Two stereographic views have been combined to capture in one image both the locomotives that were the focus of the celebration — the Central Pacific's Jupiter (left) and Engine No. 119, pride of the Union Pacific.

unto them as a gentle stream, and that mighty enterprise may be unto us as the Atlantic of Thy strength, and the Pacific of Thy love, through Jesus the Redeemer, Amen.

ALL READY NOW; THE SPIKE WILL SOON BE DRIVEN.

WE UNDERSTAND; ALL ARE READY IN THE EAST.

WE HAVE GOT DONE PRAYING; THE SPIKE IS ABOUT TO BE PRESENTED.

The final spike was slid into place. Leland Stanford was to have the honor of driving it home, with a special silver-headed maul.

THE SIGNAL WILL BE THREE DOTS FOR THE COMMENCEMENT OF THE BLOWS.

Stanford swung the hammer high above his head, brought it down — and missed. The telegrapher closed the circuit anyway: "DONE!"

In Washington, a great cheer went up from the big crowd in front of the telegraph office and an illuminated ball dropped from the dome of the Capitol. At Independence Hall in Philadelphia, the Liberty Bell was gingerly rung so that its crack would not worsen. And in San Francisco a huge banner was unfurled that proclaimed, "California Annexes the United States."

The Hayden Survey moves into the Yellowstone Valley, 1871.

Clarence King at work (above) and Ferdinand Hayden in the saddle

Lewis and Clark had begun the business of charting the region for the government, and John Charles Frémont and other army topographical engineers had continued their work.

In the 1860s and 1870s, a series of four Great Surveys, all but one of them led by civilians, would continue the job — and employ the camera to bring home to their fellow citizens back East the look of the vast region that still had not been conquered.

First Lt. George Montague Wheeler was the last of the great army surveyors. A modest soldier who believed science more important than heroics — "The day of the pathfinder has sensibly ended," he said — he managed to chart some 175,000 square miles of territory from Mexico all the way to Oregon. But his dream of completing a comprehensive map of the whole West by 1900 was dashed by the creation of the civilian United States Geological Survey in 1879.

Its first director was Clarence King, brought up as the pampered son of an old but threadbare Newport family, who nonetheless helped map the path followed by the transcontinental railroad, discovered three American glaciers overlooked even by Frémont, and survived being struck by lightning atop a Utah peak before taking up his new duties in Washington.

His successor was Major John Wesley Powell, an abolitionist minister's son from upstate New York, who volunteered for service in the Union army, lost an arm at Shiloh but stayed in the war until slavery was crushed, then taught geology at Illinois Wesleyan University before undertaking two trips down the Colorado River.

Geologist Ferdinand Hayden was small and voluble, so energetic that Indians called him "Man-Who-Picks-Up-Stones-Running," and so determinedly optimistic that when he discovered a small vein of brown coal near the little town of Laramie, he confidently announced that Wyoming would soon become a second Pennsylvania. In July of 1871, he led an expedition into the Yellowstone Valley. For more than sixty years, trappers and travelers had been returning from there with tales so wondrous that no one believed them. But the photographer William Henry Jackson accompanied Hayden, and his work made all the difference. On March 1, 1872, after viewing Jackson's pictures, Congress voted to create Yellowstone National Park, the first national park in the history of the world.

Canyon de Chelly, photographed by John Hillers for a survey led by John Wesley Powell (right) in 1869. The photographer's wagon and team are in the foreground.

The Grand Canyon of the Colorado (opposite), as seen by John Hillers's assistant during the Powell expedition. Hillers himself perches at the edge of the cliff.

Shoshone Falls on the Snake River in Idaho Territory (above), photographed by Timothy O'Sullivan during the Wheeler Survey, 1874

At one time, 30 million buffalo may have blanketed the Plains. But by the late 1860s, their numbers had already drastically declined — reduced by competition for winter fodder with the horse, by diseases carried by the emigrants' oxen and loss of grasslands to the overland trails, by hunting that had provided meat first to fur trappers and then to railroad crews, and by the buffalo-robe trade that encouraged Indians to kill more than they needed.

Still, buffalo roamed in herds beyond counting — millions upon millions of animals that to the Plains peoples represented existence itself. "Everything the Kiowas had came from the buffalo," a woman named Old Lady Horse recalled. "Their tipis were made of buffalo hides, so were their clothes and moccasins. They ate buffalo meat. Their containers were made of hide, or of bladders or stomachs. . . . Most of all the buffalo was part of the Kiowa religion. . . . The buffalo were the life of the Kiowas."

Following the lead of the Union Pacific and Central Pacific, other rail lines would soon spread across the West — the Kansas Pacific, Northern Pacific, Denver Pacific, Texas and Pacific; the Burlington and Missouri River, Denver and Rio Grande, Atchison, Topeka and Santa Fe. And as the new railroads began to move onto the Great Plains, the buffalo began to die. Now, almost anyone could shoot one: to raise money for their church, one congregation in Lawrence, Kansas, organized a buffalo excursion; three hundred people signed up for the two-day trip, blasting away from the windows of their chair car.

Foreign sportsmen came, too, including the son of the czar of all the Russias, Grand Duke Alexis Alexandrovitch. Bored with hunting in Europe, he hired an opulently furnished private train and set out for the tiny settlement of North Platte in Nebraska Territory. General Sheridan, in charge of every detail of the arrangements, selected Custer as grand marshal of the hunt and appointed the flamboyant, hard-drinking William F. Cody as his guide. Just twenty-five but already a legend in the East, where dime novels and stage melodramas exaggerating his adventures had earned him the nickname "Buffalo Bill," Cody had killed by his own count more than 4,000 buffalo as a meat hunter for the Union Pacific; his job now was to make sure Alexis got at least one.

It wasn't easy. The first kill was reserved for the grand duke, mounted on Cody's favorite horse, Buckskin Joe, and armed with an engraved revolver, made especially for him by Smith and Wesson. He fired six shots at one buffalo without hitting it, then emptied his revolver at another with the same result. Buffalo Bill handed him his own rifle, "Lucretia," then whipped the prince's horse to get him within ten feet of his target. Alexis fired at point-blank range, and a buffalo tottered and fell dead. Champagne was ordered up, a bottle for each hunter, and after it was downed the chase resumed. When the grand duke shot another buffalo, out came a second round of champagne. "I was in hopes that he would kill five or six more before we reached camp," Buffalo Bill remembered.

Alexis's last day on the Plains was especially memorable. Custer spotted a herd in the distance, and decided it would be fun to pretend the animals were Indians and lead a charge into their midst. "Boys," he shouted, "here's a chance for a great victory over that bunch of redskins on the other side of the hill!" Before they were through,

I have been on a train when the black, moving mass of buffaloes before us looked as if it stretched on down to the horizon. Everyone went armed in those days, and . . . [it] was the greatest wonder that more people were not killed, as the wild rush for the windows, and the reckless discharge of rifles and pistols, put every passenger's life in jeopardy. . . . I could not for the life of me avoid a shudder when a long line of guns leaning on the backs of seats met my eye as I entered a car. When the sharp shrieks of the train whistle announced a herd of buffaloes the rifles were snatched, and in the struggle to twist around for a good aim out of the narrow window the barrel of the muzzle of the firearm passed dangerously near the ear of any scared woman who had the temerity to travel in those tempestuous days. . . . Elizabeth Custer

some fifty buffalo lay dead on the frozen prairie. Alexis had personally killed a dozen and was so excited he grabbed Custer and kissed him.

Newspapermen reported every detail of the prince's hunt, and public interest in the gaudy show Buffalo Bill had orchestrated for his imperial guest helped persuade him to go east and try his hand at show business. If money was being made playing him onstage, Cody reasoned, he might as well get some of it himself. And the final assault on the buffalo herd would prove to be the last time George Armstrong Custer led a headlong charge "to the other side of the hill" — and survived.

Now, a different kind of buffalo hunter was heading for the Plains. Eastern manufacturers had developed new techniques for turning stiff buffalo hides into soft leather — ideal for shoes, cushions, carriage tops, and the belts that turned machinery in eastern factories. The new rail lines still spreading across the Plains meant that buffalo robes and buffalo meat could be shipped to eastern markets in much greater numbers, at far lower costs.

Plans for a railroad stop at the Arkansas River, near Fort Dodge in the heart of buffalo country, had been drawn up in July 1872, and some settlers had started moving in the next month. The first business in town was a tent saloon; an empty boxcar served as the first depot. The first train that pulled up to it in September was two hours late; it had been delayed by a buffalo herd three miles wide and ten miles long crossing the track. The residents christened their town Buffalo City, but the postmaster general in Washington vetoed their choice: Kansas already had towns named Buffalo and Buffalo Station. So, in honor of the fort nearby, they renamed it Dodge City.

"Hardly had the railroad reached there . . ." one citizen remembered, "[than the buffalo-hunting] business began; and such a business! The streets were lined with wagons, bringing in hides and meat and getting supplies from early morning to late at night. I have been to several mining camps where rich strikes have been made, but I never saw any town equal to Dodge." In just its first three months of existence, the town shipped east 43,029 buffalo hides and 1.4 million pounds of buffalo meat. That winter, more than a hundred buffalo hunters froze to death along the Arkansas River, and the Fort Dodge surgeon performed seventy amputations for frostbite.

But still more hunters turned up in the spring of 1873. In the midst of a national economic depression, buffalo hunting looked like a good thing.

Frank H. Mayer, a twenty-two-year-old Louisianan who had been a rebel bugler in the Civil War, was hanging around Dodge City that spring looking for work and excitement when he met two hunters who offered to show him their trade. "I was young. . . . I could shoot. . . . I liked to hunt. . . . I needed adventure," he remembered. "Here was it." Mayer sank everything he owned into a hunting outfit — wagons, mules, camp equipment, and firearms — and headed out onto the Plains. The buffalo didn't belong to anybody," he wrote. "If you could kill them, what they brought was yours. They were walking gold pieces."

Shooting buffalo from trains proved so easy and so popular with passengers that the Kansas Pacific found it profitable to operate its own taxidermist's department just to mount their trophies.

When I went into the business, I sat down and figured that I was indeed one of fortune's children. Just think. There were 20 million buffalo, each worth at least $3 — $60 million. At the very outside, cartridges cost 25 cents each, so every time I fired one I got my investment back twelve times over. I could kill a hun-

dred a day. . . . [T]hat would be $6,000 a month — or three times what was paid, it seems to me, the President of the United States, and a hundred times what a man with a good job could be expected to earn. Was I not lucky that I discovered this quick and easy way to fortune? I thought I was. . . .

Before long, Frank Mayer was competing with some 2,000 other marksmen to kill the buffalo of Kansas.

RAIN FOLLOWS THE PLOW

It had at first been thought that no settlers could survive anywhere on the semiarid, mostly treeless Great Plains that rolled all the way from Montana and the Dakotas south into Texas. Back in 1820, Major Stephen Harriman Long had led an exploring party across the Great Plains region of Nebraska and Colorado to the Rockies and pronounced all of it unfit for white people: "uninhabitable by a people depending on agriculture" and useful to the United States in the future only as "a barrier against too great an expansion of our population westward." Mapmakers called it "the Great American Desert," and for forty-odd years pioneers had carefully avoided settling on it.

A gigantic buffalo rifle reminds hide-hunters working out of Dodge City in 1872 that they will always find a welcome at Zimmerman's Hardware.

The Swedish immigrants, opposite, settled in Greeley County, Kansas, in the 1870s, confident that they would not have to worry about getting enough rain.

With a logic that cannot rest we are forced to this conclusion, that the agencies of civilization now in action are such as will secure a complete victory over the wilderness and waste places of western territory. The plow will go forward. God speed the plow. By this wonderful provision, which is only man's mastery over nature, the clouds are dispensing copious rains. . . . [The plow is] more powerful in peace than the sword in war, the instrument which separates civilization from savagery; and converts a desert into a farm or garden. To be more concise, Rain follows the plow.

Charles Dana Wilber, 1879

But the Homestead Act of 1862 began to change all that. It promised 160 acres of public land to any person who filed a claim, paid a ten-dollar fee, and agreed to work the property for five years. As it happened, the 1870s and early 1880s were unusually wet years in the West, and the prairies, plowed and planted for the first time, yielded bumper crops. Promoters made the most of it. The Plains might once have been desertlike, they admitted, but no longer. The climate itself, they promised, had changed for good. Some believed the presence of railroads had brought rain: "The increase of railroads," said one Colorado newspaper, "and also the increase of activity on the roads has the . . . effect of producing more showers. . . . The concussion of the air and rapid movement produced by railroad trains and engines affects the electrical conditions of the atmosphere." Others believed that the change in climate had been caused by farming itself: rain was said somehow to follow the plow.

Then, too, just a few days after the Union Pacific and Central Pacific lines met at Promontory Summit in 1869, word had come that another of the great engineering feats of the nineteenth century had been completed — the Suez Canal, linking Africa and Asia. Much of the trade between Europe and the Orient that the new western lines had hoped to carry would now never reach the United States at all, and American railroads would have to depend on domestic business to keep from going under. The competition intensified to see which lines could lure the most settlers to live along their tracks, providing business for their freight trains and buying up the 181 million public domain acres Congress had provided to the railroad corporations to encourage construction. "You can lay track to the garden of Eden," said the head of the Northern Pacific, "but what good is it if the only inhabitants are Adam and Eve?"

At the same time, as territories became states, they, too, were given federal land, and used the proceeds from selling or renting it to support their schools. Most set up promotional bureaus to lure in new settlers. "No crop to be harvested by the farmers of Kansas next summer," said the Kansas Bureau of Immigration, "will be equal in value [to] the harvest of people that may be gathered. . . . It [is] our desire to fill,

Newcomers: Members of the tennis club at Runnymede, a British colony in the middle of Kansas (left), and a flatcar filled with European immigrants being shown likely sites for farming

upon the map of Kansas, the blank space heretofore allotted to the 'Great American Desert' — that myth of the old geographers."

Most of those who came west were farmers from the midwestern states. But when the financial panic of 1873 threw thousands out of work in the East, worried industrialists hoped the promise of free land in the West would also drain off the unemployed — and with them, social unrest in the cities. One businessman suggested that factory owners without jobs to offer simply tack a copy of the Homestead Act to their plant gates: "There can be no excuse for begging in a country which offers every pauper a quarter-section of as rich land as the sun shines upon. It is more profitable to raise farmers than convicts." Others contributed to organizations — the Co-Operative Colony Aid Association of New York; the Cosmo-American Colonization and General Improvement Bureau of Philadelphia — that promised to direct the newly jobless poor from the crowded eastern cities to the open spaces of the West.

Most of these efforts came to nothing. Factory workers weren't farmers, and even those who might have wanted to try it could only rarely afford it. Land itself was cheap, but getting to it, getting started, and surviving for the five years required to get title to a homestead cost money most of them didn't have.

Prospects seemed better overseas. The Hebrew Emigrant Aid Society recruited Jewish immigrants from eastern Europe to establish farming communes in Oregon, Colorado, Kansas, and the Dakotas. The First Swedish Agricultural and Galesburg Colonization Companies started the towns of Salemsborg and Lindsborg in Kansas. Small groups of Dutch, French, Bohemian, English, and Irish families scattered across the Plains. Two hundred Scottish families settled together on the Kansas-Nebraska border. By 1875, more than half of Nebraska's 123,000 settlers were members of families headed by foreign immigrants.

The expanding railroad companies and the young western states dispatched agents to Europe to recruit settlers. In just three weeks, an agent for the Burlington railroad boasted, he had entirely filled a boat with immigrants from Liverpool, all destined for company land in the West. Nebraska's agent in Scandinavia would claim that he personally had persuaded 10,000 Swedes, Danes, and Norwegians to move to his state.

But the undisputed champion of foreign immigration agents was C. B. Schmidt of the Sante Fe Railroad in Kansas, a tireless, imaginative salesman, successful throughout Europe but especially so in Germany because he spoke the language and seemed to know by instinct just where to show up when political unrest had farmers ready to consider moving. Because of Schmidt, one person said, Kansas was "as familiar to the households of the German peasant as that of Canaan was to the Israelites in bondage." Through his efforts alone, 60,000 Germans settled along the Santa Fe route.

Then Schmidt was dispatched for the biggest prize of all — the German-Russian Mennonites. They were pacifists who had fled Prussia rather than serve in its army three-quarters of a century earlier. Promising them military exemption, the freedom to speak their own language and run their own schools, plus 175 acres of land, Catherine the Great had lured them to the Russian steppes, where they had become the best wheat farmers in the world. But in 1870, a new czar withdrew their religious privileges, and they were looking for a new home.

Armed with encouraging letters from Mennonites already in Kansas taped to his body to escape notice by the border guards, Schmidt entered Russia. As he toured the prosperous Mennonite communities, he handed out the letters, sang the praises of Kansas, and offered incentives for them to relocate — until the czar's officers chased him out.

There was plenty of competition for these able and prosperous farmers. After Canada offered them immunity from military service and free transportation if they would settle there, Kansas, Nebraska, and Minnesota all also solemnly offered to exempt them from militia duty — although they had no legal authority to do so. Everyone promised them the right to govern themselves in their own communities, to speak German in their schools, plenty of land at good prices, and easy credit.

Mennonite emissaries were taken to Washington to meet President Grant, as one of them remembered:

> In Russia, we associated a government official with a uniform and lots of lace and trimmings, and the higher ones would always have guards of soldiers at the entrances of their quarters. . . . Imagine our surprise when we reached the White House to find the portals guarded by a single colored man who did not even display a sword.
>
> Our admission and introduction to President Grant was equally simple. . . . He told us that in his younger years he had been in the habit of milking twenty cows, mornings and evenings. President Grant also told us of his early experiences on the farm and said that he could hitch up and drive a team of horses as well as ever. You who never knew life in Europe, and especially in Russia, can hardly imagine our surprise when [he] gave us the impression that it was the usual thing for the highest official of the United States . . . to do manual labor.

Secretary of State Hamilton Fish personally assured them the United States would not go to war again for at least fifty years.

In the end, although Nebraska boosters deliberately delayed the Mennonite emissaries' luggage in Lincoln so that they could be taken on a last-minute tour of their state, most of their followers finally chose to settle in Kansas, where Schmidt's Santa Fe Railroad sold them 100,000 acres in 1874 alone. Tens of thousands of other German-Russians — Catholics, Hutterites, Amish — also came to the Plains in the 1870s.

"They seem well pleased with the country," reported the Kansas *Daily State Journal.* "They wear the simple garb of the German peasant, but have well-filled wallets. The men are sturdy, healthy looking fellows. The women all wear calico gowns, with a blue handkerchief thrown over their heads, and no signs of ribbons or ear rings, or brooches, or even of wedding rings. Those articles are considered too worldly. Both men and women are very stoop shouldered which we are informed comes from hard work."

They arrived in the midst of a drought and one of the worst grasshopper plagues in Kansas history: ". . . They devoured every green thing but the prairie grass," one American-born woman homesteader remembered. "Water troughs and loosely covered wells were foul with drowned 'hoppers," another man recalled.

All honor and reverence to good men; but they and their attentions are not the only source of happiness on the earth and need not fill up every thought of woman. And when men see that women can exist without their being constantly at hand it will perhaps take a little of the conceit out of some of them.

Emmeline Wells

THE FOUNTAIN OF ALL TRUTH

Brigham Young had brought his Mormon people west in search of sanctuary from the rest of the United States. But the new transcontinental railroad now ran right through Utah and began bringing thousands of new settlers into Young's kingdom — nonbelievers who threatened his authority and deplored the Mormon practice of plural marriage. (By 1880, one out of every five citizens of Utah would be a non-Mormon.)

In 1870, some three thousand Mormon women held an "Indignation Meeting" in the Salt Lake Tabernacle, to protest against those nonbelievers who had dared criticize polygamy. One of the speakers was Emmeline Wells. "The world says polygamy makes women inferior to men — we think differently," she told the cheering crowd. "Polygamy gives women more time for thought, for mental culture, more freedom of action, a broader field of labor, . . . [and] leads women more directly to God, the fountain of all truth. . . ."

Born in Massachusetts and graduated from a select girls school, Wells had converted to Mormonism and moved to Nauvoo, where she lost her first child and was abandoned by her husband — all before the age of sixteen. She made the exodus to Utah with her second husband, a church bishop, and bore him two daughters before he died; then became the seventh wife of Daniel H. Wells, the mayor of Salt Lake City, whom she bore three more daughters. Now, she lived in her own small house with her five children, and was expected to help make up the difference whenever her husband's finances suffered. But nothing could shake her belief in plural marriage — or in giving women the vote, the other cause for which she campaigned in a newspaper for Mormon women she somehow found the time to edit.

In her push for the vote, Wells soon found a most unlikely ally. Brigham Young remained anxious about his people eventually being outnumbered — and outvoted in their own land. In Washington, a congressman urged that Utah women be given the vote, certain that they would use it to outlaw polygamy themselves.

Young needed no such urging: he knew that by adding Mormon women to the Utah voters' rolls he would strengthen his hold on the territory. On February 14, 1870, with Young's backing, the Utah territorial legislature granted women the vote. A few days later, for the first time ever in a United States territory, women cast ballots in a municipal election. Young's niece voted first, followed by one of his daughters.

Emmeline Wells never stopped urging the rest of the United States to follow the West's example. (Wyoming Territory, too, had enfranchised its women.) But she never stopped lobbying, either, on behalf of the right of every woman to remain a plural wife.

Emmeline Wells and (below) her newspaper

The polygamous family of Aaron Johnson of Springville, Utah, 1870

Neighbors passing spoke of strange happenings. A young wife awaiting her first baby, in the absence of her husband . . . had gone insane from fright, all alone in that sun-baked shanty on the bald prairie. Eggs and milk tasted of the 'hoppers and cows were drying up, somebody said. . . . A train had stalled on a curve coming out of Leavenworth on the narrow-gauge because the crushed grasshoppers greased the track so that the wheels couldn't take hold. Some of the farmers here and there began plowing their denuded corn lands for wheat, turning up the 'hopper eggs to the sun and harrowing the ground thoroughly in hope of destroying the pests as they hatched. Others said that it was wasted effort. . . . If winter didn't kill them off, it was all up with the people, there'd never be another harvest in Kansas.

To many new settlers, unaccustomed to life on the open prairie and already battered by icy winters, howling winds, and desolation, the ravenous insects were the last straw. But not for the Mennonites. "The Mennonites are not afraid of the grasshopper," the Newton *Kansan* assured its anxious readers. "He is an old acquaintance of theirs; and they kill him at once without holding mass meetings or writing complaining letters to the newspapers. With the Mennonites every year is a good year, and adds to their wealth."

Grit and patience and religious faith kept the Mennonites going. Winter wheat made them prosper. The strains of seed they brought with them from Russia flourished as no other domestic crops ever had before on the semiarid western Plains, and would soon transform them into the most productive wheat-growing region in the world. And mixed in with the wheat from Russia came weeds that adapted just as successfully as did the immigrants who brought them — corn cockle, cheatgrass, Russian pigweed, Russian knapweed, and a plant that spread so fast and ranged so widely that it became a symbol of the American West, the Russian thistle, better known as tumbleweed.

WHOA, BLUE!

The era of the Texas trail drive, ushered in by Charles Goodnight and others, would last just a little over two decades, but by the time it was over and cattle ranching had mostly moved onto the central and northern Plains, it rivaled mining as the West's dominant industry. Some 10 million head of sinewy Texas longhorns were driven north between the end of the Civil War and 1890; so many, one trail driver said, that in places the dust was knee-deep to the cattle. From the southernmost tip of Texas, the trails all pointed north — the Shawnee Trail, the Chisholm, the Stimson, the Goodnight-Loving, the Eastern, and the Western — but their destinations shifted with the market. At first, the herds were driven to mining towns in New Mexico and Colorado, and to reservations and military forts, where the government bought beef to feed its troops and the Indian peoples they were steadily subduing. But in the end, most Texas cattle were taken to the new railheads in Kansas and Nebraska, then shipped east by rail to feed the hungry workers of the cities.

For all the romance that grew up around the cattle drives almost as soon as they began, it was a distinctly unromantic business, and the workingmen who made the cattleman's profits possible labored for wages so low and under conditions so

For a man to be stove up at thirty may sound strange to some people, but many a cowboy has been so bunged up that he has to quit riding that early in life. . . . My advice to any young man or boy is to stay at home and not be a rambler, as it won't buy you anything. And above everything stay away from a cow ranch, as not many cowpunchers ever save any money and 'tis a dangerous life to live.

James Emmit McCauley

Teddy Blue Abbott (above), dressed up and slicked down after a successful trail drive in 1879, and a flash-lit photograph (right) of the changing of the cowboy guard at night, made during the 1880s. "When you add it all up," Abbott remembered, "the worst hardship we had on the trail was loss of sleep. There was never enough sleep. . . . I would get maybe five hours' sleep when the weather was nice and everything smooth and pretty, with cowboys singing under the stars. If it wasn't so nice, you'd be lucky to sleep an hour. But the wagon rolled on in the morning just the same. Sometimes we would rub tobacco juice in our eyes to keep awake. It was rubbing them with fire. I have done that a few times, and I have often sat in my saddle sound asleep for just a few minutes."

difficult and so dangerous that only a third of them were willing to undergo them more than once.

Cowboys liked nicknames — Pinnacle Jake, Mesquite Bill, Bronco Jim, Buckskin Joe, Wyoming Pete. Edward C. Abbott was known to his friends as "Teddy Blue" because, while drunk and lurching after a prostitute at a theater in Miles City, Montana, in 1881, he somehow found himself onstage. There, to cover his embarrassment and entertain his fellow cowboys in the audience, he commandeered a chair from a startled musician, straddled it as if it were his horse, and shouted, "Whoa, Blue! Whoa, Blue!" The men in the audience, not entirely sober themselves, loved it. "When I went out of that theatre that night," he remembered as an old man, "I was Blue, and Teddy Blue I have been for fifty-five years."

He was born in England and brought to Nebraska by his parents as a boy. His father let him accompany a trail drive when he was just ten years old, hoping the open air would improve the boy's frail health. "The experience," he said later, "made a cowboy out of me. Nothing could have changed me after that. . . . My family and I went separate ways, and they stayed separate forever after. My father was all for farming . . . and all my brothers turned out farmers except one, and he ended up the worst of the lot — a sheepman and a Republican." Teddy Blue made his first trail drive in 1871 and his last one — still before his twenty-fourth birthday — in 1883, going all the way from San Antonio to Montana. By that time, no one could have suspected that he was not a Texan, born as well as bred.

Like most cowboys, Teddy Blue was young (the average age was twenty-four), and slightly built — big men were too hard on the horses. Most cowboys were Texans, and many were ex–Confederate soldiers whose feelings about northerners had not improved since the Civil War. But there were Mexicans among them too, and blacks,

Riding herd in the 1880s

All in all, my years on the trail were the happiest I ever lived. There were many hardships and dangers, of course, that called on all a man had of endurance and bravery; but when all went well there was no other life so pleasant. Most of the time we were solitary adventurers in a great land as fresh and new as a spring morning, and we were free and full of the zest of darers.

Charles Goodnight

either former Texas slaves or refugees from other parts of the old Confederacy. Whatever their background, almost all the cowboys were poor — willing to work seventeen-hour days, seven days a week for up to four months, at thirty to forty-five dollars a month — and most were uncomplaining. "They had very little grub [on the trail] and they usually run out of that and lived on straight beef," one recalled. "[T]hey had only three or four horses to the man, mostly with sore backs; . . . they had no tents, no tarps, and damn few slickers. They never kicked, because those boys was raised under just the same conditions as there was on the trail — corn meal and bacon for grub, dirt floors in the houses, and no luxuries."

A drive's success depended on discipline and planning. According to Teddy Blue, most Texas herds numbered about 2,000 head with a trail boss and about a dozen men in charge — though herds as large as 15,000 were also driven north with far larger escorts. The most experienced men rode "point" and "swing," at the head and sides of the long herd; the least experienced brought up the rear, riding "drag" and eating dust. At the end of the day, Teddy Blue remembered, they "would go to the water barrel . . . and rinse their mouths and cough and spit up . . . black stuff. But you couldn't get it up out of your lungs."

They had to learn to work as a team, keeping the herd moving during the day, resting peacefully at night. Twelve to fifteen miles a day was a good pace. But such steady progress could be interrupted at any time. A cowboy had to know how to gauge the temperament of his cattle, how to chase down a stray without alarming the rest of the herd, how to lasso a steer using the horn of his saddle as a tying post. His saddle was his most prized possession; it served as his chair, his workbench, his pillow at night. Being dragged to death was the most common death for a cowboy, and so the most feared occurrence on the trail was the nighttime stampede. As Teddy Blue recalled, a sound, a smell, or simply the sudden movement of a jittery cow could set off a whole herd.

> If . . . the cattle started running — you'd hear that low rumbling noise along the ground and the men on herd wouldn't need to come in and tell you, you'd know — then you'd jump for your horse and get out there in the lead, trying to head them and get them into a mill before they scattered to hell and gone. It was riding at a dead run in the dark, with cut banks and prairie dog holes all around you, not knowing if the next jump would land you in a shallow grave.

Most cowboys had guns, but rarely used them on the trail. Some outfits made them keep their weapons in the chuck wagon to eliminate any chance of gunplay. Charles Goodnight was still more emphatic: "Before starting on a trail drive, I made it a rule to draw up an article of agreement, setting forth what each man was to do. The main clause stipulated that if one shot another he was to be tried by the outfit and hanged on the spot, if found guilty. I never had a man shot on the trail."

Regardless of its ultimate destination, every herd had to ford a series of rivers — the Nueces, the Guadalupe, the Brazos, the Wichita, the Red. A big herd of longhorns swimming across a river, Goodnight remembered, "looked like a million floating rocking chairs," and crossing those rivers one after another, a cowboy recalled, was like climbing the rungs of a long ladder reaching north.

No harder life is lived by any working man. Our comfort was nothing; men were cheap, but cattle cost money.

Andy Adams

"After you crossed the Red River and got out on the open plains," Teddy Blue remembered, "it was sure a pretty sight to see them strung out for almost a mile, the sun shining on their horns." Initially, the land immediately north of the Red River was Indian territory, and some tribes charged tolls for herds crossing their land — payable in money or beef. But Teddy Blue remembered that the homesteaders, now pouring onto the Plains by railroad, were far more nettlesome:

> There was no love lost between settlers and cowboys on the trail. Those jay-hawkers would take up a claim right where the herds watered and charge us for water. They would plant a crop alongside the trail and plow a furrow around it for a fence, and then when the cattle got into their wheat or their garden patch, they would come cussing and waving a shotgun and yelling for damages. And the cattle had been coming through there when they were still raising punkins in Illinois.

The settlers' hostility was entirely understandable. The big herds ruined their crops, and they carried with them a disease, spread by ticks and called "Texas fever," that devastated domestic livestock. Kansas and other territories along the route soon established quarantine lines, called "deadlines," at the western fringe of settlement, and insisted that trail drives not cross them. Each year, as settlers continued to move in, those deadlines moved farther west.

Sometimes, farmers tried to enforce their own, as John Rumans, one of Charles Goodnight's hands, recalled:

> Some men met us at the trail near Canyon City, and said we couldn't come in. There were fifteen or twenty of them, and they were not going to let us cross the Arkansas River. We didn't even stop. . . . Old Man [Goodnight] had a shotgun loaded with buckshot and led the way, saying: "John, get over on that point with

Isom Dart, like a good many Texas cowboys — black, white, and Hispanic — was not overly particular as to whose cattle he drove to market. He was shot dead as a rustler in 1903.

Getting comfortable: Hungry cowboys remove a thicket of spurs before settling down to dinner, 1903.

your Winchester and point these cattle in behind me." He slid his shotgun across the saddle in front of him and we did the same with our Winchesters. He rode right across, and as he rode up to them, he said: "I've monkeyed as long as I want to with you sons of bitches," and they fell back to the sides, and went home after we had passed.

There were few diversions on the trail. Most trail bosses banned liquor. Goodnight prohibited gambling, too. Even the songs for which cowboys became famous grew directly out of doing a job, remembered Teddy Blue:

The singing was supposed to soothe [the cattle] and it did; I don't know why, unless it was that a sound they was used to would keep them from spooking at other noises. I know that if you wasn't singing, any little sound in the night — it might be just a horse shaking himself — could make them leave the country; but if you were singing, they wouldn't notice it.

The two men on guard would circle around with their horses on a walk, if it was a clear night and the cattle was bedded down and quiet, and one man would sing a verse of a song, and his partner on the other side of the herd would sing another verse; and you'd go through a whole song that way. . . . "Bury Me Not on the Lone Prairie" was [a] great song for awhile, but . . . they sung it to death. It was a saying on the range that even the horses nickered it and the coyotes howled it; it got so they'd throw you in the creek if you sang it.

The number of cattle on the move was sometimes staggering: once, Teddy Blue rode to the top of a rise from which he could see seven herds strung out behind him; eight more up ahead; and the dust from an additional thirteen moving parallel to his. "All the cattle in the world," he remembered, "seemed to be coming up from Texas."

At last, the herds neared their destinations. After months in the saddle — often wearing the same clothes every day, eating nothing but biscuits and beef stew at the chuck wagon, drinking only water and coffee, his sole companions his fellow cowboys, his herd, and his horse — the cowboy was about to be paid for his work, and turned loose in town.

Several Kansas communities eventually qualified as cow towns — Abilene, Chetopa, Coffeyville, Ellsworth, Hays, Wichita, Great Bend, Caldwell, and Dodge City (after hunters destroyed the buffalo herds). Some flourished for only a season or two before the shifting quarantine line cut them off from the bawling herds and the big profits they brought to Main Street merchants. Others reaped the benefits — and endured the annual cowboy invasion — for more than a decade.

Cowboys were big spenders, and the shelves of the town stores were carefully stocked with items they especially liked. Teddy Blue remembered his arrival at one cow town:

[T]hey paid us off, and [I] bought some new clothes and got [my] picture taken. . . . I had a new white Stetson hat that I paid ten dollars for and new pants that cost twelve dollars, and a good shirt and fancy boots. Lord, I was proud of those clothes! They were the kind of clothes top hands wore, and I thought that I was dressed right for the first time in my life. . . . [When] my

Washing up, somewhere in the
Oklahoma panhandle, about 1880

sister saw me, she said: "Take your pants out of your boots and put your coat on. You look like an outlaw." I told her to go to hell. And I never did like her after that.

. . . After packing away our plunder, we sauntered around town . . . visiting the various saloons and gambling houses.

All the cow towns were wilder than their permanent residents liked. "Morally, as a class," said the Cheyenne *Daily Leader,* "[cowboys] are foulmouthed, blasphemous, drunken, lecherous, utterly corrupt. Usually harmless on the plains when sober, they are dreaded in towns, for then liquor has an ascendancy over them." The *Annals of Kansas* agreed: "When he feels well (and he always does when full of what he calls 'Kansas sheep-dip') the average cowboy is a bad man to handle. Armed to the teeth, well mounted, and full of their favorite beverage, the cowboys will dash through the principal streets of town yelling like Comanches. This they call 'cleaning out a town.'"

Bad feelings between townspeople and cowboys, Teddy Blue remembered, were exacerbated by memories of the Civil War.

Most of them that came up with the trail herds, being from Texas and Southerners to start with, was on the side of the South, and oh, but they were bitter. That was how a lot of them got killed, because they were filled full of the old dope about the war and they wouldn't let an abolitionist arrest them. The marshals in those cow towns . . . were usually Northern men and the Southerners wouldn't go back to Texas and hear people say: "He's a hell of a fellow. He let a Yankee lock him up." . . . I couldn't even guess how many was killed that way on the trail.

Dodge City is a wicked little town. Indeed, its character is so clearly and egregiously bad that one might conclude . . . it was marked for special Providential punishment. Here those nomads in regions remote from the restraints of moral, civil, social and law enforcing life, the Texas cattle drovers, . . . the embodiment of waywardness and wantonness, end the journey with their herds, and here they loiter and dissipate, sometimes for months, and share the boughten dalliances of fallen women.

Washington *Evening Star*
January 1, 1878

WILD BILL

No town had worked harder to attract the trail drives than Abilene. It had been just a cluster of a dozen log huts 140 miles west of Kansas City in the spring of 1867, when a sharp-eyed entrepreneur from Illinois named Joseph McCoy picked it to promote as the best possible shipping point for Texas cattle. He ordered a shipping yard built next to the Kansas Pacific tracks, put up a barn and a small office building, then sent an employee pounding south on horseback to intercept the herds and tell the trail bosses about the brand-new Abilene yards. Just twenty boxcars filled with cattle headed west from there that year, but the following spring Abilene shipped 75,000 head east. In 1869 and 1870 the number was 350,000, and in 1871 the total reached 700,000.

But by then, the railroads had pushed farther west, developing new cow towns, and the land around Abilene was being worked by farmers who deplored the annual influx of longhorns and the rowdy men who tore up their town each spring. In early 1871, the members of the town council, too, were weary of the cowboy horde, and saddened by the recent death of Marshal "Bear River" Tom Smith, who had refused to use his revolvers and had paid with his life for his pacifism when an angry homesteader killed him with an ax.

Sterner measures were needed, and the council voted unanimously to hire a new town marshal with no such compunctions — James Butler Hickok, or "Wild Bill." He

James Butler Hickok in his earliest-known photograph, a tintype made at Lawrence, Kansas, in 1859, and as he looked in his dangerous prime (opposite)

was the most flamboyant and among the most feared of all the gunmen who drifted from mining camps to cow towns and back again after the Civil War. He was also the teller of the tallest tales, rarely disappointing eastern newspapermen who sought him out for stories.

"I say, Mr. Hickok," the journalist Henry Morton Stanley asked him early in his career, "how many white men have you killed to your certain knowledge?"

Hickok pretended to think for a moment, then answered, "I suppose I have killed considerably more than a hundred . . . [and not] one without good cause!" The actual number he killed seems to have been fewer than ten, and his motives for killing them did not always bear close scrutiny. But he was formidable enough with a pistol that few thought it wise to challenge his claims. He was born in Troy Grove, Illinois, in 1837 and moved to Kansas in 1855, hoping to become a farmer. But he was thought tough enough to be made a town constable before he was twenty-one. He didn't stay at it — or any job — for long. In 1858, he was working at a Nebraska freight station when he shot and killed from ambush his first man, an indignant but unarmed customer who had dared demand money owed to him. Somehow, Hickok got off, claiming self-defense.

He served as a Union scout along the Missouri border during the Civil War, then became a professional gambler. Over the next few years, local newspapers chronicled events that earned him a reputation as a man it was best not to cross: "David Tutt. of Yellville, Arkansas, was shot on the public square at 6 o'clock P.M. on Friday last," reported the Springfield, Missouri, *Weekly Patriot* on July 27, 1865, "by James B. Hickok, better known in southwest Missouri as 'Wild Bill.' The difficulty occurred from a game of cards."

Four years later, on August 26, 1869, the Leavenworth, Kansas, *Times and Conservative* noted that "J. B. Hickok . . . shot one Mulrey at Hays Tuesday. Mulrey died yesterday morning. Bill has been elected sheriff of Ellis County."

"On Monday last 'Wild Bill' killed a soldier and seriously wounded another at Hays City," the Topeka *Daily Commonwealth* reported on July 22, 1870. "Five soldiers attacked Bill, and two got used up. . . . The sentiment of the community is with 'Bill,' as it is claimed he but acted in self-defense."

Hickok had already been a lawman at Hays, Kansas, when he came to Abilene. There were those who took a dim view of his private life: he roomed with a succession of prostitutes and he drank too much. "If the enthusiastic admirers of this . . . 'plainsman' could see him on one of his periodical drunks," wrote a reporter for the St. Joseph *Union*, "they would have considerable romance knocked out of them."

Wild Bill may not always have been sober, and he ran his town from the card tables inside the Long Branch Saloon, but he earned his $150 a month, nonetheless, keeping a tight lid on unruly cowboys and clearing dead dogs and horses from the streets during more tranquil times. Hickok's presence alone — along with a glimpse of his twin revolvers, pearl handles reversed to speed up his draw — was enough to intimidate all but the most drunken cowboy. "When I came along the street," one recalled, "he was standing there with his back to the wall and his thumbs hooked in his red sash. He stood there and rolled his head from side to side looking at everything and everybody from under his eyebrows — just like a mad old bull. I decided then and there I didn't want any part of him."

Abilene citizens were delighted. Hickok, said the Abilene *Chronicle*, "has posted up printed notices, informing all persons that the ordinance against carrying fire arms or other weapons in Abilene, will be enforced. That's right. There's no bravery in carrying revolvers in a civilized community. Such a practice is well enough and perhaps necessary when among Indians or other barbarians, but among white people it ought to be discountenanced."

With gun control strictly applied, the town enjoyed a somewhat nervous peace for eight months. Then, a gambler named Phil Coe, who may earlier have quarreled with Hickok over the affections of a woman, let off a couple of shots in front of the Alamo Saloon; he said he was shooting at a stray dog.

Hickok rushed to the scene, saw Coe with his revolver in his hand, and drew his own. Both men began firing. A special deputy named Mike Williams hurried round the corner to help the marshal — and ran into two of Hickok's bullets. "The whole affair was the work of an instant," the *Chronicle* reported. "The Marshal, surrounded by the crowd and standing in the light, did not recognize Williams whose death he deeply regrets. Coe was shot through the stomach, the ball coming out his back; he lived in great agony until Sunday evening; he was a gambler, but a man of natural good impulses, in his better moments."

Public sentiment was generally with Hickok, but the shooting had shocked the town, and the city council decided not to renew his contract. "He acted only too ready to shoot down, to kill outright," one citizen wrote, "instead of avoiding assassination when possible, as is the higher duty of a marshal. Such a policy of taking over justice into his own hands exemplified, of course, but a form of lawlessness."

Pressured by farmers and ordinary citizens, the Abilene town council also now voted to declare their town off-limits to the cattle drives. "Business is not as brisk as it used to be during the cattle season," the *Chronicle* admitted the next summer, "but the citizens have the satisfaction of knowing that 'hell' is more than 60 miles away."

Jobless and increasingly unsteady now with drink, Hickok began to ghost from town to town, playing cards, sometimes serving as a colorful tour guide for wealthy easterners who wanted to see something of the Wild West before it vanished.

In 1873, his old friend Buffalo Bill invited him to come east with him and tour in a melodrama, *The Scouts of the Plains.* It didn't go well. Hickok was often drunk and unable to remember his lines. He had a high girlish voice that was hard to hear, and whenever the spotlight failed to follow him closely enough, he would step out of character and threaten to shoot the stagehands. Buffalo Bill finally had to let him go when he could not be dissuaded from firing blank cartridges at the bare legs of the actors playing Indians, just to see them hop.

Soon, he was back in the West, unable to find work, drifting from cow town to mining camp, still drinking too much, and doing his best to disguise the worsening eyesight that now made his reputation as a gunfighter more and more precarious. He tried gold mining, but when it failed to make him rich he settled back into his old routine — drinking and playing poker.

He was at the Number Ten Saloon in a Dakota mining town called Deadwood one August afternoon in 1876, uncharacteristically seated with his back to the door, when a demented little man named Jack McCall slipped up behind him. McCall had evi-

Fact and fiction: The two dead cavalrymen above may have run afoul of Wild Bill Hickok at Hays City in 1870. Exaggerated reports of this and similar violent encounters helped launch him on a brief show business career as one of three stars of an 1873 melodrama, *The Scouts of the Plains* (above, right): Hickok is second from the left, his weapon unaccountably upside down. Buffalo Bill Cody is at the center, and, next to him, another showman-scout, Texas Jack Crawford. The other two buckskin-clad men in this studio photograph made in Rochester, New York, not long before Hickok left the show were friends of the players.

dently persuaded himself that Hickok was responsible for the death of a brother at Hays City, though no evidence of such a crime was ever found. He stood watching the game for a moment, then drew his revolver and fired it into the back of Wild Bill's head. Hickok died instantly, scattering his cards as he fell.

The editor of the Cheyenne *Daily Leader* offered a grudging obituary that showed how rapidly life in the West was changing:

> "Wild Bill" . . . was one of those characters developed by the onward strides of the iron horse when the "Great American Desert" was spanned by the Pacific railways. Seven or eight years ago his name was prominent in the . . . border press and if we could believe the half of what was written concerning his daring deeds, he must certainly have been one of the bravest and most scrupulous characters of those lawless times. Contact with the man, however, dispelled all these illusions, and of late, Wild Bill seems to have been a very tame and worthless loafer. . . . Years ago, before wine and women had ruined his constitution and impaired his faculties, he was more worthy of the fame which he attained on the border.

BUSINESSMEN WITH RIFLES

Frank Mayer and his competitors called themselves buffalo "runners," not hunters, but they avoided running — or even riding — after buffalo as much as possible. For efficiency's sake, the mounted chase had long since given way to a technique called "the stand," Mayer remembered:

> The thing we had to have, we businessmen with rifles, was one-shot-kills. We based our success on . . . the overwhelming stupidity of the buffalo, unquestionably the stupidest game animal in the world. . . . If you wounded the leader, didn't kill her outright, the rest of her herd, whether it was three or thirty,

would gather around her and stupidly "mill." . . . [A]ll you had to do . . . was pick them off one by one, making sure you made a dropping kill at every shot, until you wiped out the entire herd. . . . I once took 269 hides with 300 cartridges. . . .

In the East, improved rifles were specially manufactured for the trade, capable of bringing down a buffalo at better than six hundred yards. It "shoots today," one astonished bystander said, "and kills tomorrow." Individual hunters recorded kills of one hundred, then two hundred, from a single stand, pausing only to cool their overheated rifle barrels with canteens of water. When the water ran out, they urinated down the barrel and kept shooting. Orlando A. Bond, nicknamed "Brick" by his friends, killed 300 animals in a single day and 5,855 in one two-month outing, so many that he was permanently deafened by the sound of his own rifle.

Frank Mayer's favorite rifle, a Sharps, cost him $125, secondhand. It weighed twelve pounds, its barrel was nearly three feet long, and its telescopic sight was manufactured in Germany. "I was proud of that first Sharps of mine," he said. "It killed quicker . . . and it added 10 to 30 percent efficiency to my shooting." On a bet, he fired at a buffalo a half a mile away with it, and when it dropped from the shot, won a three-gallon keg of "Three Roses" whiskey.

"Where there were myriads of buffalo the year before," the commander at Fort Dodge remembered, "there were now myriads of carcasses. The air was foul with a sickening stench, and the vast plain, which only a short twelvemonth before teemed with animal life, was a dead, solitary, putrid desert." The buffalo hunters themselves, working day after day with rotting flesh, were distinctly gamey. They "didn't wash," Teddy Blue Abbott remembered, "and looked like animals. They dressed in strong, heavy warm clothes and never changed them. You would see three or four of them walk up to a bar, reach down inside their clothes and see who could catch the first louse for the drinks. They were lousy and proud of it."

All across western Kansas, the slaughter went on — an estimated 1.5 to 3 million buffalo killed in a little over two years. Buffalo skeletons, bleached by the sun, soon covered the prairies — and started still more industries. Newly arrived homesteaders augmented their income by harvesting bones. Crews of professional "bone pickers" gathered the skeletons and brought them by wagon to railroad sidings. Buffalo horns were turned into buttons, combs, knife handles. Hooves became glue. Bones were ground into fertilizer. Thirty-two million pounds of buffalo bones made their way from the Plains to eastern factories in just three years.

Some Americans grew alarmed at the extent of the slaughter, and Congress passed a bill in 1874 making it illegal for anyone to kill more buffalo than could be used for food. But President Grant allowed the law to die without his signature. Meanwhile, hunters began to talk of moving south of Kansas, onto hunting grounds reserved for the Indians. What would the government do if they shifted there? a delegation asked the commander at Fort Dodge.

"Boys," he answered, "if I were a buffalo hunter, I would hunt where the buffaloes are."

They swarmed into the Texas panhandle to harvest the southern herd, where the Indians sensed, Frank Mayer remembered, "that we were taking away their birthright

Frank H. Mayer, about the time he began shooting buffalo for a living

Cheyenne women dressing buffalo hides in 1878 (above) and a hide-hunter's camp on Evans Creek in Texas, 1874

and that with every boom of a buffalo rifle their tenure on their homeland became weakened and that eventually they would have no homeland and no buffalo. So they did what you and I would do if our existence were jeopardized: they fought. . . . They fought by stealth. They fought openly. They murdered if they had a chance. They stole whenever they could." In the summer of 1874, the Kiowa, Comanche, Arapaho, and southern Cheyenne rose up and drove out the hunters — and any other whites they came across. In response, Sheridan ordered a massive campaign against them, deploying five columns of troops to pursue the Indians relentlessly, depriving them of rest, or the opportunity to hunt. By the next spring, virtually all of the resisting bands on the southern Plains — desperate now for food — had come in to the agencies.

The buffalo hunters went back to work until both the northern and the southern herds had all but disappeared. Then, "one by one," Frank Mayer recalled, "we runners put up our buffalo rifles, sold them, gave them away, or kept them for other hunting, and left the ranges. And there settled over them a vast quiet. . . . The buffalo was gone." For his years as a buffalo runner, Frank Mayer had his wagon and outfit free and clear, and several thousand dollars in the bank. He left the Plains, married a girl in Denver, and took a job in the Rocky Mountains — hunting game to feed the miners of Leadville.

"Maybe," he recalled,

we runners served our purpose in helping abolish the buffalo; maybe it was our ruthless harvesting of him which telescoped the control of the Indian by a decade or maybe more. Or maybe I am just rationalizing. Maybe we were just a

Golgotha: buffalo skulls heaped at trackside in Detroit, Michigan, ready to be hauled to the Michigan Carbon Works, 1880s

greedy lot who wanted to get ours, and to hell with posterity, the buffalo, or anyone else, just so we kept our scalps on and our money pouches filled. I think maybe that is the way it was.

The buffalo had provided both material and spiritual sustenance to the people of the Plains. Life without it seemed inconceivable, and some began to seek some explanation for what had befallen them. Old Lady Horse remembered a story that circulated among her desperate people, the Kiowa:

The buffalo saw that their day was over. They could protect their people no longer. Sadly, the last remnant of the great herd gathered in council, and decided what they would do.

The Kiowas were camped on the north side of Mount Scott, those of them who were still free to camp. One young woman got up very early . . . and . . . peering through the haze, saw the last buffalo herd appear like in a spirit dream.

Straight to Mount Scott the leader of the herd walked. Behind him came the cows and their calves, and the few young males who had survived. As the woman watched, the face of the mountain opened. Inside Mount Scott the world was green and fresh, as it had been when she was a small girl. The rivers ran clear, not red. The wild plums were in blossom, chasing the red buds up the inside slopes. Into this world of beauty the buffalo walked, never to be seen again.

GREAT MIGRATIONS:
THE PIONEER IN THE AMERICAN WEST

JOHN MACK FARAGHER

One of the greatest mass migrations in American history began in 1815. With Indian resistance in the Mississippi Valley broken by the victories of American forces during the War of 1812, thousands of families in Pennsylvania and Virginia, Kentucky and Tennessee packed their goods and poured west into Alabama, Missouri, and Illinois. There was "good land dog-cheap everywhere," wrote English settler George Flower, "and for nothing, if you will go far enough for it." From his porch in southern Illinois, Baptist preacher John Mason Peck watched a steady westward procession of wagons, carriages, and two-wheeled carts, and fancied that "Kentucky and Tennessee were breaking up and moving to the 'Far West.'" Within five years the population of Missouri nearly tripled, and there was comparable growth all along the frontier. From 1810 to 1820 the proportion of Americans living west of the Appalachians rose from 15 to 27 percent.

Contemporaries christened this mass movement "the Great Migration," a phrase rich with historical associations. It was the name the Puritans of Massachusetts Bay gave to their Atlantic crossing of the 1630s, the name claimed by pioneers headed overland for the Far West in the 1840s, and the name historians apply to the migration of tens of thousands of black people from the rural South to the industrial North in the twentieth century.

We Americans have always had itching feet. The movement of people from one place to another is one of the most important factors in our history. Even in colonial New England, where there was a strong commitment to the value of community, high levels of migration became notable within the first fifty years of settlement. "That they might keep themselves together," Increase Mather wrote in 1676, the first Puritan colonists had been "satisfied with one Acre for each person." But "how have Men since coveted the earth," he lamented; "they that profess themselves Christians have forsaken Churches, and Ordinances, all for land and elbow-room." That pressing American need for elbowroom was so strong that by the time of the Revolution, in typical American communities in all regions of the country, at least four of every ten households packed up and left every ten years. High rates of geographic mobility have continued to characterize our national life ever since. In the world, only New Zealanders exceed Americans in their rate of mobility. We have always been a people in motion, right up to the present shift of population away from the Northeast and toward the metropolitan centers of the Sun Belt.

Mobility was particularly important in the settlement of the American West. Rates of migration in western and frontier communities were probably as high as they ever got in American experience.

In one backcountry Virginia county on the eve of the American Revolution, about two in ten families departed each year, only to be replaced by three new arrivals. Perhaps the most extreme turnover in population occurred in the mining towns of gold rush California, where only 10 or 15 percent of the people listed in the federal census of 1850 persisted to the next one ten years later. More typical western communities experienced ten-year rates of persistence of about 20 or 30 percent. Transience was one of the most important facts of pioneer life.

To bring some order to this great swirl and rush of people it helps to remember that this movement was largely of families. It is true that many single, unattached men moved west (very few single, unattached women did so). But with the exception of the gold rush and other mining booms, they tended to travel with family parties as hired hands or teamsters. These emigrating families frequently had prodigious histories of migration. "Many of our neighbors are true backwoodsmen, always fond of moving," John Woods of southern Illinois noted in 1820. Among these "extensive travelers," he wrote, "to have resided in three or four states, and several places in each state, is not uncommon." His observation is borne out by a close study of the family histories of the pioneers of the community of Sugar Creek in central Illinois, first settled during the Great Migration of 1815–20. Eight in ten families had moved from another state at least once before, and 35 percent had moved two or more times. Similarly, 78 percent of the families who participated in the Great Migration on the Overland Trail to Oregon and California in the mid-nineteenth century had made at least one previous move, many had moved several times, and a substantial minority had been almost continuously in motion.

For most moves westward, the process of decision making was not documented. The Overland Trail migration, however, provides a unique opportunity for examining the way families made those choices, for literally hundreds of men and women left journals and recollections in which they discussed, among other things, the decision to move. "Oh let us not go," Mary Jones cried when her husband John told her of his decision to relocate the family; but, she lamented, "it made no difference." Lucy Deady, daughter of an emigrant family, wrote that her despairing mother knew "nothing of his move until father had decided to go." A close study of women's overland diaries finds not a single wife who initiated the idea of moving, while nearly a third actively objected. One emigrant wife told a hired hand that "the journey for which she was bending all her energies in preparation was not in her judgment a wise business movement. But

'Wilson' wished to go, and that settled the question with her." The decision to emigrate, in short, seems to have been an example of the exercise of husbands' power.

Consider the number of "gold rush widows" left behind when tens of thousands of fevered men left their homes for western mines after 1849. "My old man has left me & has gon to Californa and took my wagon and left me and my Children in a bad situation." So Elizabeth Cress of Illinois wrote to her parents appealing for a loan to see her through the winter. But some wives simply forbade their husbands' going. "The Rolling Stone," a song popular throughout the Midwest during the 1850s, recounted such a struggle:

Since times are so hard, I'll tell you, my wife
I've a mind for to shake off this trouble and strife,
And to California my journey pursue
To double my fortunes as other men do.
For here we may labor each day in the field
And the winters consume all that summers doth yield.

Dear husband, remember your land is to clear,
It will cost you the labor of many a year.
Your horses, sheep and cattle will all be to buy,
And before you have got them you are ready to die.
So stick to your farming; you'll suffer no loss,
For the stone that keeps rolling can gather no moss.

The wife of the song, like thousands of uncounted women, succeeded in keeping her feverish husband on the farm. Other women took a different approach. When Gay Hayden came down with gold fever in early 1850, he announced to his wife, Mary Jane, that he was leaving her behind. "I was nearly heartbroken at the thought of the separation," she remembered, but she wisely adopted an aggressive defense. "We were married to live together," she declared, "and I am willing to go with you to any part of *God's foot stool* where you think you can do best, and under these circumstances you have no right to go where I cannot, and if you do you need never return for I shall look upon you as dead." And so, she concluded, "it was settled that *we* should go the next year."

Historians of the American frontier have tended to celebrate the legacy of the people called "the movers" by their contemporaries. Migration offered Americans "a gate of escape from the bondage of the past," wrote Frederick Jackson Turner, the influential historian of the American frontier. "The advance of the frontier has meant a steady growth of independence on American lines. And to study this advance, the men who grew up under these conditions and the political, economic and social result of it, is to study the *really American* part of our history." In Turner's judgment, the process of migration and resettlement, and the cultural attitudes and character they engendered, were peculiarly American, dramatically contrasting with the conservatism and persistence of traditional European societies.

In American folklore, the figure of Daniel Boone — the heroic pioneer leader of the settlement of trans-Appalachia — became the personification of this sense of possibility. "Boone used to say to me," claimed a resident of the Carolina hills, "that when he could not fall the top of a tree near enough his door for fire-wood, it was time to move to a new place." In a folktale that refers to Boone's last remove, from Kentucky to the frontier of Missouri, the old pioneer declares to a traveler, "I wanted to go where I would not be around so much by neabors," but complains that even in Missouri, "I am too much crowded." Well, how close *are* your neighbors, the man asks, and is incredulous at Boone's reply. Only twenty miles away! This sentiment was well expressed by the American poet Arthur Guiterman, whose verses were memorized by several generations of schoolchildren.

. . . Daniel Boone was ill at ease
When he saw the smoke in his forest trees.
There'll be no game in the country soon.
Elbow room! cried Daniel Boone.

. . . Ever he dreamed of new domains
With vaster woods and wider plains;
Ever he dreamed of a world-to-be
Where there are no bounds and the soul is free.
At fourscore-five, still stout and hale,
He heard a call to a farther trail;
So he turned his face where the stars are strewn;
Elbow room! sighed Daniel Boone.

Down the Milky Way in its banks of blue
Far he has paddled his white canoe.
To the splendid quest of the tameless soul
He has reached the goal where there is no goal. . . .
East of the sun and west of the moon,
Elbow room! laughs Daniel Boone.

During Boone's own lifetime his movements westward, and his lifelong love of solitude, became the stuff of folklore. But tales of his supposed wanderlust angered Boone the old man. "Nothing embitters my old age," he told a visitor a few years before his death, "like the circulation of absurd stories that I retire as civilization advances, that I shun the white men and seek the Indians, and that now even when old, I wish to retire beyond the second Alleghenies." Indeed, there was a double edge to the folklore of Boone's wanderlust, for while it celebrated migration, the very essence of American pioneering, it also raised questions about his social commitments. Boone "did not stay [in] one plase long [enough] to get acquainted," complained one of his former Kentucky neighbors; he "always lived in a world of his own." Settlers depended upon mutual assistance for survival and mistrusted men who refused to be neighborly.

Many conservative commentators likewise feared the consequences of high levels of mobility. Yale clergyman Timothy Dwight lamented in 1819 that the pioneers, "impatient of the restraints of law, religion, and morality," were "too idle, too talkative, too passion-ate, too prodigal, and too shiftless to acquire either property or char-acter." On the frontier "everything shifts under your eye," wrote Timothy Flint, another Yankee, but one who had moved west. "The present occupants sell, pack, depart. Strangers replace them. Before they have gained the confidence of their neighbors, they hear of a better place, pack up, and follow their precursors. This circumstance adds to the instability of connexions."

These perspectives call attention to the riddle of community life in the American West. What kind of communities could form with so many men and women moving in and moving out, with people constantly passing through, with the faces in the neighborhood changing so frequently? Again, a family perspective is useful. Look-ing at communities as collections not of individuals but of house-holds and families reveals considerably more social continuity than suggested by the raw data of the persistence statistics. In the commu-nity of Sugar Creek in central Illinois, for example, a quarter of the original settler families laid down roots deep enough to persist through the nineteenth century. Three-quarters of the children and grandchildren of this group chose to begin households and raise children of their own in the local community. Over time kinship ties became increasingly important. In 1830 about one in five heads of household shared his surname with the heads of at least two other households; thirty years later that proportion had doubled.

By marrying locally and building family alliances, these genera-tions of "stickers," as the western historian Wallace Stegner called them, strengthened their influence within the local community. Sev-en in ten children and better than half the grandchildren of those original families found spouses among others who had lived in the community for ten years or more. Although in part these were the choices forced upon people by life in a small and relatively isolated community, the practice of what some have called "sibling-exchange marriage" suggests that there was considerable deliberation at work here. A significant mi-nority of marriages among the descendants of original fami-lies took place among sibling sets, the brothers and sisters of one family marrying the broth-ers and sisters of another. Such marriage patterns seem strange today, but were commonplace in the nineteenth-century countryside, and are still a fact of life in some regions. "My three daughters married Ed's three sons," one Appalachian woman told a sociologist in the 1960s; "ain't nothing that brings a family together like

that." Sibling exchange accounted for nearly one in five of the mar-riages within the group of original families in Sugar Creek.

Families practicing intermarriage stood a much better chance of retaining their original grants by combining their resources with others, facilitating the concentration of real property. In 1838 mem-bers of these families controlled nearly 90 percent of the local arable land. Twenty years later, although their proportional strength in the community had greatly declined, they continued to hold over half the land. Today, more than a century and a half after the area was first settled during the Great Migration, the descendants of some two dozen of those original families continue to live in the Sugar Creek area, and control at least 10 percent of the land.

The riddle of community in the American West is resolved, then, by recognizing the coexistence of both the "movers" — the transient majority who farmed for a time before pushing on — and the "stick-ers" — the men and women who persisted on the land and rooted themselves in the community during the first decades of settlement, intermarried with each other, and passed their farms on to their chil-dren. The westward movement is the story of the choices of families in both groups. Long ago this was recognized by the early-nineteenth-century Illinois writer James Hall. "The settlers are not always in motion," Hall wrote. "They remain for years in one spot, forming the mass of the settled population, and giving a tone to the institutions of the country; and at each remove, a few are left behind, who cling permanently to the soil, and bequeath their landed possessions to their posterity." As much as mobility, posterity and landed posses-sions, family, and land shaped the character of western communities.

During the second half of the nineteenth century the direction of American expansion shifted from the countryside to the city. The West was popularly known as the land of wide-open spaces, but by the 1890s the typical westerner lived in an urban oasis like Omaha, Denver, or San Francisco. The American West included the fastest-growing cities in the na-tion, and by 1890 had be-come more heavily urban than any other region except the Northeast. When we think of the astounding growth of nineteenth-century American cities, most of us think of the flood of immigration from abroad; yet the single most im-portant source of the expand-ing population of western cities came from the country-side. With the expansion of the commercial economy, farming and ranching became a signifi-cantly more capital-intensive

The J. H. Byington family, Utah, 1870

business. After the Civil War a western settler needed an average of a thousand dollars to purchase land, the equipment necessary to work it, and the transportation to get the family there. Although railroads and land speculators continued to promote the West as a safety valve for the urban working class, as the "free range" disappeared and the number of tenant farmers and hired hands grew larger, it is more accurate to say that it was the cities that provided the safety valve for *rural discontent.* As one historian has put it, for every industrial worker who became a farmer, twenty farm boys moved to the city.

This is relatively well known. Less so is the fact that for every twenty farm boys, there were in the late nineteenth century perhaps twenty-five or thirty farm girls moving from the rural to the urban West. The prominent place of young, unattached women in the migration from farm to city marks it as significantly different from the process that settled the countryside. While a great many families came to the city from American farms, the great majority of the migrants were unmarried young people, and there seem to have been many more migrating women than migrating men. Many studies of short-distance migrations from country to city, throughout the world, confirm that young women predominate in these movements. Throughout the West they left home at a considerably greater rate than their brothers. One study of rural households found that among middling to poor farmers, only four in ten daughters as compared to seven in ten sons remained on the land. Apparently, when the resources of the family were not sufficient to provide for all the children, daughters were the most likely to migrate. Another study found a persistence rate of only 31 percent among the daughters of Minnesota farmers, compared to 46 percent for sons. Evidence of the greater movement of young women also exists at the other end of the trail. In Chicago, which was the Mecca for young people from Indiana to Kansas and beyond, native-born young women began to outnumber native-born young men during the 1880s, and over the next forty years the female proportion of this group continued to rise. As the westward movement shifted from country to city, young women were prominent among the new urban pioneers.

What accounted for the greater number of women choosing the city over the country? In the opinion of many contemporaries, a lack of opportunity pushed them out. "I hate farm-life," says a young wife in Hamlin Garland's *Main-Travelled Roads,* published during the 1890s. "It's nothing but fret, fret, and work the whole time, never going any place, never seeing anybody but a lot of neighbors just as big fools as you are. I spend my time fighting flies and washing dishes and churning. I'm sick of it." Farm and ranch women themselves added to the chorus of complaint. "Isolation, stagnation, ignorance, loss of ambition, the incessant grind of labor, and the lack of time for improvement by reading, by social intercourse, or by recreation of some sort are all working against the farm woman's happiness and will ultimately spell disaster for the Nation," one wife wrote. "In my opinion," declared another, "the worst feature of farm work is too much work and too little pleasure. No wonder young folks leave the farm." Rural women generally agreed that they suffered from the drudgery of household and outside labor, that male attitudes kept them from full participation in public and community life, and that lack of educational and vocational opportunity bound them to the fate of their mothers.

A letter from a rural woman, published in *The Farmer's Voice* in 1912, warned of the growing dissatisfactions of the country daughter: "She isn't going to 'stay put,' but will get out where she can earn some money of her very own, to buy the little things so dear to the hearts of girls; and she will not be questioned and scolded over every little expenditure." The progressive reformer Martha Foote Crow, in a 1915 study, *The American Country Girl,* warned that "if the home cannot be made happy and the work in the farmhouse cannot be made interesting, if her fair share of incentive as a human being in the common round of life cannot be assigned to her, if her part in the complex structure of the farmstead cannot be put upon an equitable basis, if the universal happy fortune of woman cannot be seen to shine as a goal in the long service of the farmstead, why, she will have none of it!" Another reformer lamented that practically the only alternatives to marriage for country girls were teaching district school and leaving home to go to the city. The emancipation of women still had far to go in the country. In the view of most contemporaries, it was the lingering tradition of rural patriarchy that pushed young women from the farm.

But perhaps even more compelling than the push of the country was the pull of the city, which represented the hope of a better life for many women. "It is the girl with ability," one observer noted, "who dares to migrate to the city." The conditions of country life, echoed another, "tend to create gradually a strong revolt on the part of girls of vigorous personality." Many contemporaries emphasized the hopes of women migrants. "Women find in cities greater opportunities for partial or entire self-support," wrote a social scientist in 1895, "while the scope for employment afforded them by country life is much less." In the city a new sense of possibility could develop from the freedom afforded by wage work outside the household. Abraham Bisno, a union organizer among Chicago's women cloak makers, found that women fresh from the rural family "appreciated the opportunity of working a limited number of hours and earning money. Though their wage was small, they considered it large." It was, Bisno declared, "a historic revolution in their lives." With work in the public world, wrote one observer, the perspective of the young rural migrant changes: "the world is bigger than she knew and there are other ways of living than those she has been taught to accept. A new attitude toward life begins to develop, manifested in a little more self-assertion and a desire 'to do as other girls do.' Gradually she comes into her own world of hopes and ambitions in which the parents have little part."

One of the important dimensions of urban work was the extent to which it allowed young migrant women money of their own, a means to determine their own affairs. Many of the working women who continued to live with their families, and brought their wages home to their mothers, attempted to squeeze out a small allowance for their own needs. A federal study of 1909 found that working girls often kept the extra income they earned from tips or overtime. One young woman, asked in her mother's presence how much she could save each week for herself in this way, replied, "Oh, about $1.50." Surprised, the mother exclaimed, "Why, Nellie, you don't do any such thing." "Yes, I do," Nellie answered, "but I never told you." This pattern encouraged girls doing piecework to speed up their own routines so they could earn a little something for themselves. "As there is often a difference of two or three dollars a week between what she accepts as her limit and what she can do 'on a spurt,'" reported one social worker, "the temptation to earn more money may be accepted at a frightful cost of nervous energy."

As early as the 1880s, young working girls in San Francisco, Denver, and cities all over America were spending relatively substantial sums on clothes, makeup, and amusements. After the working day, wrote one investigator, girls sought excitement at the dance halls and the theater, later at the movies, or simply by strolling the streets with their companions and enjoying the scene. "Those who faithfully hold to a difficult and uncongenial occupation, bringing home the entire wage to the family and submitting to an almost patriarchal control in other matters," she wrote, "will demand a freedom in the use of the evening before which their parents are helpless."

Most unmarried working women in western cities resided with families, but the number living on their own increased greatly as the nineteenth turned to the twentieth century. In Chicago about 20 percent of white working women lived on their own in the early 1890s; by 1909, according to one survey, nearly half of them were living on their own. Many country women in western cities for the first time found rooms in the "newcomer" homes of charitable organizations like the YWCA, but few of them chose to live there for long. Social workers often held suspicious attitudes about working girls, and regulations about visitors, "lock-up," and "lights-out" alienated many young women, who stayed only until they could find other accommodations. If she had her way, a worker in one of the organized homes told a reporter, the women in her care would be more closely supervised, but, she admitted, this was impossible because of the freedom demanded by young business girls. From the 1880s to the 1950s the Harvey chain of restaurants along the Santa Fe line in Kansas, Colorado, and New Mexico hired thousands of single women to serve hungry travelers and tourists. Harvey Girls lived in company dormitories, but were free to do as they pleased after work. In the words of a popular tune of 1907:

O the pretty Harvey Girl beside my chair,
A fairer maiden I shall never see.
She was winsome, she was neat, she was gloriously sweet
And she was certainly good to me.

Few single working women could afford their own apartments. Most settled for furnished rooms, in the words of one young Los Angeles migrant of the 1920s, "a place where we can unpack our trunk, anchor our electric iron, and hang our other blouse over the chair." The demand for rooms, for freedom and independence in living arrangements by young people living and working in the city, led to the growth of rooming house districts in all the major cities of the West. In San Francisco, Portland, Denver, and Chicago such districts became little bohemias, dominated by young people interested in culture and politics. According to one study of Chicago, the West Side rooming house district was filled with "genuine Americans, most of them men and girls under thirty, who have come to Chicago from towns and country districts of Illinois, and from Wisconsin, Michigan, and other neighboring states, most of whom lead irregular lives and very few of whom are found in families."

As this last line suggests, there was considerable fear that naive and innocent young country girls would be ruined by their urban experience. The migrating girl, warned Martha Foote Crow, "exchanged the safe and kindly surroundings of the rural home for the dangerous conditions of the city, its unregulated contacts, its promiscuity and its perils, and its loneliness in the midst of strangers." Were these the same young women that Crow described as understanding the limitations of country life and acting hopefully to create new opportunities of their own? Somehow the contradiction between the two images got lost in the anxiety of social change. Surely young working women faced challenges. "A girl has to be some sport to work in this joint," said a Portland waitress who told of sexual harassment by customers and fellow workers. But things may have been worse down on the farm; according to a recent study of late-nineteenth-century migrating women, many reported fleeing sexual abuse at home. Certainly few women drifted into sin in the cities. Most worked for a time, then married and raised children. But into those marriages they carried a set of expectations very different from those of their mothers, the result of their several years of independence.

These young migrating women were the urban pioneers of the West. Historians of the changing manners and morals of women have generally focused on the middle and upper classes. But close attention to the choices of migrating country girls suggests that it was they who took the lead in creating new opportunities for twentieth-century women. Jane Addams, the founder of Hull House in Chicago, and a sensitive observer of the city, wrote in 1909 that "through the huge hat, with its wilderness of bedraggled feathers, the girl announces to the world that she is here. She demands attention to the fact of her existence, she states that she is ready to live, to take her place in the world." Let us give these young urban pioneers their appropriate place, side by side with the forty-niners and the migrating family in the drama of the Great Migrations.

Mammoth Hot Springs,
Yellowstone Valley

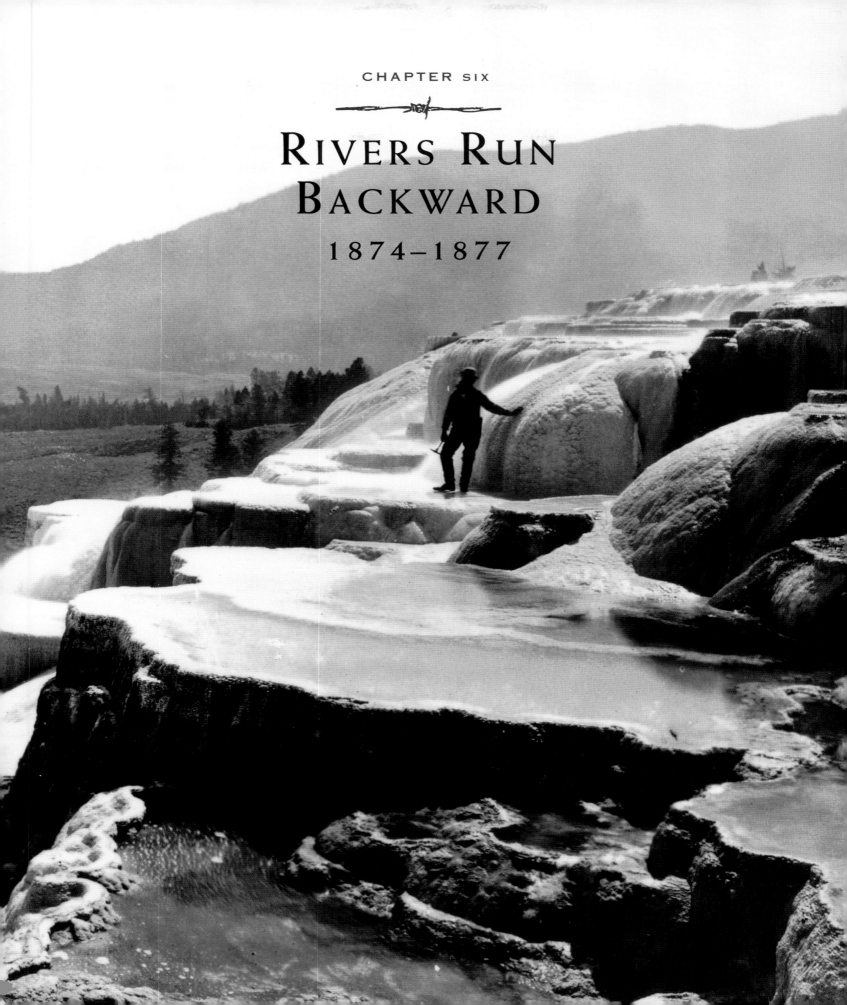

CHAPTER SIX

RIVERS RUN
BACKWARD

1874–1877

By 1874, the railroads had changed much of the West forever, opening whole regions to settlement, transforming the lives of those who already lived there, helping the United States to consolidate its authority. But some stubbornly held out against the American transformation. In their desert stronghold, the Mormons found themselves again besieged and sought to survive by sacrificing one of their own for the greater good, while two great Indian leaders refused to abandon lands they believed should be theirs alone, scored astonishing triumphs, and then discovered that there was no way to get away from the Americans.

George Armstrong Custer with the Black Hills bear he claimed as his own. "I have reached the highest rung on the hunter's ladder of fame," he wrote his wife. "I have killed my grizzly." In reality, he had had a good deal of help from backup bullets fired into the animal by his Cree scout Bloody Knife (left) and Captain William Ludlow (right).

In the summer of 1874, two long columns — more than a thousand soldiers, a hundred wagons, sixty-one Arikara scouts, and three newspapermen — marched out of Fort Abraham Lincoln on the Missouri and started southwest across the Great Sioux Reservation. They were officially looking for a site on which to build a fort from which the army could keep an eye on the Lakota who lived around the Red Cloud and Spotted Tail agencies.

But they were also looking for gold. For half a century now, Americans had scoured the West in frantic search of it. California, Oregon, Washington, Nevada, Montana, Colorado, Arizona, New Mexico — all had already been made to yield up much of their treasure. Now, rumors held that the Black Hills, too, were full of gold. But they were technically off-limits to gold-seekers, part of the Great Sioux Reservation promised to the Lakota in perpetuity in the treaty of Fort Laramie of 1868.

That was no longer going to matter. "As the Christian looks forward with hope and faith to that land of pure delight," said the editor of the Bismarck *Tribune,* "so the miner looks forward to the Black Hills, a region of fabulous wealth, where the rills repose on beds of gold and the rocks are studded with precious metal. . . . [T]he time has come when the entire army could not much longer keep the country from being over-run by the invincible white man — by the hardy pioneer."

George Armstrong Custer rode at the head of the expedition. His destruction of Black Kettle's Cheyenne on the Washita in 1868 — and his own colorful published accounts of this and other exploits — had made him the army's most celebrated Indian fighter. Now, the Black Hills expedition promised Custer still more of the excitement and adventure he craved. "We have discovered a rich and beautiful country," he wrote to his wife. "I have been Commanding Officer and everything else, especially guide." Custer helped blaze the trail, shot at the deer and pronghorn antelope that stopped to watch him pass, and wrote it all up for the New York *World.* And in French Creek, a narrow stream that wound through a glade, which one of his topographical engineers named "Custer Park," his men found gold — not a real bonanza, but enough to persuade his troopers to line up shoulder to shoulder along the creek to try their luck at panning, more than enough to inspire wild-eyed stories in the local press of pay dirt "from the grass roots down."

"This immense section," wrote the editor of the Bismarck *Times,* "bids fair to become the new El Dorado of America." Gold-hungry whites would soon swarm in and begin banging together a dozen mining camps — Lead City, Washington, Blacktail, Golden Gate, Deadwood — and Custer City. Whites now called the path Custer's columns had followed the "Freedom Trail."

The Lakota called it the "thieves' road." They kept their distance as Custer's columns invaded their sanctuary, but they were deeply disturbed. They professed a spiritual attachment to the Black Hills and considered them uniquely sacred to their tribe, though they had only relatively recently wrested them from other Indian peoples. But the Black Hills also had practical meaning for them: the Hunkpapa holy man Sitting Bull called them a "food pack," by which he meant that their valleys were alive with small game, their slopes covered with trees for fuel, ideal for winter camp. Once the Black Hills were lost to the white man, he believed, it would no longer be possible to sustain the old ways any longer. And as far as Sitting Bull was concerned, those ways were the only ones by which a true Lakota could live. "I will remain what I am until I die," he said, "a hunter, and when there are no buffalo or other game I will send my children to hunt and live on prairie mice, for where an Indian is shut up in one place his body becomes weak."

Some 30,000 Lakota, Arapaho, and Northern Cheyenne now drew rations at the five agencies. But another 3,000 Lakota, along with some 400 Cheyenne — whites called them all "Non-Treaties" — spent much of the year in the unceded hunting grounds that extended west, beyond the reservation, to the Bighorn Mountains.

If I were an Indian, I often think that I would greatly prefer to cast my lot among those . . . who adhered to the free open plains, rather than submit to the confined limits of a reservation, there to be the recipient of the blessed benefits of civilization, with its vices thrown in without stint or measure.

George Armstrong Custer

Custer's columns advancing into Castle Creek valley in the Black Hills, 1874

Gall, Hunkpapa Lakota, who would fight with special fervor at the Little Bighorn armed only with a hatchet because, he remembered, army bullets had killed his two wives and three of his children and "my heart was bad that day"

Custer's camp at Hiddenwood Creek in the Black Hills, not far from the spot where his men found gold

Some of them wandered still farther, to raid white settlements in Montana Territory and to harass their old enemies, the Crow. And when in 1872 surveying parties for the Northern Pacific tried to chart a route through the Yellowstone Valley, they had been attacked by them, again and again.

They had many leaders — Black Moon, Four Horns, Gall, Crow King, Black Eagle, Rain-in-the-Face, American Horse, and Crazy Horse, the daring Oglala who had helped lure Captain Fetterman and seventy-nine of his men to their death back in 1866. But the man to whom even these veteran fighters often looked for guidance was Sitting Bull. He was born about 1831 on the Grand River at a place the Lakota called Many Caches because of the pits for storing food they had dug there, and he would devote much of his life simply to ensuring that his people had enough to eat.

He counted his first coup at fourteen during a raid on the Crow, and led the Strong Heart warrior society, whose members ascribed their triumphs in battle against the Crow, Assiniboin, and Shoshone to the extraordinary power of his visions. No one had earned a greater reputation for bravery. Once, in the midst of a fight with soldiers guarding a railroad crew on the Yellowstone, he strolled out between the lines with two warriors and calmly sat down. Then, with bullets whizzing all around him, he filled his pipe, smoked it slowly, passed it back and forth to his companions until the bowl was empty, then reamed it out and walked away from the fighting.

Crow King, who would lead his own Hunkpapa Lakota band in the Custer fight

Rain-in-the-Face, Oglala Lakota, whom Custer had once arrested for the murder of three men on the Yellowstone River. After escaping from his captors, he too would battle Custer at the Little Bighorn.

He was an implacable opponent of accommodation. "Look at me!" he once shouted to a group of Assiniboin who had made their peace with whites. "See if *I* am poor, or my people, either. The whites may get me at last, as you say, but I will have good times till then. You are fools to make yourselves slaves to a piece of fat bacon, some hard-tack, and a little sugar and coffee."

Sitting Bull's name was meant to describe an intractable buffalo bull, on its haunches but still resolute in the face of danger. That resolution would soon be tested.

By the winter of 1875, some 15,000 miners had crowded into the Black Hills, in violation of the treaty with the Lakota. It was the army's task to drive them out. But there were far too many. "I have been captured and sent out of the Hills four times," one resolute prospector said. "I guess I can stand it as long as they can." "We owe the Indians justice and fair play," said the Chicago *Inter-Ocean*, "but we owe it to civilization that such a garden of mineral wealth be brought into occupation and use."

Another solution had to be found. A Senate commission was sent west, prepared either to lease the Black Hills from the Lakota or to pay $6 million for them if the Indians were willing to sell them outright. Twenty thousand Lakota came to meet with the commissioners, but Sitting Bull, Crazy Horse, and other defiant bands stayed away entirely, unwilling even to discuss selling their most sacred place. They sent a messenger named Little Big Man to express their scorn. He rode into the council on horseback, with three hundred warriors, all painted for battle and chanting a new song:

> Black Hills is my land and I love it
> And whoever interferes
> will hear this gun.

Little Big Man waved his Winchester at the commissioners and shouted, "I will kill the first chief who speaks for selling the Black Hills," then wheeled his horse and led his warriors away.

The senators plunged ahead, regardless. "You should bow to the wishes of the Government which supports you," their chairman told the assembled chiefs. "Gold is useless to you, and there will be fighting unless you give it up."

Chief Spotted Tail of the Brulé responded first. He evidently saw the sale as inevitable — there were too many whites to be resisted — but he wanted to set the highest possible price. "As long as we live on this earth, we expect pay . . ." he said. "The amount must be so large that the interest will support us. . . . If even only two Indians remain, so long as they live they will want to be fed, as they are now."

Red Cloud gave more specifics. He was proving as formidable in negotiation as he had been skilled at war.

> . . . I want seven generations ahead to be fed. . . . These hills out here to the northwest we look upon as the head chief of the land. My intention was that my children should depend on these hills for the future. I hoped that we should live that way always. . . . I want to put the money that we get for the Black Hills at interest among the whites, to buy with the interest wagons and cattle. . . . For

Two brand-new mining camps — Custer City (above, left), named in honor of the man whose expedition discovered gold, and Deadwood — sprawl across the Lakota hunting grounds. "I want to hunt in this place," Sitting Bull warned whites. "I want you to turn back from here. If you don't, I'll fight you."

Opposite: Sitting Bull, 1884

I will remain what I am until I die, a hunter, and when there are no buffalo or other game I will send my children to hunt and live on prairie mice, for where an Indian is shut up in one place his body becomes weak.

Sitting Bull

seven generations to come I want our Great Father to give us Texas steers for our meat. I want the Government to issue for me hereafter, flour and coffee, and sugar and tea, and bacon, the very best kind, and cracked corn and beans and rice and dried apples . . . and tobacco, and soap and salt and pepper for the old people. . . . I want a sow and a boar, and a cow and a bull, and a hen and cock, for each family. I am Indian and you want to make a white man out of me. I want some white men's houses at this agency to be built for the Indians. I have been into white people's houses, and I have seen nice black bedsteads and chairs and I want that kind of furniture . . . a saw-mill, . . . a mower and a scythe. Maybe you white people think that I ask too much . . . but I think those hills extend clear to the sky — maybe they go above the sky, and that is the reason I ask so much. . . .

For three full days, as other chiefs echoed Red Cloud's demands and then added to them, the commissioners grew more and more disheartened — the Lakota's speeches were "of so extraordinary a character," they wrote later, "as to make it manifest that it was useless to continue the negotiations. . . . The Indians place a value on the hills far beyond any sum that could possibly be considered by the Government." Congress should therefore simply "fix a fair equivalent . . . taking into account all the circumstances surrounding them, and the value of the Hills to the United States," and then present that arrangement to the Lakota as a "finality."

To increase the pressure, Congress threatened to withhold food until the Lakota capitulated. President Grant secretly ordered the army to ignore the miners' intrusions. The Interior Department demanded that the non-treaty bands be compelled to abandon the unceded hunting grounds and come into the agencies by January 31, 1876. Sitting Bull, Crazy Horse, and the others refused.

Sometime in the early spring of 1876, Sitting Bull had climbed to a hilltop to commune with the spirits. In his vision, a great dust storm swirled down upon a small white cloud that resembled a Lakota village. Through the whirlwind, Sitting Bull could see soldiers marching. There was a great storm and the cloud was swallowed up for a time, but it emerged intact and the dust storm disappeared. It was an encouraging vision.

In the spring of 1876 the Lakota needed encouragement — the United States Army was about to move against them. In his far-off Chicago headquarters, General Philip Sheridan had already drawn up a plan that would send three columns of soldiers to drive the Lakota into the agencies, a plan that had worked against the Cheyenne eight years earlier and in the Red River campaign against the southern Plains tribes. One column, led by Brigadier General George Crook, was to move north from Fort Fetterman; another, under Colonel John Gibbon, would march east from western Montana, while Custer and the Seventh Cavalry drove west from Fort Abraham Lincoln.

Custer was in his element: "General George A. Custer, dressed in a dashing suit of buckskin, is prominent everywhere . . ." a correspondent for the New York *Herald* reported. "The General is full of perfect readiness for a fray with the hostile red devils, and woe to the body of scalp-lifters that comes within reach of himself and brave companions in arms."

His command included 566 enlisted men and 31 officers. Some venerated their commander, among them three of his own brothers, a nephew, and a reporter for a New York newspaper who could be counted on to issue admiring progress reports. But others loathed him, including his second-in-command, Major Marcus A. Reno, who had once schemed to supplant Custer as commander, and Captain Frederick W. Benteen, an alcoholic whose hostility extended beyond Custer to most of the other officers in the Seventh Cavalry.

None of the commanders knew precisely where Sitting Bull and his followers were, but they believed one column or another would find and destroy them. "I have given no instructions . . ." wrote General Sheridan. "Each column will be able to take care of itself [while] chastising the Indians, should it have the opportunity."

A private in Custer's Seventh left a letter behind for his sister:

Dear Sister,
. . . The Indians are getting bad again. I think we will have some hard times this summer. The old chief Sitting Bull says that he will not make peace with the whites as long as he has a man to fight. . . . As soon as I get back [from] the campaign I will write you. That is, if I do not get my hair lifted by some Indian.
From your loving brother,
T. P. Eagan

On June 6, some 3,000 Lakota and Cheyenne were camped along Rosebud Creek. There they held their most sacred ritual — the sun dance. Sitting Bull slashed his arm a hundred times as a sign of sacrifice, then had a new vision. In it, the soldiers came again to attack his people — "as many as grasshoppers," he said — but this time they

General George Crook, a veteran Indian fighter, was first assigned the hopeless task of clearing prospectors from the Black Hills, then fared poorly against the Lakota and the Cheyenne at the battle of the Rosebud. Later, he would redeem himself subduing the Apache in the Southwest.

were upside down, their horse's hooves in the air, their hats tumbling to the ground as they rode into the Lakota camp. The soldiers were coming again. He was sure of it. But this time, his people would be ready for them.

Eleven days later, on the morning of June 17, General Crook's column stopped to brew coffee on the bank of the Rosebud. Crook and his officers began a leisurely game of whist. Suddenly, some five hundred Sioux and Cheyenne warriors attacked Crook's force, which was twice the size of their own. Sitting Bull was too weak from the sun dance to fight, but he urged the young men into battle.

In a fierce, desperate fight that boiled on for more than six hours, Crook was saved in part by his Crow and Shoshone allies, who twice scattered the attackers by riding through their ranks. The general declared the battle of the Rosebud a victory because the Indians withdrew from the battlefield, but it had really been a standoff, and it had signaled something new in Plains warfare. Until now, Indian fighting had largely been a matter of pursuit and surprise. This time, the Lakota and Cheyenne had been the first to attack and had more than held their own against a far larger force. Crook thought it best to withdraw. The Lakota and Cheyenne moved north onto Crow lands and set up a new camp along a winding stream they called the Greasy Grass. Whites called it the Little Bighorn.

Six troopers from the Seventh Cavalry, photographed at Fort Lincoln, before Custer's last campaign began

On June 21, Custer met on the Yellowstone River with Gibbon and their superior, Brigadier General Alfred Terry. They knew nothing of Crook's retreat.

Terry's Arikara scouts told him that Sitting Bull was now camped somewhere in the valley of the Little Bighorn. He ordered Gibbon to march up the Yellowstone and Bighorn to block its mouth. Meanwhile, Custer and the Seventh Cavalry were to hurry up the Rosebud, where, if they could locate the Indians, they would attack them from the south and drive them toward Gibbon and annihilation.

As Custer began his march, Terry called out to him, "Now Custer, don't be greedy, but wait for us."

"No," Custer said, laughing as he rode off, "I will not."

Custer's scouts were Crow, eager to defend their lands against the Lakota, and he was delighted with them. "They are magnificent-looking men," he wrote to his wife, "so much handsomer and more Indian-like than any we have ever seen, and jolly and sportive; nothing of the gloomy, silent red-man about them. . . . [T]hey said they had heard that I never abandoned a trail; that when my food gave out I ate mule. That was the kind of man they wanted to fight under; they were willing to eat mule, too."

Fearful Sitting Bull would elude him, Custer pushed his column hard under a merciless prairie sun — twelve miles the first day, thirty-three the second, twenty-eight the third. The men began to grumble about the man they privately called "Hard Ass." They found the Indians' trail, but evidently did not grasp the full meaning of the fresh layers of pony and travois tracks that crossed and recrossed it.

In fact, during the last few days, 3,000 more Indians — angered by the ongoing white invasion of the Black Hills, eager to return to their old ways — had left their agencies to join Sitting Bull. The encampment now stretched for three miles along the river. In it were more than 6,000 Indians — Hunkpapa, Oglala, Miniconjou, Sans Arc, as well as Blackfoot Sioux and Northern Cheyenne. Almost 2,000 of them were

Curly, one of Custer's Crow scouts, said to have been the first man to bring news of what had happened at the Little Bighorn to the outside world

warriors. "There were more Indians . . ." a Cheyenne woman named Kate Big Head recalled, "than I ever saw anywhere together. . . . The chiefs from all the camps decided we should move down the Little Bighorn River to its mouth . . . and kill antelope in the great herds they had seen there. The plan was to stay at this camp but one night, and go on down the valley the next day."

On the evening of June 24, Sitting Bull made his way to a ridge that overlooked the camp and the Bighorn Valley beyond. There, he made offerings to the Creator and prayed for the protection of his people.

> *Wakantanka,* pity me. In the name of the [people] I offer you this peace-pipe. Wherever the sun, the moon, the earth, the four points of the wind, there you are always. Father save the [people], I beg you. . . . We want to live. Guard us against all misfortune. . . . Pity me.

The next day was June 25, a Sunday, cloudless and hot. Custer's Crow scouts spotted the village from a distant hilltop and called Custer up to have a look. Even with a telescope, he was unable to see much more than a white blur on the valley floor, but the Crow warned him that there were enough Indians to fight for many days.

Custer just laughed: "I guess we'll get through them in one day," he said. His only concern was that he had already been spotted, that unless he attacked right away, the Indians would split up and flee in so many different bands that he could never stop them. There was no time to send men ahead to reconnoiter. He knew nothing of the terrain, could not tell how many Indians awaited him, but he was evidently not worried. It had been a surprise attack that had allowed him to destroy Black Kettle's Cheyenne on the Washita nine years earlier, after all, and a victory here seemed just as likely.

He ordered Captain Benteen, with 125 men, south to seek out a ridgeline from which to survey the valley and make sure no hostiles were behind him. Then, he hurried toward the Little Bighorn. When he saw dust rising over a ridge just ahead of him he was sure it meant that the Indians were already on the move.

It was now or never. Some forty warriors appeared, then began racing back toward their camp. Custer ordered Major Marcus Reno and three companies — 140 men — to pursue them, promising he would be right behind.

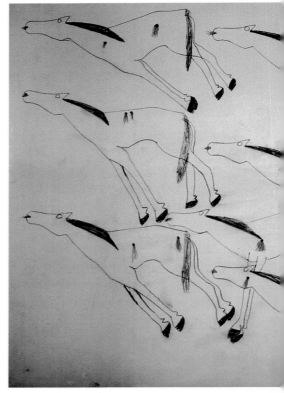

"It was somewhere past the middle of the afternoon," Kate Big Head recalled, "and all of us were having a good time. We found our women friends bathing in the river and we joined them. Other groups . . . were playing in the water. . . . Two Sioux boys came running toward us. They were shouting, 'Soldiers are coming!' We heard shooting. We hid in the brush."

Reno's men crossed the river, formed a thin skirmish line, and began firing into one edge of the village, assuming that Custer would quickly reinforce them. But he did not come and they were soon outnumbered. Reno's men held until a Lakota bullet struck the head of Bloody Knife, an Arikara scout, splattering his brains over Reno's face. Then, he shouted to his men to fall back into a grove of cottonwoods.

From her hiding place in the brush near the river Kate Big Head could see little. But she could hear what was happening:

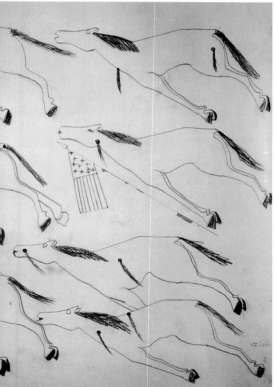

The Custer fight, as remembered by Red Horse, Miniconjou Lakota

The sounds of the shooting multiplied. . . . We heard women and children screaming. Old men were calling the young warriors to battle. Young men were singing their war songs. . . . We heard the sounds of battle change from place to place. It seemed the white men were going away, with the Indians following them . . . shooting and beating them.

More warriors swarmed out of the village. Reno ordered his men to retreat. The soldiers were falling into the village, just as Sitting Bull's dream had suggested they would. "Indians covered the flat," the Cheyenne Two Moons remembered. "They began to drive the soldiers, all mixed up — Lakota, then soldiers, then more Lakota, and all shooting."

The soldiers struggled across the swift-running river and tried to clamber up the riverbank. Those who made it did their best to find cover in the thick grass, and began to fire back. And still there was no sign of Custer. He had changed his plan, turning northwest and leading his five companies of 210 men toward a ridge that overlooked the village, apparently convinced the Indians were fleeing from Reno and that by charging down into it, he could cut them off. But when he got to the crest and saw for the first time the size of the village spread out below, a Crow scout named White-Man-Runs-Him remembered, he "looked whiter than ever."

Custer's Crow scouts began to sing their death songs. Custer told them they could go. They had found Sitting Bull's camp for him; that was enough.

He scribbled a note in pencil and sent his bugler back to deliver it to Benteen, in charge of the ammunition train: "Come on, Big Village. Be Quick. Bring packs. Hurry." Then he waved his hat to rally his troops and led them down toward the encampment, firing as they rode.

Kate Big Head left the brush and ran toward her teepee, but "[b]efore I got to my home lodge all [the warriors] were riding wildly back . . . through the camps. It appeared they had been beaten and were running away. But I soon learned what had happened. I heard a Cheyenne old man calling out: 'Other soldiers are coming! Warriors, go and fight them!'" Cheyenne warriors led by Lame White Man, Hunkpapa Lakota under Gall, and Oglala under Crazy Horse rode out together to turn back these new attackers.

"It appeared there would be no end to the rushing procession of warriors," Kate Big Head remembered. "They kept going, going, going. I wanted to go, too. . . . I had seen other battles in past times. I always liked to watch the men fighting."

The soldiers stopped at the sight of the advancing line of warriors, milled around for a moment, then began a headlong retreat toward the summit of a long, high ridge. The Indians noticed that the legs of the men and the horses trembled as they staggered onward. Some were simply exhausted. Others seemed terrified.

"I called to my men," Low Dog remembered. "'This is a good day to die: follow me.' We massed our men, and that no man should fall back, every man whipped another man's horse and we rushed right upon them."

"Little Bird and I were after one certain soldier . . ." a Cheyenne named Wooden Leg recalled. "We were lashing him and his horse with our pony whips. It seemed not brave to shoot him. . . . He pointed back his revolver, though, and sent a bullet into

Little Bird's thigh. . . . I whacked the white man . . . on his head with the heavy elk-horn handle of my pony whip. The blow dazed him. I seized the rifle strapped on his back . . . he fell to the ground. I did not harm him further. I do not know what became of him. The jam of oncoming Indians swept me on."

Scattered across the slope, Custer and his men dismounted and tried to defend themselves as best they could, firing into the swirl of ponies and warriors. Then, Crazy Horse and his Oglala rode down upon them. One by one, Custer's companies were wiped out. "As we rushed upon them the [soldiers] dismounted to fire," Low Dog recalled, "but they did very poor shooting. They held their horse's reins on one arm while they were shooting, but their horses were so frightened that they pulled the men all around and a great many of their shots went up into the air and did us no harm."

Another Lakota warrior, White Bull, remembered the fury of the fighting — and the pleasure he took in it:

> I charged in. A tall, well-built soldier . . . saw me coming. . . . [W]hen I rushed him, he threw his rifle at me without shooting.
>
> We grabbed each other and wrestled there in the dust and smoke. He hit me with his fists on the jaw and shoulders, then grabbed my long braids with both hands, pulled my face close and tried to bite my nose off. I yelled as loud as I could to scare my enemy, but he would not let go. Finally, I broke free.
>
> He drew his pistol. I wrenched it out of his hand and struck him with it three or four times on the head, knocked him over, shot him in the head and fired at his heart. . . .
>
> *Ho hechetu!* That was a fight, a hard fight. But it was a glorious battle, I enjoyed it. . . .

After a little while, "[t]he shots quit coming from the soldiers," Wooden Leg recalled. "Warriors who had crept close to them began to call out that all of the white men were dead. . . . All of the Indians were saying these soldiers . . . went crazy and killed themselves. I do not know. I could not see them. But I believe they did so. . . ."

And Kate Big Head, watching from the hillside, "saw several different ones of the soldiers not yet quite dead. The Indians cut off arms or legs or feet of these, the same as was done for the entirely dead. . . . Some of the women mourning for their own dead, beat and cut the dead bodies of the white men."

The fighting, one warrior remembered, had lasted no longer than a hungry man needed to eat his dinner. Almost one-third of Major Reno's command were killed before Benteen and his men finally arrived to relieve them. But all of the men in Custer's command now lay dead — 209 soldiers, along with the newspaper reporter whom Custer had brought along to write up his exploits. Only his Crow scouts had managed to get away. It was the greatest Indian victory of the Plains wars.

According to Kate Big Head, two Cheyenne woman found Custer's body:

> The women . . . pushed the point of an awl into each of his ears, into his head. This was done to improve his hearing, as it seemed he had not heard what our chiefs in the South had said when he smoked the pipe with them. They told him

The Custer fight, as recalled by
Amos Bad Heart Bull, Oglala Lakota

then that if ever afterward he should break that peace promise and should fight the Cheyennes the Everywhere Spirit surely would cause him to be killed. . . . I often have wondered if, when I was riding among the dead where he was lying, my pony may have kicked dirt upon his body.

The next day the great encampment broke up. The Indians set the grass afire to mask their passage with smoke. Some 8,000 Lakota and Cheyenne separated into bands and started for the Bighorn Mountains. They had won the Custer fight, had killed the man who had invaded the Black Hills and most of his command. It had been his last stand, but it would prove to be their last stand, as well.

At Fort Abraham Lincoln, the wives of the officers of the Seventh Cavalry knew nothing of what had happened to their husbands. Their chief concern was the steady, wearying heat:

Our only pleasure after the torrid day [one remembered] was to gather on someone's porch in the long twilight, enjoy what little music we could muster, and try to forget our worries and the devilish mosquitoes. Many among us had sweet voices, and while I played the guitar everyone sang. . . . Then, glancing across the parade ground, we noticed small groups of soldiers talking excitedly together, and several people came running toward us, faces set and wild-eyed. One was Horn Toad, the Indian scout, who gasped in short, sharp sentences, "Custer killed. Whole command killed."

The guitar slipped from my knees to the floor, the pink ball of knitting fell out of Charlotte Moylan's hands, the letter lying idly in Mrs. Benteen's lap fluttered over the rail and onto the . . . lawn. . . .

Americans were celebrating their centennial that summer, proud of one hundred years of independence, and the news that George Armstrong Custer and 263 men of his command had been killed by Indians was greeted with simple disbelief. How could such a thing possibly have happened? they asked. How could mere Indians with names that sounded absurd to eastern ears — Low Dog, Crazy Horse, Sitting Bull — have defeated so celebrated a soldier?

General Philip Sheridan, the architect of the plan that had ended in disaster, was so humiliated that he denied for a time that there really was a "Sitting Bull," assuring the press that the alleged name was just a Sioux phrase that meant "hostile Indians."

Sitting Bull had not joined the fighting at the Little Bighorn, but across the nation, he was now believed to be the Indian who had beaten the army. Others were convinced Sitting Bull couldn't really be an Indian at all — since no Indian could outgeneral a white man. Or that he was an Indian dropout from West Point, "the red Napoleon."

"Who slew Custer?" asked the New York *Herald.* "The celebrated peace policy of General Grant, which feeds, clothes, and takes care of their noncombatant force while men are killing our troops . . . [and] the Indian Bureau, with its thriving agents and favorites as Indian traders, and its mock humanity and pretense at piety — *that* is what killed Custer."

Price 25 Cents.

MASSACRED

GEN. CUSTER AND 261 MEN THE VICTIMS.

NO OFFICER OR MAN OF 5 COMPANIES LEFT TO TELL THE TALE.

3 Days Desperate Fighting by Maj. Reno and the Remainder of the Seventh.

Full Details of the Battle.

LIST OF KILLED AND WOUNDED.

THE BISMARCK TRIBUNE'S SPECIAL CORRESPONDENT SLAIN.

Squaws Mutilate and Rob the Dead

Victims Captured Alive Tortured in a Most Fiendish Manner.

What Will Congress Do About It?

Shall This Be the Beginning of the End?

It will be remembered the the Bismarck Tribune sent a special correspondent with Gen. Terry, who was the

Aftermath: news of the Custer disaster as it first appeared in the Bismarck *Tribune* on July 6, 1876, and (above, right) three of Custer's Crow scouts photographed among the gravestones of Custer's men, many years after the battle.

Sheridan promised Custer would be avenged, and fresh blue columns were soon crisscrossing the Powder River country in pursuit of the bands that had split up after the Custer fight. One by one, they were forced to surrender. There were simply too many soldiers to fight, too few buffalo left to feed their women and children. In the spring of 1877, even Crazy Horse came in with fifteen hundred Oglala, laying down his rifle as a token of peace. By September, he would be dead, bayoneted in the back while under guard.

Congress took away the Black Hills and another 40 million acres of land from the Lakota by obtaining the signatures of non-hostile chiefs and headmen and ignoring the provision of the 1868 Fort Laramie Treaty that required the vote of three-quarters of all adult males before any changes could be made. Indians who had had nothing to do with the warfare were disarmed.

Sitting Bull alone held out. He and his followers were now beyond the reach of American troops, across the border in Canada, which he called the "Land of the Grandmother," in honor of Queen Victoria. When General Alfred Terry traveled north to offer him a full pardon on the condition that he settle at an agency, Sitting Bull angrily sent him away again. "This country is my country now," he told the general, "and I intend to stay here and raise people to fill it. We did not give our country to you; you stole it. You come here to tell lies; when you go home, take them with you."

For thirty years, Brigham Young had attended to every possible detail of life in Mormon Utah. "I feel like a father with a great family of children around me, in a winter storm," he once told his people, "and I am looking with calmness, confidence and patience, for the clouds to break and the sun to shine, so that I can run out . . . and say, 'Children, come home. . . . I am ready to kill the fatted calf and make a joyful feast to all who will come and partake.'"

But now he felt besieged. Congress was trying once again to assert control over Utah. A new law gave federal courts, not local ones, jurisdiction over criminal cases in the territory, and one of the first actions of the federal prosecutors was to arrest Young's devoted follower John D. Lee for murder in the matter of the Mountain Meadows Massacre, twenty years earlier. He and the other Mormon participants had taken a blood oath that they would never reveal what had really happened, church officials blamed the Paiute for the massacre, and for nearly twenty years non-Mormons had struggled in vain to force a full accounting.

But the memory of the massacre continued to haunt Utah, and even among some of the faithful pressure had slowly grown to find and prosecute the guilty so that the church as a whole might be exonerated. In 1870, Brigham Young excommunicated John D. Lee, and in 1872 he urged him to disappear into the wilderness. Lee gave up his home and business. With one of his eleven wives, he fled deep into Arizona, where the Mormons were starting new colonies. Then, he settled with another wife at the mouth of the remote Paria River, just north of the Grand Canyon, and started a ferry business across the Colorado. Church officials always sent him warning if lawmen were in the area, so that he could hide out until they were safely gone. With the exception of a few Mormons headed to Arizona, his only visitors were Indians, outlaws, and explorers.

Still, he remained steadfast in his devotion to Brigham Young. "It is told around for a fact that I could tell great confessions and bring in Brigham Young and the heads of the church . . ." he wrote. "[But] I will not be the means of bringing troubles on my

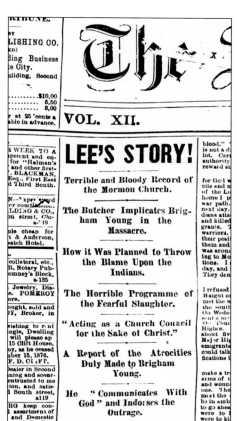

Exile's return: "Lonely Dell" (left), the home at Jacob's Pool in Arizona Territory to which Brigham Young banished John D. Lee after the Mountain Meadows Massacre, and Lee's confession issued after he was sentenced to death in 1877

Last look: John D. Lee (seated on coffin, left) just before his execution and (above) after the firing squad had done its work

people, for . . . this people is a misrepresented and cried-down community. Yes, a people scattered and peeled . . . and if at last they did rise up and shed the blood of their enemies, I won't consent to give 'em up."

As Lee awaited trial federal prosecutors offered him money and leniency if he would implicate others, including Young. Lee refused: "I chose to die like a man," he said later, "rather than to live as a villain." Orders went out from Salt Lake City that no Mormon should testify against him. None did, and when the four gentiles on the jury found Lee guilty, the eight Mormons were unanimous for acquittal. Across the nation, the case became a symbol for everything Americans despised about Mormonism, and pressure mounted for the government to strip Brigham Young and the church of its authority in Utah.

In the second trial everything changed. This time, since the prosecutors concentrated their attack on John D. Lee alone, Brigham Young ordered Mormons to cooperate: all the blame for the tragedy was to be placed on the shoulders of one man. Witnesses now testified that the killing had been Lee's idea and Lee's alone.

All the members of the jury were Mormons. All now voted to convict. Under Utah law, Lee was allowed to choose whether he wished to be shot, hanged, or beheaded. He chose a firing squad.

On March 23, 1877, he was escorted to the site of the massacre and seated on a coffin so that he might be photographed. He made arrangements for each of the two wives who remained true to him to get a copy of the picture, then rose and spoke to the little crowd that had turned out to see him die:

> I am ready to die. . . . I do not fear death, I shall never go to a worse place than I am now in. . . . I do not believe everything that is now being taught and practiced by Brigham Young. I do not care who hears it. . . . I studied to make this man's will my pleasure for thirty years. See, now, what I have come to this day! I have been sacrificed in a cowardly, dastardly manner. . . . Sacrifice a man that has waited upon them, that has wandered and endured with them in the days of adversity, true from the beginnings of the Church! And I am now singled out and am sacrificed in this manner! What confidence can I have in such a man! I have none, and I don't think my Father in heaven has any. . . .

I regret leaving my family; they are near and dear to me. These are things which touch my sympathy, even when I think of those poor orphaned children.

I declare I did nothing designedly wrong in this unfortunate affair. . . . I do not fear death, I shall never go to a worse place than I am now in. . . .

Having said this, I feel resigned. I ask the Lord, my God, if my labors are done, to receive my spirit.

Then Lee shook hands with his executioners, and handed his hat and overcoat to a friend. His last words were to the firing squad: "Center my heart, boys. Don't mangle my body."

No one else was ever indicted for the Mountain Meadows Massacre.

Brigham Young toward the end of his life. "He has been the brain, the eye, the ear, the mouth and hand for the entire people of the Church," said one of the eulogists at his funeral. "Nothing was too small for his mind; nothing was too large."

Brigham Young was failing badly now. Rheumatism had so crippled him that he had to be carried on a chair during his ceaseless inspection tours. Then, while passing through the town of Ephraim, a Scandinavian convert darted into the street and berated him for having sacrificed John D. Lee: "Oh, you Cheat!" he shouted, shaking his fist. "Oh Church Fraud! You coward to forsake your tools! You are the man that they should have hung instead of Lee!" The man was pulled away. Young said nothing, but his hands gripped the seat of his coach until his knuckles turned white.

On August 23, 1877, he was seized by sudden terrible stomach pains. For six days, surrounded by his huge family, he floated in and out of consciousness. Then, on August 29, 1877, he called out the name of Joseph Smith, his predecessor as prophet of the church, and died. It would be nearly three decades before his people were rewarded with the statehood he had sought, and to get it they had to forswear the policy of plural marriage he had defended so hard.

Even in death, Brigham Young remained in charge. He was laid in a redwood coffin of his own precise design, fashioned "two or three inches wider than is commonly made for a person of my breadth and size . . . to have the appearance that if I wanted to turn a little to the right or left I should have plenty of room to do so. . . ." Twenty-five thousand Mormons filed past his bier inside the still-unfinished Salt Lake Tabernacle before his remains were placed in a stone vault overlooking his desert city. Jedediah Grant, one of Young's closest advisers, tried to convey to the readers of the New York *Herald* something of what Brigham Young had meant to his people:

I can't undertake to explain Brigham Young to your Atlantic citizens, or expect you to put him at his value. Your great men Eastward are to me like your ivory and pearl handled table knives, balance[d] handles, more shiny than the inside of my watch case; but, with only edge enough to slice bread and cheese or help spoon victuals, and all alike by the dozen, one with another.

Brigham is the article that sells out West with us — between a Roman cutlass and a beef butcher knife, the thing to cut up a deer or cut down an enemy, and that will save your life or carve your dinner every bit as well, though the handpiece is buckhorn and the case a hogskin hanging in the breech of your pantaloons.

You, that judge men by the handle and the sheath, how can I make you know a good *Blade?*

A TOUGH BUNCH

"I was a boy during the Civil War," one rueful western regular remembered, "and there was an army camp near and I guess I soaked in some of the game, for later, every time I got Spiflicated I wanted to enlist. . . . [I] . . . thought it would be like the volunteers during the Civil War . . . but I found out the mistake. The Regular Army was a tough bunch in those days."

The western army had an impossible job — policing some two and half million square miles of land between the Missouri and the eastern slope of the Sierras. There were never more than 15,000 men, scattered among one hundred forts and outposts, yet they were somehow expected to defend settlers, ranchers, miners, railroad crews; keep thousands of Indians confined to their reservations — and keep tens of thousands of whites out of Indian lands.

But even though army pay was low — just thirteen dollars a month — steady jobs were scarce during the economic slump that followed the Civil War, and army ranks were soon filled with immigrants, some of whom could speak almost no English. There were drifters, too: men with assumed names; men escaping bad marriages — or the law. "Some of the recruits [I joined with]," one recalled, "had no doubt served in some penitentiary before enlisting, and I shouldn't wonder that some went back to their old prisons as a haven of rest and decent treatment."

Promotions were rare, and riddled with politics. Discipline was severe; men were flogged for minor infractions, locked up in log stockades, suspended by their thumbs, made to sit for hours on a wooden horse.

The climate added to the soldiers' woes. "Everything dries," one man wrote during a tour of duty at Fort Yuma in Arizona Territory. "Men dry; chickens dry; there is not juice left in anything. living or dead, by the close of summer. . . ."

A regular army private named Comfort had this formal portrait made on a rare trip to town.

The parade ground at Old Camp Grant, Arizona Territory. "Some of what are called military posts," General William Tecumseh Sherman wrote, "are mere collections of huts made of logs, adobes or mere holes in the ground, and are about as much forts as prairie dog villages might be called forts."

Sleeping it off: Whiskey wa the soldier's curse. Forty men out of every thousand were hospitalized for alcoholism — and that was only those whose drinking had actually rendered then unfit for service.

Victuals: Army food was almost always unpalatable, sometimes inedible. Hardtack — flour-and-water biscuits — delivered to the Seventh Cavalry at Fort Hays was six years old and had to be shattered with a hammer.

Officers tent, Seventh Infantry, somewhere on the Plains

Troopers in buffalo coats struggle to keep warm at Fort Keogh in Montana Territory, 1879.

Chickens hatched at this season, as old Fort Yumers say, come out of the shell already cooked."

Winter on the northern Plains was just as bad: "I am now wearing two flannel and a buckskin shirt," one soldier reported, "one pair of drawers, trousers of buckskin and a pair of army trousers, two pairs woolen socks, a pair of buffalo overshoes and big boots, a heavy pair of blanket leggins, a thick blouse and heavy overcoat, a heavy woolen cap that completely covers my head, face and neck except nose and eyes — and still I am not happy."

Most regulars never met an Indian in battle. Some never saw any Indians at all. Boredom was all the men could depend upon, three to five years of it. They quarreled, drank, pitted red ants against black ants just to stir things up.

Disease was the worst killer. In one two-year period, the Seventh Cavalry lost thirty-six men to Indians — and fifty-one to cholera. And desertion rates were understandably high. "I want to get out of the army honorable," one soldier wrote home, "but if I can't get out otherwise I will give the cursed outfit the 'Grand bounce.' I can not endure them much longer. None but a menial cur could stand the usage of a soldier of the army today in America."

Officers and their wives and children take time out from croquet at Fort Bridger in Wyoming Territory, 1873.

FIGHT NO MORE, FOREVER

Of all the Indian tribes in the West, none had a longer record of unbroken friendship with the United States than the Nez Percé. They had saved Lewis and Clark and their companions from starvation in the autumn of 1805, and when their neighbors, the Cayuse, had risen up against Marcus and Narcissa Whitman and other whites in 1847, they had refused to join them. During the early 1860s, when thousands of whites in search of gold crowded onto land that was theirs by a treaty signed in 1855, they had remained resolutely peaceful. And when in 1863 the government sought to purchase all but about 10 percent of their land and persuade them to move onto what was left, a narrow strip of land along the Clearwater in Idaho, most had reluctantly agreed. Many converted to Christianity, wore white men's clothes, and took up farming and stock raising.

But several bands resisted. One had its home in the beautiful Wallowa Valley of eastern Oregon and was led by a chief called Old Joseph. He had been the first Nez Percé to be baptized by the missionary Henry Spalding, but had soon grown so disillusioned with the white man's faith and with his incessant demands for Indian lands that he refused to sign the new treaty and tore up his copy of the Gospel of Saint Matthew, which Spalding had translated for him. His people had signed no agreement to sell their land, he maintained, and he saw no reason to give it up. The Nez Percé were now split in two: Christians versus non-Christians, treaty supporters versus treaty opponents. "It was these Christian Nez Perces who made with the government a thief treaty," a man from Old Joseph's band named Yellow Wolf remembered. "Sold to the government all this land. . . . Sold what did not belong to them. We got nothing for our country. None of our chiefs signed that land-stealing treaty. . . . Only Christian Indians and government men."

President Grant himself agreed that Joseph's band could not legally be moved and by executive order even set aside part of the valley for them in 1873, but local whites were so exercised by this action that it was rescinded. Whites poured into the valley. Killings of Indians went unpunished. Still, the Nez Percé refused to retaliate. Old Joseph died and leadership of his band fell to his sons, *Ollokot*, known for his bravery and skill at buffalo hunting, and *Hin-mah-too-yah-lat-kekht* — Thunder Rolling from the Mountains — known to whites as Young Joseph and responsible for the daily welfare of his people.

Faced with increasing tension between the Nez Percé and the invading whites, the government finally decided in 1876 to compensate the Wallowa Nez Percé for their lands and then make sure they, and all the other non-treaty bands, moved. General Oliver Otis Howard was dispatched to get the job done. He had lost an arm at the Civil War battle of Seven Pines and won the Medal of Honor; after the war, he ran the Freedmen's Bureau to help emancipated slaves, founded Howard University for African-Americans, and negotiated a peace between the United States and the Apache leader Cochise in Arizona. He was as pious as he was unyielding.

Joseph tried to explain to the general what the valley meant to him. It was the place where his ancestors were buried, he said. He had promised his late father never to abandon it. "Do not misunderstand me . . . [and] my affection for the land. I never said the land was mine to do with as I chose. The one who has the right to dispose of

My father was the first to see through the schemes of the white men. He said, "My son . . . [w]hen I am gone . . . [y]ou are the chief of these people. Always remember that your father never sold his country. You must stop your ears whenever you are asked to sign a treaty selling your home. . . . My son, never forget my dying words. This country holds your father's body. Never sell the bones of your father and mother." I pressed my father's hand and told him I would protect his grave with my life. . . . A man who would not love his father's grave is worse than a wild animal.

Chief Joseph

Chief Joseph, photographed in 1877 at the end of his astonishing journey

it is the one who has created it. I claim a right to live on my land, and accord you the privilege to live on yours."

Howard, whose sympathies were with the Nez Percé and who was ordinarily a patient man, soon wearied of Joseph's protests: "We do not wish to interfere with your religion," he told the chiefs, "but must talk about practicable things. Twenty times over you repeat that the earth is your mother. . . . Let us hear no more, but come to business at once."

Howard gave all the non-treaty bands an ultimatum: accept compensation for their lands and move to a reservation at Lapwai, in Idaho, or his soldiers would force them in. They had just thirty days to comply. To avoid war, the non-treaty chiefs reluctantly began moving their people to the reservation. "I knew I had never sold my country," Joseph remembered, "and that I had no land in Lapwai; but I did not want bloodshed. I did not want my people killed. I did not want anybody killed. . . . I said in my heart that, rather than have war, I would give up my country. I would give up my father's grave. I would give up everything rather than have the blood of white men upon the hands of my people."

It was slow going. There were cattle and horses to round up. The Snake River was still swollen by melted snows. The young men particularly resented giving up their homeland without resisting, and when Joseph's band met up with those led by White Bird and Toohoolhoolzote, three young warriors, full of whiskey and eager for revenge, slipped away and murdered four whites whom they believed guilty of crimes against their people.

Joseph and the other chiefs realized immediately what the killings meant: soldiers would be coming, and for the first time in their history, the Nez Percé and the United States would be at war. Joseph still wanted to talk with Howard: the actions by the young men had not been sanctioned by anyone. "I would have given my own life if I could have undone the killing of white men by my people . . ." Joseph said. "I saw that war could not then be prevented. . . . I knew we were too weak to fight the United States. We had many grievances, but I knew that war would bring more." But the other chiefs overruled him and another unsanctioned raid in which seventeen settlers were killed made further talks irrelevant. The non-treaty bands headed for the Salmon River.

Howard sent Captain David Perry and the Mount Idaho Volunteers after them, and confidently wired his superiors: "Think we will make short work of it." When the volunteers neared the Nez Percé encampment at White Bird Canyon on the Salmon, the Indians sent out a party under a white flag, still hoping somehow to avoid bloodshed. The volunteers opened fire, anyway. It was a bad mistake. "It was just like two bulldogs meeting," Yellow Wolf recalled. "Those soldiers did not hold their position ten minutes. Some soldiers . . . were quickly on the run. Then the entire enemy force gave way. . . . We counted 33 dead soldiers. We did no scalping. We did not hurt the dead. Only let them lie."

Just three Nez Percé warriors had been wounded in the battle, and their companions had captured sixty-three rifles and stores of ammunition. "I have been in lots of scrapes," one army scout remembered, but "I never went up against anything like the Nez Percés in all my life." News of the stunning defeat at White Bird Canyon, less than

Our fathers gave us many laws, which they had learned from their fathers. . . . They told us to treat all men as they treated us; that we should never be the first to break a bargain; that it was a disgrace to tell a lie; that we should speak only the truth. . . . We were taught to believe that the Great Spirit sees and hears everything, and that he never forgets. This I believe, and all my people believe the same.

Chief Joseph

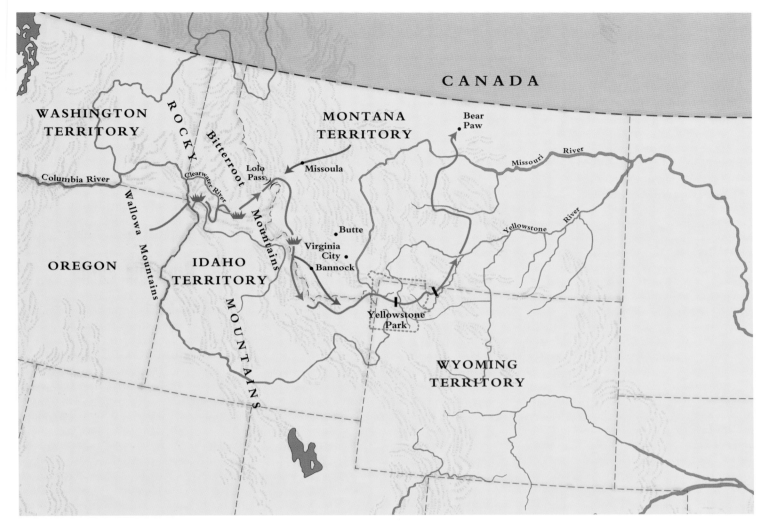

The flight of the Nez Percé and some of the battles and skirmishes they survived along the way

a year after Custer's death at the Little Bighorn, shocked the country. Howard called for more troops and set out in pursuit of the Indians.

Meanwhile, the Nez Percé leaders debated what to do next, finally agreeing with a war chief named Looking Glass to head east, out of Idaho. In Montana, he said, the white people would not bother them. And the Nez Percé's Indian allies, the Salish and the Crow, would surely shelter them along the way. They could hunt buffalo until a peace was negotiated for their return. As they began moving east, there were about seven hundred of them — only two hundred were warriors, the rest were women, children, and old people, with their horse herd and belongings, all in Joseph's care. For the next three months, the Nez Percé would lead the United States Army on one of the most remarkable pursuits in American military history.

On July 3, they wiped out an army scouting party of thirteen men that got too close. The next day, Independence Day, they fought off an attack at an old stage stop called Cottonwood. A week later on the Clearwater River they killed thirteen more of Howard's men. "They fought as well as any troops I ever saw," Howard said. Then, the Indians began climbing the Bitterroots, following the same trail that had brought Lewis and Clark to them three-quarters of a century earlier.

Howard also wired ahead to Montana so that troops would be sent to block their exit from the mountains. "There are high mountains and a narrow pass where the [Montana] soldiers were camped," Yellow Wolf remembered:

They had built a long log barricade across the trail. That was the trail we had thought to travel. I saw Salish Indians at the soldiers' fort. They seemed quite a bunch. All had white cloths tied on arm and head . . . so as not to shoot each other. So the soldiers would know they were not Nez Perces. They were helping the soldiers. Always friends before, we now got no help from them. . . . No help any time. Here, another body of soldiers came upon us and demanded our surrender. We refused. They said, "You can not get by us." We answered, "We are going by you without fighting if you will let us, but we are going by you, anyhow."

The outnumbered soldiers let the Indians pass without firing a shot. Local citizens derided their strongpoint as "Fort Fizzle."

The Nez Percé turned south, along the Bitterroot River, meticulously paying for all the food and supplies they obtained from the settlers they happened upon. "We bought provisions and traded stock with white men there," Joseph remembered. "We understood that there was to be no more war. We intended to go peaceably to the buffalo country, and leave the question of returning to our country to be settled afterward." But in the towns of Missoula, Butte, Bannack, and Virginia City terrified citizens demanded army protection.

On an elevated plateau ringed by mountains, called the Big Hole, the war chief Looking Glass convinced the weary Indians they could rest for several days. Howard, he said, was now too far behind for them to worry about. But Colonel John Gibbon, who had pursued Sitting Bull's Lakota the year before, had meanwhile assembled all the available soldiers in western Montana — 163 regular infantrymen and 34 volunteers — and begun to track the unsuspecting Nez Percé. "The trail led us along the bluffs overlooking the brush-covered valley . . ." Gibbon recalled, "and as we moved stealthily forward I could hear a cautious whisper, 'there they are — look!' . . . and the main camp of our enemies was as plainly in sight as the dim starlight permitted. . . . The troops attacked at dawn."

"It must have been about three o'clock in the morning, just before daylight, when I heard it — a gun — two guns! . . ." Yellow Wolf remembered. "I lay with my eyes closed. Maybe I was dreaming? I did not [know] what to do! Then I was awake. . . . Then came three volleys from many rifles, followed by shouting of soldiers." In the first moments, between sixty and ninety Indians were cut down — more than half of them women and children, many killed before they could kick free of their blankets. "It was not good to see women and children lying dead and wounded," Yellow Wolf recalled:

Wounded children screaming with pain. Women and men crying, wailing for their scattered dead! The air was heavy with sorrow I would not want to hear, I would not want to see, again. About ten warriors had been killed when the tepees were fired on before anyone was armed. All this was seen. The chiefs now called to the warriors to renew the fighting where the soldiers had hidden themselves.

Independent Extra

Big Hole Battle.

Gibbon Makes a Desperate Fight and is Overpowered.

LOGAN & BRADLEY KILLED

Gibbon and three Lieutenants Wounded.

" Help! Help!! Send us all the Relief you. We are Cut off from Supplies."

FIRST DISPATCH.
Big Hole, August 9; 1877.
To Governor Potts –
Had a hard fight with the Nez Perces, killing a number and losing a number of officers and men. We need a doctor and

A breathless dispatch in the Helena *Independent* gives the first news of the battle at the Big Hole and suggests a Nez Percé victory over Colonel John Gibbon's forces.

Looking Glass, the war chief who helped direct the Nez Percé retreat, photographed by William Henry Jackson in 1871, six years before the tribe was driven to desperation

The furious warriors regrouped and drove the soldiers from the camp. Gibbon suddenly found himself on the defensive, digging in on a wooded hillside while the Nez Percé pinned his men down with their fire. Twenty-nine soldiers were killed, forty more were wounded, including Gibbon himself. Lieutenant James H. Bradley, the first soldier to discover the bodies of Custer and his men a year earlier after the Little Bighorn battle, was among the dead.

The Nez Percé moved south now, back into Idaho, then turned east again. Angered over the loss of women and children at the Big Hole, some of the younger warriors began to disregard their leaders' urgings of restraint. Ranches along the way were raided, and some civilians murdered.

Howard — now ridiculed daily in the press for his inability to stop the Nez Percé — continued his dogged pursuit, and nearly caught up to them at Camas

The Grand River in the heart of Yellowstone National Park, through which the Nez Percé retreat passed in 1877. This view was made during the Hayden Survey six years earlier by William Henry Jackson.

Meadows, just west of the Wyoming border. But Nez Percé raiders stole his mule herd, and stalled him once again. He and General Sherman exchanged heated telegrams:

> [To General William T. Sherman. From General Oliver O. Howard. Sir:] My command is so much worn by over fatigue that I cannot push it much further. . . . I think I may stop near where I am, and in a few days work my way back to Fort Boise slowly.

> [To General Oliver O. Howard. From General William T. Sherman.] That force of yours should pursue the Nez Perces to the death, lead where they may. . . . If you are tired, give the command to some young energetic officer, and let him follow them. . . . No time should be lost.

> [To General William T. Sherman. From General Oliver O. Howard.] Sir: You misunderstood me. I never flag. . . . You need not fear for the campaign. Neither you nor General McDowell can doubt my pluck and energy. My Indian scouts are on the heels of the enemy. . . . We will move in the morning and will continue to the end.

While the soldiers bickered, the Nez Percé slipped back into Idaho, then turned east again, toward the Yellowstone plateau, which only five years earlier had been set aside as a national park. William Tecumseh Sherman himself had assured tourists they were in no danger: Indians, he said, were too superstitious to venture near the geysers.

"I was camped in the Lower Geyser Basin," a visitor named John Shively remembered. "I was eating my supper, and on hearing a slight noise, looked up, and to my astonishment, four Indians, in war paint, were standing within ten feet of me, and twenty or thirty more had surrounded me. . . ."

The Nez Percé swept into the park without a pause. On August 24, a scouting party came upon a party of ten tourists from Montana. The chiefs ordered them released, but some of the warriors wanted to avenge the killing at the Big Hole. "A pistol shot rang out," a woman named Emma Cowan remembered, "my husband's head fell back, and a red stream trickled down his face from beneath his hat. The warm sunshine, the smell of blood, the horror of it all, a faint feeling and all was blank."

"Emma fainted, then," another woman recalled, "and I jumped and screamed and ran in and out among the Indians and horses. The Indians ran after me, and one caught me by the throat and choked me. I bore the prints of his fingers on my neck for two weeks. As he loosened his hold I had the satisfaction of biting his fingers."

Before things could get any worse, a war leader named Red Scout intervened: "I had not the heart to see those women abused. I thought we had done them enough wrong. . . . Poker Joe and I prevented other injuries being done the party."

The Indians moved on, still hoping to find sanctuary among their longtime friends, the Crow.

The army, meanwhile, now believed it had the Nez Percé surrounded. Six companies of soldiers under Colonel Samuel D. Sturgis blocked the Clark's Fork River. Five

It gave us no pleasure to see our wagons overhauled, ransacked and destroyed. . . . We did not appreciate the fact that the Indians seemed to enjoy the confiscated property. One young chap dashed past us with several yards of pink mosquito bar tied to his horse's tail. A fine strip of swansdown, a trophy from Henry Lake, which an ugly old Indian had wrapped around his head turban fashion, did not please me either.

Emma Cowan

The women were not insulted. Can the white soldiers tell me of one time when Indian women were taken prisoners, and held three days and then released without being insulted?

Chief Joseph

The Nez Percé had hoped that Crow warriors like these men, photographed in 1890, would help shelter them from the whites. When they failed to do so and turned up fighting alongside their pursuers, the Nez Percé leaders feared that the end was near.

more guarded the Shoshone River. Still more troops were positioned north of the park, and Howard, with the largest force, was slowly coming through it from the west.

Somehow, the Nez Percé eluded them all. Sturgis finally caught up with them at Canyon Creek on the Yellowstone River, but couldn't stop them. His Crow scouts, however, engaged them in running skirmishes, killing some stragglers and stealing horses. This was an especially bitter blow for the Nez Percé. "Crows! . . ." Yellow Wolf remembered:

Many snows the Crows had been our friends. But now . . . [they had] turned enemies. My heart was just like fire. . . . I do not understand how the Crows could think to help the soldiers. They were fighting against their best friends! Some Nez Perces in our band had helped them whip the Sioux who came against them only a few snows before. This was why Chief Looking Glass had advised going to the Crows, to the buffalo country. He thought Crows would help us, if there was more fighting.

The Nez Percé were alone. With the hope of finding friends and sanctuary on the northern Plains gone, they fastened on one last chance for escape. Sitting Bull had found safety in Canada. They would head north across Montana to join him. At first it seemed nothing could stop them. They crossed the Yellowstone River, then the Musselshell, and finally, in late September, the Missouri, where they easily drove off a detachment of troops at Cow Island and helped themselves to an army supply depot.

They had now come more than seventeen hundred miles across some of the most rugged terrain in North America; fought in seventeen engagements against more than two thousand soldiers and Indian scouts; suffered hardships, disappointments, and the loss of loved ones. But they had beaten or eluded every army sent against them, and Canada — and freedom — were now only forty miles away. Howard, they knew, was more than two days' march behind them, and so before crossing the border the Nez Percé stopped to camp on Snake Creek near the Bear Paw Mountains.

"No white men were seen by scouts ahead," Yellow Wolf remembered:

> We guarded the back trail, but saw no signs of soldiers. We knew the distance to the Canadian line. Knew how long it would take to travel there. But there was no hurrying. . . . With horses' feet mostly sick and lots of grass, the chiefs ordered, "We camp here until tomorrow forenoon." . . . We knew General Howard was more than two suns back on our trail. It was nothing hard to keep ahead of him. . . .

But for nearly two weeks, Colonel Nelson A. Miles, who had taken over Custer's old command, had mercilessly pushed the Seventh Cavalry all the way from eastern Montana to intercept the Nez Percé. With him rode Lakota and Cheyenne warriors, who just a year before had defeated the Seventh at the Little Bighorn but had little affection for the Nez Percé. Now, they rode into the Nez Percé camp at a full gallop. "The Nez Percés were quietly slumbering in their tents," Miles remembered, "evidently without a thought of danger. . . . When the charge was made . . . [t]he tramp of at least 600 horses over the prairie fairly shook the ground, and, although a complete surprise to the Indians in the main, it must have given them a few minutes' notice, for as the troops charged against the village the Indians opened a hot fire upon them."

Despite the complete surprise, the Nez Percé warriors repulsed one attack — then a second, and a third. They killed or wounded fifty-three of the soldiers, but all their horses had been driven off. Both sides dug rifle pits. The weather turned colder. Snow started falling. Looking Glass was killed. Then, night fell, Yellow Wolf remembered:

> Most of our few warriors left from the Big Hole had been swept as leaves before the storm. Chief Ollokot, Lone Bird, and Lean Elk were gone. . . . A young warrior, wounded, lay on a buffalo robe dying without complaint. Children crying with cold. No fire. There could be no light. Everywhere the crying, the death wail. . . . I felt the coming end. All for which we had suffered lost! Thoughts came of the Wallowa where I grew up. Of my own country when only Indians were there. Of tepees along the bending river. Of the blue, clear lake, wide meadows with horse and cattle herds. From the mountain forests, voices seemed calling. I felt as dreaming. Not my living self.

Sunday, September 30th, 1877. Reveille at 2 o'clock a.m. The moon and stars shine in a clear sky, the air is chilly. We march as soon as we can see to move. A wolf serenades us at our first halt by the side of a stream. We soon come upon the broad Indian trail. Our Cheyenne and Sioux undergo a sudden transformation: they are painted, stripped for a fight, on their favorite chargers. . . . They are bounding over the plain on either side of the column, which is now in rapid motion. To be astride a good horse, on the open prairie, rifle in hand . . . [as] one of four hundred horsemen, galloping on a hot trail, sends a thrill through the body which is seldom experienced.

Major Henry Remsen Tilton
Seventh Cavalry

For five more days, the siege went on. A few Nez Percé slipped behind the lines and straggled into Canada. Sitting Bull welcomed them, but would send no force to help the others. Their last hope of rescue was gone.

Under a white flag, Miles opened negotiations. Since most of their chiefs were dead, Joseph was selected to talk with him. The general told Joseph that if he and his men turned over their weapons, they would be allowed to return home in the spring.

> I knew that we were near Sitting Bull's camp [Joseph remembered,] and I thought maybe the Nez Percés who had escaped would return with assistance. . . . My people were divided about surrendering. We could have escaped from Bear Paw Mountain if we had left our wounded, old women and children behind. We were unwilling to do this. We had never heard of a wounded Indian recovering while in the hands of white men. . . . I could not bear to see my wounded men and women suffer any longer; we had lost enough already. General Miles had promised that we might return to our own country with what stock we had left. I thought we could start again. I believed General Miles, or I never would have surrendered.

On the afternoon of October 5, Joseph rode out to the foot of a bluff on the prairie. Miles and General Howard were waiting for him. "Joseph threw himself off his horse," an officer noted, "draped his blanket about him . . . and with a quiet pride, not exactly defiance, advanced toward General Howard and held out his rifle in token of submission. Howard gestured for him to hand it over to General Miles."

"I am tired of fighting," Joseph told Howard, through an interpreter:

> Tell General Howard I know his heart. What he told me before, I have in my heart. I am tired of fighting. Our chiefs are killed. Looking Glass is dead. Toohoolhoolzote is dead. The old men are all dead. It is the young men who say "Yes" or "No." He who led the young men is dead. It is cold, and we have no blankets. The little children are freezing to death. My people, some of them, have run away to the hills, and have no blankets, no food. No one knows where they are — perhaps freezing to death. I want to have time to look for my children, and see how many of them I can find. Maybe I shall find them among the dead. Hear me, my chiefs! I am tired. My heart is sick and sad. From where the sun now stands I will fight no more, forever.

Joseph and his people were loaded onto a riverboat and sent down the Missouri River toward Fort Abraham Lincoln in Dakota Territory, where they expected to spend the winter. But while they were on the way, the promise that Miles and Howard had made, that the Nez Percé would be allowed to return to their home country, had been overruled by General Sherman:

> [The war with the Nez Percé] was one of the most extraordinary Indian wars of which there is any record. The Indians throughout displayed a courage and skill that elicited universal praise. They abstained from scalping; let captive women go free; did not commit indiscriminate murder of peaceful families, which is usual, and fought with almost scientific skill. . . . Nevertheless, they would not settle down on lands set apart for them . . . and when commanded by proper

authority, they began resistance by murdering persons in no manner connected with their alleged grievances. . . . They should never again be allowed to return to Oregon.

When the Nez Percé arrived at the fort, its cannon boomed a greeting, and the steam engine of a Northern Pacific train blasted its whistle three times. They had never seen a train before and began a mournful song. It sounded, one onlooker said, like a "death chant." Then they were loaded onto the train.

They were not going home, they were now told, but far away, into exile in Oklahoma's Indian Territory. "We were not asked if we were willing to go," Chief Joseph remembered. "We were ordered to get into railroad cars."

Joseph and 337 others were taken to the northeast corner of Indian Territory in Oklahoma. There, they soon began to fall sick. Sixty-eight died in the first year alone. Soon, they had a cemetery set aside solely for infants, with one hundred graves. They called the place of their exile *Eeikish Pah,* which meant both "the hot place" and "hell."

General Miles continued to promote the exiles' cause. But white settlers in Joseph's homeland in the Wallowa Valley adamantly opposed his return. Even some of the Nez Percé on the Idaho reservation considered Joseph and his band troublemakers who should be kept away.

To plead for his people, Chief Joseph went to Washington. He met with President Rutherford B. Hayes, and in Lincoln Hall, near the Capitol, spoke to a gathering of congressmen, cabinet members, and businessmen.

I have shaken hands with a great many friends, but there are some things I want to know which no one seems able to explain. I cannot understand how the Government sends a man out to fight us, as it did General Miles, and then breaks his

A Presbyterian missionary (back row, second from right) and some of her Nez Percé charges on the Lapwai reservation to which Joseph and his band had refused to go

What I heard those generals and chiefs say, I have always remembered. But those generals soon forgot their promises. Chief Joseph and his people were not permitted to return to their own homes. We were not captured. It was a draw battle. . . . We expected to be returned to our own homes. This was promised us by General Miles. That was how he got our rifles from us. It was the only way he could get them.

Yellow Wolf

Joseph and members of his family, photographed during their confinement in Oklahoma

word. Such a Government has something wrong with it. . . . If the white man wants to live in peace with the Indian he can live in peace. There need be no trouble. Treat all men alike. Give them all the same law. Give them all an even chance to live and grow. All men were made by the same Great Spirit Chief. They are all brothers. The earth is the mother of all people, and all people should have equal rights upon it.

The speech prompted praise and sympathy all across the nation, but nothing changed. Joseph and his band still could not go home.

WILDERNESS AND THE WEST

T. H. WATKINS

In the late summer of 1861, a young man sat in a rowboat and watched in awe while much of an entire western forest went up in flames. His name was Samuel Clemens, a tramp newspaperman and sometime riverboat pilot who had come west earlier that summer as companion to his brother, Orion, the newly appointed secretary to the governor of Nevada Territory (carved off from Utah Territory earlier that year, after the discovery of huge deposits of silver in the mountains north of Carson City had given Nevada a claim to its own identity). Before wandering up to the mining region to see what they could see, Sam and a companion decided to spend the rest of the summer of 1861 loitering about the shores of Lake Tahoe up in the Sierra Nevada. It was an interlude of splendid isolation in the heart of one of the most compellingly beautiful wild areas on the planet, and the two young men embraced it gratefully. "The forest about us was dense and cool," Clemens remembered in *Roughing It* (1872), writing now as Mark Twain,

> the sky above us was cloudless and brilliant with sunshine, the broad lake before us was glassy and clear, or rippled and breezy, or black and storm-tossed, according to Nature's mood; and its circling border of mountain domes, clothed with forests, scarred with land-slides, cloven by cañons and valleys, and helmeted with glittering snow, fitly framed and finished the noble picture. The view was always fascinating, bewitching, entrancing.

Listen now to what the young nature lover soon did to the beauty he had described so elegantly. He left a cook fire unattended briefly one evening, and before he could get back to it a vagrant gust of wind had sent sparks into the tinderlike pine needles of the forest floor. When the resulting flames reached a stand of summer-dry manzanita, the resulting explosion of heat sent the two young men into their rowboat and out onto the lake. "Within half an hour," Twain wrote,

> all before us was a tossing, blinding tempest of flame! It went surging up adjacent ridges — surmounted them and disappeared in the cañons beyond — burst into view upon higher and farther ridges, presently — shed a grander illumination abroad, and dove again — flamed out again, directly, higher and still higher up the mountain-side — threw out skirmishing parties of fire here and there, and sent them trailing their crimson spirals away among remote ramparts and ribs and gorges....

Every feature of the spectacle was repeated in the glowing mirror of the lake! Both pictures were sublime, both were beautiful; but that in the lake had a bewildering richness about it that enchanted the eye and held it with the strongest fascination.

It is not Twain's carelessness that we find startling today; many forest fires still begin with some camper's runaway cookfire. It is his attitude toward the whole business that mystifies us. Smokey the Bear would weep large ursine tears over such a spectacle, and even the most hidebound fire ecologist probably would offer some barbed observations regarding human stupidity as being an unnatural and inappropriate substitute for lightning as the prime cause of environmentally correct forest fires. But in Twain's eyes, for all his infatuation with the scenery of the forested mountains, the fire was a grand entertainment, remembered without so much as a passing phrase of remorse for all that he had sent to perdition. His description of the event was the raucous celebration of a Hannibal-indoctrinated frontier mentality that sees even the most beautiful land essentially as something subservient to human needs, no quarter given, no regrets expressed.

That mentality represents the oldest and most dominant philosophical strain in the history of the settlement of the West. It is a perception that sees the land mainly as a resource, a commodity to be used to fuel national dreams of progress and an ever-growing gross national product, as well as personal dreams of security, wealth, and power. The perception hardly was confined to the West, of course; it already had flamed through most of the land east of the Big River, with consequences (erosion-caused flooding in the timber-stripped Appalachians, for example, or farmed-out soils in New England) that were beginning to be understood, though fitfully. But there seemed to be so *much* beyond the wide Missouri — so *much* land, so *many* forests, so *many* rivers, so *enormous* a population of wild creatures, so *thick* a crust of treasure-laden rock formations — that for sensibilities already profligate with hope it seemed it all would last forever. It could not last, and much of it did not last, and most of what was lost will never be reclaimed: native prairie grasses plowed under and replaced by millions of acres of wheat and corn and other commercial species; forests scythed off the slopes of scores of mountains in nearly every major range in the West; grasslands in the deserts of the Southwest and the High Plains of the Dakotas and mountain meadows everywhere eaten down to their nubby roots by millions of cattle and sheep; wild rivers converted into plumbing systems by dams and poisoned by runoff from smoking industrial mining complexes and agribusiness farms the size of Balkan nations; urban conurbations oozing everywhere, linked by habitat-fragmenting highway systems and kept alive by rapidly dwindling supplies of water, while plant and animal species are eased ever closer to the abyss of extinction.

A familiar litany, and usually an angry one, as if most of those who created this imperfect world west of the Mississippi had been nothing more than bands of wild-eyed Visigoths laying waste with ax, plow, and cement, dancing, like Twain, before the flames of their vandalism, then moving on. It leaves out of the equation those whom Wallace Stegner has called "the stickers," the men and women who came to make a life in the West, not to take what they could from it and leave it the poorer for their passage. It was the stickers who gave the region the best that was in it, after all: resiliency, community, humor, and hope, all of it forged in that difficult arena where human character is tested.

Still, there were Visigoths enough, opportunists and entrepreneurs who used both the land and the people in it with such arrogant disregard that historian Vernon L. Parrington would call their era the time of "the Great Barbecue" and Bernard DeVoto would describe the West as the "Plundered Province." Like the story of what our culture did to the Native American cultures that lay in its path, the story of what happened to the land provides a dark counterpoint to the brimming excitement of the western adventure. But even as the driving force of settlement was puncturing and peopling and plundering the land, there was another, paradoxical sensitivity developing — more slowly and never so completely as that which shaped the essential history of the West, to be sure, but one that nevertheless was not without its own excitements, its own shades of color, its own heroes and heroines. It was an idea, as one of its historians has characterized it, and it was called wilderness.

In March of 1862, just about seven months after Mark Twain set fire to much of the Tahoe Basin in the Sierra Nevada, a seriously ill Henry David Thoreau sat at the writing desk of his house in Concord, Massachusetts, and gave the final polish to an essay called "Walking." When done, he sent it off to *The Atlantic Monthly*, where it was accepted immediately. On May 6, he died, and "Walking," appearing in the June 1862 issue of the magazine, became the first posthumously published work produced by the nineteenth century's most recognized natural philosopher. It is a pity Thoreau did not live to see the essay given the luminosity of print, for it proved to be one of the most enduring pieces he ever wrote, one whose insights into the natural order of things carry a special weight when applied to the West.

Not that Thoreau ever saw anything of the land that lay beyond the wild Missouri. Red Wing, Minnesota, was as far west as he ever got, and that only briefly a few months before his final illness. But if he had not seen the West, he somehow knew it in his New England bones, and it spoke to him of something crucial to the spiritual and physical well-being of the human species. When he went out of the house for a walk, he wrote, he instinctively turned in a westerly direction.

The future lies that way to me, and the earth seems more unexhausted and richer on that side. . . . Eastward I go only by force; but westward I go free. . . . I believe that the forest which I see in the western horizon stretches uninterruptedly toward the setting sun. . . . Let me live where I will, on this side is the city, on that the wilderness, and ever I am leaving the city more and more and withdrawing into the wilderness. I should not lay so much stress on this fact if I did not believe that something like this is the prevailing tendency of my countrymen. I must walk toward Oregon, and not toward Europe.

But there was more to this instinct than just a vague cultural yearning to escape Europe's intellectual and psychological bonds, Thoreau believed. The movement was like that of a compass's arrow trembling always in the direction of magnetic north; he turned west, toward the wilderness, he thought, because he was drawn there by a connection that was as irresistible as it was poorly understood. "The West of which I speak," he went on, "is but another name for the Wild; and what I have been preparing to say is that in Wildness is the preservation of the World." The presence of uncorrupted wildness, he believed, enriched both the physical and spiritual needs of the human societies that pocketed and threatened to overwhelm it, and to ignore or destroy that connection would be to diminish not merely the character of human life, but its chances of survival. And, as he had suggested even before "Walking" was published, it might be as necessary as it was desirable to save some of the wild. Why not, he had asked in an 1858 essay, set aside "national preserves" in which "the bear and panther, and some even of the hunter race [by which he meant Indians], may still exist, and not be 'civilized off the face of the earth' . . . ?" In "Walking," he had attempted to set forth some of the compelling reasons for such preservation.

For the most part, Thoreau's posthumous thesis fell upon uncomprehending ears, and it would be more than another two generations before his message would be understood in its deeper meanings. Still, there already was concern about what the engines of progress had so far accomplished in the way of environmental damage, and some worry about consequences. If few were yet talking about the preservation of wilderness as an abstract aesthetic or ethical notion, some people, at least, were beginning to see the links between a healthy, productive natural world and the continuing survival of American civilization. The polymathic George Perkins Marsh — linguist, architect, historian, folklorist, former Vermont fish commissioner, and U.S. ambassador to Italy — for example, pointed back in time to lost civilizations and found in them cautionary tales. In *Man and Nature; or, Physical Geography as Modified by Human Action* (1864), he declared that "man has too long forgotten that the earth was given to him for usufruct alone, not for consumption, still less for profligate waste." The systematic disregard of that responsibility, he said, had made of the ancient Fertile Crescent "an assemblage of bald mountains, barren, treeless hills and Swampy and malarious plains," while the marbled relics of vanished Greek and Roman civilizations were surrounded by "a desolation almost as complete as the moon." And here in the United States, he feared, we were in all ignorance repeating the same mistakes, "breaking up the floor and wainscoting and doors and window frames of our dwelling, for fuel to warm our bodies and seethe our pottage. . . ." He called for stewardship based on the lessons of the past and, like Thoreau, embraced the idea of setting aside a reserve of "American soil . . . as far as possible, in its primitive condition."

President Theodore Roosevelt and John Muir
(fifth and seventh from left) at Yosemite National Park, 1903

portfolio, he was given government support for a survey of the lands of the Colorado Plateau, embracing much of what is now southern Utah and northern Arizona, as well as portions of Nevada, Colorado, and New Mexico.

Powell, for all his experience of wild country, was no Thoreau. He was here to see what resources the plateau might hold and how the land might otherwise be put to human use. But he was a sublimely rational man, and among the things he learned in the nearly seven years of the survey was that because there was so little water available in most of the land west of the Mississippi Valley, the traditions of settlement exemplified by the Homestead Act were simply not appropriate. Land laws would have to be reshaped, he said, with land units drawn larger and water rights guaranteed to all settlers in order to prevent the monopoly of both land and water. The system of rectilinear surveys that had marched across most of the eastern landscape should be scrapped beyond the Mississippi and the boundaries of states and territories be redrawn to conform to geographic, not political, imperatives. All current land laws, including the Homestead Act, should be suspended until surveys were completed to identify all available irrigation sites, as well as whatever timber, mineral, and other resources the land might hold. Above all, if agriculture was to survive here, irrigation was going to be necessary — and even irrigation had its limits.

Marsh's audience was hardly bigger than that enjoyed by Thoreau even in the East. And as Twain's unenlightened celebration of casual destruction suggests, out in the West, where a lot of pottage already was being seethed to a fare-thee-well, virtually no one was listening. True, Congress had given the Yosemite Valley to the state of California to be used as a park "for public use, resort and recreation," and in 1872 would establish 2.2 million acres of the upper Yellowstone River region as "a public park or pleasuring ground for the benefit and enjoyment of the people" — the first national park in our history, if one does not include Hot Springs, Arkansas, set aside forty years earlier for the presumed medicinal value of its waters. But the Yosemite and Yellowstone reserves were made possible largely because these areas were perceived to have no particular economic value. They were the exceptions that tested the rule, and the rule was still unfettered use.

This was no more true at any time than in the years immediately following the Civil War, when the full surge of settlement began to spill across the Mississippi and Missouri rivers, encouraged by such laws as the Homestead Act of 1862 and the plethora of land laws that followed it, each patterned on assumptions derived from experience in the humid and subhumid lands east of the isohyetal line that divides the portion of the country getting twenty inches or more of rain every year from that which gets less — which includes most of the West, once described by historian Walter Prescott Webb as a "semi-desert with a desert heart." This, Major John Wesley Powell announced in 1878, had been a mistake. The one-armed major, who lost his right arm at the battle of Shiloh, was a largely self-trained scientist and explorer who had reached some considerable fame after leading an expedition down the Green and Colorado rivers and through the Grand Canyon in 1869. With that accomplishment as his

Powell's *Report on the Lands of the Arid Region of the United States* flew in the face of expectations and was ignored by the Congress that had authorized it, as was a similar public lands commission report that followed it a couple of years later. By the 1890s, however, tens of thousands of Homestead entries had gone bust, done in by the realities of which Powell had warned, while land and water monopoly by a few plagued most of those homesteaders who had not gone under. A great cry for irrigation to supply "a million forty-acre farms" now arose in the West. Can't be done, Powell said. "Gentlemen," he told an Irrigation Congress in 1893 when it showed interest in the Colorado River as one source of water for those million little farms, "you are piling up a heritage of conflict, for there is not enough water to supply the land!" Never mind: then as now, it was the boomers and the boosters who controlled both the economy and the politics of the West, and the boomers wanted irrigation dams. In 1902, Congress passed the Newlands Act, creating the Reclamation Service (later renamed the Bureau of Reclamation), and put the federal government in the dam-building business. An antimonopoly provision in the law stipulated, among other things, that no one could receive water from any federally constructed reservoir for more than 160 acres and that all recipients must live on the land and work it personally. This provision was systematically ignored by the beneficiaries of federal water and never seriously enforced by the Bureau of Reclamation, whose officials knew perfectly well that Congress would rise up and stifle the attempt, and as one western river after another was relentlessly plugged over the next half century, fewer and fewer nonresident individuals and corporate entities ended up in control of more and more land.

Powell died before witnessing the final perversion of his vision for the rational settlement of the West. The ideas of another rational man of the era had better fortune. He was Gifford Pinchot, trained by Germans in the then embryonic field of silviculture and forest management and as early as the beginning of the 1890s recognized as this country's leading — which is to say, nearly only — professional forester. His work as a "consulting forester" was at first confined to private forests, like those owned by George W. Vanderbilt on his Biltmore estate in North Carolina, but his ambitions were capacious enough to include the entire 200 million acres of federally owned forests in the West (including Alaska).

Most of those lands certainly were in need of stewardship. Many had already been mutilated. Even legitimate timber companies had the habit of abusing such laws as the Timber and Stone Act, clear-cutting their federal grant lands and moving on before establishing final title. In 1866, so much damage already had been done in both Washington and Colorado to cause the surveyors general of the two territories to recommend that the government sell the forests that remained while it still had something left to sell.

The government did not sell the forests, but such depredations did enable a small contingent of reformers in Congress to win passage of the Forest Reserve Clause in 1891, a law that gave the president authority to withdraw federal forest regions from land-claim filings. President Benjamin Harrison withdrew 13 million acres immediately, and at the end of his second term President Grover Cleveland withdrew another 21 million. In 1896, Cleveland also formed a National Forest Commission, a body whose members traveled from state to state in the West to determine the condition of the forests. Among the members was young Gifford Pinchot, and he helped to write much of the language for legislation that grew out of the commission's investigations. The legislation, passed in 1897, was called the Forest Organic Act, and it stipulated that the forest reserves had been established "to improve and protect the forest . . . for the purpose of securing favorable conditions of water flow, and to furnish a continuous supply of timber for the use and necessities of citizens of the United States." A Forestry Division was created in the Department of the Interior, the agency then in control of the public forests. Pinchot was appointed to head the division, and eight years later the Progressive-minded President Theodore Roosevelt persuaded Congress to pass the Forest Transfer Act, which took responsibility for the forests out of Interior and put it in the Department of Agriculture. Shortly thereafter, the forest reserves became "national forests," the Forestry Division of the Interior Department became the U.S. Forest Service of the Department of Agriculture, and Gifford Pinchot was appointed chief forester of the United States. By the time a political conflict with President William Howard Taft caused his resignation in 1910, Pinchot had fashioned the Forest Service into one of the most dedicated federal agencies in government, and the National Forest System had grown to 148 million acres (later withdrawals and purchases would bring the total to what it is today: 191 million acres).

What about wilderness in the equation, then? As a concept separate from utilitarian values, it simply did not exist in the minds of Powell, Pinchot, and most of the other Progressive spirits who were striving so hard to give the concept of stewardship political and legal validity. They were, Pinchot would later say, practicing "conservation," a term he always claimed he had invented and that he unquestionably defined more precisely than anyone before or since: "Conservation means the wise use of the earth and its resources for the lasting good of man. Conservation is the foresighted utilization, preservation, and/or renewal of forests, waters, lands, and minerals for the greatest good of the greatest number for the longest time." The concept's unadorned anthropocentrism limited its philosophical scope; it left no room for the notion that at least some enclaves of the natural world might best be left entirely alone.

Still, it should be remembered that without the accomplishments of utilitarian conservation, particularly with regard to the forests, there might have been precious little left to preserve. One of the preservationists who would have been willing to concede that point — indeed, his lobbying of President Theodore Roosevelt had gone a long way toward helping to establish the U.S. Forest Service and put Pinchot at its head — was John Muir, who had met and learned to respect Pinchot while serving with him on the 1896 National Forest Commission. Muir, born in Scotland, raised in Wisconsin, and seduced at an early age by the mysteries of nature, found himself drawn more and more to an almost visceral love of all Creation for its own pure sake and of wilderness as Creation's most joyful trove of fascination and knowledge. "In God's wildness," he would write in 1890 in a deliberate reprise of Thoreau, "lies the hope of the world — the great fresh unblighted, unredeemed wilderness." With that as yet unstated and inchoate love circulating throughout his wiry Scottish being, he had turned his back on a career in manufacturing in the Midwest in 1867, walking a thousand miles to Florida and, after a season of illness, taking a ship bound for California in 1868.

There, he hired on as a herder of sheep ("hooved locusts," he would come to call them) in the Sierra Nevada and soon encountered the Yosemite Valley. He was dumbstruck with awe. Here was nature at its most sublime, wilderness given its greatest celebration, and except for a ten-year stint running his family's farm in the San Joaquin Valley, Muir would spend most of the rest of his life delving into and writing about the secrets of the valley and of the mountains in which it lay, the Sierra Nevada, the "Range of Light," as he called it. Along the way, Muir became the best-known and most articulate spokesman for the necessity of the wilderness, the unofficial leader of a tiny preservation movement whose philosophy combined romantic literary notions of a lost Eden and the ostensibly noble savages who had inhabited it; elaborate aesthetic traditions of natural beauty; a conviction that American history and character had been largely shaped by the wilderness that had challenged the growth of our civilization, and that wildness should be honored as a kind of artifact of our own past; and, among a few like Muir himself, the almost mystical belief that the essence of the wild was in them, that humans were inextricably bound up in its mysteries and enlarged by its power.

Muir's growing fame and mystical certainties were turned to a practical end when it became clear that the State of California, into whose care the valley had been placed in 1864, was allowing it to be degraded by sundry entrepreneurs. Encouraged by eastern nature enthusiast Robert Underwood Johnson, who offered the pages of his influential *Century* magazine, Muir bent his writing talents and his passions to a campaign to have the valley returned to the federal government and declared a national park. That effort succeeded in 1890, and in 1892 the now prototypical environmental activist joined with Johnson and a few like-minded California friends to form the Sierra Club. The organization's general goal was the preservation of the wild country of the Sierra Nevada, but its specific goal soon became to add the meadows and forests in the ring of high country surrounding the Yosemite Valley to Yosemite National Park. That effort, too, succeeded, in 1905. In the meantime, Muir and the club cheered the creation of Sequoia, General Grant, Mount Rainier, and Crater Lake national parks, and would cheer again as Mesa Verde, Petrified Forest, Grand Canyon, Zion, Olympic, and Glacier were added to the National Park System, either as full-fledged parks or as national monuments, each to be preserved, in the words of the 1916 National Parks Organic Act, "unimpaired, for the enjoyment of future generations."

What with the forests finally in the hands of intelligent management and parks being established as never before in

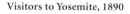

Visitors to Yosemite, 1890

American history, the deliberate preservation of the wild might have seemed well on its way toward becoming an accepted part of the country's land policy in the West. Not quite yet. In 1901, the city of San Francisco petitioned Congress for the right to dam the Tuolumne River in the Hetch Hetchy Valley of the Sierra Nevada. Congressional permission was necessary, for the Hetch Hetchy Valley lay in the heart of Yosemite National Park. The city wanted to eliminate its dependence on a private water monopoly by establishing its own supply, an ambition the civic-minded Progressive movement could be expected to support — and indeed, Gifford Pinchot became one of the project's most vigorous champions. Congress granted its permission, but Muir, who considered the Hetch Hetchy Valley to be even more beautiful than the Yosemite Valley, violently opposed its destruction, however worthwhile the cause. Congress and the dam promoters, he wrote President Roosevelt early in the conflict, were demonstrating "the proud sort of confidence that comes of good sound irrefragable ignorance," and for twelve years one secretary of the interior after another refused to authorize the building of the dam, while Congress never followed its permission with enabling legislation. That stalemate ended in 1913 when Franklin K. Lane, former city attorney for San Francisco and an important supporter of Woodrow Wilson's 1912 presidential campaign, was appointed secretary of the interior. As good a Progressive as Gifford Pinchot and an even better friend of San Francisco, Lane promoted the Hetch Hetchy project and in December 1913 Congress passed enabling legislation.

The conflict had split even the Sierra Club, most of whose members, after all, were Progressive San Franciscans who, while they may have loved Yosemite, wanted to see their citizens freed of the dead hand of monopoly. The conflict saddened the last years of the club's founder, and the final defeat in 1913, most believed, broke his heart. The seventy-five-year-old Muir cursed "this dark damn- dam-damnation," and a little over a year later was dead.

In the Hetch Hetchy conflict, Muir and the nascent wilderness movement had come smack up against the fact that while some landscapes might assuredly be saved from exploitation, the dominant view still held that no piece of land, however beautiful, was better than any apparently superior human use that might be made of it. Wilderness preservation was not yet an idea whose time had come, but it was a good deal closer than a despairing Muir might have imagined. Even as the controversy over Hetch Hetchy developed, preservation sentiment began to simmer in the mind of another wilderness philosopher in the making. His name was Aldo Leopold, a dedicated and practical-minded ranger in Pinchot's utilitarian Forest Service, and in 1909 and 1910 he spent a lot of time packing into the wild country of Apache National Forest in New Mexico, surveying the boundaries of the forest, checking on the condition of the land, monitoring the grazing of sheep and cattle, taking stock of the timber "inventory," and chasing game poachers.

And on at least one occasion, killing wolves. He and a crew had stopped to eat lunch on some rimrock in the Blue Range when they noticed an old female wolf below them, surrounded by cavorting pups. Without a second thought, Leopold and his crew whipped out their rifles and began pumping bullets into the little pack. They then clambered down the rocks to see how well they had done their work. The mother was still alive when they approached her, Leopold remembered many years later:

> We reached the old wolf in time to watch a fierce green fire dying in her eyes. I realized then, and have known ever since, that there was something new to me in those eyes — something known only to her and the mountain. I was young then, and full of trigger-itch; I thought that because fewer wolves meant more deer, that no wolves would mean hunters' paradise. But after seeing the green fire die, I sensed that neither the wolf nor the mountain agreed with such a view.

That moment in the Blue Range was an epiphany that would nourish a growing conviction in Leopold that sooner or later a line would have to be drawn between what human beings merely thought they needed to manage and what they truly needed to save: wilderness. Conviction soon became passion, and just ten years after Muir's death Leopold would persuade his superiors in the Forest Service to establish the 500,000-acre Gila Wilderness, the first federal wilderness area in our history. In another eleven years he would join with forester Robert Marshall to help found the Wilderness Society, and even while a gaggle of New Deal planners transformed the river basins of the Tennessee, the Colorado, the Columbia, and the Missouri with concrete, electricity, and irrigation, and the machinery of World War II and the booming postwar years bloated the urban enclaves that pocked the wide-open spaces of the West, a reborn wilderness movement would forge the protocols of preservation and offer them to the Congress and the people with increasing skill and persuasiveness.

And on September 3, 1964, President Lyndon B. Johnson would take pen in fist and in the Rose Garden of the White House sign the Wilderness Act, which, in order "to secure for the American people of present and future generations the benefits of an enduring resource of wilderness," established "a National Wilderness Preservation System to be composed of federally owned areas designated by Congress as 'wilderness areas' . . . administered for the use and enjoyment of the American people in such manner as will leave them unimpaired for future use and enjoyment as wilderness."

This, then, is what we have done with at least some of the best of the land beyond the wide Missouri in the 130 years since Mark Twain celebrated the fiery spectacle he created on the shores of Lake Tahoe: an idea that had been little more than a suspicion then has now been sanctified by law to provide a more durable legacy than the burned-over lands and sensibilities left by all the years of boom and bust.

It has not been a perfect transformation. While the National Wilderness Preservation System has grown to more than 104 million acres, virtually every acre of each new wilderness area has been placed in the system only after years of agitation among wilderness advocates, reluctant land-managing agencies, presidential administrations whose dedication to the wilderness idea has run the gamut from enthusiastic endorsement (Carter) to open opposition (Reagan), national corporations and small-town entrepreneurs who remain unconvinced that the measure of the West should be taken in anything but greenbacks or their equivalent, and the politicians who service their needs and parrot their philosophies.

Still, it is important to listen to the names as they ring on the tongue, for they reverberate triumphantly with an ineffable westernness: Comanche Peak, Lizard Head, Escudilla, Superstition, Gates of the Mountains, Great Bear, Bosque del Apache, Black Canyon, High Uintas, Indian Heaven, Coyote Mountains, Fishhook, Powderhorn, Jedediah Smith — and hundreds more, talismans carved by law to stand forever as testimony to this nation's commitment to turn its back on much of the history of the West, to pause in the midst of careless enthusiasms fired by transient dreams of wealth just long enough to leave for future generations "an enduring resource of wilderness."

Winter roundup

CHAPTER SEVEN

THE GREAT
DIE-UP

1877–1887

By 1877, the American conquest of the West was nearly complete; for every Indian in the West, there were now nearly forty whites, homesteaders had plowed up the plains that had once nourished the buffalo, and, as the Indian wars drew to a close, the last obstacles to complete American domination seemed to drop away. From now on, there would be less and less room for those who didn't conform to American ways. But then, in one savage winter the newcomers would learn just how "wild" the West could really be — and that no matter how many of its native people were subdued, conquest of the western landscape could never be complete.

In the autumn of 1872, a thirty-year-old Union veteran named Uriah Wesley Oblinger left his rented farm in Onward, Indiana, and set out by wagon with his brother and two brothers-in-law for eastern Nebraska. After years of working for other people, all four hoped to rise in the world by establishing homesteads of their own. They were not alone. "There is a heavy emigration this fall," Uriah wrote home. "The wagons are going in our direction by the hundreds, the people tell us. . . . We meet a good many coming east that have been out and located and are going to move permanent in the spring."

Uriah Oblinger was part of one of the greatest migrations in history. Nearly 2 million people moved out onto the prairies and the plains in the 1870s, lured in large part by the theory that rain followed the plow. The populations of Colorado and Nebraska doubled. South Dakota's, Montana's, and Wyoming's tripled. In 1880, North Dakota had 37,000 non-Indians within its borders; by 1890, there would be five times as many more.

Oblinger's wife, Mattie, and infant daughter, Ella, were to wait until he sent for them, but he wrote to them as often as he could:

Fillmore County, Nebraska. Dear Wife & baby: . . . I can get along well enough through the week, but when Sunday comes I feel a little lonesome without you. . . . I am hunting a home for us where we can enjoy ourselves without . . . being bothered doing as other people says whether it is my interest or not. . . .

Give baby a kiss — yes, 2 of them — and take one yourself.

Well I suppose the first question you would ask me now would be how do you like Nebraska. [Mattie,] . . . you can see just as far as you please here, and almost every foot in sight can be plowed. . . .

The longer I stay here, the better I like it. There are . . . mostly young families, just starting in life the same as we are and I find them very generous, indeed. We will all be poor here together.

[Wife,] you must not get out of heart because people try to discourage you. . . . When they tell you we have nothing to live on, just tell them we can raise larger vegetables here than Indiana can grow to save her neck. . . .

It would take Oblinger a while to find the homestead he wanted — "all the good ones are taken up," he told his wife — and he finally settled on a parcel that had been

claimed by another man who had returned to the East without ever working it. "There is not a square inch of it but is as rich as cream and can be plowed," he wrote, "and I can stand almost anywhere on it and see it all."

Throughout the long winter, Uriah hauled ice and railroad ties in Lincoln at three dollars a day to pay the lawyer who did the paperwork that legitimized his claim and to save up for his little family's passage west.

> [W]hen the bachelors in Nebraska all get women it will fill up rapidly . . . or at least it ought to, for there are a number of men here who have homesteads . . . & nearly all have a "bird" in view as soon as they can get a cage ready. As for me I will build my cage soon and then send for my birds to come. I want you to cook, wash, iron, scrub, bake, make & mend — and do many things too numerous to mention. I'm getting tired of sleeping with bachelors, [even] if they are your brothers.

In May, Uriah Oblinger's nine-month wait finally ended. Mattie and Ella, along with a crate containing all their worldly goods and another filled with live chickens, arrived at the Crete depot aboard the morning train. Uriah took them to their new home, built from blocks of prairie sod cut with his own hands.

Soon, Mattie Oblinger and her daughter, too, were sending letters east.

> May 19th, 1873
> Dear Mother and Father,
> At home in our house and a sod at that! . . . We moved in last Wednesday — Uriah's birthday — It is not quite so convenient as a nice frame, but I would as soon live in it as the cabins I have lived in. . . . I ripped our wagon sheet in two, have it around the sides and have several papers up. . . . It looks real well. . . . The only objection I have is that we have no floor yet. . . .

Uriah and Mattie Oblinger, with their firstborn child, Ella, probably photographed in Indiana before Uriah set out for the West

January 26, 1874

Dear Grandpa,

I have learned my letters and can spell. I will be ready for more books pretty soon. I can spell Ax & Cat & Dog & Girl off the book when Pa or Ma give it out to me. I love to spell so well. I bother Pa and Ma considerable to get them to learn me. . . . I am learning "Twinkle, twinkle, Little Star." Grandma, I know you would learn me if I was at your house.

Lots of love and kisses . . .
Ella Oblinger

July 5th, 1874

[W]e have just come in from the truck patch and found the gophers had about cleaned the peas off all the vines. They hull the peas out and leave the pods so it looks as though they were full yet. [But] our squash vines are full of bloom and watermelon too, and we had cucumbers sliced for breakfast. We brought in beets just now that measured one foot in circumference and potatoes almost as large as a goose egg . . . so . . . just step in this fall and see if we don't have enough of the substantial for any Dutch family to eat!

Mattie

November 24th, 1874

. . . Mr. Macbeth [a neighbor] buried their babe yesterday. Died of the whooping cough. Was about nine months old and they have another child that is very poor with it. . . . They are very poor folks and like the rest of us, see pretty hard times, and it seems hard to see their child taken away, but I suppose it is all for the best as it is the Lord will remove those that He sees fit to remove from earth to Heaven.

Mattie

There was no well — the Oblingers hadn't the money to have one dug — and water had to be hauled from a nearby stream. Cooking pots and tin dishes were washed with sand. Twice, grasshoppers swooped down to devour their crops. A prairie fire burned down the nearest schoolhouse and would have destroyed their home, too, if Uriah hadn't plowed a circle around it to keep the flames from reaching the roof. Still, he refused to be defeated: "What a pleasure it is to work one's own farm," he wrote, "for you can feel that it is yours and not for someone else. I would rather live as we do than have to rent and have someone bossing us as we used to do."

August 8th, 1876

. . . Mother, you said in your letter for us to keep a stiff upper lip. . . . Well, that is no trouble for us any more, for we have had to keep a stiff upper lip so much since we have been here that they have about grown stiff. . . . It has kept us scraping and gathering pretty close to keep agoing, but we have managed so far not to go in debt one cent this summer. Uriah is going to town tomorrow afternoon and I want to send a little butter and potatoes and corn and pickles to get some groceries. Credit is pretty hard for anyone to get in Sutton and we have learned he is a poor customer to deal with and the least we have to do with him

The Chrisman sisters of Custer County, Nebraska, four daughters of a wealthy and calculating rancher who built each of them three small shacks like this one in which they took turns living. By so doing he was able to claim title simultaneously to a dozen 160-acre homesteads.

that much better off we are. We will have to get some calico for the girls' dresses or we will have to grease and go naked.

Mattie

September 10, 1876

. . . I suppose you would like to know if we have been grasshoppered again. They were here several days pretty thick and injured the corn considerable. Some fields they stripped the blades all off and other pieces stripped partly. They nibbled the end off most all the ears and ate off all the silks so it will not fill out. Nebraska would have had a splendid crop if the grasshoppers had stayed away a while.

Mattie

Things did not get easier for the Oblingers — or their fellow homesteaders. The series of unusually heavy rains that had fed the notion that rain followed the plow eventually ended. Many places on the High Plains emptied almost as fast as they had filled with farmers. It was becoming clear that the generous-sounding 160 acres of

Solomon D. Butcher, shown above in front of the crumbling dugout in which he rode out his first Nebraska winter, came west to Custer County from Virginia in 1880. He abandoned homesteading after only two weeks, attended medical school but never got a degree, and opened a post office and photographer's studio in the brand-new town of Walworth only to watch the community die as drought drove farmers from the land. Then, he hit upon the scheme that kept him and his family fed and much later made him one of the West's best-remembered photographers: chronicling the history of his county and selling prints of his pictures to its citizens . His photographs — some published here for the first time— constitute an unrivaled record of the fierce odds homesteaders faced and the fierce pride they took in what they'd done.

The family of Ike Bentley (second from right), near Sargent in Custer County, Nebraska, 1887. Bentley's father (third from left) — remembered in Solomon Butcher's records only as "Grandpa Bentley" — had seen a lot of American history: long before heading west, he had fought in the War of 1812.

Mr. and Mrs. L. N. Beager
exchange wedding
vows on the open prairie
north of West Union,
August 13, 1889.

The family of Orson
Cooley, near Coolytown
Post Office, 1887. Mrs.
Cooley had been married
before back in Wisconsin,
lost her husband after
bearing him two sons, and
then wrote to a Nebraska
newspaper asking if a
widow could make a living
on the prairie. Mr. Cooley,
himself a widower, began
writing to her, they were
eventually married, and
she brought her boys
west to live. The Cooleys'
own child, perched here
on Father's lap, did not
survive infancy, but the
boys grew up to inherit
their stepfather's farm.

The home of the Reverend and Mrs. E. Eubank (seated), Clear Creek, 1888. He was the first minister in Custer County, and she was the first schoolteacher.

John Spellmeyer of Sumner offered a special sort of testimony to the fertility of Nebraska. He and his wife (third from left) had sixteen children, including the three sets of twins on the porch, the last of which came into the world at about the same time the family cow produced triplets.

In March, 1884 . . . I took a pre-emption on Spring Creek. I'll never forget that first night out there. After supper I went outdoors and stayed so long that my sister came out to look for me. She found me crying and I told her that it was the worst-looking country I had ever seen and that we had little enough in Iowa but this was worse. She said it wasn't bad, and I would soon get used to it. That was the only time I ever cried in Custer County.

Mrs. Joanna Hickenbottom Jensen

Prairie style: In 1887, the one-room sod structure (above) in Cummings Park served as schoolhouse for twenty-eight pupils of every age and size, while the comparatively elegant soddy (left) in the southwestern section of the county boasted plastered and whitewashed recesses for the doors and windows and a dinner bell attached to the windmill that on a clear day could be heard for miles.

Not everyone in Custer County was comfortable with the pioneer life. When Solomon Butcher visited the David Hilton homestead (far left) south of Weissert in 1887, Mrs. Hilton insisted on having the pump organ that was her most prized possession pulled out into the yard so that no one back East would see that she and her husband were still living in a sod house.

Success stories: G. W. Farmer of Mena grew 6,000 bushels of corn in 1902, according to Butcher's notes: "No state in the Union but Nebraska has such cribs of corn."

Nothing came easy in Custer County. A veteran farmer named Swain Finch demonstrated how he used a branch to beat the grasshoppers off his crops — and then made sure Butcher drew a suitably daunting swarm of insects onto the glass photographic plate before printing his picture.

A farmer named Gillette and his family (left), dressed in their best clothes, pretend to be on their way way to harvest their wheat, 1886.

John J. Downey (standing at center in the photograph at right) came to Dale Valley in Custer County in 1887 with two mules and twelve dollars. He built his family a sod house, went to work, and seventeen years later was a prosperous farmer and stock-raiser and the owner of the handsome house shown above.

FREE GROUND

In 1877, the last federal troops were withdrawn from the South, Reconstruction collapsed, and new state laws began to restrict the rights of freed slaves. Blacks found themselves once again under the power of their former masters. Black colonization committees were formed all over the South, seeking some means of escape. Some favored emigrating to the African republic of Liberia, or northward into Canada.

To others, the open spaces of the West seemed to offer more immediate hope. Benjamin "Pap" Singleton was an ex-slave from Tennessee who believed himself appointed by God to rescue his people. He had fled from his masters more than a dozen times during slavery, and ran a station on the Underground Railroad. But he had finally become convinced that there was no future for African-Americans unless they left the South and formed their own independent communities in the West. He flooded the South with handbills.

Those who answered his call called themselves "Exodusters" because, like the Old Testament Hebrews, they believed their salvation lay in reaching a promised land. Soon, blacks were scattered all across Kansas, and their hopeful letters home were being read aloud in black churches.

Then, in the spring of 1879, a rumor raced through African-American communities throughout the Deep South. The federal government had set aside all of Kansas for former slaves, the story went, and would provide every black family that could get there with free land and five hundred dollars. It wasn't true, but it was enough to convince some 6,000 people to start west. Some went by riverboat as far as St. Louis. Others, too poor to pay their passage, walked the whole way.

By 1880, more than 15,000 African-Americans had migrated to Kansas, most of them living on farms or in small communities like Juniper Town, Dunlap, and Rattlebone Hollow. Nicodemus, in western Kansas, was the largest settlement, home to 700 settlers from Kentucky. Some whites welcomed the newcomers. Others shunned them, or tried to drive them away. Many Exodusters returned to the South, defeated by the harsh climate of the Plains. But most stayed, or tried again still farther west.

"When I landed on the soil [of Kansas]," one man named John Solomon Lewis remembered, "I looked on the ground and I says, 'This is free ground.' Then I looked on the heavens and I says, 'Them is free and beautiful heavens.' Then I looked within my heart and I says to myself, 'I wonder why I was never free before?' I said, 'Let us hold a little prayer meeting . . . on the river bank.' It was raining but the drops fell from heaven on a free family, and the meeting was just as good as sunshine. We was thankful to God and we prayed for those who could not come.

"I asked my wife did she know the ground she stands on. She said, 'No.'

"I said, 'It is free ground,' and she cried for joy."

Benjamin "Pap" Singleton (below) and some of the Exodusters who answered his call, waiting for a steamboat to carry them westward

The family of Jerry Shores (seated, second from right), a former slave who made his home near Westerville in Custer County, 1887. Not all black newcomers were met with hostility: the Shores family, one white woman who lived nearby remembered, "were as fine neighbors as any one would want."

free land for which the homesteaders had come west was insufficient on the semi-arid plains.

The Oblingers held on, had two more daughters, Stella and Maggie. By early 1880, Mattie was about to give birth to still another baby.

January 11, 1880

. . . Uriah is repairing the minutes of the last Literary Society which was held last Saturday night. They have some big times debating. The question for next Saturday night is "Resolved that Intemperance causes more sorrow than war." . . . I go once in a while to hear them spout.

We had rather a nice time [over the holidays]. . . . We had a Christmas tree at the schoolhouse. It was something new for this neighborhood. Every thing went off nice and agreeable. We had a Norway spruce evergreen tree. It looked nice filled with presents for the little ones and some for the old ones. Uriah played Santa Claus but the little ones most all knew him. . . .

Mattie

January 12th, 1880

Dear Grandpa and Grandma: I must tell you how I spent Christmas. We all went to a Christmas tree on Christmas eve and each of us girls got a new red oil calico dress . . . and a doll and Uncle Giles put a book on the tree for Stella and me and each one of us girls got a string with candy and raisins on it.

From your grandchild,
Ella Oblinger

February 27th, 1880. The Lord called for [my] Sister Mattie this evening at 4:15 o'clock . . . and she is now resting with the angels in Heaven.

She was confined Tuesday evening about 4 o'clock and about 8 o'clock she took a fit very sudden and never spoke after the first one. The doctors were compelled to perform a surgical operation by relieving her of the child. The child is also dead and will be buried with her some time Sunday.

Uriah said he could not stand to write now. I don't know what he will do yet. It's left him and his three little girls in a sad condition — without a Mother.

Giles S. Thomas

Dear Father and Mother: I try to bear the trouble cheerfully, though the task is hard at times. . . . This season has not been a success with me in farming. . . . Crops and prices are so poor that it is making times pretty close here. . . . I hardly know how to manage. . . .

Uriah did everything he could think of to hold on to his farm and what was left of his family. He rented out his land, hired himself out to plow other people's fields, but nothing worked. Finally, he abandoned his homestead and moved back east, to Minnesota, where his family was now living. There, he remarried and had three more daughters, before returning to the Plains to start over in Nebraska, then Kansas, then Nebraska again, where he rented a parcel of land not far from his first homestead and finally broke his health trying once more to make a go of it. He spent the last few months of his life being cared for by his daughter, Ella, the same girl, now grown, he had once been so eager to bring out to Nebraska with her mother.

A HARD TIME I HAVE

By the spring of 1881, the Indians who had occupied the lands that Americans and Europeans were now settling so fast had all but lost their struggle to remain free. The Lakota and Cheyenne bands that had wiped out Custer and his command were now living at or near the agencies. Only Sitting Bull and fewer than two hundred of his followers, many of them members of his own family, remained defiant, in Canada. But the Canadian tribes had wearied of sharing their depleted hunting grounds with Sitting Bull's band, and Canadian officials had come to see his presence as a political embarrassment. "We began to feel homesick for our own country where we used to be happy," a young Lakota named Black Elk recalled. "The old people talked much about it and the good old days before the trouble came. Sometimes I felt like crying when they did that."

Finally, on July 19, 1881, having been promised a full pardon, Sitting Bull led a handful of his hungry people south across the border to Fort Buford and gave up. "I

Mattie Oblinger with Ella (right) and Maggie

A Nebraska settler named Harvey Andrews and his wife tend the grave of their infant daughter, Victoria, carefully planted with pine seedlings and protected by a picket fence, 1887.

The life my people want is a life of freedom. I have seen nothing that a white man has, houses or railways or clothing or food, that is as good as the right to move in the open country, and live in our fashion.

Sitting Bull

Lakota who had surrendered to the army going aboard the steamboat that would take them to the Standing Rock agency in the spring of 1881

surrender this rifle to you through my young son," he told the commanding officer, "whom I now desire to teach in this manner that he has become a friend of the Americans. I wish him to learn the habits of the whites and to be educated as their sons are educated. I wish it to be remembered that I was the last man of my tribe to surrender my rifle. This boy has given it to you, and he now wants to know how he is going to make a living."

Sitting Bull still wanted the right to cross back and forth into Canada at will, to have a reservation of his own on the Little Missouri, near the Black Hills, and to hunt wherever he wished. But the Lakota were now surrounded by newcomers — immigrants from Russia, Germany, Denmark, Sweden, as well as the eastern states — who were building homes on what had once been Lakota lands. Whites now filled the Black Hills; cattle grazed on their foothills.

The soldiers granted none of Sitting Bull's requests. They ordered him to go to the Standing Rock reservation hundreds of miles to the east, instead, and to live there as

Lakota receiving government rations

his people lived. There, he was reunited with his daughter, and wept to see again those who had fought alongside him at the Little Bighorn. But he also gave an interview to a reporter in which he breathed some of the old defiance.

> When I came in I did not surrender. I want the government to let me occupy the Little Missouri Country. There is plenty of game there. I want to keep my ponies. I can't hunt without ponies. I want no restraint. I will keep on the reservation, but want to go where I please. I don't want a white man over me. I don't want an agent.

The army was jittery that Sitting Bull might lead another uprising. Soldiers herded him and 167 followers back onto the steamboat at bayonet point, and steamed farther down the river to Fort Randall, where they were to be kept indefinitely as prisoners of war. The army had already broken its promises to him. There, the Lakota were made to pitch their teepees and wait. He asked to be allowed to go to Washington and see the Great Father, demanded to know how long he would have to stay apart from his people, and received no satisfactory answer to either request. To pass the long hours, Sitting Bull painted scenes from his own life as gifts for individual soldiers who had been kind to him, and charged curiosity-seekers for his autograph, one dollar for ladies, five for men. He and his small band spent twenty months in lonely exile at Fort Randall before the army felt secure enough to permit them to return to Standing Rock and start new lives as wards of the government.

Sitting Bull came back to his people on May 10, 1883 — and entered a world unlike any he had ever known. The power of the chiefs had largely been broken. Their fate was now in the hands of an Indian agent, James McLaughlin, who was himself married to a half-Lakota woman but determined to transform the lives of her people.

Antagonists: Sitting Bull (above, at center) and James McLaughlin (the bearded civilian at the table) were at loggerheads almost from the moment the holy man arrived at Standing Rock. Each struck the other as imperious and unyielding. Below, the two men awkwardly flank the rock formation resembling an Indian woman with a child on her back that gave the agency its name. Sitting Bull had opposed moving it to this new site near McLaughlin's headquarters; the agent had done it anyway, and then held a dedication ceremony.

He considered Sitting Bull vain and boastful and was wary of having him under his charge. The leader who whites believed had conquered Custer was to be treated merely as one more mouth to be fed, McLaughlin said; just one more body to be clothed.

The Lakota lived in log cabins now, as well as teepees, and they were expected to farm. Even Sitting Bull eventually found himself at work, hoe in hand.

When a delegation of senators visited the agency in August of 1883, with a plan for opening part of the reservation to white settlement, Sitting Bull protested bitterly.

"Do you know who I am?" he demanded of the commissioners. "I want to tell you that if the Great Spirit has chosen any one to be the chief of this country, it is myself."

The senators had no patience with him. "You were not appointed by the Great Spirit," John Logan of Illinois replied. "Appointments are not made that way . . . you have no following, no power, no control, and no right to any control. . . . If it were not for the Government you would be freezing and starving today in the mountains."

Just across the Grand River from his cabin, Sitting Bull could see the spot where he had been born into an entirely different world. To fill the empty hours, he composed his own song. "A warrior I have been," he sang. "Now it is all over. A hard time I have."

BARBARIANS

In October of 1871, an eager and ambitious young Chinese named Chung Sun arrived in California. He carried six hundred dollars with him, and dreamed of starting a tea plantation in southern California. But in Los Angeles he found himself caught up in a riot. It started as a quarrel between two Chinese factions over a woman, but quickly turned into an armed struggle between the small Chinese community and the rest of the city. "For two days," a reporter wrote,

> that portion of the city cursed by the presence of the Mongols was in a state of war. . . . Chinatown, wholly surrounded, was in a state of siege. Mounted men came galloping from the country — the *vaquero* was in his glory, and the cry was *"Carajo la Chino!"* . . . A young Israelite, heavy-framed and coarse-featured, and a German known as "Dutch Charley" were prominently active and cruel. "Crazy" Johnson seemed to represent all Ireland; while Jacques, a Frenchman, shirtless and hatless and armed with a cleaver . . . was the fire-fiend of the occasion — time and again Chinatown was ablaze — and Jacques with his cleaver was always found pictured in the glare.

Before it was over, at least twenty-three Chinese immigrants had been hanged or stabbed or dragged or shot to death, and Chung Sun had been beaten and robbed of his savings.

By the time of his arrival, more than 300,000 Chinese had entered the country, the vast majority of them west of the Mississippi. They had begun coming to California during the gold rush of 1849, and now could be found in every corner of the West. They dug irrigation ditches and planted vineyards in Sonoma, operated laundries and restaurants, established fishing fleets up and down the coast.

But in 1877, depression gripped the country. In the East, there were strikes, lockouts, riots that left scores dead, factories and rail yards demolished. Western workmen joined the protests, too, denouncing the railroads and the wealthy men who owned them. But they also came to believe they had

Damage done by an anti-Chinese riot in Seattle, Washington

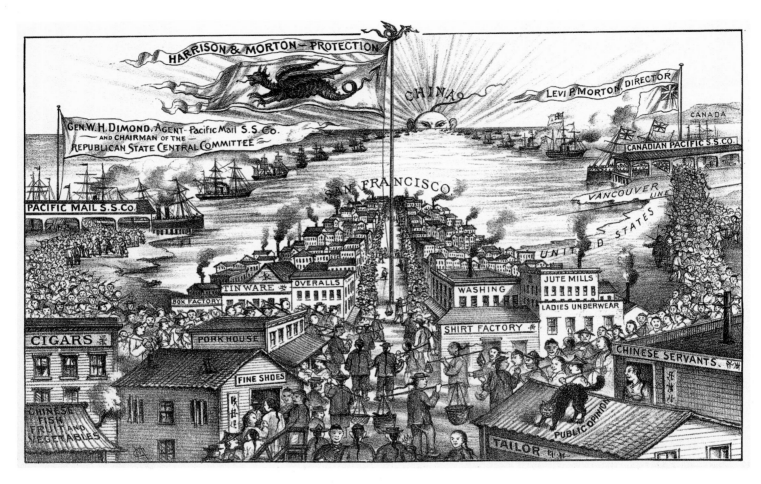

A Democratic cartoonist accuses the Republicans of favoring an all-Chinese California, 1889.

another enemy — the Chinese with whom they were forced to compete for what little work there was.

The San Francisco workers' best-known spokesman was an Irish-born merchant sailor named Denis Kearney, a failure at the cartage business, who blamed what he called "the interests" for all his troubles. He helped found the Workingmen's Party and hoped to use anti-Chinese feeling to win political power. "We intend to try and vote the Chinaman out, to frighten him out, and if this won't do, to kill him out," he boasted, "and when the blow comes we won't leave a fragment for the thieves to pick up. . . . The heathen slaves must leave this coast, if it costs 10,000 lives. . . ."

Kearney was eventually jailed — and later abandoned politics to sell real estate. His party fell apart, but the anti-Chinese feeling it had helped foster only intensified. Anti-Chinese riots erupted throughout the West. In Rock Springs, Wyoming, whites murdered twenty-eight Chinese, and drove out hundreds more. In Tacoma, state militiamen had to be called in to restore order. The Chinese in Seattle were rounded up, pushed onto boats, and forced out to sea.

The Los Angeles riot had left Chung Sun penniless. He made his way north to the little town of Watsonville, where he managed to find a job digging ditches and laying a gas line for $1.50 a day.

> I left the loved and ever-venerated land of my nativity to seek [in the United States] that freedom and security which I could never hope to realize in my own. . . . I hope you will pardon my expressing a painful disappointment. The

ill treatment of [my] own countrymen may perhaps be excused on the grounds of race, color, language, and religion, but such prejudice can only prevail among the ignorant. . . . [B]eing a man of education and culture I am capable of other work than digging in the streets, but my philosophy teaches me, any useful work is more honorable than idleness. I shall therefore, with patience, continue to dig with an abiding hope for something better. . . .

But when the ditch was finished, Chung Sun could not find another job. No one would hire him. And in 1882, western politicians and labor unions persuaded Congress to pass the Chinese Exclusion Act.

The year before the law was enacted, nearly 40,000 Chinese entered the United States. The next year, just 23 were allowed in.

Even the 1882 act failed to placate anti-Chinese sentiment in the West. "This Oriental octopus [of coolieism] . . . this herculean of all gigantic evils . . . from the shores of Asia . . . embraces within it explosives more deadly than dynamite . . ." said Senator John H. Mitchell of Oregon.

[It] depresses labor, corrupts morals, debases youth, makes merchandise of personal freedom and female virtue, mocks at justice, defies law, dwarfs enterprise, obstructs development, chains personal liberty, destroys personal freedom, menaces the public peace, invades domestic tranquility, endangers the public welfare, converts whole sections of beautiful American cities . . . into squalid, wretched, crime-smitten, and leperous spotted habitations of the lowest and most debased classes of the pagan mongol. . . .

More discriminatory statutes followed, barring Chinese laborers from entering the country, forbidding even the thousands who had gone home on visits the right to return, requiring longtime Chinese residents to carry certificates of eligibility to remain in the United States.

Meanwhile, Chung Sun moved on to San Francisco, then set sail for home. But before he left he wrote up his stay for a California newspaper:

[Americans] have no purely national settlement in anything. . . . [T]here is no uniform mode of dress or manner of living; no system, regularity or order . . . but all is a jumble of confusion and a labyrinth of contradictions. . . . [I]n civility, complaisance, and polite manners [Americans] are wholly wanting and are very properly styled barbarians.

THE DUDE

At two in the morning on September 8, 1883, a twenty-four-year-old New York assemblyman stepped down from the train at the Little Missouri River in the heart of Dakota Territory. His name was Theodore Roosevelt and he had already earned a reputation for himself back East as a noisy but energetic reformer. Now, he had come west to shoot a buffalo before the species vanished — and to build himself up after a bout of cholera.

He seemed the quintessential dude — shrill, nearsighted, Harvard-educated, wheezing with asthma, and insistent upon being called "Mr. Roosevelt." Still, despite day after day of rain so cold that even his guide urged him to abandon the chase, he

[Westerners] value good government and have a remarkable faculty for organizing some kind of government, but they are tolerant of lawlessness which does not directly attack their own interests. Horse-stealing and insults to women are the two unpardonable offenses; all others are often suffered to go unpunished. . . . [The leading newspaper of a considerable western city], commenting on one of the train robberies that had been frequent in the state, observed that so long as the brigands had confined themselves to robbing the railway companies and the express companies of property for whose loss the companies must answer, no one had greatly cared, seeing that these companies themselves robbed the public; but now that private citizens seemed in danger of losing their personal baggage and money . . . something ought to be done.

James Bryce

Frank and Jesse James with tools of their trade, shortly after the Civil War

On January 31, 1874, the Iron Mountain Express rolled into the tiny Missouri hamlet of Gads Hill, where a signal flag at the station brought the train to a halt. Expecting to meet a new passenger, the conductor stepped down — only to be greeted by five men holding cocked pistols and wearing white sheets.

The bandits took over the train, emptied its safe of two thousand dollars, and then demanded money and jewelry from the passengers. They announced theatrically that the poor would be exempt. They would steal only from those who didn't have the calluses of a workingman. But in the end, no one's wallet was spared. Before riding away, one of the robbers handed the conductor a note and asked that it be given to the newspapers. It was a press release, written in advance, with all the details of the robbery filled in, except for a blank space for the amount of money stolen:

THE MOST DARING ROBBERY
ON RECORD.
The southbound train on the Iron Mountain railroad was boarded here this evening by five heavily armed men and robbed of __ dollars. The robbers arrived at the station a few minutes before the arrival of the train and arrested the station agent and put him under guard, then threw the train on the switch. The robbers were all large men, none of them under six feet tall. They were all masked and started in a southerly direction after they had robbed the express. They were all mounted on fine, blooded horses. There is a hell of an excitement in this part of the country.

The James-Younger gang had struck again.

Frank and Jesse James and the four Younger brothers were all products of the sectional violence that had plagued the Kansas-Missouri border since the 1850s. They had themselves ridden with guerrilla bands during the Civil War, more interested in looting and killing civilians than in fighting Union forces, and their families had felt the full brunt of the Union forces who turned western Missouri into the "Burnt District." Kansas raiders murdered the Youngers' father and burned their home. Federal militia jailed the James boys' mother for spying.

Frank James, who had taken part in William Quantrill's butchery of unarmed men at Lawrence, Kansas, was tall, big boned, and quiet. He enjoyed reading Shakespeare and the essays of Francis Bacon. Because of his book learning, some people suspected he was the gang's strategist.

But it was Frank's younger brother who became the gang's best-known member. He was vain about his looks, rarely drank or smoked, never swore in the presence of women, and was devoted to his mother. He had become a Confederate guerrilla at seventeen, was wounded three times, and in one skirmish personally killed the Union commander — some said by slitting his throat. Jesse James, said his leader, Bloody Bill Anderson, "is the keenest . . . fighter in the command."

After the war, other Confederates had gone home and back to work. The James and Younger brothers kept right on stealing and killing — and used the war's bitter, lingering passions as their excuse. They robbed banks and trains on a regular basis, killed cashiers, engineers, innocent bystanders — then hid out among their Missouri neighbors, who considered railroads and banks hated symbols of northern oppression.

The gang had an influential public defender — John Newman Edwards, a prominent Missouri editor and unreconstructed Confederate in whose florid reports the outlaws were always victims of Yankee mistreatment, not ruthless outlaws but modern Robin Hoods. Theirs, he wrote, was the "Chivalry of Crime."

Having given up hope that local authorities could stop the gang, an association of bankers turned to the nation's most celebrated private investigator, Allan Pinkerton, founder of Pinkerton's National Detective Agency, whose slogan was "We never sleep."

But in the James gang and their protective neighbors, the Pinkertons more than met their match. When one detective disguised himself as an itinerant farmhand and applied for work on the James farm, he was found on the roadside the next

Pinkerton agents acted as Union spies during the Civil War, and afterward helped break up labor unions and chased embezzlers and robbers for the railroads. The term "private eye" was inspired by their symbol.

morning, shot in the head and chest. A few days later, two more Pinkerton agents were gunned down in a shootout that also killed John Younger.

Then, just as local public opinion was beginning to turn against the gang, the Pinkertons reversed it once again. On the night of January 26, 1875, they quietly surrounded the James home in Kearney, Missouri. Believing Frank and Jesse were inside, they tossed a canister through a window — only a flare, the Pinkertons later claimed; a grenade, according to the Jameses. "I was blown against the ceiling and heard a tremendous report," their stepfather said. "Outside I heard several hurrahs, then the groans of my little boy and the agonized cries of my wife, who told me her right arm was blown to pieces." Archie Peyton Samuel, Frank and Jesse's nine-year-old half-brother, was dead. Their mother's arm, shattered by the explosion, had to be amputated later that night.

Newspapers across the nation condemned the Pinkertons for the bombing. The Missouri legislature called for an official investigation and nearly passed a bill giving the James and Younger brothers amnesty. A local grand jury even indicted Allan Pinkerton for murder, though he was never arrested or formally charged.

A few months later, a neighboring farmer suspected of having harbored a Pinkerton man before the raid was shot down at his doorstep. Others were warned that they would share his fate if they cooperated with lawmen.

Around the same time, the first book appeared devoted entirely to the exploits of the James and Younger gang. There would be many more in the years to come.

But by the early 1880s, the gang's fortunes started to sour. An attempted bank robbery in Northfield, Minnesota, ended in disaster when angry townspeople opened fire on the bandits. Three gang members were killed. The three Younger brothers — Cole, Jim, and Bob, all severely wounded — were captured, tried, and sentenced to life imprisonment.

Frank and Jesse James escaped. Then, in the summer of 1881, two trains were robbed in western Missouri. Two men were killed, and two more brutally beaten. For Missouri's governor, Thomas Crittenden, it was the last straw. He spread the word that any gang member who surrendered and turned witness against the brothers would be given clemency. And he offered ten thousand dollars for Frank or Jesse James — dead or alive.

Robert Ford was a new recruit to the gang and had never taken part in a robbery, although his older brother, Charley, had helped hold up a train. On April 3, 1882, the Ford brothers came to Jesse's house in St. Joseph, Missouri, where he was living with his wife and two children under the assumed name of Thomas Howard.

"Between eight and nine o'clock this morning while the three of us were in a room in Jesse's house," Robert Ford would tell a lawman that evening, "Jesse pulled off his coat and also his pistols, two of which he constantly wore, and then got up onto a chair for the purpose of brushing dust off a picture. While Jesse was thus engaged, Charley winked at me, so I knew he meant for me to shoot. So, as quickly as possible, I drew my pistol and aiming at Jesse's head, which was not more than four feet from the muzzle of my weapon, I fired, and Jesse tumbled headlong from the chair on which he was standing and fell on his face. . . ."

The Fords rushed from the house, telegraphed Governor Crittenden that they had killed Jesse James, and turned themselves over to the police. Two weeks later, they pleaded guilty to murder, were sentenced to hang, and were immediately pardoned by the governor. But the Fords never got to enjoy their reward money. Songs glorified Jesse and mocked them as cowards. Former friends shunned them. Charley Ford became despondent and committed suicide. Bob Ford went on tour with a stage show, reenacting the shooting every evening. The big crowds that turned out to see him do it booed as often as they cheered. He began to drink heavily, wandered the West, finally settled down in the mining town of Creede, Colorado, opened a tent saloon, and was shot to death there after a quarrel.

Zerelda James Samuel, Jesse's fiercely protective mother, insisted that his body be buried in the yard at the family home. For twenty-five cents, visitors were allowed to see the tombstone and listen to Mrs. Samuel tell stories glorifying her son and condemning the Fords. For an extra quarter, she would give the tourists a pebble from the grave site, which she kept restocked from a nearby streambed.

Six months after Jesse James's death, his older brother, Frank, turned himself in. "I have known no home," he said. "I have slept in all sorts of places — here today — there tomorrow. . . . I am tired of this life of taut nerves, of night-riding and day-hiding, of constant listening for footfalls, cracking twigs and rustling leaves and creaking doors; tired of seeing Judas on the face of every friend I know — and God knows I have none to spare — tired of the saddle, the revolver and the cartridge belt. . . . I want to see if there is not some way out of it." A sympathetic Missouri jury refused to convict him.

The James-Younger gang lived on in people's imaginations. Rumors spread that Bob Ford had somehow shot someone else, that Jesse James was still alive. In less than a year, a neighboring farmer reported seeing Jesse James in the flesh, and Jesse's son would later count twenty-six imposters. Even while Frank James was alive, a farm worker in Washington claimed to be the real Frank James.

Dime novels about the James gang proliferated, too — and placed them in the most improbable locales: *Jesse James Among the Mormons, Jesse James in New York, Jesse James at Coney Island*. Critics blamed the books for the rising rate of juvenile crime in eastern cities, and for a time the postmaster general refused to deliver them.

For his part, Frank James never again turned to crime. He worked as a race starter at county fairs, as a shoe salesman, a livestock importer, a doorman at a burlesque house, even a department store detective. He eventually returned to the James family farm and carried on his mother's tradition of leading tours for a price. As he grew older, he developed a fear that his corpse would one day be disturbed by grave robbers and left instructions that he was to be cremated and his ashes kept out of the reach of any thief — in a bank vault.

JOHN WESLEY HARDIN

The son of a Methodist minister who named him for the founder of his faith, John Wesley Hardin was bright and personable and articulate enough to have succeeded in the law or politics. Instead, he became the most feared gunfighter in Texas. In the showy autobiography he was working on when he died, he claimed to have killed forty-four men, and he may actually have killed twenty — including one man, shot through the wall of his room at the American Hotel in Abilene, Kansas, whose only of-fense had been to disturb Hardin's sleep. "They tell lots of lies about me," he said. "They say I killed six or seven men for snoring. Well, it ain't true. I only killed one man for snoring." He had accounted for four men — an ex-slave and three federal troopers sent to arrest him for his murder — before he was sixteen, and would spend ten years on the run from federal authorities, hiding out among relatives scattered across central Texas, before he was finally arrested and sent to jail in 1874 for killing a deputy sheriff. He opened a law office in El Paso after he got out of prison, but was rarely sober enough to practice, and was eventually shot from behind by a policeman whose life he had threatened.

BLACK BART

Charles Boles (below) had lived a full life as a farmer, Union soldier, and prospector before he took to robbing Wells, Fargo stagecoaches in California in 1879. Before he was through, he would hold up twenty-eight stages, wearing a black hood and leaving behind handwritten verse signed "Black Bart" to mock his pursuers.

> Here I lay me down to sleep
> To wait the coming 'morrow.
> Perhaps success, perhaps defeat,
> And ever lasting sorrow.
> But come what may I'll try it on,
> My condition can't be worse,
> If there's money in that box,
> 'Tis money in my purse. . . .

He might have continued stealing and versifying for years had he not dropped a hand-kerchief, which a shrewd San Francisco detective traced to him by its Chinese laundry mark.

BELLE STARR

Myra Belle Shirley, a farmer's daughter from Scyene, Texas, could not seem to get enough of outlaws or the outlaw life. She was first the mistress of Cole Younger, then of another bank robber, Jim Reed. After he was shot and killed, she helped run a horse- and cattle-stealing ring with a Cherokee named Blue Duck (shown here), then married another Cherokee rustler, Sam Starr, and became notorious as Belle Starr, "the Bandit Queen." She served six months in jail with her hus-band, and after he was killed in a barroom brawl in 1886, took up with still another Indian outlaw named Jim Tully. Three years later, an unknown gunman shot her from her horse.

THE DALTONS

Hubris: The three Dalton brothers were Coffeyville, Kansas, boys who decided in 1892 to set a new record by simultaneously robbing two banks in their own hometown. It was not a good idea. Townspeople recognized them and opened fire: four local citizens were killed in the crossfire, but so were two of the Daltons — Bob and Grat, whose corpses are being held up here for the photographer — and the third was badly wounded and spent fifteen years in prison.

BILLY THE KID

He was remembered as Billy the Kid, but his real name was Henry McCarty, and he was born in a New York slum, the son of a widowed Irish laundress who moved to New Mexico to try to cure the tuberculosis that quickly killed her. Small and slight, her orphaned son began his life of crime at fifteen, pilfering a tub of butter from a rancher and clothes from a Chinese laundryman; graduated to stealing horses and rustling cattle; broke out of three jails; and in 1877 shot and killed his first man, a bullying blacksmith who had dared make fun of his girlish looks.

A few weeks later, he signed on with one of two rival armies of gunmen about to go to war over just who in Lincoln County should profit from supplying beef and other provisions to army posts and Indian reservations. It was a bloody business that lasted for nearly two years. McCarty — now calling himself William H. Bonney — played a prominent part in it. And his faction lost.

Legend had him killing twenty-one men before his twenty-first birthday. He seems actually to have killed just four, but when the fighting finally ended and Governor Lew Wallace offered a general amnesty to all who had taken part, Billy was exempted from it because a sheriff had been among his victims. He tried to win himself a pardon by turning in old friends for new crimes committed since the shaky peace was established — but then was told he would have to stand trial for murder, anyway.

Between crimes, Billy was evidently amiable and outgoing. "You appear to take it easy," a reporter told him once, as he smiled for the crowd that had come out to see him momentarily locked up.

"Yes," the Kid answered. "What's the use of looking on the gloomy side of everything? The laugh's on me this time." A sympathetic lawman let him get away again, and he returned to his old profession — cattle rustling.

Then, local ranchers, tired of losing cattle to him, helped elect a local bartender named Pat Garrett sheriff (below), with orders to hunt him down. On the night of July 13, 1881, Garrett cornered him in the darkened bedroom of a ranch where he'd taken refuge and shot him dead. He was just twenty-one.

Within a year there were eight novels about him in the bookstores, plus a spurious but bestselling biography written by the man who killed him.

found and shot his buffalo. And he fell in love with the Dakota Badlands — and with the prospect of quick riches its grassy slopes seemed to offer virtually free of charge. Before he returned home that fall, Theodore Roosevelt had invested nearly $14,000 in a herd of cattle.

Roosevelt was just one of hundreds of eager entrepreneurs then hoping to cash in on the beef boom on the northern Plains. Everything seemed to suggest it was a sure thing. "A good-sized steer when it is fit for the butcher market will bring from $45 to $60," boasted the *Breeder's Gazette*. "The same animal at its birth was worth but $5. He has run on the plains and cropped the grass from the public domain for four or five years, and now, with scarcely any expense to its owner, is worth forty dollars more than when he started on his pilgrimage. . . ."

The government was buying more than 50,000 head of western cattle a year, solely to feed the Indian tribes now confined to reservations. Railroads with refrigerated cars could now ship western beef all around the world. By 1881, 110 million pounds were being exported each year to England alone.

And all one needed to do was buy a herd and turn it loose on grasslands that seemed as limitless as the profits they promised. "Cotton was once crowned King," wrote a western newspaper editor, "but *grass* is now." Marshall Field, the Chicago dry goods king, invested. So did William K. Vanderbilt, the railroad magnate, and Joseph Glidden, the manufacturer of barbed wire. Fortune-seekers from England, Scotland, and Europe invested, too, after reading newspaper stories that proclaimed profits of forty cents on the dollar routine. "Rich men's sons from the East were nothing new as far as I was concerned," Teddy Blue Abbott remembered. "The range in the eighties was as full of them as a dog's hair of fleas, and some of them were good fellows and some were damn fools."

But for Theodore Roosevelt, the West was much more than a chance to get rich; it was also a chance to escape the sorrows of his private life. In 1884, after his mother and wife died within hours of one another, he returned to the Badlands to deal with his grief in long, solitary rides:

> Nowhere, not at sea, does a man feel more lonely than when riding over the far-reaching, seemingly never-ending plains. . . . Nowhere else does one feel so far off from mankind; the plains stretch out in deathless and measureless expanse, and as he journeys over them they will for many miles be lacking in all signs of life. . . . Black care rarely sits behind a rider whose pace is fast enough.

Over the course of three summers on his Dakota ranches, Roosevelt hunted, rounded up cattle, and reveled in the rugged landscape and equally rugged life. When a drunken cowboy, a revolver in each hand, cursed and called him "four eyes," he knocked him senseless with his fists. And when three squatters stole his rowboat, he set out with two friends to track them down, carrying copies of *Anna Karenina* and the poetry of Matthew Arnold for campfire reading. Roosevelt captured all three thieves and drove them forty miles on foot to the town of Dickinson to stand trial.

Then, in the autumn of 1886, he decided to return to New York to run for mayor and to court Edith Carow, the childhood sweetheart who would become his second wife. In the West, Roosevelt had transformed himself. "Here," he said later, "the romance of my life began."

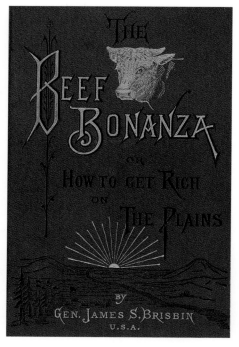

THE
BEEF
BONANZA
OR
HOW TO GET RICH
ON
THE PLAINS

BY
GEN. JAMES S. BRISBIN
U.S.A.

FRIENDS OF THE INDIAN

In the autumn of 1883, the same year Sitting Bull was reunited with his people, a group of white people gathered at the Mohonk Mountain House in upstate New York to make decisions that would change his life and the lives of all the Indian peoples of the West. They were clergymen, social workers, lecturers on moral topics, government officials who had fought hard against corruption, and although some of them had never met an Indian, they were convinced they knew how to bring the first Americans into the mainstream of American life.

Indians were "vanishing," they believed, victims of white mistreatment, but also of their own benighted tribal nature. "The Indian," said Merrill Gates, the president of Amherst College, "must be made to be intelligently selfish . . . [got] out of . . . blankets and into trousers — and trousers with a pocket in them, and a pocket that aches to be filled with dollars."

Theodore Roosevelt (opposite) the fledgling ranchman in 1885, and one of the books that made limitless profits in cattle raising seem plausible. "The beef business," its author assured his readers, "cannot be overdone."

Policy for the Indians of the West was largely set in the East, and much of it was made by the self-styled Friends of the Indian, who met annually at the Mohonk Mountain House in upstate New York.

In the classrooms of the Riverside Indian School at Anadarko, Oklahoma Territory, seen here in 1901 — and in scores of other schools backed by eastern reformers at the turn of the century — Native American children were taught to abandon tribal ways.

Indians had first been removed from their lands, then herded onto scattered reservations. Now, if the Friends of the Indian had their way, they were no longer to be Indians at all. The reformers would first see to it that the youngest generation was transformed as rapidly as possible. Indian children as young as five were to be taken from their families and sent halfway across the continent to school, to the United States Indian Training and Industrial School at Carlisle, Pennsylvania. There, Captain Richard Henry Pratt ran a boarding school whose purpose was to teach them useful skills while making them forget their Indian ways. It was his task, he said, to make the Indian a member of a "new social order" and "to do this we must recreate him, to make him a new personality."

Indian children were punished if they dared speak the languages their parents had taught them, were forbidden to dance or to sing their religious songs. "Our belongings were taken from us," remembered a Blackfoot boy who made the journey, "even the little medicine bags our mothers had given us to protect us from harm. Everything was placed in a heap and set afire."

Within twenty years, there were 24 other off-reservation schools like the one at Carlisle — and 81 boarding schools and 147 day schools on the reservations themselves. All shared the same goal. "Education," said one reformer, "should seek the disintegration of the tribes.... They should be educated, not as Indians, but as Americans." (In the end, however, the Indian schools taught another lesson, as well: that no matter what tribe they belonged to, they were all Indians and needed to begin thinking of themselves in those terms.)

The assault on tribal culture extended beyond the schools. Even on the reservation, parents and old people were ordered to abandon their faith, put behind them all their religious customs. Men were to give up all but one wife — though what was to be done with those they discarded was never made clear. The Lakota were not even supposed to keep the ritual bundles that allowed the spirits of those who had died to be released. "The white people made war on the Lakotas to keep them from practicing their religion . . ." a warrior named Short Bull recalled. "The white people wish to make us cause the spirits of our dead to be ashamed."

Lakota boys on their arrival at Carlisle (left) and after the process of "civilizing" them had begun

MEDICINE FLOWER

Frank Cushing (top, in the dark clothing), taking part with other Zuni bow chiefs in the War God Ceremony, and (above) wearing a costume of his own creation, part-Navajo, part-Spanish

The Zuni of New Mexico had been among the first Indians of the West to meet a European — the explorer Coronado, who had stormed Hawikuh pueblo in 1540. Three and a half centuries later, they looked out from their mesa top and saw a very different group of explorers approaching. They represented the first expedition of the newly formed U.S. Bureau of Ethnology, sent to survey Indian tribes as quickly as possible, on the belief that Native Americans and their customs were on the verge of disappearing.

With them was a frail but eager twenty-two-year-old named Frank Hamilton Cushing, who had been fascinated by tales of Indians ever since discovering an arrowhead near his home in central New York as a boy. To the shock of his eastern companions — and to the surprise of the Zuni — Cushing immediately moved into one of the Indian's homes and announced he intended to stay. The best way to understand Indians, he said, was to live the way they did. The expedition hurriedly moved on, but Cushing remained.

He learned the Zuni language, cooking and pottery making; grew his hair long and had his ears pierced; adopted Zuni clothing and a Zuni name — Medicine Flower. With the help of his friend Pedro Pino, an aging patriarch of the pueblo, Cushing studied the Zuni's sacred ceremonies, which for centuries they had kept secret from outsiders.

"The Zuni faith . . ." [he wrote,] "is as a drop of oil in water, surrounded and touched at every point, yet in no place penetrated or changed inwardly by the flood of alien belief that descended upon it. . . . [The Zuni] adjusts other beliefs and opinions to his own, but never his own beliefs and opinions to others. . . . In religious culture, the Zuni is almost [the same] as ere his land was discovered."

The Zuni permitted Cushing to learn the rituals of their sacred priesthood of the bow, but only after he went through the lengthy and torturous initiation it required — including days of fasting, sitting motionless on a hill of fire ants, and taking an enemy's scalp.

After word spread in the East that a white man had been initiated into the Zuni tribe, tourists began showing up. They wanted to become members, too, they said, and asked how much they had to pay for the initiation fee.

Cushing was now an influential member of his tribe. He took part in their councils, joined war parties against Apache and Navajo raiders, and justified it all to startled Indian agents:

> Mr. Galen Eastman
> U.S. Indian Agent
> Navajo Indian Agency
> Fort Defiance, Arizona Territory
>
> Sir: It is quite true that I fired, not twice, but three times into two different bands of horses belonging to the Navajo Indians. It is possible that, as I intended, I killed one or two of them, although of this I cannot be certain. . . . Rest assured, sir, that . . . when all of our grievances are set right by the Navajos, we shall be then very ready to say amen, and to act all things aright on our side.
> Very respectfully, Your Obedient Servant,
> F. H. Cushing,
> 1st War Chief of Zuni
> U.S. Ass't Ethnologist

Cushing quarreled with missionaries and Indian agents intent on changing their charges. His warrior society tracked down two horse thieves — one a Mexican, one an American — and killed them. And after he exposed a scheme by relatives of a powerful U.S. senator to build a ranch on valuable Zuni land, his superiors finally ordered him back to Washington. He had been sent to study the Zuni, not become one.

Cushing died in 1900. In 1938, fifty years after he left Zuni pueblo, an archaeologist reported that older Zuni people still wondered why their good friend Medicine Flower had never returned.

MONEY OUT OF WIND

To the casual visitor, Los Angeles in the 1870s seemed much as it had always been — a largely Hispanic farming town, with a population of fewer than 10,000. Without either a railroad or an opening to the sea, it seemed likely forever to be dwarfed by San Francisco to the north.

But life for its inhabitants had already begun to change. Political power had long since passed from the old, landed *Californio* families into the hands of the Anglos, who now insisted that the town's original inhabitants remain within barrios. The schools no longer taught Spanish. Bullfights and bear-baiting had been outlawed, replaced by baseball as the city's most popular sport.

Then, the Southern Pacific Railroad was persuaded to build a line right into Los Angeles — and around the town's chief rival, San Diego. The Atchison, Topeka and Santa Fe followed in 1886, and the two lines began a fare war. At its frenzied height, passengers buying excursion tickets could make it all the way to Los Angeles from St. Louis for as little as one dollar.

The pace of change accelerated overnight. Now, easterners and midwesterners, drawn by reports of warm sunshine, fresh air, and cheap land began arriving in larger and larger numbers, 120,000 in 1887 alone. "Hell, we're giving away the land," one promoter said. "We're selling the climate."

"The crazy part of it was started by professional boomers flocking from Kansas City, Chicago, St. Paul, San Francisco . . ." another man recalled, "showing the natives

Hilario Ybarra and his family, Main Street residents of late-nineteenth-century Los Angeles

Mexican American citizens stroll around the plaza that was the heart of the original Los Angeles, 1893.

By the time the costumed Mexican caballeros above paraded down Main Street as part of a fiesta celebration in 1901, their pueblo had been engulfed by a sprawling, mostly Anglo city (below) and they were considered relics of a distant and romantic past.

It has been a sore subject ever since that I did not buy Southern California when I was there last March and sell it out the same month. I should have made enough money to pay my railway fare back . . . and had money left to negotiate for one of the little States on the Atlantic coast.

Charles Dudley Warner

Salesmanship: Thanks to ceaseless advertising, one frustrated San Jose booster wrote in 1885, "the average eastern mind conceives of California as a small tract of country situated in and about Los Angeles. The mines, parks, vineyards, and redwood forests are all thereabouts. . . ."

Los Angeles fields and farms: looking toward the Hollywood Hills, 1900

how to make money out of wind. . . . Farmers began to neglect their farms and go into town-lot speculation. . . . It became far more dignified for the owner of town-lots that were advancing in value by the day to buy his eggs from Iowa, his chickens from Kansas City, his pork from Chicago . . . than to bother with raising them."

Speculators poured in, so many the hotels ran out of beds and rented them bathtubs to sleep in. They staged picnics and circuses and barbecues to pull in the customers, sometimes offering dubious title to house lots in new communities that existed only on paper. "[N]ot one in ten [buyers] had ever seen the place," one man remembered, "and not one in ten intended to live there."

In just thirty months, sixty new towns were founded in Los Angeles County, including Avalon, Burbank, Glendale, Pasadena, Pomona. Many of the new communities died not long after they were born, but by the end of the decade, Los Angeles's population was five times what it had been in 1880.

Northwest of town, a pious speculator from Ohio named Horace Henderson Wilcox began subdividing ranch land into town lots for what he hoped would be a model community. Liquor and vice would be permanently barred, and Wilcox offered a free plot to any congregation willing to put up a church. His wife named the new town for a friend's country house back home in Ohio — Hollywood.

HELL WITHOUT THE HEAT

By the summer of 1886, the supposedly risk-free cattle business was in trouble on the northern Plains. Seven and a half million hungry cattle were now competing for grasses that every year grew less plentiful from overgrazing. In some places where it had once taken just five acres of land to support a steer, it now took more than ninety. Big herds of voracious sheep were beginning to move across the landscape, too, devouring everything in sight, and farmers were advancing as well, turning the grasslands into fields, building fences, driving cattle from their crops.

Ranchers formed stockmen's associations to fight back. They bought and sold congressmen, ran down rustlers, slaughtered sheep wholesale — and put up fences of their own, claiming vast areas for themselves, then defending them with armies of hired gunmen.

Meanwhile, beef prices were dropping. The summer of 1886 was hot and dry. On the overgrazed ranges, the cattle grew thin and weak.

Then came winter. "In November we had several snowstorms," Teddy Blue Abbott, who had followed the beef business north from Texas, remembered, "and I saw the first white owls I have ever seen. The Indians said they were a bad sign, 'heap snow coming, very cold.' . . . It got colder and colder. . . . It was hell without the heat."

On the northern Plains it began snowing on November 13, 1886, and did not stop for a month. The cattle struggled to stay alive, nosing through the snow in search of what little grass remained. January 1887 was the coldest month anyone on the northern Plains could recall. The snow fell so hard during one seventy-two-hour blizzard, a survivor wrote, that "it seemed as if all the world's ice from Time's beginnings had come on a wind which howled and screamed with the fury of demons."

Across the Plains, the unsheltered, helpless cattle began to die. Some, too weak to stand, were simply blown over by the savage wind. Others, their feet frozen into the ice, died like statues. Teddy Blue Abbott remembered doing all he could to save them:

It was all so slow, plunging after them through the deep snow. . . . The horses' feet were cut and bleeding from the heavy crust, and the cattle had the hair and hide wore off their legs to the knees and the hocks. It was surely hell to see big four-year-old steers just able to stagger along. It was the same all over Wyoming, Montana, and Colorado, western Nebraska, and western Kansas.

When the snow and ice finally began to melt, cattlemen understood for the first time the magnitude of what had happened. Dead animals were everywhere, hundreds of thousands of them, sprawled across the hillsides and along fence lines, heaped at the bottom of coulees, where the snow had trapped them, swollen and bobbing in the rushing rivers. "[I saw] a grim freshet pouring down the river valley as no man had ever seen before or would see again . . ." a rancher remembered, "countless carcasses of cattle were going down with the ice, rolling over and over as they went, sometimes with all four stiffened legs pointed skyward. For days on end, tearing down with the grinding ice cakes, went Death's cattle roundup."

Ranchers scoured the prairies for survivors. "The first day I rode out," one remembered, "I never saw a live animal." Cattlemen would remember the winter of 1886–87 as the "Great Die-Up." Many eastern investors now withdrew what was left of their

Aftermath: Snow slowly retreats from a Montana ranch.

funds. Foreign ranchers packed up and went home. In the end, the only men who made much money on the northern cattle ranges that spring were scavengers, gathering bones to sell to fertilizer companies.

Like the homesteaders who had learned that their mere presence could not change the climate of the West, the ranchers who had rushed in during the beef bonanza had learned they could not ignore it. The great days of the open range were coming to an end. From now on, cattlemen would have to feed their herds in winter. Theodore Roosevelt had remarried and was in Europe on his honeymoon when the storm hit. He hurried west as soon as he got back to see how bad the damage was. "The losses are crippling," he wrote.

> For the first time I have been utterly unable to enjoy a visit to my ranch. I shall be glad to get home. In its present form, stock-raising on the plains is doomed and can hardly outlast the century. The great free ranches . . . mark a primitive stage of existence as surely as do the great tracts of primeval forests, and like the latter must pass away before the onward march of our people . . . and we who have felt the charm of the life, and have exulted in its abounding vigor and its bold, restless freedom . . . must also feel real sorrow that those who come after us are not to see, as we have seen, what is perhaps the pleasantest, healthiest and most exciting phase of American existence.

A GUNPOWDER ENTERTAINMENT

Among those who had sought to avenge George Armstrong Custer in the summer of 1876 had been Buffalo Bill Cody, back scouting for the army between theatrical engagements. On July 17, while wearing one of his stage costumes — a black velvet outfit modeled after those worn by Mexican vaqueros, with a scarlet sash, silver embroidery, and lace at the collar and cuffs — he helped lead a troop of cavalry within sight of a small band of Cheyenne warriors.

Buffalo Bill arrives at Chehalis, Washington, aboard his private car in 1915, still the idol of every American schoolchild after nearly half a century on the road.

Vaquero, cowboy, and Indian (left), leading figures in Buffalo Bill's epic of the West.

"The most animated equestrian spectacle ever seen." The people eagerly lined up (above) to see the show in 1900 happen to be Chicagoans, but when they passed through the entrance they saw much the same astonishing performance as the people of Omaha (below) drank in two years later. Even members of the show's cast (right) could not seem to get enough of it.

By the time this advertisement went up in France in 1905, Cody's face was so universally recognizable that the only legend the poster maker had to print was "Je Viens" — "I am coming" — to pull in big Parisian crowds.

COL. W.F. CODY

JE VIENS

There was a fight. One chief fell, a bullet through his skull. Cody took his scalp and mailed it to his own sister — who fainted when she opened the parcel. The Cheyenne's name had been Yellow Hair, but a newspaperman reported it as Yellow Hand, and that name stuck. The story grew with the telling until the Cheyenne had challenged Cody to hand-to-hand combat and when the duel was over a triumphant Cody had shouted, "The first Scalp for Custer!"

It was just the latest in a long litany of embroidered tales that attached themselves to Cody, some his own handiwork, most created by others. "There being but little prospect of any more fighting," he wrote later, "I determined to go East as soon as possible to organize a new 'Dramatic Combination,' and have a new drama written for me, based upon the Sioux war. This I knew would be a paying investment, as the Sioux campaign had excited considerable interest."

Cody had done a good many of the things a young man could do in the West — he'd been a wrangler, expressman, gold-seeker, buffalo hunter, ranchman, army scout, winner of the Medal of Honor for valor against the Cheyenne. And he had a natural talent for drawing attention to himself. Teddy Blue Abbott remembered working briefly for him as a cowboy:

The perennial finale of Cody's show (right) and the cast of the 1908 version sitting for a collective portrait in front of Wanamaker's Manhattan department store (below). The Russian Cossack with his shaggy hat at the left was a comparatively late addition to Cody's Congress of Rough Riders of the World.

Buffalo Bill was a good fellow, and while he was no great shakes as a scout as he made the eastern people believe, still we all liked him, and we had to hand it to him because he was the only one that had brains enough to make that Wild West stuff pay money. I remember one time he came into a saloon in North Platte, and he took off his hat and that long hair of his that he had rolled up under his hat fell down on his shoulders. It always bothered him, so he rolled it back under his hat again and Brady the saloon man, says: "Say, Bill, why the hell don't you cut the damn stuff off?" And Cody says: "If I did, I'd starve to death."

But Cody was also unhappily married to a woman who understandably objected to his fondness for young actresses; he was very often drunk between performances, and he seemed unable to resist dubious investment schemes that kept him perpetually on the brink of bankruptcy.

None of this mattered to the eastern audiences who saw him as the living embodiment of every frontier virtue. The five-act melodrama called "Buffalo Bill's First Scalp for Custer" had no "head or tail," he recalled, "and it made no difference at which act we commenced the performance. . . . It afforded us, however, ample opportunity to give a noisy, rattling, gunpowder entertainment . . . which seemed to give a general satisfaction."

The stage eventually proved too confining for Cody, and in 1883, he launched "Buffalo Bill's Wild West — America's National Entertainment," an outdoor extravaganza that featured live elk and buffalo, genuine cowboys in spotless outfits roping steers and playing music, authentic Indians attacking a real stagecoach, and a deeply affecting — and totally fictional — tableau in which Cody arrived at the Little Bighorn too late to save Custer and his command from disaster. Even Libbie Custer came to see it several times. It ran for three decades, imprinting its own version of the West on the minds of an entire generation, at home and overseas.

Buffalo Bill backstage after a New York appearance toward the end of his long career. When he died in 1917, a procession of 3,000 motorcars would follow the hearse to his tomb high above Denver, Colorado. Even in death, he remained an attraction.

In 1885, Sitting Bull joined Cody's entourage. He was paid $50 a week, a bonus of $125 for signing on, and the right to profit directly from the sale of autographs and pictures of himself. The aging chief was required only to ride around the arena once a show, doing his best to ignore the boos of Custer's admirers, and afterward, to sign his name for the awed visitors who came to peer at him in his teepee. Sitting Bull liked Cody — who presented him with a handsome hat and the gray horse he'd ridden in the show as gifts — and during an appearance in Washington, D.C., he managed to shake hands with President Grover Cleveland, an event that he took to be evidence that he was still considered a great chief.

But he spent just four months with the Wild West show. He had seen enough of whites, and could not understand why beggars were left to drift about the streets of big cities. He gave much of his pay away to newsboys and hoboes he encountered on the tour, and when he got back to Standing Rock, he used the money he had left to provide feasts for his friends, much to the disgust of agent James McLaughlin: "He is . . . too vain and obstinate to be benefitted by what he sees and makes no good use of the money he thus earns."

Now, the aging medicine man was once again back in the land of his birth, living quietly with his two wives, five children, and a nephew named One Bull, whom he had adopted as his son. He refused to give up either of his wives and rejected Christianity, but he sent his children to a Congregational day school run by a woman missionary, convinced that in the future all Lakota children would need to be able to read and write. "We were always good friends personally," she remembered, "but he hated Christianity and found great satisfaction in taking my converts back into heathendom while of course I felt equal satisfaction in converting his heathen friends."

Soon after he returned to his cabin on the Grand River, he had another of his mystical visions about the future. In 1876, one had warned him that white men were pursuing the Lakota. Another had predicted that Custer's soldiers at the Little Bighorn would fall into the village, upside down. His new vision was equally clear. Wandering alone near his home one morning, he watched a meadowlark flutter down onto a hillock. Then the bird spoke to him, saying, "Your own people, Lakotas, will kill you." Sitting Bull had faith in his visions; they had always proved true in the past.

THE AMERICAN WEST
AND THE BURDEN OF BELIEF

N. SCOTT MOMADAY

I.

West of Jemez Pueblo there is a great red mesa, and in the folds of the earth at its base there is a canyon, the dark red walls of which are sheer and shadow stained; they rise vertically to a remarkable height. You do not suspect that the canyon is there, but you turn a corner and the walls contain you; you look into a corridor of geologic time. When I went into that place I left my horse outside, for there was a strange light and quiet upon the walls, and the shadows closed upon me. I looked up, straight up, to the serpentine strip of the sky. It was clear and deep, like a river running across the top of the world. The sand in which I stood was deep, and I could feel the cold of it through the soles of my shoes. And when I walked out, the light and heat of the day struck me so hard that I nearly fell. On the side of a hill in the plain of the Hissar I saw my horse grazing among sheep. The land inclined into the distance, to the Pamirs, to the Fedchenko Glacier. The river which I had seen near the sun had run out into the endless ether above the Karakoram range and the Plateau of Tibet.

— The Names

When I wrote this passage, some years ago, it did not seem strange to me that two such landscapes as that of northern New Mexico and that of central Asia should become one in the mind's eye and in the confluence of image and imagination. Nor does it seem strange to me now. Even as we look back, the partitions of our experience open and close upon each other; disparate realities coalesce into a single, integrated appearance.

This transformation is perhaps the essence of art and literature. Certainly it is the soul of drama, and historically it is how we have seen the American West. Our human tendency is to concentrate the world upon a stage. We construct proscenium arches and frames in order to contain the thing that is larger than our comprehension, the plane of boundless possibility, that which reaches almost beyond wonder. Sometimes the process of concentration results in something like a burden of belief, a kind of ambiguous exaggeration, as in the paintings of Albert Bierstadt, say, or in the photographs of Ansel Adams, in which an artful grandeur seems superimposed upon a grandeur that is innate. Or music comes to mind, a music that seems to pervade the vast landscape and emanate from it, not the music of wind and rain and birds and beasts, but Virgil Thomson's "The Plow That Broke the Plains," or Aaron Copland's "Rodeo," or perhaps the sound track from *The Alamo* or *She Wore a Yellow Ribbon.* We are speaking of overlays, impositions, a kind of narcissism that locates us within our own field of vision. But if this is a distorted view of the West, it is nonetheless a view that fascinates us.

And more often than not the fascination consists in peril. In *My Life on the Plains,* George Armstrong Custer describes a strange sight:

> I have seen a train of government wagons with white canvas covers moving through a mirage which, by elevating the wagons to treble their height and magnifying the size of the covers, presented the appearance of a line of large sailing vessels under full sail, while the usual appearance of the mirage gave a correct likeness of an immense lake or sea. Sometimes the mirage has been the cause of frightful suffering and death by its deceptive appearance.

He goes on to tell of emigrants to California and Oregon who, suffering terrible thirst, were deflected from their route by a mirage, "like an *ignis fatuus,*" and so perished. Their graves are strewn far and wide over the prairie.

This equation of wonder and peril is for Custer a kind of exhilaration, as indeed it is for most of those adventurers who journeyed westward, and even for those who did not, who escaped into the Wild West show or the dime novel.

For the European who came from a community of congestion and confinement, the West was beyond dreaming; it must have inspired him to formulate an idea of the infinite. There he could walk through geologic time; he could see into eternity. He was surely bewildered, wary, afraid. The landscape was anomalously beautiful and hostile. It was desolate and unforgiving, and yet it was a world of paradisal possibility. Above all, it was wild, definitively wild. And it was inhabited by a people who were to him altogether alien and inscrutable, who were essentially dangerous and deceptive, often invisible, who were savage and unholy — and who were perfectly at home.

This is a crucial point, then: the West was occupied. It was the home of peoples who had come upon the North American continent many thousands of years before, who had in the course of their habitation become the spirit and intelligence of the earth, who had died into the ground again and again and so made it sacred. Those Europeans who ventured into the West must have seen themselves in some wise as latecomers and intruders. In spite of their narcissism, some aspect of their intrusion must have occurred to them as sacrilege, for they were in the unfortunate position of robbing the native peoples of their homeland and the land of its spiritual resources. By virtue of their culture and history — a culture of acquisition and a history of conquest — they were peculiarly prepared to commit sacrilege, the theft of the sacred.

Even the Indians succumbed to the kind of narcissism the Europeans brought to bear on the primeval landscape, the imposition of a belief — essentially alien to both the land and the peoples who inhabited it — that would locate them once again within their own field of vision. For the Indian, the mirage of the ghost dance — to which the concepts of a messiah and immortality, both foreign, European imports, were central — was surely an *ignis fatuus,* and the cause of frightful suffering and death.

II.

George Armstrong Custer had an eye to the country of the Great Plains, and especially to those of its features that constituted a "deceptive appearance." As he stealthily approached Black Kettle's camp on the Washita River, where he was to win his principal acclaim as an Indian fighter, he and his men caught sight of a strange thing. At the first sign of dawn there appeared a bright light ascending slowly from the skyline. Custer describes it sharply, even eloquently:

> Slowly and majestically it continued to rise above the crest of the hill, first appearing as a small brilliant flaming globe of bright golden hue. As it ascended still higher it seemed to increase in size, to move more slowly, while its colors rapidly changed from one to the other, exhibiting in turn the most beautiful combinations of prismatic tints.

Custer and his men took it to be a rocket, some sort of signal, and they assumed that their presence had been detected by the Indians. Here again is the equation of fascination and peril. But at last the reality is discovered:

> Rising above the mystifying influences of the atmosphere, that which had appeared so suddenly before us and excited our greatest apprehensions developed into the brightest and most beautiful of morning stars.

In the ensuing raid upon Black Kettle's camp, Custer and his troopers, charging to the strains of "Garry Owen," killed 103 Cheyenne, including Black Kettle and his wife. Ninety-two of the slain Cheyenne were women, children, and old men. Fifty-three women and children were captured. Custer's casualties totaled one officer killed, one officer severely and two more slightly wounded, and eleven cavalrymen wounded. After the fighting, Custer ordered the herd of Indian ponies slain; the herd numbered 875 animals. "We did not need the ponies, while the Indians did," he wrote.

In the matter of killing women and children, Custer's exculpatory rhetoric seems lame, far beneath his poetic descriptions of mirages and the break of day:

> Before engaging in the fight orders had been given to prevent the killing of any but the fighting strength of the village; but in a struggle of this character it is impossible at all times to dis-

criminate, particularly when, in a hand-to-hand conflict such as the one the troops were then engaged in the squaws are as dangerous adversaries as the warriors, while Indian boys between ten and fifteen years of age were found as expert and determined in the use of the pistol and bow and arrow as the older warriors.

After the fighting, too, Black Kettle's sister, Mah-wis-sa, implored Custer to leave the Cheyenne in peace. Custer reports that she approached him with a young woman, perhaps seventeen years old, and placed the girl's hand in his. Then she proceeded to speak solemnly in her own language, words that Custer took to be a kind of benediction, with appropriate manners and gestures. When the formalities seemed to come to a close, Mah-wis-sa looked reverently to the skies and at the same time drew her hands slowly down over the faces of Custer and the girl. At this point Custer was moved to ask Romeo, his interpreter, what was going on. Romeo replied that Custer and the young woman had just been married to each other.

In one version of the story it is said that Mah-wis-sa told Custer that if he ever again made war on the Cheyenne, he would die. When he was killed at the Little Bighorn, Cheyenne women pierced his eardrums with awls, so that he might hear in the afterlife; he had failed to hear the warning given him at the Washita.

In the final paragraph of *My Life on the Plains,* Custer bids farewell to his readers and announces his intention "to visit a region of country as yet unseen by human eyes, except those of the Indian — a country described by the latter as abounding in game of all varieties, rich in scientific interest, and of surpassing beauty in natural scenery." After rumors of gold had made the Black Hills a name known throughout the country, General (then Lieutenant Colonel) George Armstrong Custer led an expedition from Fort Abraham Lincoln into the Black Hills in July and August 1874. The Custer expedition traveled six hundred miles in sixty days. Custer reported proof of gold, but he had an eye to other things as well. He wrote in his diary:

> Every step of our march that day was amid flowers of the most exquisite colors and perfume. So luxuriant in growth were they that men plucked them without dismounting from the saddle. . . . It was a strange sight to glance back at the advancing columns of cavalry and behold the men with beautiful bouquets in their hands, while the headgear of the horses was decorated with wreaths of flowers fit to crown a queen of May. Deeming it a most fitting appellation, I named this Floral Valley.

In the evening of that same day, sitting at mess in a meadow, the officers competed to see how many different flowers could be picked by each man without leaving his seat. Seven varieties were gathered so. Some fifty different flowers were blooming in Floral Valley.

Imagine that Custer dreamed that night. In his dream he saw a man approaching on horseback, approaching slowly across a meadow full of wildflowers. The man drew very close and stopped, sitting straight up on the horse, holding Custer fast in his gaze. There could be no doubt that he was a warrior, and fearless, though he flourished no scalps and made no signs of fighting. His unbound hair hung below his waist. His body was painted with hail spots, and a white bolt of lightning ran down one of his cheeks, and on his head he wore the feathers of a red-backed hawk. Except for moccasins and breechcloth he was naked.

"I am George Armstrong Custer," Custer said, "called Yellowhair, called Son of the Morning Star."

"I am Curly," the man said, "called Crazy Horse."

And Custer wept for the nobility and dignity and greatness of the man facing him. And through his tears he perceived the brilliance of the meadow. The wildflowers were innumerable and more beautiful than anything he had ever seen or imagined. And when he thought his heart could bear no more, a thousand butterflies rose up, glancing and darting and floating around him, to spangle the sky, to become prisms of the sun. And he awoke serene and refreshed in his soul.

George Armstrong Custer sees the light upon the meadows of the Plains, but he does not see disaster lurking at the Little Bighorn. He hears the bugles and the band, but he does not hear or heed the warning of the Cheyenne women. All about there is deception; the West is other than it seems.

III.

In 1872, William Frederick Cody was awarded the Medal of Honor for his valor in fighting Indians. In 1913, U.S. Army regulations specified that only enlisted men and officers were eligible to receive the Medal of Honor, and Cody's medal was therefore withdrawn and his name removed from the records. In 1916, after deliberation, the army decided to return the medal, having declared that Cody's service to his country was "above and beyond the call of duty."

Ambivalence and ambiguity, like deception, bear upon all definitions of the American West. The real issue of Cody's skill and accomplishment as an Indian fighter is not brought into question in this matter of the Medal of Honor, but it might be. Beyond the countless Indians he "killed" in the arena of the Wild West show, Cody's achievements as an Indian fighter are suspect. Indeed, much of Cody's life is clouded in ambiguity. He claimed that in 1859 he became a pony express rider, but the pony express did not come into being until 1860. Even the sobriquet "Buffalo Bill" belonged to

Lakota, ca. 1900

William Mathewson before it belonged to William Frederick Cody.

Buffalo Bill Cody was an icon and an enigma, and he was in some sense his own invention. One of his biographers wrote that he was "a man who was so much more than a western myth." One must doubt it, for the mythic dimension of the American West is an equation much greater than the sum of its parts. It would be more accurate, in this case, to say that the one dissolved into the other, that the man and myth became indivisible. The great fascination and peril of Cody's life was the riddle of who he was. The thing that opposed him, and perhaps betrayed him, was above all else the mirage of his own identity.

If we are to understand the central irony of Buffalo Bill and the Wild West show, we must first understand that William Frederick Cody was an authentic western hero. As a scout, a guide, a marksman, and a buffalo hunter, he was second to none. At a time when horsemanship was at its highest level in America, he was a horseman nearly without peer. He defined the plainsman. The authority of his life on the Plains far surpassed Custer's.

But let us imagine that we are at Omaha, Nebraska, on May 17, 1883, in a crowd of 8,000 people. The spectacle of the "Wild West" unfolds before us. The opening parade is led by a twenty-piece band playing "Garry Owen," perhaps, or "The Girl I Left Behind Me." Then there comes an Indian in full regalia on a paint pony. Next are buffalo, three adults and a calf. Then there is Buffalo Bill, mounted on a fine white horse and resplendent in a great white hat, a fringed buckskin coat, and glossy thigh boots. He stands out in a company of cowboys, Indians, more buffalo, and the Deadwood Stage, drawn by six handsome mules, and the end is brought up by another band, playing "Annie Laurie" or "When Johnny Comes Marching Home." Then we see the acts — the racing of the pony express, exhibitions of shooting, the attack on the Deadwood Stagecoach, and the finale of the great buffalo chase. Buffalo Bill makes a stirring speech, and we are enthralled; the applause is thunderous. But this is only a modest beginning, a mere glimpse of things to come.

What we have in this explosion of color and fanfare is an epic transformation of the American West into a traveling circus and of an American hero into an imitation of himself. Here is a theme with which we have become more than familiar. We have seen the transformation take place numberless times on the stage, on television and movie screens, and on the pages of comic books, dime novels, and literary masterpieces. One function of the American imagination is to reduce the American landscape to size, to fit that great expanse to the confinement of the immigrant mind. It is a way to persist in our cultural being. We photograph ourselves on the rim of Monument Valley or against the wall of the Tetons, and we become our own frame of reference. As long as we can transform the landscape to accommodate our fragile presence, we can be saved. As long as we can see ourselves on the picture plane, we cannot be lost.

Arthur Kopit's play *Indians* is a remarkable treatise on this very subject of transformation. It can and ought to be seen as a tragedy, for its central story is that of Buffalo Bill's fatal passage into myth. He is constrained to translate his real heroism into a false and concentrated reflection of itself. The presence of the Indians is pervasive, but he cannot see them until they are called to his attention.

BUFFALO BILL: Thank you, thank you! A great show lined up tonight! With all-time favorite Johnny Baker, Texas Jack and his twelve-string guitar, the Dancin' Cavanaughs, Sheriff Brad and the Deadwood Mail Coach, Harry Philamee's Trained Prairie Dogs, the Abilene County Girls' Trick Roping and Lasso Society, Pecos Pete and the —

VOICE: *Bill.*

BUFFALO BILL: (Startled.) Hm?

VOICE: Bring on the Indians.

BUFFALO BILL: What?

VOICE: The *Indians.*

BUFFALO BILL: Ah . . .

Solemnly the Indians appear. In effect they shame Buffalo Bill; they tread upon his conscience. They fascinate and imperil him. By degrees his desperation to justify himself — and by extension the white man's treatment of the Indians in general — grows and becomes a burden too great to bear. In the end he sits trembling while the stage goes completely black. Then all lights up, rodeo music, the glaring and blaring; enter the Rough Riders of the World! Buffalo Bill enters on his white stallion and tours the ring, doffing his hat to the invisible crowd. The Rough Riders exit, the Indians approach, and the lights fade to black again.

At five minutes past noon on January 10, 1917, Buffalo Bill died. Western Union ordered all lines cleared, and, in a state of war, the world was given the news at once. The old scout had passed by. Tributes and condolences came from every quarter, from children, from old soldiers, from heads of state.

In ambivalence and ambiguity, Cody died as he had lived. A week before his death, it was reported that Buffalo Bill had been baptized into the Roman Catholic Church. His wife, Louisa, was, however, said to be an Episcopalian, and his sister Julia, to whom he declared, "Your church suits me," was a Presbyterian. Following his death there was a controversy as to where Cody should be buried. He had often expressed the wish to be buried on Cedar Mountain, Wyoming. Notwithstanding, his final resting place is atop Mount Lookout, above Denver, Colorado, overlooking the urban sprawl.

IV.

DECEMBER 29, 1890

Wounded Knee Creek

In the shine of photographs
are the slain, frozen and black

on a simple field of snow.
They image ceremony:

women and children dancing,
old men prancing, making fun.

In autumn there were songs, long
since muted in the blizzard.

In summer the wild buckwheat
shone like fox fur and quillwork,

and dusk guttered on the creek.
Now in serene attitudes

of dance, the dead in glossy
death are drawn in ancient light.

On December 15, 1890, the great Hunkpapa leader Sitting Bull, who had opposed Custer at the Little Bighorn and who had toured for a time with Buffalo Bill and the Wild West show, was killed on the Standing Rock reservation. In a dream he had foreseen his death at the hands of his own people.

Just two weeks later, on the morning of December 29, 1890, on Wounded Knee Creek near the Pine Ridge agency, the Seventh Cavalry of the U.S. Army opened fire on an encampment of Big Foot's band of Miniconjou Sioux. When the shooting ended, Big Foot and most of his people were dead or dying. It has been estimated that nearly 300 of the original 350 men, women, and children in the camp were slain. Twenty-five soldiers were killed and thirty-nine wounded.

Sitting Bull is reported to have said, "I am the last Indian." In some sense he was right. During his lifetime the world of the Plains Indians had changed forever. The old roving life of the buffalo hunters was over. A terrible disintegration and demoralization had set in. If the death of Sitting Bull marked the end of an age, Wounded Knee marked the end of a culture.

I did not know then how much was ended. When I look back now from the high hill of my old age, I can still see the butchered women and children lying heaped and scattered all along the crooked gulch as plain as when I saw them with eyes still young. And I can see that something else died there in the bloody mud, and was buried in the blizzard. A people's dream died there. It was a beautiful dream. . . .

—Black Elk

In the following days there were further developments. On January 7, 1891, nine days after the massacre at Wounded Knee, a young

Sioux warrior named Plenty Horses shot and killed a popular army officer, Lieutenant Edward W. Casey, who wanted to enter the Sioux village at No Water for the purpose of talking peace. The killing appeared to be unprovoked. Plenty Horses shot Casey in the back at close quarters.

On January 11, two Sioux families, returning to Pine Ridge from hunting near Bear Butte, were ambushed by white ranchers, three brothers named Culbertson. Few Tails, the head of one of the families, was killed, and his wife was severely wounded. Somehow she made her way in the freezing cold a hundred miles to Pine Ridge. The other family — a man, his wife, and two children, one an infant — managed to reach the Rosebud agency two weeks later. This wife, too, was wounded and weak from the loss of blood. She survived, but the infant child had died of starvation on the way.

On January 15 the Sioux leaders surrendered and established themselves at Pine Ridge. The peace for which General Nelson A. Miles had worked so hard was achieved. The Indians assumed that Plenty Horses would go free, and indeed General Miles was reluctant to disturb the peace. But there were strong feelings among the soldiers. Casey had been shot in cold blood while acting in the interest of peace. On February 19, Plenty Horses was quietly arrested and removed from the reservation to Fort Meade, near Sturgis, South Dakota.

On March 27, General Miles ordered Plenty Horses released to stand trial in the federal district court at Sioux Falls. Interest ran high, and the courtroom was filled with onlookers of every description. The Plenty Horses trial was one of the most interesting and unlikely in the history of the West. Eventually the outcome turned upon a question of perception, of whether or not a state of war existed between the Sioux and the United States. If Plenty Horses and Casey were belligerents in a state of war, the defense argued, then the killing could not be considered a criminal offense, subject to trial in the civil courts.

General Nelson A. Miles was sensitive to this question for two reasons in particular. First, his rationale for bringing troops upon the scene — and he had amassed the largest concentration of troops in one place since the Civil War — was predicated upon the existence of a state of war. When the question was put to him directly, he replied, "It was a war. You do not suppose that I am going to reduce my campaign to a dress-parade affair?" Second, Miles had to confront the logically related corollary to the defense argument, that, if no state of war existed, all the soldiers who took part in the

Nachez, son of Cochise, Chiricahua Apache, 1883

Wounded Knee affair were guilty of murder under the law.

Miles sent a staff officer, Captain Frank D. Baldwin, to testify on behalf of Plenty Horses' defense. This testimony proved critical, and decisive. It is a notable irony that Baldwin and the slain Casey were close friends. Surely one of the principal ironies of American history is that Plenty Horses was very likely to have been the only Indian to benefit in any way from the slaughter at Wounded Knee. Plenty Horses was acquitted. So too — a final irony — were the Culbertson brothers; with Plenty Horses' acquittal, there was neither a logical basis for nor a practical possibility of holding them accountable for the ambush of Few Tails and his party.

We might ponder Plenty Horses at trial, a young man sitting silent under the scrutiny of curious onlookers, braving his fate with apparent indifference. Behind the mask of a warrior was a lost and agonized soul.

As a boy Plenty Horses had been sent to Carlisle Indian School in Pennsylvania, the boarding school founded by Richard Henry Pratt, whose obsession was to "kill the Indian and save the man." Carlisle was the model upon which an extensive system of boarding schools for Indians was based. The boarding schools were prisons in effect, where Indian children were exposed to brutalities, sometimes subtle, sometimes not, in the interest of converting them to the white man's way of life. It was a grand experiment in ethnic cleansing and psychological warfare, and it failed. But it exacted a terrible cost upon the mental, physical, and spiritual health of Indian children.

Plenty Horses was for five years a pupil at Carlisle. Of his experience there he said:

I found that the education I had received was of no benefit to me. There was no chance to get employment, nothing for me to do whereby I could earn my board and clothes, no opportunity to learn more and remain with the whites. It disheartened me and I went back to live as I had before going to school.

But when Plenty Horses returned to his own people, they did not fully accept him. He had lost touch with the old ways; he had lived among whites, and the association had diminished him. He rejected the white world, but he had been exposed to it, and it had left its mark upon him. And in the process he had been dislodged, uprooted from the Indian world. He could not quite get back to it. His very being had become tentative; he lived in a kind of limbo, a state of confusion, depression, and desperation.

At the trial Plenty Horses was remarkably passive. He said nothing, nor did he give any sign of his feelings. It was as if he were not there. It came later to light that he was convinced beyond any question that he would be hanged. He could not understand what was happening around him. But in a strange way he could appreciate it. Indeed he must have been fascinated. Beneath his inscrutable expression, his heart must have been racing. He was the center of a ritual, a sacrificial victim; the white man must dispose of him according to some design in the white man's universe. This was perhaps a ritual of atonement. The whites would take his life, but in the proper way, according to their notion of propriety and the appropriate. Perhaps they were involving him in their very notion of the sacred. He could only accept what was happening, and only in their terms. With silence, patience, and respect he must await the inevitable.

Plenty Horses said later:

I am an Indian. Five years I attended Carlisle and was educated in the ways of the white man. . . . I was lonely. I shot the lieutenant so I might make a place for myself among my people. Now I am one of them. I shall be hung and the Indians will bury me as a warrior. They will be proud of me. I am satisfied.

But Plenty Horses was not hanged, nor did he make an acceptable place for himself among his people. He was acquitted. Plenty Horses lived out his life between two worlds, without a place in either.

Perhaps the most tragic aspect of Plenty Horses' plight was his silence, the theft of his language and the theft of meaning itself from his ordeal. At Carlisle he had been made to speak English, and his native Lakota was forbidden, thrown away, to use a term that indicates particular misfortune in the Plains oral tradition, where to be "thrown away" is to be negated, excluded, eliminated. After five years Plenty Horses had not only failed to master the English language, he had lost some critical possession of his native tongue as well. He was therefore crippled in his speech, wounded in his intelligence. In him was a terrible urgency to express himself — his anger and hurt, his sorrow and loneliness. But his voice was broken. In terms of his culture and all it held most sacred, Plenty Horses himself was thrown away.

In order to understand the true nature of Plenty Horses' ordeal — and a central reality in the cultural conflict that has defined the way we historically see the American West — we must first understand something about the nature of words, about the way we live our daily lives in the element of language. For in a profound sense our language determines us; it shapes our most fundamental selves; it establishes our identity and confirms our existence, our human being. Without language we are lost, "thrown away." Without names — language is essentially a system of naming — we cannot truly claim to be.

To think is to talk to oneself. That is to say, language and thought are practically indivisible. But there is complexity in language, and there are many languages. Indeed, there are hundreds of Native American languages on the North American continent alone, many of them in the American West. As there are different languages, there are different ways of thinking. In terms of what we call "worldview," there are common denominators of experience that unify language communities to some extent. Although the Pueblo peoples of the Rio Grande valley speak different languages, their experience of the land in which they live, and have lived for thousands of years, is by and large the same. And their worldview is the same. There are common denominators that unify all Native Americans in certain ways. This much may be said of other peoples, Europeans, for example. But the difference between Native American and European worldviews is vast. And that difference is crucial to the story of the American West. We are talking about different ways of thinking, deeply different ways of looking at the world.

The oral tradition of the American Indian is a highly developed realization of language. In certain ways it is superior to the written tradition. In the oral tradition words are sacred; they are intrinsically powerful and beautiful. By means of words, by the exertion of language upon the unknown, the best of the possible — and indeed the seemingly impossible — is accomplished. Nothing exists beyond the influence of words. Words are the names of Creation. To give one's word is to give oneself, wholly, to place a name, than which nothing is more sacred, in the balance. One stands for his word; his word stands for him. The oral tradition demands the greatest clarity of speech and hearing, the whole strength of memory, and an absolute faith in the efficacy of language. Every word spoken, every word heard, is the utterance of prayer.

Pacer's Son, Kiowa Apache

Thus, in the oral tradition, language bears the burden of the sacred, the burden of belief. In a written tradition, the place of language is not so certain.

Those European immigrants who ventured into the Wild West were of a written tradition, even the many who were illiterate. Their way of seeing and thinking was determined by the invention of an alphabet, the advent of the printed word, and the manufacture of books. These were great landmarks of civilization, to be sure, but they were also a radical departure from the oral tradition and an understanding of language that was inestimably older and closer to the origin of words. Although the first Europeans venturing into the continent took with them and held dear the Bible, Bunyan, and Shakespeare, their children ultimately could take words for granted, throw them away. Words, multiplied and diluted to inflation, would be preserved on shelves forever. But in this departure was also the dilution of the sacred, and the loss of a crucial connection with the real, that plane of possibility that is always larger than our comprehension. What follows such loss is overlay, imposition, the distorted view of the West of which we have been speaking.

V.

My children, when at first I liked the whites,
My children, when at first I liked the whites,
I gave them fruits,
I gave them fruits.
— Arapaho

Restore my voice for me.
— Navajo

The landscape of the American West has to be seen to be believed. And perhaps, conversely, it has to be believed in order to be seen. Here is the confluence of image and imagination. I am a writer and a painter. I am therefore interested in what it is to see, how seeing is accomplished, how the physical eye and the mind's eye are related, how the act of seeing is or can be expressed in art and in language, and how these things are sacred in nature, as I believe them to be.

Belief is the burden of seeing. And language bears the burden of belief rightly. To see into the heart of something is to believe in it. In order to see to this extent, to see and to accomplish belief in the seeing, one must be prepared. The preparation is a spiritual exercise.

In order to be perceived in its true character, the landscape of the American West must be seen in terms of its sacred dimension. "Sacred" and "sacrifice" are related. Something is made sacred by means of sacrifice; that which is sacred is earned. I have a friend who wears on a string around his neck a little leather pouch. In the pouch is a pebble from the creek bed at Wounded Knee. Wounded Knee is sacred ground, for it was purchased with blood. It is the site of a terrible human sacrifice. It is appropriate that my friend should keep the pebble close to the center of his being, that he should see the pebble and beyond the pebble to the battlefield and beyond the battlefield to the living earth.

The history of the West, that is, the written story that begins with the record of European intervention, is informed by tensions that arise from a failure to see the West in terms of the sacred. The oral history, the oral tradition that came before the written chronicles, is all too often left out of the equation. Yet one of the essential realities of the West is centered in this still living past. When Europeans came into the West they encountered a people who had been there for untold millennia, for whom the landscape was a kind of cathedral of their spiritual life, the home of their deepest being. It had been earned by sacrifice forever. But the encounter was determined by a distortion of image and imagination and language, by a failure to see and believe.

George Armstrong Custer could see and articulate the beauty of the Plains, but he could not see the people who inhabited them. Or he could see them only as enemies, impediments to the glory for which he hungered. He could not understand the sacred ceremony, the significance of the marriage he was offered, and he could not hear the words of warning, nor comprehend their meaning.

Buffalo Bill was a plainsman, but the place he might have held on the picture plane of the West was severely compromised and ultimately lost to the theatrical pretensions of the Wild West show. Neither did he see the Indians. What he saw at last was a self-fabricated reflection of himself and of the landscape in which he had lived a former life.

The vision of Plenty Horses was that of reunion with his traditional world. He could not realize his vision, for his old way of seeing was stolen from him in the white man's school. Ironically, just like the European emigrants, Plenty Horses attempted by his wordless act of violence to persist in his cultural being, to transform the landscape to accommodate his presence once more, to save himself. He could not do so. I believe that he wanted more than anything to pray, to make a prayer in the old way to the old deities of the world to which he was born. But I believe too that he had lost the words, that without language he could no longer bear the burden of belief.

The sun's beams are running out
The sun's beams are running out
The sun's yellow rays are running out
The sun's yellow rays are running out

We shall live again
We shall live again
— Comanche

They will appear — may you behold them!
They will appear — may you behold them!
A horse nation will appear.
A thunder-being nation will appear.
They will appear, behold!
They will appear, behold!
— Kiowa

Leadville, Colorado, ca. 1890

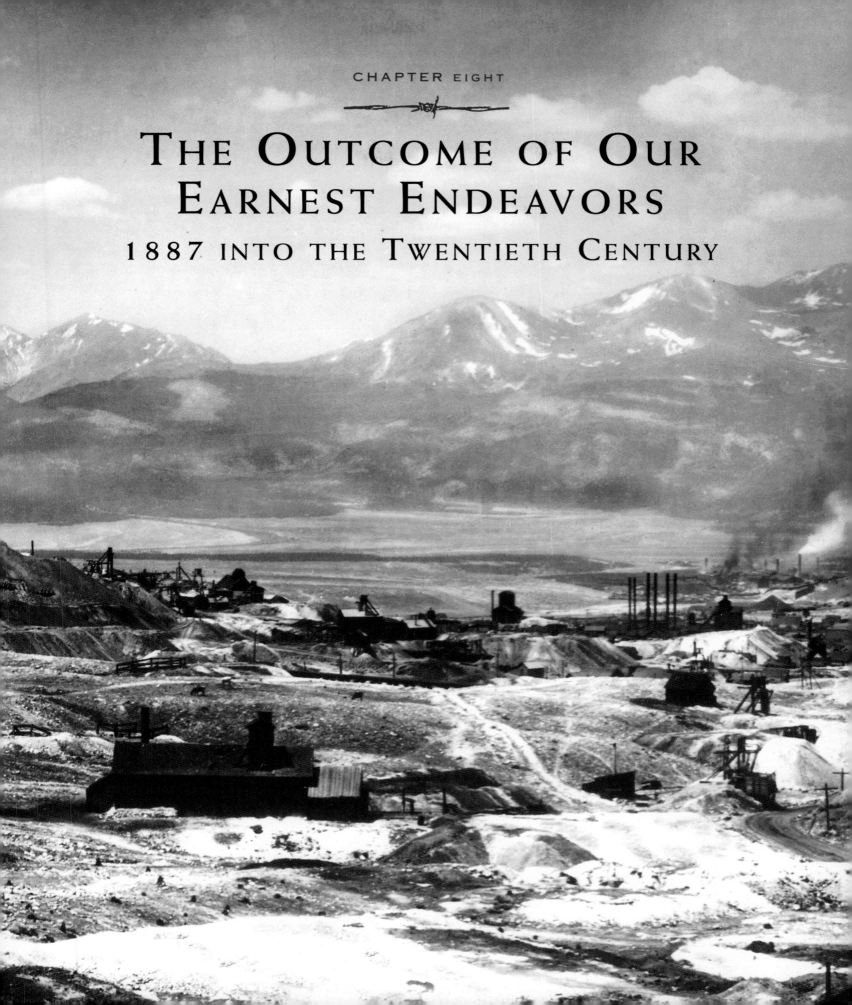

CHAPTER EIGHT

THE OUTCOME OF OUR EARNEST ENDEAVORS

1887 INTO THE TWENTIETH CENTURY

In 1893, the four hundredth anniversary of the arrival of Columbus in the New World was celebrated in Chicago. The World's Columbian Exposition was so large, so ambitious, so self-congratulatory, that it took an extra year just to get everything ready. There were 63 million Americans in 1893. Twenty-four million tickets to the fair were sold. More people attended it than had ever attended any other single event in the history of the world. Their pride was understandable. In a span of less than fifty years, the United States had stretched its boundaries to the Pacific and altered everything in its path. The conquest of the West that had begun with Coronado at last seemed complete. But beyond the fairgrounds, beyond Chicago, in the real West, for every frontier story that was coming to an end, another one began.

In the spring of 1889, two determined middle-aged women arrived at the Nez Percé reservation in Lapwai, Idaho. They had been active in the temperance and women's rights movements and were now deeply committed to a new cause.

Jane Gay, fifty-nine, from New Hampshire, had nursed Union soldiers during the Civil War, had published a book of poems, and was accustomed to hard work and attention to detail, having been a clerk for seventeen years in the dead letter office of the postal service. To document her time with the Nez Percé, she had learned the art of photography.

Her companion, Alice Fletcher, fifty-one, was the former secretary of the Association for the Advancement of Women and a skilled performer on the lecture circuit. After visits to the Plains to study the ceremonies of the Lakota, Ponca, and Omaha tribes, she had become a pioneer in the emerging field of ethnology. Among the Friends of the Indian, who gathered each summer at Lake Mohonk, Fletcher was one of the relatively few who had ever actually gone west to meet Indians, and so her opinions were given special weight and she had become the group's most visible — and effective — lobbyist in passing the Dawes General Allotment Act of 1887.

It was meant, said the head of the Lake Mohonk Conference, to be "a mighty pulverizing engine for breaking up the tribal mass." The act provided for each reservation to be surveyed, and each head of a family to be given 160 acres of farmland or 320 of grazing land. Then, once each family had its allotment, the remaining tribal lands were to be declared "surplus" and opened up for homesteading. Tribal ownership — and the tribes themselves — were meant simply to disappear.

"The Indian may now become a free man," Alice Fletcher said; "free from the thraldom of the tribe; free from the domination of the reservation system; free to enter into the body of our citizens. [The Allotment Act] may therefore be considered as the Magna Carta of the Indians of our country." She and other reformers favored the new policy because it seemed the fastest way to force Indian peoples to become like other Americans. Land speculators liked it, too. Indians themselves were not consulted.

On behalf of the Bureau of Indian Affairs, Fletcher had already implemented allotments in Nebraska among the Omaha and Winnebago. Now, she would divide up the lands of the Nez Percé, the nation's oldest friends in the West. "If I believe in anything for the Indians, I believe in allotment . . ." she said. "I always help the progressive Indians first. It helps to break the dead monotony of the tribe. . . . [P]erhaps one third will make successful farmers, another third will make a scramble, . . . and the other third will be a miserable worthless lot. But I do not believe in keeping all the others back for this fraction. I have always had to coerce a few, and I rather enjoy it."

Fletcher's strong will — as well as her physical resemblance to Queen Victoria — prompted her companion to refer to her privately as "Her Majesty." The Nez Percé came to call her the "Measuring Woman." She had her work cut out for her at Lapwai. The first Nez Percé she settled among simply refused to cooperate. Fletcher and Gay — along with a surveyor and an interpreter — then relocated to another part of the reservation, nearer a group of Christian Nez Percé more willing to comply.

Even there, Fletcher wrote, it was "the worst struggle of my life." Jane Gay recalled an early meeting with tribal leaders:

> [She] explained what she had called them together to hear: explained the land allotment, the meaning of citizenship and her wish that the whole people would see the wisdom of the great change that she had come to bring upon them. . . .
>
> Still a silence. . . . The Interpreter read the law and then sat down and waited. A little stir arose among the people, . . . and at length one man stood up, a tall, broad-shouldered fellow with . . . an air of authority about him. . . . He said, "We do not want our land cut up in little pieces; we have not told you to do it. . . . We are content to be as we are." And a groan of assent ran along the dark line of Sphinxes as the old man drew his blanket about him. . . .
>
> . . . "Our people are scattered," [said] another. "We must come together and decide whether we will have this law."
>
> [She told] them that there is nothing for them to decide; they have no choice. The law must be obeyed. . . .

Whites — anxious for the "surplus" lands to be opened, and just as anxious that the Indians not be allotted the prime parcels — came to call, hoping to persuade Fletcher to see things their way. "Already we have been called upon by a delegation of cattlemen," Gay wrote,

> who desire to know what the Allotting Agent proposes to do about their "rights" upon the Reservation. They seem to be utterly ignorant of the intent of the Severalty Act. . . . Her Majesty . . . explained that it was her sworn duty to place the Indians upon their best lands. . . . The men are evidently non-plussed, for, as they mounted their horses [I] heard one mutter, "Why in thunder did the Government send a woman to do this work? We could have got a holt on a man."

Chief Joseph and Alice Fletcher, the "Measuring Woman," on the Nez Percé reservation in Idaho, 1890. Joseph was willing to take an allotment, but only if it were granted to him in the Wallowa Valley, where his father was buried. Fletcher could do nothing for him, but she thought him "a most interesting blending of the old and the new."

Chief Joseph came to pay a visit to the "Measuring Woman," too. After his long flight from the army in 1877, he had been exiled to Oklahoma, and then finally allowed to return to a reservation in eastern Washington — but not to his beloved Wallowa Valley. Using a new device — a wax cylinder — Fletcher convinced the old chief to record one of his traditional songs. But she could not talk him into taking an allotment at Lapwai.

> If you tie a horse to a stake, [he asked,] do you expect he will grow fat? If you pen a man on a small spot of earth, and compel him to stay there, he will not be contented, nor will he grow and prosper. I have asked some of the great white chiefs where they get their authority to say to that man that he shall stay in one place, while he sees white men going where they please. They can not tell me.

Jane Gay was impressed by Joseph's dignity and his determination: ". . . He will have none but the Wallowa valley, from which he was driven; he will remain landless and homeless if he cannot have his own again. It was good to see an unsubjugated Indian. One could not help respecting the man who still stood firmly for his rights, after having fought and suffered and been defeated in the struggle for their maintenance." (Joseph remained unsubjugated to the end and died in 1904, without ever seeing his beloved valley again.)

Fletcher went back to work:

> It requires all Her Majesty's tact to avoid open conflict, [Gay continued,] for she is constantly meeting decided opposition . . . old men whose splendid obstinacy is invincible; who refuse to take their quota of land on principle, holding to their tribal right to roam at will all over the Reservation. It is of no use to explain to them that the world is so rapidly filling with people that no tribe can longer hold unused land against the clamor of a multitude of homeless men and women; that the earth, in a sense, belongs to all that are upon it and that no man can be allowed to claim more than he can use for his own benefit or for that of others; that no treaty could be enforced that sought to hold

Between two worlds: Alice Fletcher (top, at work) felt herself caught between "the greed of the whites" and the reluctance of the Nez Percé (shown gathered in council above) to give up any part of their land.

back the living tide that had set in upon this continent; that any tribe of Indians that stood out against that flood would be overwhelmed. . . . Nor is it worthwhile to try persuasion upon the chiefs who, Her Majesty says, "oppose because land in severalty breaks up completely their tribal power and substitutes civilization and law."

Fletcher kept at it for four years, and when she was finished had made over 2,000 Nez Percé allotments — some 175,000 acres. Then she and Jane Gay returned to Cambridge, Massachusetts, where Fletcher had been awarded a lifetime fellowship at Harvard's Peabody Museum. "In the week's journey [home] across the continent,"

SOONERS

By the mid-1880s, the biggest single area in the West suitable for farming and still largely untouched by white settlement was Indian Territory. Representatives of some fifty-five tribes now called it home, but there were large tracts within it upon which no one lived.

One of these — 2 million empty and unassigned acres — was called "the Oklahoma District," and the army was soon kept busy driving from it armed parties of squatters from Kansas who called themselves "Boomers." Furious lobbying eventually succeeded where invasion failed, and Congress finally voted to buy out all Indian claims to the Oklahoma District.

On the morning of April 22, 1889, some 100,000 eager Boomers surrounded it, waiting for the signal to storm in and stake their claims.

At precisely noon, the bugles blew and the Boomers started forward. "The last barrier of savagery in the United States was broken down," said a reporter for *Harper's Weekly*. "Moved by the same impulse each driver lashed his horses furiously; . . . each man on foot caught his breath and started forward."

Some pedaled bicycles. Others jumped aboard special Santa Fe trains that steamed along slowly so as not to give their passengers too great an advantage over those on foot.

Many headed for the sites of new towns about to be born: Oklahoma City, Stillwater, Kingfisher, Norman — and Guthrie, which was to become the provisional territorial capital. There, a wild scramble began to stake claims on parcels of land, but the choicest lots had already been taken by settlers — known as "sooners"— who had illegally slipped through the army lines the night before. "Men who had expected to lay out the town-site were grievously disappointed at their first glimpse of their proposed scene of operations," a reporter noted. "The slope east of the railway at Guthrie

station was [already] dotted white with tents and sprinkled thick with men running about in all directions."

Others staked claims in what turned out to be the middle of the streets and had to be driven out later by armed marshals. By nightfall, all 1.92 million acres of land in the district had been claimed, and Guthrie was a tent city with 15,000 residents.

By noon of the following day, the new citizens of Guthrie began choosing their mayor. It wasn't easy. There were two candidates and no ballots. Two lines were formed and each man's vote was tallied, but so many voters ran to the back of the line to vote again that the whole business had to be done over.

Everything was improvised. A blacksmith saw the need for a dentist, declared himself one, and advertised his skills by hanging the teeth he extracted on a string outside his tent. Three men without a cent between them simply exchanged worthless notes for $10,000, declared capitalization of $30,000, and opened a bank. Deposits were kept in a potbellied stove until they could afford to buy a vault. An elderly woman named Button Mary, who had already performed the same function in other western towns, opened for business, sewing buttons back on bachelors' shirts for ten cents each. Within five days, wood-frame buildings were being banged together along Main Street. And by the time Guthrie was five months old, it had a hotel, three newspapers, three general stores — and fifty saloons.

Within a little over a year, the Oklahoma District became Oklahoma Territory. In the next few years, five more "runs" would open up all but a few scattered patches of Indian Territory to settlement. But in the end, when Oklahoma became a state in 1906, it was Oklahoma City that became the state capital. Guthrie was left out in the cold.

The last — and largest — of the Oklahoma land rushes gets under way (above) on September 16, 1893. Within hours some 6 million acres of land — the so-called Cherokee Outlet — had been carved up among nearly 100,000 newcomers.

Guthrie going up: the land office (left), where claims were registered; two armed sooners (opposite, left) whose weapons ensured that no one dared jump their claim to a choice site between the land office and the depot; and Hilarity Roost or Boomers Retreat (opposite, right), to which all of Guthrie's brand-new citizens were cordially invited once they'd completed their onerous paperwork

Gay wrote as they were packing up, "we shall have time to review the outcome of our earnest endeavors, so far as it has been revealed to us. But if it has been well for us, and well for the Indian . . . is not for us to know. We can only leave the question among the unsolvable, whose multitude grows ever greater as life goes on."

In 1895, the remaining half million unallotted acres of Nez Percé tribal land were declared surplus and opened for homesteading. Two thousand whites rushed in to file claims on the first morning alone. By 1910, there would be 30,000 whites within the Nez Percé reservation — and just 1,500 Nez Percé. "It will only be a few generations," the government Indian agent predicted, "before the tribe is extinct." All across the West, the story would be the same. Before the Dawes Act, some 150 million acres still remained in Indian hands. Within twenty years, two-thirds of that land would be gone, too.

RELICS

During his long life, Mariano Guadalupe Vallejo had fought California Indians on behalf of Spain, commanded *Californio* troops for Mexico, welcomed the Americans to the Pacific coast — and then watched as they dispossessed him of his lands and ignored his culture. While many of his children adjusted well to the new, American California, Vallejo worried that the legacy of his people was being forgotten. His father had been one of the first settlers of San Francisco, yet now the city's schools taught French and German, but not Spanish. Immigrants from other countries, he complained, were "fawned upon while we Californios are despised. . . . If the Californios could all gather together to breathe a lament, it would reach Heaven as a moving sigh which would cause fear and consternation in the Universe! What misery!"

If the Californios could all gather together to breathe a lament, it would reach Heaven as a moving sigh which would cause fear and consternation in the Universe! What misery!

Mariano Guadalupe Vallejo

Mexican American mine workers somewhere in the Southwest, 1890s

An agricultural workers' encampment in southern California, ca. 1900. As Mexican Americans left their own village lands to make their homes in cities, many still found themselves in the countryside at harvesttime, gathering crops belonging to others.

He was hounded by lawyers, plagued by debts. "Everyone is money-mad," he said. "Everyone barks, cries, and whines for it." His once vast estate was reduced to fewer than three hundred acres. With his wife, Benicia, Vallejo now lived in a New England–style cottage in Sonoma that he called Lachryma Montis — Tear of the Mountain. But he sometimes visited his old adobe home near Petaluma, now decaying from neglect. "I compare that old relic with myself . . ." he wrote, "ruins and dilapidation. What a difference between then and now. Then, youth, strength and riches; now age, weakness and poverty."

Friends petitioned Congress for a pension for the old man, recognizing "his kindness to immigrants and his noble conduct" during California's transition from Mexican to American rule. But before any action could be taken, Vallejo died on January 21, 1890.

By then, hundreds of Mexicans were crossing the border into the United States every month. Some were escaping political turbulence and crushing poverty. Others were lured by the promise of jobs — working in mines, on the railroads, or in the farm fields and orange and lemon groves made possible by irrigation. Their reasons for coming north were more or less the same as those that drove Americans west:

"My intention is to get a good job and save some money and start out for myself," said one, "for one can make good money and there is always work."

In the next thirty years, 1.5 million men, women, and children — 10 percent of the population of Mexico — would come north in pursuit of that dream, following many of the same routes once taken by Coronado and the conquistadors.

WOUNDED KNEE

In 1890, the United States undertook the last census of the nineteenth century. Back when some of the Americans counted in that census had been born, everything west of the Mississippi lay beyond the boundaries of the nation. Now, after a rush of statehood ceremonies that brought Montana, Washington, North and South Dakota, Idaho, and Wyoming into the Union in the space of two years, only Utah, Arizona, New Mexico, and Oklahoma remained as territories.

Nearly 17 million people lived between the Mississippi and the Pacific — three times the population of the entire nation when Thomas Jefferson completed the Louisiana Purchase in 1803 and propelled his countrymen toward the western sea. "This census completes the history of a century," wrote the man who directed it; "a century of progress and achievement unequaled in the world's history." Nearly 2 million square miles had been "redeemed from wilderness and brought into the service of man."

No Indian people anywhere in the West now lived freely on their own land — and even the lands on which they were now forced to huddle were being broken up under the Allotment Act.

Lakota lands had yet to be allotted, but a commission headed by General George Crook had managed, by playing the chiefs off against one another, to talk them into giving up some 9 million acres, nonetheless.

Sitting Bull had done everything he could to keep his people from signing away their land. "[The whites] will try to gain possession of the last piece of ground we possess," he warned them. "Let us stand as one family as we did before the white people led us astray." In the end, he was ignored. Afterward, a reporter asked him how the Indians felt about losing their lands. "Indians!" he said. "There are no Indians left but me!"

Pawnee ghost dancer's shirt

The Lakota had been assured they would continue to receive the rations their previous treaties guaranteed them. But as soon as the commission left for the East, Congress cut appropriations for all reservation Indians everywhere. Rations were drastically reduced. It was a dry summer and the crops failed. Children went hungry. There were epidemics of measles, influenza, and whooping cough. "They made us many promises," one old man said, "more than I can remember, but they never kept but one; they promised to take our land and they took it."

That same summer, reports began to filter in from reservations all over the Plains of a new religion that seemed to promise a revival of the old ways. Its

Wovoka (top), the Paiute shaman whose message of renewal was entirely peaceful, and Kicking Bear, the Lakota who brought a more militant version of it to Standing Rock

prophet was a Paiute named Wovoka, and the gospel of salvation he proclaimed, filled with Christian as well as Indian elements, was simple:

> My brothers, I bring to you the promise of a day in which there will be no white man to lay his hand on the bridle of the Indians' horse; when the red men of the prairie will rule the world. . . . I bring you word from your fathers the ghosts, that they are marching now to join you, led by the Messiah who came once to live on earth with the white man but was killed by them.

Men and women were first to purify themselves and forswear alcohol and violence. "You must not hurt anybody or do harm to anyone," Wovoka said. "You must not fight. Do right always." Then they were to dance in a large circle, chanting and appealing to the spirits of their ancestors. If their faith was strong enough, Wovoka promised, the old world of their fathers would return, the whites would vanish, the buffalo would cover the earth again.

It was called the "ghost dance," and James Mooney, director of the Bureau of American Ethnology, understood its appeal:

> When the race lies crushed and groaning under an alien yoke, how natural is the dream of a redeemer . . . who shall return from exile or awake from some long sleep to drive out the usurper and win back for his people what they have lost. The hope becomes a faith and the faith becomes the creed of priests and prophets, until the hero is a god and the dream a religion, looking to some great miracle of nature for its culmination and accomplishment.

One day that autumn, a Miniconjou from the Cheyenne River agency came to see Sitting Bull. His name was Kicking Bear and, with his brother-in-law, Short Bull, he had returned from a train trip to the Far West where he had seen the prophet Wovoka and learned from him of the great renewal that was coming the following spring. The dancing had already begun at Cheyenne River and Rosebud and Pine Ridge, Kicking Bear said; Sitting Bull's people at Standing Rock should start dancing, too.

Sitting Bull was concerned that the whites would send soldiers to stop the dancing. Kicking Bear reassured him. If the dancers dressed as Wovoka had told them to dress — in white shirts, painted with special symbols — no bullet could harm them. This was no part of Wovoka's teaching, and Sitting Bull remained skeptical, but he agreed to let Kicking Bear stay and teach the ghost dance to the people of Standing Rock.

They sang as they danced, "Mother, hand me my sharp knife,/Mother, hand me my sharp knife,/Here come the buffalo returning —/Mother, hand me my sharp knife." And they sang, "Mother, do come back!/Mother, do come back!/My little brother is crying for you —/My father says so!"

At all the Lakota agencies, people began to dance. Some moved out of their cabins into teepees, as in the old days. Children abandoned their schoolrooms, one Pine Ridge pupil recalled.

> That part about the dead returning was what appealed to me. To think I should see my dear mother, grandmother, brothers, and sisters, again! . . . Soon fifty of us, little boys, about eight to ten, started out across country . . . almost thirty

The only known photograph of the Lakota ghost dancers at Pine Ridge, made by a small-town photographer, J. E. Meddaugh, in September of 1890, when whites still considered the new ceremony merely a curiosity

miles. There on the Porcupine Creek thousands of Lakota people were in camp. . . .

The people, wearing the sacred shirts and feathers, . . . formed a ring. We [boys] were in it. All joined hands. Everyone was respectful and quiet, expecting something wonderful to happen. . . . The leaders beat time and sang as the people danced, going round to the left in a sidewise step. Occasionally, someone . . . fell unconscious into the center and lay there "dead." After a while, many lay about in that condition. They were now "dead" and seeing their dear ones. As each one came to, she, or he, slowly sat up and looked about, bewildered, and then began wailing inconsolably.

Although most Indians had nothing to do with the ghost dancers, some Indian agents grew frightened. To them, the mysterious dancing and the boasts about magic shirts that could not be pierced by bullets sounded like warnings of war.

No one was more frightened than Daniel Royer, agent at Pine Ridge. A political appointee, utterly ignorant of his charges and so often alarmed by them that the Lakota called him "Young Man Afraid of Indians," he was sure he was about to be attacked. On November 12, 1890, he wired the army for help: "Indians are dancing in the snow and are wild and crazy. . . . We need protection and we need it now. The leaders should be arrested and confined at some military post until the matter is quieted, and this should be done at once."

General Nelson A. Miles was dispatched with 5,000 troops, including the Seventh Cavalry, the successor to Custer's old command. Scores of reporters came along, too, eager to cover a new Indian war. No one was sure what Miles planned to do. Miles wasn't either. The West had changed since he had last waged war there. "It would be unwise to say anything at this time," he told reporters. "Anything I might say would be telegraphed over the country. Indians now have young men who read English perfectly well, and they no longer depend upon runners to take their news from camp to camp. They utilize the mails, and keep posted with regard to current events affecting their interests."

The ghost dancers at Pine Ridge and Rosebud, frightened that the soldiers had come to attack them, fled to a remote plateau surrounded by cliffs that nervous whites began calling "the Stronghold."

At Standing Rock, Sitting Bull now actively encouraged his people to dance. Nothing that might lead to a return to the old ways should be overlooked — and no one, white or Lakota, was to interfere with the practice of their faith. His old enemy, agent James McLaughlin, now became convinced that Sitting Bull was the "high priest and leading apostle of this latest absurdity." If he were removed from the scene, McLaughlin concluded, the whole business might just blow over. A message from Lieutenant Bull Head of the Oglala police provided him with the excuse he needed to act:

Coup de grâce: Sergeant Red Tomahawk (center) of the Lakota police fired the fatal bullet into Sitting Bull's head.

Sitting Bull has received a letter from the Pine Ridge outfit asking him to come over there, as God was to appear to them. Sitting Bull's people want him to go, but he has sent a letter to you asking for your permission, and if you do not give it he is going to go anyway; he has been fitting up his horses for a long ride and will go on horseback in case he is pursued. [I] would like to arrest him at once before he has the chance of giving them the slip. . . .

When McLaughlin heard that Sitting Bull was planning to leave Standing Rock to join the ghost dancers in the Pine Ridge stronghold, he determined to stop him. Forty-three Indian policemen were sent to do the job. Two troops of cavalry were to follow along at a distance, so as not to make a bad situation worse. They were to intervene only if the police ran into trouble.

Early in the morning of December 15, 1890, Lakota policemen burst into Sitting Bull's house and ordered him to his feet. His wives began to wail. The police pushed him toward the door. Lieutenant Bull Head and an officer named Shave Head grabbed his arms, and Sergeant Red Tomahawk walked behind as they started toward the wagon that was to carry the prisoner back to the agency.

But Sitting Bull's followers were now awake. They began to taunt the police. One of Sitting Bull's adopted sons urged his father to resist. Sitting Bull slowed, apparently unsure what to do.

The police shoved him toward the wagon. One of his supporters, a man named Catch-the-Bear, raised his rifle and fired into Lieutenant Bull Head's side. As the policeman fell, he fired his revolver into Sitting Bull's chest. At the same time, Red Tomahawk put a bullet through his head. The cavalry rushed in, and when it was all over, Sitting Bull and eight of his followers lay dead. The last of his visions had come true; his own Lakota people had killed him.

Four Indian policemen were also dead, and two more mortally wounded. One of them, Shave Head, later asked agent McLaughlin if he had done well. The agent nodded that he had. Then he asked for a Catholic priest so that he might be married to his wife in the church before he died.

Sitting Bull's grieving followers, fearful now that the soldiers would attack them, hurried toward the Cheyenne River reservation, where they joined a Miniconjou band led by a chief named Big Foot. He had once been an enthusiastic ghost dancer but was now ill with pneumonia, and no longer certain that the world would truly be transformed in the spring. Red Cloud and other chiefs, seeking to avoid further trouble with the soldiers who now seemed to be swarming everywhere, asked him to bring his band in to Pine Ridge and see if there weren't some way to reconcile things before more blood was shed.

General Miles misunderstood what was happening. Convinced that Big Foot's Miniconjou, their numbers swollen by refugees from Sitting Bull's band, intended to make a stand in the stronghold, he ordered his men to intercept them.

Colonel John Forsyth and the Seventh Cavalry caught up with Big Foot near Porcupine Creek three days after Christmas. Big Foot rode in a wagon, too sick even to sit up but with a white flag above his head as evidence that he meant no harm to anyone.

The soldiers transferred him to an army ambulance and then led his band down to a little creek called Wounded Knee for the night. There were 120 men and 230 women and children. The soldiers distributed rations. An army surgeon did what he could for Big Foot. But the soldiers also posted four Hotchkiss guns on the top of a rise overlooking the camp. If there was trouble their shells would tear through the whole length of the encampment. Big Foot and his people could not possibly get away. Both sides were sure of it. The Lakota would be disarmed the next day.

"The following morning there was a bugle call," a Lakota named Dewey Beard remembered. "Then I saw the soldiers mounting their horses and surrounding us. It was announced that all men should come to the center for a talk. . . . Big Foot was brought out of his tent and sat . . . and the older men were gathered around him. . . ."

Colonel Forsyth asked Big Foot if his people had any arms. A few were handed over and placed in a pile. They were old weapons, for the most part.

Forsyth demanded to know where the Indians' repeating Winchesters were hidden. Big Foot denied they had any. Forsyth ordered his men to search the whole village. As his troops began moving from teepee to teepee, confiscating knives and axes from the women, and sometimes seizing a repeating rifle, a reporter named Charles Allen noted something else: ". . . eight or ten Indian boys dressed in the gray school uniforms of that period. The fun they were having as they played 'bucking horse,' 'leap frog,' and similar games, carried the mind for a fleeting moment back to the days of boyhood."

Then, a medicine man began to dance, pausing from time to time to throw pinches of dust into the air. "Do not fear," he shouted to the warriors, "but let your

We tried to run but they shot us like we were buffalo. I know there are some good white people, but the soldiers must be mean to shoot children and women.

Louise Weasel Bear

Three of the four breech-loading Hotchkiss guns that did such deadly work at Wounded Knee

hearts be strong. Many soldiers are about us and have many bullets, but I am assured the bullets cannot penetrate us. . . . If they do come toward us, they will float away like dust in the air."

"He was an orator of the first water," Charles Allen recalled. "Every gesture and body movement flowed rhythmically. . . . Suddenly, scooping up a handful of dirt he tossed it scattering in the air, and with eyes turned toward heaven, implored the Great Spirit to scatter the soldiers likewise. I remarked to some troopers nearby that if the man were an ordained minister of some Christian church he would convert the world."

A soldier spotted a rifle beneath one man's blanket. Forsyth ordered him disarmed. The soldiers did not know the man was deaf and snatched impatiently at his blanket. He pulled away, raising the rifle above his head. "If they had left him alone he was going to put his gun down . . ." Dewey Beard remembered. "They grabbed him and spun him in the east direction. He was still unconcerned even then. . . . They came on and grabbed the gun. Right after there was a report of a gun, quite loud."

Snow blanketed Wounded Knee after the shooting stopped, and 146 dead Lakota were left where they had fallen for three days, then buried in a mass grave on the top of the hill from which the Hotchkiss guns had fired into their camp.

The soldiers opened fire with rifles, revolvers, struggled hand to hand, then the Hotchkiss guns began to hurl exploding shells into the teepees. The Lakota did their best to fight back. "I was badly wounded and pretty weak, too," Dewey Beard recalled. "I looked down the ravine and saw a lot of women coming and crying. . . . I saw soldiers on both sides of the ravine shoot at them until they had killed every one of them. . . . One woman was crying, 'Mother! Mother!' She was wounded under her chin, close to her throat and the bullet passed a braid of her hair and carried some of it into the wound. Her mother had been shot down behind her."

When the shooting finally stopped, perhaps 250 Lakota — men, women, and children — were dead. "It was a thing to melt the heart of a man, if it was stone," said one soldier, "to see those little children with their bodies shot to pieces. . . ."

Charles Allen had watched it all in horror:

While the officers moved among the bodies, feeling that it might not be in order for a civilian to join them, I walked around east of the guards viewing the sad spectacle. On reaching the corner of the green where the schoolboys had been so happy in their sports but a short time before, there was spread before me the saddest picture I had seen or was to see thereafter, for on that spot of their playful choice were scattered the prostrate bodies of all those fine little Indian boys, cold in death. . . . The gun-fire [had] blazed across their playground in a way that permitted no escape. They must have fallen like grass before the sickle.

Dead, too, were twenty-five soldiers.

Wounded Lakota and wounded troopers alike were loaded onto army wagons and taken to the Holy Cross Episcopal Church at Pine Ridge, its walls still hung with Christmas decorations. "Pews were torn from their fastenings and armsful of hay fetched by Indian helpers," a nurse remembered. "Upon a layer of this we spread quilts and blankets taken from our own beds. The victims were lifted as gently as possible and laid in two long rows on the floor — a pathetic array of young girls and women and babes in arms, little children, and a few men, all pierced with bullets."

"A young girl," another nurse recalled, "who had a ghost shirt on underneath her clothes [said,] 'They told me if I put this on the bullets would not go through and I believed them. Now see where we are.'"

The fighting stuttered on for nearly two weeks. When angry warriors set agency buildings afire in retaliation for the killing at Wounded Knee, Colonel Forsyth led the Seventh Cavalry in pursuit, clumsily failed to secure the surrounding hillsides, and suddenly found himself surrounded by angry Lakota, just as Custer had been fifteen years before. This time, however, troops of the all-black Ninth Cavalry came riding to the rescue.

Some 4,000 ghost dancers remained at large, including 1,000 warriors, all huddled together in one big village. Miles, who blamed Forsyth for the slaughter at Wounded Knee, was determined not to have more such killing if he could help it. He surrounded the village, then drew the noose tight slowly enough to give the Indians plenty of time to think about the folly of further resistance.

Finally, on January 15, 1891, the ghost dancers surrendered. Kicking Bear, the man who had brought news of the ghost dance to the Lakota agencies, was one of the last to turn over his rifle to General Miles.

THE OWENS RIVER IS OURS

Between 1890 and 1904, the population of Los Angeles mushroomed from 50,000 to nearly 200,000. There was already too little water in dry years to keep the city parks green, and it seemed clear that Los Angeles could not grow much further without some new source of supply. But Los Angeles had to grow — its whole economy was based on frenzied boosterism. "If Los Angeles runs out of water for one week," warned the head of its Water Department, William Mulholland, "the city within a year will not have a population of 100,000 people. A city quickly finds its level, and that level is its water supply."

And the water Los Angeles wanted was 250 miles away, across the Sierra Nevada in the Owens River that wound through a high valley 250 miles northeast of Los Angeles. It was home to several thousand small ranchers who had dug canals to irrigate their apple orchards and fields of hay and alfalfa with snowmelt from the Sierras.

In September of 1904, two strangers traveled through the valley. They were careful not to identify themselves, but one was Fred Eaton, a shrewd financial operator and former mayor of Los Angeles.

The other was William Mulholland himself. An Irish immigrant, he'd served briefly as a merchant seaman, tried lumberjacking and panning for gold, then joined the privately owned L.A. Water Company as a lowly ditch-tender. A big man with infinite energy and a remarkable memory — he is said to have committed to memory the location of every pipe and valve and fire hydrant in the city system — he was made superintendent just eight years later, when the city bought the company and began to run it on its own. Mulholland believed rivers existed only to be used: if it were left up to him, he once said, he would have the Yosemite Valley carefully photographed and then "build a dam from one side of that valley to the other and *stop the goddamned waste.*"

The people of the Owens Valley were optimistic that year. The brand-new federal Bureau of Reclamation had promised to improve the irrigation system that made their farms possible. But Mulholland and Eaton had other plans. Mulholland believed he could build a system of aqueducts and siphons and tunnels that would take Owens River water right through the Sierras and on into Los Angeles — provided he got the funds.

Eaton hurried to Washington and quietly helped convince the Bureau of Reclamation to abandon its plan to aid the Owens Valley: the water would benefit many more people if it could be moved to Los Angeles, instead. Then, he went back to the valley and, posing as an eccentric but enormously wealthy rancher, began buying up land and water rights. In cooperation with a clandestine syndicate of investors — unknown even to Mulholland — he also bought up large tracts in the still-dry San Fernando Valley, where plans called for a vast reservoir from which water would one day be sold to farmers.

Mulholland and Eaton then persuaded the city's voters to pass the largest bond issue in the history of the United States up to that time — $23 million. "Owens River is ours," said the Los Angeles *Times,* "and our business now is to hustle and bring it here and make Los Angeles the garden spot of the earth and the home of millions of contented people."

The dreamer and his dream: William Mulholland (above) and some of the mules that outperformed tractors and kept his project moving across the Mojave Desert

At last, William Mulholland could get to work. Neither personal profit nor politics ever interested him: once, asked if he wanted to run for mayor, he answered that he'd sooner give birth to a porcupine — backward. He lived only to build, and now faced an engineering challenge that rivaled those faced by the builders of the transcontinental railroad and the Suez Canal. Fifty-three tunnels had to be blasted through the mountains; 500 miles of trails and roads had to be built; 120 miles of railroad track laid; 170 miles of power lines brought in from two specially built power plants. Five thousand to 6,000 men had to be fed and housed and doctored while they inched their way across the Mojave Desert — immigrant Irishmen, Greeks, Austrians, Serbians, Hungarians, Italians, and grizzled veterans of the West's gold and silver strikes, a few of whom had worked the Comstock Lode before the Civil War. The 110-degree heat spoiled food moments after it was cooked. Blowing sand destroyed twenty-eight Caterpillar tractors that had to be replaced by fifteen hundred mules. Forty-three men died in the six years it took to finish the job.

But finally, on November 5, 1913, before a huge crowd at Exposition Park, valves were turned and Owens River water rushed down the spillway for the first time. "There it is!" said Mulholland. "Take it!" Thanks largely to Mulholland, Los Angeles soon surpassed San Francisco to become the biggest and most powerful city in the West.

The Owens Valley never recovered from its loss. "Ten years ago this was a wonderful valley," Will Rogers wrote in 1923, "with one quarter of a million acres of fruit and alfalfa. But Los Angeles had to have more water for its Chamber of Commerce to drink more toasts to its growth, more water to dilute its orange juice and more water for its geraniums to delight the tourists. . . ."

The first water from the Owens River cascades down the last sluiceway of the Los Angeles aqueduct and into the San Fernando Valley, November 5, 1913.

SEEING EDEN

The first quarter century of the world's first national park, Yellowstone, did not go smoothly. Just five years after the park was established in 1872, Chief Joseph's Nez Percé had raced through Yellowstone, killing several tourists along the way.

In 1882, during an expedition through the park, General Phil Sheridan had discovered the park's minimal management in shambles. Poachers were indiscriminately slaughtering the wildlife — 4,000 elk in one winter alone and buffalo, whose heads were worth three hundred dollars apiece because there were so few left. Sheridan also learned that a company run by the Northern Pacific Railroad was being granted monopoly rights to develop the park at a ridiculously low rent.

Launching a national campaign to protect the wildlife and keep the park under federal control, Sheridan brought President Chester A. Arthur to Yellowstone the next year.

In 1886, the army took over. It supervised Yellowstone for the next thirty-two years, brought poaching under control, and with the help of breeding stock from Charles Goodnight's private herd in Texas, helped save the buffalo from extinction.

Meanwhile, more and more people were coming to view Yellowstone's marvels. By the turn of the century, tourist traffic was increasing throughout the West. Ranchers who for years had freely hosted eastern friends seeking a taste of western life began accepting payment for their hospitality, and the dude ranch was born. Elegant hotels went up, too — on the rim of the Grand Canyon, in the Rockies, in Yellowstone itself. And still the visitors kept coming, eager to see for themselves the West they had only read about till now.

In 1913, after intense lobbying by the new American Automobile Association, cars were permitted for the first time in Yosemite National Park. Two years later, they entered Yellowstone. The number of visitors to both parks immediately doubled. To help cope with them all, Congress created the National Park Service in 1916. Eventually, tourism would become the biggest industry in the West.

Well-shaded hikers at rest on the Minerva Terrace, Yellowstone, 1888

20 REAL PHOTOGRAPHS 50c

FOR YOUR ALBUM

FOR YOUR FRIENDS

YOSEMITE NATIONAL PARK

I heard the other day that a question has been raised as to whether automobiles should be admitted in the Yosemite Valley. May a word be permitted on that subject? If Adam had known what harm the Serpent was going to work, he would have tried to prevent him from finding lodgment in Eden; and if you stop to realize what the result of the automobile will be in that wonderful, that incomparable valley, you will keep it out. . . . Do not let the Serpent enter Eden at all.

James Bryce, 1912

Seeing Yosemite from the comfort of one's parlor (opposite, bottom) and from horseback (above)

The first automobiles chug their way into Yosemite, 1913.

WHY IN HEAVEN'S NAME THIS HASTE?

Gentlemen, why in heaven's name this haste? You have time enough. No enemy threatens you. No volcano will rise from beneath you. Ages and ages lie before you. Why sacrifice the present to the future, fancying that you will be happier when your fields teem with wealth and your cities with people? In Europe we have cities wealthier and more populous than yours and we are not happy. You dream of your posterity; but your posterity will look back to yours as the golden age, and envy those who first burst into this silent, splendid Nature, who first lifted up their axes upon these tall trees and lined these waters with busy wharves. Why, then, seek to complete in a few decades what [took]

the other nations of the world thousands of years. . . ? Why do things rudely and ill which need to be done well, seeing that the welfare of your descendants may turn upon them? Why, in your hurry to subdue and utilize Nature, squander her splendid gifts? . . . Why hasten the advent of that threatening day when the vacant spaces of the continent shall all have been filled, and the poverty or discontent of the older States shall find no outlet? You have opportunities such as mankind has never had before, and may never have again. Your work is great and noble; it is done for a future longer and vaster than our conceptions can embrace. Why not make its outlines and beginnings worthy of these destinies. . . ? James Bryce

Smoke belching from the smelters that surrounded Butte, Montana (above), was so thick that one perpetually blanketed neighborhood was called "Seldom Seen."

Undergrowth ablaze after lumbermen clear-cut a slope in Washington State, about 1900

On October 20, 1905, the Rawlins-to-Lander stagecoach rattled north toward the Sweetwater River in Wyoming. Al Dougherty, a hardened veteran of the lonely trail, held the reins. He had been driving the same route during the terrible winter of 1886–87, when a blizzard stranded him and a young woman passenger. Before help finally arrived, the woman froze to death, and Dougherty was so frostbitten that he lost six fingers, half of one foot, and all of the other. His nickname now was "Peggy."

This day his passenger was twenty-three-year-old Ethel Waxham, daughter of a prominent Denver physician and a recent graduate of Wellesley College, where she had studied classical literature, learned four languages, and earned a Phi Beta Kappa key. She dabbled in poetry, enjoyed amateur theatricals, and was voraciously curious about the world. During one school vacation, she had volunteered for work in the slums of New York City. "I do not want to see one side of life only, but many," she explained to a friend. And she soaked up experience:

> Peggy Dougherty . . . is tall and grizzled. They say that when he goes to dances they make him take the spike out of the bottom of his wooden leg. Our way lay up to Crook's Gap, the coldest part of the road where the night before, the thermometer had registered zero. . . . [Y]e gods, how he could swear. We switched him off to telling stories of the cold winter of '86 and the old times. . . . "The winters have not been so severe lately," he said. "No," said [another passenger], "and we haven't had a blizzard this summer."

Now, she had accepted her first full-time job: as the teacher in a one-room school in the isolated center of Wyoming, in a county named Frémont, in honor of the pathfinder who had first mapped it in the 1840s.

> At last we saw the little school house of logs, fourteen by sixteen with a good [sod] roof, almost flat coming low over the sides. . . . The whole was put up, I believe, at an original expenditure of seventy-five dollars. . . . We soon had the place swept out and arranged, brought in the books that we had carried over,

Miss Ethel Waxham as she looked at Wellesley College shortly before heading west in search of adventure

The Rawlins-to-Lander stage, with Peggy Dougherty holding the reins. "Ye gods," Ethel Waxham noted, "how he could swear."

and set the traps for the mountain rats that had left traces of themselves over the place. . . . The door has had some passerby's six shooter emptied into it.

She had seven students, ages eight to sixteen, and lived with a ranch family, and so soon became acquainted with the customs of a place where the nearest neighbor lived miles away, and Lander, the closest "city" — population 1,000 — was visited just once a year. She took it all in, with what one friend called "her combination of strength and the gentlest charm — welded by that flashing mind."

People passing, we call company. Sometimes no one comes by for days. Sometimes many pass. A Mormon boy . . . Old Hanley . . . [and] Ted Abra, one of the roustabouts. . . . He enjoys the reputation of being cattle thief and horse wrangler. Roy McLaughlin is another of the gang. They went by once with about fifty head of horses. . . .

Bill [Bruce] is an Irishman. . . . He has a childlike gentleness and drollery of manner that is either innocence itself or simulated. He came over to this country and found a five-dollar gold piece on the sidewalk. "Come over, Brothers," he wrote home. "It's all true." Later, he got a job of carrying bricks. "Come over, Brothers," he wrote again. "All I have to do is to carry bricks up to the fourth floor in a hod and the man up there does all the work."

Among those who began showing up with considerable regularity, despite the fact that his home was an eleven-hour ride away, was a sheep rancher named John Galloway Love.

Ethel Waxham out riding near her parents' home in Denver

John Galloway Love

Mr. Love is a Scotchman about thirty-five years old. At first sight he made me think of a hired man, as he lounged stiffly on the couch, in overalls, his feet covered with enormous red and black-striped stockings edged with blue around the top, that reached to his knees. . . . His face was kindly, with shrewd blue twinkling eyes. A moustache grew over his mouth, like willows bending over a brook. But his voice was most peculiar and characteristic. Close analysis fails to find the charm of it. A little Scotch dialect, a little slow drawl, a little nasal quality, a bit of falsetto once in a while, and a tone as if he were speaking out of doors. There is a kind of twinkle in his voice as well as in his eyes, and he is full of quaint turns of speech, and unusual expressions. For he is not a common sheepherder, [it is said,] but a mutton-aire, or sheep baron.

He was born on a Wisconsin farm to Scottish parents. His mother died shortly after his birth, and his father, a professional photographer and lecturer, had taken him back to Scotland, then died when the boy was only ten. After a few years in an orphanage, he joined his four older sisters in Custer County, Nebraska, where they had each taken homesteads and also worked as schoolteachers. He was a bright boy — he could recite by memory Sir Walter Scott's "The Lady of the Lake" in its entirety — but also high-spirited.

Expelled from the University of Nebraska in 1891 for a foolish prank, he invested his savings in two horses and a buggy, and headed for Wyoming. When his horses died after drinking poisoned water, Love walked a hundred miles to the Sweetwater country. There, he had worked as a sheepherder and cowboy, and, some said, had also been a friend of the outlaw Butch Cassidy. In any case, after seven straight years of living on the range, without a roof over his head, Love had decided to start his own ranch on a treeless stretch along Muskrat Creek. Why, a friend asked, had he chosen "that God-forsaken lonesome place"? "Because," Love answered, "it has lots of room and that is what I want." President Theodore Roosevelt had signed Love's papers under the new Desert Land Act, granting him outright ownership of 640 acres and, because of the water on it, effective control of a thousand square miles, as well. He had big dreams for his land — thousands of sheep and cattle, irrigated grain fields, and hay meadows and fruit orchards.

Now he had another dream as well. Nearly from the moment he first saw her, he wanted Ethel Waxham for his wife. But he was not her only suitor, and when he proposed marriage, she refused, and thought no more about it. When the school year ended, she returned home, and entered the University of Colorado for a master's degree. But memories of the seven months she had spent in the wilds of Wyoming were rarely far from her mind.

I know a land where the gray hills lie
Eternally still, under the sky,
Where all the might of suns and moons
That pass in the quiet of nights and noons
Leave never a sign of the flight of time
On the long sublime horizon line —

And a steady stream of letters from John Love kept those memories fresh:

It is a cruel country as well as a beautiful one. Men seem here only on sufferance.

Ethel Waxham

An isolated Wyoming ranch, about 1908

Muskrat, Wyoming.
September 12, 1906
Dear Miss Waxham,

. . . [When I received your letter] I lay awake . . . out in the sagebrush curled up in my buggy robes and thought and studied astronomy. . . . You have no idea how pleased I was to hear from you and it is beyond my pencil to express the satisfaction I felt. Thank you very much for the picture. It does not flatter you any, but at the same time it is very lifelike. . . .

Of course it will cause many a sharp twinge and heartache to have to take "no" for an answer, but I will never blame you for it in the least and I will never be sorry that I met you. . . . I know the folly of hoping that your "no" is not final, but in spite of that knowledge, in spite of my better judgment, and in spite of all I can do to the contrary, I know that I will hope until the day that you are married. Only then I will know that the sentence is irrevocable. . . .

Yours Sincerely,
John G. Love

John Love's sheep wagon (above) and one of his hired hands (opposite) hard at work on one of the two dams Love hoped would turn his ranch into a garden

November 12, 1906
Dear Miss Waxham,

. . . I know that you have not been brought up to cook and labor. I have never been on the lookout for a slave and would not utter a word of censure if you never learned or if you got ambitious and made a "batch" of biscuits that proved fatal to my favorite dog. I honestly believe that I could idolize you to such an extent as to not utter a harsh word. "Little girl," I will do my level best to win you and will be the happiest mortal on earth if I can see the ring that I wear on my watch chain flash on your finger. It has never been worn by or offered to another. . . .

We had one very hard storm and several herders lost their lives but that I think was their own fault.

February 15, 1907
Dear Mr. Love,

I am fortunate in having two letters from you to answer in one. . . . [T]he days have been comparatively dull. . . . I am too busy for dances here, if I care to go, which I do not. They are prosaic affairs in the boys' fraternity houses — not at all like the "Hailey Ball!" . . . The seven months I spent at the ranch I would not exchange for any other seven months in my life. They seem shorter than seven weeks, even seven days, here.

Dear Miss Waxham,

. . . I for one am glad that your curiosity led you to drift up here to Wyoming and now my supreme desire in life is to persuade you to come back. . . .

In 1907, Ethel received her degree in literature, having written her thesis — "The Dramatic Theory and Practice of Maurice Maeterlinck" — in both French and English. She took a job teaching Latin at a private school in Wisconsin for a year; returned home to be in charge of her father's household; then, in 1909, went to Pueblo, Colorado, as a high school teacher.

Everywhere she went, John Love's letters continued to follow her, steadily weakening her defenses, friendship slowly warming into something else:

April 3, 1909
Dear Mr. Love —
There are reasons galore why I should not write so often. I'm a beast to write at all. It makes you — (maybe?) — think that "no" is not "no," but "perhaps," or "yes," or anything else. . . .

> Good wishes for your busy season from E. W.
> P.S. I like you very much.

October 12th, 1909
Dear Miss Waxham,
. . . I am once more in debt, but if my season of bad luck has come to an end and the winter is not too severe, I will come out with flying colors in the spring. . . . Your picture nicely framed now adorns the wagon. . . .

Meanwhile, through unending labor and with the same determination with which he kept at his courtship, Love continued to develop his ranch. Sheep, cattle, and horse herds grew, then declined, then grew again depending on the whims of weather and markets. To water the grain fields, gardens, and fruit orchards that were still only dreams, he began work on two dams and a long irrigation ditch. All the work had to be done by hand and by horse. He had no dam-building experience, so he consulted government bulletins, the *Encyclopaedia Britannica,* and any passerby with advice to give. He scoured the countryside for abandoned buildings, too, dismantled them, and moved them to his ranch. A saloon, an old hotel, and other buildings from two former stage stations became bunkhouses, sheds, barns, a blacksmith shop on Muskrat

Creek. Around what had once been a hotel dining room, he constructed the large main house. For logs, he had to travel a hundred miles to the Wind River Mountains, then haul them back by wagon. Each trip for a load of twenty took two weeks.

After four years, he was finally ready to try again to persuade Ethel to marry him.

October 25th, 1909

Dear Miss Waxham,

. . . There is no use in my fixing up the house anymore, papering, etc., until I know how it should be done and I won't know that until you see it and say how it ought to be fixed. If you never see it, I don't want it fixed, for I won't live here. *We* could live very comfortably in the wagon while *our* house was being fixed up to suit you if you only would say yes.

January 1, 1910

Dear Mr. Love,

. . . Suppose that you lost everything that you have and a little more; and suppose that for the best reason in the world I wanted you to ask me to say "yes."

What would you do?

E.

January 11, 1910

Dear Miss Waxham,

. . . *Hope* is far far from being dead yet, "little girl." I have lost over twenty thousand dollars in the last forty days. If I lose another twenty thousand, hope will still live and not even be very feeble. . . . If I were with you, I would throw my arms around you and kiss you and wait eagerly for the kiss that I have waited over four years for.

Finally, in the spring of 1910, Ethel Waxham agreed to be John Love's wife. Many years later, their son David remembered family stories of their honeymoon:

When my father was sure that my mother was going to marry him he had a sheep wagon built especially to his order. And that was to be the honeymoon sheep wagon. . . . They were married on June 20th, 1910 and it was pretty hot, so they started out for the mountains and from then on there is a blank in our knowledge. Mother rarely discussed it except uh, in times of crisis. And my father never discussed it. But apparently it rained a great deal. The horses got away and they were marooned and never got to the mountains. So the honeymoon was not a romantic success.

I AM NOT AFRAID

By 1900, there were 76 million Americans, more than 20 million of them living in the West. But the number of Native Americans had dropped to only 237,000 — the smallest number the continent had held since the coming of the first Europeans.

"The field of research is speedily narrowing," wrote the explorer and pioneer anthropologist John Wesley Powell, "because of the rapid change in the Indian population now in progress; all habits, customs, and opinions are fading away; even languages are disappearing; and in a very few years it will be impossible to study our North American Indians in their primitive condition except from recorded history."

My little son grew up in the white man's school. He can read books, and he owns cattle and has a farm. He is a leader among our Hidatsa people, helping teach them to follow the white man's road.

He is kind to me. We no longer live in an earth lodge, but in a house with chimneys; and my son's wife cooks by a stove.

But for me, I cannot forget our old ways.

Buffalo Bird Woman

Buffalo Bird Woman (left), her hair cut short in mourning for her husband, and her daughter-in-law, Sioux Woman, prepare prairie turnips.

Since the time they had sheltered Lewis and Clark during the winter of 1804, the Mandan and Hidatsa had been forced to move twice, each time farther up the Missouri. Smallpox and the Lakota had first driven them north during the 1830s. Then the federal government insisted they abandon their communal life, centered on earth lodge villages, and spread out onto individual parcels of land. One by one, families left their villages, and as they departed their lodges were dismantled to prevent them from returning.

Among the last to leave was the extended family of *Waheenee-wea,* Buffalo Bird Woman. She had been born in 1840, the granddaughter of an important Hidatsa medicine man named Missouri River, from whom she learned the traditions of her people. "My old grandfather," she remembered, "taught me of the spirits. . . . 'Not all the spirits are good,' he said. 'Some seek to harm us. The good gods send us buffaloes, and rain to make our corn grow. But it is not well to provoke the gods. My little granddaughter should never laugh at them or speak of them lightly.'"

Buffalo Bird Woman never forgot that admonition.

As a gift, her mother had taught her the ceremonies for making an earth lodge — a special skill that earned her many robes from other families. She learned to weave baskets and mats, make pots from clay, decorate robes with paint and porcupine quills, and was rewarded for her work with a beaded belt of which she said she was as proud "as a war leader of his first scalp."

Buffalo Bird Woman's family moved onto land that her brother had selected while fasting for a vision. It was on a hill the Hidatsa called *Awatahesh,* "hill by itself," and came to be known as Independence.

Her people were told to build square cabins. Building a house was now a man's job — and no longer sacred. But as a link with their past, her husband, Son of Star, placed a buffalo skull over the door, and set their stove in the center of the house, where an earth lodge fire would once have been.

For Buffalo Bird Woman it was not the same: "I think our old way of raising corn is better than the new way taught us by white men," she told a visitor. "Last year, our agent held an agricultural fair . . . and we Indians competed for prizes for the best corn. The corn which I sent to the fair took the first prize. . . . I cultivated the corn exactly as in the old times, with a hoe."

She spoke only her native language, shunned the clothing of white people, and when her husband died in 1906, mourned in the traditional way: she cut her hair short and wore it loose, and sliced off the tip of her little finger. "Sometimes at evening I sit," she said,

> looking out on the big Missouri. The sun sets, and dusk steals over the water. In the shadows I seem again to see our Indian village, with smoke curling upward from the earth lodges; and in the river's roar I hear the yells of the warriors, the laughter of little children as of old. It is but an old woman's dream. Again I see but shadows and hear only the roar of the river; and tears come into my eyes. Our Indian life, I know, is gone forever.

As a young man, Buffalo Bird Woman's brother, Wolf C. Chief, had hunted buffalo, become a successful warrior, learned sacred songs, and gone on vision quests — all in hopes of becoming a leader of his people. But unlike his sister, who resisted change, Wolf Chief was quick to adopt new ways, not just to survive, but to succeed. "My people often talk against me," he said, "& laugh & say 'That man wants to be a white man.' . . . [But] I want to be strong & go forward. . . ."

At thirty, he had decided to learn the white man's language: "When Indians come to a white man's store for bacon and think [he] cannot understand them, they make signs like a flat curled up nose for pig and go 'unh-unh' — grunting. But when I go to a store I say 'bacon' and get it right away."

Soon, he opened his own store, but when the reservation agent's brother decided to get into the business, Wolf Chief was pressured to close it. Instead, he wrote to the commissioner of Indian affairs in Washington.

> My Dear Sir:
> . . . The present Agent John S. Murphy bothered me in every way to keep me from keeping a Store. He did not do a single act that will encourage me in this. . . . I think it's [an] honorable way of making my living. . . . I wish you sent me a copy of Reservation laws so that I will read it and be not troublesome to my agent and to this office.
>
> > Yours respectfully,
> > Mr. Wolf C. Chief

A federal inspector was dispatched. Eventually, the agent's brother had to close his store. Wolf Chief's doors stayed open. He kept writing letters to Washington, more than a hundred before he was through — on his own behalf, and that of his people.

Wolf Chief as he looked when he was a thirty-year-old warrior (above), and, at right, waiting on a customer in the store he successfully insisted he had the right to run

Fort Berthhold, Dakota Territory, March, 1882.
To the Great Father [Chester Arthur]:
My name is Wolf Chief. I am poor. My agent is bad . . . he tells lies. . . . [He] says I am bad bec[a]use I write. . . .

December, 1888.
Dear Great Father [Grover Cleveland]
. . . I want to speak for my people. . . . [T]he frost came and now we have no crop at all and we do not know what we will do this winter for food. . . . We have no more buffalo and very few deer left. If you . . . do not help us we don't know how we [are] going to get along. I wish you would write me and tell me what you are going to do.

April 29th, 1891.
President [Benjamin] Harrison, President of the United States at Washington, D.C.
My Dear Friend Sir: Our school houses [are] very old indeed. No good white man [would] keep children in such bad and dangerous buildings. At a little blow of wind the houses might fall down, killing every child. . . . I wish that the school houses be removed [and new ones built]. . . . I am trying to be like a white man and am learning the best I can. . . . Please, I wish to hear from you soon on this matter. I am your friend.

Wolf Chief eventually converted to Christianity, and donated ten acres of land for a chapel close to his cabin. But in an old earth lodge near his house was the sacred medicine bundle that had belonged to his grandfather, Missouri River. The two human skulls wrapped in a blanket had been passed along for generations, used to invoke the help of spirits in war, in hunting, and especially in bringing rain.

Missionaries and Indian agents had urged Wolf Chief to destroy the sacred bundle. He had refused, out of respect for his ancestors. But no member of the special Waterbuster clan — the Hidatsa group responsible for the bundle's ceremonies — would come forward to take responsibility for it, and Wolf Chief grew worried that neglecting the medicine bundle while he practiced Christianity would anger both his old gods and his new one. In 1907, he sold the relic to an anthropologist who placed it in a New York museum.

Shortly before she died, Buffalo Bird Woman cooperated with an anthropologist, explaining her people's ways so that they might be remembered in the future. Her son, Edward Goodbird, who had converted to Christianity, did the translations:

I have changed my ways and become Christian, but that one way I have not changed. When poor people and hungry old people come for food, I cannot refuse them. I am sure that Jesus fed people when He was on earth.

Wolf Chief

Whenever the white man treats the Indian as they treat each other, then we will have no more wars. We shall all be alike — brothers of one father, and one mother, with one sky above us and one country around us, and one government for all. Then the Great Spirit Chief who rules above will smile upon this land . . . and . . . all people may be one people. Hin-mah-too-yah-lat-kekht has spoken for his people.

Chief Joseph

A mixed world: dinnertime at the home of a Crow family in Montana in 1910

Opposite: Independence Chapel, built in 1910 entirely through the donations and labor of Wolf Chief's Indian friends and neighbors and presided over by his nephew, Edward Goodbird, the son of Buffalo Bird Woman

White men think it strange that we Indians honored sacred bundles; but I have heard that in Europe men once honored relics, the skull, or a bone, or a bit of hair of some saint, or a nail from Jesus' cross; that they did not pray to the relic, but thought that the spirit of the saint was near; or that he was more willing to hear their prayers when they knelt before the relic. In much the same way, we Indians honored our sacred bundles.

Wolf Chief, meanwhile, kept writing letters to Washington up to his death in 1934. His last one — to President Franklin Roosevelt's commissioner of Indian affairs — described the drought that was turning the plains into a dust bowl. Shortly after his death, the Hidatsa Waterbuster clan petitioned the Museum of the American Indian for the return of the sacred medicine bundle that Wolf Chief had sold. In 1938, in one of the first instances in which sacred Indian objects were returned to the people who revered them, it was sent back to the tribe.

That summer, rain fell again on the plains.

I WILL NEVER LEAVE YOU

After their honeymoon, John and Ethel Love had returned to the ranch on Muskrat Creek. Seventy miles from the schoolhouse where she had once taught, it was more remote, more treeless, more immense than anything Ethel had ever seen before. "We live the ranchiest kind of ranch life . . ." Ethel wrote. "The sheer alone-ness of it is unique — never a light but one's own, at night. No smoke from another's fire in sight. . . ." In an area the size of Rhode Island, the Loves were the only inhabitants.

During their first winter together, John lost 8,000 sheep and 50 cattle. Ethel lost a baby. But they managed to complete one dam near the ranch headquarters, nonetheless, and to begin work on a larger one downstream.

The next winter was the worst since the Great Die-Up of 1887, and Ethel, pregnant again, left John alone and went home to Denver to have the baby under her father's care. She and the infant, a son, had just returned when the spring floods began.

Black clouds, thunder and lightning showed heavy rains up the creek, although we had only showers about the house. All that afternoon John had been chanting happily, "Roll, Jordan, Roll," in anticipation of water to fill the small reservoirs, already nearly empty, in front of the house, and partly fill the large one down the creek, on which he had had men working for many months. I fed the baby and went to bed about nine o'clock.

Then Jordan rolled. I heard John shout, "The creek's coming down." A suddenly increasing roar of water charged the air, while I pulled my bathrobe around me, stepped into my sandals, and picked up the baby, asleep in his blan-

Life with the Loves: glimpses from a family album

kets. When I reached the back door, water was up to my knees. John lifted the baby and myself in his arms and, water swirling about us, carried us up the slippery hill behind the house.

They tried to sleep that night in the sheep wagon in which they'd spent their honeymoon.

At daylight we returned to the house. Stench, wreckage and debris met us. The flood had gone. Its force had bust open the front door and swept a tub full of rain water into the dining room. Chairs and other furniture were overturned in deep mud. Mattresses had floated. . . . Kitchenware, groceries and silverware were filthy. . . . It rained every day for a week. . . . Later, when John's office desk could be opened, we found the largest drawer full of a tangled mass of roots and sprouts a foot or two long. The envelopes of garden seeds had disintegrated.

Bankers from Lander showed up, surveyed the damage, and brusquely announced that they were foreclosing on Love's livestock loans:

The aftermath came quickly. Buyers arrived to take over the sheep, sheep wagons, dogs and equipment. Cowboys rode to collect the string of saddle

horses. . . . The boys gathered the hundred and fifty head of cattle. John paid his own cowboys, and they departed. Ranch work stopped.

Before he left, the childless banker asked, "What will you do with the baby?"

"I think I'll keep him," I said.

All of John Love's dreams seemed shattered. Everything he'd promised his wife had fallen through; he told her she had every right to leave him. She said, "I will never leave you."

They went back to living in a sheep wagon while they cleaned out the flood wreckage and began rebuilding. A second son, David, was born, and by the next year, the big dam downstream was finished. It was the largest irrigation project ever built in Wyoming without government funds.

"That summer we had a lulling sense of satisfaction and anticipation . . ." Ethel remembered, "awaiting a real test of the dam's strength. The sky in the west was blackened by a hail storm. . . . It filled the dam, overflowing the spillway. Under the pressure the dam burst. . . . John salvaged five loads of rye and more of winter wheat. . . . This was all he had to show for his years of expensive effort on the dam. 'Love's Labor Lost,' was his summary."

John Love was forty-three years old. He still had his land and his family, but that was all. He hired himself out as a common sheepherder for forty dollars a month and started over again. Ethel concentrated on the children — three, now that a daughter had been born. "I have been busy trying to get some raw material in shape for you teachers," she wrote to her Wellesley College newspaper. "And this report is late because the raw material has been teething."

Beside the pleasure of watching the . . . babies' development, I had the contrasting daily struggle with what I thought of to myself as the three damned D's — dirt, dishes, and diapers. . . . We keep open house for all who pass. . . . "When did you eat last?" is the correct greeting.

Their son David remembered one dinner guest:

A chap named Bill Grace. He had been rather lively as a young man and killed somebody and had been sent to the penitentiary for it. But he was a decent sort and, as my father said, the man needed killing anyway.

We little boys — we were about ten or eleven years old — were in a kind of awe to be in the presence of this murderer and it just happened that one day he was at the ranch we had found an enormous rattlesnake. It was five feet nine inches without the head. That's a big rattlesnake and it was beautiful and we skinned it out because we wanted the skin. And we saw all this beautiful meat and we thought, well, it will make a good supper, so we brought it in and mother took the bones out of it and creamed it and served it on toast. And we boys were told not to say anything about this being rattlesnake meat, because it might offend Bill. So, we didn't but we couldn't really quite stay away from the thought and so we were talking about rattlesnake meat and how good it could be. And Bill Grace struck his fist on the table and he said, "If anybody fed me rattlesnake meat I would kill 'em." And there was a dead silence, and then

John Love at seventy-six, photographed in the doorway of his ranch house just before he and his wife left it for the last time

mother passed the plate of rattlesnake meat and said, "Have some more chicken, Bill."

Ethel taught the children their lessons around an old gambling table their father had salvaged from a ghost town. There was no electricity or indoor plumbing, but the house was filled with books to be read by the light of kerosene lamps.

There were still more setbacks. The great Spanish influenza epidemic of 1919 that ravaged eastern cities found its way to the Loves' ranch. John and David very nearly died. Then fire destroyed one of the ranch buildings. Hopes for sudden wealth during a Wyoming oil boom ended in disappointment. One year, shipping cattle to Omaha ended up costing Love twenty-seven dollars more than he received for them in sale. Disease took another herd of sheep. A bank failed, and with it went the family savings.

John and Ethel Love stayed on their ranch for thirty-seven years, and watched their children grow, go off to college, and succeed. One became a chemist, another a design engineer, the third a geologist.

Finally, illness and old age forced them to leave their ranch for good. In the car that drove them away for the last time, Ethel pronounced herself satisfied. "At least," she said, "I left it clean for the next people."

John Love died in 1950. Ethel joined him nine years later.

Looking back many years later, their son David thought that in their determination to endure in spite of everything his mother and father were typical of many of the men and women who settled the West. The winter of 1919 had "pretty much wiped us out," David remembered, and influenza had so weakened him and his father that each had had to teach himself to walk again. "I can still remember us standing together, each leaning on the other, this six-year-old boy and the fifty-year-old man, and his saying, 'Well, laddy, even we can make it.' So, of course, we did."

MONUMENT VALLEY

DAYTON DUNCAN

A few years ago, I stopped at Monument Valley, a place on the border between Arizona and Utah that I have always considered one of the West's most breathtakingly beautiful spots, and one of its most symbolic. I was near the end of a particularly long and grueling road trip and needed a short rest to gather my thoughts before moving on. A spectacular sunset, I figured, would do the trick, and few places can top Monument Valley when the evening shadows begin to lengthen.

It was a late-fall afternoon, and the desert air was about to be freshened by one of those storms unique to the West — the kind you can see coming toward you for hours, even though it's moving fast, a series of billowy cumulous clouds, each one trailing angled tentacles of rain like some giant Portuguese man-of-war migrating across the sky. I watched in sunlight as the clouds approached, felt the wind change and the temperature drop when the shadows reached my spot, then a spattering of rain and the pungent scent of damp sagebrush, and then sunlight again as the cloud migration floated on indifferently toward the next horizon.

The brief storm settled the dust and cleared the way for an especially stunning sunset. Rising mysteriously from the flat desert floor of Monument Valley are immense buttes of red sandstone. Each monolith is individually distinct, mutely telling its own story of both timelessness and change, in which the rise and fall of human civilizations are subjects too puny and too hurried to consider, compared with the vaster, ceaseless struggle between wind, rock, and water that created the buttes aeons ago. If the gods had a sacred graveyard, this would be it. The buttes would be their tombstones, their etched epitaphs faded over so much time, decipherable only in certain light.

As the sun lowered, the rocks turned to burnt orange, then blood red, then shades of purple that seemed to change by the minute. The slanting sunlight cast shifting shadows across the valley and threw every eroded notch and line on the buttes' sides into sharp relief. There was a remarkable clarity to the light, but it was restless, like a supernatural flashlight moving steadily from point to point to read hieroglyphic inscriptions that spoke of time in millions of years.

Then the colors turned deeper and softer, and the light slowly dimmed until the buttes became coal-black silhouettes against a cobalt sky. The stars popped out. A coyote howled. I was ready to go home.

When I remember that sunset, I see myself alone in Monument Valley, silent and awestruck, just me and the ageless, primal elements. But in truth, I wasn't alone at all.

At least three busloads of tourists — Japanese and Germans mostly — had been there the same afternoon, enjoying the same scenery and listening to tour guides explain Indian customs. On the valley floor, a scattering of cars and RVs moved over dirt roads, stopping occasionally while people in expensive hiking boots got out to snap a photograph. The highway leading into the valley was lined with tents and booths of Navajo offering curios that ranged from expensive pottery and turquoise jewelry to cheap beads and toy tomahawks with rubber blades.

In two locations, commercials were being made with the monuments as a backdrop. One of them featured a shiny new car, the other a gorgeous model who would emerge from a trailer from time to time, have her picture taken in an elegant dress, and then go back inside to change outfits and do it all again. (When I returned home, I started counting the advertisements I saw that were set in Monument Valley: Estée Lauder perfume, Guinness beer, IBM typewriters, specially designed running shoes, two or three automobiles, Marlboro cigarettes, and an 18-karat-gold watch available only in New York, Bal Harbour, and Palm Beach. The cover of a fashion magazine, using high-tech photo-imaging to merge the features of beautiful women to create what it called "today's all-American beauty," displayed her exquisitely morphed face looming in front of three of the valley's distinctive buttes. When I saw a television commercial for Oscar Mayer weiners that showed a vehicle shaped like a hot dog driving across Monument Valley, I quit counting.)

And of course there were Navajo in the valley. Not just those selling tourist curios or leading pony rides over the dunes, but families that tend small herds of sheep, cart their water from wells and streams by hand, and live in hogans tucked away along the bottom of some butte, several strata below the poverty line. Perhaps they had a rusting pickup truck parked outside, a pack of cigarettes and some hot dogs inside — but little else even remotely resembling the multitude of products constantly promoted for sale to the rest of the world using the powerful mystique of Monument Valley, their home, as the come-on.

It was probably only by chance that a Hollywood movie crew wasn't also there with me. In 1938, John Ford came to Monument Valley and filmed *Stagecoach,* a western that won him an Academy Award, made a star out of one its young actors, John Wayne, and turned the valley into the location of choice for Ford and other filmmakers, whether or not their storylines actually matched the locale. Monument Valley has served as Tombstone, Arizona, for *My Darling Clementine* and as Lincoln, New Mexico, for *Billy the Kid* and *Young Guns.* In *Fort Apache,* the cavalry chases Apache through the buttes. In *She Wore a Yellow Ribbon,* it's tribes from the Great Plains they're after, and in one scene a cavalryman crests a dusty sand dune and points to something in the distance, which the next shot reveals to be a huge buffalo herd filmed in some other part of the West. Comanche are the enemy in *The Searchers,* one of my personal favorites, which pretends that Monument Valley is part of the Texas cotton belt. A Swedish settler, whose every other statement seems to be "yumpin' yiminy," complains to John Wayne about how hard it is to get a crop to grow, but Wayne's too busy trying to track down the tribe that captured his niece to point out that the homesteader might have better luck planting cotton in a place that gets more than six inches of rain a year.

John Ford's stagecoach takes one of several on-screen turns around the Mittens in Monument Valley.

In more recent films, Michael J. Fox was transported through time to Monument Valley to reach his past; Thelma and Louise drove a convertible through it in an attempt to escape from theirs. In either case, the valley itself proved inescapable, much like its image in modern times. I have no way to verify this, but I believe that the cumulative result of all the movies and commercials is that Monument Valley is immediately recognizable to virtually everyone in the nation, perhaps much of the world, even though few people could name it and fewer still have actually been there in person. It has become the visual symbol to conjure the West and all it represents. For most people, in fact, it *is* the West, a mythic place that exists as much in the imagination as in reality.

There's nothing particularly new in that. From its beginning, the story of the West has in great part been the story of different people seeing whatever it was they wanted to see there, often to the exclusion of harder truths and messier realities. It's as if the vast canvas of the western spaces has been some epic Rorschach inkblot test, with each people imposing on it their own individual or collective dreams, hopes, and desires. Some have looked at the majestic landscape and seen objects of reverence and worship; some have seen a warehouse with stockpiles of treasure available on a first-come, first-served basis. People have seen the West as the place to lose themselves, or find themselves; to save others' souls, and sometimes risk their own; to get rich, get lucky, or get away; to chase adventure and court danger; to be brave and free or left alone. The West is where the trickster Coyote created the *Nimipu* — the "real people" — and corn crops listened like children to the singing of women. It has been the Seven Cities of Gold or the Great American Desert, Zion or the Heart of Heathen Darkness, Across the Wide Missouri and Home on the Range, that spot just over the horizon where the sunsets are always golden and rain follows the plow. For some the West was (and is) a fresh start and new beginning. For others it is (and was) the last, best place.

The only thing that's changed is that somehow, through the wonders of mass entertainment, mass advertising, and mass media, Mon-ument Valley's image now compresses all those various and contradictory western dreams — and expresses them all in a visual shorthand of, say, thirty seconds.

If I tended to block out the presence of everyone else during my sunset reverie at Monument Valley, then I was also not alone. Those German and Japanese tourists, no doubt, had come with certain expectations, perhaps to see more sand, rock, sky, and horizon than their homelands could ever provide; and they probably focused most of their attention toward whatever it was that they had spent so much money and traveled so far to see. The commercial crews, I'm sure, carefully adjusted their camera angles to make sure that the tourists, vendors, and especially any hogans with rusty pickups were not in their final frames. The Navajo may have viewed the scene with the same combination of nonchalance and complex, deeply freighted emotions that all people have when looking at their home. They may have seen the tourists, camera crews, and people like me as intruders in that home, outsiders chasing — and exploiting — foolish fantasies. But they may also have seen us through the prism of their own dreams of getting ahead, seen us not as individual people but as a resource whose tourist dollars and permit fees might help them improve their lives in those hogans and shacks that most of us so studiously screened from our selective vision of Monument Valley.

An important part of the reality of the West is the dream — or more accurately, the dreams — of the West. Its history can only be understood with that in mind. And the same is true of the present. Separating myth and dream from reality is as impossible now as ever. They are distinguishable, but inseparable.

As a journalist and writer of history, I am by nature most interested in fact. But what I have learned in the West is that facts — reality — are often driven by dreams. I learned this again, in compressed form, at Monument Valley. The tour buses, the shiny car, the rusting pickups were facts. The fuel that made them all go was dreams. I was in the midst of many people that sunset. *And* I was alone in my dream.

All places have their own coordinates of latitude and longitude, their own topographical idiosyncrasies, their own particular look and feel that set them apart from all other locations. With its signature buttes and sweeping vistas, Monument Valley just happens to have this spatial distinctiveness in spades. It cannot be mistaken for any other place.

But I also believe that places exist not only in space, but in time. When I visit a location, I feel that I'm standing not just at an intersection of map lines, but at many intersections from the past as well. I don't mean this in some soft and fuzzy, New Age sense of "channeling" with previous incarnations. I mean that history can be read in books and told in stories, but it can also be read in the land. And in the West, because of the wide-open spaces, the general sparsity of rain, and a variety of other reasons, those marks from history seem more accessible and stark, like the exposed layers of sediment on a butte's cliffside at sunset. They make the past, and its role in shaping the present, more palpable.

Tucked away in corners of Monument Valley are the elaborate ruins of the Anasazi, a civilization that once dominated the Four Corners region. The Anasazi hit their peak of population in the eleventh century, about the same time William the Conqueror invaded England. Three centuries later (still before Columbus "discovered" the New World) their major cities and villages had been abandoned, and the ancestors of the Navajo — believed to have taken over after migrating south from Canada — were already referring to them and their mysterious relics as "the ancient ones." One of the best Anasazi ruins in Monument Valley is called the House of Many Hands, built in the recess of an overhanging cliff. On the cliff walls are hundreds of faded, white-paint handprints, put there more than five centuries ago for reasons no one fully understands. Not far away, in Canyon de Chelly, I've seen more of them on canyon walls, as well as primitive drawings of people and animals. The early Navajo painted the rocks, too. One cave drawing depicts a pitched battle with the Ute. Another shows a man on a horse, bearing a lance and the Christian cross.

No one, it seems, has been immune to the impulse to leave some evidence of their individual passing through the west. Juan de Oñate inscribed his name on El Morro Rock in New Mexico as he searched for a water route to the Pacific in 1605, adding that he — not the king of Spain — was paying for the expedition. In 1743, as the Vérendryes explored South Dakota for the same fabled Northwest Passage on behalf of France, they buried a lead tablet bearing their names. From 1804 to 1806, as Meriwether Lewis and William Clark pursued the same myth and became the first American citizens to see the West, Clark was particularly prone to the inscription habit. He carved his name on cottonwoods along the Missouri River. He left it on evergreens along the Clearwater and Snake and overlooking the mouth of the Columbia. And near the banks of the Yellowstone, in the only inscription of his still visible today, he etched his name in a sandstone outcropping that he named Pompey's Pillar in honor of Sacagawea's infant son, who had accompanied the expedition to the sea. Seventy years later, soldiers under the command of George Armstrong Custer scratched their names on the same outcropping. When I visited Pompey's Pillar in the 1980s, I noticed a family of four sneaking to a secluded nook in the rock, where they added their names to the hundreds already there.

Such sites cover the West: petroglyphs and rock art from people whose names and customs we will never know; Indian paintings telling stories of ancient battles and animals that talked; thousands of names of American pioneers chiseled into the rounded hump of Independence Rock during the Great Migration and gold rush. In a way, they all could be considered graffiti. To me, they're the simplest and most direct thread connecting the succession of human presence over the ages. I've driven hundreds of miles out of my way to see them. They seem somehow endearing and poignant, an understandable and absolutely human response to such an immense and timeless landscape. In their own ways, they seem to say, "I was here. I count for something, too. Remember me." And although I have always resisted the urge to put my own name next to theirs, I have placed my hand on their handprints or rubbed my fingers across their inscriptions, reaching across time to people who once stood at this same precise spot.

At South Pass in Wyoming, and other places along the main Overland Trail, I have seen wagon ruts left more than a hundred years ago. The missionary Narcissa Whitman, the land-hungry Sager family, the scout Kit Carson, the Mormon prophet Brigham Young, and the forty-niner William Swain passed this way. Each one pursued different dreams, yet the dreams led them all — and so many thousands more of their countrymen — in the same direction, west, and through this same gentle saddle in the otherwise impenetrable Rockies. It does not take an overactive imagination to stand in those ruts and seem to hear the creak of ox yokes from wagon after wagon after wagon, to sense a restless nation on the move, or to feel a moment of anticipation knowing that the slope on the other side at last leads to the Pacific.

At Sand Creek in eastern Colorado, one fall afternoon I visited the place where Colonel John Chivington and his volunteers massacred the peaceful Cheyenne village of Black Kettle in 1864. Not surprisingly, the site is not as well marked for travelers as South Pass — it's part of a privately owned ranch, not public land — but after two stops for directions I found it easily enough off a gravel road. I clambered down a steep embankment to the dry creek bed, lined with cottonwoods, and walked across toward the other side, where the Indian village had been. Chivington's men would have come this same way and encountered an old chief named White Antelope, the first of his tribe to have visited Washington, D.C., and received a peace medal from the President. The morning of the attack, he was wearing the medal and flying an American flag over his teepee, and when the shooting started White Antelope had run forward and shouted "Stop, stop!" in English. The soldiers paid no attention. As the rest of the village scattered for their lives, White Antelope stood in the center of camp, his arms folded, singing his death song:

Nothing lives long,
Except the earth and the mountains.

Some two hundred Cheyenne were slaughtered that morning, most of them women and children. White Antelope had been one of the first to fall. His ears and nose were cut off by one of the volunteers;

someone took his scalp; his scrotum was removed and put to use as a tobacco pouch. No one knows what became of the presidential peace medal he was wearing.

When I crossed Sand Creek, I saw a lone cottonwood towering by itself from the dusty, broken ground. As I approached, an eagle suddenly lifted from one of the middle branches — noiseless, but startling in its emergence. It flapped slowly, up and away, and then, riding an updraft, began circling higher and higher directly above me. The circles got smaller as the eagle gained altitude. He became a tiny dot overhead. I stood motionless the whole time, hardly breathing, squinting in the sun to follow him, knowing that, with his vision, he was looking right in my eye. Then the dot became even smaller, merged with the sky, and disappeared. My breath returned in a gulp, and so did my awareness of sound. A wind swept down the creek, rustling the cottonwood leaves. The cicadas in the trees started rasping, answered by the dry clatter of grasshoppers on the range. It sounded like the shaking of several hundred Indian gourds in a solemn ceremony. Or one very large rattlesnake. I couldn't stay there any longer. By the time I had climbed the creek bank to reach my truck, my heart was pounding, and I immediately drove away.

I would have stopped at the nearest town to have a cup of coffee and try to recompose my nerves, but it was one of those places that exist more on the map than in reality — a dying Plains village a half-step away from becoming a ghost town. There were only a few houses standing, most of them unoccupied, no café or gas station. In the center of town stood a big, two-story brick building, the last evidence that someone had once held grand dreams for the place. The building looked as if a bomb had hit it. The windows were all shattered, the roof had collapsed, part of the second story had crumbled into the ground floor, and tumbleweeds had rolled in through a broken door and piled up inside. The town's name was Chivington. I kept on driving, telling myself that nothing lives long, only the earth and the mountains.

In John Ford's movie *Stagecoach,* which first brought the image of Monument Valley to a worldwide audience, the fictional journey begins against the backdrop of the Mittens, one of the valley's most distinctive landmarks. The stage passengers include a salesman and a gambler, a corrupt banker and a drunken doctor, a proper lady and a prostitute, a sheriff and an impulsive, though brave and good-hearted outlaw named Ringo, played by John Wayne. Each one has his or her own private reason for needing to get to Lordsburg, farther west, as quickly as possible. They ford a swirling river, stay at two or

Poster for *Stagecoach,* 1939

three stage stops, narrowly survive an Indian attack, face other hardships and danger together, bicker with one another, and then coalesce as a group (except for the banker). Finally they reach their destination, which a close viewer would recognize as a movie set somewhere near the base of the Mittens in Monument Valley. In reality — though not in the story — they're back where they began.

Ford, I'm sure, had the most practical of reasons for this. He probably had a tight budget, and since he was in this terrific location that nearly *begs* to be filmed, he shot as much footage in the same place as he felt he could get away with. Besides, he probably figured, few people would notice; or, if they're as wrapped up in the story as I always am, even fewer would be bothered by it.

In fact, I've come to enjoy the fact that on one level *Stagecoach*'s journey seems to be a long and arduous straight line, while on another, unintentional level it turns out to be a circle. Like so many other things I associate with Monument Valley, it condenses another lesson I have learned in the West. *Stories* have a definite beginning and an end; *history* doesn't. And yet the way we most vividly remember and tell history — from gathering around campfires in the oldest times to reading a book or watching television in the present — is through stories. Stories are usually linear. But history can be circular, unending, returning to essentially the same place again and again like a song with many verses but the same refrain. Some Native Americans have always contended that history revolves this way, referring to a Sacred Hoop or large Medicine Wheel.

Many of my experiences in the West have turned out to be the pursuit of stories that circled back in time, linking past and present in both direct and oddly dizzying ways. At a place called Hovenweep (a Ute word for "deserted valley"), I once camped in the midst of some Anasazi ruins and marveled at clusters of buildings, some of them several stories high, built in the crevices and alcoves of steep cliffs. It seemed a most unlikely — and difficult — spot in which to erect such complex structures. I wondered which fact would astonish their architects and masons the most: that their work would still be standing after five hundred years, or that their civilization would not be. The next day I went to Tickaboo, Utah, where a uranium-processing plant had been built during a big boom in the nuclear market in the 1980s. Tickaboo had been laid out in eager anticipation of the hundreds of people expected to move in and go to work. But the uranium bubble had burst, the completed plant never opened for business, and no one ever showed up to buy house lots. When I stopped, Tickaboo was a grid of paved streets and sidewalks, some fire hydrants and junction boxes for underground utilities —

and nothing more. A western ghost town without even abandoned buildings, without even ghosts.

On the Nevada-California border, I once watched a modern gold mine in operation. It was not the first mining boom the place had experienced. A century and a half earlier, some forty-niners were in such a rush to reach California that they ventured with their wagon train out onto the scorching alkali flats of the hemisphere's lowest, driest, and hottest spot. When it nearly killed them, they named it Death Valley.

In the early 1900s, another mining boom touched Death Valley. Much of it turned out to be fraudulent — stock sold in nonexistent mines with the knowledge that no one in the East would ever dare come to such a forbidding place to check out his or her investment in person. But there were some legitimate finds. One touched off a human stampede that included a man pushing a wheelbarrow loaded with supplies across seventy-five miles of desert (jackasses, even at the inflated price of five hundred dollars each, had been sold out). It also gave birth to the town of Rhyolite, which in six short months was transformed from a barren patch of rock to the home of twenty-five hundred rainbow-chasers. There were 50 saloons, 16 restaurants, 19 hotels, 6 barbers, and 1 public bath. At four hundred dollars a ton, ice fetched a higher price than gold ore. Rhyolite, like the boom that spawned it, went under in less than a decade.

When I was there in 1990, all that was left of the town were a few shells of buildings, protected from final destruction as a national historic site. But a new gold boom was under way, swelling the population — and driving up the prices — in the nearby town of Beatty. On the outskirts of Rhyolite, a mining company using dynamite, massive bulldozers, and giant trucks was steadily tearing down a small mountain. The low-grade ore is crushed and soaked in cyanide to separate microscopic amounts of gold from the waste rock, which is then piled up like a pyramid where a mountain once stood. Aside from the newer technology — and its capacity to alter the landscape in ways the gold rushes of 1849 and 1900 never dreamed of — history was repeating itself.

History's wheel had also turned full circle in places I visited on the Great Plains portions of Texas, Oklahoma, and Colorado. There I met farmers who had invested heavily in center-pivot irrigation systems to bring up water from the underground Oglala aquifer, so they could grow corn and cotton in places that don't get enough rain for either one. As grasslands were turned into fields of cash crops, money flowed like water, and both seemed endless. They even called the circling sprinklers "Wheels of Fortune." Then the aquifer's water level dropped and the cost of the gasoline running the pumps tripled. Hundreds of farmers went bust, and the small towns that relied on their business dried up.

In the very same places, I talked to old people who had lived through the Dust Bowl of the 1930s. Their parents had moved onto the Plains during a great wheat bonanza during World War One, when good crop prices and a string of wetter-than-usual years had resulted in thousands of acres of grasslands being plowed up. Then

drought hit, and the exposed topsoil was lifted into dark clouds stretching from horizon to horizon. People told me of sitting inside their homes with washcloths over their mouths so they could breathe without choking on the dust that engulfed everything. They talked of high noons turned dark, of shoveling paths through sand drifts to reach dying cattle, and of dry winds that eventually swept away two-thirds of their county's population.

And before all *that,* in the 1880s, the same area had experienced homesteaders arriving by the thousands, persuaded by land promoters and even some university professors that their very act of settling the Plains would alter its climate. People who would have considered an Indian performing a rain dance a superstitious savage nonetheless believed that the vibrations of railroad engines, the atmospheric disturbances created by larger concentrations of population, and most of all the simple plowing of virgin prairie brought more rain. Not just an occasional storm, of the kind the medicine man with his chant and his drum might claim credit for, but a permanent change toward a moister Plains. Dry times drove most of them off their land before 1890. Rain, it turns out, does *not* follow the plow. But, as those who followed in their footsteps proved, hope is the West's most reliable crop, a hardy perennial that grows with or without irrigation.

I don't remember the first time I ever saw the endless sweep of the Plains — I was too young at the time — but I'll never forget re-experiencing the moment with my wife, Dianne, a New Englander accustomed to horizons foreshortened by humped mountains, to roads that wind through canopies of trees, and to a scale of landscape in which twenty miles can seem like a considerable distance. On her first trip to the West, she flew out to meet me in Great Falls, Montana, arriving at night. At dawn the next morning, we set out by car. The Plains are absolutely treeless here. On the flattest parts, to the east and north, unfenced wheat fields stretch toward Canada, 120 miles away. If you look in that direction, the only thing that prevents you from seeing the small station at the border crossing is the curvature of the earth. A little to the west, the Plains begin undulating — short-grass rangeland that gently rolls and swells until it crashes into the massive ramparts of the northern Rockies, which you can see from a distance of nearly a hundred miles. Overhead was a clear bowl of azure sky covering a perspective that encompassed in one view a landmass roughly equivalent to Dianne's home state of Vermont. For hours, she rode in rapt silence.

It was a personal exposure to an immensity of sky and land and nature beyond all experience, beyond expectation, almost beyond imagination. But it was nothing new. Coronado's men had felt the same emotion — part awe, part uneasiness — when they marched toward Quivira in the 1540s and entered into a sea of grass they feared might swallow them without a trace. A little emigrant girl, trudging across the Plains in a covered wagon three hundred years later, woke up each morning crying inconsolably. Her parents asked her why. "We will never get to Oregon," she sobbed, "if we come back and camp in the same place every night." Across the centuries, every explorer, every pioneer, every traveler has experienced some variation of the same stunned response. So much sky. Such yawning distances. Such a humbling moment to discover oneself so insignificant compared with such a vast, indifferent landscape. I've read it in diaries, journals, and letters dating back to the start of recorded history in the West. I've heard it at gas stops on the interstate. And I've seen it in my wife's wide-open eyes.

Sometimes, I have encountered places where it seemed the wheel of history had rotated halfway, turning old stories upside down. In southern Utah, I met a man who had moved into a remote canyon in the 1970s, trying to escape modern society and live apart with his multiple wives and expanding family. After an armed confrontation with federal officials over a homesteading claim, he had been forced from his sanctuary, and his houses had been bulldozed. But now he was mayor of a growing, if still tiny town on the main highway — and supplemented his income with government consulting contracts on emergency management. One hundred years earlier, under intense and persistent pressure from the federal government, the Mormon Church had renounced one of its most distinctive features: plural marriage. But this mayor made no secret that he was a polygamist. Everyone in town — in fact, in the state — knew it. And although the Mormons had excommunicated him, no one representing the government seemed inclined to prosecute him, least of all the town attorney, who happened to be one of his nine wives.

Near Monument Valley, I followed a young Navajo political leader who was mounting a campaign to bring electricity, running water, passable roads, telephone service, and other amenities that most of us take for granted to his corner of the reservation. In essence, he was leading an Indian "uprising," but the goal was to catch up with — not slow down — the white man, and the method was ballots instead of bullets. In an old hogan, some tribal elders conferred with a federal mediator, assigned to monitor the upcoming election after some tense incidents between Indians and whites over voter registration. The elders spoke no English so the translations took a long time and the meeting went late into the night, lit by kerosene lamps that hissed as they burned. The next day we went to a gathering of environmental activists, where we listened to a lively discussion about whether merely *hiking* in a wilderness might cause too much damage to it. My friend had come hoping to raise some money for his campaign. Instead, he was asked why his people still cut down cedar trees on a mesa that was being designated as wilderness. For the same reason they had been cutting down those trees for centuries, he answered — for heat.

As we drove one day over the washboard roads he wanted paved, we listened to a tribal radio station broadcasting some campaign commercials in Navajo. During the news reports, the only words I recognized were "George Bush," "Saddam Hussein," "Bureau of Indian Affairs," and then, just before the music started, "Dolly Parton." Later, at a two-day powwow, he handed out leaflets that said *Niha whol zhiizh* ("It's our turn"). They showed a water spigot, a modern house, a road grader, and the symbol of a Democratic ballot being put in a voting box. The powwow featured traditional Native American dancing, a rodeo, and a "mud bog" competition in which souped-up trucks with oversized tires try to speed through a short stretch of desert that has been transformed by fire hoses into a man-made swamp. My friend took a break from campaigning to win the rodeo's bareback riding event. But his two brothers, the reigning all-Indian mud bog champions at the time, lost at the powwow to a white man driving a truck called "Custer's Revenge."

No one disputes that the West has held a unique grip on our nation's and the world's imagination, yet no one knows for certain why. There are as many theories as there are historians and social scientists. But I believe that one of the most important factors is the West's unique landscape. It is the screen onto which so many dreams have been projected, the stage on which so many human dramas have been enacted. Those dreams and dramas, in themselves, are not unique. Greed, folly, inquisitiveness, love, courage, ambition, and hope — these have always been elemental to the human story. They are timeless. Each generation reenacts them anew. The Sacred Hoop whirls, the Wheel of Fortune spins, the stagecoach rolls out — and they all eventually return to where they began and start all over again.

What separates those same stories when they occur in the West is the landscape. It exposes everything to a harsher, clearer light. It, too, seems elemental and timeless. And, as a projection screen for the looping reels of human history, it is, well, *monumental.*

And that is why Monument Valley is one of the most appropriate symbols of the West. I've felt it every time I've been there — and especially during that magic sunset after a storm. In every direction, I could see into the folded layers of time. Through the gullies ran streams of water tinged red from the tiny bits of soft stone that the rain had washed off the buttes, continuing a slow, steady process that began before humans walked the planet. In the House of Many Hands, the Anasazi homes and eerie wall paintings spoke of a past civilization that flowered and withered in the time the buttes might have eroded less than an inch. Some of the Navajo I could see were wearing headbands and bright print skirts and tending sheep the way their ancestors had done in the nineteenth century; others were busy trying to bring their people the basic accoutrements of the twentieth century, hopefully before the onset of the twenty-first. There were buses and cars and RVs, tourists hoping to buy some piece of their own vision of the "Old West." There were advertisers plugging into the same dream, making commercials to sell the West's mystique like a bar of soap. And we were all there together, a mixture of different times and different dreams, united at least in the thought that this particular spot of earth was someplace special.

Monument Valley's story is the West's story, and the West's story is everyone's story. In Monument Valley, the past and the present stand side by side. People come and go, repeating what seem to be arcs on the circle of a never-ending story. But nothing lives forever, only the earth and the mountains.

Camera Club at
General Sherman Tree
in the Mariposa Grove,
California

ACKNOWLEDGMENTS

Beginning early in the nineteenth century, Americans dreamed of a railroad that would span the continent, but it could not be undertaken by one individual, or one company — the distances were too vast, the terrain too daunting, the costs prohibitive — and it was only when the government got involved that the dream became a reality. Much the same thing could be said about directing and producing a twelve-and-a-half-hour film series on the history of the West: no individual filmmaker could do it alone, no one company could manage it, and only a partnership between corporations, foundations, and the government enabled it to be "built," hour by hour, shot by shot, frame by frame. Our PBS series *The West,* and this illustrated history that grew out of it, were realized because an extraordinary collection of dedicated men and women invested their heart and soul in telling the western story.

This project would not have happened without the guidance and unwavering support of Ken Burns, our Executive Producer and Senior Creative Consultant. Ken first conceived the series, and throughout the more than five years we worked on the films, he was our principal creative collaborator. He brought his uncompromising standards, intuitive sense of storytelling, and boundless energy to every aspect of the series production. It was because of his pioneering work in the field of historical documentary filmmaking that *The West* came into existence, and it is because of his ongoing support and advice that it exists today.

More than anyone else, my co-producers are responsible for this project's completion. For five years they sustained me through all of its vicissitudes and all of its victories. Jody Abramson oversaw virtually every aspect of *The West*'s production, and in every area brought her competence, composure, and impeccable professionalism to bear. She was one of the first people to come on board, and she never failed me or the rest of the staff. Whether it was a complex technical task or a painful administrative one, Jody met every challenge that was thrown at her head-on, and helped shape the series and make the films stronger. Documentaries such as this one are chaotic by nature, and it was Jody's remarkable good humor, good instincts, and good Yiddish that kept us all together.

Michael Kantor was in many ways *The West*'s trail boss, managing the immense logistical and technical demands of filmmaking with a steadiness and sure-handedness that was extraordinary. In addition to his role as a co-producer, time and again Michael shouldered responsibilities no one else could manage — master of our computers and editing facilities, coordinator of our voice-over sessions, and most remarkable of all, post-production supervisor for twelve and a half hours of film. And yet, while juggling all of these managerial roles, Michael never stopped contributing to the film's creative lifeblood — on location, in the voice-over studio, and in the editing room.

Like the explorers Lewis and Clark, our writers, Geoffrey C. Ward and Dayton Duncan, brought an amazing combination of skills to their endeavor, and like the leaders of the Corps of Discovery, they agreed to "share the command . . . and the hardships." Films like *The West* are filled with words — words from diaries and letters, from newspapers, journals, and editorials — but most of all they are filled with words that form a unifying narration out of an infinite number of possible stories, themes, and ideas. Geoff and Dayton crafted that story, in draft after draft, never flagging in their determination to see the history of the West clearly and honestly, never hesitating to embrace difficult stories and make them work in the dramatic context of a documentary film.

Geoff brought his inexhaustible love of history to our project, but he also brought a keen appreciation of the limitations that filmmaking places on the writer's craft. Time and again he allowed the pictures to tell the story, recognized how little needed to be said to make the message clear. And his words that survived stand as eloquent testimony to his skill as a writer for the screen.

Dayton joined this project over coffee in a café in Norcatur, Kansas (population 189), in the summer of 1991. Since that day, he traveled thousands of miles as our Consulting Producer, sharing with us his innate feel for the western landscape and his sensitive understanding of western people. Like any group of easterners heading west, at the outset of this project we were in need of a guide, and no mountain man or army scout could have served us better than Dayton. He introduced us to the realities of the West's geography, climate, and social customs, and perhaps most important of all, showed us how to find the best rib-eye steak — in Santa Fe or Cheyenne, Durango or Dodge.

Once drafted into service as a co-writer, Dayton became a full partner in the scripting process. For him, perhaps more than for any other member of this project, *The West* has been a labor of love, and throughout the long years of research and writing, editing and reediting, his commitment to see this film through — and his determination to tell the complex history of the West in a new and lasting way — has been a source of inspiration to us all.

Victoria Gohl was the Associate Producer and director of all of the visual research for the series. In all my experience in historical documentaries, I have never seen anyone throw herself into her work with such all-consuming enthusiasm. It is rare for archivists, private collectors, and curators to know, or long remember, an associate producer, even less common for them to actively seek *her* out, ask *her* advice, and see *her* as a kindred spirit, but this was Victoria's reception across the country. The film and this book have been immeasurably enriched by the unpublished, undiscovered, or merely unnoticed collections that have found their way to us because of her research and her reputation.

The West's scripts went through more than twenty complete drafts, and Michelle Ferrari brought her rigorous editor's eye to our scripting process, while qualifying the hundreds of books needed to write the script, uncovering new collections of letters in archives, and managing the historical research that was such an important part of the film's content. She also brought a clear and consistent focus to the arduous task of film research at archives throughout the country.

For nearly two years, Suzanne Seggerman organized our production trips with unfailing energy and skill, and helped initiate the archival film research process. Jeff Dupré not only organized our office with great efficiency and almost unfathomable good cheer, but also served as a fast-learning Production Coordinator during our final year of shooting. Sarah Bingham served with great distinction as our Production Secretary, before heading off to a new career in Great Britain, and our bookkeeper Maureen Dougherty brought an attention to our checkbook that made our funders sleep more soundly. Near the end of the project, photo research assistance was provided by Linda Hattendorf and Allison Ross with such intelligence and efficiency we wished we had discovered them years before.

It is perhaps a truism that documentaries are made in the editing room, but there is truth in truisms. We edited *The West* for more than twenty-eight months, and the team that we assembled deserves a special place in the film's honor roll. The Supervising Editor was Paul Barnes, one of the most accomplished film editors of our generation. A veteran of countless documentary film credits, including the *Civil War* and *Baseball* series, Paul braved an arduous weekly commute from Walpole, New Hampshire, to New York City and brought his calm yet passionate eye to our editing room. Throughout the long schedule, he set a memorable example of the myriad ways in which a talented editor can transform a film, while also providing the guidance and experience that our ever-expanding editing staff required. Most of all, Paul provided me with an unforgettable lesson in the ways an editor can both support a director and challenge him to do his best work.

The three principal editors, Richard Hankin, Michael Levine, and Adam Zucker, made *The West* what it is, chapter by chapter, scene by scene, and they brought to that task an overabundance of enthusiasm and humor, as well as a keen understanding of the editor's craft. Their persistent attention to detail and their keenly observant insights influenced this film profoundly. Their assistant editors — Laura Congleton, George O'Donnell, Keir Pearson, and Jay Pires — tirelessly administered to our AVID editing systems, often working the graveyard shift to meet our ever-shrinking editing deadlines, but still managed to contribute creative ideas to the editing process. In the eye of the storm, Hope Litoff and Vanessa Cochran managed our editing room with energy and inimitable style.

We are also grateful to our sound editors, Ira Spiegel, Marlena Grzaslewicz, Jacob Ribicoff, and Missy Cohen, who brought such subtlety and nuance to our sound design, to Lou Verrico and our friends at A&J Recording in New York, and Scott Greiner at Transmedia in San Francisco, for attending to our voice-over work in the studio, and to Bill Nisselson, Dominick Tavella, and Lee Dichter at Sound One, who made our mix come out so well.

Once again Buddy Squires brought his remarkable skills as a cinematographer to bear on one of our projects, helping us record the many moods of the western landscape. Evocative imagery is what you expect from Buddy, and he always delivers, but what is never included in his job description is the wellspring of creative advice that he willingly shares whenever he is not behind

J. J. Reilly's Stereoscopic View Tent in Yosemite

the camera. His patient wisdom helps you get the most out of every day of shooting. Buddy was joined by another gifted cinematographer, Allen Moore, who journeyed to some of the most remote parts of the West on our behalf (including Devils Tower, Wyoming, for several subzero nights) and always managed to return with images of great beauty and power. Both of our cameramen were often assisted by the irrepressibly good-natured and talented Anthony Savini, who also drove more than 30,000 miles of the West in our trusty Chevy Suburban.

Teese Gohl composed, orchestrated, arranged, and conceived our musical score, and masterfully incorporated a wide variety of musical traditions into a unified whole, while Jay Ungar and Molly Mason, Jacqueline Schwab, Andy Tierstein, Dennis Yerry, Ken Littlehawk, Dane LeBeau, Ellsworth Brown, and Melvin Youngbear played music from those various traditions with precision and pride. And Courtney Little made our recording sessions run smoothly, even in the blizzard of '96.

The West's narration is Peter Coyote's, and for more than twenty days in the studio Peter brought his skill as an actor and keen sense of language to bear on our film. Time and time again he made our narration come alive with his gift for drama and storytelling, and he often caught problems with our script, then helped us fix them. Peter is a person who clearly loves history and loves his work, and he made my job directing the narration a challenge, a learning experience, and a damn good time!

Our maps were painstakingly created by Deborah Freer, of Geosystems Global Corporation, and animated with great technical skill and almost superhuman patience by Rob Issen, of the Tape House, Computer Ink & Paint, Inc. Alex Gatje created our distinctive title design.

Throughout the making of the series, we had the advice and counsel of a panel of academic consultants whose eye for historical detail kept our stories clear and our chronology on track. Four scholars — David Gutiérrez, Patricia Nelson Limerick, N. Scott Momaday, and Richard White — gave us consistent, often sharp criticism for almost four years, and labored hard to understand the peculiarities of historical filmmaking and to serve our project and our subject fairly and honestly. They deserve our special thanks. These four were joined by an admirable group of historians and writers who shared their knowledge of the West with us, including Alan Brinkley, William Cronon, R. David Edmunds, William K. Everson, John M. Faragher, Yvette Huginnie, Alvin Josephy, Clara Sue Kidwell, Howard R. Lamar, Henrietta Mann, Gail Nomura, Joseph Porter, James P. Ronda, Robert M. Utley, T. H. Watkins, James Welch, and Laura Wilson.

The West was a partnership between Insignia Films and two other producing organizations, Florentine Films and WETA-TV, Washington, D.C. Once again we are grateful to the always cheerful and supportive Walpole, New Hampshire, crew of Florentine Films: Pam Baucom, Camilla Rockwell, Suzanna Steisel, Patty Lawlor, Susan Butler, Brenda Heath, Kevin Kertscher, and Shannon Robards. Our thanks as well to the wonderful staff at WETA, our coproduction partner and presenting station to the PBS system, especially Sharon Rockefeller, Phylis Geller, David Thompson, Noel Gunther, Lin Lloyd, Rick Heiman, Jay Phillips, Elise Adde, and Mary Schultz.

This handsome volume exists because of the interest and enthusiasm of our publishers at Little, Brown and Company, especially our insightful editor, Bill Phillips. The elegant design was created by Wendy Byrne, who calmly sifted through our archives and created a book that is a remarkable reflection of the film's spirit and intention. Her quiet skill and taste are visible on every page. She was assisted in the research and photo selection by Victoria Gohl, who tackled her first book project with the same determination she brought to our film. We also relied on the steady hand of Carl Brandt, who was present at this book's creation and helped us see it through to the very end.

The West Film Project was lucky enough to have Jim Kendrick as its attorney and to benefit from his wise counsel. Ed Weisel's careful guidance kept our books balanced and made sure we came out on the right side of the ledger in the end. Every frame of *The West*'s negative was developed and processed by Tim Spitzer, Al Pierce, and Joe Monge at Du Art, and managed with precision by Elliot Gamson at Immaculate Matching. Every frame was cut with steady hands and steadier nerves by Noelle Penraat. John Dowdell made that negative look wonderful transferred to videotape, and Mark Polyocan helped us navigate through the complicated postproduction process with his gifted staff at the Tape House.

Of course, no film of this magnitude could ever arrive on the screen without the support of underwriters who share a commitment to education, the mission of public television, and the importance of promoting and understanding our nation's past. *The West* was made possible by generous grants from The Public Broadcasting System, The Corporation for Public Broadcasting, The National Endowment for the Humanities, the Arthur Vining Davis Foundations, and The General Motors Corporation.

Standing behind these organizations were people whose talent and vision helped bring the series to the screen. Phil Guarascio and Luanna Flocuzio at GM, Skip Roberts and Tricia Kenney at N. W. Ayer & Partners, Sandy Heberer and John Wilson at PBS, Don Marbury at CPB, Jim Dougherty at the NEH, and Max King Morris and Jonathan Howe at the Arthur Vining Davis Foundations.

And I would like to add a special note of thanks to David and Jane Love, whose family story concludes our series and this book. David shared his parents' remarkable letters with us, gave us wonderful photographs of their family's life on their ranch in Wyoming, and provided one of the most emotional and inspiring on-camera interviews I have ever recorded. I am also indebted to his daughters, Frances Love Froidevaux and Barbara Love, who made available to us their own research already collected for their superb memoir about their grandparents, *Lady's Choice.* I believe that the story of this remarkable family, with its combination of endurance, love, and undying hope, profoundly reflects the essence of the western experience.

In the end, five years is a long time to work on any creative endeavor, and inevitably there are individuals whose kindness and generosity are overlooked in the passage of time. I hope the many friends of this project will not forget how much we relied on them for their advice and how grateful we are for their support.

Finally, I would like to thank Anne Symmes, who more than anyone else helped me make it through the last year of this project, and the Board of Directors of Insignia Films — Daniel C. Esty, David O. Ives, John T. Sughrue, and Robert A. Wilson — for their steadfast encouragement and understanding, without which my job would have been impossible.

Stephen Ives

SELECTED BIBLIOGRAPHY

In preparing this book and film series we consulted a great many sources, far too many to list here. But we do want to acknowledge those that meant the most to us. We are grateful to the authors and editors of all of them; any errors uncovered, either onscreen or in these pages, are our own.

Abbott, E. C., and Helena Huntington Smith. *We Pointed Them North: Recollections of a Cowpuncher* (Norman, 1939).

Ambrose, Stephen E. *Crazy Horse and Custer* (New York, 1975).

Arrington, Leonard. *Brigham Young: American Moses* (Urbana, 1986).

———. *The Mormon Experience: A History of the Latter-day Saints* (New York, 1979).

Ballantine, Betty, and Ian Ballantine (editors). *The Native Americans: An Illustrated History* (Atlanta, 1993).

Beilharz, Edwin A., and Carlos V. Lopez (translators and editors). *We Were 49ers!: Chilean Accounts of the California Gold Rush* (Pasadena, 1976).

Billington, Ray Allen, and Martin Ridge. *Westward Expansion* (New York, 1982).

Branch, Edward Marquess, et al. (editors). *Mark Twain's Letters. Volume 1 (1853–1866)* (Berkeley, 1989).

Brooks, Juanita. *The Mountain Meadows Massacre* (Norman, 1950).

Carter, Harvey Lewis. *Dear Old Kit: The Historical Christopher Carson* (Norman, 1968).

Chen, Jack. *The Chinese of America* (New York, 1980).

Connell, Evan S. *Son of the Morning Star* (San Francisco, 1984).

Covey, Cyclone (editor and translator). *Cabeza de Vaca's Adventures in the Unknown Interior of America* (Albuquerque, 1961).

Daniels, Roger. *Asian America: Chinese and Japanese in the United States Since 1850* (Seattle, 1988).

Dary, David A. *The Buffalo Book: The Full Saga of the American Animal* (Chicago, 1974).

———. *Cowboy Culture: A Saga of Five Centuries* (Lawrence, 1981).

De Bruhl, Marshall. *Sword of San Jacinto* (New York, 1993).

Dillinger, William C. *The Gold Discovery: James Marshall and the California Gold Rush* (Sacramento, 1990).

Duncan, Dayton. *Out West: An American Journey Along the Lewis and Clark Trail* (New York, 1987).

Egan, Feral. *Frémont: Explorer of a Restless Nation* (Reno, 1985).

Emmons, David M. *The Butte Irish: Class and Ethnicity in an American Mining Town, 1875–1925* (Urbana, 1990).

———. *Garden in the Grasslands: Boomer Literature of the Central Great Plains* (Lincoln, 1971).

Faragher, John Mack. *Daniel Boone* (New York, 1992).

Gilman, Carolyn, and Mary Jane Schneider. *The Way to Independence: Memories of a Hidatsa Indian Family, 1840–1920* (St. Paul, 1987).

Goodrich, Thomas. *Bloody Dawn: The Story of the Lawrence Massacre* (Kent, Ohio, 1991).

Gutiérrez, Ramon A. *When Jesus Came the Corn Mothers Went Away* (Stamford, 1992).

Haley, J. Evetts. *Charles Goodnight: Cowman and Plainsman* (Boston, 1936).

Hoig, Stan. *The Battle of the Washita: The Sheridan-Custer Indian Campaign of 1867–69* (Lincoln, 1976).

———. *The Sand Creek Massacre* (Norman, 1985).

Holliday, J. S. *The World Rushed In: An Eyewitness Account of a Nation Heading West* (New York, 1981).

Hutton, Paul Andrew (editor). *The Custer Reader* (Lincoln, 1992).

Jackson, Donald (editor). *Letters of the Lewis and Clark Expedition with Related Documents, 1783–1854.* 2 vols. (Urbana, 1978).

Jeffrey, Julie Roy. *Converting the West: A Biography of Narcissa Whitman* (Norman, 1991).

Josephy, Alvin M. *The Nez Perce Indians and the Opening of the Northwest* (Lincoln, 1965).

———. *The Patriot Chiefs* (New York, 1958).

Kraus, George. *High Road to Promontory: Building the Central Pacific Across the High Sierra* (Palo Alto, 1969).

Lamar, Howard R. (editor). *The Reader's Encyclopedia of the American West* (New York, 1977).

Lavender, David. *Let Me Be Free: The Nez Perce Tragedy* (New York, 1992).

Lazarus, Edward. *Black Hills, White Justice* (New York, 1991).

Limerick, Patricia Nelson. *Legacy of Conquest: The Unbroken Past of the American West* (New York, 1987).

Limerick, Patricia Nelson et al. (editors). *Trails: Toward a New Western History* (Lawrence, 1991).

Long, Jeff. *Duel of Eagles: The Mexican and U.S. Fight for the Alamo* (New York, 1990).

Love, Barbara, and Frances Love Froidevaux (editors). *Lady's Choice: Ethel Waxham's Journals and Letters, 1905–1910* (Albuquerque, 1993).

Malone, Michael P. *The Battle for Butte* (Seattle, 1981).

Mark, Joan. *Stranger in Her Native Land: Alice Fletcher and the American Indians* (Lincoln, 1988).

Marks, Paula Mitchell. *Precious Dust: The American Gold Rush Era: 1848–1900* (New York, 1994).

Mayer, Frank H., and Charles B. Roth. *The Buffalo Harvest* (Denver, 1958).

McKittrick, Myrtle M. *Vallejo, Son of California* (San Francisco, 1944).

McPhee, John. *Rising from the Plains* (New York, 1986).

Milner, Clyde A. II et al. (editors). *The Oxford History of the American West* (New York, 1994).

Moulton, Gary E. (editor). *The Journals of the Lewis and Clark Expedition* (Lincoln, 1986).

Nabokov, Peter (editor). *Native American Testimony: A Chronicle of Indian-White Relations from Prophecy to the Present, 1492–1992* (New York, 1991).

Nelson, Howard J. *The Los Angeles Metropolis* (Dubuque, 1983).

Painter, Nell Irvine. *Exodusters: Black Migration to Kansas After Reconstruction* (New York, 1976).

Pitt, Leonard. *The Decline of the Californios* (Stamford, 1961).

Prucha, Francis Paul. *The Great Father: The United States Government and the American Indians* (Lincoln, 1984).

Rawls, James J. *Indians of California: The Changing Image* (Norman, 1984).

Ronda, James P. *Lewis and Clark Among the Indians* (Lincoln, 1984).

Rosenbaum, Robert J. *Mexicano Resistance in the Southwest: The Sacred Right to Self-Preservation* (Austin, 1981).

Russell, Don. *The Lives and Legends of Buffalo Bill* (Norman, 1973).

Sanborn, Margaret. *Mark Twain: The Bachelor Years* (New York, 1990).

Schlissel, Lillian. *Women's Diaries of the Westward Journey* (New York, 1982).

Schlissel, Lillian et al. (editors). *Far from Home: Families of the Westward Journey* (New York, 1989).

Stands in Timber, John, and Margot Liberty. *Cheyenne Memories* (New Haven, 1967).

Stegner, Wallace. *The Gathering of Zion: The Story of the Mormon Trail* (New York, 1964).

Stratton, Joanna L. *Pioneer Women: Voices from the Kansas Frontier* (New York, 1981).

Takaki, Ronald. *A Different Mirror: A History of Multicultural America* (Boston, 1993).

Thompson, Erwin N. *Shallow Grave at Waiilatpu: The Sagers' West* (Portland, 1985).

Twain, Mark. *Roughing It* (New York, 1962).

Unruh, John D., Jr. *The Plains Across: The Overland Emigrants and the Trans-Mississippi West, 1840–60* (Urbana, 1979).

Utley, Robert M. *Cavalier in Buckskin: George Armstrong Custer and the Western Military Frontier* (Norman, 1988).

———. *Frontier Regulars: The United States Army and the Indian, 1866–1891* (New York, 1973).

———. *Frontiersmen in Blue: The United States Army and the Indian, 1848–1865* (New York, 1967).

———. *The Indian Frontier of the American West, 1846–1890* (Albuquerque, 1984).

———. *The Lance and the Shield: The Life and Times of Sitting Bull* (New York, 1993).

———. *The Last Days of the Sioux Nation* (New Haven, 1963).

Vestal, Stanley. *Joe Meek: The Merry Mountain Man* (Lincoln, 1952).

Weber, David J. *The Mexican Frontier, 1821–46: The American Southwest Under Mexico* (Albuquerque, 1982).

Weber, David J. (editor). *Foreigners in Their Native Land* (Albuquerque, 1973).

———. *The Spanish Frontier in North America* (New York, 1992).

Weems, John Edward. *Dreams of Empire* (New York, 1971).

West, Elliott. *Growing Up with the Country: Childhood on the Far Western Frontier* (Albuquerque, 1989).

White, Richard. *It's Your Misfortune and None of My Own: A History of the American West* (Norman, 1991).

———. *The Roots of Dependency: Subsistence, Environment, and Social Change Among the Choctaws, Pawnees and Navajos* (Lincoln, 1983).

Williams, John Hoyt. *A Great and Shining Road* (New York, 1988).

———. *Sam Houston* (New York, 1993).

INDEX

Figures in italic type refer to illustrations.

Mr. and Mrs. O. C. Smith being photographed at Echo Canyon during the building of the Trans-Mississippi Railroad, ca. 1868

Camp Curry Souvenir Shop, Yosemite Valley

ILLUSTRATION CREDITS

Each credit lists source, negative number (when one exists), and photographer/artist last name (where one is known). When there is more than one credit for a page the images will be listed clockwise from top left.

INSTITUTION ABBREVIATIONS

AC   Amon Carter Museum
AHC   American Heritage Center, University of Wyoming
BAL   The Bancroft Library
BBHC   Buffalo Bill Historical Center
BL   Beinecke Rare Book and Manuscript Library, Yale University
BYU   Brigham Young University
CAH   Center for American History, University of Texas at Austin
CAP   Society of California Pioneers
CHS   California Historical Society
CSHS   Colorado State Historical Society
CSL   California State Library
DPL   Denver Public Library, Western History Department
GG   Greg Gibbs Collection
HL   The Henry E. Huntington Library
ISHS   Idaho State Historical Society
JMW   John McWilliams Collection
Joslyn   Joslyn Art Museum
KC   Kansas Collection, University of Kansas Libraries
KSHS   Kansas State Historical Society
LAPL   Los Angeles Public Library
LBHB   Little Big Horn Battlefield National Monument
LDS   Church of Jesus Christ of Latter-day Saints Archives Division
LOC   Library of Congress — Prints and Photographs Division
Loves   J. David Love Family
MHS   Montana Historical Society
MI   Matthew R. Isenburg Collection
MNHS   Minnesota Historical Society
MNM   Museum of New Mexico
MPM   Milwaukee Public Museum
NA   National Archives
NAA   National Anthropological Archives, Smithsonian Institution
NHS   Nebraska State Historical Society
NMAA   National Museum of American Art, Smithsonian Institution
NMAI   National Museum of the American Indian
NP   Nez Perce National Historical Park
NYHS   New-York Historical Society
NYPL   New York Public Library
OH   Oregon Historical Society
OM-A   The Oakland Museum Art Department
OM-H   The Oakland Museum History Department
PP   Peter E. Palmquist Collection
SA   Stephen Anaya Collection

SC Seaver Center for Western History Research, Natural History Museum of Los Angeles County
SL Department of Special Collections, Stanford University Libraries
TXL Archives Division, Texas State Library
UNP University of Nebraska Press
UOK Western History Collections, University of Oklahoma Library
UPRR Union Pacific Museum Collection
USC University of Southern California, Department of Special Collections
USHS Utah State Historical Society
WDC Division of Cultural Resources, Wyoming Department of Commerce
WS William L. Schaeffer

PHOTOGRAPHERS, ARTISTS, AND OTHER ABBREVIATIONS

Abert, James W.; **Anderson**, George Edward; **Anderson**, John A.; **Baker & Johnston**, Charles S. & Eli; **Baker**, Isaac Wallace; **Barry**, David F.; **Bastida**, Ignacio de la; **Beaman**, E.O.; **Bell**, William A.; **Bierstadt**, Albert; **Bodmer**, Karl; **Butcher**, Solomon; **Cameron**, Evelyn; **Carter**, Charles W.; **Catlin**, George; **Chapman**, John Gadsby; **Choate**, John N.; **Choris**, Ludovik; **Compton**, Alma W.; **Currier**, Nathaniel; **Curtis**, Edward Sheriff - most images from NAI: *North American Indian*, 20 volumes and 20 S supplementary folios. **Deas**, Charles; **DeBry**, Theodor; **D'Heureuse**, R.; **Fennemore**, James; **Fouch**, John H.; **Gardner**, Alexander; **Gay**, Jane; **Goff**, Orlando S.; **Grabill**, John C.H.; **Hart**, Alfred A.; **Haynes**, Frank Jay; **Hillers**, John K.; **Huddle**, William H.; **Huffman**, Layton Alton; **Hunter**, Elliott W.; **Illingworth**, William H; **Jackson**, William H.; **Kane**, Paul; **Kinsey**, Darius; **Kirkland**, Charles D.; **Lamb**, Adrian; **L'Ouvrier**, Paul; **McArdle**, Henry Arthur; **McClintock**, Walter; **McClure**, Lewis; **Martinez**, Juan de; **Matteson**, Sumner; **Meddaugh**, J. E.; **Miller**, Alfred Jacob; **Moon**, Karl; **Morledge**, Charles D.; **Morrow**, Stanley; **O'Sullivan**, Timothy; **Peale**, Charles Wilson; **Prettyman**, William S; **Reilly**, John J.; **Remington**, Frederic; **Rhinehart**, Frank A.; **Robertson**, George; **Russell**, Andrew J.; **Sherman**, F.M.; **Steele**, F.M.; **Stimson**, Joseph E.; **Throssel**, Richard; **Traeger**, George; **Vance**, Robert; **Vespucci**, Juan; **Vollmer**, H. D.; **Vroman**, Adam Clark; **Watkins**, Carlton E.; **Wilson**, Gilbert; **Wittick**, Ben; **Wright**, Jefferson

Endpapers: WS, Russell.
ii-iii: MHS. v: LOC #USZ62-49148, Curtis, NAI-S V8 #256. vi: JMW; OM-A #A-84.2.1; JMW; LDS #P 100 42. vii: Museum Fine Arts Houston #92.444. viii: SC #4670. ix: OM-A #68.94.1, Baker. x: MHS #946-434. xi: BBHC #P.69.2088. xii: MHS #981-096, Huffman. xiii: BYU, Anderson. xiv: What-com Museum #7978, Kinsey. xvi: MPM #43953, Matteson.

THE NORTHERN MYSTERY

1: BL #F805, McClintock. 3: Hispanic Society of America #K42, Vespucci. 4-5: BL #Taylor 192, DeBry. 7: AC #P198.27.38, O'Sullivan. 8-9: SC #V-879, Vroman. 10-11: BL #Zc16 T29 +978ga, Gardner; DPL #F20285, Rhinehart; LOC #USZ62-109747, Moon. WDC #457, Stimson; NAA #1784, Hillers; NAA #42,021, Baker & Johnston. 12: NHS I396:1-4; BL #ZZc12 907cua, Curtis NAI-S Vol 2 #72; LOC #USZ62-106280, Curtis NAI Vol 6 P88. 13: LOC #USZ62-113091, Curtis; SC V-648, Vroman; LOC #USZ62-101197; LOC #USZ62-83603, Curtis. 14-15: LOC #USZ62-47017, Curtis NAI Vol 10 P243; National Archives of Canada #PA37756; American Museum of Natural History #32960; LOC #USZ62-111291, Curtis. 16: LOC #USZ62-113085, Curtis; MPM #112055, Matteson; NAA #54663; NHS C951.8:2-9. 17: BL, Curtis NAI-S Vol 7 #249; NHS A:547-222, Anderson; LOC-Rare Books #USZ62-47017, Curtis NAI-S Vol 16, # 563. 18: British Museum Library, Martinez. 19: University of Glasgow Library. 20: Canyon de Chelly National Monument; School for American Research, Karl Kernberger. 22-23: SC #V-947, Vroman. 24: LOC #USZ62-109374, Hillers. 26: New Phoenix Sun Corp. 28: NMAI #1/6745. 29: LOC #USZ62-40310, Curtis; NAA #3404-A, Bell. 30: NMAI #12/2147. 31: NAA #1535, Beaman. 32: BL #EEcd 815d, Choris; Mission Santa Barbara. 33: OM-H, Coronelli. 34: Both Mission San Fernando, Norman Neuerberg. 35: Joslyn Tab. 16, Bodmer. 36: Both Independence National Historical Park by Peale, #40 & #30. 39: BL #WA MSS 303-4. 40: Both BL #Zc10 807 gac. 41: Joslyn #NA 118A, Bodmer. 42: BL #WA MSS S897. 43: Joslyn, Bodmer. 44-45: ISHS #63-221.223B. 46: American Philosophical Society #871. 49: LOC #USZ62-3283, Hennepin. 51: LOC #USZ62-104344. 52: Old Mission Santa Ines, Jim Frank.

THE MOST AVID NATION

54-55: LDS #C-188, Carter. 57: Charles Terrill. 58: Shelburne Museum #27.1.5-18, Deas. 59: Joslyn, Miller. 60-61: BL #Zc74870vib; AHC, Miller. 62: BL #WA MSS S498 Box 1 File13. 64: Both GG. 65: Both JMW. 66-67: Both BL #Zc50844gr Vol 1 Copy 1, Didier; BL #Zc50848uqa Copy 2, Abert. 69: CAH #Young TX Map; NYHS #1878.3, L'Ouvrier. 70: RW Norton Art Gallery #311, Catlin. 71: San Jacinto Museum of History, Chapman. 72: CAH #CT0004, Bastida; Daughters of the Republic of Texas Library; TXL #1979/86-1, Wright. 73: CAH. 74: Both Joslyn by Bodmer #NA117 & R16. 75: CAH #CT0034. 76-77 Both TXL 1989/154-1 & 1990/139-1, McArdle. 78: UOK Rose #105; TXL 1990/18-1, Huddle. 79: All NMAA #'s 1985.66 145, 146, 311 by Catlin. 80: OH #87847B; Whitman College. 82: LOC Map Div US West Inds 1:2, 625,000. 83: Houghton Library, Harvard University ABC 18.3.2 Vol 1. 84: Philbrook Museum of Art; UOK Phillips #1459. 85: CSL #550-1. 86-87: National Cowboy Hall of Fame, Bierstadt. 88: BAL #1963.2.1536-D; CSL. 89: California Department of Parks & Recreation #70-02; BAL #1963.2.831-D. 91: Both Whitman College. 92-93: NA #57-HS-277. 94: DPL #F3226. 96: OH #11167. 97: Both Museum of Ontario, Kane. 99: Both LOC #USZ62-14734 & #USZ62-31528. 101: National Portrait Gallery #71.43, Lamb; LDS #P145. 102: LDS #P1300/135. 103-104: Both Church of Jesus Christ of Latter-day Saints Museum of Church History and Art. 105-106: Both USHS #917.81. & #917.8 P24. 108: GG; LOC #LC-BH-8201-8. 109: AC #79.33. 110-111: BL Mexican War; CAP; GG. 113: NP #0226. 115: DPL #F29210. 117: Whyte Museum, Banff #V469/2771.

SEEING THE ELEPHANT

118-119: SA. 120: Mrs. Philip Kendall Bekeart. 121: BAL, Watkins/Vance; BL #AN.33.N5.C128. 122: OM-A #A68.90.2, Currier; Museum City of New York. 123: Museum City of New York #57.300.31. 124: Both BL WA MSS 96 F Box 2. 125: Great Lakes Maritime. 126: BAL #1963.2.1418Fr. 127: MI. 128: Both BL WA MSS 96 F Box 2. 129: USHS #92.P4. 131: NYHS #67962. 132: PP, Reilly. 133-134: MI. 135: PP. 136-137: MI; CSL; JMW; MI. 138-140: SA. 141: Gary W. Ewer; JMW; Mark Koenigsberg. 142-143: JMW; SA; MI; MI. 144-145: CAP #C002950. 146: Mrs. Philip Kendall Bekeart. 147: MI. 148: CSL. 912149: WS. 150-151: Greg French; BAL Mackay #105. 153: LOC Maps #US-NW-1851. 156: Peter Shearer; BAL Picture Drawer #16894 (36), D'Heureuse. 158-159: All LDS #P100/6, #P914, #P11. 160-161: BAL Mackay #95. 162-163: BAL Mackay #49; CAP #C004282; CHS #6-G. 165: Porter Historical Society. 167: SC #3516. 170: LAPL #S-000-947-120.

A HELL OF A STORM

172-174: All KSHS B, Doy, John. 175: Watkins Community Museum #CS3118.288.40.1. 176: KSHS #B Lovejoy. 177: LDS #P574. 178: USHS #979.2P.13.5. 179: Brownsville Historical Association. 180: WS; WS; JMW. 181: UOK, Rose #937; NAA #1746-A-6; GG. 182: CSL. 184: DPL MC1367. 186: Both NA by O'Sullivan #77-KW-140 & #77-KS-1-13. 187: GG. 188: GG; LOC #B8172-1976; AC-Mazzulla Collection. 189: GG. 190: State Historical Society of Wisconsin WHi(X3)33609, LOT 4645; GG. 191: State Historical Society of Wisconsin WHi(X3)33609, LOT 4645. 192: Linda Harper; State Historical Society of Missouri. 193: KSHS #FK2.D4.2X*1. 194: All KC RHPH 87.5, RHPH 18K:108:D, RHPH 18K:51. 195: KSHS #FK2.D4.L53 1865*1. 196: NAA #79,4274. 198: MNM #7151; NA #111-SC-

William Henry Jackson photographing on Glacier Point, Yosemite Valley, 1880s

87976. 199: CSHS #F1897. 200: CSHS #WPA 834. 201: MNM #9829. 202-203: AHC #TP566. 204-211: KSHS #44, Gardner, #C.50*1, #FK2 S3W.71 EP1*1. 212: University of California, Santa Cruz.

THE GRANDEST ENTERPRISE UNDER GOD

214-215: OM-H #78, Russell. 216: University of Southern Mississippi. 217: Mariners Museum #P820. 218: OM-H #91, Russell. 219: UPRR #H-5-3, Russell. 220: OM-H #234, Russell. 221: UPRR #H-5-61, Russell. 223-229: All OM-H by Russell, #59, #S-176, #S-267-A, #37-b, #23, #55. 231: NAA #3237-A, Bell. 233: LBHB #562. 236: NA #111-SC-87316; NAA #7713305. 237: UOK Campbell #78, Gardner. 238: BL #Zc16D1 +872ga, Gardner. 241: Panhandle-Plains Historical Museum #PH 1 1980-251/24. 242-243: AC; NA #111-SC-87978. 244: Mead Kibbey, E&HT Anthony & Co. 245-247: All SL by Hart, #317, #327, #255, #239. 248-249: Charles Schwartz, Watkins. 251: BL #WA MSS S-1294 S 3 B10 F153. 252: BL WA Photos 27. 254-255: All SL by Hart, #356 & #358-359 (composite). 256: NA #57-HS-114, Jackson; DPL #F20301; Eastman House #GEH 9312.29043, O'Sullivan. 257: NA #57-PS-87, Hillers; DPL #F45231. 258: Both NA #57-PS-61, Fennemore, & #106-WB-304, O'Sullivan. 260-261: UOK, Campbell #1667. 262: LOC #USZ62-42305. 263: Charles Schwartz. 264-265: KSHS #FK2.F2.D73 Zim*1, #FK2.G8.2E.SW*3. 266-267: KSHS #FK2.H2.R65.A.1891*1; KC #RH PH P1924.1. 269: LDS #P100/2882; LDS; BYU #4596507, Anderson. 271: University of Oklahoma Press; LOC #USZ62-36143, Steele. 272-273: LOC #USZ62-55222,

Steele. 275: DPL #F21407; DPL #F26839, Sherman. 276-278: KSHS #F596*27 & #B, Hickok*10. 279: BBHC #P.71.659.2. 280-281: KSHS #FK2.E3.H77*22; DPL #F20368. 282: Sage Books, CO. 283: TXL #1/112-6, Robertson; NAA #3701, Morrow. 284: Detroit Public Library. 287: DPL #F12921, Compton.

RIVERS RUN BACKWARD
290-291: CSHS #WHJ 1190 F24157, Jackson. 292: South Dakota State Historical Society, Illingworth. 293: NYPL #NYPG 90-F80, Illingworth. 294: NYPL #NYPG 90-F80, Illingworth; NAA #3189-B-10, Barry. 295: Both DPL by Barry, #B920, #B156. 296: LOC #USZ62-12281, Palmquist & Jergens. 297: Both NHS by Illingworth, #B774-37, #B774-54. 298: HL. 299: BL #Uncat WA MSS US Army 7th Cavalry Box 3, Goff; James S. Brust, MD, Fouch. 300-301: Both NAA by Red Horse, #CT 72.3934 & #CT 72.3940. 302-303: Both UNP by Amos Bad Heart Bull. 304: Bismarck *Tribune;* AHC #TP633, Throssel. 305: LDS; USHS #728.P2. 306: LDS #P1300/648; NHS #R539-39:2. 307: LDS #P1700/4347. 308: NA #111-SC-88717; NA 106-WB-100, Hillers; MHS #H-3067, Haynes. 309: AC #P1989.7.2; NA #111-SC-82497; MHS #981-359; NA #111-SC-88170. 311: James S. Brust, MD, Fouch. 314: MHS - Library. 315: NAA #2953-A, Jackson. 316-317: Huntington Library, Jackson. 319: AHC #T192, Throssel. 322: Schlesinger Library, Radcliffe College. 323: Washington State Historical Society #1.01, 001. 326: Yosemite Museum #RL-13. 724. 328: MHS #H-2080, Hunter.

THE GREAT DIE UP
330-331: BBHC #P67.279. 333: NHS #012:1-2. 335: NHS #B983-1053, Butcher. 336-337 Both NHS, Butcher, #B983-1216 & #B983-2938a. 338: Both NHS, Butcher, #B983-2182 & #B983-1221. 339: Both NHS, Butcher, #B983-1402 & #B983-1906a. 340-341: All NHS, Butcher, #B983-3137, #B983-73 & #B983-1694. 342: All NHS, Butcher, #B983-2026, #B983-3208 & #B983-1007. 343: Both NHS, Butcher, #B983-1552a & #B983-1552. 344: KSHS #B Singleton*3; LOC #USZ62-26365. 345: NHS #B983-1231, Butcher. 346: NHS 012:1-4. 347: NHS #B983-2567, Butcher. 348: MHS, Huffman Stereo Collection. 349: NAA #56630. 350: Both DPL, Barry, #B751 & #B754. 351: University of Washington #1678. 352: BAL #1963.21477. 354: DPL #F27468. 355: Pinkerton's. 356: Charles Terrill Collection; CSL; Oklahoma Historical Society #4631. 357: Oklahoma Historical Society #8957; NA #111-SC-93354; DPL #F24121. 358: Brown Brothers; BL #Zc10 881br. 359: Mohonk Mountain House. 360: UOK Phillips #436. 361: NAA, Choate, #125 & #195. 362: NAA #78-12294 & #22E. 363: SC #3061. 364: SC #2873. 365: HL Pierce #1185; SC #3000. 366-367: SC #4637 & #1109. 369: MHS

PaC 90-87 35-8, Cameron. 370: Jack Rannert; BBHC #P.69.750. 372-373: BBHC #MS47; BBHC #P.69.1918; BBHC #1.69.442; WDC #1846, Stimson. 374-376: All BBHC #P.69.54 & #1.69.2165. 376 & #P.6.454. 379: NHS A547:1:81, Anderson. 381: MNM #15901, Wittick. 382: NHS #R539:18-2.

THE OUTCOME OF
OUR EARNEST ENDEAVORS:
384-385: DPL #McL934, McLure. 387: ISHS #3771, Gay. 388: ISHS #63-221-24, Gay. 388-389: MHS #955-986, Gay. 390-391: All UOK Cunningham#182, Prettyman; Swearingen#113; Swearingen #103; Cunningham #106. 392: WDC, Stimson. 393: SC #4170. 394: NMAI #2/1133. 395: NAA#1659-A; LOC #USZ62-40973. 396: NHS Private Collection, Meddaugh. 397: DPL #B835, Barry. 399: LOC #USZ62-11974, Grabill. 400-401: NHS #W938-47, Traeger & Morledge. #403: USC #5; Los Angeles Department of Water & Power #121. 404-405: USC #063. 406: MHS #H-1946, Haynes; Ted Orland Collection. 407: LOC #USZ62-97453; Yosemite Museum. 408: LOC #USZ62-113600; Whatcom Museum, Kinsey. 409-411: J. David Love Family. 412-413: WDC #3781, Stimson. 414-415: J. David Love Family. 417: MNHS #42845, Wilson. 419: State Historical Society of North Dakota #8820; MNHS #9562-A, Wilson. 420: MNHS Wilson Album #V-78-1913 9480-A, Wilson. 421: NAA #4644, Throssel. 422-425: J. David Love Family. 427: Museum of Modern Art. 429: Bruce Herschenson, Plains MO.

432: LOC #USZ62-63510. 434: PP, Reilly. 439: OM #S-591, Russell. 442: Ted Orland. 444: DPL #F7527. 445: BBHC #P.69.2054. Endpaper: WDC

CONTRIBUTORS

DAYTON DUNCAN is the cowriter of the script on which this book is based. He is also a journalist and the author of several books, including *Out West: American Journey Along the Lewis and Clark Trail* and *Miles from Nowhere: Tales from America's Contemporary Frontier.*

JOHN MACK FARAGHER is a professor of history at Yale. He is the author of *Women and Men on the Overland Trail,* for which he received the Frederick Jackson Turner Award, and *Daniel Boone: The Life and Legend of an American Pioneer.*

DAVID GUTIÉRREZ is a member of the history faculty at the University of California, San Diego. He is also the author of *Walls and Mirrors: Mexican Americans, Mexican Immigrants, and the Politics of Ethnicity,* and editor of *Between Two Worlds: Mexican Immigrants in the United States.*

JULIE ROY JEFFREY is Elizabeth Connelly Todd Professor of History at Goucher College. She is the author of *Frontier Women: The Trans-mississippi West, 1840–1880,* and *Converting the West: A Biography of Narcissa Whitman.*

PATRICIA NELSON LIMERICK is professor of history at the University of Colorado at Boulder and author of *Legacy of Conquest: The Unbroken Past of the American West.*

N. SCOTT MOMADAY is a poet, playwright, painter, Pulitzer Prize–winning novelist, and professor of English and American literature. He is the author of many books, including *House Made of Dawn, The Way to Rainy Mountain,* and *Circle of Wonder.*

T. H. WATKINS is the editor of *Wilderness* magazine and the author of many books about the human and natural history of the West. His *Righteous Pilgrim: The Life and Times of Harold L. Ickes 1874–1952* won the Los Angeles *Times* book prize in 1991.

RICHARD WHITE is a professor of history at the University of Washington and the author of *It's Your Misfortune and None of My Own: A New History of the American West.*

A NOTE ABOUT THE AUTHOR

GEOFFREY C. WARD, historian, former editor of *American Heritage* magazine, and writer of more than sixty hours of historical documentaries for public television, is coauthor of *The Civil War: An Illustrated History* and *Baseball: An Illustrated History* as well the principal writer for the television series on which they were based. He is also the author of five other books, including *A First-Class Temperament: The Emergence of Franklin Roosevelt,* which won the 1989 National Book Critics Circle Award for biography and the 1990 Francis Parkman Award of the Society of American Historians.

Production still of mock battle scene during the filming of *The Indian Wars,* produced by Buffalo Bill Cody in 1913

FILM CREDITS

THE WEST

A FILM BY
Stephen Ives

WRITTEN BY
Geoffrey C. Ward and
Dayton Duncan

PRODUCED BY
Stephen Ives
Jody Abramson
Michael Kantor

SENIOR PRODUCER
Ken Burns

SUPERVISING EDITOR
Paul Barnes

EDITED BY
Richard Hankin
Michael Levine
Adam Zucker

NARRATED BY
Peter Coyote

VOICES
Victor Aaron, George Aguilar,
Adam Arkin, Philip Bosco, Matthew
Broderick, Tantoo Cardinal,
Keith Carradine, John Cullum,
Blythe Danner, Ossie Davis, Laura Dern,
Hector Elizando, Peter Gallagher,
Gilly Gilchrist, Murphy Guyer,
Julie Harris, Derek Jacobi, Cherry Jones,
Gene Jones, Stephen Lang, Ben Lin,
Becca Lish, John Lithgow, Ken Littlehawk,
Amy Madigan, Mary Stuart Masterson,
Charlie McDowell, Zahn McLarnon,
Walt McPherson, Russell Means,
Arthur Miller, Esai Morales,
Martin Moran, Tom Nellis, Larry Pine,
Tony Plana, George Plimpton,
Murray Porter, Michael Potts, Robert
Prosky, Pamela Reed, Jason Robards,
Tim Sampson, Miguel Sandoval,
August Schellenberg, Gary Sinise,
Jimmy Smits, Sheila Tousey, John Trudell,
Daniel Von Bargen, Terry Waite,
Eli Wallach, M. Emmet Walsh,
Fred Ward, Andy Weems, B. D. Wong

MUSIC BY
Matthias Gohl

DIRECTOR OF PHOTOGRAPHY
Buddy Squires with
Allen Moore

CONSULTING PRODUCER
Dayton Duncan

ASSOCIATE PRODUCER
Victoria Gohl

SCRIPT AND FILM RESEARCH
Michelle Ferrari

PRODUCTION MANAGER
Suzanne Seggerman

PRODUCTION COORDINATOR
Jeffrey Dupré

PRODUCTION SECRETARY
Sarah Bingham

BOOKKEEPING
Maureen Dougherty

ASSISTANT EDITORS
Laura Congleton, George O'Donnell,
Keir Pearson, Jay Pires

APPRENTICE EDITOR
Hope Litoff

SUPERVISING SOUND EDITOR
Ira Spiegel

SOUND EDITORS
Marlena Grzaslewicz
Jacob Ribicoff

MUSIC EDITOR
Missy Cohen

SOUND RECORDISTS
Michael Kantor, Michael Becker,
Doug Cameron, Peter Drowne,
Steve Longstreth, Dale Lynn,
Bruce Pearlman, Bob Silverthorne,
Swain Wolfe

ADDITIONAL CINEMATOGRAPHY
Ken Burns, Jon Else,
Mead Hunt, Kevin Kertscher,
David Pickner, Dyanna Taylor

ANIMATION PHOTOGRAPHY
Rob Issen
Peter Longauer
The Frame Shop, Edward Joyce
and Edward Searles

ASSISTANT CAMERA
Steve Bannister, Ulli Bonnekamp,
Justin Fonda, Roger Haydock,
Molly O'Brien, Rita Roti,
Anthony Savini, Brett Wylie

RESEARCH ASSOCIATES
Nick Davis, Bronwyn Emmet,
Mia Gallison, Jan Grenci,
Linda Hattendorf, Allison Ross

CONSULTANTS
Alan Brinkley, R. David Edmunds,
William K. Everson, John M. Faragher,
David Gutiérrez, Yvette Huginnie,
Alvin Josephy, Clara Sue Kidwell,
Howard R. Lamar,
Patricia Nelson Limerick,
Henrietta Mann, N. Scott Momaday,
Gail Nomura, Joseph C. Porter,
James P. Ronda, Robert M. Utley,
T. H. Watkins, James Welch,
Richard White, Laura Wilson

ADDITIONAL RESEARCH
Nancy Bernard, Brian Bibby, Russell
Frank, Jane Jordan, Tina Klein, Jack
McDermott, Robin Richman

POSTPRODUCTION ASSISTANTS
Vanessa Cochran
Courtney Little

STILL PHOTOGRAPHY
Paul Christensen
Robert Burgess
Peter Palmquist
Brad Townsend

DIGITAL ENHANCEMENT
Christensen Carver Digital

NEGATIVE MATCHING
Immaculate Matching
Noelle Penraat Incorporated

MAPS
Deborah Freer
Geosystems Global Corporation

RERECORDING ENGINEER
Dominick Tavella
Sound One

TITLE DESIGN
Alexandra L. Gatje

VOICE-OVER RECORDING
Lou Verrico, A & J Recording Studios, Inc.
Scott Greiner, Transmedia
Jeff Robeff, Interlock Audio Post

AMERICAN FOLK MUSIC
Jay Ungar
Molly Mason
Andy Stein
John Kirk
L. E. McCullough
Andy Tierstein

SOLO PIANO
Jacqueline Schwab

NATIVE AMERICAN MUSIC
Dennis Yerry
Bernard Cottonwood
Luke Dubray
James Fall
Ken Littlehawk
Louis Moffsie
Sherry Blakey-Smith
Butch Brown
Charlie Smith
Johnny Smith
Larry Swalley
Melvin Youngbear
Darryl Ironwing Zephier

ADDITIONAL MUSIC
Matthias Gohl, Peter Calo, Richard
Martinez, Nana Vasconcelos

MUSIC CONSULTANTS
Dennis Yerry
Andy Tierstein

NATIONAL PUBLICITY
Owen Comora Associates

SPECIAL THANKS
Daniel C. Esty
David O. Ives
John T. Sughrue
Robert A. Wilson

THANKS
Celie's Waterfront Bed & Breakfast;
Eric Altman, Film Video Denver;
Pam Tubridy Baucom;
J.S. Canner & Company, Inc.;
Custer County Historical Society;
Durango and Silverton Railroad;
Peggy Frank; J. S. Holliday;
Gary Keller, South Dakota Film
Commission; Bertha Kucera;
Duane Lammers, Triple 7 Ranch;
Howard Lay; Bill Lindstrom,
Kathy Landau; Wyoming Film
Commission; Mike McCone,
California Historical Society;
Barbara Love; David and Jane Love;
Frances Love Froidevaux; Dan Markoff;
Nannies Unlimited, Los Angeles;
Toby Shimin; Sterling Memorial Library,
Yale University; Lonie Stimac, Montana
Film Commission; Anne Symmes;
University of Oklahoma Press; Annette
Windhorn, University of Nebraska Press;
Dr. Deward E. Walker, Jr. ; and Lucy

A Coproduction of Insignia Films and
WETA-TV, Washington,
in Association with
Florentine Films
and
Time-Life Video & Television

FOR WETA
Sharon P. Rockefeller, President and CEO
Phylis Geller, Executive-in-Charge
David S. Thompson, Project Director
Mary Schultz and
Cecily Van Praagh, Promotion

SENIOR PROGRAM CONSULTANT
Geoffrey C. Ward

EXECUTIVE PRODUCER
Ken Burns

Copyright 1996
The West Film Project, Inc./Greater
Washington Educational
Telecommunications Association, Inc.